HUMAN GEOGRAPHY

PEOPLE, CULTURES, AND LANDSCAPES

HUMAN GEOGRAPHY

PEOPLE, CULTURES, AND LANDSCAPES

Ronald E. Nelson • Robert E. Gabler • James W. Vining
Western Illinois University

SAUNDERS GOLDEN SUNBURST SERIES

Saunders College Publishing
Harcourt Brace College Publishers

Fort Worth Philadelphia San Diego New York
Orlando Austin San Antonio Toronto
Montreal London Sydney Tokyo

Text Typeface: Times Roman
Compositor: CRWaldman Graphic Communications
Acquisitions Editor: John Vondeling
Developmental Editor: Nanette Kauffman
Managing Editor: Carol Field
Project Editor: Martha Brown, Sarah Fitz-Hugh
Copy Editor: Deborah K. Hardin
Manager of Art and Design: Carol Bleistine
Art Director: Robin Milicevic
Art and Design Coordinator: Sue Kinney
Photo Research: Sue C. Howard
Text Designer: Nanci Kapel
Cover Designer: Robin Milicevic
Text Artwork: Tasa Graphic Art, Inc./Tijeras, N.M.
Text Illustration: Mona Mark
Director of EDP: Tim Frelick
Production Manager: Carol Florence
Marketing Manager: Sue Westmoreland

Cover Credit: Mona Mark

Printed in the United States of America

Human Geography

ISBN 0-03-024514-0

Library of Congress Catalog Card Number: 94-067522

4567890123   069   10 987654321

(Facing page) *In the less developed world, children—like this young Latin American taking a break—are commonly part of the labor force.*

PREFACE

These are exciting times for geographers in the United States. American society is beginning to recognize the value of geography and appreciate the skills and insights of people trained in the discipline. The leadership in global affairs assumed by the United States, the intricate involvement in international business of American corporations, and participation by the United States in decisions and actions to reverse the world's environmental deterioration are among the most important reasons the nation is discovering that geographical information, concepts, and skills are of great value to it at this time.

After decades of neglect in American schools, the study of geography is now undergoing a major rejuvenation at all educational levels. The National Geography Bee and "Geography Awareness Week" have become highly publicized annual events. Research in geography is being conducted and published by more scholars than ever before. College graduates with degrees in geography are beginning to find a growing variety of exciting employment opportunities. Geography in the United States is enjoying a repositioning from the shadows into the full sunlight of the educational landscape. We are proud to potentially help that process with the development of this new geography textbook.

Rationale and Objectives

HUMAN GEOGRAPHY: *People, Cultures, and Landscapes* is an introductory college-level text in human geography. It also should serve successfully as a beginning cultural geography textbook. We have chosen HUMAN GEOGRAPHY for our title, however, because the scope of the book is broader than the subfield of cultural geography as we interpret it. (Some geographers see the content of human and cultural geography as nearly identical.)

We are keenly aware that the vast majority of those who use this book will be general-education students enrolled in lower-division courses. These students typically have little or no formal background in geography and may never take another geography course in their college careers. It is toward this majority that we have aimed this book.

From the usual subject matter of human geography, we have selected several major issues of global importance—including population growth, cultural and ethnic conflict, economic development, expanding urbanization, and environmental deterioration—to emphasize in the book. In most chapters, we have focused on differences between the less developed and the more developed countries (probably the most significant division of the world at present). In order to develop these topics, we have omitted from the text certain others, such as aspects of popular culture, that often are included in books of this genre. These omitted topics, to us, seem less essential to the needs of the general-education student than the ones we have chosen to emphasize.

Although geography majors and minors constitute a minority of the students enrolled in most introductory human geography courses, we have also considered their needs in our organization of this book. For majors and minors, the introductory human geography course normally serves as a prerequisite for more specialized upper-division courses. The latter most often are courses on historical geography, political geography, cultural geography, population geography, economic geography, settlement geography, and urban geography. We feel that our book should adequately prepare students for such specialized courses. Limited to a single chapter, our coverage of languages and religions may seem relatively brief. However, we feel there is less need to prepare students for advanced courses on these topics. Rarely do geography curricula, even in the most comprehensive universities, include offerings on the geography of languages or the geography of religions at the present time.

The fact that so few college-educated Americans in the past have acquired even a vague familiarity with the nature of geography has motivated us to provide a general survey of the development, scope, and tools of geography in Chapter 1. The inclusion of this material should help dispel the persistent notion that memorization of such trivia as capital cities, highest mountains, and longest rivers is the essence of geography.

We designed Chapter 2, "The Human Habitat," with two objectives in mind. First, we concluded that a survey of major components of habitat would further the comprehension of human geography by most introductory students, especially those with no prior preparation in physical geography. Second, we felt the inclusion of this chapter would help convey the fact that geography is a unified field with strong linkage between the subdisciplines of human geography and physical geography.

Nearly all prior introductory human geography textbooks have paid little or no attention to two of the most important contemporary global issues: illegal narcotics and the role of women. (For example, see Tamar Mayer, "Consensus and Invisibility: The Representation of Women in Human Geography Textbooks" in *The Professional Geographer,* November 1989, pp. 397–409.) We have attempted to fill this gap by providing thorough coverage of both topics, particularly in Chapters 10 and 11.

As is customary in contemporary textbooks, we have provided case studies and certain specialized information in boxes distributed throughout the text. They appear as two series: *Cultural Landscapes* and *The Geographer's Notebook.* A variety of features of cultural origin that exist on the earth's surface are presented in the *Cultural Landscape* boxes; information on geography, some of its approaches, and some of its more unusual topics are included in *The Geographer's Notebook* series.

Pedagogy and Features

A concern expressed by many instructors of introductory-level courses is that the textbooks often give the students so much information that it can be difficult for them to discern the central ideas from the more subordinate facts. We have addressed this matter and hope that our attempt at a solution will be suitable. To this end, practically every section within each chapter of HUMAN GEOGRAPHY begins with a special set of general statements and questions for the student to think about while reading. This interactive pedagogy, which we refer to as *Thoughtful Reading,* is designed to focus students' reading and to guide them to ask geographic questions, without being condescending or appearing as a rigid system of instruction and learning.

Cultural Landscapes Boxes The frequent appearance of *Cultural Landscapes* boxes throughout the text

signifies the importance of each concept and its widespread use in human geography.

The Geographer's Notebook boxes focus on some of the methods, approaches, and concerns of geographers and on topics that are especially unusual, current, and interesting to students.

With the *Thought Questions* that wrap up both the *Cultural Landscapes* and *The Geographer's Notebook* boxes we hope to stimulate students to cultivate informed opinion and geographic perspective.

Every chapter ends with definitions of *Key Terms,* listed in the order of their appearance in the chapter—that is, the key terms are juxtaposed according to conceptual rather than alphabetical relationship. A glossary at the end of the text provides an alphabetical reference of key terminology.

End-of-chapter *Review Questions* focus attention on the main ideas and concepts contained in the chapter and refrain from the type of question that draws on an ability to memorize raw facts.

Acknowledgments

To identify in a limited amount of space all those who, in one way or another, have contributed to this book is unfortunately an impossible task. Our organization and selection of material in the book have been influenced by our contacts over many years with students in our classes, with colleagues in our department and university, and with fellow workers in the geography profession. Although most will go unnamed here, our indebtedness to them is substantial.

We gratefully acknowledge the input of fellow geographers who served as reviewers of our initial outline and of all or parts of the manuscript, providing helpful criticism and offering suggestions to strengthen the book. They include:

S. Reza Ahsan, Western Kentucky University
Thomas D. Anderson,
   Bowling Green State University
Sarah Bednarz, Texas A & M University
L. Carl Brandhorst,
   Western Oregon State College
Brock Brown, University of Colorado, Boulder
James R. Curtis, Oklahoma State University
James L. Davis, Western Kentucky University
Dorothy W. Drummond,
   Indiana State University
Gary S. Elbow, Texas Tech University

Adrian Esparza,
  Indiana University, Bloomington
Thomas O. Graff, University of Arkansas
Elizabeth Hovinen,
  Georgia Institute of Technology
James B. Kenyon, University of Georgia
William A. Koelsch, Clark University
James Kus, California State University, Fresno
Thomas A. Maraffa,
  Youngstown State University
Richard McClusky,
  State University of New York, Geneseo
Norman T. Moline, Augustana College
David J. Nemeth, University of Toledo
Brian Osborne, Queen's University
Gregory Rose, Ohio State University, Marion
James W. Scott, Western Washington University
Roger M. Selya, University of Cincinnati
Everett G. Smith, Jr., Oregon State University
Ingolf Vogeler,
  University of Wisconsin, Eau Claire
Morton D. Winsberg, Florida State University

Any errors or deficiencies that remain in the book are the responsibility of the authors alone.

The people at Saunders College Publishing Company have been more helpful and patient than we had any right to expect. We are deeply grateful to John Vondeling for providing us with the opportunity to prepare the book. Nanette Kauffman, Martha Brown, and Sarah Fitz-Hugh have been ingenious and dedicated editors; we owe them many thanks for their ideas and efforts. Also, we wish to thank art director Robin Milicevic, who made valuable contributions to the visual appeal of the book, and production manager Carol Florence.

Our calls for photographs of specific subjects not in our own collections largely were fulfilled by photo researcher Sue C. Howard, who managed to locate an amazing assortment of slides and prints. We also are indebted to many of our colleagues and friends for other photographs that appear in the book. They include Siyoung Park, A. R. Longwell, Norbert Archbold, Richard Rieck, John Simmons, Cindy Hare (all of Western Illinois University), Robert J. Sager (Pierce College), R. Lynn Bradley (Belleville Area College), and Frederick L. Bein (Indiana University-Purdue University, Indianapolis). In addition, we were fortunate to have access to the slide collection of the late Donald Marshall of Western Illinois University.

All of the maps and line drawings reflect the skillful work of Karen and Dennis Tasa of Tasa Graphic Arts, Inc. The Western Paragraphic Projection used for world maps throughout the book was developed by our colleague, Fred C. Caspall, of Western Illinois University.

We are particularly thankful for the assistance of Charles F. Gritzner, a specialist in cultural geography at South Dakota State University, who contributed some of the text that appears in Chapter 3. Also, Jeffrey A. Nelson prepared material on the three case studies that are included in Chapter 6.

We have been most fortunate to have Pam Hines and Cindy Hare available for word processing duties, and Scott Miner to assist with photographic and cartographic matters. Sandy Nelson proofread nearly all of the text and saved us from a number of grammatical oversights.

Finally, we wish to acknowledge the patience and understanding of our spouses, Sandy Nelson, Mary Ellen Gabler, and Peggy Vining, who now fully understand what it means to be a "book widow."

—R.E.N.
R.E.G.
J.W.V.

CONTENTS OVERVIEW

CONTENTS

Chapter 3

Culture and Culture Regions

Chapter 4

Cultural Diversity: Languages and Religions

Chapter 10

Societies and Livelihoods in the Less Developed World   356

Chapter 13
Cities and Urbanization: Patterns and Trends

The geography students in the accompanying photograph are conducting a field exercise and learning about the value of maps. Geographers also find photos taken from the air and imagery obtained by artificial satellites to be helpful tools for certain types of field investigations. Field work for geographers commonly involves recording data and plotting observations on maps and photos for later analysis in the office or laboratory.

Students enrolled in their first college-level geography course usually find it to be different from—and more interesting than—what they expected. They soon discover that geography involves far more than simply memorizing locations and facts. As they progress through the course and begin to discover explanations for patterns displayed on maps and photographs of the earth's surface, as they acquire an understanding of fundamental differences in the lifestyles of people from one region to another, and as they evaluate possible solutions to problems associated with humankind's use of physical environments, most students find geography to be exciting and rewarding.

As we will describe in Chapter 1, the character of modern geography has evolved over a long history. Encompassing the earth's varied physical environ-

PART 1

GEOGRAPHY AND GEOGRAPHERS

(Robin Milicevic)

ments, human inhabitants, and the associations of people with their environment, the subject matter of geography overlaps the physical and social sciences. It is not subject matter, however, that distinguishes geography from other fields of study. Instead, the uniqueness of geography is its emphasis on spatial analysis—the examination of such variables as the distributional patterns, arrangements, and diffusions of phenomena over the space of the earth's surface—as a means of finding answers to questions and solutions to problems. This spatial approach requires skillful use and interpretation of maps, photographs, and imagery obtained from artificial satellites.

With their proficiency in spatial analysis and the use of maps and similar investigational tools, geographers often find employment in governmental agencies and private businesses. Their work assignments often involve a variety of practical problems associated with such matters as human use of land and resources, environmental issues, economic development, and the provision of social services. Many geographers also are employed as teaching professionals because their discipline is widely regarded as essential in the education of all people.

CHAPTER 1

GETTING TO KNOW GEOGRAPHY

The dominant idea in all geographical progress is that of terrestrial unity.

—Paul Vidal de la Blache

The spatial approach of geography enables us to account for the presence of this native American in southwestern United States. (Joe Sohm/The Image Works)

Have you ever examined a map of a foreign country and wondered what life is like in that part of the world? Have you ever been curious about how the cultural traits of people—their languages, religious beliefs, political ideologies, economic practices, technological accomplishments, and social traditions—vary from place to place in the world? Have you ever noticed the association of certain kinds of land use with particular terrain or climatic conditions? Are you concerned about human-induced environmental changes and alarmed by evidence of environmental deterioration? Do you follow international affairs in the news and find them intriguing? Are you preparing for a career that will involve travel, trade, planning, resource utilization, or interactions with foreign cultures? If you answer "yes" to any of these questions, you can expect to find the study of geography to be fascinating, exciting, and rewarding. Students often comment at the end of their first geography course on how much they learned about the world and how interesting they found geography to be. For some students, this new interest leads to selecting geography as a major and to an eventual career in the field.

Many students are attracted to geography because of its broad scope and its integration of many different components of the world. Geography is a **holistic** discipline; its study encompasses an unlimited variety of phenomena, processes, and events on or near the earth's surface. Elements of the natural (physical) environment as well as aspects and activities of the human population, individually or in some combination, may be studied by a geographer. Solving a geographic problem commonly requires synthesizing a number of interrelated variables. Because these variables usually are distributed over a broad area, a geographer is likely to plot them on a map in order to study their associations with one another. This contrasts with the investigating procedure of scholars in many scientific fields who commonly use microscopes to enlarge their objects of study. Also, they usually isolate their objects of study in a laboratory in order to analyze them in the absence of influence from other variables. The geographer's "laboratory" is the surface of the earth—or at least a selected part of it—and a map, rather than a microscope, is likely to be the main instrument for carrying out a geographical investigation.

This first chapter is designed to familiarize the reader with the discipline of geography; it is designed especially for a student enrolled in his or her first college-level course. We briefly trace the development of geography and explain its general structure and some of its basic concepts. We also provide information on the main characteristics and uses of maps, as well as other tools frequently employed in geographic studies. Our orientation and examples will reflect the focus of this book on introductory human geography. To conclude the chapter, we will survey some of the main career opportunities in geography for the benefit of students who find themselves attracted to the field.

THE DEVELOPMENT OF GEOGRAPHY

➤ Geography is one of the oldest fields of study; in Western civilization, its origins can be traced to the writings of early Greek and Roman scholars.

Why was knowledge of geography so important among early scholars?

What were some important contributions of the ancient Greeks to the field of geography?

For more than 3000 years people have been involved in geographic inquiry, often simply to satisfy their curiosity about the nature of places beyond their homeland. Curiosity about places on the earth's surface appears to be a ubiquitous human characteristic that has stimulated the study of geography for millennia and continues to do so today. People wonder what the landscape and life are like in different locations and raise questions about the conditions and circumstances that have led to variations in lifestyles from one place to another. Over much of its history, geography largely was devoted to descriptions of places. Since the first half of the nineteenth century, however, geography has become more analytical and scientific in its approach. Let us examine how the old descriptive geography has evolved into a modern analytical discipline. Our focus will be on the development of geography in the Western world and particularly in the United States. The geographical accomplishments of scholars in China and other parts of the Eastern world have been substantial, but we will not mention them further because they have had little influence on American geography.

Geography's Early Roots

Among the earliest contributors to the development of geography were many of the scholars and travelers of classical Greece and Rome. Over several centuries, geographical knowledge was expanded by early Greeks and Romans as they traveled throughout lands on the margin of the Mediterranean Sea and toward the interior of adjacent continents. They often measured distances along their routes, recorded the location of places they visited, and wrote descriptions of areas and people they observed. Perhaps the most famous of the early Greek explorers was Aristotle's pupil Alexander the Great (356–323 B.C.), who traveled with his army as far east as the valley of the Indus River in southern Asia (Fig. 1.1). Alexander's accounts of his travels contributed a great deal to Greek knowledge of the world.

Greek scholars helped establish the early foundations of geography in a number of other ways. For example, some speculated about the causes and consequences of place-to-place differences in climate and divided the earth into the now familiar torrid, temperate, and frigid zones. Although today we criticize these zones because they are an overgeneralization of climatic patterns, the ancient Greeks demonstrated amazing theoretical skill by postulating their existence. Even with no first-hand knowledge of the Southern Hemisphere, the Greeks theorized that its climatic patterns should be symmetrical with those in the Northern Hemisphere. Natural occurrences such as volcanic eruptions and the annual floods of the Nile River also attracted the attention of Greek scholars and led them to suggest possible explanations for these events. In addition, Eratosthenes (ca. 273–192 B.C.) and Posidonius (135–50 B.C.) devised schemes for determining the circumference of the earth, and a number of other Greeks worked on the problems of systematically locating places and accurately mapping the earth's surface. Ptolemy was the most prominent Greek cartographer; his famous map of the world as it was known by the ancient Greeks is reproduced here (Fig. 1.2). Eratosthenes even originated the word *geography*, basing it on the root words *geo* (the earth) and *graphein* (to write about or describe).

Descriptive Geography

➤ Geography, for most of its history, largely has been a descriptive field.

What was the important role of Moslem scholars in geography during the Middle Ages?

How were the great European explorations of the fifteenth and subsequent centuries linked to descriptive geography?

To whom has descriptive geography been particularly valuable?

During the long period of the Greek and Roman Empires and for many centuries afterward, scholars wrote descriptions of selected parts of the world as their principal geographic accomplishment. Among the Greeks, Strabo (ca. 64 B.C.–A.D. 20) became famous for his *Geography*—a seventeen-volume work that was filled mostly with descriptions of the world as it was known in his time. Moslem scholars and travelers also added to the fund of descriptive geographies from the seventh through the fourteenth centuries with accounts of their travels and areas that they visited in Asia and Africa. By building on earlier work by the Greeks, the Moslems filled an important chapter in the history of geography. Although this was a period of great accomplishments by the Moslems, in Europe it was the "Dark Ages"—an interval of little progress in European scholarship that extended for several centuries following the disintegration of the Roman Empire. Work in geography and other academic fields was generally neglected by Europeans during this time.

By the fifteenth century, however, dramatic change was underway. Europeans initiated a period of exploration that brought them to all parts of the world and vastly expanded their geographic knowledge. Ships and their crews under the command of such notables as Christopher Columbus (1451–1506), Vasco da Gama (1469–1524), Ferdinand Magellan (1480–1521), and James Cook (1728–1779) established European contact with the other inhabited continents (Fig. 1.3) and paved the way for many other explorers to follow. The result was an enormous flow back to Europe of information for geographers to use in preparing maps and descriptions of various parts of the world.

By developing in this manner, the field of geography became closely linked to descriptive accounts involving written and mapped information about places. Descriptive geography was of great value to many people, especially military officers, diplomats,

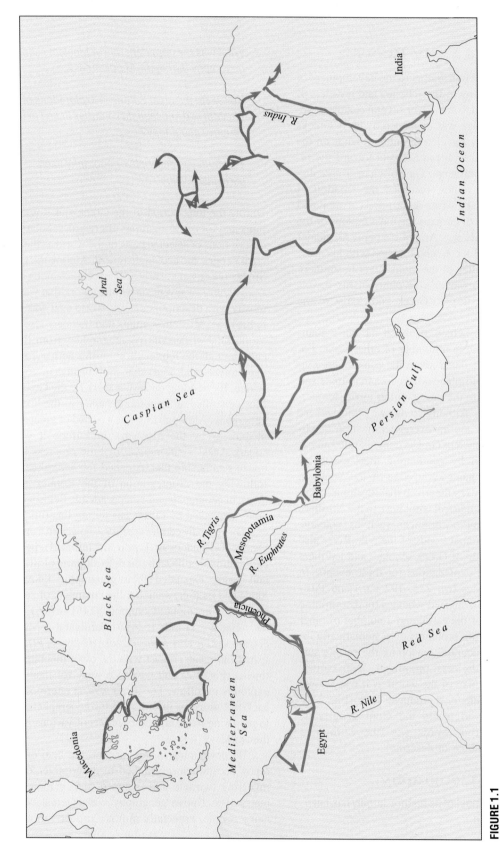

FIGURE 1.1

The routes of Alexander the Great. With his army, Alexander conquered and explored much of southwestern Asia and parts of Africa in the fourth century B.C. The information he acquired about these areas was an important addition to Greek knowledge of the world at that time.

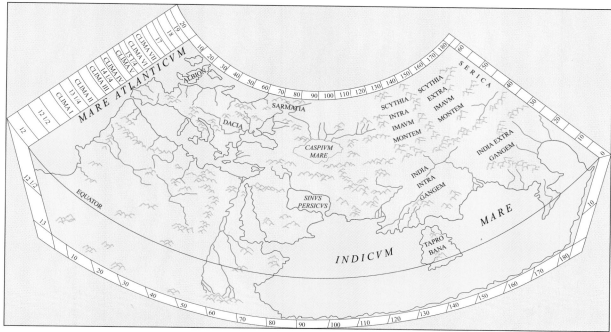

FIGURE 1.2

A map of the world, prepared by Ptolemy in the second century A.D.

individuals engaged in international trade, and others involved in travel and exploration. The close association of geography and description of places from this early period of scholarship is still evident in many ways. For example, in many libraries today the collection of geography books continues to be filed under the heading of ''Description and Travel.'' Also, in current popular games and contests, the ''geography'' questions asked are nearly always about a descriptive characteristic of a place or area. It is clear that the general public and even many professionals in other fields are unaware of major changes in the nature of geography that have come about since the early nineteenth century. Although descriptive geographies (sometimes written by nongeographers) continue to be published, a far more complex analytical and theoretical geography has evolved over recent generations.

The Emergence of Modern Geography

➤ The beginning of modern geography often is associated with the work of Alexander von Humboldt and Carl Ritter.

How did the careers of Humboldt and Ritter differ?

How did their work result in changes in geographical study?

The careers of two German scholars, Alexander von Humboldt (1769–1859) and Carl Ritter (1779–1859), often are identified as a transition between the old descriptive geography and modern analytical geography (Fig. 1.4). Independently, both of these scholars attempted to master an enormous amount of information about the world—information gathered by Humboldt primarily during extensive field study and by Ritter from other scholars and authorities. Humboldt's travels were in various parts of Europe, the tropical and mountainous environments of South and Central America, and in Russia as far as Siberia. On these journeys, Humboldt recorded innumerable scientific measurements of such things as elevation, temperature, and magnetism, and he gathered thousands of specimens of plants and other materials for later study. Humboldt's experiences and study led him to recognize the interconnectedness of nature's great variety of elements, a key concept in modern geography. By lecturing and writing on his ideas and observations,

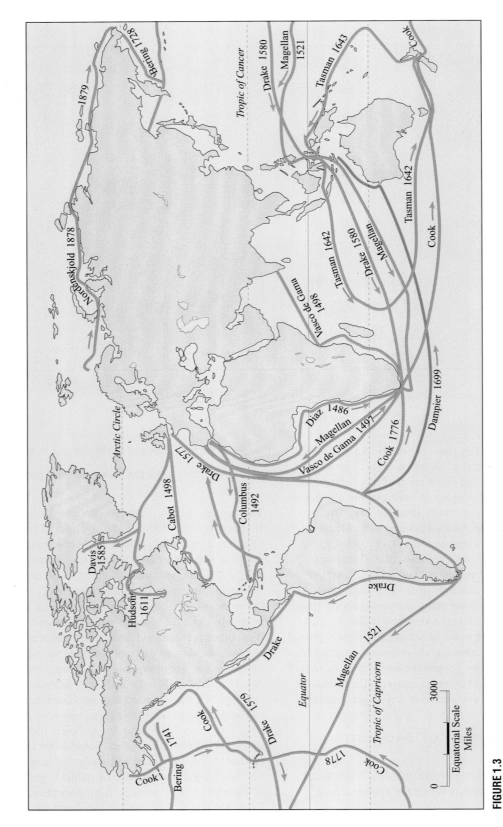

FIGURE 1.3

The routes of selected European explorers from the fifteenth to the eighteenth centuries. During this Age of Exploration, Europeans acquired a vast amount of new information about the world.

(a)   **(b)**

FIGURE 1.4

(a) Alexander von Humboldt (Stock Montage, Inc.) and (b) Carl Ritter (Culver Pictures, Inc.) were highly influential geographic scholars in nineteenth-century Europe. In their work, both recognized that the components of nature are interrelated.

Humboldt became one of Europe's best-known scientists of the nineteenth century. His five-volume work entitled *Kosmos*, published between 1845 and 1862, was the capstone of his career.

Carl Ritter traveled much less than Humboldt, but he also recognized that there is "unity in the diversity" of nature. Ritter focused his scholarship on understanding the interconnections of phenomena on the surface of the earth and revealed his ideas in regional studies. He is best known for a series of nineteen volumes on Africa and part of Asia, published between 1817 and 1859, which he entitled *Erdkunde*. As a professor of geography, Ritter influenced and stimulated many students—a number of whom became prominent geographers during the last half of the nineteenth century. Among Ritter's followers were some who used his title *Erdkunde* (science of the earth) in their efforts to restrict geography to the study of the physical earth. Although it led to considerable debate, this narrow definition of geography was not widely accepted even in Germany. In fact, a German scholar

named Friedrich Ratzel (1844–1904) became one of the pioneers in the study of the human element in geography.

By employing in their work the concept of unity in diversity—the idea that all components of an area are interconnected—Humboldt and Ritter showed how geography could be analytical rather than merely descriptive. Although descriptions of places may have considerable value, analysis of interrelationships among the various components of an area can lead to a higher level of understanding.

Habitat, People, and Culture

➣ An important aspect of modern geography has been attempts to comprehend the associations of people and their habitat.

What is environmental determinism, and how did it become popular in geography during the late nineteenth and early twentieth centuries?

What alternatives were proposed to displace environmental determinism in geographical studies of the relationships between people and their physical environment?

An important facet of the development of modern analytical geography has been the attempts by geographers to comprehend the associations of people with their **habitat** or physical environment. Over many centuries, travelers and scholars came to recognize that the relationships between people and their environmental surroundings differed from place to place and from time to time. Both European and American scholars helped focus modern geography on these relationships.

Friedrich Ratzel became impressed early in his career by the apparent influence of the physical environment on human beings and the course of history—ideas that he included in the first edition of his book *Anthropogeographie* (1882). These ideas spread among geographers in Europe and were carried to the United States where they were accepted enthusiastically. During the late nineteenth and early twentieth centuries, some geographers even concluded that the physical environment *controls* human activities and accomplishments. This interpretation of the relationship between people and their habitat, now called **environmental determinism**, was popular especially among American geographers prior to the 1920s. Ratzel, however, modified his emphasis on environmental influence in a later version of his *Anthropogeographie* (1891).

Geography departments were established in American colleges and universities usually as an outgrowth of geology, much as they were established in European universities. The first faculty members in those departments often were geologists who had become interested in the interconnection between the physical earth and its human inhabitants. The most prominent and influential of the American geologists-turned-geographers was William Morris Davis (1850–1934), a professor at Harvard. Geography, in Davis's interpretation, was the study of "inorganic control and organic response"—clearly the view of an environmental determinist.

Professor Ellen Churchill Semple (1863–1932), who had studied under Ratzel and introduced his early ideas into American scholarship, also was among those most responsible for the popularity of environmental determinism in American geography prior to

the 1920s (Fig. 1.5). Both Semple and Davis influenced many students in their classrooms, and Semple particularly was effective in expressing ideas of environmental control with her colorful writing. The opening sentences of her widely read book, *Influences of Geographic Environment* (1911), are often quoted to show her skill in expressing deterministic ideas:

> Man is a product of the earth's surface. This means not merely that he is a child of the earth, dust of her dust; but that the earth has mothered him, fed him, set him tasks, directed his thoughts, confronted him with difficulties that have strengthened his body and sharpened his wits, given him his problems of navigation or irrigation, and at the same time whispered hints for their solution.

By contrast, geographers in France during the late nineteenth and early twentieth centuries generally were not impressed by ideas of the environmental determinists. Under the leadership of Paul Vidal de la Blache (1845–1918), French geographers did pioneer work in human geography and concluded that the physical environment offers people a variety of possibilities from which to select ways of using their habitat. The selection from among the possibilities, according to Vidal, is made by the inhabitants according to their *genre de vie* (way of life or culture). This interpretation of the relationship of people with their habitat, called **possibilism**, eventually found greater acceptance than environmental determinism among geographers.

By the 1920s, a number of geographers in the United States also were vigorously criticizing environmental determinism and offering alternative ideas. These critics pointed out the tendency of determinists to view the world only in terms of cause and effect and noted that the answers of the determinists to questions regarding the relationships of humans and their environment were predetermined and unvarying. Harlan Barrows (1877–1960) of the University of Chicago offered the alternative of "geography as human ecology," an appeal to focus geographic studies on human *adaptations* to environmental conditions. Carl Sauer (1889–1975), a geographer at the University of California, Berkeley, proposed another alternative. He advocated that geographers turn their investigations to how groups of people, within the framework of their culture, have transformed the natural landscapes into **cultural landscapes**. Working with colleagues in history and anthropology, Sauer became the generally ac-

(a)

(b)

FIGURE 1.5

(a) William Morris Davis (Courtesy of Harvard University) and (b) Ellen Churchill Semple (Courtesy of Clark University) were early twentieth-century geography professors at major universities in the United States. Both contributed to the popularity of environmental determinism and influenced many students.

knowledged leader in the development of cultural geography in the United States. His program of study was dedicated to examining the visible works of cultural groups that occupy an area—the buildings, fields, lines of transportation, settlements, and other features that collectively form the cultural landscape and give distinctiveness to individual areas. (See *Cultural Landscapes: Carl Sauer and the Cultural Landscape.*)

The long-term focus of geographers on place-to-place variations in the associations of people with their habitat has been enriched over the past century by growing recognition of the dynamic role of culture. Later chapters in this book will reflect the importance now assigned to culture as a geographic variable.

GEOGRAPHY: A SPATIAL DISCIPLINE

➤ On the basis of its spatial approach, geography is generally considered to be a unique field of study.

How does geography differ from history and from other academic fields?

Can geography be regarded as a science?

In view of the many changes in emphases and reorientations in geography over the centuries, and considering the great variety of topics that are examined by geographers today, is it even possible to claim that geography is a unified field with a central aim and purpose? Immanuel Kant (1724–1804), a German philosopher who also lectured on geography, pointed out in his lectures that geography and history cannot be classified with other fields of learning that have different origins. History is the study of things as they occur in time; it employs a *chronological approach.* Geography is the study of the earth; it uses a *spatial approach.* Thus, geography and history are distinctive fields of learning because of *how* they go about studying things, not *what* things they study. Both are *holistic* disciplines that make no attempt to limit their subject matter. In contrast, most other traditional fields of learning are classified and defined on the basis of their subject matter or on what segment of reality they study. Although generations of geographers have attempted to refine definitions of their field, none has yet provided a more logical or generally accepted rationale for the place of geography in the realm of learning than did Kant in the eighteenth century. (See *The Geographer's Notebook: Pattison's Four Traditions of Geography.*)

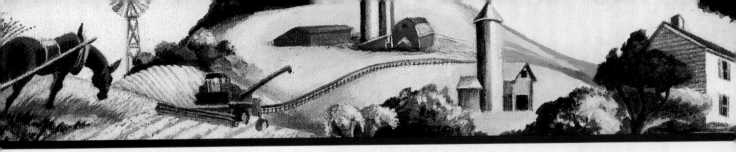

CULTURAL LANDSCAPES

Carl O. Sauer and Cultural Landscapes

Cultural landscapes are segments of the earth's surface that show evidence of human activity. In the process of occupying an area, people change the appearance of the landscape by such actions as altering the original vegetation; plowing the soil and planting crops; constructing buildings, fences, and roads; establishing towns and cities; rearranging the natural drainage; and even resculpturing the land surface by excavating some sites and filling others. Visible results of these activities—such as agricultural fields, roads, structures, settlements, canals, and landfills—are the individual features of cultural landscapes.

The principal scholar responsible for promoting the concept of cultural landscapes in American geography was Carl O. Sauer (1889–1975). Born in Missouri to parents of German heritage, Sauer obtained some of his formal education in Germany. His early life, however, was spent primarily in the American Middle West, and he completed a doctoral degree in geography at the University of Chicago in 1915. Most of Sauer's lengthy career as a geography professor was at the University of California, Berkeley, where he enjoyed close professional associations with colleagues in anthropology and history. Soon after arriving in Berkeley, he published a monograph, ''The Morphology of Landscape'' (1925), that subsequently had great influence because it turned the attention of many geographers to studies of cultural landscapes. Sauer

also focused much of his work on early human societies, the origins of agriculture, European exploration and colonization in the Americas, and the impact of human activities on the environment. His pioneering and innovative work in cultural geography led to widespread recognition of Sauer as one of the discipline's greatest scholars.

In contrast to ''natural'' landscapes that are formed by the processes of nature, cultural landscapes

Carl Sauer (Courtesy of the University of California, Berkeley)

are artificial in the sense that they are created by human processes. In fact, elements of an area's natural landscape usually are substantially altered or even destroyed as a cultural landscape is created. The transformation of natural landscapes into cultural landscapes has been going on throughout human history; now the imprint of human activity is evident over vast areas. Some geographers express doubt that a pristine natural landscape remains in any part of the world. It is probable that even in remote and uninhabited areas, such elements as the natural vegetation and surface materials have been altered in character. For example, we know that certain types of human-created pollution can be transported by winds and currents in the atmosphere and affect areas that are far removed from the source of the pollution.

The form and function of cultural landscape features have important diagnostic value to a geographer because they reflect the nature of the culture that created the features. By examining such things as (1) the spatial arrangement of fields, roads, and buildings and (2) architectural styles, building materials and techniques, and intended function of structures, the geographer can learn a great deal about the culture or cultures that have occupied an area. A culture's technological abilities and skills, level of economic development, religious beliefs, social structure, goals, and aspirations often are evident in the landscape. Furthermore, because cultural landscape features often remain long after the demise of the people who created them, it often is possible to reconstruct the character of an earlier culture through study of the landscape.

Carl Sauer recognized that a cultural landscape evolves over time and that comprehension of a present landscape requires careful examination of developments in the past. In his interpretation, it is the functioning of people within the framework of their culture over time that brings about transformation of a natural landscape into a cultural landscape. In the case of an area that has been inhabited for a lengthy period, particularly if two or more different cultural groups have been involved, the present cultural landscape can be complex and challenging to interpret.

THOUGHT QUESTIONS

1. The rural Middle West was the setting for most of Carl Sauer's experiences during the early part of his life. Do you believe that a person who has grown up in a rural environment is more likely to be sensitive to landscape changes than someone who has lived only in a city? Why or why not?

2. How is the level of technology possessed by a group of people likely to influence the cultural landscape it creates?

3. Is there a structure in the cultural landscape where you live that no longer serves the function for which it was originally intended? If so, what was its original function and for what purpose is it used now? Can you think of a use for the structure that would be more valuable than its current one?

4. Is there a cultural landscape feature in your area than can be associated with a particular cultural group? If so, explain how.

Geography is becoming recognized increasingly as a spatial science—a science that has as its primary responsibility the recognition and explanation of spatial patterns. But is geography a science in the same sense as the "hard" sciences that seek to identify universal laws and employ theory and the scientific method in their investigations? The approach of scholars in such sciences often is identified as **nomothetic**, meaning that the eventual objective is to discover scientific laws. Studies that employ the scientific method are carried out in a deductive manner; that is, hypotheses are formulated based on theory and then tested against real world evidence. Although many geographers forcefully argue for a nomothetic geography, others (usually those less concerned about the recognition of their field as a hard science) are more comfortable with the **idiographic** approach, which begins with study of individual phenomena and progresses inductively to general conclusions. It remains to be seen if geography eventually will become established as a hard science. There seems little doubt, however, that both nomothetic and idiographic approaches will continue to be employed in geographical studies for many years.

THE SUBFIELDS OF GEOGRAPHY

➤ Although geography is unified by its spatial approach, the field commonly is divided along subject matter lines.

What are geography's broadest subfields and how do they differ?

Although it is important to recognize that geography is a unified field on the basis of its spatial approach, it has become commonplace to divide the discipline along the lines of its subject matter. Thus *physical geography* and *human geography* are widely recognized as the discipline's broadest subfields (Fig. 1.6). This division makes evident the fact that geography is associated with both the physical sciences and the social sciences. Physical geography involves applying the geographic approach in study of the physical earth or natural environment. Similarly, human geography involves applying the geographic approach in examining the world's human population, including the great variety of human attributes and activities. The subject matter in physical and human geography usually is investigated topically (i.e., by individual topic). However, *regional geography* offers the alternative of stud-

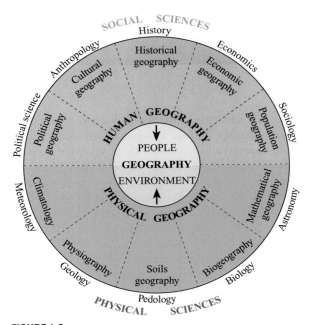

FIGURE 1.6

The subfields of geography. This diagram identifies the main subject matter areas within human geography and physical geography and shows closely related disciplines in the social sciences and the physical sciences.

ying physical and human subject matter within the setting of a particular region of the world.

Regional Geography

➤ Regional geography provides an important alternative to topical studies in geography.

What is a region?

How do uniform regions and functional regions differ?

To the geographer, a **region** is not merely an arbitrarily chosen area. Rather, it is a carefully defined and delimited segment of the earth's surface that has one or more unifying criteria. Two types of regions are generally recognized: *uniform* (or *homogeneous*) *regions* and *functional* (or *nodal*) *regions* (Fig. 1.7). Uniform regions are defined by a criterion that prevails with generally the same intensity throughout the region. A good example is a political region, such as a state or country, in which a particular governmental

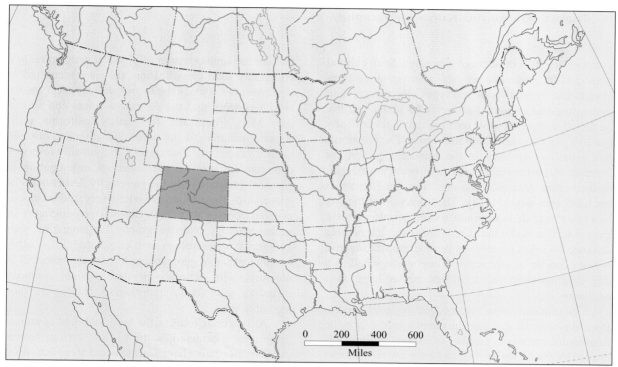

a) A Uniform Region — The State of Colorado

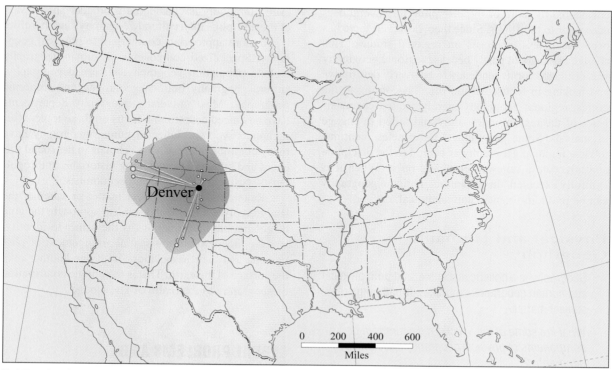

b) A Functional Region — The Tributary Area of Denver

FIGURE 1.7

Example maps of (a) a uniform region and (b) a functional region. How do these two types of regions differ?

system is in effect throughout the region. Such cultural criteria as language and religion or environmental elements like vegetation or soil types also can serve to define uniform regions. Functional or nodal regions, on the other hand, involve territory that is functionally tied to a place (node) within the region. The functional link usually is strongest in the immediate vicinity of the node and decreases in intensity toward the margins of the region. One example of a functional region is the trade area around a city. The attraction of the city as a place to trade is strongest among people who live closest to that node and decreases as the intervening distance becomes greater. As these examples suggest, regions can be of any scale. Some are as small as a city neighborhood, while others are as large as a continent.

Geographers have engaged in regional studies from the time of the ancient Greeks to the present. Regional studies by a number of French geographers tutored by Paul Vidal de la Blache are among the most elegant of those prepared in the twentieth century. In the United States, regional geography generally was considered the core of the discipline for several decades prior to the 1960s. Since then, however, there has been much less emphasis on regional studies. This change came about partly because regional geography was criticized for its tendency to be overly descriptive and lacking in focus. All too often, according to the critics, regional geography merely recited characteristics of the region under study and failed to engage in analysis. Some geographers nevertheless continue to view regional geography as central to the discipline and advocate a renewed emphasis on it. When it is skillfully executed, they point out, regional geography can be problem-oriented and analytical.

Physical and Human Geography

➤ Geography is a holistic discipline, and both physical and human geography embrace a broad range of subject matter.

What are some of the specialized courses in or components of physical geography and human geography?

The topical approach traditionally employed in both physical and human geography involves focusing attention on individual subject matter components. It is, of course, the various components of the physical earth that are the subject matter of physical geography. In a commonly used classification, they are identified as the *lithosphere* (land), the *hydrosphere* (water), the *atmosphere* (air), and the *biosphere* (plant and animal life). More specifically, the earth's landforms, soils, mineral resources, water bodies, weather and climate, natural vegetation, and wildlife, individually or in any combination, may be the object of investigation in physical geography. In the geography departments of universities, these topics are intensively studied in specialized courses with such titles as physiography or geomorphology, hydrogeography, biogeography, soils geography, meteorology, and climatology. It is obvious that physical geographers have many interests in common with scholars in the physical sciences, including geologists, hydrologists, biologists, and meteorologists.

As this book reflects, the broad subfield of human geography is centered on the world's various human populations, their characteristics, and their activities. Some geographers use the alternate title of "cultural geography" for this subfield. Human geography, however, commonly is considered a broader subdivision of the discipline than cultural geography, and therefore it is a more appropriate counterpart to physical geography. Specialized components of human geography include population geography, historical geography, cultural geography, political geography, and economic geography. Most university geography departments have advanced courses that focus on these topics. Geographers who specialize in human geography have many common interests with scholars in the social sciences and humanities, including historians, anthropologists, political scientists, and economists.

Regardless of the subject matter or whether the study involves a regional or topical approach, the goal of geographic investigations is the same: to identify, analyze, and explain the spatial arrangement of phenomena and their associations with one another over the surface of the earth. That is the unique contribution of geography to the realm of knowledge.

GLOBAL PROBLEMS AND HUMAN GEOGRAPHY

➤ The study of human geography is a means of gaining a solid understanding of some of the most critical problems in the world today.

What are some critical world problems that are linked to the study of human geography?

How can knowledge of human geography help identify solutions to these global problems?

In addition to being a major subfield of the discipline of geography, human geography is also an excellent vehicle for analyzing many of the world's most severe problems. The subject matter of human geography encompasses these problems, and the spatial approach and holistic character of geography are especially helpful in investigating them. Many experts in a variety of fields agree that among the most pressing contemporary global problems are the following:

1. *Population Growth* Many authorities have concluded that the world's most critical problem is the burgeoning growth of human population. Now estimated to total about 5.5 billion, world population at its current rate of growth will double the present total in about 40 years. Of course, some parts of the world are more heavily populated than others, and some have much higher rates of increase in human numbers than others. Programs to control population growth have been implemented in many countries, but often the methods of restricting growth are resisted by people for various cultural reasons. One approach to easing the population problem is increasing food production or improving the availability of food in the world's troubled areas. But to accomplish this is extremely difficult because areas with critical population problems also tend to be economically poor and therefore are unable to afford these means of increasing food supplies.

2. *Cultural and Ethnic Conflict* Another serious problem in many parts of the world is conflict between two or more human groups that occupy the same or nearby areas or countries. These conflicts usually are the consequence of differences in traditions, religious beliefs, languages, political ideologies, or economic opportunities. Other causes are historical events, sometimes ones in the distant past. Long-standing animosity between adjacent groups of people often is the basis for such developments as revolutions, civil wars, political fragmentation, and changes in government. A few contemporary examples are the conflicts in the Middle East, the recent political fragmentation of the former Soviet Union, and civil war in the former Yugoslavia.

3. *Economic Development* On the basis of major differences in their level of economic development, the world's countries are effectively divided into two groups: the wealthy and the poor. The wealthy or developed countries (DCs) are ones that have diversified and modernized their economies to increase their output of goods and services and provide their general population with a relatively high standard of living. In contrast, the poor or less developed countries (LDCs) continue to rely on traditional livelihoods—usually agriculture. For a variety of reasons, they have not adequately improved their economic output to significantly raise the living standard of their people. Their failure to at least match the economic growth of the wealthy countries has resulted in a widening gap between the two groups. The importance of this contrast in economic development is accentuated by the fact that the poor countries constitute nearly four-fifths of all countries in the world and contain more than three-fourths of the world's population. Many authorities interpret this maldistribution of wealth as a serious threat to global stability and urge the establishment of programs to accelerate economic development in the poor countries.

4. *Expanding Urbanization* Problems of many types—housing, employment, traffic congestion, pollution—are the consequences of ongoing growth of cities throughout the world. The most rapid urbanization at present is in countries troubled by high rates of population growth. In the past, migrations to other lands have been a means of escaping local and regional population pressures. Today, however, there are far fewer opportunities and much greater obstacles for potential migrants—particularly when the move is to another country. Often the only available alternative for people in overpopulated rural areas is to move to a city within their own country. This, in turn, has caused enormous crowding and associated health and welfare problems in the urban centers of these countries.

Pattison's Four Traditions of Geography

In an article published in the *Journal of Geography* in 1964, William Pattison (b. 1921) noted that the several attempts by prominent American geographers to define the field seemed to be excessively narrow or restrictive in character. In truth, geographers generally have refused to restrict the nature and scope of their work to make it conform to these definitions. Nevertheless, according to Pattison, geographic studies do exhibit a broad consistency, a unity that can be recognized in "a small number of distinct but affiliated traditions" in the profession. Pattison, a professor of geography at the University of Chicago for most of his career, specified four traditions that are "of great age and have passed into American geography as parts of a general legacy of Western thought." A brief summary of each follows.

1. *The Spatial Tradition* The spatial focus of geography has been widely recognized since Immanuel Kant called attention to it in the eighteenth century. From the time of its earli-

est practice, geography has dealt with such spatial attributes as the location, direction, distance, and extent of features on the earth's surface. Modern geographers have expanded this tradition in studies of spatial interactions (i.e., the movement of phenomena across the space separating places on the earth's surface) and the spatial arrangements (or geometry) of phenomena on the surface. The discovery of regularities in spatial interactions and arrangements on maps has led to the development by modern geographers of theories and models that deal with the causes of such patterns.

2. *The Area Studies Tradition* Examination of the content and characteristics of areas, or regions, is a tradition in geography that also

The Spatial Tradition: Transportation on the Rhine River. (R. Gabler)

The Area Studies Tradition: An agricultural region in the Nebraska Sand Hills. (R. Gabler)

The Man–Land Tradition: Valley settlements in the Alps.
(R. Gabler)

The Earth Science Tradition: The Grand Teton Mountains.
(R. Gabler)

can be traced to classical time—especially to the work of Strabo. Modern geographers, in their effort to comprehend the complexity of regions, have continued to perfect techniques of regional study. Although not emphasized as much now as in earlier decades, regional studies are still considered by many geographers to be a very important part of their discipline.

3. *The Man-Land Tradition* This terminology used by Pattison was standard at the time that he wrote. However, the current sensitivity to gender discrimination demands a different title, such as the human-environment tradition. The associations of people and their natural environment have attracted the interest of geographers over many centuries. Although this tradition was blemished by some geographers who advocated environmental determinism, it experienced a twentieth-century rejuvenation as others recognized the dynamic role of cul-

ture in the relationships of people with their habitat.

4. *The Earth Science Tradition* One can accurately say that geography has always involved study of the physical earth—its landforms, atmosphere, water bodies, and other physical components. This is apparent in the close association of geography with geology over time. As late as the nineteenth century some European geographers maintained that the subject matter of their field should be restricted to the physical earth. Despite the later development of human geography and establishment of close ties with disciplines in the social sciences, geography's reputation as an earth science remains strong.

THOUGHT QUESTIONS

1. Can you identify possible linkages of the four traditions that might unify all work in geography?
2. Do these four traditions conform with what you expected to find emphasized in geography? If not, how do they differ from your expectations?

5. *Environmental Deterioration*   Human health and well-being and even the survival of many organisms are being threatened by a host of stresses on the physical environment. Called on to support an ever-increasing population and substantial improvements in living standards in many areas, the earth has been seriously abused by accelerating exploitation of its resources and the creation and careless handling of hazardous wastes. The depletion of soils and certain minerals, the reduction of forests, the pollution of air and water, and the formation of acid rain have become severe environmental problems in a variety of regions. Particularly disturbing is the increasing evidence of deterioration in the ozone layer in the upper atmosphere and of global warming, both of which seem to be closely linked to certain aspects of air pollution. The ozone layer is critical to life on earth because it regulates the amount of ultraviolet radiation that reaches the surface. Increased human exposure to ultraviolet radiation resulting from ozone layer deterioration is expected to cause more skin cancer in the future. If global warming persists, accompanying changes in the nature and pattern of climates most likely will disrupt the present spatial arrangement of human livelihoods and settlements. Implementing effective solutions to environmental problems obviously is of extreme importance to all humanity.

The scope of this book is not limited to these five problems, but they are carefully explored in turn in several of the following sections and chapters.

THE USE OF MAPS AND OTHER TOOLS OF GEOGRAPHY

➤ A globe is the only true representation of the earth, but maps have served for centuries as the principal tool of geographers.

What conditions contributed to the inaccuracy of early maps, including those from the Middle Ages?

Why is a globe more accurate than even a modern map of the world?

Among the tools and techniques used in geographic studies, some are shared with other sciences. For example, computers commonly are used now in all disciplines for such purposes as organizing, storing, retrieving, analyzing, and displaying information and data. Also, idealized models are employed in several fields, including geography, as a means of applying theory to real world situations. Scholars have devised a wide variety of models, including ones that deal with such topics as population growth, economic development, and patterns of land use. It is in the frequent and varied use of maps and remote sensing imagery, however, that geographic studies usually are different. For the examination of phenomena that occur on the surface of the earth, maps have served for centuries as the principal tool of geographers. During recent decades, aerial photographs and imagery of the earth's surface obtained by space vehicles have come to be extremely valuable alternatives to maps.

We cannot be certain when maps were first devised and used by humans, but it was undoubtedly thousands of years ago. Of course, early maps were extremely crude by modern standards and had limited usefulness. Because of early mapmakers' restricted knowledge about the world beyond their immediate location and their lack of precise instruments, the maps that they produced were grossly inaccurate. In Europe even as late as the Middle Ages, a period when religion dominated intellectual activity, very crude *T-O maps* were prepared to portray the earth (Fig. 1.8). Within the circular margin of the typical T-O map were the three continents known at that time (Europe, Asia, and Africa), and these land areas were separated by the Mediterranean, Red, and Black Seas, which together roughly form the letter ''T.'' These maps were ''oriented'' toward Jerusalem and the East where paradise was assumed to exist. Reasonably accurate maps of large areas did not appear until the sixteenth century, and the practice of publishing collections of maps together as atlases began at about the same time.

The accumulation of vast amounts of information by explorers during the following centuries and the eventual precise surveys of land areas with scientific instruments have made possible the highly accurate maps available for use and study by recent generations. The preparation of maps is a subfield of geography called **cartography**. In the past, cartographers drafted maps entirely by hand. Now, however, maps commonly are prepared mechanically, making particular use of computers.

A map is defined as a graphic representation of all or part of the earth's surface, drawn to scale. Because the earth has the general shape of a *sphere*, only a globe can approach complete geometric accuracy in portraying the surface of a planet. When the curved surface of the earth is represented on a flat map, geometric distortion is inevitable. Nearly all maps consequently contain a degree of inaccuracy; the only possible exception is maps of very small areas that have a negligible amount of surface curvature. A cartographer can minimize or confine the distortion in a map of a large area, when it is desirable to do so, by manipulating the **map grid** formed by *parallels* and *meridians*.

Map Projections

➤ The effectiveness of a map depends on the selection of an appropriate projection.

What three important properties should be considered when selecting a map projection?

The arrangement of a map's grid is called a **map projection** because a simple means of transferring the par-

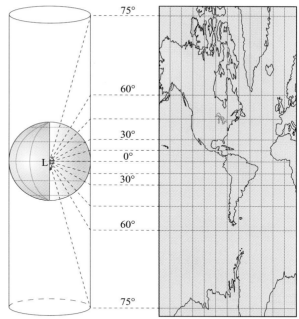

L – Light source in center of globe

FIGURE 1.9

Projecting a globe's grid to a flat surface with a light source is a nonmathematical means of establishing the pattern of parallels and meridians for a map.

FIGURE 1.8

An example of a T-O map from medieval Europe. With such maps we can judge the powerful influence of religion and the limited knowledge of the world among most Europeans during the Middle Ages.

allels and meridians of a globe onto a flat surface is by projecting them with a light source as illustrated in Figure 1.9. Many different projections are now available for use, including some that have been designed mathematically. It is important to remember that no single projection can accurately preserve the characteristics of the grid on a globe. In evaluating a projection, the following questions need to be asked:

1. Is it an equal-area projection (Fig. 1.10a)? That is, does the projection allow areas throughout the map to be shown in the same ratio as they exist on the earth's surface? An equal-area projection is particularly important if the map is to be used for showing worldwide distributions.

2. Does the projection allow the *shapes* of land areas to be accurately retained on the map? Conformal projections (Fig. 1.10b) have this quality, which is valuable for educational purposes because it facilitates recognizing the areas.

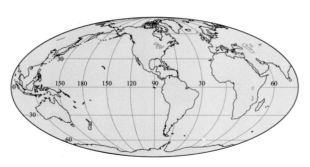

a) Mollweide (equal area)

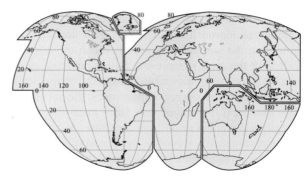

b) Western Paragraphic (conformal)

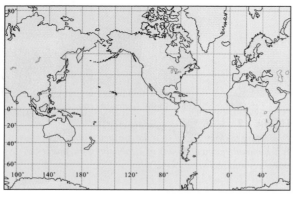

c) Mercator Projection

FIGURE 1.10

Examples of (a) an equal area, (b) a conformal projection, and (c) the Mercator projection. Each projection has properties that make it appropriate for some types of maps but not others.

3. Does the projection allow a line of constant direction to appear as a straight line on the map (Fig. 1.10c)? A projection with this quality is valuable when the map is to be used for purposes of navigation.

It is impossible for any one projection to incorporate all three of these properties; no "ideal" projection exists. It is necessary, therefore, that the cartographer select a projection with the qualities that allow the most accurate rendering of the map with regard to the map's eventual use.

Determining Locations

➤ When using a map for locational purposes, we may determine either the mathematical location or the relative location of a place or feature.

How is the most precise mathematical location obtained?

Why is relative location likely to be more valuable to a geographer?

Maps have become commonplace in our society and now are used not only by geographers in their study and research, but by people in many activities. Almost everyone uses road maps; they are probably more frequently consulted than any other type of map. We also see maps daily in newspapers and television reports to illustrate places in the news. Whether used by a layperson or a professional geographer, then, maps are an important means of obtaining and recording information, making comparisons and showing relationships between places, and carrying out a variety of analyses.

Undoubtedly maps are consulted most often to simply determine the location of a place or feature on

a) Parallels

b) Meridians

FIGURE 1.11

(a) Parallels identify latitude or position relative to the Equator, and (b) meridians identify longitude or position relative to the Prime Meridian.

servatory in Greenwich, England. Like the Prime Meridian, other lines of longitude (also called *meridians*) extend from pole to pole on the globe (Fig. 1.11b). Thus, each meridian is only a half-circle, as opposed to the full circle formed by parallels. Because latitude and longitude involve segments of circles and half-circles, *degrees* are used as the unit of measurement.

The mathematical location of the city of Memphis, Tennessee, for example, is 35° north latitude and 90° west longitude (Fig. 1.12). Remember that latitude is the identification of a position relative to the Equator and longitude is the expression of position relative to the Prime Meridian. No two places share the same latitude–longitude position on the globe; only Memphis is located at 35° N, 90° W. (On maps of relatively large areas, such as the United States, the use of degrees alone is satisfactory to identify location. On maps of small areas, however, greater precision is possible in locating features like farmsteads, buildings, and the intersection of streets.) If a higher degree of accuracy is desired in locating a feature on the earth's surface, the measurement can make use of minutes as a subdivision of degrees (one degree = 60 minutes) and seconds as a subdivision of minutes (one minute = 60 seconds). The symbol ′ is used for minutes and ″ for seconds. For example, city hall in Memphis has a mathematical location of 35°08′55″ N, 90°03′04″ W.

Although mathematical location is valuable information for certain purposes, we consult maps more often to determine the **relative location** of a place or feature. A map can show us that Atlanta, Georgia, is located in the southern Appalachian Mountains, that Chicago, Illinois, is near the southern end of Lake

the earth's surface. We can find the precise **mathematical** or **absolute location** of a place or feature by using the map's grid. Mathematical location is expressed in terms of latitude (position relative to the Equator) and longitude (position relative to the Prime Meridian). The Equator, a complete circle on the globe that forms the circumference equidistant from the North Pole and South Pole, is the 0° line of latitude. On a globe (but not necessarily on a map), other latitude lines are parallel with the equator; therefore, they often are referred to as *parallels* (Fig. 1.11a). The *Prime Meridian*, which serves as the 0° line of longitude, was selected by international consensus in 1884 as the north–south line passing through the Royal Ob-

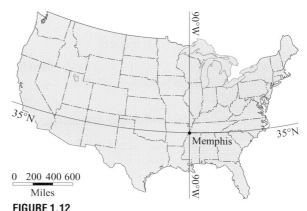

FIGURE 1.12

The mathematical location, or latitude and longitude, of Memphis, Tennessee.

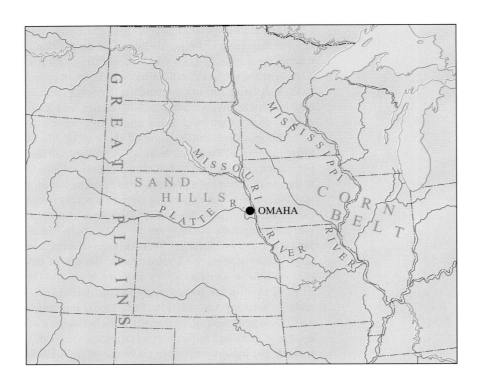

FIGURE 1.13

The relative location, or regional setting, of Omaha, Nebraska.

Michigan, and that Omaha, Nebraska, is in the western Corn Belt (Fig. 1.13). All three of these examples are expressions of relative location—that is, the location of a place relative to a larger or more generally known area or feature. Relative location is employed commonly in geography because it can suggest possible spatial and functional relations (for example, the role of Omaha as a processing center for agricultural products from the western Corn Belt).

Determining Distances

➤ A scale is the means by which a map can be used to determine the distance between places on the earth's surface.

What are three common methods of indicating the scale of a map?

Another common use of maps is the determination of *distance* between places on the earth's surface. We usually consult a map when we need to learn the distance between our home and the hometown of a new friend, between Chicago and Tokyo, or between Los Angeles and Honolulu, for example. To measure dis-

tances on a map, we must employ the **map scale**. Each map is drawn to scale in order to represent proportionally and accurately the earth's surface. The scale of a map is the means by which we are able to convert the distance between two points on the map into the distance between the same two points on the earth's surface. The scale of any given map may be indicated in one of three ways (Fig. 1.14): (1) a *verbal scale* is a statement printed on the map that explains how a particular distance on the map is to be converted into distance on the earth's surface. An example is ''one inch to ten miles,'' meaning that a distance of one inch on the map is equivalent to ten miles on the surface of the earth. (2) A *linear scale* is merely a line or bar divided into segments that represent an indicated distance on the earth's surface. (3) A *fractional scale* may appear on the map as a numerical ratio (e.g., 1:250,000) or a fraction (e.g., 1/62,500). When a fractional scale is applied, it is important to remember that the same unit of measure must be used when comparing distance on the map with distance on the earth's surface. For example if the scale is 1:250,000, a distance of one *inch* on the map represents a distance of 250,000 *inches* on the surface of the earth.

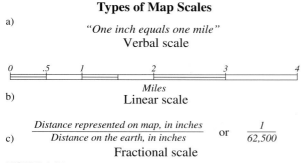

Types of Map Scales

a)

"One inch equals one mile"
Verbal scale

b)

Miles
Linear scale

c)

$$\frac{Distance\ represented\ on\ map,\ in\ inches}{Distance\ on\ the\ earth,\ in\ inches} \quad or \quad \frac{1}{62,500}$$

Fractional scale

FIGURE 1.14

Examples of (a) a verbal scale, (b) a linear scale, and (c) a fractional scale. At least one type of scale identification is an essential feature of every map.

Maps with little detail that represent large areas, such as a continent or the entire world, commonly are identified as *small-scale maps*; those that show small areas with much detail, such as the downtown area of a city with individual streets and buildings, are called *large-scale maps*. In recalling this distinction, it is helpful to remember that 1/30,000,000—a scale appropriate for a map of a continent—is a smaller fraction than 1/10,000, which might serve as the scale for a map of an urban business district. In addition to its role in the determination of distances, scale obviously governs the degree of informational detail that can be portrayed on a map.

Examining Distributions

➤ Maps allow us to examine the pattern, density, and dispersion of phenomena as they are distributed over the earth's surface.

How do choropleth, isoline, and dot maps differ in their portrayal of geographic distributions?

In geography, maps are particularly valuable for examination of the spatial distribution of phenomena over the earth's surface. The distribution of population, mineral resources, precipitation, and per capita income are a few examples of the great many things that a geographer might examine on a map. The mapped distributions of phenomena pose questions and suggest possible answers of a geographical nature. Often a question raised by the distribution of one phenomenon can be answered at least partially by the distribution of another. The distributional characteristics

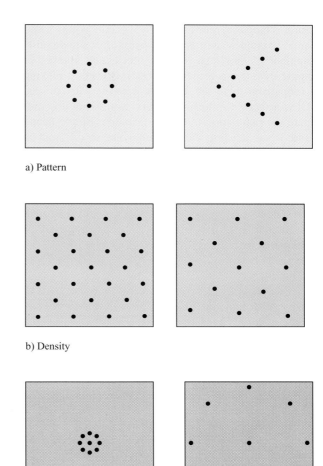

a) Pattern

b) Density

c) Dispersion

FIGURE 1.15

The distribution of phenomena on maps can be identified in terms of (a) pattern, (b) density, and (c) dispersion.

that we examine on a map are *pattern*, *density*, and *dispersion*. (See Fig. 1.15.)

The pattern may be random or have some recognizable geometric arrangement, such as linear, rectangular, or circular. For example, the distribution of towns along a railroad may be linear, the arrangement of rural fields in Iowa may be rectangular, and the rural subscribers to a metropolitan newspaper may be distributed in a circular pattern. The density of a phenomenon is based on how frequently it occurs within a unit area. Examples are number of people per square mile, number of buildings per city block, and number of apple trees per acre. Density often is used in making comparisons between different areas that vary in size. Obviously, it would not be very worthwhile to compare the population totals of states like Rhode Island and Texas because the two areas are so different in size; on the other hand, if we compare the population density (number of people per square mile) it is possible to arrive at more meaningful conclusions. The third distributional characteristic, dispersion, refers to the spacing of the phenomena. Again, a unit area, such as a square mile or a city block, must be employed for comparison purposes. Within the unit area, the mapped phenomena may range from widely dispersed to highly agglomerated.

Three types of maps that commonly are used to show geographic distributions are *choropleth*, *isoline*, and *dot maps*. The character of the distribution and the nature of the data available to the cartographer will

help determine which type is selected. Each involves the application of a different cartographic technique.

The choropleth map employs a range of colors, shades, or patterns to differentiate areas according to each area's quantity of the phenomenon being represented (Fig. 1.16a). The quantities usually are grouped into classes (for example, 0–9, 10–19, 20–29, . . .), with each represented on the map by a unique shade, color, or pattern. The usual practice is for higher quantities to be represented by darker shades, colors, or patterns, and for lower quantities to be indicated by lighter shades, colors, or patterns. Choropleth maps are particularly amenable to portraying distributions by political areas, such as the number of Methodist churches per county or the number of members of Congress per state. In such maps, the distributional detail is governed by the size of area selected.

The isoline map shows distributional patterns by means of a system of lines, each of which joins points on the map of equal value (Fig. 1.16b). If the map portrays the distribution of annual precipitation, for

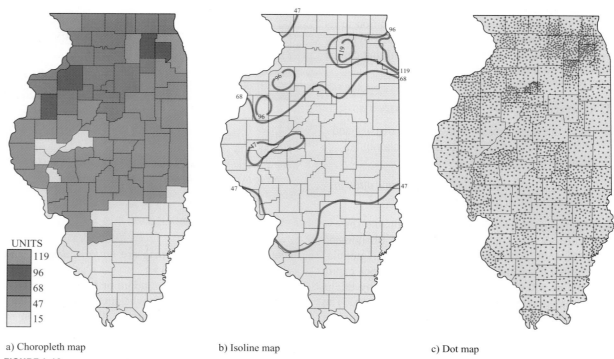

a) Choropleth map   b) Isoline map   c) Dot map

FIGURE 1.16

Examples of three kinds of maps: (a) choropleth, (b) isoline, and (c) dot.

example, one line may connect all points that received 30 inches of precipitation, the next line may run through all points that received 32 inches, and so on. To enhance the visual impact, the cartographer may use a range of colors, shades, or patterns to fill the spaces between adjacent isolines. An advantage of the isoline map is that it shows gradients in the distribution pattern. A steep gradient (that is, a relatively abrupt change over a horizontal distance) is indicated when the isolines are closely spaced, and a gradual gradient is represented by wide spacing of the isolines. In most cases, an isoline map provides more detail of the distribution pattern than a choropleth map.

The dot map is a particularly effective means of portraying geographic distributions (Fig. 1.16c). If the distribution involves a relatively small number of items, it may be possible for each dot to represent a single item and be placed on the map precisely where that item occurs. When the number of items is large, however, it becomes necessary to have each dot represent a selected quantity (e.g., one dot represents 50 people, or one dot represents 20 houses) and be placed in a representative location on the map. A dot map may employ dots of only one size or it may use dots of several sizes with each larger dot representing a proportionally greater quantity of items.

Although not as commonly used as choropleth, isoline, and dot maps, *three-dimensional maps* provide a visually impressive alternative means of representing distributions (Fig. 1.17). Their preparation is a good

deal more complicated and, to be effective, they must be carefully designed. Unlike conventional maps, which represent the earth's surface as seen from directly above, three-dimensional maps must have the perspective of the viewer carefully determined. If successfully executed, these maps usually can be interpreted more easily than alternative types.

In recent years, geographers increasingly have become aware of the role of *mental maps* in the spatial behavior of people and their perceptions of places. People formulate mental maps in their heads, based on their experiences, attitudes, beliefs, and even rumors. Mental maps may be highly subjective and may depart greatly from reality. Yet people commonly make decisions on their routes of travel, on destinations for vacations and business, and on places to avoid based on their mental maps. For individuals with faulty mental maps, substantial unnecessary costs in travel time and energy consumed, together with apprehension and poor decisions, may result (Fig. 1.18). The improvement of a student's mental maps may be one of the most valuable benefits derived from a geography course.

Remote Sensing Imagery

➤ In addition to maps, remote sensing imagery is an increasingly valuable tool for geographic studies.

What is remote sensing and what type of images does it provide?

Technological development during the twentieth century has given geographers a variety of new materials to use along with maps in studying the surface of the earth. These materials are mostly images of parts of the earth's surface that have been obtained by instruments (sensors) aboard aircraft and spacecraft. The process of obtaining these images is called **remote sensing** because of the relatively great distance between the sensors and the earth's surface. Remote sensing imagery is highly varied in character, and new uses for it are continuing to be discovered.

The earliest remote sensing images available for use by geographers were photographs taken with cameras aboard aircraft. From about 1930 until the present, aerial photographs have given us an alternate means of locating phenomena on the earth's surface, examining patterns of land use, determining the spatial extent of environmental pollution, and carrying out other geographical tasks. With overlapping pairs of air pho-

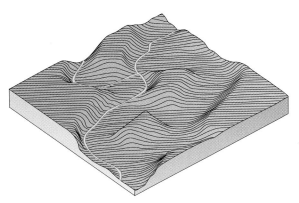

FIGURE 1.17

An example of a three-dimensional map. The viewer's perspective must be carefully chosen for this type of map to be effective.

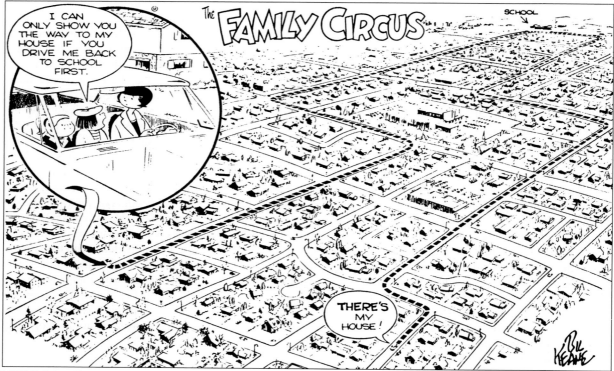

2-13 1972, The Register and Tribune Syndicate

FIGURE 1.18

This cartoon illustrates how a mental map can influence human behavior. (Reprinted with special permission of King Features Syndicate.)

tos taken from different angles, we are able to study the land surface in three dimensions through the lenses of a stereoscope (Fig. 1.19). In recent years, the versatility of aerial photography has been increased by the development of *infrared* film. An advantage of infrared photography is that atmospheric haze does not obscure the subject. The detection of disease in crops and other plants commonly involves the use of infrared photos because in them only healthy plants appear in a bright red color (Fig. 1.20).

Since 1960 artificial satellites orbiting the earth have provided even more remote platforms from which to obtain images of the planet. From distances between several hundred to more than 20,000 miles above the earth, these orbiting spacecraft have provided spectacular views of the earth's surface (Fig.

1.21). In addition to standard and infrared photographs, satellite images are obtained by a variety of other devices including *thermal scanners*, *multispectral scanners*, and *radar*. Because of its ability to penetrate darkness, cloud cover, and vegetation, radar is particularly versatile in detecting terrain irregularities and cultural features on the earth's surface.

Geographers have made generous use of images from data recorded by LANDSAT satellites since 1972. Data obtained by multispectral scanners aboard these satellites are processed by computers to obtain images of the earth's surface. Such images can be extremely valuable for such purposes as detecting land-use changes, resources, and environmental pollution. Many new uses for satellite imagery of the earth undoubtedly will be discovered in the future.

FIGURE 1.19
A stereoscope allows the viewer to see features on overlapping air photos in three dimensions. (Scott Miner)

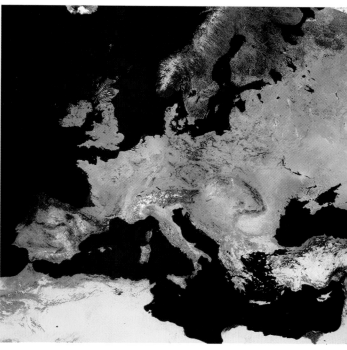

FIGURE 1.21
A satellite image showing a view of part of the earth's surface from space. (DRA/Viesti Assoc., Inc.)

FIGURE 1.20
An infrared photograph is particularly valuable for examining the condition of vegetation in an area. (Alan Mercer/Stock Boston)

Geographic Information Systems

➤ A relatively new tool for performing geographical tasks, called geographic information systems (GIS), is extremely versatile and powerful.

What does GIS involve? What type of tasks can it perform?

The computer, another product of recent technological development, has become an extremely valuable new tool in geography. With a computer and appropriate software, a geographer can process a vast amount of spatial data with amazing speed. To accomplish the same tasks manually would be extremely difficult, if not impossible. The preparation of maps by computer (computer cartography) is especially valuable not only because it saves a great deal of time, but because it allows enormous flexibility in map design and content.

A new field, **geographic information systems** (GIS), has emerged from the blending of computer cartography and data base management by computer. GIS typically involves the processing of large amounts of spatial data from a variety of maps, remote sensing imagery, and similar sources to solve a problem or perform a task. A computer can store data and later retrieve it for updating, manipulating, and analysis. A computer can also change the data in form to facilitate different types of analysis, which can then be displayed in tabular or map form. A geographer might use GIS, for example, to perform the task of selecting possible sites in a given city for the location of a new industry. Necessary characteristics of the site as specified by the industry might be (1) land zoned for industry, (2) an available area of 10 to 15 acres, (3) land with a slope of less than 3 percent, (4) a multi-lane highway within two miles, and (5) city water and sewer service available. Drawing on its data bases, the computer could identify all possible sites that meet this combination of criteria and prepare a map showing the location of the sites within the city. GIS has a wide variety of potential applications in geography, and rapidly it is being adopted for use in many other fields.

CAREERS IN GEOGRAPHY

➤ An education in geography can prepare students for a remarkable variety of careers in education, business, and government.

Why are geographers so versatile in the jobs they can fulfill?

What types of employment for geographers are traditional and where do the newer opportunities exist?

Geographers presently have a variety of careers open to them, but that has not always been the case. Until recent years, nearly all college-trained geographers became teachers. Those with an undergraduate or master's degree typically found employment as teachers at the elementary and secondary school levels, and those who obtained a doctorate usually assumed faculty careers in a college or university. Teaching remains an important career alternative for geographers in the United States, even though geography at all education levels now is given only a minor role in the curriculum. However, efforts to increase the emphasis on geography in the schools are underway as a consequence of growing public concern over the extent of geographic ignorance in American society. In addi-

tion, a "back to the basics" movement in many schools is a positive trend for more geography in the curriculum. With these developments, we can anticipate a need for more geography teachers in the future.

Before committing themselves to a teaching career, however, individuals should conduct a careful and objective assessment of their personal qualities and ambitions. Successful teaching requires a mastery of subject matter and a variety of skills and attributes: communication skills, motivational skills, patience, compassion, and a genuine interest in young people. In addition to teaching duties, college and university professors also commonly are expected to conduct research projects and publish their findings in scholarly journals and books. In the past, when almost all geographers with advanced degrees were employed as professors, nearly all research in geography was accomplished by college and university faculty; this is no longer the case now that more geographers are engaged in careers outside of education.

A growing number of employment opportunities in business and government agencies has provided career alternatives for geographers who are not attracted to teaching. Travel agencies, export-import companies, mining and petroleum companies, the real estate departments of major banks, land development corporations, and firms that conduct market analyses are a few of the businesses that employ geographers. Governmental agencies, such as environmental protection agencies, departments of conservation, the National Forest and National Park Services, and the National Weather Service are also sources of employment for geographers. Agencies engaged in planning optimal land use, whether in urban centers or rural areas, have found geographers to be valuable employees. Many geographers who have acquired training in cartography and remote sensing while in school are now employed by the federal government, particularly at the Defense Mapping Agency. Because potential employers in business and government commonly have little familiarity with modern geography, it may be necessary for job-seeking geographers to take the initiative in searching out vacancies they might fill and to explain their skills and training in employment applications and interviews.

The curricula of geography departments in universities across the country have been revised during recent years to better equip students for careers in business and government. In most cases, this has involved emphasis on courses in applied geography, and many geography departments have developed internship programs for their students. The internship commonly is spent with a business firm or government agency that may be a possible source of permanent employment for the student who performs well.

Employers commonly find geographers to be capable of working effectively on a variety of tasks. Geographers are trained to be familiar with a broad range of knowledge encompassing both the physical environment and its human inhabitants and to employ both synthesis and analysis in solving problems. Most geographers also are proficient in the use of a variety of analytical tools, including maps, air photos, artificial satellite imagery, and computers. The versatility that geographers are able to bring to the workplace is a most valuable professional asset.

KEY TERMS

Holistic A focus on the whole rather than individual parts. **4**

Habitat The environment inhabited by humans or other organisms. **10**

Environmental determinism A conviction that the activities and attainments of humans are highly influenced or controlled by one or more elements of the physical environment. **10**

Possibilism A belief that the physical environment offers people a variety of possibilities from which to select ways of using their habitat. **10**

Cultural landscape A landscape or area containing material features that are the consequence of human activity. **10**

Nomothetic The focus of a field of study on identification of scientific laws. **14**

Idiographic The focus of a field of study on description of unique phenomena rather than identification of scientific laws. **14**

Region A specific part of the earth's surface that is defined or delimited by one or more criteria. **14**

Cartography The art and science of map construction. **20**

Map grid The network of parallels and meridians (or similar lines) on a map or globe. **21**

Map projection On a map, the orderly arrangement of parallels and meridians to facilitate representation of the earth's curved surface. **21**

Mathematical (absolute) location The location on a globe or map of a place or feature by latitude and longitude. **23**

Relative location The location of a place or feature in relation to an adjacent or nearby place or feature that may be more prominent or generally known. **23**

Map scale The ratio of distance on a map to the distance it represents on the earth's surface. **24**

Remote sensing The gathering of information about the earth by use of relatively distant instruments, usually cameras and radar devices aboard aircraft and space vehicles. **27**

Geographic information systems (GIS) Programs to perform tasks and solve spatial problems by use of computer cartography and data base management. **29**

REVIEW QUESTIONS

1. What prompted people to first study geography? What were some contributions to the field made by scholars in ancient Greece?

2. What was the nature of geographic study up until the nineteenth century? What two scholars are closely associated with the emergence of modern geography? How did their work differ from that of earlier geographers?

3. What is *environmental determinism*? What prompted its development and who were its leading proponents? Why has the idea of environmental determinism been abandoned in geography?

4. How does *possibilism* differ from environmental determinism? What other alternatives to environmental determinism were advocated by some American geographers?

5. How did Immanuel Kant's classification of fields of learning distinguish geography from history and from other academic disciplines? Why is geography referred to as the spatial science?

6. In conducting a scholarly investigation, what is the difference between a *nomothetic* and an *ideographic* approach? Which is most closely associated with the ''hard sciences''?

7. What is a *region*? What two major types of regions are recognized by geographers? How do they differ?

8. What are the major subdivisions or specialized courses within physical geography? Within human geography? What goals do they all have in common?

9. What major global problems are especially appropriate as subject matter within human geography? What aspects of human geography contribute to the investigation of these problems?

10. What is *cartography*? How is a map defined? What three important properties should be considered when evaluating or selecting a map projection?

11. How is the *mathematical* or *absolute location* of a place determined from a map? How does *relative location* differ from *absolute location*?

12. What is scale and in what three ways may it be represented on a map? How is scale related to measuring distance on a map? What is meant by *small-scale* and *large-scale maps*?

13. How are pattern, density, and dispersion involved in the examination of geographic distributions? How do *choropleth*, *isoline*, and *dot maps* show geographic distributions?

14. What are mental maps? In what ways might faulty mental maps lead to poor decision making?

15. In what ways have remote sensing and geographic information systems improved the study of human geography?

16. In the past, what profession provided most of the employment opportunities for college-educated geographers? What additional opportunities are available today?

AN INTERVIEW WITH LAURA HARTWIG, CARTOGRAPHER

Laura Hartwig   *As a master cartographer for GeoSystems, R.R. Donnelley & Sons Company located in Lancaster, Pennsylvania, Laura Hartwig produces maps for encyclopedias, museums, travel publications, textbooks, and many other uses. "Every project is a new challenge," she says of her work. "Every day is different, because I do something new every day."*

Ms. Hartwig was born in 1956 in Milwaukee, Wisconsin. She became intrigued by archeology as a child, when her family visited the ancient cliff dwellings of Mesa Verde, Colorado.

In 1977, she earned an undergraduate degree in anthropology from the University of Wisconsin at Milwaukee, where she also received a master's degree in the same discipline in 1981. A few years later, she decided to become a cartographer. "Cartography was always the part of anthropology that I had enjoyed the most," she explains. She received her master's degree in cartography through a program in the department of geography at the University of Wisconsin at Madison in 1986. (Brian Christopher)

How did your interest in cartography develop?

I originally wanted to be an archeologist, ever since I was 10 years old. My interest developed after my family and I went on a trip to Mesa Verde, Colorado, when I was about 8 or 9 years old. While we were there, we saw all of the old cliff dwellings that had once been inhabited by Native Americans. I was fascinated by it.

As a university student, I originally intended to get a Ph.D. in anthropology. But by the time I had finished my first master's degree in 1981, the job market for anthropologists was quite poor. Cartography was always the part of anthropology that I had enjoyed the most. After all, once you dig up an artifact, you have to map the site where you found it and determine your exact location on the earth.

The department of geography at the University of Wisconsin had a good cartography program, and I was eligible for in-state tuition, so I decided to give it a shot!

Tell me about your job at GeoSystems.   What do you do?

One major responsibility I have is to manage different map-making projects for the company. In this capacity, I interact with the company's customers whenever they have questions about the design or specification of maps we are making for them. I help them decide, for example, how best to illustrate landforms, continents, or cities. I ask them how they want the final map to look, and I answer any questions they might have about sources or content for the map.

My responsibilities also include production work, where I actually design and lay out maps.

Finally, I then make sure everything is ready and in place for the printing process.

What kinds of maps do you prepare?

GeoSystems makes a wide range of maps. We have made maps for telephone directories, for textbooks, and for travel publications. We also prepare "Bible" or religious maps, which might illustrate, say, the life of Jesus, showing where Jesus walked on earth.

The company provides maps for *World Book Encyclopedia.* We also work for the U.S. National Parks Service, making the park folders that you might use to find your way along a hiking trail. GeoSystems has even completed maps for publication in *National Geographic Traveler Magazine.*

A customer might call me and say, "We are publishing a Grade Six textbook on American History." My colleagues and I would then decide how we should design the maps. We offer the customer as much design assistance and guidance as necessary. Much of my work involves educating the customer about cartography on a day-to-day basis.

> "My favorite project was making maps to illustrate American wars for the West Point Museum. It was really fun because the colonels . . . left the research up to my colleagues and me. It was great to be given that kind of artistic freedom."

Many people at GeoSystems focus on producing digital map products based on geographic information systems, or GIS technology. (A GIS system is a computerized database and spatial analysis tool that allows researchers to investigate, for example, physical features, human settlement patterns, environmental problems, and other issues from a geographical perspective.)

What methods do you use to complete your maps?

GeoSystems maintains an extensive source library, which includes reference materials such as atlases, flat maps, encyclopedias, and geographic dictionaries. We also have base maps that provide us with basic information about where national boundaries, shore lines, and other geographic markers are located. Relief art work, which shows the elevations of land surface, is another component of our maps. If a customer says, "We would like to order a map of Africa, and we want all of the mountains to be shown in relief," we can do that using the artwork that we have on hand.

Many of our information sources were created by the U.S. government. The Central Intelligence Agency (CIA), for instance, produced a number of the base maps that we use. We also use information from the *National Atlas of the United States.*

A finalized map can be provided to the customer either in film format—which can be transferred to printing plates for publication—or in digital format, on a computer disk. Virtually all of our new work these days is being completed on a computer, but we can output our maps in either format.

Do you ever need to travel to distant continents, to prepare maps "from scratch," based on field research?

I wish I did! [She laughs.] No, we usually do not travel in order to complete our maps. We might make telephone calls to foreign countries to verify specific geographic landmarks. I might call the tourism bureau or the chamber of commerce in the city of Atlanta, for example, to find out precisely where a monument is located, but I probably would never travel to the monument site.

A cartographic editor at GeoSystems is responsible for keeping me up-to-date on political events or other factors that could affect the map of a particular region. They conduct extensive research to make sure that our information is accurate. Some of these staff members speak various languages, so that they can communicate with geographers in other countries.

You have worked on many different projects for GeoSystems. What was your favorite project?

My favorite project was making maps to illustrate American wars for the West Point Museum. It was a brand-new museum, part of the U.S. Army's Military Academy in West Point, New York. I was invited to attend the opening of the exhibit, which was very exciting.

To complete the assignment, I worked with a number of West Point colonels who had backgrounds in military history. It was really fun because the colonels would just say, "Please make me a map to show the battles of the Viet Nam war." They left the research up to my colleagues and me. It was great to be given that kind of artistic freedom, to create maps which were totally "ours."

My maps show the battlefields of 12 different wars, including the American Revolution, the Civil War, the War of 1812, the French and Indian wars, World War II, and World War I. Each map is about four feet wide and four feet long. Because they are such large-scale maps, we were able to include a great deal of special information, such as a timeline, on each one. When you are working on a map for a textbook, you cannot incorporate that much detail into the images.

Your job seems very demanding. Is it stressful?

It is true that I have a high-pressure job, but it is also very rewarding for me. At GeoSystems, we are constantly working under tight deadlines, which we absolutely must meet because our customers need to meet their printing schedules. My colleagues and I end up working a lot of evenings and weekends, and we always work on more than one project at a time. But I enjoy working at a fast pace. It is always exciting.

> "Cartographic skills are technical, yet it is a discipline which is very creative and artistic at the same time."

How did you work your way up to the position of master cartographer?

In 1986, my first job title after college was "graphics coordinator" for a major publishing company. I served as a kind of "filter" between the company's production staff and their editors. The job involved writing map specifications, which were basically a set of instructions to tell a cartographic company what basic pieces of information and what images should be included on the map. While writing specifications can be challenging, I missed the more creative side of cartography: the actual design and production work.

Well, as part of that job, I often dealt with a cartographic company called Donnelley Cartographic Services, which later became GeoSystems. I joined Donnelley as a cartographer in 1987. I have been here ever since.

Now, instead of writing instructions for a cartographer, I carry out those instructions.

What types of courses did you have to complete as part of your cartography education?

I had to take various mathematics courses, plus remote sensing, cartographic design, computer programming, and a variety of geography courses. The geography courses covered topics such as weather and climate, landforms, methods of geographic investigation, and the history of American settlement patterns. An anthropology course on surveying and mapping was also useful.

Many university geography programs offer cartography as a specialty. The University of Wisconsin treats cartography almost as a separate field, deserving of its own intensive course of study.

To supplement my course work, I worked for three years in the university's cartography laboratory, which gave me hands-on experience.

Do cartographers need to be artistically inclined?

I think it helps to have a little "artistic flair." Cartographic skills are technical, yet it is a discipline which is very creative and artistic at the same time. This kind of work requires a knowledge of geography, history, and current events, as well as social sciences and computer skills. The best cartographers have a flair for graphic design.

Has the field of cartography changed since you were in school?

Yes! It is amazing how much the technology has changed. When I first took cartography courses in the early 1980s, I learned to make maps using pen-and-ink drafting techniques. Today, I work on a computer all day long. The discipline has changed incredibly quickly.

Just about all of our new assignments these days are output in a digital format. I create maps on a computer, using a commercially available graphics software package called Adobe Illustrator. I input various pieces of information to this software, which works well for cartography.

Do you think students will be able to find jobs as cartographers in the future?

We will always need new maps, and we will always need to update our existing maps. In fact, various regions of the world have never been mapped very well for many purposes—to show information on a region's economy, linguistics, history, climate, vegetation, and so forth.

Every time I complete a map, I always learn something. Every project is a new challenge. Every day is different because I do something new every day.

People engaged in the basic task of food production illustrate the interplay of habitat and culture that is a central theme in human geography. In the accompanying photograph a volunteer of the Peace Corps is teaching a small group of farmers from an economically disadvantaged country a new farming technique. As the farmers learn, their culture is undergoing change that can be expected to result in an alteration of their farming practice—their association with the natural environment—in the immediate future.

In our study of human geography it is necessary that we examine at an early stage major components of the natural environment (Chapter 2)—such as land-

forms, climate, soils, and vegetation—that together make up much of the human habitat. These components, which vary in character over the surface of the earth and are themselves the objects of study in physical geography, of course are critical to the welfare and lifestyle of the humans who inhabit each part of the planet. It is these elements of their habitat that people must rely on and must exploit if they are to attain any degree of affluence. Geographers have learned that the associations of people with their habitat are delicate, complex, and different from one location to another. To comprehend the nature of these associations and their spatial variations, our familiarity

PART 2

HABITAT AND CULTURE

must extend beyond the habitat and encompass human culture as well.

Whatever the assortment and character of an area's environmental components, it is the culture of those who inhabit the area that guides their interpretation, evaluation, and utilization of those components. The attitudes, goals, beliefs, technical skills, and other cultural traits of people influence the processes of human occupance and utilization of the habitat. Over time, cultures can change, and with each change there may be a significant alteration in ways that people make use of their environments. In Chapter 3 we examine the concept of culture and then survey the

world's major culture regions—extensive parts of the earth's surface in each of which distinctive human life-styles have evolved—in order to identify important differences in human cultures and explain how these differences have come about. In Chapters 4 and 5, we focus on languages, religions, and political systems to comprehend their paramount importance in accounting for the world's cultural diversity. We will find that the bases for most conflicts between groups of people usually can be traced to one or more of these three major components of culture.

CHAPTER 2

THE HUMAN HABITAT

All the world's a stage, and all the men and women merely players. They have their exits and their entrances and one man in his time plays many parts.

—William Shakespeare
(*As You Like It*, Act II, Scene 7)

Deserts are rigorous human habitats. This Berber tribesman is among the few people who have adapted to the arid western Sahara.
(S. Smith/The Image Works)

41

As the most successful playwright of his era Shakespeare was chiefly concerned with the actions of men and women, their desires and concerns, the roles they played throughout their lives, and their relationships with the important places and events of their time. In addition, the Bard of Avon never overlooked the importance of the stage. The settings for each of his plays always create specific moods, are important to the plot, and help to explain the actions of his characters. In much the same way the human geographer must take into consideration the stage settings, the countless and varied habitats or environments in which human societies exist and carry out their activities.

Every place on the earth has a unique physical environment or stage setting. Among the most important elements of that environment are the long-term conditions of the atmosphere, the character and appearance of the topography or landforms, the nature of the associated plant and animal life, and the resources such as soils or minerals available to support agriculture or industry. As humans have come to occupy all but the most severe of the earth's environments they have learned to adapt to and often modify each new set of environmental conditions. The activities and cultural traits of people reflect those human/environment relationships. In many cases the successes or failures of entire nations or societies have depended on how well humans have learned to protect as well as to exploit the environments in which they live.

In this chapter we will survey the major components of the human habitat. First, we will examine global environmental patterns, particularly the distribution of major landform and climatic types. We will discuss environmental processes only insofar as they are necessary to explain these distributional patterns. Second, we will identify the close links among the various components of the natural environment. Third, and most important, we will illustrate some of the intricate associations of people with their habitats. It will become obvious in later chapters that most of the major topics in human geography cannot be fully understood without some prior knowledge of the environmental characteristics of the places people occupy.

THE PLANET EARTH

➤ Despite the billions of galaxies in the universe and the countless numbers of potential solar systems, according to our present knowledge, human life exists only on planet earth.

What characteristics of earth enable it to support human life?

What does this suggest about our "stewardship" of the planet?

The universe is so vast and complex that, at first glance, the earth would seem to be an exceedingly ordinary and insignificant celestial body moving through space as merely one member of an unremarkable solar systsem. But clearly this is not the case. As far as we know, earth is the only home to life as we define it. Such life is totally dependent on the precise combination of environmental conditions, including temperature ranges, moisture supplies, and surface materials, that are found on the earth. It is mathematically probable that other solar systems contain planets similar to the earth, but as far as this solar system is concerned, the earth is unique. No other planet has the same orbital period or distance from the sun; together with the nature of the earth's rotation these characteristics regulate the heating of the earth and determine earth temperatures. Most significant is the fact that the earth is the only planet with an abundant supply of water.

The Water Planet

➤ Within our solar system, earth is the only planet with an abundant supply of water.

What functions does water perform as an element of the physical environment?

How is the availability of fresh water important to human activity and settlement?

Within the temperature ranges on earth, water can exist in all three states of matter—as a solid, a liquid, and a gas. To an observer in a high-altitude jetliner or an orbiting satellite the abundance of water on earth in the three states is readily apparent (Fig. 2.1). The world's oceans are obviously liquid water; the clouds covering portions of the earth are water droplets that reached the upper levels of the atmosphere as water vapor; the snow and ice covering high mountains and polar regions are water in the solid state. The amount of water in the earth environment totals more than a billion cubic kilometers (Table 2.1). Over 97 percent is stored as salt water in the oceans. The largest percentage of fresh water is stored as ice in glaciers or as

FIGURE 2.1

Ice, snow, and ocean water. The coast of Greenland from the air, photographed through a vapor-filled atmosphere. (R. Gabler)

TABLE 2.1	Storage Reservoirs for the Earth's Water	
Location		**Percentage of Total Hydrosphere**
Oceans		97.1
Ice Caps and Mountain Glaciers		2.24
Deep Ground Water		0.306
Shallow Ground Water		0.306
Freshwater Lakes		0.009
Saline Lakes		0.008
Soil Root Zone		0.0018
Stream Channels		0.0001

underground water. Only an exceedingly small proportion of water (less than .05 percent) is circulating as part of the **hydrologic cycle.** The hydrologic cycle is the name given to the movement of water as it is evaporated at the earth's surface, is condensed in the atmosphere to form clouds, and then falls to earth again as some form of precipitation (Fig. 2.2).

It is impossible to exaggerate the importance of water on earth. Although some living things can survive without air, none can survive without water. Wa-

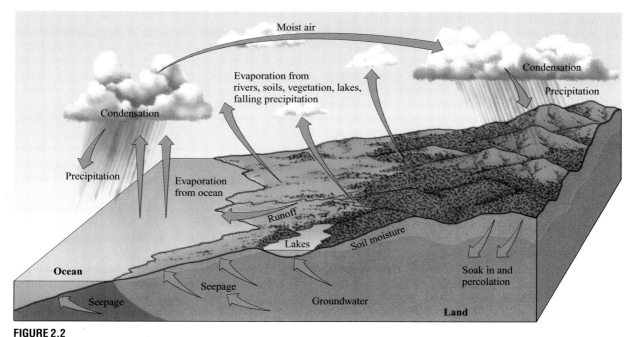

FIGURE 2.2

The hydrologic cycle. The earth's water supply is cycled endlessly between the atmosphere, the soil, subsurface storage, lakes and streams, plants and animals, glacial ice, and the principal reservoir— the oceans.

ter is necessary for photosynthesis, for cell growth, for protein formation, for the development of soils, and for the absorption of nutrients by plants and animals. Water provides homes for many plants and animals in the earth's diverse aquatic environments—lakes, rivers, ponds, swamps, estuaries, and the world's oceans. Furthermore, about two-thirds of human body weight is water.

Some of the effects of water on earth are not easy to discern. Because of the chemical structure of water it is able to combine with or dissolve a great variety of other substances. In fact it is such a universal solvent that it is rarely found in a pure state. Even rain is filled with impurities picked up in the atmosphere. Indeed, without these impurities water vapor would not condense and neither clouds nor precipitation would occur. Rainwater often contains dissolved carbon dioxide from the air and reaches the ground as a weak form of carbonic acid. Hence both groundwater and surface streams alter landforms by dissolving rock particles. In addition, running water serves as the major erosion and transportation agent of solid earth materials in both humid and arid regions (Fig. 2.3).

As will be evident in later chapters, the availability or scarcity of fresh water has had an enormous impact on human geography. Human migrations and settlements are dependent on water supplies. Water is essential to agriculture, and where water is in short supply, irrigation becomes a necessity. Modern industry could not survive without water. For example, it takes 10 gallons of water to make 1 gallon of gasoline; 250 gallons of water to make 1 pound of paper; and 300 gallons to make 1 pound of steel. The average household in a technologically advanced nation uses more than 1000 gallons of water a day. Water is a major source of power and provides almost the total electricity needs of some small nations—for example, Switzerland. In addition, water serves as the least expensive method of transporting bulk commodities and is the major medium for disposal of sewage and industrial wastes. The reader should note that within this last statement there is a clear message: Water pollution is an ever-present danger, and to maintain life on the planet, humans must protect their fresh water supplies.

Oceans and Continents

➤ Oceans cover nearly three-fourths of the earth and particularly dominate the Southern Hemisphere, whereas the continental land masses are more concentrated in the Northern Hemisphere.

What resources can be obtained from within and beneath the oceans?

How has human use of the oceans changed since the Age of Exploration?

The World Ocean   A glance at the globe reveals that water and land are unequally distributed over the face

(a)   (b)

FIGURE 2.3
(a) The silt-laden Colorado River above the Grand Canyon, and (b) the Colorado River as it flows through the gorge below Hoover Dam. Compare the river at the two locations. What problem does this suggest for Lake Mead, which is behind Hoover Dam? (R. Gabler)

of the earth. The world ocean covers more than 70 percent of the earth's surface. Most geographers divide this vast expanse of water into four separate bodies. The Arctic Ocean is usually included in this separation, even though it is little more than an ice and land-locked sea. The three other principal water bodies are the Pacific, Atlantic, and Indian Oceans. As Table 2.2 indicates, the Pacific Ocean is the largest at approximately 64 million square miles (166 sq km). The Atlantic is half that size at about 32 million square miles (83 million sq km), and the Indian Ocean is a fraction smaller at nearly 28 million square miles (73 million sq km) in area. The Arctic Ocean is far smaller at 5 million square miles (13 million sq km).

The oceans vary greatly in depth as well as size. Both the Pacific and Indian Oceans have average depths of 13,000 feet (4000 m) or more; the Atlantic has an average depth of nearly 12,000 feet (3700 m); but the average depth of the Arctic Ocean is only 5000 feet (1500 m). More significant is the fact that the ocean floors are not smooth plains but actually contain differences in elevation that are greater than those found on the continents. There are basins, mid-ocean ridges, trenches, and isolated mountain peaks that have great influence on ocean depths from place to place

(Fig. 2.4). Challenger Deep, located in the Marianas Trench of the South Pacific, is 36,198 feet (11,033 m) *below* sea level. This vertical distance is more than 1 mile (2 km) greater than that of the earth's highest mountain, Mt. Everest, which rises 29,028 feet (8048 m) *above* sea level.

Throughout history humans have turned to the oceans as a source of food and certain mineral resources, and as avenues of trade and transportation. The distribution of marine life is influenced most by the fact that dissolved nutrients are mainly concentrated near the ocean floor, whereas sunlight penetrates to a maximum depth of approximately 400 feet (120 m). Because both sunlight and nutrients are essential to the growth of plankton (the organisms at the lowest level of the marine food chain), major commercial fishing areas often are located in coastal areas or submerged portions of the **continental shelves.** In other instances the surface mixing of warm and cold ocean currents or the vertical upwelling of deep ocean waters will bring dissolved nutrients into contact with solar energy and create the conditions necessary for the concentration of marine organisms.

The actual production of minerals from the ocean is limited, although salt has been obtained through the

TABLE 2.2 The Earth's Major Features

Oceans

	Area (sq mi)	Mean Depth (ft)
Pacific	64,190,000	13,420
Atlantic	32,420,000	11,730
Indian	27,950,000	13,090
Arctic	5,100,000	3,910

Continents

	Area (sq mi)	Lowest Point (ft)		Highest Point (ft)	
Asia	17,100,000	Dead Sea	−1312	Everest	29,028
Africa	11,690,000	Lake Assal	−512	Kilimanjaro	19,340
North America	9,370,000	Death Valley	−282	McKinley	20,320
South America	6,880,000	Valdés Peninsula	−131	Aconcagua	22,834
Antarctica	5,100,000	—		Vinson Massif	16,864
Europe	4,020,000	Caspian Sea	−92	Elbrus	18,510
Australia	2,970,000	Lake Eyre	−52	Kosciusko	7,310

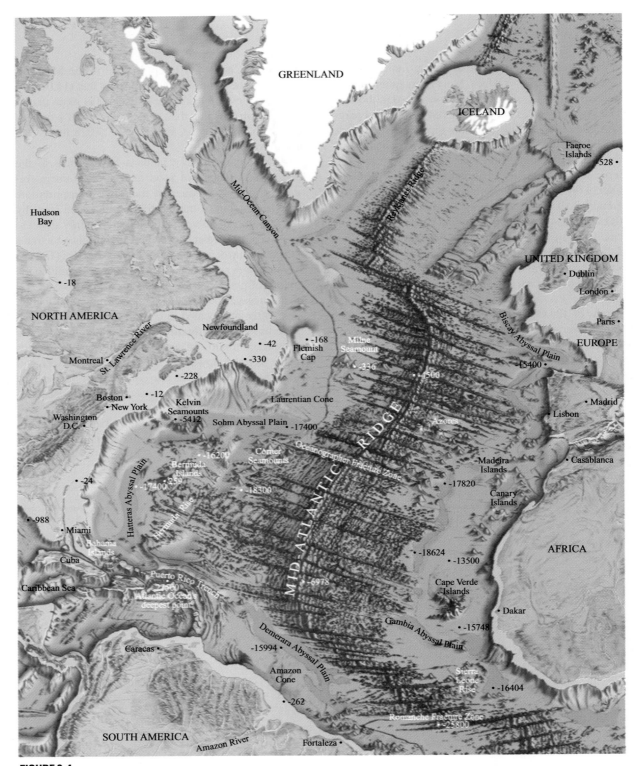

FIGURE 2.4

A diagram of the floor of the Atlantic Ocean, showing such features as the Mid-Atlantic Ridge, the Puerto Rico Trench, numerous seamounts, and the continental shelf and slope of the surrounding continents. (Courtesy of Aluminum Company of America)

evaporation of sea water since humans first settled coastal areas. In addition to salt, bromine and magnesium are produced in commercial quantities. Bromine is an important constituent in gasoline, and magnesium, originally used in various incendiary devices, has become a major alloy metal. Undoubtedly the most important resource in the oceans is the water itself. The production of fresh water from salt water through *desalinization* has increased greatly in recent years and has even become a necessity with expanding populations in certain desert nations such as Kuwait and Israel.

The most important mineral resources associated with the oceans comes not from ocean water but from the continental shelves beneath the water. In earlier periods of earth history, organic debris collected in oxygen-poor environments in certain areas along continental margins. As was the case with interior locations, this debris slowly altered into deposits of petroleum and natural gas. To meet the demands of an energy-hungry world, petroleum geologists have been turning more and more to these off-shore deposits (Fig. 2.5). Oil and gas fields have been identified along the Gulf Coast of the southwestern United States; along the coast of southern California; in the North Sea; off the shores of Peru, Venezuela, and Colombia; in the Mediterranean Sea and Persian Gulf; around Africa's Gulf of Guinea; in the seas near Indonesia; and off the coasts of Australia. More than one-third of the world's oil comes from beneath the sea.

The oceans have had a significant impact on human history. Before the European Age of Exploration only the most daring of travelers braved the stormy seas or followed the perilous inland routes to make contact with people in other lands. Isolation was the rule, not the exception that it is in modern societies. Quite different cultures developed on the various land masses separated by huge expanses of intervening sea. As technology advanced and modern vessels replaced the early sailing ships, the ocean barriers were breached by sea lanes. Today all but a small portion of the bulk commodities that enter world trade move on the oceans.

Despite the significance of the world ocean, however, it is the land masses of the earth that comprise the stage for most of human geography. Since humans live on land it is axiomatic that the landform features, climates, and resources of the continents have the greatest significance to human activities and events.

FIGURE 2.5

An offshore oil drilling platform. Rigs such as this one are used to tap the rich oil and natural gas deposits along favored continental margins. (Schlumberger, Inc.)

Continents   Look again at Table 2.2; we note that Asia is by far the largest continent. If it were not for the arbitrary separation of Europe and Asia along the Ural Mountains, the combined Eurasian landmass would be nearly twice the size of the second largest continent, Africa. After Africa and the midsized continents of North America, South America, and Antarctica come the smallest continents, Europe and Australia. If you study the globe for a moment, you will note that much of the area covered by the continents lies north of the Equator. This is why the Northern Hemisphere is often referred to as the *land hemisphere* and the Southern Hemisphere is called the *water hemisphere.*

Each continent exhibits a remarkable variety of physical landscapes, climatic characteristics, and natural resources. Although it may be true that Asia has much of its land area in highlands and Australia presents primarily an arid environment, it is of limited value to generalize by continent about characteristics of the physical environment. It is much easier to understand the nature, distribution, and relationships with humans of such elements as landforms and climates if we examine each in its turn. We will commence with a brief survey of landforms.

EARTH LANDFORMS

➤ Major landform types may be differentiated on the basis of local relief and the steepness of slopes.

What are the distinguishing characteristics of plains, plateaus, hills, and mountains?

Earth landforms come in an enormous variety: flat plains, rolling hills, deep canyons, broad valleys, isolated peaks, scattered dunes, and towering mountains. There is so much variety, in fact, that it is difficult to classify landforms or place them into groups for purposes of generalized discussion. Each landform is unique and differs from all others in one or more characteristics such as height or depth, amount of sloping land, size, shape, mode of origin, or surface material. (See *The Geographer's Notebook: Glaciation.*) Of all these characteristics, probably the easiest to distinguish are differences in elevation in a given area, often called **local relief**, and the amount of land in steep or gentle slopes. In fact, these two characteristics may be used to identify the most generalized landform types. Plains, for example, are distinguished by minimal local relief and gentle slopes, while mountains are recognized by their steep slopes, peaked summits, and maximum local relief. In between these two extremes are hills and plateaus (also called tablelands). Hills have less significant sloping land, rounded summits, and far fewer differences in elevations than mountains, and plateaus are characterized by few slopes but significant local relief produced by deep river canyons, bordering escarpments, or occasional isolated hills or mountains rising above the plateau surface.

Landform Potential

➤ In the human evaluation of landform types, societies determine their preferences on the basis of perceived advantages and disadvantages.

What are possible advantages and disadvantages for societies of each landform type?

Which type has been most preferred in history and why?

Each major landform type has been evaluated for its advantages and disadvantages by those humans who have considered it as a place to live. Humans can be found in almost every kind of landscape—the slopes of Mt. Kilimanjaro, the plateau of Tibet, the hills of the German Black Forest, the plains of the agricultural heartland of North America. However, it is clear from a comparison of world maps showing population distribution and physical landscapes that most societies have come to prefer certain landform characteristics to others.

Plains In most societies, the majority of people consider gently sloping or nearly level land the most desirable landform characteristic. Plains with their gentle slopes and minimal local relief make some of the most productive agricultural regions in the world. This is especially true of alluvial plains and plains of recent glacial deposition where rich, young soils are the most favorable to agriculture, and where the land can support the greatest human population concentrations. When plains have both climate and soil conducive to agriculture, as in the midwestern plains area of the United States, as much as 80 to 90 percent of the land may be cultivated, leaving only about 10 to 20 percent for houses, towns, roads, barns, and woodlots (Fig. 2.6). The nearly level surface of plains also permits

FIGURE 2.6
The American Midwest, with farms and fields stretching to a nearly flat and featureless horizon. This region's combination of terrain, soil, and climate is among the most favorable in the world for agriculture. (R. Gabler)

the development of good transportation systems because there are few obstacles to bypass or overcome by roads, railroads, or canals. Therefore, plains also are conducive to contact between human populations and the spread of ideas, culture, and trade.

Because plains are attractive for so many aspects of human development, the majority of the world's population lives in these regions. Coastal plains, such as those of Denmark and the Netherlands, alluvial plains such as those of India's Ganges River or China's Huang He (Yellow River), and delta plains such as that of the Nile in Egypt, are especially attractive because they tend to have highly productive soils and nearby waterways to provide easy transportation.

There are also certain potential drawbacks to plains regions. In coastal, alluvial, and delta regions, the advantages of fertile soil and easy water transportation may be offset by the hazard of frequent floods. Plains also offer little protection from invasion. Belgium, the Netherlands, and Poland are examples of plains regions that often have been invaded by hostile foreign armies. Furthermore, many vast plains are totally desolate. The world's major deserts generally encompass large areas of plains. The Sahara, the Gobi, the Arabian, and the Australian deserts collectively include hundreds of thousands of square miles that are of little or no use to humans at the current time. Interior plains in tropical wet climates such as the Amazon Basin and plains in tundra areas are also currently of little value for human habitation. Therefore, surface configuration alone is a poor predictor of an area's potential as a human habitat.

Mountains   In contrast to plains, mountainous regions usually have been considered difficult habitats outside of tropical latitudes. Poor mountain soils, cold climates—particularly at higher elevations—and problems of thin atmosphere severely limit the use of mountains for agriculture. The same is true for the excessive run-off, rapid erosion, steep slopes, and exposed rocks that are common in mountainous areas (Fig. 2.7). Mountains also form barriers to population expansion, transportation, trade, communication, and the spread of ideas and cultures. The Rocky Mountains and the Sierra Nevada, for example, limited the westward expansion of population in the United States until the middle of the nineteenth century, when the lure of gold and other riches encouraged humans to find passes through the mountains or to make long detours around them. Of the many passes now known to cross the 450-mile length of the Sierra Nevada, only one—Donner Pass—remains open year-round, and even it is sometimes closed for a few days during major snowstorms. The Alps have many famous passes that channel the land transportation between northern and southern Europe: Brenner Pass, Simplon, St. Bernard, St. Gotthard, and now the Mont Blanc Tunnel. Some of these have been especially important during times of war, as far back as the early days of the Roman Empire.

FIGURE 2.7

The northern Rocky Mountains in Alberta, Canada. The active glaciers, steep mountain slopes, and narrow valleys discourage agriculture. (R. Gabler)

Glaciation

Can you imagine a sheet of ice that is several thousands of feet thick and extends over an area of five million square miles? That is the magnitude of the ice cap, or glacier, that presently covers nearly all of the Antarctic continent. In the Northern Hemisphere, most of Greenland remains covered by a large glacier and a number of smaller islands along the Arctic coast of North America and Eurasia have ice caps. In addition, the peaks of many of the world's highest mountains (even including some near the Equator) have accumulations of permanent ice and snow. As indicated in Table 2.1, present-day glaciers represent a little more than 2 percent of the earth's total water supply.

While current glaciers are impressive features, they actually are only the small remaining remnants of vast ice sheets that covered much of North America and Eurasia during a period of earth history called the *Pleistocene Epoch*. Since the beginning of the Pleistocene about two million years ago, there have been at least four times when glaciers spread over large parts of these land masses from centers in central Canada, northern Europe, and northeastern Russia. The accompanying map shows the maximum extent of the Pleistocene glaciers; the chart indicates the approximate time of the glacial and interglacial stages. Names given to the glacial stages, from the earliest to the most recent, are the *Nebraskan*, *Kansan*, *Illinoian*, and *Wisconsinan*. (In Europe, the corresponding stages are called the *Günz*, *Mindel*, *Riss*, and *Würm*.) Somewhat cooler global temperatures and greater precipitation during these periods allowed for the accumulation of snow and its compression into ice in the centers from which the glaciers spread. The last ice sheet, the Wisconsinan or Würm, melted and withdrew from land areas that it covered only about 10,000 to 15,000 years ago.

Because of their great mass and strength as they advanced over the earth's surface, glaciers were able to drastically alter the preglacial landforms and relocate tremendous amounts of surface materials. In some areas, generally those areas relatively close to the centers of glacial formation, the moving ice was a powerful agent of erosion, capable of wearing down preglacial mountains and hills and excavating large basins in the surface. The surface materials—rocks, gravel, sand, and soil—picked up by the ice during erosion were later deposited mostly near the margin of the glaciated area, in association with melting and withdrawal of the ice. In some cases these materials were deposited in a generally uniform blanket to create *till plains*, but in others their deposition was irregular and resulted in the formation of low hills or ridges called *moraines*. Great quantities of meltwater from the ice also helped alter the land surface by means of erosion and deposition of materials. Although features

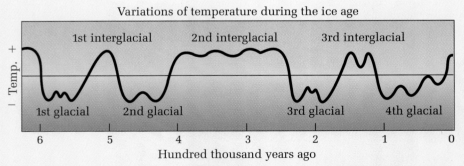

Variations of temperature during the ice age

During the Pleistocene, temperature variations caused at least four major ice advances, called glacials, and retreats, called interglacials. The last major advance ended only 10,000 years ago.

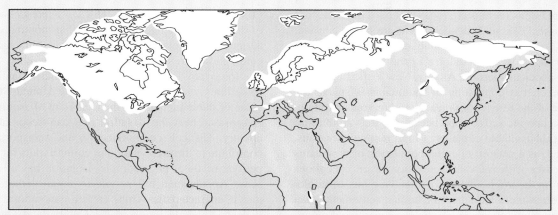

Maximum extent of glaciation in the Northern Hemisphere during the Pleistocene. Much of North America and Eurasia was covered by enormous ice sheets.

of erosion and deposition from earlier glacial stages can be identified on the present landscape in some areas, those from the Wisconsinan stage generally are more evident.

Another consequence of Pleistocene glaciation was a fluctuation in the level of the world's seas and oceans. In comparison with the level during interglacial time, sea level was at least 300 feet (91 m) lower when a portion of the earth's water supply was "locked up" in the great ice sheets on the land. Under these conditions, less water was able to flow from the land into the seas and ocean basins to replace that lost by evaporation. The resulting drop in sea level exposed more land around the margins of the continents and created temporary *land bridges* between land masses that were separated at other times by narrow water bodies. These land bridges were of great importance in facilitating prehistoric human migrations. In Chapter 7 we will discuss migrations involving Pleistocene land bridges and the displacement of prehistoric people by the expansion of glaciers.

THOUGHT QUESTIONS

1. Do you think it is more likely that current glaciers are expanding or retreating? By what means might a person determine if glacial expansion or retreat is underway?
2. If the earth's present glaciers completely melt, what environmental and human consequences would you expect?
3. Do you think it is possible that human activities might influence the length of time until the next glacial stage? How?

Because mountains are such effective barriers, the passes through them become vitally important to humans. Consequently, most population centers in mountainous regions are located at gaps or at the foot of passes. Examples of such towns are Reno, Nevada; Salt Lake City, Utah; Albuquerque, New Mexico; Innsbruck, Austria; Andorra in the Pyrenees; and in less spectacular terrain, Albany, New York. In general, however, the population of mountains is sparse because of the restrictions on agriculture, transportation, and economic activity and because of the variable and often inhospitable climates of high mountain regions. In fact, as a general rule, the population of mountains decreases with increased elevation. Rare exceptions occur in the tropics, where highland regions are cooler and often more attractive for human settlements than the hot, wet, lowlands. Examples of populated mountain regions in the tropics occur in Colombia, Peru, East Africa, Malaysia, New Guinea, and the foothills of the Himalayas.

The same factors that isolate areas often help protect them from invasion. Switzerland is a classic example. It is unlikely that this small country could have maintained its neutrality so successfully through many European and two world wars without the mountains that protect it, despite the excellent reputation of the Swiss military. Unfortunately, isolation is not always the deciding factor in a nation's survival. The most remote and mountain-guarded of the world's populations, the Tibetans, have been all but absorbed by the Chinese over the past three decades, despite the protection their mountainous region would seem to provide.

It should be pointed out that even the *presence* of nearby mountains can be a major asset to human settlements. Mountains often are regions of substantial precipitation, and much of the snow that falls in the higher elevations is stored and subsequently provides water throughout the year to semiarid regions nearby. Mountain streams and rivers can be harnessed for hydroelectric power and provide plentiful water for irrigation and urban needs in nearby areas. For example, the run-off of California's Sierra Nevada crosses the state's vast Central Valley and is channeled by pipeline, canal, and aqueduct to supply the urban populations of both the San Francisco and Los Angeles areas. Many cities are located on the great rivers kept flowing by the run-off from nearby mountains: Calcutta and Delhi on the Ganges in India, Baghdad on the Tigris, Cairo on the Nile, Shanghai on the Yangtze (Chang Jiang), and Vienna and Budapest on the Danube.

Other Major Landforms Hill lands present many of the same challenges to humans that mountains do, although to a lesser degree. In rugged hill country, communities are often isolated from each other. They are forced to become more self-sufficient and are sometimes wary of outsiders. In the United States, some of the inhabitants of the Ozarks in Missouri and Arkansas reflect the isolation that can occur in hill country. Difficult communication and transportation contribute to the preservation of cultural traits for long periods of time. For example, isolation has allowed some Appalachian hill people to retain certain language characteristics from earlier generations. The dialect of people living in the Cumberland Hills of Appalachia includes words common in eighteenth-century English, but unheard elsewhere today. The Appalachian hill people have also been able to preserve folk music passed from previous generations.

Agriculture is difficult in hill country, although not as limited as it is in mountain regions. There are poor soils, the constant threat of erosion, and a scarcity of level land. Still, farming persists, despite the obstacles, and crops are grown especially in the flatter "bottom lands" along streams (Fig. 2.8). In heavily pop-

FIGURE 2.8
This field in a narrow valley is typical of the farming in Kentucky's Appalachian hill country. (R. Gabler)

ulated areas, as in Europe and Asia, terraced hills produce a surprising variety of orchard and field crops. Where growing seasons are short, grazing is often more successful than the cultivation of crops. In the United States, the vast areas of hills that occupy the eastern part of the country are partly covered by state and national forests.

The human activities on plateaus depend on diverse local conditions. The steep cliffs, canyons, ravines, and escarpments of plateaus always present severe problems to transportation, communication, trade, and migration. It is often difficult, if not impossible, to get from one part of a plateau to another across a canyon. In addition, the few rivers in plateau regions are often full of rapids and waterfalls that are difficult to navigate. Thus, they too fail to provide easy transportation routes. Plateau areas commonly are associated with aridity because many are located in continental interiors or lie on the leeward side of higher mountains. Because of these conditions, agriculture is difficult at best, and these regions are not usually marked by dense human settlements. The exceptions, again, occur in the wet tropical climates where higher elevations provide some relief from the constant heat and humidity. Thus, the plateau regions of eastern Africa were prime areas of European settlement during the colonization of the African continent by European nations, and continue to be relatively well populated.

Landform Distribution

➤ The distribution of the earth's landforms is best explained by tectonic plate theory.

How does the movement of tectonic plates help us to understand the location of major earth landforms?

Why is an understanding of plate movement of interest in human geography?

A first glance at Figure 2.9, showing the distribution of major landform types of the earth, would seem to indicate that landforms with steep slopes and landforms with gentle slopes are arranged haphazardly from continent to continent. However, with a map projection centered on the North Pole such as that in Figure 2.10, one can see the alignment of landform features and the interconnection of the major landmasses despite their separation by vast expanses of ocean. Mountain ranges radiate in several directions from the

knotted mass of the Pamirs in south central Asia. To the south and east they extend through the Himalayas and the Kunlun Shan of Tibet to the Indo-Chinese peninsula, the Pacific Islands, and eastern Australia. To the north and east major ranges include the Tien Shan, Great Altai, and Stanovoy before the chain is briefly interrupted by the Bering Sea. The mountain chain then turns southward through the Alaskan Ranges, the Rocky Mountains and Coastal Ranges of North America, the highlands of Mexico and Central America, and the Andes of South America. To the west of the Pamirs, highlands extend through the Hindu Kush Range and the plateaus of Iran and Turkey and then split in the eastern Mediterranean to include (on the north) the Balkans, Alps, and other ranges of central Europe, and (on the south), the Atlas Mountains of Africa.

It is apparent that the oceans are generally bordered by highlands and the interiors of the continents are most often occupied by plains of low to moderate relief. In Eurasia the North European Plain extends eastward to the Russian steppes and central Siberia, broken only by the low ranges of the Urals. The drainage basin of the Mississippi River is joined by the Hudson Bay Lowland to the north and the Atlantic-Gulf Coastal Plain to the south to form continuous plains through North America. Practically all of interior Australia is an arid plain. The Amazon Basin and the plains to the south, associated with the Rio de la Plata and its tributaries, occupy much of inland South America. Even in Africa, which has a large portion of its landmass well above sea level, much of the Sahara Desert in the north and parts of the south are rolling plains of moderate relief.

The Shifting Earth   The major land configurations of the earth have been well mapped since the latter days of the European Age of Exploration, but until quite recently earth scientists have been unable to agree on the reasons for their locations. Many processes associated with mountain building such as crustal folding, volcanism, and the upthrusting of crustal blocks along great cracks or faults, have been studied for centuries, but few scientists have ever accepted one set of theories to explain these earth phenomena. This is no longer the case today; nearly all earth scientists now support the theory of **plate tectonics**, which has revolutionized the study of the solid earth just as the theory of evolution revolutionized the study of life on earth more than a century ago.

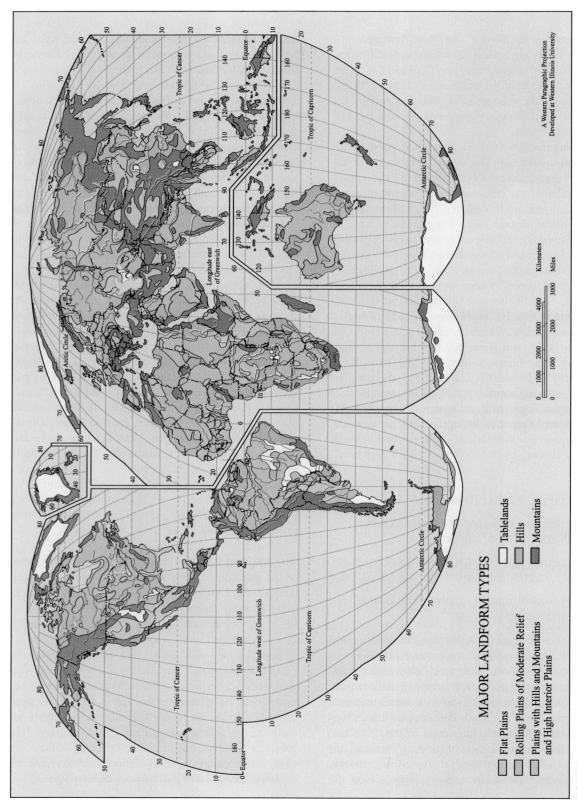

MAJOR LANDFORM TYPES

- Flat Plains
- Rolling Plains of Moderate Relief
- Plains with Hills and Mountains and High Interior Plains
- Tablelands
- Hills
- Mountains

A Western Panagraphic Projection
Developed at Western Illinois University

Kilometers
Miles

FIGURE 2.9

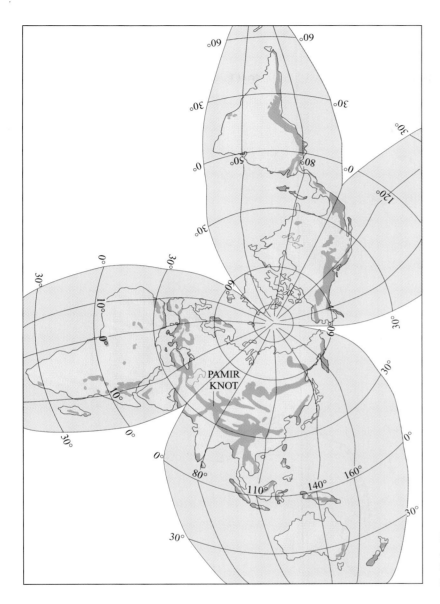

FIGURE 2.10

Mountain ranges extend outward from the Pamir Knot in Asia to the most distant parts of the other continents.

Tectonic plate theory maintains that the outer portion of the solid earth, termed the *lithosphere*, consists of as many as twenty rigid plates moving about the earth's surface as distinct units (Fig. 2.11). Seven are considered major plates and are of continental or oceanic proportions. Although the largest, the Pacific Plate, consists primarily of heavier oceanic rock, portions of the lighter continents are deeply imbedded in the surfaces of all other major plates and are carried along by plate movement. In general, the major plates are moving at exceedingly slow rates away from mid-ocean ridges where new crustal material is added from deep within the earth through intense volcanic activity.

Along their common boundaries, the lithospheric plates either pull apart, slide past one another, or collide with incredible force. Movement is at most a few inches a year, but in millions of years the earth's crust can be thrust upward in mountain ranges thousands of

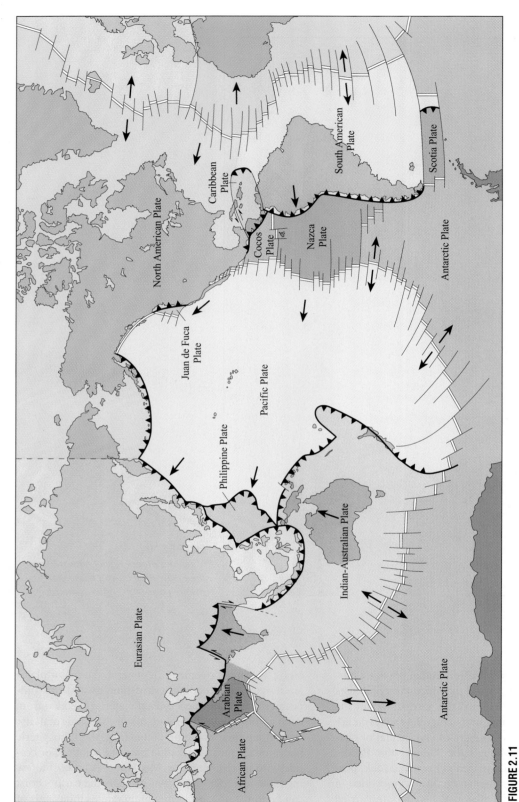

FIGURE 2.11

The earth's major tectonic plates and their general direction of movement. Most tectonic activity occurs along the plate boundaries where plates separate, collide, or slide past one another.

North American Plate

Caribbean Plate

South American Plate

Scotia Plate

Cocos Plate

Nazca Plate

Antarctic Plate

Juan de Fuca Plate

Pacific Plate

Philippine Plate

Indian–Australian Plate

Eurasian Plate

Antarctic Plate

Arabian Plate

African Plate

feet above sea level. Although significant crustal activity takes place with diverging or lateral plate movement, the greatest changes take place when crustal plates come together. When plates composed primarily of heavier oceanic rock meet lighter continental plates, for example, the oceanic plate descends within the earth and creates deep oceanic trenches along the margins of the continent (Fig. 2.12). As the crustal rocks reach zones of great heat and pressure, they melt, and the molten material moves upward along fissures and zones of crustal weakness. Where it reaches the surface, volcanic peaks and ranges form, like the Cascades in Washington and Oregon or the Andean volcanoes in South America.

Where two continental plates collide, massive rock folding and crustal block movement occur, rather than volcanic activity. This causes crustal thickening and again major mountain ranges may form. The Him-

alayas, the Tibetan plateau, and other high Eurasian ranges were formed in this way where the continental Indian plate collided with Eurasia some 40 million years ago. In addition, the Alps were formed when the African plate moved against Eurasia. Thus, the plate boundary zones mark the locations of the more spectacular landforms on our planet: high mountain ranges, erupting volcanoes, and deep ocean trenches.

Perils along Plate Boundaries   Other than to explain the distribution of landforms, why are human geographers interested in the location and movement of the earth's lithospheric plates? The answer lies in the coincidence of plate boundaries with two of the earth's great *hazard zones*, those of earthquakes and those of volcanic activity. There are few things in nature more cataclysmic or destructive to human life and property than the violently shaking earth or the erupting vol-

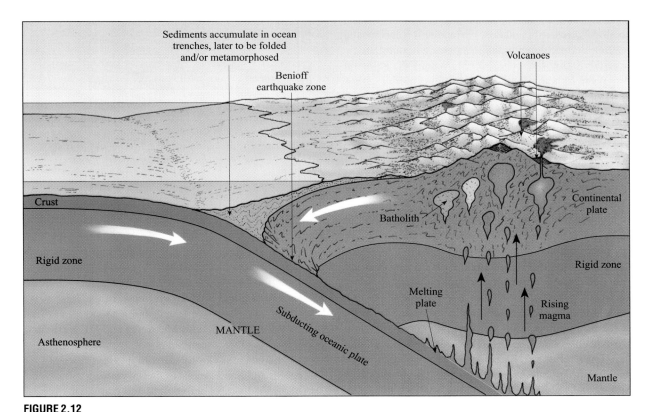

FIGURE 2.12
When a denser, heavier oceanic plate collides with a lighter continental plate, the oceanic plate descends (subducts) beneath its lighter neighbor. This leads to the formation of an ocean trench and adjoining volcanic landform features.

cano. Earthquakes occur when pressure builds along fracture zones (*faults*) in the solid crust as great crustal blocks are forced past one another by the movement of the lithospheric plates. When pressure reaches the point at which sudden slippage occurs, tremendous energy in the form of shock waves is transmitted through the crust.

Most earthquakes originate deep within the earth and are not felt on the surface. But the effects of major earthquakes that are felt can be devastating, especially to those surface areas directly above the crustal movement. Most of us can recall vividly the "World Series earthquake" of 1989 in the San Francisco Bay area, which caused billions of dollars in property damage and was responsible for the death of more than 60 persons. But this is a minor event compared with the Peruvian earthquake in 1970 that collapsed entire villages and obliterated others under enormous avalanches of rock and ice falling from Andean peaks. More than 50,000 people lost their lives.

Volcanoes can be just as destructive. When Mt. Vesuvius in Italy erupted suddenly in A.D. 79, the associated gases, ash, and dust buried the Roman coastal resorts of Herculaneum and Pompeii, claiming an estimated 20,000 lives (Fig. 2.13). When Mt. Pelée on the West Indian island of Martinique literally blew apart in 1903, the resulting firestorm rushed down the mountain slope and in a few minutes killed all but one person in a city of 30,000. And although the loss of life was small by comparison (more than 60), the 1980 eruption of Mt. St. Helens in the Cascade Range of southern Washington reminded all of us in the United States that no one living in a volcanic region is immune from a natural disaster.

Why do humans live in hazard zones, risking life and property on the odds that cataclysmic events will not occur while they are in residence? First, the odds are in their favor. Even though earth history does repeat itself, and certain volcanic regions and fault zones are more active than others, earth processes move slowly, and as generations come and go, the memory of the preceding disaster fades with the years. Second, most people who live in hazard zones may feel that they have no other choice. It was the home of their parents and grandparents, it is where they make their living, and they may be unfamiliar with other locations. Third, and perhaps most important, there are often excellent reasons for living with the unpredictable tectonic event. The climatic conditions of the Andean highlands, for example, are far superior to the geolog-

FIGURE 2.13

The villas of a restored Herculaneum provide evidence of the affluence exhibited by wealthier citizens in an early Roman civilization. The arches below the villas are part of stone boathouses that mark the former coastline. (R. Gabler)

ically safer tropical lowlands nearby. The volcanic rocks of Hawaii, Indonesia, and the Philippines consistently renew the fertility of the soils in these hot, wet regions in which agriculture is normally limited by quick removal of plant nutrients. In the same way, thriving vineyards are found along the slopes of recently erupted volcanoes Mt. Aetna and Mt. Vesuvius, near the Mediterranean Sea.

Then there is California with its great cities of Los Angeles and San Francisco, literally sitting astride one of the world's most active fault and earthquake zones. No one knows when the "big one," the truly devastating earthquake, will occur, but everyone agrees that it will happen—some day. For most Californians, it is a matter of weighing the climate, the scenery, their careers, and their lifestyle against the perils of residing in a hazard zone. The state observes the strictest building codes in the nation, remains fully prepared for the next tremor, conducts business as usual, and awaits its fate.

Human Alteration of Landforms

➤ At least since the beginning of sedentary agriculture, humans have modified physical landscapes to suit their needs.

Why has human alteration of landforms increased so rapidly since the beginning of the industrial period?

What consequences of human modification of landforms are positive? What are negative?

Although the changes humans make in the natural landscape are minute compared to the sum total of changes made by natural forces, on a local level human alterations of natural landforms can be highly significant. This is especially true when we consider that for thousands of years humans have been altering the land as they have engaged in agriculture, forestry, grazing, mining, and building construction. Agriculture is undoubtedly the oldest of human activities that significantly have affected landforms. Deforestation for agricultural purposes has greatly accelerated soil erosion, especially in the tropical and middle latitudes. Erosion is pronounced in some parts of Europe where woodlands have been widely destroyed, and it is especially conspicuous in areas along the Mediterranean Sea where overgrazing has been a major problem.

Many farming societies have terraced hill and mountain slopes to create additional agricultural space while attempting to keep erosion at a minimum. Such terraces can be found in Asia where the terraces are flooded to grow paddy rice (Fig. 2.14), in Peru, on the slopes of the Andes, in Lebanon, and to a lesser extent in Greece and Italy in the Mediterranean basin. In all of these regions the agricultural terraces create a truly spectacular landscape. Looking up at them from below, one sees only the terrace faces; looking down from above, all that is visible are green fields, orchards, or rice paddies. Humans also have drained lakes, marshes, and tidelands, as in the polders of the Netherlands, and along Florida's Gulf Coast to create additional agricultural lands. By these means, people have modified the shorelines of the land masses and

FIGURE 2.14
Rice terraces high in the Himalayas of the state of Sikkim in India. The photo was taken at the time of the dry winter monsoon, after the rice had been harvested. (R. Gabler)

increased their productive land area. (See *Cultural Landscapes: Polders of the Netherlands.*)

Overgrazing by herds of domesticated animals has accelerated erosion throughout the occupied world. Severe erosion can create deep gullies where land once was level or gently sloping. These gullies may in turn lower the water table and thereby affect vegetation in general.

Modern construction carried on by humans has significantly affected not only the form of the land, but also the associated soils, vegetation, and animal life. Construction of a modern superhighway is a good example. If you have ever watched a crew build a superhighway, you will have observed that the workers dig out the land, fill it in, flatten it out, change streambeds, build bridges, and finish everything off with an icing of concrete or asphalt. It is estimated that in the United States, where the automobile has reigned supreme for decades, there is one linear mile of road for every square mile of land. Not only does a superhigh-

CULTURAL LANDSCAPES

Polders of the Netherlands

Polders are flat-lying segments of land that formerly were beneath the sea and are now exposed only because of human modification of the physical landscape. Without these alterations—building dikes to hold back the water, installing drainage tiles, constructing canals, using pumps to remove water from the land, and sometimes adding landfill (new soil material)—the flat land that comprises the polders would be under water. The new land is a cultural landscape because it would not exist without purposeful and well-organized human activity. Polders have been built in brackish deltaic areas and coastal marshes in many countries around the world, but they are most closely associated with the Netherlands. Approximately half of the total area of the Netherlands consists of polders and the canals that separate them. No other European nation has more artificial land.

The earliest inhabitants of what is now the Netherlands resorted to building mounds to elevate their homes above the marshes and provide protection from the encroaching sea. Perhaps as early as the eighth or ninth century the citizens worked for greater protection by building dikes; by the fourteenth century several parts of the coastal zone were surrounded by dikes constructed to protect against sea or river flooding. During the Middle Ages, people in this lowland part of Europe also began transforming peat bogs into productive land by extracting the peat (precoal organic deposits), and adding fertilizers. In the twelfth century the windmill was first used for pumping water over the dikes. By the end of the sixteenth century, the Dutch were using their huge windmills extensively and effectively to drain the polders. Constructing canals and using windmills, they began draining inland lakes during the seventeenth century, forming new polders that had been below sea level by as much as 20 feet (6.2 m).

The most ambitious single reclamation undertaking in the Netherlands has been the Zuider Zee project, begun in the 1920s. Construction teams built a dike across the mouth of the Zuider Zee, a marine inlet of the North Sea, and freshwater accumulation behind the dike created a lake named Ijsselmeer (after the major river that flowed into it). Once the Dutch established the freshwater lake, they began draining segments of it to create new polders. The first reclamation project, completed in 1930, added almost 50,000 acres (20,250 ha) of new farmland to the nation's land resources. Other Zuider Zee reclamation projects implemented in the Ijsselmeer since 1930 have increased the total amount of new land to over 400,000 acres (162,000 ha). One more large addition is possible and could add another 100,000 acres (40,500 ha), but already the Zuider Zee project has been of huge importance by providing 10 percent of the nation's total farmland. By the year 2000 as many as half a million people will be settled on the new farms and in the cities of the Ijsselmeer polders.

A farm in the old polders of the Netherlands. (R. Gabler)

The layout of the polderlands greatly influences landholdings and settlement patterns. In the new lands of the Ijsselmeer district, landholdings of 60 to 148 acres (24 to 65 ha) are laid out in rectangular parcels bounded by canals or drainage ditches. Farmsteads are located on these holdings, producing a dispersed settlement pattern. Towns and cities have been established at regular intervals to act as service centers for the surrounding rural areas. In the older polderlands of the nation, rectangular properties defined by artificial waterways also are typical, but the size of holdings is more irregular. Many farmers live in a dispersed fashion in these areas, while others have arranged their farmsteads into linear hamlets on dikes and along roads. Windmills, although now rapidly disappearing, still pump water over dikes in older polders; most pumping, however, is now accomplished by electric or diesel engines.

Once reclaimed from beneath the sea, the soils of new polderlands initially have such a high salt content that they commonly must be "flushed" in order to make them agriculturally productive. The flushing process diverts freshwater onto the land; its subsequent drainage carries away the excessive salt, a process that may require as long as several years. After the flushing is accomplished and the soils are adequately drained, the new polders become some of the best agricultural lands in the Netherlands. On well-drained polderlands, the soils yield large harvests of small grains (wheat, rye, oats), sugar beets (for sugar extraction), fodder beets (for cattle feed), fruits, vegetables, and horticultural specialties such as cut flowers, potted plants, and flower bulbs. (The Netherlands leads the world in the production of flower bulbs.)

Government-planned farmsteads in the Ijsselmeer polders. (R. Gabler)

Much of the intensive horticultural production is accomplished in huge greenhouses. The polderlands that are not well drained most commonly are used for pasture to support dairy cows. Black and white Dutch cows, closely related to the Holstein breed, dot the landscape and account for the nation's leading agricultural exports—meat, milk, butter, and cheese. However, agriculture produces only about 20 percent of the total exports for this modern, industrialized nation.

THOUGHT QUESTIONS

1. Can you think of any areas where the natural landscape has been as completely converted into a cultural landscape as the Dutch polderlands? How do these examples differ from the polderlands?

2. If you had been a member of the Dutch Parliament, how would you have determined which farmers should occupy the rich new agricultural lands created by the Ijsselmeer project?

3. In comparison with older reclaimed areas, the newest Dutch polders have a much lower percentage of land dedicated to crop farming. Why do you suppose this is so? What other uses might be made of the land?

way, or any road for that matter, visibly alter the natural shape of the land, it also alters the character and quality of the land by disturbing the soil, water drainage, and vegetation.

The changes in landforms and the environment caused by urbanization are even more significant. A city has acres of land covered with concrete, tar, asphalt, steel, drainage grates, and manhole covers. Except for small preserved parkland areas, the natural landscape of the urban center is almost completely obscured. Often even the original shape of the land—the mounds and the depressions—has been eliminated by the bulldozer and, as in highway construction, such modification of the natural landscape affects the entire environmental complex; soils, vegetation, and animal life are altered or even totally eliminated. Urbanization also triggers erosion in surrounding areas. All the precipitation that formerly percolated into the soil now falls on concrete, asphalt, steel, and glass. It is drained into storm sewers that funnel into streams that are not accustomed to such heavy flows. The rush of the water results in streambed deepening or scour, which triggers bank collapse, and the newly scoured-out sediment is deposited downstream, causing additional problems there.

Other examples of human alteration of landforms include the end products of constructing dams, extracting resources, disposing of waste, draining wetlands, and modifying coastal areas. An especially harmful example is open-pit mining, which has turned productive, gently sloping farmland into a maze of barren hills and water-filled craters. Shaft mining has produced huge banks of waste and spoils wherever valuable mineral products are exploited. Each new dam, together with the reservoir behind it, changes the course of a river, fills valleys, and drowns floodplains. So many depressions throughout the United States have been filled with the solid products of human waste that new sites for waste disposal are at a premium. The alteration of wetlands and coastal areas has threatened water supplies; permanently damaged wildlife; changed the nature of shorelines; added new lands for industry, housing, and recreation in some areas; and in others led to the deterioration of some of our most scenic coastal regions. Only the great forces of the earth can create new mountain chains, or erode hill lands to plains, but humans have had a significant impact on the land as they have superimposed their cultural landscapes on the face of the earth.

THE EARTH ATMOSPHERE

➤ In addition to containing gases necessary for plant and animal life, the atmosphere makes possible environmental variations in the form of climate and weather.

How are climate and weather differentiated?

Why is climate often the dominant element of a habitat?

The solid earth is surrounded by an atmosphere that extends as far as 6000 miles (9600 km) into space. This mixture of gases is essential to life as we know it on earth. In addition to containing the oxygen that humans and other animals breathe and the carbon dioxide necessary for photosynthesis and plant growth, the atmosphere serves to regulate the receipt and transfer of solar energy, therefore maintaining livable temperatures at the earth's surface. The ozone layer of the atmosphere screens out dangerous amounts of ultraviolet radiation. Most meteors never reach the earth because they are burned by friction as they pass through the atmosphere.

Conditions within the atmosphere change dramatically with altitude, and humans are affected by these changes. The further one moves above the earth's surface, the thinner the atmosphere and the lower the atmospheric pressure becomes. Jetliners must have pressurized cabins to provide ground-level pressure conditions and to protect passengers from lack of oxygen and low temperatures. In the lowest layer of the atmosphere, termed the **troposphere**, where most human activity takes place, temperatures decrease at a nearly uniform rate with increasing altitude. This produces the significantly different environmental conditions that prevail between lowlands and highlands throughout the world. The troposphere is also the atmospheric layer where water vapor, dust particles, and—unfortunately—much of the human-generated air pollution is concentrated.

Within the troposphere the air is in constant motion. There are broad circulation patterns, fueled by solar energy and governed by the planetary relationships that exist between the earth and the sun, that produce varied atmospheric conditions from place to place at the earth's surface.

Geographers use the terms **climate** and **weather** when describing atmospheric conditions at a given lo-

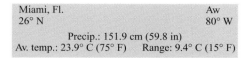

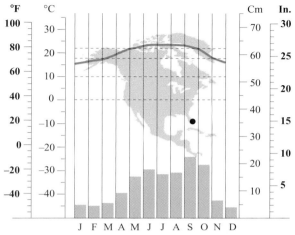

FIGURE 2.15

A graph illustrating the climate of Miami, Florida. The curving line on the graph shows average temperatures, and the individual bars show average precipitation for each month of the year.

cation. Climate is a summation of the conditions one might expect throughout the year whereas weather is an expression of the conditions that exist at a particular moment in time. For example, when northerners travel to Florida in January, they do so because they know the southern United States has a mild winter *climate* (Fig. 2.15). However, when a mass of cold Arctic air moves out of Canada it may bring freezing temperatures as far south as Florida and the *weather* at that time can be downright chilly.

Types of climate and weather are differentiated by stating the conditions of the various characteristics or elements of the atmosphere. Of primary importance among the elements are temperature and precipitation (rain, snow, sleet, hail). Of secondary importance are atmospheric pressure and wind. The climate of a particular location might be discussed in terms of such characteristics as annual totals and seasonal patterns of precipitation, monthly averages and seasonal extremes of temperature, prevailing wind directions, and annual patterns of atmospheric pressure. On the other

hand, a weather observer might report current temperature, wind direction and velocity, atmospheric pressure, and whether it is sunny, cloudy, or raining. In either case the atmospheric elements tell the story.

Human geographers are interested in the earth's varied climates because climate is a fundamental characteristic of the physical environment with which all societies must deal. Because climate has great influence on other aspects of the environment, including landforms, it is usually the dominant element that characterizes a human habitat. Although each location on earth has its own unique combination of climatic elements, there are enough similarities from place to place that geographers can group the world's climates into broad zones or regions based on the dominant elements of temperature and precipitation. However, before we consider climatic regions, let us briefly examine the dominant climatic elements for a better understanding of their distribution.

Solar Energy and Temperature Distribution

➤ Earth–sun relationships are of primary importance in accounting for the distribution of temperatures on earth.

How does the receipt of solar energy in the Northern and Southern Hemispheres vary over the course of a year?

How do land masses and oceans influence temperature distributions?

The annual dynamics of the atmosphere and the distributional patterns of all the climatic elements can be traced to the unique relationships between the earth and the sun. Figure 2.16 shows familiar diagrams illustrating how the inclination of the earth's axis during the earth's annual orbit around the sun causes the direct rays of the sun to shift north and south of the Equator as the year progresses. Receipt of solar energy (and hence temperature) varies by latitude because of this movement. As an example, at the time of the June **solstice** (about June 22) the direct rays of the sun have reached their maximum northern latitude ($23\frac{1}{2}°$ N). It is also on this date that the days are longest in the Northern Hemisphere. This combination of direct rays, which concentrate solar energy over small areas, and long days produces maximum receipt of solar energy,

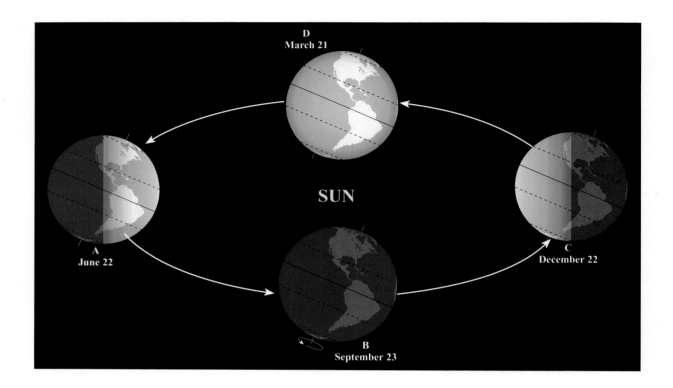

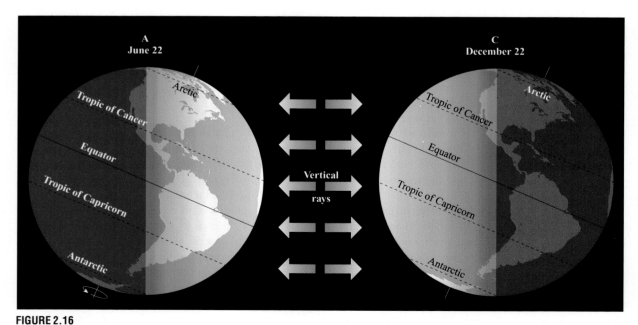

FIGURE 2.16

Geometric relationships between the earth and the sun at the time of maximum shifts of the direct rays of the sun north and south of the Equator (the June and December solstices). Note the differing day lengths and angles of the sun's rays during summer and winter in the Northern and Southern Hemispheres.

higher temperatures, and summer in the Northern Hemisphere.

In contrast, in the Southern Hemisphere low-angle sun rays and short days at the June solstice produce minimum receipt of solar energy, lower temperatures, and winter. At other dates through the year the direct sun rays are striking at other latitudes between $23\frac{1}{2}°$ N and $23\frac{1}{2}°$ S and maximum incoming solar radiation (*insolation*) shifts back and forth between Northern and Southern Hemisphere. The shifting pattern of insolation during the year produces six distinct latitudinal temperature zones (Fig. 2.17). In the Northern Hemisphere the Tropic of Cancer and the Arctic Circle may be used as the dividing lines of these zones. The area between the Equator and the Tropic of Cancer is the north tropical zone. Here insolation and temperatures are always high but are greatest when the direct rays of the sun are over the Northern Hemisphere. This occurs between the March and September **equinoxes** (about March 21 and September 23).

The north midlatitude zone is the wide band between the Tropic of Cancer and the Arctic Circle. In this belt, insolation is greatest at the June solstice when the sun reaches the highest noon altitude and the pe-

riod of daylight is longest, and it is least at the December solstice (about December 22) when the noon sun is low in the sky and the days are short. It is in this midlatitude zone where temperatures vary greatly through the year and there are distinct seasons.

The north polar or Arctic zone extends from the Arctic Circle to the North Pole. In this zone insolation and temperatures are low throughout the year except for a brief summer when the noon sun is highest in the sky and when the sun will be continuously above the horizon for twenty-four hours during one or more days of the season.

In the same way, there are the south tropical zone, the south midlatitude zone, and the south polar or Antarctic zone separated by the Tropic of Capricorn and the Antarctic Circle in the Southern Hemisphere. These areas receive their greatest and least amounts of insolation and experience their highest and lowest temperatures at opposite times of the year from the northern zones.

Figure 2.18 provides an illustration of temperature distribution near the times of the December and June solstices, the extreme periods of temperature conditions on earth. (The months of January and July are mapped because there is a lag of atmospheric temperature maxima and minima behind shifts in receipt of insolation.) The maps illustrate average sea level temperature by means of lines called *isotherms* that connect points of equal temperature. Note that what is first apparent on both maps is the general tendency of the isotherms to run in an east–west direction, similar to the parallels of latitude. This is to be expected since insolation varies with latitude. Despite seasonal differences, temperatures are at a maximum near the Equator and at a minimum near the poles in both January and July.

Another feature of the two maps is a product of changing insolation as the sun shifts north and south across the Equator between the two solstices. Note that when the direct rays of the sun are striking near the Tropic of Capricorn in January, the temperatures over the Southern Hemisphere are at their highest; in July, when the direct rays are near the Tropic of Cancer, Southern Hemisphere temperatures are lowest. Australia, for example, has places with average temperatures of 90° F (30° C) or more in January but in July the average temperatures are much lower. This makes sense, of course, because in the Northern Hemisphere seasons are the reverse of those in the Southern Hem-

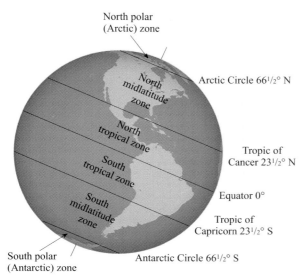

FIGURE 2.17

The line of the Equator, the Tropic of Cancer, the Tropic of Capricorn, and the Arctic and Antarctic Circles define six latitudinal zones that have distinctive characteristics of insolation.

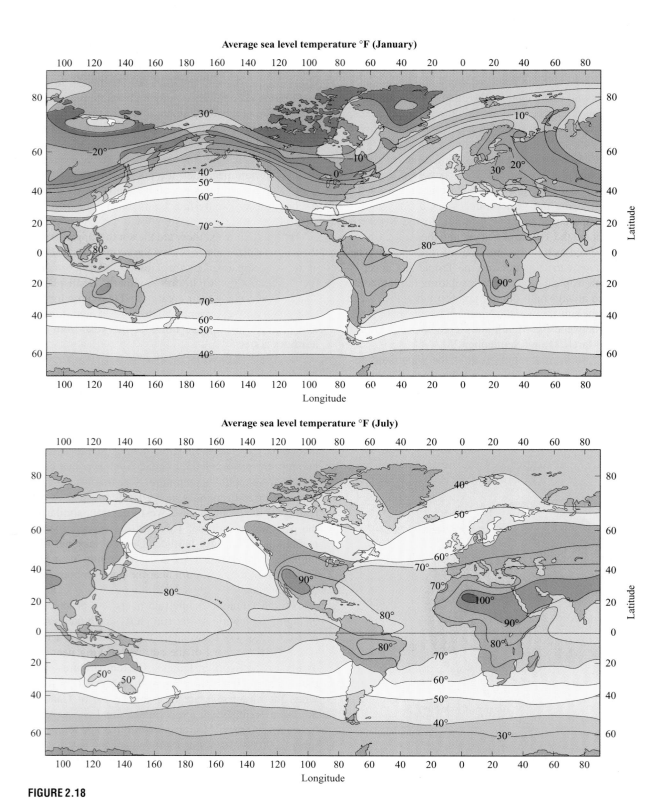

FIGURE 2.18

Average sea level temperatures (°F) in January and July.

isphere; in the Northern Hemisphere temperatures are lowest in January and highest in July.

Finally, note that temperatures are much hotter in summer and colder in winter over the continents than over the oceans. This is especially true in the Northern Hemisphere, which contains the largest land masses. This characteristic of atmospheric temperatures is a direct result of the fact that land heats and cools much more rapidly than water. It is important to remember when considering climate at a given latitude that temperature extremes are found in the interiors of continents and more moderate temperatures are found near the oceans.

Patterns of Precipitation

➤ Global patterns of precipitation reveal a great range between desert areas and zones of maximum precipitation.

What are the typical locations of the world's major desert areas and zones of heaviest precipitation?

What factors influence the distribution of precipitation?

A world map of average annual precipitation illustrates that the availability of moisture from place to place over the earth varies as much as temperature (Fig. 2.19). What may be most important to humans (and may come as a surprise to students who have not previously studied the map) are the vast areas of the earth that have limited potential for human use because of a lack of moisture. Because the original source of most of the earth's precipitation is the world ocean, the nearer to continental interiors one looks the drier the atmospheric conditions generally become. This is especially true in the upper-middle latitudes wherever north–south trending highlands block the generally west-to-east movement of moist oceanic air. In both North and South America major arid regions (generally between 10 and 20 inches or 25 and 50 centimeters per year) are found to the lee of mountain ranges between 40° and 65° latitude. On the west coasts, humid conditions are limited to narrow coastal zones. In contrast, note that in western Europe the lack of north–south highlands allows moist air to penetrate far inland.

The earth's greatest deserts and adjacent semiarid regions are located both north and south of the Equator in the general vicinity of the Tropic of Cancer and the Tropic of Capricorn. Throughout much of the year in

these latitudes there are large cells of high atmospheric pressure along the western coasts of the continents. The descending and diverging movement of the atmosphere in these cells creates conditions that are the direct opposite of those that produce clouds and precipitation. The Australian, Namib, Kalahari, and Atacama deserts of the Southern Hemisphere, as well as the Thar, Arabian, Sahara, and Sonoran deserts of the Northern Hemisphere are all associated with subtropical cells of high pressure. They share the cloudless skies, relentless sunshine, high daytime temperatures, and cool nights characteristic of deserts in these latitudes.

The large areas of low precipitation poleward of the Arctic and Antarctic circles are not technically considered deserts or semiarid regions. Even though they receive exceedingly low amounts of precipitation, rates of evaporation in the cold polar air are so low that these regions actually experience a surplus of moisture. They are of little value for most human activity, not because of insufficient precipitation but because of the short growing seasons and their low temperatures during most of the year.

Further examination of Figure 2.19 reveals that there are two broad latitudinal zones of significant precipitation. The zone of heaviest precipitation lies astride the Equator and extends for some distance poleward where coastal regions face moist, steady winds blowing onshore from the tropical oceans. The equatorial zone of rainfall, referred to as the *doldrums* or *intertropical convergence* (ITC), is situated where winds moving away from the high pressure cells of both hemispheres converge. The converging air rises, the air is cooled, water vapor in the air condenses, clouds form, and heavy precipitation results. The ITC includes much of northern South America, west-central Africa, the major tropical Pacific Islands, and the peninsular extensions of southern Asia. The zone of heavy rainfall extends well poleward in south Asia as low pressure develops over the continent during the summer months. Air laden with moisture is drawn by the lower pressure centers into India, southern China, and the lands in between, as far as the interior mountain ranges.

The second zone of precipitation lies in the upper-middle latitudes and extends inland from both west and east coasts until the dry climates of the continental interiors are reached. This is the zone of westerly winds (wind moving generally west to east across the continents). In the Southern Hemisphere, little land is

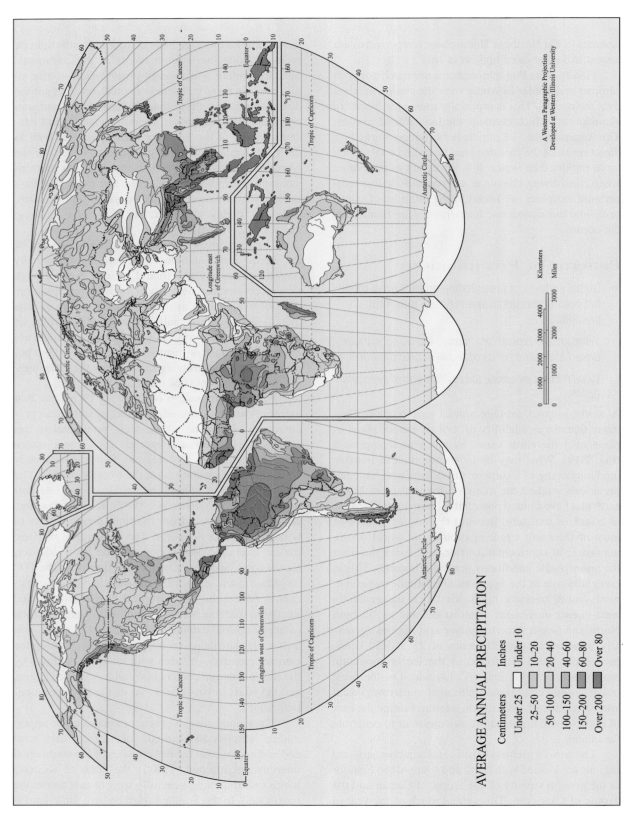

AVERAGE ANNUAL PRECIPITATION

Centimeters   Inches
Under 25   Under 10
25–50   10–20
50–100   20–40
100–150   40–60
150–200   60–80
Over 200   Over 80

A Western Paragraphic Projection
Developed at Western Illinois University

FIGURE 2.19

located in these latitudes and significant rainfall is limited to southern Chile, New Zealand, and extreme southern Australia. In the Northern Hemisphere this is the zone where cold polar air drifting southward meets warm moist air flowing northward from the tropical oceans. Where the contrasting air comes together, cyclonic storms develop and form the basis for daily weather changes. The precipitation associated with these storms is reinforced in summer along eastern coasts by moisture-bearing winds flowing inland from the warm oceans. As expected, rainfall amounts decrease both poleward and toward continental interiors as distance from the sources of moisture increases.

Variety in Climate

➤ Classifying the world's varied climates into specific types helps us understand their global distribution, associations with other environmental elements, and potential as human habitats.

What are the world's various climatic types and their typical locations?

Which climatic regions are most densely populated, and what are their apparent attractions?

What seems to explain population concentrations in some of the other climatic regions?

As we have observed from our review of temperature and precipitation distribution, there is infinite variety in each of the atmospheric elements. There is so much variety that, as background for human geography, it is helpful to generalize some climatic data and reduce the infinite number of worldwide climatic variations by combining elements with similar statistics. Through this procedure, called *classification*, we can identify a relatively small number of groups or types of climate. Each climatic type is significantly different from all others in the classification system, but all places that represent a given type have climatic characteristics that are similar.

When choosing a classification system, geographers are interested in the map that results when the distributions of the various types within the system have been plotted. Figure 2.20 is a world map of climatic types from a classification system originally developed in the early 1900s by a German scientist, Wladimir Köppen (1846–1940), but modified on numerous occasions since then. There are distinct advantages to the **Köppen classification**. It establishes precise statistical parameters or boundaries that

differentiate one climatic type from another. It uses not only readily available data concerning averages and totals of temperature and precipitation but also takes into consideration seasonal distribution. In addition, the boundaries of the system were selected to conform to boundaries between important natural vegetation types.

The world map of climates shows that each climatic type is distributed in a recurring pattern governed by latitude and continental position. There are five major climatic groups, four of which—humid tropical, humid mesothermal (mild winter), humid microthermal (severe winter), and polar—are differentiated on the basis of temperature. The fifth, arid climates, is distinguished by moisture deficiency that is determined by formulas that take into consideration not only total precipitation but evaporation rates as well. Note that because of low evaporation rates the polar climates are not considered to be moisture deficient even though they receive little precipitation. Note also that the many **microclimates** of mountains and other high elevation landforms are mapped together in a separate group labeled highlands.

Bear in mind when examining the map in Figure 2.20 that the climatic variations between regions are greatest for places near the centers or cores of each region. The boundaries between regions that appear as lines on the map are actual zones of transition where the climatic statistics between one place and another change gradually. Boundaries fluctuate as temperature and precipitation vary from year to year, and it is impossible to determine exactly when you have crossed from one climatic type to another as you travel the earth's surface.

The Humid Tropics The Köppen classification uses letter symbols to identify the individual climatic types within the system. Each letter represents a specified characteristic or range of either temperature or rainfall. However, as the legend of Figure 2.20 indicates, there are also descriptive names (the use of which will be sufficient for the purposes of our discussion) associated with the various climates. The humid tropical climates, therefore, include the *tropical rainy* or *rainforest*, the *tropical monsoon*, and the *tropical savanna* types. Table 2.3 summarizes the location, characteristics, and related features of these three climates.

With their location either within or adjacent to the tropics, the humid tropical climates have no winter season and temperatures are high throughout the year.

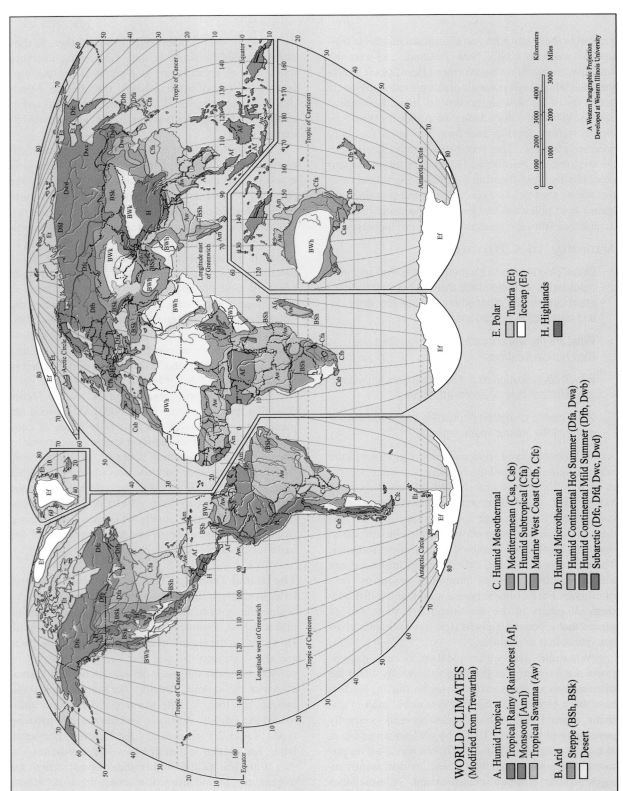

WORLD CLIMATES
(Modified from Trewartha)

A. Humid Tropical
  Tropical Rainy (Rainforest [Af],
  Monsoon [Am]
  Tropical Savanna (Aw)

B. Arid
  Steppe (BSh, BSk)
  Desert

C. Humid Mesothermal
  Mediterranean (Csa, Csb)
  Humid Subtropical (Cfa)
  Marine West Coast (Cfb, Cfc)

D. Humid Microthermal
  Humid Continental Hot Summer (Dfa, Dwa)
  Humid Continental Mild Summer (Dfb, Dwb)
  Subarctic (Dfc, Dfd, Dwc, Dwd)

E. Polar
  Tundra (Et)
  Icecap (Ef)

H. Highlands

A Western Paragraphic Projection
Developed at Western Illinois University

FIGURE 2.20

TABLE 2.3	The Humid Tropical Climates		

Name	Location	Characteristics	Features
Tropical Rainforest	Amazon R. Basin, Zaire (Congo) R. Basin, east coast of Central America, east Coast of Brazil, east coast of Madagascar, Malaysia, Indonesia, Philippines	Constant high temperatures; equal length of days and nights; low (3–5° F) annual temperature ranges; evenly distributed heavy precipitation; high amount of cloud cover and humidity	Multi-storied broad-leaf evergreen forest, treetops form a thick canopy; jungle where light penetrates, climbing and flying animals, reptiles, and insects; shifting native agriculture; commercial plantation agriculture of rubber and cacao; major soil erosion and depletion where farming or ranching is attempted, exceptions are on volcanic soils and river floodplains
Tropical Monsoon	Coastal areas of southwest India, Sri Lanka (Ceylon), Bangladesh, Myanmar (Burma), southwestern Africa, Guyana, Surinam, French Guiana, northeast and southeast Brazil	Heavy high-sun rainfall, (especially with orographic lifting), short low-sun drought; 3–10° F annual temperature range, highest temperature just prior to rainy season	Forest vegetation with fewer species than tropical rainforest grading to jungle and thorn forest in drier margins; iron-rich soils; rainforest animals with larger leaf-eaters and carnivores near savannas; paddy rice
Tropical Savanna	Northern and eastern India, interior Myanmar (Burma) and Indo-Chinese peninsula; northern Australia; borderlands of Congo (Zaire) R., south central Africa; interior regions of Brazil (Campos) and Venezuela llanos; western Central America, south Florida, and Caribbean Islands	Distinct high-sun wet and low-sun dry seasons; rainfall averaging 30–60 in.; highest temperature ranges for Humid Tropical Climates	Grasslands with scattered, drought-resistant trees, scrub, and thorn bushes; fluctuating water table, leached soils, and compacted layers of metallic oxides (laterites) common in the subsoil; iron-rich soils on wetter margins; brown grassland soils on drier margins; large herbivores, carnivores, and scavengers

An average temperature of 64.4° F (18° C) for the coldest month was selected as the boundary for these climates because above this temperature vegetative growth and reproductive cycles are not influenced by cold. All three climates have annual rainfall amounts that exceed **evapotranspiration** (the combined rates of evaporation and transpiration), but anticipated totals and seasonal distribution of rainfall vary widely among the three types. The tropical rainforest climate has copious rainfall that is well distributed throughout the year. Although there are periods of maximum rainfall, no month averages below 2.4 inches (6 cm) of precipitation. The tropical monsoon and tropical savanna climates, on the other hand, are characterized by dry seasons of varying length, although rainfall totals for some tropical monsoon locations may be higher than those for some tropical rainforest locations.

The tropical rainforest climate is characterized by constantly high temperatures, days and nights of nearly equal length, low annual temperature ranges, evenly distributed heavy precipitation, and high amounts of both cloud cover and humidity. This is consistent with its year-round location within the dol-

(a)

(b)

(c)

FIGURE 2.21

(a) Tropical rainforest climate: clearing land for shifting agriculture in Jamaica. (R. Gabler) (b) Tropical monsoon climate: seed bed for paddy rice farming utilizing monsoon rainfall, West Bengal, India. (R. Gabler) (c) Tropical savanna climate: grazing zebras in the savanna grasslands of an East African game preserve. (Donald Marshall Collection)

drums or ITC bordering the Equator. As Figure 2.20 shows, there are also some areas of tropical rainforest—as in Central America, South America, and the island of Madagascar—along coasts facing persistent winds carrying moisture from the oceans throughout the year.

The most common natural vegetation of the tropical rainforest climate is the multi-storied, broad-leaf evergreen forest that is the climate's namesake (Fig. 2.21). The forest is made up of many species whose tops form a thick, almost continuous cover that pre-

vents much of the sunlight from reaching the ground and produces a forest floor with little undergrowth. The relationship between the soils of the tropical rainforest and the vegetation is so close that there exists a nearly perfect ecological balance between the two. The trees of the rainforest supply the soils with the nutrients the trees need for growth. As leaves, flowers, branches, and trunks fall to the ground, and as roots die, the numerous soil animals and bacteria act on them, transforming the organic matter into usable nutrients. However, when the forest is cleared for human

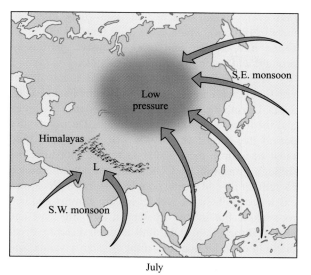 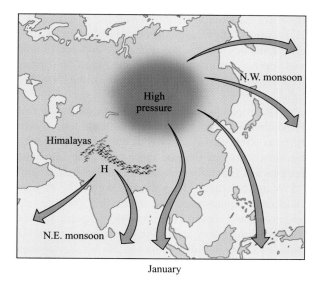

FIGURE 2.22

Seasonal changes in surface wind direction that create the Asiatic monsoon system. The onshore flow of tropical humid air in summer usually results in heavy precipitation; the offshore flow of dry continental air in winter creates the "dry monsoon" and drought conditions in southern Asia.

use, there is rapid deterioration of soil fertility. Even if the land is abandoned and new vegetation flourishes, there is little chance that the true rainforest will return.

With a few notable exceptions, such as along river floodplains or in areas of volcanic soils, tropical rainforest regions are among the earth's least inhabited climates. In addition to limitations on continuous agriculture, there is the discomfort associated with ever-present heat and humidity, the constant battle with countless insects that thrive in the absence of cold and drought, and serious health hazards for inhabitants. Human parasites and disease-carrying insects abound. Malaria, yellow fever, and sleeping sickness are a constant threat in the tropics, especially to visitors from the middle latitudes who have not developed immunity to such diseases. In the past native populations have been subsistence hunters and gatherers or have practiced shifting agriculture—clearing and farming small fields for a few years until fertility is diminished, and then moving to a new area. Today, however, as populations are rapidly increasing in less developed tropical nations, the forests are being considered a new frontier to be permanently settled. (Details of this recent development are included in Chapter 14.)

The tropical monsoon climate is primarily a poleward extension of the tropical rainforest climate, and in Figure 2.20 the two climates are mapped together. The relatively short, dry, low-sun season (when the noon sun is lowest in the sky) and the heavy rainfall that accompanies the high-sun season (when the noon sun is highest in the sky) of the monsoon climate are associated with pressure changes and shifts in wind direction that occur over southern Asia (Fig. 2.22). There is an outflow of dry air from interior Asia during the low-sun season and a strong movement of moist tropical air from the oceans to the Indian subcontinent and southeast Asia during the high-sun season. The seasonally heavy rainfall is most significant along coastal areas of India, Myanmar (Burma), and Bangladesh, although a modified monsoon effect occurs in restricted coastal areas of Africa and South America as well.

The wet and dry seasons of the monsoon climate are extremely important to the inhabitants of India and southeast Asia. Most of the people living in those areas are farmers and their major crop is rice, the staple food for millions of Asians. Much of the rice is irrigated and grown in flooded fields or paddies, so the monsoon rains are essential to its growth. (Refer to Fig. 2.21.) Harvesting of the rice, on the other hand, must be done during the dry season. The difference between famine and survival for many people in the monsoon regions depends on the arrival and departure of the monsoon rains.

The tropical savanna climate is one of the few that is dominated by seasonal contrasts in climatic conditions as atmospheric zones shift north and south with the direct rays of the sun during the year. Savanna regions are generally centered inland between 5° and 15° N and S latitude. They usually border the tropical rainforests equatorward and the earth's great deserts and associated semiarid lands toward the poles. During the high-sun season, atmospheric conditions resemble those of the humid doldrums and during the low-sun season these regions experience the almost cloudless skies and aridity of the Equatorward-shifting high pressure cells. Precipitation patterns vary considerably; savanna locations close to the rainforest may have

rain every month and annual totals may reach 70 inches (180 cm), whereas the drier margins of the savanna have longer and more intensive periods of drought and much lower annual rainfalls.

The typical savanna vegetation is a mixture of grasslands with trees, scrub, and thorn bushes (Fig. 2.21). During the wet periods the grasslands are green and the trees are covered with foliage. During the dry period the grass turns dry, brown, and lifeless, and most trees drop their leaves to reduce moisture loss through transpiration. Conditions are not well suited to agriculture and native populations live a precarious existence. Soils in the wet season are gummy and water-soaked, but in the dry season they are hard and almost impenetrable. Rainfall is unpredictable, especially in the drier margins of the African savanna, and famine is a clear danger during drought periods. Even though most savanna regions make poor pasture lands at least part of the year, animal husbandry can support limited populations where more nutritious subtropical

TABLE 2.4 The Humid Mild Winter Climates

Name	Location	Characteristics	Features
Mediterranean	Central California; central Chile; Mediterranean Sea borderlands, Iranian highlands; Capetown area of South Africa; southern and southwestern Australia	Mild, moist winters, hot, dry summers inland with cooler, often foggy coasts; high percentage of sunshine; high summer daily temperature range; frost danger	Summer drought-resistant (sclerophyllous) vegetation; low, tough brush (chaparral); scrub woodlands; varied soils, severe erosion in Old World regions; winter-sown grains, olives, grapes, vegetables, citrus, irrigation farming
Humid Subtropical	Southeastern United States; southeastern South America; coastal southeast South Africa and eastern Australia; eastern Asia from northern India through south China to southern Japan	High humidity; summers like humid tropics; frost with polar air masses in winter; precipitation 25–100 in. decreasing inland; monsoon influence in Asia	Mixed forests, some grasslands, pines in sandy areas; strongly leached iron-rich soils; high production with continuous fertilization; rice, wheat, corn, cotton, tobacco, sugar cane, citrus
Marine West Coast	Coastal Oregon, Washington, British Columbia, and southern Alaska; southern Chile; interior South Africa; southeast Australia and New Zealand; northwest Europe	Strong oceanic influences; mild winters, mild summers, low annual temperature range; heavy cloud cover; high humidity; frequent cyclonic storms, with prolonged rain, drizzle, or fog; 3–4-month frost danger or period	Naturally forested, green year round; strongly leached humus-poor soils; root crops, deciduous fruits, winter wheat, rye, pasture, and grazing animals; coastal fisheries

grasses have been introduced or herders are free to migrate with the rains.

Mild Winter Environments   There are three distinctly different humid mesothermal or humid mild winter climates (Table 2.4). Although each has a summer season and a mild winter, there are significant contrasts in summer temperatures and rainfall characteristics among the three. The *Mediterranean* climate has hot summers inland and mild summers along coastal areas. Because of its west coast location, it also experiences summer drought associated with the same high-pressure cells that influence the location of the low-latitude deserts. During the winter season the high pressure moves equatorward and Mediterranean regions receive modest rainfall as westerly winds shift into the lower-middle latitudes to bring moisture from the oceans.

The unusual challenge to inhabitants of the Mediterranean climate is the distribution of precipitation—enough in winter to exceed annual losses from evapotranspiration but little or none during the normal summer growing season. The natural vegetation reflects the wet–dry seasonal pattern (Fig. 2.23). During the rainy winters the native grasses are lush and green but during the summer drought they turn lifeless and brown. Many of the larger plants have tough surfaces; shiny, thick leaves that resist moisture loss; and deep roots to help combat aridity. Some hillsides were originally covered by low, scrubby bushes, like the manzanita in California that grew together in an almost impenetrable tangle. Fires are a common occurrence

(a)

(b)

(c)

FIGURE 2.23

(a) Mediterranean climate: the shimmering white buildings and nearby golden fields of Granada, Spain, on a blistering hot midsummer day. (b) Humid subtropical climate: The Japanese mix homes and fields on every parcel of level land on the crowded mountainous island of Honshu. (c) Marine west coast climate: An isolated farmstead in the Scottish highlands reflects the stormy marine climate of the British Isles. (R. Gabler)

FIGURE 2.24
The charred remnants of a late summer brush fire that swept up from the canyon below and engulfed this half-million-dollar home in the Hollywood hills above Los Angeles. (R. Gabler)

in the dry grass and brush during the summer season (Fig. 2.24).

Despite the climatic drawbacks, grazing of sheep, goats, and other animals is widely practiced on sloping land in Mediterranean regions; the lowlands are farmed wherever rainfall is sufficient or water for irrigation is available. Grains like wheat and barley are winter-sown and other agricultural products, such as grapes, figs, and olives, are well suited to the moist winters and dry summers. California, with fertile valleys for growing fruits, vegetables, tree crops, and flowers, is probably the most agriculturally productive of the Mediterranean regions. It is also the one that has best exploited its warm sunny climate to attract new industries, millions of additional inhabitants, and countless tourists in recent decades.

As the world map of climates indicates, the *humid subtropical* climate occupies the east coasts of continents in nearly the same latitudes (20°–40° N and S) as the Mediterranean climate is located along the west coasts. These two climates have similar temperature

ranges, but they differ significantly in rainfall distribution. As a result of moist tropical air that flows into the humid subtropics during the summer, these regions do not experience the seasonal drought of the Mediterranean lands. Summers are marked by high humidity and frequent convectional showers reminiscent of the humid tropics that lie equatorward.

Vegetation thrives in humid subtropical regions with the abundant rainfall, high temperatures, and long growing seasons (Fig. 2.23). Before human occupance of these regions there were forests of broad-leaf deciduous trees, pine forests on sandy soils, and mixed forests. In the drier interiors forests gave way to grasslands that required less moisture. Some forests remain and are exploited for timber, fuel, and other wood products, but in general these regions are used for their enormous agricultural value. They have been farmed intensively for both subsistence crops, such as rice and wheat in Asia, and commercial crops, such as cotton and tobacco in the United States. When we consider that this is the characteristic climate of south China as well as of the most densely populated portions of both India and Japan, we realize that this climatic region supports far more human beings than any other.

There are risks associated with the human occupance of the humid subtropics, however. Severe storms, especially hurricanes and typhoons, often cause great property damage and sometimes many deaths. The high precipitation totals in wetter areas carry the threat of soil erosion and soil depletion through the removal of plant nutrients by groundwater. The old cotton and tobacco belt of the southern United States has suffered major soil exhaustion and severe erosion problems. Similar conditions face the subsistence farming regions of northern India. Only exceptional care has conserved the soil resource in China and other parts of eastern Asia. Numerous parasites and insects are another problem for crops, livestock, and humans alike. In addition, people often find the humid subtropical summer an uncomfortable experience. This handicap is offset in developed areas by the use of air conditioning and by the advantages of humid subtropical winters for vacation and retirement, but such is not the case in less developed regions of Asia and South America.

The third mild winter climate is labeled the *marine west coast*, although highland areas in certain eastern portions of southern Africa and South America have summers cool enough to match the statistical description for the climate. The typical location is between 40° and 60° N and S latitude on islands, along coasts, or situated inland in the path of prevailing winds from the west. Because of the moderating influence along these west coasts of moist maritime air flowing off the adjacent oceans, summers are mild to cool and winter months all average above freezing far poleward of locations toward the interiors of the continents. Modest precipitation occurs throughout the year and the most consistent climatic characteristics are heavy cloud cover, high humidity, and frequent cyclonic storms with prolonged rain, drizzle, or fog.

As a human habitat the marine west coast climate offers many of the advantages shared by the other mild winter climates. The small annual temperature ranges, moderate winter temperatures, long growing seasons, and abundant precipitation all favor plant growth (Fig. 2.23). Although the soils are not naturally rich in plant nutrients, highly successful agriculture is carried out with the use of either natural or commercial fertilizers. Grains, such as wheat, barley, and rye; root crops, such as potatoes, beets, and turnips; fruits, such as apples and pears; and both berries and grapes all do well in this environment. Some of the earth's greatest forests once covered most areas of marine west coast climate. Only remnants remain in Europe in carefully managed upland areas, as most European forests were cut centuries ago for timber or to clear land for agriculture. The greatest remaining reserves are found along the Pacific coast of North America where there are large stands of fir, spruce, and pine. For those people who have learned to accept the clouds, fog, drizzle, and the damp cold of winter, marine west coast climatic regions have proven to be hospitable and highly productive habitats.

Severe Winter Environments   As can be seen in Figure 2.20 the humid microthermal or severe winter climates are all situated in the Northern Hemisphere. The explanation is apparent; these are the humid midlatitude climates that owe their existence to location in the interior of continents at great distances from the oceans that serve to moderate atmospheric temperatures. No large land masses exist in the upper-middle latitudes of the Southern Hemisphere. However, in the Northern Hemisphere between latitudes 35° and 40° and the polar climates surrounding the Arctic Ocean, much of northern and eastern North America and Eurasia are occupied by either the *humid continental hot summer*, the *humid continental mild summer*, or the *subarctic* climate (Table 2.5).

The three severe winter climates have much in common. Although precipitation in microthermal regions decreases both poleward and with distance inland from the nearest coasts, there is sufficient moisture to support forests or rich grasslands where forests do not prevail. All three microthermal climates experience significant snow cover that stays on the ground longer both poleward and toward the continental interior. Each also experiences the variable and unpredictable nature of weather associated with the cyclonic storms that move at irregular intervals from west to east in the upper-middle latitudes throughout the year.

The microthermal climates are differentiated by regional characteristics related to temperature, such as the length and severity of both winter and summer and the length of the growing season, as well as the human activities associated with these characteristics. The length and severity of summer and the length of the growing season decrease poleward throughout the microthermal climates, and the length and severity of winter increase. The humid continental hot summer climate usually has subfreezing winter temperatures for significant periods of time, but in July and August there are often hot spells when heat and humidity rival that of the humid subtropics. Since the introduction of air conditioning in the United States, the ''cooling bills'' of summer now match the ''heating bills'' of winter. The growing season varies from as much as 200 days equatorward to as little as 140 days poleward. This climate comprises the heartland of the agricultural midwestern United States, where corn, soybeans, beef cattle, and hogs are the most common commodities (Fig. 2.25). Wheat, barley, and other grains are especially important in European and Asian regions.

In contrast with its equatorward counterpart, the humid continental mild summer climate rarely experiences long periods of high temperatures in summer and is characterized in winter by regular invasions of cold Arctic air that brings successive days or weeks of clear skies and frigid temperatures. Growing seasons are shorter by 1 to 3 months, averaging 90 to 130 days. Agriculture is still important but farmers must rely on quick-ripening grains, grazing animals, orchard products, and root crops. Spring wheat or other spring-sown grains must be raised and, if corn is grown, it is harvested green for fodder. In Europe, potatoes, beets, turnips, and cabbages are especially common. Dairy products are major sources of farm income in Europe as well as in such areas of the United States as New

TABLE 2.5 The Humid Severe Winter Climates

Name	Location	Characteristics	Features
Humid Continental Hot Summer	Eastern and midwestern United States from Atlantic Coast to the one-hundredth meridian; east central Europe; northern China, Manchuria, northern Korea, and Honshu	Hot, often humid summers; occasional winter cold waves; rather large annual temperature ranges; weather variability; precipitation (20–45 in.) decreasing inland and poleward; 140–200-day growing season	Broad-leaf deciduous and mixed forest with moderately leached soils in wetter areas; grasslands with fertile dark-colored humus-rich soils in drier areas; "corn belt," soybeans, hay, oats, winter wheat
Humid Continental Mild Summer	New England, the Great Lakes region, and south central Canada; southeastern Scandinavia; eastern Europe, extensive region through Russia and bordering republics to central Asia; northeastern China and east coastal Asia; Hokkaido	Moderate summers; long winters with frequent spells of clear, cold weather; large annual temperature ranges; variable weather with less total precipitation than further south; 90–130-day growing season	Mixed or coniferous forest; moderately leached soils in wetter areas; grasslands, highly fertile humus-rich soils in drier areas; spring wheat, corn for fodder, root crops, hay, and dairying
Subarctic	Northern North America from Newfoundland to Alaska; northern Eurasia from Scandinavia through most of Siberia to the Bering Sea and the Sea of Okhotsk	Brief, cool summers; long, bitterly cold winters; largest annual temperature ranges; lowest temperatures outside Antarctica; low (10–20 in.) precipitation; unreliable 50–80-day growing season; permanently frozen subsoil (permafrost) common	Northern coniferous forest (taiga); strongly acidic soils; poor drainage and swampy conditions in warm season; experimental vegetables and root crops

England, New York, and Wisconsin. Humid continental mild summer climate often coincides with recently glaciated regions. The combination of comfortable summer temperatures, beautiful forests, snow-covered slopes in winter, and crystal-clear lakes left by glacial erosion has made New England and the upper Midwest major tourism and recreation areas (Fig. 2.25).

Finally, in the subarctic climatic regions the summers are so short and cool and the winters so long and bitterly cold that there is little hope for agriculture. The growing season averages 50 to 70 days and frost may occur even during June, July, and August. Permanent settlements have developed for politically strategic purposes or to exploit mineral deposits, but the most common human activity is hunting, fishing, and trap-

ping by native populations. Seemingly endless tracts of spruce, fir, and pine occupy enormous areas, generally untouched by humans (Fig. 2.25). Logging is unimportant because of small tree size or because the wood for paper or pulp is too distant from world markets.

Arid Lands Aridity is one of earth's greatest challenges to human settlement and, as was indicated in our discussion of world patterns of precipitation, large areas of each middle latitude continent suffer from insufficient moisture. The classification on which Figure 2.20 is based recognizes two distinct climatic types, *desert* (arid) and *steppe* (semiarid). Both desert and steppe are identified on the basis of the relation be-

(a)

(b)

(c)

FIGURE 2.25
(a) Humid continental hot summer climate: a bumper crop on an Illinois Corn Belt farm. (R. Gabler) (b) Humid continental mild summer climate: autumn colors bordering a New Hampshire lake, an attraction for visitors from throughout the eastern United States. (R. Gabler) (c) Subarctic climate: this rapidly sinking rail line provides evidence of obstacles to human occupance of the Canadian subarctic with its permanently frozen subsoil. (U.S. Dept. of the Interior, Geological Survey)

tween precipitation and potential evaporation. In the desert climate the amount of precipitation received is less than half the potential evaporation. In the steppe climate the precipitation is more than half of the potential evaporation but less than the total.

The deserts of the world are core areas of aridity, usually surrounded by steppe regions that receive slightly greater precipitation (Fig. 2.26). Both climates owe their existence to location in areas of persistent high atmospheric pressure with descending, diverging

air, or to location close to continental interiors protected from oceanic sources of moisture by distance or intervening highlands. Both range from the tropics to the upper-middle latitudes (Table 2.6). The tropical arid lands experience average annual temperatures above 64.4° F (18° C) whereas many middle latitude arid regions have long, cold winters.

Although deserts and steppes share their common reasons for existence and similar locations, they present strikingly different landscapes and quite separate

WORLD DESERT AND STEPPE REGIONS

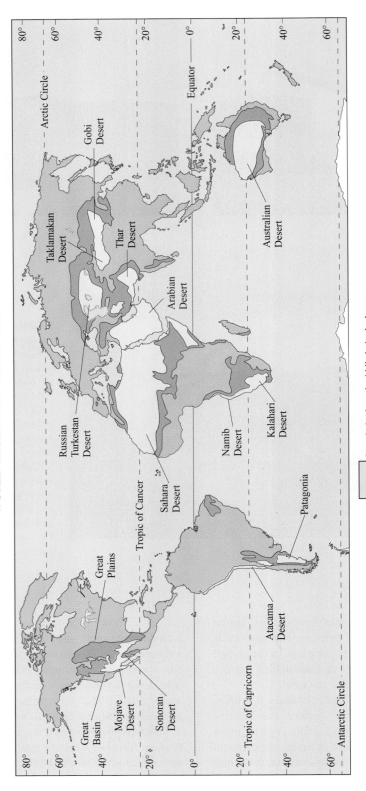

Low latitude and middle latitude deserts

Low latitude and middle latitude steppes

FIGURE 2.26

The world's arid lands.

| TABLE 2.6 | The Arid Climates | | |

Name	Location	Characteristics	Features
Desert	Coastal Chile and Peru, southern Argentina, southwest Africa, central Australia, Baja California and interior Mexico, North Africa, Arabia, Iran, Pakistan, and western India (tropical and subtropical); inner Asia, and western United States (midlatitudes)	Aridity; low relative humidity, irregular and unreliable rainfall; highest percentage of sunshine, highest daily temperature range, highest daytime temperature; windy conditions	Year-round, drought-resistant (xerophytic) vegetation; often barren, rocky, or sandy surface; desert soils, excessive salinity; usually small, nocturnal or burrowing animals; nomadic herding, irrigated agriculture where water is available
Steppe	Peripheral to deserts, especially in Argentina, northern and southern Africa, Australia, central and southwest Asia, and western United States	Semiarid conditions, annual rainfall distribution similar to nearest humid climate; temperatures vary with latitude, elevation, and distance from oceanic sources of moisture (continentality)	Dry savanna (tropics) or short grass vegetation; highly fertile dark-colored soils; grazing animals in vast herds, predators, and smaller animals; ranching, dry farming

challenges to the humans who seek to occupy them (Fig. 2.27). The deserts are stark and forbidding environments with vast areas of bedrock, gravel, or sand and only sparse drought-resistant vegetation. Deserts are lands of extremes—extreme drought, maximum daytime temperatures, high amounts of insolation throughout the year, and great daily temperature ranges. The little precipitation that does fall in desert regions is both irregular and unreliable. An enormous cloudburst might bring more precipitation in a single

(a)

(b)

FIGURE 2.27

(a) Desert climate: the barren landscape of the Mojave Desert in southern California. (b) Steppe climate: grasses of the Nebraska Sand Hills support sleek cattle where herds of American bison once roamed. (R. Gabler)

rainfall than has been recorded in months or even years. Likewise, the skies could remain cloudless for months. For these reasons deserts have had limited human occupance.

For the most part desert people traditionally have been hunters and gatherers, nomadic herders, and subsistence farmers wherever there was a reliable water supply. However, given a sufficient source of water from *exotic rivers* (rivers that bring water from outside the region) like the Nile, Colorado, Tigris-Euphrates, and Indus, desert regions can be agriculturally productive. The river floodplain soils are little leached and rich in plant nutrients. With careful irrigation and flushing of soils to prevent excessive salinity, desert oases have become significant producers of commercial crops for export to other regions.

Steppes involve most of the earth's great grassland regions, often covered by rich soils and originally teeming with a variety of wildlife. In North America this was the realm of the bison and antelope and in Asia the domain of wild horses. Farmer and herder alike have been attracted to the fertile grasslands, but not without cost to both humans and the environment. As in deserts, precipitation is highly variable. A series of wetter years inevitably will be followed by a period of drought. Those who attempt to farm the semiarid steppes may have bountiful harvests for a time, but if irrigation or special ''dry farming'' methods are not applied, they ultimately will be forced to abandon the land to the relentless wind and blowing topsoil. And in the drier portions of the steppe climate, overgrazing

by domesticated cattle, sheep, and goats is an almost universal problem.

Polar Regions   The two polar climates share a common obstacle to human use; they are too cold throughout the year to permit the agriculture or other human activity that would support significant populations. The polar climates are found in the highest latitudes, usually poleward of the Arctic and Antarctic Circles. These are regions with a net annual radiation loss— that is, they give up more energy through earth radiation each year than they receive from the sun. The only reason they do not become progressively colder is because winds transport heat into polar regions from warmer climates closer to the Equator. Polar climates also have low annual precipitation because the latitudes they occupy are dominated by the descending air associated with high atmospheric pressure. However, these climates are classified as humid because precipitation still exceeds potential evaporation in the cold polar air.

Polar climates are subdivided into the *tundra* and the *ice-cap* types (Table 2.7). Of the two, tundra is the less restrictive environment. Its warmest month averages above freezing, although frost is possible on any date. Another glance at Figure 2.20 reveals that, with the exception of the Antarctic Peninsula, the tundra climate borders the Arctic Ocean. Maritime influences are strong enough to moderate both winter and summer temperatures so that annual temperature ranges are less than those of the subarctic climate. Because

TABLE 2.7	The Polar Climates		
Name	**Location**	**Characteristics**	**Features**
Tundra	Arctic Ocean borderlands of North America, Greenland, and Eurasia; Antarctic Peninsula; some polar islands	Summerless; at least 9 months average below freezing; low evaporation; precipitation usually below 10 in.; coastal fog; strong winds	Tundra vegetation; thin, young, poorly drained soils; permafrost; swamps or bog conditions during brief, cool summers; life most common in nearby seas; Inuit populations; mineral and oil resources
Ice-cap	Antarctica; interior Greenland; permanently frozen portions of the Arctic Ocean and associated islands	Summerless; all months average below freezing; world's coldest temperature; extremely meager precipitation in the form of snow; evaporation even less; gale-force winds	Ice- and snow-covered surface; no vegetation; no exposed soils; only seal life or aquatic birds; scientific exploration

growth of even the hardiest tree species requires monthly temperatures that average 50° F (10° C) or higher, the tundra regions are treeless (Fig. 2.28). However, during the damp and chilly summer there is sufficient surface thawing to allow for the growth of

mosses, lichens, grasses, and shrubs. Unfortunately, this thawing constitutes a further problem because the subsoil remains permanently frozen. The tundra in summer soon becomes a morass of lakes, marshes, swamps, and bogs.

The ice-cap climate is situated primarily in Antarctica and Greenland. It has no month that averages above freezing. There may be some thawing when the sun is above the horizon, but this climate constitutes what is essentially a frozen and lifeless environment. Wildlife from the surrounding oceans may visit from time to time, but the main value of these lands to humans is either scientific or strategic (Fig. 2.28). Permanent research stations have been established in Antarctica by several nations, and the strategic importance of this continent is so widely recognized that all nations have voluntarily given up their claims to territorial rights in exchange for cooperative exploration in behalf of all humankind.

THE IMPACT OF CLIMATE

➤ Although climate is an extremely important component of the physical environment, humans nevertheless have the potential to overcome climatic limitations or handicaps.

How may a society's level of technology influence its evaluation of and associations with the physical environment?

We noted in Chapter 1 that some early geographers (the environmental determinists) were inclined to exaggerate the influence of climate and other aspects of the physical environment on human activity. Perhaps we could better understand why they held such ideas if we lived when they did—at a time when most of the world's people lived at a subsistence level, technology was poorly developed, and only a few nations had made significant progress toward industrialization. To people who are poorly equipped to deal with environmental conditions, the environment is likely to be viewed as a powerful force that has a great effect on their lives and daily activities.

With industrialization, modernization, and the rapid growth of technology, the human–environment relationship has changed. Humans have proven capable of overcoming climatic and other environmental limitations and handicaps. As we will explain in Chapter 14, there also is growing evidence that human ac-

(a)

(b)

FIGURE 2.28

(a) Tundra climate: Tundra landscapes, like this one in northern Alaska, are almost impossible to cross during the thaws of a brief summer season. (R. Gabler) (b) Ice-cap climate: Argentina's research base in Antarctica. (William E. Ferguson, Nature Photography)

tivity may be altering climate to the detriment of future generations and societies. Clearly, the association between human beings and the characteristics of the climates in which they live is a close one, and it is contantly changing.

Climate and Agriculture

➤ Among human activities closely associated with climatic conditions, agriculture is particularly important.

What factors, in addition to climate, account for present global agricultural patterns?

We have reiterated the direct association of climate and agriculture at many points. Each crop or farm product is best suited to certain conditions of temperature and precipitation. Since the beginnings of sedentary farming, humans have discovered through trial and error which plants and animals native to their climatic regions give the greatest promise of a reliable food supply. But many living things can thrive under a variety of climatic conditions. As a result humans have introduced and adapted farm products that were not native to the climatic region in which they lived. What has emerged is a worldwide pattern of agriculture that is closely associated with climate but is influenced greatly by cultural preference and technological development.

In several climatic types agriculture is severely limited or nonexistent. Growing seasons are of insufficient length in the subarctic and polar climates. Farming in desert regions depends on irrigation and an adequate water supply. Much of the humid subtropics now is of little use for continuous farming because unwise cropping practices and heavy rainfall have eroded the soil and removed soil nutrients.

However, in parts of the tropical climates and throughout the more humid middle latitude climates specific crop patterns have emerged. Rice is the staple of the diet for millions of people in the humid tropical lowlands of south Asia. Dairying, hay production, and the raising of various root crops characterizes the marine west coast regions of western Europe. Corn, soybeans, hogs, and beef cattle are common agricultural commodities of the humid continental hot summer climate of the American Midwest. The temperature/rainfall characteristics of the Mediterranean climate are so unusual that a crop combination involving winter-sown grains, olives, grapes (wine production), citrus,

and various vegetables, soft fruits, and nuts can be found in each region where the climate is located.

Climate, Vegetation, and Soils

➤ Climate, vegetation, and soils have strong natural associations with one another.

How are the earth's four major biomes related to temperature and precipitation?

In what ways are soil-forming processes influenced by climatic conditions?

The climate/agriculture relationship is but one obvious demonstration of the natural associations among climate, vegetation, and soils. Figure 2.29 illustrates the relationships to temperature and precipitation of the earth's four major plant communities (**biomes**): forest, grassland, desert, and tundra. In the tropics the biomes grade from rainforest to monsoon forest, to scrub forest, to savanna, and to desert with decreasing rainfall. In the middle latitudes the progression is from forest to woodland, to chaparral (Mediterranean woodland), to grassland, and finally to desert. The subarctic regions are dominated by coniferous forest (*taiga*) and the only vegetation in the Arctic is tundra. However, even in these two latter regions the biomes are affected by precipitation amounts. As precipitation decreases in the subarctic and arctic, the individual plants grow smaller and farther apart.

Although other factors—such as the local bedrock or transported parent material from which the soil is formed, the slope of the land and soil drainage, or organic activity—may be of greater importance locally, on a global scale the soil-forming processes are dominated by the climatic elements. A soil process termed *laterization* occurs in humid tropical and subtropical climates where high temperatures and abundant precipitation produce rapid breakdown of rocks and decomposition of minerals. There is little or no organic debris (*humus*), and heavy accumulation of iron and aluminum compounds occurs in the subsoil. Where forest vegetation remains, the soluble nutrients released in the weathering process are quickly absorbed by the vegetation, which eventually returns them to the soil where they are reabsorbed by other plants. This rapid nutrient cycle prevents the total removal of basic material, so the soil is only moderately acidic.

In cool moist climates *podzolization* is a critical soil-forming process. With lower temperatures the ac-

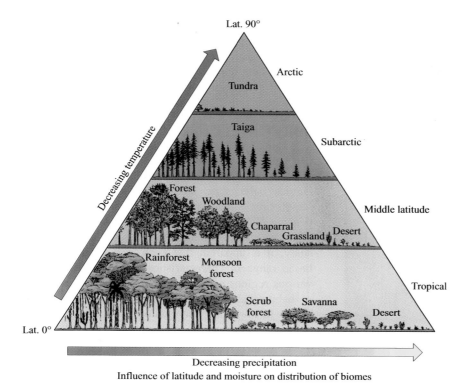

Lat. 90°

Arctic

Tundra

Taiga

Subarctic

Decreasing temperature

Forest

Woodland

Middle latitude

Chaparral

Grassland   Desert

Rainforest   Monsoon
forest

Tropical

Scrub
forest   Savanna

Desert

Lat. 0°

Decreasing precipitation

Influence of latitude and moisture on distribution of biomes

FIGURE 2.29

*The distribution of the earth's
major biomes as they are related
to temperature (latitude) and the
availability of moisture. Within
the tropics and middle latitudes
there are distinctly different
biomes as total biomass decreases
with decreasing precipitation.*

tivity of microorganisms is reduced and humus accu-
mulates, usually at the surface of the soil. Most of the
soluble basic material as well as aluminum and iron
compounds are removed by strongly acidic soil water.
Coniferous trees are the typical vegetation where podzolization is most common, and the acidic nature of
the needles they drop contributes to the acidic quality
of the soils. As a further illustration of the close association between climate-controlled vegetation and
soils, it is difficult to say whether the soil is acidic
because of the vegetative cover or whether the vegetative cover is adapted to the acidic soil.

The third climate-related soil-forming process is
termed *calcification*. Calcification occurs in climates
where evapotranspiration exceeds precipitation and
grassland vegetation prevails. With little precipitation
and low soil moisture, basic material is not removed
from the soil and it tends to accumulate near the surface. Calcification is enhanced by the fact that grass
uses calcium, drawing it up from the lower soil layers
and then returning it to the soil when the grass dies.
The grasses and their dense root networks provide
large amounts of organic matter to the soil, which is

typically mixed deep into the soil by the numerous
animals found there. Hence midlatitude grassland soils
are rich both in bases and in humus and are among the
world's most productive agricultural soils.

Other Climatic Effects

In addition to indirect effects through agriculture,
soils, and vegetation, the atmospheric elements have
direct impacts on human populations that are literally
too numerous to mention. Consider such atmosphere-
related phenomena as hurricanes, floods, ice storms,
blizzards, and tornadoes (Fig. 2.30). Each can result
in significant property damage and possible loss of
life. Of less dramatic nature, but involving much
greater numbers of people, is the migration of humans
with the seasons; examples are ''snowbirds'' from the
northern United States and Canada traveling south to
Florida to escape the cold of winter, well-to-do Indians
fleeing to the highlands of the Himalayas to avoid the
worst heat of the Calcutta summer season, and African
herders following the rain and greener pastures as the
wet and dry seasons come and go in the savanna.

FIGURE 2.30

The devastation from Hurricane Andrew in southern Florida, August 24, 1992. Andrew was the costliest natural disaster in U.S. history, with more than $20 billion in damages. (Frank Siteman/Stock Boston)

Moreover, almost taken for granted are the human adjustments to climate in terms of clothing and housing. Without question, climate is a fundamental part of the physical environment with which people, at whatever level of civilization, must continue to contend.

OUR COMPLEX HABITAT

Our survey in this chapter of the earth's various environmental elements leads to an obvious conclusion: Human habitats are exceedingly complex systems. Landforms, climate, vegetation, soils, and other components of habitats exist in enormous variety. Even when we classify them into types to facilitate their study, it is apparent that each type encompasses a broad range of characteristics and is represented in various regions of the world. The different elements of habitats also are intricately interrelated; each is linked in important ways with all other elements to create an environmental system that is delicately balanced. In every part of the world, the human inhabitants are able to find within the environmental complex a combination of perceived opportunities and obstacles for their way of life. To avoid catastrophic disruption of the balanced environmental system, people must employ wisdom and caution as they exploit opportunities and confront obstacles of their habitats.

KEY TERMS

Hydrologic cycle   The exchange of water between the earth's surface and atmosphere in a general cycle involving evaporation, condensation, precipitation, and runoff.   **43**

Continental shelf   The extension of a continental block beneath the shallow margins of an adjacent sea or ocean   **45**

Local relief   The difference in elevation between the highest and lowest points of land in a specified area.   **48**

Plate tectonics   The independent movement and deformation of segments (plates) of the earth's crust.   **53**

Troposphere   The lowest general layer of the atmosphere; most weather activity occurs in this layer.   **62**

Climate   The accumulated weather over a relatively long period in a place or region, usually expressed in terms of averages and deviations from the norm.   **62**

Weather   The condition of the atmosphere at a specific place and time.   **62**

Solstice   The date when the noon sun is vertical at the Tropic of Cancer (about June 22) and at the Tropic of Capricorn (about December 22).   **63**

Equinox   The date (approximately March 21 and September 23) when the noon sun is vertical at the Equator and on which the periods of daylight and darkness are of equal length over the entire earth.   **65**

Köppen classification A widely used classification of climates developed by Wladimir Köppen. **69**

Microclimates The climates of relatively small areas or precise locations. **69**

Evapotranspiration The transfer of water at the earth's

surface into water vapor in the atmosphere by the combination of evaporation and transpiration. **71**

Biomes Major terrestrial ecosystems, such as tropical rainforests or grasslands. **84**

REVIEW QUESTIONS

1. What characteristics of its physical environment make the earth unique and supportive of life as we know it?

2. Why is the earth termed the water planet? What is the hydrologic cycle and what effects does it have on the physical environment?

3. What examples can you cite that illustrate the impact of the availability of fresh water on human geography?

4. What is the significance to humans of the size and location of the earth's oceans and continents?

5. What is the definition of local relief, and how can local relief and the steepness of slopes be used to distinguish major landform types?

6. What are some of the advantages and disadvantages for human occupance of plains, mountains, hill lands, and plateaus?

7. Where, in general, are the earth's plains and mountains located in respect to their position on the continents? How is this explained by the theory of plate tectonics?

8. What is meant by a hazard zone? How are both the volcano and earthquake hazard zones related to the movement and present distribution of the earth's lithospheric plates?

9. What are some of the beneficial and some of the detrimental effects of human alteration of landforms? What human activities have been most responsible for transforming the physical landscape?

10. What is the difference between the climate of a given location and the weather of the location? What characteristics or elements of the atmosphere are used when describing a location's climate and weather?

11. Why is climate usually the dominant element that characterizes a human habitat? Why are data on temperature and precipitation used to group the world's climates into broad zones or regions?

12. How do earth–sun relationships influence the general distribution and seasonal changes of temperature on the earth? How do locations in the interior of a continent and near an ocean coast affect temperatures?

13. Where are the earth's great deserts and semiarid regions, and what factors influence their location? In what latitudes are the earth's humid regions and what explains their location?

14. What are the three climates of the humid tropics, and how do they differ from one another? What limitations to human occupance exist in each of the three? What factors explain the concentrations of population that exist in each?

15. How and why does the Mediterranean climate differ from the humid subtropical climate? How have humans taken advantage of the characteristics of each?

16. In what way does continental location explain the characteristics of the marine west coast climate? How would you evaluate this climate as a human habitat?

17. What are the three severe winter climates of the upper-middle latitudes? What do they have in common and how are they distinguished from one another? How do these distinctions account for differences in human activity among the three?

19. How do the definitions of desert and steppe climates differ? What contrasts in the physical landscape are reflected in these differences? Why does human occupance of steppes often involve greater risks than the occupance of deserts?

19. Why do tundra and ice-cap climatic regions offer the least potential as human habitats? What human activity is most likely in these regions?

20. What are the natural associations between climate, vegetation, and soils? How are the earth's four major biomes related to temperature and precipitation? What soil-forming processes are related to climate?

CHAPTER 3

CULTURE AND CULTURE REGIONS

*The significance . . . of the physical and biotic features
of the habitat is a function of the attitudes, objectives,
and technical skills of [the inhabitants].*

—Preston E. James

*This Latin American girl at holy communion illustrates the role of culture
in accounting for regional variations over the earth.* (Stock, Boston)

89

The associations of people with their habitat are more intricate and variable than the environmental determinists of earlier generations recognized. As we noted in Chapter 1, the environmental determinists persisted in concluding that the physical environment controls human activities, progress, and attainments. Modern human geographers, however, are now aware of the critical and dynamic role of culture in human/environment relationships. As individuals and groups of people evaluate the elements of their habitat, identify environmental resources, and choose ways of using the environment and solving environmental problems, they rely on their *culture*. Culture provides direction, guidance, orientation, opportunities, and limits as humans interpret their habitat, make decisions, and exploit the available resources.

WHAT IS CULTURE?

➤ Human culture consists of all those traits acquired by people through both formal and informal learning processes.

How does popular use of the term culture *differ from its technical meaning?*

What is the difference between formal and informal learning?

In order to understand **culture** as an object of geographical investigation, it is essential to be aware of technical definitions of the term. "Culture" is a common word with a variety of meanings. In popular usage, culture often is associated with the fine arts. For example, a Shakespearean play or a concert by a symphony orchestra is likely to be identified as a cultural event. A refined or educated person may be regarded as cultured; in contrast, a crude, ill-mannered person who has poor taste may be regarded as an uncultured person. As used by geographers and other social scientists for technical purposes, the term *culture* is interpreted quite differently.

It has long been common in the social sciences to identify culture as "a way of life," or *genre de vie* in the words of the French geographer Paul Vidal de la Blache. As indicated in the quotation at the beginning of this chapter, the American geographer Preston E. James employed more specific terms in referring to culture as "the attitudes, objectives, and technical skills" of a people. Modern definitions of culture in

this sense tend to emphasize that culture is an ensemble of human traits acquired through learning processes.

Both formal and informal learning processes are involved in the dissemination of culture. For example, informal learning occurs as a child interacts daily with parents, siblings, and playmates, and as adults share ideas, beliefs, attitudes, and skills with one another. Formal learning processes, on the other hand, are more structured and usually involve teacher–student interaction in the setting of a school or other institution. By such learning activities, cultural transfer can occur throughout an individual's lifetime and from one generation to the next.

Cultural Traits

➤ Cultural traits are the individual components of a cultural complex. A group of people that is distinguishable by its possession of a unique assortment of cultural traits may be called a society or a cultural group.

What three categories encompass most cultural traits?

Is there a difference between cultural groups and ethnic groups?

How do racial traits differ from cultural traits?

Every human being is born into a cultural environment that includes customs, beliefs, attitudes, goals, technology, and material possessions, as well as the means to communicate or transmit these characteristics or **cultural traits** from individual to individual and from generation to generation. We might regard cultural traits as the building blocks of culture. They are the individual components that together form the cultural complex.

Cultural traits are numerous and varied, but we can group most of them into three categories. (1) *Sociological traits* are those involved in the interaction between an individual and other members of a group (e.g., family, gang, school, or church) within the society. These traits include the laws, regulations, rules, and standards that societies and groups adopt to regulate or govern the behavior of their members. (2) *Ideological traits* are associated with a society's belief systems. They include the society's philosophies, convictions, beliefs, faiths, myths, and legends, as well as the means by which these are communicated. Particularly important among these traits are religious and political ideologies. (3) *Technological traits* are the tools, techniques, and skills possessed by a society and used to provide food, clothing, housing, material goods, defense, and entertainment. A society's technological traits are closely linked to the character and level of its economic development. We need to keep in mind that the cultural traits in all three of these categories do not exist in isolation; they are interrelated parts of a whole and each influences the others.

A society that differs from all others in terms of the unique assortment of cultural traits it possesses is often called a **cultural group**. A cultural group also may be identified as an **ethnic group**, but these two terms are not precisely synonymous because racial characteristics may be involved in the identification of an ethnic group. It is important to point out that culture and race are fundamentally different concepts. Cultural traits, as we have stated, are acquired through learning, but racial traits (including skin color, facial features, stature, and the character of hair) are biological characteristics that are inherited. Although a racial group may acquire certain distinguishing cultural traits, members of different races can share the same cultural characteristics and thus belong to the same cultural group (Fig. 3.1).

FIGURE 3.1

A single cultural group may contain members of different races. Culture involves learned characteristics, whereas racial traits are inherited. (Daemmrich/Stock Boston)

Material Culture and Cultural Landscapes

➤ Material culture consists of the physical objects created by people as they engage in their way of life. These objects are components of the cultural landscape.

How are material culture and nonmaterial culture related?

By what means have natural landscapes been converted into cultural landscapes?

Closely associated with **nonmaterial culture**—the various learned attributes including attitudes, beliefs, goals, language, and technological skills that we described in the previous section—are objects of **material culture**. The physical items produced by people as they engage in their particular way of life, including their clothing, houses, places of worship, crops, roads, monuments, and even textbooks, are objects of material culture. It is important to recognize that items of material culture reflect the nonmaterial culture of the individual or group who created them. Whether it is a suit of clothes, a building, or a crop field, every item of material culture produced by an individual or group has incorporated into it some of the attitudes, goals, and skills (i.e., the nonmaterial culture) possessed by the individual or group. While both nonmaterial and material culture are important in geography, field studies are likely to be focused on material culture because it is more conspicuous on the landscape. For example, a building of worship (material culture) is more readily discerned than the religious faith (nonmaterial culture) it serves. (See *The Geographer's Notebook: The Geography of Housing*.)

Material culture on the earth's surface reflects human activity and is displayed in *cultural landscapes*. People long have been the dominant agent of environmental change. Few places on the face of the earth remain untouched and unaltered by direct or indirect human influence. Distinct cultural imprints on the landscape have emerged as humans have used and modified the earth's habitats. Some of the most visible features of the cultural landscape have resulted from human modifications of natural vegetation, plant and animal husbandry, resource utilization, the division of land, and the construction of settlements and transportation lines. Cultural landscapes display lesser or greater alterations of the original natural landscape depending, to a considerable degree, on the level of tech-

The Geography of Housing

Among the innumerable elements of material culture, none has attracted greater attention among geographers than the structures built by people to meet their housing needs. *Folk housing*—the dwellings of a society's common people—has been the usual focus of attention because it is more representative than the ostentatious housing of the elite. As prominent and relatively durable features of the cultural landscape that contribute to distinctive spatial variations over the earth, houses are of geographic significance. Important place-to-place differences can be noted in the architectural style and floor plan of houses, as well as in the building materials and techniques employed in their construction. By combining such characteristics, geographers have identified different *house types* that facilitate generalization about spatial patterns.

Houses also have important diagnostic value to the geographer. The characteristics of houses can indicate a great deal about their inhabitants' way of life and associations with the natural environment. Furthermore, the spatial patterns houses exhibit can provide a means of determining past routes of migration by certain culture groups and can serve an important role in delimiting (determining the extent of) culture regions.

The building material and architectural details of houses, for example, may reflect local environmental conditions and problems. Available resources usually will influence whether most folk houses in an area are built primarily of stone, brick, wood, adobe, grass, or some combination of materials. Houses with steeply pitched roofs are typical of areas with heavy precipitation, and particularly of those with deep snow accumulation. The rare precipitation in desert areas, on the other hand, may allow structures to be built with flat roofs. Housing in tropical deserts commonly is distinguished by thick walls made of stone, brick, or adobe material in a light color to reflect solar rays and help moderate interior temperatures. Of course, the scarcity of wood in desert environments as well as in semiarid grasslands encourages the use of alternative building materials. The construction of houses on stilts is common in areas where floods are frequent and where circulation of air beneath the floor is desired to cool the interior.

While we may tend to regard houses as relatively permanent features, in a number of societies temporary shelters are typical. This is particularly true of nomadic livestock herders of the Old World deserts, whose housing consists of tents that can be quickly assembled and disassembled to accommodate the frequent movement of these people to new grazing lands. Although groups in the rainy tropics that engage in shifting cultivation do not move as frequently as nomads, the usual housing suggests that it will be abandoned as soon as local soil resources are exhausted. Units in the mobile home parks of North America also are a form of temporary housing, although some owners may use them as permanent residences.

Geographers have been able to reconstruct past routes of migration and identify the boundaries of culture regions by mapping the occurrence of specific house types and their characteristics. This investigation is based on the tendency of individual cultural groups to employ distinctive architectural styles and building practices in constructing their housing. Once generally adopted by the group, these familiar housing characteristics commonly were transplanted to new areas by members of later generations as they migrated ever farther from their cultural hearth area. The relative durability of houses, usually surviving their builders, has aided the reconstruction of past human spatial patterns when other evidence has disappeared.

THOUGHT QUESTIONS

1. What are some means of adapting or altering housing now underway in the United States to conserve energy? Are there any regional variations in these efforts? What are they?

2. Do you feel that it is probably more difficult now than in the past to use housing as a means of differentiating culture regions within the United States? Why or why not?

3. Can you suggest any evidence other than housing that might be used to trace past human migrations?

FIGURE 3.2

A view of Tokyo. In some urban settings the natural landscape is almost completely obscured by buildings, streets, parking lots, and other elements of material culture. (R. Gabler)

nology possessed by the people. Tribal groups occupied by hunting and gathering may make so few landscape changes that their impact is scarcely noticeable. Industrial-urban societies, on the other hand, can so completely cover an area with concrete and steel that little of the natural environment remains evident (Fig. 3.2).

CULTURAL CHANGE

➤ Cultural change may be initiated within a society or introduced from external sources.

By what means may a culture change from within the group?

What processes may result in cultural change from outside the group?

Because cultures are dynamic and continually changing, the geographer must be alert to any modifications that may result in new spatial patterns or alterations in human associations with the natural environment. Change tends to be relatively infrequent among isolated and traditional societies. However, modern industrial-urban societies are likely to place a high value

on new ideas and skills and thereby experience frequent change.

Change can occur in a culture as a consequence of developments within the group or as a result of contacts with representatives of other cultures. Within every group of substantial size there are creative individuals who, through their original ideas, inventions, and innovations, stimulate fundamental cultural change. Consider, for example, the impact on American culture of Thomas Jefferson's ideas about democratic government, Thomas Edison's invention of the light bulb, and Henry Ford's innovations in automobile manufacturing.

A group's culture also may change as a result of contact with a different cultural group. Such change can be forced on a weaker group by a stronger one as a consequence of war, conquest, or colonization. On the other hand, such friendly contact between groups that goes along with the establishment of alliances, the conduct of trade, and the exchange of tourists also can lead to cultural change. One group may adopt another's ideas, techniques, practices, and technology if they are perceived to improve on those previously held.

Cultural change can occur in varying degrees. **Acculturation** takes place when one group merely assumes some of the cultural traits of another (Fig. 3.3). When a group changes so completely that its culture is no longer distinguishable from that of another, the process is called **assimilation**. If the interaction of two or more groups results in each one enriching or im-

FIGURE 3.3

An example of acculturation, the adoption of a trait from another culture. (Charles Gupton/Stock Boston)

proving its culture by the adoption of traits of the other, that process is described as **cross-cultural fertilization**.

Cultural Diffusion

➤ By means of diffusion processes, cultural traits are spread from one location to another.

What conditions or circumstances might facilitate cultural diffusion?

What might retard it?

How does a culture hearth come about?

The spread of cultural traits from their points of origin to new locations is a function of **diffusion**. The dominance of the Roman Catholic Church in Latin America and the English language in Australia, as well as the cultivation of maize (corn) in Africa and the presence of Chinatown in San Francisco, are consequences of cultural diffusion. As a general rule, accelerated rates of cultural change and growth tend to occur in those locations in which historical, locational, or social factors have been conducive to the steady flow and exchange of ideas through diffusional processes. By

the same token, the more isolated a cultural group is from other peoples or from exposure to new ideas, the more stagnant it will be.

An area that has been a rich source of cultural traits diffused to other locations is called a **culture hearth**. The world's primary culture hearths (Fig. 3.4) coincide with the areas of the earliest human civilizations. Some of the ideas, institutions, technologies, and goods from these centers of early cultural advancement spread to other areas and regions over many centuries. Additional secondary culture hearths developed later in time at other locations.

During the colonial period of North America, for example, four secondary culture hearths were established (Fig. 3.18). European settlers in the Middle Colonies discovered that Indian corn was an excellent feed for their livestock. As a result, pioneers from the area carried this idea across the Appalachians, into the Ohio River Valley, and eventually into the farmlands of the Middle West. Diffused in this way, the practice of raising corn primarily to feed livestock became the central economic activity on nearly every Middle Western farm. Many other cultural practices from these secondary hearths were diffused to various parts of North America in a similar way.

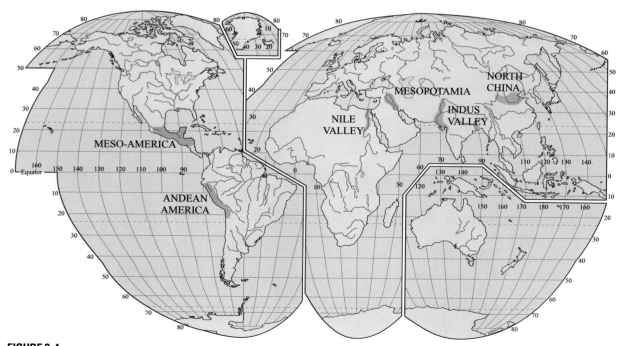

FIGURE 3.4

The world's primary culture hearths. These areas were major centers of early cultural development.

Cultural Revolutions

➤ Cultural changes since Paleolithic time that have had particularly far-reaching consequences are the Agricultural, Industrial, and Democratic Revolutions.

Which of these revolutions remain underway at the present time?

What kinds of cultural developments initiated each of these revolutions?

The examination of cultural history confirms that fundamental changes in the way of life of human groups in the past have been exceedingly slow, often extending over many generations or centuries. *Cultural revolutions*, those dramatic changes influencing most facets of life, in fact have been quite rare. Those designated by Preston E. James and other geographers as having the greatest impact are the **Agricultural Revolution**, the **Industrial Revolution**, and the **Democratic Revolution**. The Agricultural Revolution, initiated about 10,000 years ago, often is used to mark the separation of the **Paleolithic Period** (Old Stone Age) from the **Neolithic Period** (New Stone Age). The Industrial and Democratic Revolutions, underway only since the eighteenth century, have yet to spread to all of the world's societies. As a result, they often are identified as modern or contemporary cultural revolutions.

The Agricultural Revolution   Plant domestication and the somewhat later domestication of animals were the central technological advancements of the Agricultural Revolution. These developments made it possible for Neolithic peoples to engage in a more intensive form of economic activity and a more sedentary lifestyle than did their Paleolithic predecessors, who apparently practiced a seminomadic lifestyle in order to survive by hunting, gathering, and fishing. Although the earliest experiments in plant domestication probably were undertaken thousands of years earlier, the major centers of early agriculture developed no more than about 10,000 years ago. Agriculture was so rare and restricted in area in 8000 B.C. that the livelihood of almost all humans on earth at that time was still based on hunting, gathering, and fishing. By the beginning of the Christian era, however, the vast majority of people were farmers.

Carl Sauer, the American geographer most noted for studies of early agriculture, suggested that the initial domestications were probably in regions of great diversity of plant species—the subtropics and tropics.

He also argued that agriculture did not *originate* in major river valleys, even though such areas as Mesopotamia and the Nile Valley were among the first centers of concentrated farming. According to Sauer, more likely sites of the earliest agriculture were forested hill lands, which had better drainage and soft, easy-to-dig soils. We cannot be absolutely certain about the area where the first plant domestications occurred, of course. Sauer favored locations in Southeast Asia, but most other authorities have concluded that it was in Southwest Asia. It seems certain that agriculture did not originate in only one place and diffuse from there to all other areas. Instead, plant domestications appear to have been carried out in a number of regions during a fairly short span of human history.

Figure 3.5 designates the principal regions of early agriculture and identifies several of the main domestications accomplished in each. It is clear that some plants were domesticated in more than one center. Also, it is noteworthy that several of the regions of plant domestication also include areas in which domestications of major livestock animals occurred. It is interesting to note that neither of the two regions of early agriculture in the Americas were important centers of animal domestication. (See *Cultural Landscapes: The Sacred Cattle of India.*)

By the beginning of the Christian era, a considerable amount of diffusion of domesticated plants and animals had been accomplished in southern Asia, China, Africa, and Europe. Diffusion into Europe was from the eastern Mediterranean area. After the fall of the Roman Empire, agricultural diffusion was slowed, but later Arab traders were active in the process. Fifteenth- and sixteenth-century European explorers initiated the exchange of crops and domesticated animals between the Old World and the New World, and soon a more complex agriculture emerged in all of the world's agrarian areas.

The Industrial Revolution   During the eighteenth century the second major cultural revolution got underway. This new development, which first appeared in Great Britain and soon spread to the mainland of Europe, was the Industrial Revolution. A number of innovations in manufacturing procedures and inventions of mechanical devices marked the beginning of the Industrial Revolution. These developments dramatically increased the human ability to do work and raised the level of efficiency in the production of goods.

Many of the early industrial innovations and inventions led to improvements in textile manufacturing,

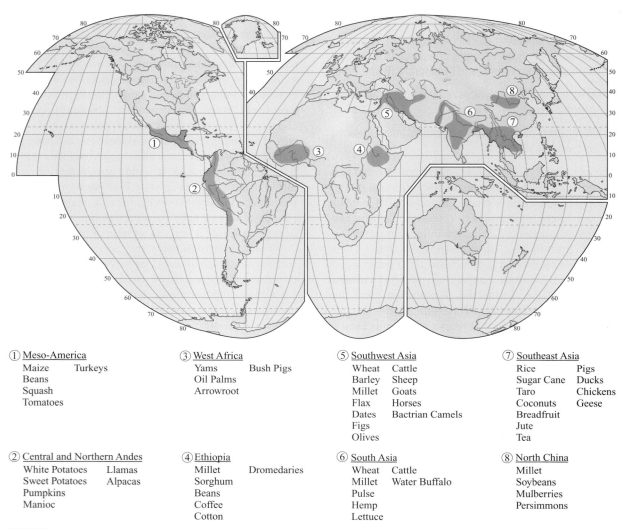

FIGURE 3.5

Regions of early agricultural development. The domestication of plants and the establishment of crop raising by people in these regions were major cultural advancements.

① Meso-America

Maize	Turkeys
Beans	
Squash	
Tomatoes	

② Central and Northern Andes

White Potatoes	Llamas
Sweet Potatoes	Alpacas
Pumpkins	
Manioc	

③ West Africa

Yams	Bush Pigs
Oil Palms	
Arrowroot	

④ Ethiopia

Millet	Dromedaries
Sorghum	
Beans	
Coffee	
Cotton	

⑤ Southwest Asia

Wheat	Cattle
Barley	Sheep
Millet	Goats
Flax	Horses
Dates	Bactrian Camels
Figs	
Olives	

⑥ South Asia

Wheat	Cattle
Millet	Water Buffalo
Pulse	
Hemp	
Lettuce	

⑦ Southeast Asia

Rice	Pigs
Sugar Cane	Ducks
Taro	Chickens
Coconuts	Geese
Breadfruit	
Jute	
Tea	

⑧ North China

Millet
Soybeans
Mulberries
Persimmons

metallurgy, and sources of power. It is understandable that textile manufacturing was among the first to be improved by mechanization; the demand for inexpensive cloth was widespread, but the spinning and weaving of fibers had required much labor and patience prior to the eighteenth century. Then came a series of inventions in Britain that greatly improved the efficiency of textile production: the "flying shuttle" in 1733, the spinning jenny in 1764, the spinning water frame in 1769, the spinning mule in 1779, and the power loom in 1785. These inventions led to the establishment of new textile mills in various parts of the country and enabled Britain to become the dominant producer and distributor of textiles in the early industrial period. Also, in eighteenth-century Britain and

other parts of Western Europe, several improvements in iron-making procedures led to the production of improved metals. Particularly important for the smelting of iron was the perfection of a process to convert coal into coke by Abraham Darby in 1709. Other developments were the invention of *puddling* (a process to make iron more malleable) and of the rolling mill.

The steam engine, the product of several inventors including James Watt, who patented it in 1769, was especially important to early industrialization because it was a versatile and dependable source of inanimate power. Waterwheels and windmills had been used for several centuries as sources of inanimate power, but they were undependable because of variations in stream flow and wind velocity and they were restricted to specific sites. The steam engine, fueled by wood, charcoal, and eventually coal, was a much more versatile device. It rather quickly was adapted to a variety of tasks, including propelling ships and boats, pulling trains, pumping water, and powering machinery in mills and factories. Transportation, mining, and manufacturing activities were vastly improved in efficiency by use of the steam engine, which was the dominant source of power until the internal combustion engine early in the twentieth century.

From Europe industrialization spread to the United States and Canada during the nineteenth century and to the former Soviet Union, Japan, Australia, and a few other areas more recently. In each case, industrialization was accompanied by accelerated rates of resource exploitation, technological growth, an increase in wealth, and basic changes in population trends and settlement patterns. Most of the world's people, however, occupy regions that have not yet been transformed by industrialization; they share little in the world's wealth, live in rural settings, and depend on agriculture for their livelihood. These contrasts between the world's industrially developed nations and those that are less developed will be examined in most of the following chapters of this book.

The Democratic Revolution   Like its industrial counterpart, the Democratic Revolution originated in Western Europe, particularly Great Britain and France, about two to three centuries ago. This movement was a reaction against special privilege and the absolute authority of monarchs and aristocrats. It was energized by new ideas regarding the rights of individuals and personal freedoms that were expressed in the American Declaration of Independence and by the leaders of the French Revolution. According to Preston E. James, the Democratic Revolution focused on five rights and freedoms of the individual: (1) the right to equal treatment before the law; (2) the right to protection from arbitrary acts by those in authority; (3) the right of representation in government; (4) the right to expression by secret ballot; and (5) the right to free access to information and open discussion of public issues. The Democratic Revolution also put forth the idea that the authority to govern should not be based on inheritance or membership in a privileged class but rather on the consent of those being governed. Of course, throughout the years these ideas were vigorously opposed by aristocrats and others who expected to benefit from maintaining the status quo. Rights often have been gained only through bitter struggle.

The spread of the Democratic Revolution from Western Europe to other regions has been furthered by the abandonment of colonial control and its replacement by independent governments. The United States and most other former colonies in the Americas obtained their independence relatively early, during the late eighteenth and early nineteenth centuries. In parts of Asia and most of Africa, on the other hand, colonialism persisted until after World War II. The transition from colonial control to independence in these areas has not been accompanied by the adoption of democratic principles by all governments; however, totalitarian regimes are finding themselves under growing pressure to reform their systems.

The defeat of fascism during World War II and the recent abandonment of communism in Eastern Europe and the former Soviet Union are the most important events in paving the way for further expansion of democracy. Fascism, communism, and other ideologies that promote totalitarian societies obviously have not been completely eliminated, and many millions of people still lack individual rights and freedoms. Nevertheless, democracy is a powerful movement and the Democratic Revolution is making significant gains in the contemporary world.

THE WORLD'S CULTURE REGIONS

➤ Dividing the inhabited world into major culture regions makes it easier to generalize about global cultural patterns.

How does a regional classification scheme aid our study and understanding of the world?

Why is it best to regard regional boundaries as transition zones rather than sharp lines?

The **culture region** concept is useful to geographers and other social scientists because it provides a means of identifying, classifying, and better understanding the complex mosaic of people's varied ways of thinking, living, and working within their spatial context. Classifications are as important to social scientists as to natural scientists, for only by grouping similar things together can knowledge be effectively assembled and conveyed. Without a regional classification scheme we would have to abandon meaningful generalizations about world areas and present information by means of case studies in which every case is unique. It is important to recognize that each place on earth is truly unique, but emphasizing the uniqueness rather than the similarity of places is not an effective method of advancing understanding.

CULTURAL LANDSCAPES

The Sacred Cattle of India

Had they never been domesticated, cattle would be a part of the natural landscape; since their domestication more than 7000 years ago, however, they have comprised a part of the cultural landscape in many parts of the world. Domesticated cattle and other livestock were a part of the cultural landscape of the Indian subcontinent at least as early as 2500 B.C. Today India has more cattle than any other nation—more than 200 million head, or about one-fourth of the world's total. That would be merely a noteworthy fact of economic geography were it not for the influence of religion.

Hinduism, the dominant religion in India, forbids the killing of cattle and most other animals. This prohibition is related to the Hindu belief in reincarnation. According to Hindu faith, following death all creatures may have their soul reborn in the body of another. Hindus believe the soul of a human most likely will return in the body of a cow. As a consequence, cattle are considered sacred; a cow can be milked or used to pull a plow or perform other work, but it cannot be slaughtered and consumed as food. Privately owned sacred cattle and others that are ''common cattle'' (owned by people in general), therefore, are allowed to wander throughout the rural areas of India and even in the towns and cities. Three other bovines are also considered sacred—the water buffalo, the yak, and the mithan. India has tens of millions of water buffalo, but the yak and the mithan are relatively uncommon.

Debate over the degree to which sacred cattle influence the agrarian economy of India has been under way for decades. No one questions the fact that cattle are an integral part of the rural economy, but opinion is divided over whether their benefits exceed their liabilities. Both cattle (principally the Brahman and zebu varieties) and water buffalo are major contributors to milk production; the water buffalo accounts for more than half of India's milk production. Critics argue, however, that the country's milk requirements could be better satisfied by modern dairying based on selective breeding. Because that involves the slaughter of undesirable animals, the modern approach to milk production holds little appeal to conservative Hindus. Bovines also continue to be very important for plowing, grinding grain, pulling carts, and other tasks. In the opinion of many experts, however, India possesses far more animals than are required for these purposes.

Another benefit of India's huge livestock population is its production of hundreds of millions of metric tons of dung annually. Dung is the country's principal source of agricultural fertilizer and of domestic fuel. No one can argue against the sacred cow in this regard, since India is fuel-poor, and most farmers cannot afford chemical fertilizers.

Some critics argue that the health of the Indian people is adversely affected by accepting the sacredness of cattle and by the spread of this concept in recent decades. Before Indian independence in 1947, these critics point out, slaughtering accounted for half of all cattle that died, whereas by the 1960s only 5 percent were killed to be butchered for meat. Most beef consumption in India today is by non-Hindu ethnic minorities and by Hindus of the lowest caste (known as untouchables); even meat-eating among the untouchables is declining as they seek upward mobility in a society that frowns on the practice. Those who criticize the concept of the sacred cow point out that a large proportion of the cattle that die of natural causes are buried or become carrion for dogs or vultures, to the detriment of Indian nutrition.

Cattle are a ubiquitous component of the cultural landscape in India, where they are regarded as sacred by the Hindu population. Most are untended and allowed to roam freely over the countryside.

Other criticisms of the lack of livestock control in India are that it allows for no scientific management and that it permits wandering animals to trample crops, overgraze, induce soil erosion, and interfere with transportation and other human activities. The fact that a benefit offsets each liability ensures that the debate will continue. Because religion lies at the heart of the matter, and because a people's religious beliefs must be respected, it is a debate that will remain, for a long time to come, fruitless.

THOUGHT QUESTIONS

1. With a much higher proportion of Indian cattle slaughtered prior to 1947 than since, one might conclude that these animals became even more sacred during the second half of the twentieth century than before. Do you feel that this is a valid conclusion? Why or why not?

2. Do you think that cattle will be considered sacred by most of the people of India in the year 2050? Why or why not?

3. If there had never been sacred cattle in India, how do you think that country would be different today?

Our survey of the world's major culture regions in the remainder of this chapter is intended to provide an opportunity for the reader to acquire general familiarity with broad cultural patterns before proceeding to more detailed information in following chapters. Even this brief examination of culture regions can be helpful in gaining an appreciation of the myriad of customs, beliefs, and practices of different human groups around the world. In becoming knowledgeable about the ideas and practices of different cultural groups we are likely to find reason to abandon any tendency to think of them as wrong, bizarre, or threatening.

The culture regions that we identify in this chapter are similar to other geographic regions in that they are based on arbitrary criteria. Considering the great diversity of cultural criteria worldwide, it is understandable that scholars often disagree on the number and spatial extent of culture regions. Another point to keep in mind is that few clearly defined lines of cultural demarcation exist. It is best, therefore, to regard boundaries separating adjacent regions as transitional

zones of cultural intermixing rather than as sharp lines on a map. An example of such a transition zone is the border area between the United States and Mexico, where Anglo and Hispanic cultures have become intermixed. Less arbitrary are some cultural boundaries that have been determined by physical barriers separating human groups. These include water bodies, mountain ranges, and deserts. In addition, zones with little or no population are often effective boundaries between cultures.

For the purposes of our general survey, we have divided the inhabited world into nine major culture regions (Fig. 3.6). We will identify certain cultural characteristics that give identity and unity to each region and help distinguish it from the others. However, the vast extent of each region results in a certain amount of cultural diversity. The division of our first-order regions into smaller second- and third-order regions would be a method of attaining greater cultural homogeneity within each. For example, the Oriental Culture Region could be broken into Indic, Eastern Asian, and Southeastern Asian subdivisions that in-

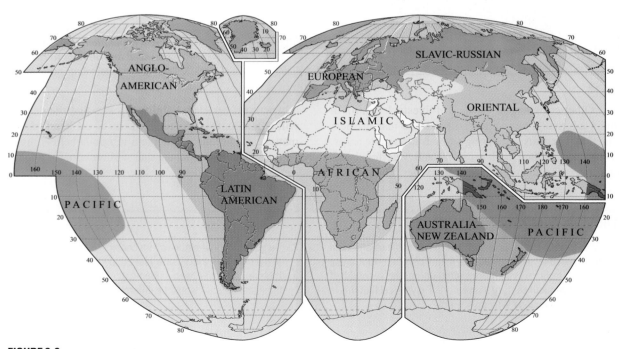

FIGURE 3.6

Major culture regions of the world. Each region possesses a unique record of cultural development and a distinctive combination of cultural characteristics. The regional boundaries often are zones of cultural intermixing rather than sharp separations of cultures.

dividually would exhibit less variation in human life-styles. In fact, if our primary goal were to identify regions with the highest degree of cultural homoge-neity possible, we would need to subdivide these units again and again. The result would be a world map showing a complex mosaic of very small culture regions that would not serve satisfactorily for our pur-pose of conducting a general survey. The major culture regions that we examine here may lack a high degree of homogeneity, but they will adequately serve our needs in conducting a global survey.

We will begin our survey with regions in the Old World—the African, Islamic, Oriental, and European culture regions. To complete the survey, we will ex-amine the Slavic-Russian, Latin American, Anglo-American, Australia–New Zealand, and Pacific cul-ture regions, all of which have been influenced to an important degree by the diffusion of European culture. At least since the fifteenth century, the spread of Eur-opean culture into these regions has altered—and in some cases even erased—many native (aboriginal) cultural practices and patterns.

The African Culture Region

> Africa, one of the world's major culture regions, has the longest record of human occupance and the widest assortment of serious contemporary problems.

Why did Africa become known as the "Dark Continent?"

How did European colonialism contribute to many of Africa's current problems?

What have been other causes of African problems?

Although social scientists are not in complete agree-ment, the prevailing interpretation of the archaeolog-ical record places the ancestors of modern humans in equatorial East Africa where they appear to have evolved more than 3 million years ago. Much later—about 2000 years ago—native African culture reached a peak in the Sudan, a broad transitional belt that spans the continent and separates the Sahara Desert and rain-ier areas to the south. Trans-Sahara caravan traders and Arab peoples who swept into the Sudan as fervent missionaries for the spread of Islam as early as the latter half of the seventh century fostered cultural dif-fusion into the region. Powerful kingdoms, with rather high levels of cultural attainment, flourished here.

They included Ghana, Bornu, Mali, Songhai, Hausa, and Fulani.

Throughout most of history, however, the peoples inhabiting Africa south of the Sahara Desert have suf-fered cultural impoverishment imposed by isolation. A combination of physical barriers—the arid Sahara, steep escarpments and mountains near the coasts, rapids and falls on rivers leading into the interior, and dense tropical vegetation along the low-latitude coasts—effectively prevented penetration of the re-gion by outsiders. Only during recent centuries have African cultures become known to the outside world. The contact of outsiders—Europeans and Arabs—with Africa led to a slave trade that eventually in-volved the removal of millions of Africans for en-slavement in other lands, mostly the Americas.

Unifying characteristics of this region include a predominantly negroid population, preindustrial sub-sistence economies, lingering problems fostered by European colonial control, and extremely complex ethnic and linguistic diversity.

European Colonialism and Its Aftermath
Throughout much of the region, traditional cultural practices were changed little by European colonial control (Fig. 3.7). Many contemporary problems can be attributed to the fact that European powers during

FIGURE 3.7
Despite European colonialism in Africa, many traditional African ceremonies and practices have survived. (Donald Marshall Collection)

the colonial period divided Africa among themselves with little, if any, consideration for existing African cultural patterns. The Europeans neither involved African peoples in democratic governmental processes nor did they train Africans to become active participants in self-government and twentieth-century industrial and commercial activity.

In those instances where change in native cultures was imposed by Europeans, it often was detrimental. Many native cultural institutions were subjugated without being replaced by acceptable and viable alternatives. In the postcolonial period, faced with the sudden responsibility of self-government, many African countries seem to be hopelessly divided by lingering conflicts between historically antagonistic tribal groups, unable to govern themselves through democratic means or to develop their own resources and other economic potentials.

Economic and Political Problems   At present, most Africans are engaged in low-yielding economic activities. Hunters and gatherers such as the Pygmies of the Congo Basin and the Bushmen of the Kalahari Desert subsist on a ''feast or famine'' diet much the way their ancestors did many thousands of years ago. In portions of eastern and southwestern Africa, highly specialized herding societies have evolved (e.g., the Hottentot, Masai, and Watusi). In wet tropical parts of the continent, however, herding is precluded by the presence of the tsetse fly that transmits deadly *nagana* disease to livestock (Fig. 3.8). Here, using only the primitive digging stick, hoe, and machete as implements, farming peoples raise a variety of root crops (manioc, yams, sweet potatoes) and grain crops (millets, corn). Among farmers who have focused on the production of cash crops (cotton, peanuts, coffee, cacao, oil palm), very few have prospered. The introduction of modern forms of technology has not yet resulted in large-scale alterations of agriculture in Africa. Soil compaction and soil erosion, as well as persistent droughts, are problems hindering progress in agriculture. Not only is agriculture showing little or no improvement, but per capita food output in most African countries has declined in recent decades.

Furthermore, the peoples of Africa have been unable to make up for the poverty of their agriculture with industrialization. The lack of industrial technology, fossil fuels, and investment capital, together with an inadequate transportation system, have contributed to this low level of industrial development. In part be-

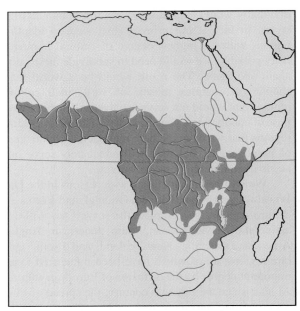

FIGURE 3.8
Areas infested by the tsetse fly. A disease-carrying insect, the tsetse fly has restricted livestock herding in much of tropical Africa.

cause of this limited industrialization, the population of Africa is predominantly rural. Nearly all countries are heavily in debt, and their economic problems are exacerbated by some of the world's highest rates of population growth. Most Africans live in great poverty, are poorly educated, and have inadequate health care. Malnutrition is common, tropical diseases cause much suffering, and HIV/AIDS has become a health problem of epidemic magnitude.

The people in many countries of this region have been victimized by authoritarian government leaders who have deprived them of their civil rights and looted their national treasuries. Serious political instability exists within and between countries; coups d'état, intertribal frictions, and international conflicts are common.

African states undoubtedly will continue for some time to be plagued with many problems: a rather impoverished material culture, the colonial heritage and its legacy, a relatively meager resource base with only scattered deposits of fossil fuels and industrial metals, the lack of native technology and capital required to achieve substantial economic growth, chronic overpopulation and unemployment in many areas, and conflicts that arise from instability within many of the primary institutions. These problems are compounded by widespread impatience and rapidly rising expectations held by many Africans who have now turned their backs on traditional lifestyles and want to see their homelands modernized.

The Islamic Culture Region

➤ The Islamic culture region has been distinguished by the formation of early civilizations; major cultural developments, including establishment of the Jewish, Christian, and Islamic religions; and persistent human conflict.

What were primary and secondary civilization hearths in this region?

How did the Islamic faith become dominant throughout most of the region?

How has religion been a factor in conflicts, and what other factors have contributed to strife in the region?

As the name implies, the Islamic culture region is unified by adherence to the Islamic faith of the vast majority of its population. From its core in the Middle East, the region extends westward across North Africa and northeastward into parts of central Asia. Although it is mostly climatically arid and contains some of the world's most extensive deserts, this has been a region of cultural innovation, growth, and diffusion for thousands of years. About 10,000 years ago nomadic groups of people, previously engaged in hunting and gathering, began establishing sedentary lifestyles made possible by the domestication of plants and development of crop agriculture. Within a few thousand years, the domestication of animals provided people of the region with additional economic security and a new source of power and mobility. Cultural growth also was stimulated in the region by the diffusion of traits in and through this crossroads location at the junction of three continents.

Several civilizations with roots in this setting exerted a cultural influence that extended far beyond the region's geographic limits. Mesopotamia, occupying the fertile valley between the Tigris and Euphrates Rivers (in what is now the country of Iraq), and the lower Nile Valley of Egypt were the primary hearths of major cultural development long before the dawn of the Christian Era. Secondary hearths emerged in Phoenicia on the eastern shore of the Mediterranean Sea, Persia (now Iran), Palestine, and Arabia.

Cultural and Economic Developments Early cultural developments within these hearths include many agricultural techniques, particularly ones involving irrigation; the harnessing of wind, water, and animal power; the wheel and the plow; and advances in metallurgy. Nonmaterial culture traits that originated here include alphabet-based forms of writing, mathematics, astronomy, social and political ideologies, and three major monotheistic religions (Judaism, Christianity, and Islam). The earliest known sedentary human settlements—villages, towns, and cities—also were established in these areas.

By means of a series of conquests and diffusions, the Islamic faith was brought from the Arabian Peninsula to all parts of the region over several centuries following the death of the prophet Mohammed in A.D. 632. In fact, Islam spread far beyond the boundaries we have drawn around the Islamic culture region. A large proportion of the world's Islamic population today live in a number of countries outside the region. In most cases, they constitute a minority among larger groups, but in Bangladesh, Indonesia, and Malaysia they form the majority.

Traditional economic activity in the Middle East and North Africa has focused on three types of endeavors: sedentary oasis farming where water is available, pastoral nomadism, and commerce involving the movement of goods by water or caravan. Throughout history, nomadic herders and individuals engaged in trade have constituted only a small percentage of the population; the vast majority have been oasis farmers (Fig. 3.9). Mesopotamia and especially the Nile Valley have supported great concentrations of farmers for thousands of years. Nomadism has drastically declined in importance over recent decades. Alternative occupations in towns and cities are more attractive than the rigors associated with frequent movement of livestock from one grazing area to another in the desert. Furthermore, governments have encouraged or forced nomads into permanent settlements. In some cases, this has been for the purpose of exerting political control over the nomadic groups, or to prevent problems that might arise when nomads cross international boundaries.

With the discovery of oil in the vicinity of the Persian Gulf in 1908 and subsequently in other areas, the region acquired an escalated economic and polit-

FIGURE 3.9
Irrigation farming in the Nile Valley of Egypt. Using water from the Nile River, Egyptian farmers have worked the soils here for about five thousand years. (Robert Caputo/Stock Boston)

ical importance. About two-thirds of the world's oil reserves are here, with one-fifth in Saudi Arabia alone. Development of the oil fields has provided new jobs, created a small middle class, and contributed to urban growth, but it has not brought diversified economic development nor has it eliminated the gap between the rich and poor. Much of the oil wealth has been channeled into the build-up of military machines and into the personal bank accounts of the elite. Also, only a fraction of the region's countries possess significant oil deposits; most suffer from a shortage of natural resources.

Persistent Conflict   Conflict has been a persistent characteristic of the region for most of its history. In fact, it was in part by means of conquest that Islam was spread across the region. Other conflicts accompanied the formation of empires, European colonialism, the two world wars, struggles for political independence, and political revolutions. Since World War II the most bitter struggle and the one of greatest significance to the region and to the world has been waged between the Jewish state of Israel and neighboring Islamic countries. The stage for this hostility was set in 1948 when Israel was formed from part of the Arab-dominated territory of Palestine, which had been administered by Britain. The Arabs believed that Palestine was rightfully Arab territory, and the existence of Israel was vigorously opposed. After a series

of military engagements, Israel not only managed to survive but even extended the area under its control as it captured parts of the surrounding Arab countries. With large-scale foreign aid and investment capital, especially from the United States, Israel has become a highly developed nation with a powerful military establishment. Its Arab adversaries, although larger and more populated, have had few successes in their ongoing confrontations with Israel.

The most recent major conflicts in this strife-plagued region have included a revolution in Iran during 1978–1979; a military intervention, beginning in 1979 and lasting for nearly a decade, by the Soviet Union in Afghanistan where a communist government was facing widespread rebellion; a costly war between Iran and Iraq extending through most of the 1980s; and Iraq's conquest of Kuwait in 1990 and subsequent defeat only a few months later by a U.S.-led coalition of forces to liberate Kuwait. For the inhabitants of the Islamic culture region, peace and stability have been extremely elusive.

The Oriental Culture Region

➤ A huge population, cultural development in isolation, reliance on an agrarian economy, and a tendency to look to the past for security have characterized the Oriental culture region.

What have been some of the main cultural developments in the Orient?

How does the agrarian economy reflect the high ratio of people to available farmland?

How have the people of this region traditionally adapted to hardship and uncertainty?

Encompassing South, Southeast, and East Asia, the Orient is homeland to more than half the world's population. China and India together account for nearly 2 billion people, while even some of the region's relatively small nations have populations that exceed 100 million. Nevertheless, extensive parts of the Orient—those with little agricultural potential because they are too dry or too rugged—have never been inhabited by significant numbers of people. As a consequence, the Orient has striking contrasts in population densities.

Isolation and Cultural Evolution   Until recent centuries, the way of life of Asiatic peoples remained virtually unknown to Westerners. Not only were they physically separated from the remainder of the world's population by water bodies, high mountains, deserts, and great distance, but some of the Asian cultures adopted isolationist policies. The diffusion of outside culture traits into most of the Orient therefore was both late and very selective. Increased contact with outside societies has greatly accelerated cultural exchange over recent generations, however.

With the exception of industrialization, cultural evolution within the Orient exhibits many parallels to that of Western civilization. Plant and animal domestication, practiced as early as 10,000 years ago, provided an early foundation for cultural development in several centers ranging in location from India to northern China. Early developments in the arts, technology, mathematics, astronomy, and medicine also kept pace with those in the Western world during comparable time periods. As late as the thirteenth century, the Venetian traveler Marco Polo (ca. 1254–1324) returned to Mediterranean Europe from China and astounded listeners with his tales of Chinese cultural developments. They included the use of coal, gunpowder, the magnetic compass, paper, wood-block printing, and paper money.

Agrarian Domination The economy of the Orient continues to be overwhelmingly agrarian. Agricultural villages, supported by subsistence peasant farming and home crafts, are the most common places of residence. The very high ratio of people to available farmland requires intensive farming techniques that include an enormous amount of hand labor, terracing, extensive use of human and animal wastes as fertilizer, and widespread irrigation. Land often is put to multiple use; for example, grain (especially rice), vegetables, fish, and waterfowl commonly are produced on the same plot. The cultivation of rice is as widespread as environmental conditions will allow, and rice lands are the most valued agricultural areas. A long history of food shortages and famines, usually caused by floods and droughts, has been interrupted recently by some success in modernizing agriculture. The improvements have involved construction of dams for water control and increased irrigation, and the introduction in some areas of modern forms of technology. Even without mechanization and the use of agricultural chemicals, however, parts of the Orient account for some of the world's most productive farming.

On the oceanic fringe of the Orient are a number of burgeoning metropolitan areas, including the city-

FIGURE 3.10
The appearance of modern Singapore reflects the city's development into one of the most prosperous industrial and commercial centers of the Orient. (Stock Boston)

states of Hong Kong and Singapore (Fig. 3.10), that have become thriving industrial-commercial centers. Their early development, and in some cases even their origin, can be attributed to the influence of Western traders and European colonial activity. Industrialization now is underway on at least a limited scale in most countries of the region, but only Japan has risen to prominence as an industrial-commercial giant on a level with the Western powers.

Overpopulation, hunger, poverty, illiteracy, and a general lack of well-being and individual freedoms are among the region's most serious problems, some of which have persisted for many generations. For much of modern time, Oriental people have endured tragic warfare and political instability associated with European colonialism, Japanese expansionism, and the spread of communism.

Adjustments to Hardship With long exposure to hardship and uncertainty, many people in the Orient have looked to the past for security—a trait that is apparent in their worship of ancestors and rigid adherence to traditions. They have followed a course of social conformity, as in Chinese obedience to the teachings of Confucius and the quotations of Mao Zedong and in the Indian adherence to the Hindu caste system, which dictates one's life-long social position, status, employment, and opportunity. Also, many

FIGURE 3.11
Practicing transcendentalism in the Orient.
(Cary Wolinsky/Stock Boston)

groups have relied on transcendentalism (Fig. 3.11) as a release from painful reality (e.g., their belief in nirvana), or have held an abiding belief in a life hereafter (e.g., karma; reincarnation).

Most of the region's people exhibit a fatalistic outlook and adjust to hardship, misfortune, and institutional change with little outward expression of resentment. India adopted a democratic form of government under the direction of British colonialists, the Chinese accepted communist ideology and discipline after Mao Zedong's successful revolution and the founding of the People's Republic of China in 1949, the Japanese have undergone revolutionary cultural transformation since adopting the concepts and technologies associated with industrialization, and the Indo-Chinese seem to have developed an almost stoic countenance in response to repeated cultural invasion and military conflict.

The future of the Orient will surely rest on the degree to which the problems of overpopulation, poverty, and human well-being can be addressed within the framework of stable social, economic, and political institutions.

The European Culture Region

➤ Europe has been a particularly dynamic culture region for many centuries, serving as a hearth for many developments and spreading European culture to most parts of the world.

What elements of culture did the Romans introduce into various parts of their empire prior to the Dark Ages?

How did western Europe become the first industrial power and center of democratic society in the modern world?

How has European unification progressed since World War II?

Although small in area, the European culture region is complex and dynamic. For more than 2000 years it has been a hearth of technological innovation, social advancement, and many other forms of human accomplishment (Fig. 3.12). Through their commercial and colonial activities, Europeans have spread elements of their culture to most of the world during recent centuries, with great impact on native societies.

Cultural Antecedents and European Accomplishments Many antecedents to European cultural development can be traced to the Nile Valley and southwestern Asia. By the fifth millennium B.C., Neolithic peoples had begun migrating westward from Asia, bringing with them the practices of crop agriculture and livestock herding. The earliest European civili-

FIGURE 3.12
The world's only commercial supersonic aircraft, the Concorde is a recent example of European technological accomplishment. Production of the Concorde was a joint venture by France and the United Kingdom.
(Robert Rothe/Stock Boston)

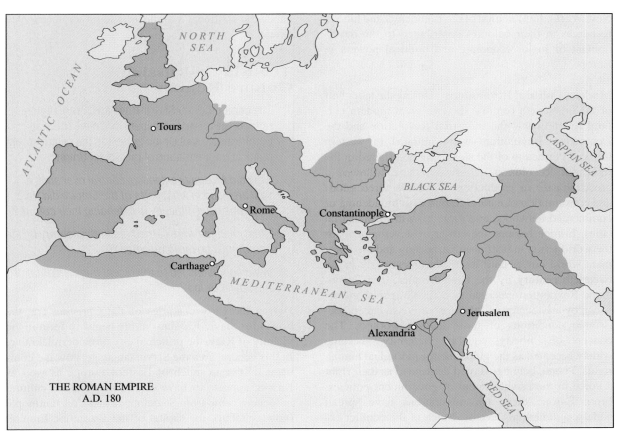

FIGURE 3.13
The cultural influence of Rome extended throughout the Roman Empire by the end of the fourth century A.D.

zation emerged with the Minoans on the island of Crete about 2800 B.C. During the first millennium B.C., concepts of civilized living spread to sedentary agricultural peoples inhabiting islands within and lands adjacent to the Aegean Sea. Greece became a major culture hearth from which a distinctly European way of life was to emerge and diffuse elsewhere.

With the decline of the Greek civilization, the Roman Empire emerged as the dominant cultural force on the continent. By the end of the fourth century A.D. the influence of Rome reached throughout the Mediterranean area and extended northwestward as far as Great Britain (Fig. 3.13). Through military conquest, building cities, and developing a network of roadways to facilitate communications, the Romans made a lasting cultural imprint throughout their empire. Signifi-

cant contributions include the Latin language, Christian religion, concepts regarding law and politics, agricultural and technological practices, and the establishment of numerous cities. Roman dominance was broken by disruptions of its political and military strength, owing particularly to a series of invasions by Germanic tribes from the east. For several centuries thereafter, European culture slumbered through what has been called the Dark Ages.

Beginning with the fifteenth century voyages of discovery, the focal point of power and influence shifted to the Iberian peninsula and gradually to other countries facing the Atlantic. Exploration, first by Spain and Portugal, and later by England, France, and the Netherlands, led to the formation of colonial empires and the migration of millions of Europeans to the

New World. Exploitation of environmental and human resources in their colonies contributed to the development of major economic and political powers in Europe.

Modern Cultural Revolutions During the latter half of the eighteenth century, the two great modern cultural revolutions—the Industrial Revolution and the Democratic Revolution—were initiated in western Europe. Perfection of the steam engine ushered in the Industrial Revolution. Afterward, there followed a great increase in production of manufactured goods and consumption of natural resources, a broadening of commercial networks, and rapid growth of industrial cities. Europe became the center of development for the world's first industrial-urban society and the dominant world power until its displacement early in the twentieth century by the United States. The Democratic Revolution emerged as a revolt against governance by aristocracy and the oppressive social and economic conditions of most factory workers. The concept of "liberty, equality, fraternity" became widely accepted as the guideline for individual human rights. People being governed demanded as their right a voice in the establishment of government policies. From Europe these two revolutions have spread widely, although not evenly. Much of the conflict experienced in the world today can be traced to differing viewpoints on human rights and to the varying degrees to which societies have become involved in industrialization.

Strength Through Unification During recent decades, after centuries of debilitating conflict and the tragedies of two world wars, European states have exhibited a tendency to seek greater economic and political strength through interdependence. Former disadvantages associated with the intricate political fragmentation of the continent are being overcome. The European Community, developed in stages over the decades after World War II, has emerged as the dominant agency for integration of national economies and governments. For most of the postwar period, the main barrier to European integration was the "Iron Curtain," established to isolate the communist countries of Eastern Europe. With the virtual collapse of communism in this area since 1989, the opportunity has opened up for Western European states to reach out to their Eastern European counterparts and ad-

vance the continent's unification to an unprecedented extent.

The Slavic-Russian Culture Region

➤ The contemporary Slavic-Russian culture region reflects the long-term expansion of the Russian Empire and Soviet Union as well as the recent abrupt political fragmentation of the Soviet Union.

How did Moscovy extend its control over such a vast area and in what parts of the Empire did the Russians have difficulty in extending their culture?

What changes were carried out in the country by the communist government after 1917?

What conditions led to the recent fragmentation of the Soviet Union?

During the early centuries of the Christian era, the hearth for Slavic-Russian culture began to form in the vicinity of Kiev, the principal city of modern Ukraine. In this general area the Slavic language, now the dominant tongue in much of Eastern Europe as well as Russia, appears to have originated. Outside cultural influences came from Scandinavia and Constantinople (now Istanbul), the capital of the Byzantine Empire, with which Kievan Russians participated in a trading network during the Middle Ages. Particularly important among the cultural acquisitions from Constantinople was the Orthodox Christian faith, adopted by Kiev in the tenth century and continued to the present as a central element of Russian life. Another source of cultural input was the Tatars, a varied group of nomads from central Asia, who pushed westward through the steppe grasslands of southern Russia and held control over that area until the fifteenth century. At that time, the center of Russian culture had shifted northward to Moscovy, a city-state in the vicinity of the headwaters of the Volga River.

Evolution of the Russian Empire From the fifteenth through the nineteenth centuries, under the direction of a series of czars, Moscovy extended its control by exploration and conquest over a vast area and thereby created the Russian Empire (Fig. 3.14). The empire extended from Eastern Europe to the Pacific Ocean and temporarily included Alaska in North America. With this territorial expansion, Slavic-

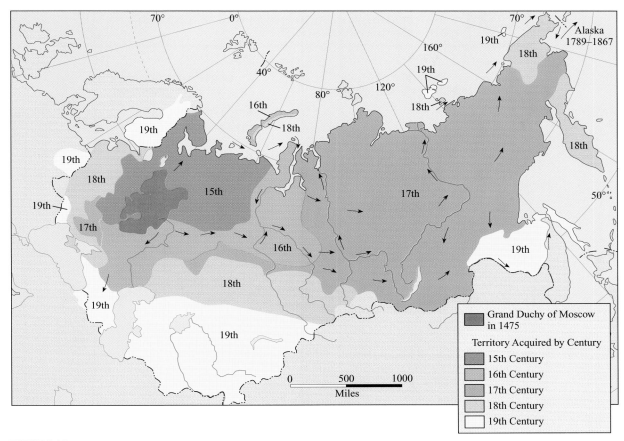

FIGURE 3.14

The formation of the vast Russian Empire was underway at the time colonial empires were being established by the major European countries.

Russian culture diffused from Moscovy and eventually became dominant over much of the empire. However, substantial parts of the empire were inhabited by other ethnic groups of considerable strength, especially Islamic peoples along the southern margin; here the Russians had only limited success in extending their culture.

To an important degree, the cultural makeup of the Russian Empire was influenced by its insular position within the huge Eurasian landmass. Isolated from neighboring civilizations by enormous distances and environmental barriers, it failed to significantly benefit from their accomplishments. Ideas emanating from China, India, and Mediterranean Europe seldom reached the Russians. Even though Peter the Great (1672–1725), a czar impressed by developments in

Western Europe, imported much Western technology, traditional lifestyles in Russia were virtually unaffected by ideas from the West until the present century. Only gradually did the Russians begin to accept the concepts and technologies fostering industrialization. Ideas pertaining to democratic government and the rights of individuals were rejected, first by the czarist regimes and then, after 1917, by the communist government.

The Soviet Union and Communism   Following the Bolshevik Revolution in 1917, the territory and cultural patterns of the empire were transformed into the Union of Soviet Socialist Republics (Soviet Union). The new communist government established several Soviet Socialist Republics (also called Union Repub-

TABLE 3.1 Ethnic Composition in the Union Republics of the Former U.S.S.R.	
Republic (in descending order of total population)	**Largest Ethnic Groups** (percent of total population)
Russia	Russian (83), Tatar (4)
Ukraine	Ukrainian (74), Russian (21)
Uzbekistan	Uzbek (69), Russian (11)
Kazakhstan	Russian (41), Kazakh (36)
Belorussia (Belarus)	Belorussian (79), Russian (12)
Azerbaijan	Azerbaijani (78), Armenian (8)
Georgia	Georgian (69), Armenian (9)
Tadzhikistan	Tadzhik (59), Uzbek (23)
Moldavia (Moldova)	Moldavian (64), Ukrainian (14)
Kirghizia (Kyrgyzstan)	Kirghiz (48), Russian (26)
Lithuania	Lithuanian (80), Russian (9)
Turkmenia (Turkmenistan)	Turkmen (68), Russian (13)
Armenia (Hayaston)	Armenian (90), Azerbaijani (8)
Latvia	Latvian (54), Russian (33)
Estonia	Estonian (65), Russian (27)

lics) with each bearing the name of a major ethnic group. The number of Union Republics eventually reached fifteen (Table 3.1) as the U.S.S.R. absorbed the Baltic States of Latvia, Lithuania, and Estonia during the World War II period. The unifying element in this multiethnic, culturally diverse ensemble of republics was Karl Marx's communist ideology as adopted and implemented by the Soviet leaders V. I. Lenin (1870–1924), Joseph Stalin (1879–1953), and their successors. That ideology encompassed the suppression of religion, the collectivization of farmlands, and the elimination of private ownership of all property and facilities involved in economic production.

All aspects of economic planning and activity in the Soviet Union were directed by communist bureaucrats who exercised strong centralized control. Under this system agriculture suffered immensely, both from the resistance of farmers to the collectivization of their land and from the government's policy of exploiting agriculture to support industrial growth. The emphasis on industry primarily was for the purpose of developing a strong military machine (Fig. 3.15); consumer goods were generally neglected. Poor worker incentives generally resulted in less than enthusiastic effort and inferior workmanship. Recognizing the inherent

weaknesses of this system, then President Mikhail Gorbachev (b. 1931) began experimenting with its restructuring in the late 1980s.

Political Fragmentation   In addition to initiating economic and social democratization at home, President Gorbachev refused to use military force to prevent the simultaneous abandonment of communism by the Soviet Union's satellite states in Eastern Europe. These changes in the established order resulted in an erosion of Gorbachev's support; some old-line communists charged that he was dismantling the system while other critics complained that he was not implementing change fast enough. Sensing the opportunity to regain their freedom, the Baltic Republics declared their independence. In short order the other Union Republics took similar action, and by the end of 1991 the U.S.S.R. had completely disintegrated. A vague ''Commonwealth of Independent States'' was proclaimed as a means of retaining some link among the former Union Republics, but it seems to have generated little enthusiasm among the republics.

With this fragmentation of their political system, only those parts of the former Soviet Union that are linked by other cultural traits remain in the Slavic-

FIGURE 3.15

The Soviet Union's military power regularly was put on display during parades prior to the country's disintegration in 1991. (Jasmin/GAMMA)

Russian culture region (Fig. 3.6). The region, therefore, generally encompasses the territory of Russia, Ukraine, and Belarus (formerly Belorussia). The other former Union Republics have been transferred to adjacent regions with which they have greater cultural affinity; thus the predominantly Islamic populated areas are now elements of the Islamic culture region, and the Baltic States—Latvia, Lithuania, and Estonia—as well as Moldova (formerly Moldavia) are included in the European culture region. Because of the intricate cultural patterns of the small states in the Trans-Caucasus area (Azerbaijan, Armenia, and Georgia), it is best dealt with as a transition zone between first-order culture regions.

The Latin American Culture Region

➤ The Latin American culture region is most distinguished by the colonial superimposition of Iberian traits over native Indian civilizations that developed in pre-Columbian time.

What were the objectives of Spanish and Portuguese colonists in Latin America, and what principal cultural traits did they introduce?

Why is land reform needed in Latin America, and to what extent has it been implemented?

What changes in attitudes and lifestyles are underway in Latin America today?

Latin America is that portion of the Americas to the south of the United States. Included are 32 sovereign states and several Caribbean Islands that are territories or dependencies of France, the Netherlands, the United Kingdom, and the United States. Also included is French Guiana, now the only mainland country in Latin America that is not independent. (It is, like French Polynesia, an overseas department of France.) Some Latin American states (e.g., Haiti, Honduras, and Guyana) are among the poorest in the world, while others—especially Mexico, Brazil, and Argentina—are in early stages of industrialization and have realized significant economic diversification in recent years. Some countries are very large—Brazil is almost as large as the United States—and well endowed with resources. Others, especially ones in the Caribbean, are small and have little resource variety.

The Iberian Imprint   The dominant cultural imprint on Latin America is that of the Iberian countries, Spain and Portugal, with few exceptions. It has been said that the Spaniard came to the New World not as a permanent settler but in search of "glory, God, and gold," not necessarily in that order. The Portuguese, on the other hand, came to colonize vast tracts of land for the benefit of the mother country. Certainly, the differing attitudes and objectives of western Europeans (especially the British) in Anglo-America and of Ibero-Europeans in Latin America during the initial stages of colonization had a dominant influence on the contrasting economic, social, political, and settlement patterns that developed within these two culture regions. The Iberians brought to Latin America the Catholic religion, which continues to exert a strong influence on the modern population. They brought the Portuguese and Spanish languages, which soon replaced most of the indigenous languages. The Iberians introduced European systems of land ownership and inheritance. Iberian architecture, arts, and a host of customs, attitudes, and perceptions also were diffused to Latin America (Fig. 3.16). The introduction of European plants and animals made possible new diets and new ways of accomplishing work. Among the most unfortunate introductions were disease organisms from Europe that brought death to millions of the

FIGURE 3.16
The Spanish architecture of the older building is in striking contrast to the newer structures around it in this scene of Mexico City. (A. R. Longwell)

native peoples. Even so, portions of Latin America retained, to a much greater degree than Anglo-America, an important aboriginal population and culture. Indians and mestizos (people of mixed Indian and European ancestry) dominate the populations of most Middle American countries as well as the northern and central Andean countries.

Economic and Social Reform From colonial times until the present, the ownership of land has been a measure of great economic and social significance in Latin America. *Minifundia* (small properties) account for most landholdings; only a few people own *latifundia* (large properties). Although there are many millions of small farmers who own their land, millions of others are still peons doing wage labor on the large estates. Land reform implemented by governments during recent decades has increased dramatically the number of small farmers and reduced the number of peons. Many of the small farmers, however, are as poor as they were before as peons.

People employed in manufacturing are largely in Argentina, Brazil, and Mexico; most Latin American countries have only a small manufacturing sector and the service sector is not well developed except for government. The development of manufacturing in Argentina, Brazil, and Mexico has been aided by substantial foreign investment in these nations.

Changing attitudes and lifestyles are evident throughout Latin America today as traditional insti-

tutions collapse in the wake of industrialization and democratic ideology. Reactions to each often have been violent (Fig. 3.17). The Roman Catholic Church, long regarded as the dominant social institution in Latin America, recently has begun to play an active role in social reform. However, many people regard such activities as threatening to the status quo and beyond the ecclesiastical purview. With industrialization a small but vocal middle class has emerged to challenge time-honored social, economic, and political practices, including the tradition in some countries of government by dictatorship and, in most countries, of the vested interests of the landed aristocracy. Death rates have been reduced significantly during the past three decades, and rapid population growth rates have become a serious problem. During the same period, illiteracy rates have been greatly reduced—one of the few favorable trends. As yet, economic growth has been unable to keep pace with demographic trends, and there remain broad disparities within and between countries in wealth, health, opportunity, and individual well-being. Unemployment, poverty, and malnutrition continue to be major problems, especially in rural areas. Throughout most of Latin America, the 1990s is a time of rising expectations, impatience, and cultural adjustment to changing institutions.

FIGURE 3.17
Public demonstrations, some punctuated by violence, have been common events for many years in Latin America. (Martin Thomas/GAMMA)

The Anglo-American Culture Region

➤ The Anglo-American culture region is characterized by a diversified population caused by enormous immigration from various parts of the world and by its leadership in advancing the Democratic and Industrial Revolutions.

How have the source regions of immigrants to Anglo-America changed over time?

What have been important consequences of the human diversity in Anglo-America?

How has the global leadership of Anglo-America been challenged in recent decades?

Encompassing the territory of Canada and the United States, the region of Anglo-America represents both an extension and expansion of European culture. European religions and languages were effectively transplanted to this part of the New World, as were the central ideas and technologies associated with the Democratic and Industrial Revolutions. Nowhere have the impacts of these two cultural developments been more profound than in Anglo-America. Immigrant populations of diverse backgrounds seeking political stability, economic security, and individual freedom and well-being have advanced the principles and derived the benefits of both revolutions.

European Settlement and Human Diversity   European settlers began the establishment of colonies in the region's Atlantic coastal zone at the turn of the seventeenth century. Early culture hearths were formed by French settlers in the lower valley of the St. Lawrence River, by predominantly English-speaking peoples in New England and the Southern Colonies, and by northern Europeans of various nationalities in the Middle Colonies (Fig. 3.18). The initial Hispanic footholds in Florida and the Southwest were eventual casualties of subsequent expansion by the increasingly dominant Anglo culture. From the outset, European settlement flourished at the expense of the region's aboriginal population, which was neither as culturally advanced nor as numerous as that in Latin America. (The native population of Anglo-America was less than 2 million at the time of initial European settlement; it quickly dropped to even smaller numbers with the introduction of European diseases.) Although early European colonists adopted from native agricultural-

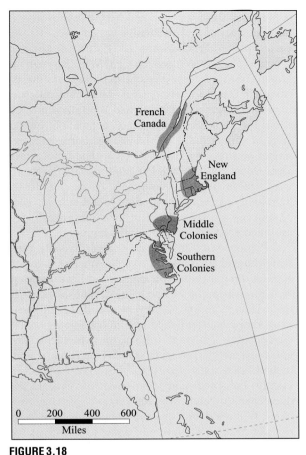

FIGURE 3.18

The four culture hearths established in colonial Anglo-America. Distinctive culture traits from each of these areas were diffused to other parts of the region.

ists certain techniques of cultivation and crops (most importantly, maize or corn), the native Indian cultures generally were either subdued or forced to occupy some of the continent's most isolated and marginal lands as Europeans spread westward.

Substantial variety has been injected into the European-dominated culture of Anglo-America by the arrival of people with other backgrounds. To meet the growing need for workers that accompanied the development of commercial production of tobacco and cotton in the Southern Colonies, landowners imported slaves of African ancestry. As it spread across the South with expansion of plantation agriculture, the institution of slavery stimulated heated controversy in the young nation and eventually was terminated by the Emancipation Proclamation of President Abraham Lincoln (1809–1865) and the Civil War. Through migration from the rural areas of the South, during the twentieth century many African-Americans relocated in urban centers of the North and West; they now account for 12 percent of the U.S. population. Further cultural variety has accompanied the burgeoning immigration since the 1960s of Asians and Latin Americans. Most concentrated in California and the Southwest, these recent immigrants have yet to be thoroughly assimilated into the general culture. Their presence is clearly evident in their languages, religions, and economic impact on the region.

Regions with cultural and racial diversity often suffer human frictions, and Anglo-America is no exception. Prejudice and discrimination have been unfortunate aspects of American life despite the adoption of legislation meant to prevent it and the efforts of many individuals, officials, and groups to promote human equality. Although serious, these problems have not threatened government stability or national unity in the United States. In Canada, however, the predominantly French-speaking province of Quebec has threatened to secede from the English-speaking provinces. Without doubt, this cultural conflict poses a serious obstacle to the future of unified Canada.

Global Influence and New Challenges   For most of the twentieth century, Anglo-America has exercised enormous global influence based on its economic, political, and military strengths. A combination of large territorial size, abundant natural resources, human skills, and technology have supported the development of a highly productive agricultural and industrial complex (Fig. 3.19). Economic growth also has been bolstered by a reliable flow of capital, ever-expanding domestic and foreign markets, excellent transportation and communication systems, and comparative social and political stability. Anglo-Americans have made their economic, political, and military presence felt throughout much of the world as they have attempted to ensure the security of their own way of life and foster the diffusion of those institutions that have proven so successful in the American experience.

Since the height of Anglo-America's dominance at the conclusion of World War II, several challenges to its global importance and way of life have surfaced. First was the ''Cold War''—the military threat posed

FIGURE 3.19
The enormous productivity of Anglo-American farmers has been aided by their highly mechanized operations. (R. Gabler)

by the Soviet Union and its communist allies—which persisted until the disintegration of the U.S.S.R. in 1991. Economic challenges accompanied the postwar industrial development of Japan and the growing economic significance of the European Economic Community. Perhaps the greatest challenges for Anglo-America in the future will be stresses on the environment and shrinking supplies of available resources. To maintain its high standard of living, the region has consumed resources at a rate totally disproportionate to its population. With many domestic resources dwindling and international sources increasingly costly or unreliable, there is no assurance that supply can continue to meet demands. It remains to be seen if Anglo-Americans can respond to such challenges in ways that fulfill their expectations while still being acceptable to other members of the global community.

The Australia–New Zealand Culture Region

➤ The sparse population of the Australia–New Zealand culture region has vigorously retained British culture and succeeded in developing a prosperous economy.

What important elements of British culture predominate in Australia–New Zealand today?

How are the economies of Australia and New Zealand similar and how do they differ?

The culture region formed by Australia and New Zealand possesses greater cultural homogeneity than any other in our survey. In their history, heritage, economy, and world outlook, the two countries are strikingly similar.

The Colonial Heritage   Despite the great distance separating them from Europe, Australia and New Zealand have vigorously retained British culture in particular and European orientation in general. They have accomplished this by maintaining close political and commercial ties with Britain and by implementing strict immigration policies that have effectively prevented settlement in the region of people lacking European ancestry. Only in recent years have they significantly reoriented their trade and eased their immigration restrictions.

Prior to the discovery of Australia and New Zealand by European navigators, both had been inhabited by aboriginal peoples for thousands of years. The native Australians, or Aborigines, were driven into the interior of the country (the Outback) by English colonizers (Fig. 3.20). The Maori, the native people of New Zealand, more vigorously resisted encroachment by the British and eventually were defeated in a bloody

FIGURE 3.20
Aborigines in the Outback of Australia comprise only a tiny fraction of the present population in Australia. (Viesti Associates, Inc.)

war during the 1860s. The two aboriginal groups today represent small ethnic minorities; the Aborigines comprise about 1 percent of the population of Australia, and the Maori represent approximately 9 percent of the population of New Zealand.

During the late eighteenth and early nineteenth centuries, the British used Australia as a penal colony for criminals and other social undesirables. New Zealand was not used for the same purpose, although in most other regards the history and settlement of the two countries are very much alike. Both countries have a background of British colonization, British heritage, and British culture. Their governments and educational systems are based on those of Great Britain. Almost all Australians and New Zealanders speak English, and the Anglican Church (Church of England) is strong in both countries. Throughout most of their histories, Australia and New Zealand had economies closely linked to that of Britain. Since World War II, however, as they have industrialized, both have established more important economic ties with other nations, especially the United States and Japan.

Economic Diversification   Agriculture has long been an important sector of the total economy of both countries, despite several environmental limitations, especially Australia's extensive arid climate. Australia has a well-developed sheep and cattle ranching industry, and dairy farming also is important. Crop farming emphasizes wheat production, and Australia is a major exporter. New Zealand's economy is even more completely based on agriculture. From the time of the first European settlement here, the production of mutton and wool for export to Europe has been a major economic activity. Dairy farming produces butter, cheese, and milk solids for the export market (Fig. 3.21). New Zealand's lack of a wheat belt is perhaps the main difference between its agricultural economy and that of Australia.

After long domination by agriculture, the economies of Australia and New Zealand have become more diversified with high development of the industrial and service sectors. Although Australia is now more industrialized and urbanized than New Zealand, the standard of living in both countries is far above the world norm. But despite their well-developed economies, Australia and New Zealand have little voice in world affairs because of their relative isolation and small populations of only 17 million and 3 million, respectively.

FIGURE 3.21

A New Zealand dairy farm. Dairy products are a major part of New Zealand's exports. (Cameramann Int'l., Ltd.)

The Pacific Culture Region

➤ The Pacific culture region, consisting of thousands of predominantly tropical islands sparsely populated by native peoples, has experienced significant cultural transformation since initial European contact a few centuries ago.

When and how did the original inhabitants reach these Pacific islands?

In what ways have Europeans and other foreigners stimulated a cultural transformation of the region?

There are more than 10,000 islands in the Pacific, an ocean that covers more than 40 percent of the earth. Because Japan, the Philippines, Taiwan, Indonesia, and New Zealand are island countries that are closely associated with the Asian mainland or (in the case of New Zealand) with Australia, we have excluded them from the Pacific culture region. Also excluded are such high-latitude islands as the Aleutians and Sakhalin that are integral parts of other nations. Our definition of the region therefore consists of predominantly tropical islands that commonly are divided into three groups: (1) *Melanesia*, the southwestern portion of the region; (2) *Micronesia*, the islands of the western and central Pacific lying mostly north of the Equator; and (3) *Polynesia*, lying mostly south of the Equator in the southeastern portion of the region (Fig. 3.22). Most of the Pacific islands are very small. Together they form the least populated culture region in the world; their inhabitants do not represent even one-half of 1 percent of the world's population.

Government systems vary widely in the Pacific culture region. Eight islands and island groups, all former British colonies, are now sovereign (Table 3.2). The *raison d'être* of some of these nations is weak, considering their tiny populations and scant resources. Other islands are territories, and still others are de-

Sovereign States (all former British territories)	**Territories**	**Dependencies**
Fiji	Christmas Islands (Australia)	American Samoa (United States)
Kiribati	Cocos Islands (Australia)	French Polynesia (France)
Nauru	Cook Islands (New Zealand)	Guam (United States)
Papua New Guinea	Heard and McDonald Islands (Australia)	Johnson Atoll (United States)
Solomon Islands	Niue (New Zealand)	Midway Islands (United States)
Tonga	Norfolk Island (Australia)	New Caledonia (France)
Tuvalu		Northern Mariana Islands (United States)
Western Samoa		U.S. Trust Territory of the Pacific (Marshall Islands, Micronesia, Palau)
		Wake Island (United States)
		Wallis and Futuna Islands (France)

TABLE 3.2   Political Status of Pacific Islands

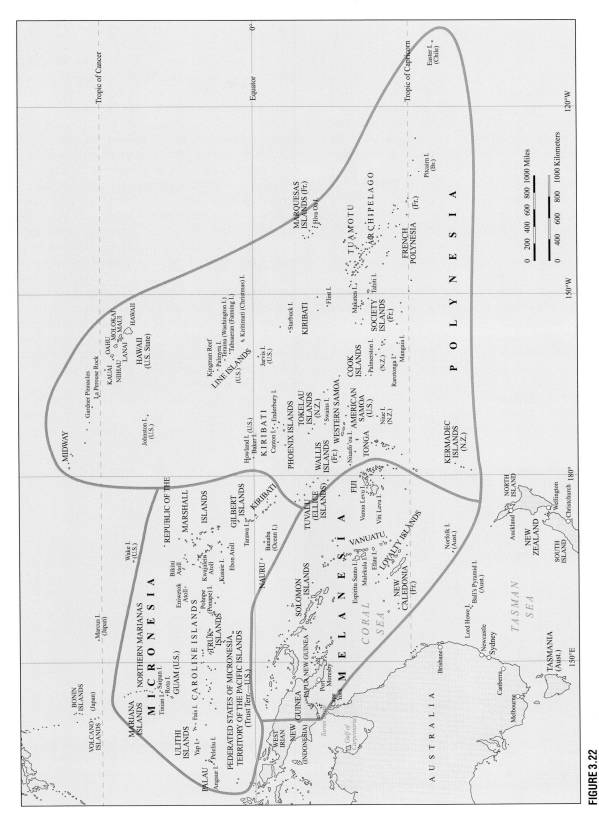

FIGURE 3.22

The major island groups of the Pacific are Melanesia, Micronesia, and Polynesia.

pendencies. Following a coup, the military was in control in Fiji in 1990.

Native People and Their Traits   Thirty thousand years ago no one lived on any of the Pacific islands. Initial settlement began a few thousand years later with the first inhabitants arriving from Indonesia and the Asian mainland. These early migrations involved people of varied racial stock, and they entailed island-to-island boat trips of as much as 50 miles (80 km). The post-Pleistocene rise of the sea to its present level some 10,000 years ago effectively isolated the native population of the Pacific from the remainder of humanity until the age of European exploration. Two or three thousand years ago, skilled seafaring aboriginal peoples began populating the smaller, more remote islands. These islanders made the longest sea voyages accomplished by humans up to that time and retained that record long after.

The native peoples of the Pacific region were racially and culturally fragmented. In Melanesia people of black or dark brown skin color combined hunting and fishing with primitive forms of subsistence agriculture. Lighter-skinned Micronesians and Polynesians were primarily subsistence farmers who augmented their starch diet of sweet potatoes and taro with skilled fishing and the raising of pigs. None of the cultures developed a written language or metallurgy. They were quite skilled, however, in working with wood, stone, and cloth, and in many respects developed extremely complex social systems.

Foreign Economic and Cultural Impact   Pacific cultures were unknown to Europeans until the voyages of discovery, and in the few centuries since their discovery some of the islands have experienced great cultural transformation. Foreign-owned corporations have established coconut and sugar cane plantations on some of the islands, and as a consequence many people have abandoned subsistence agriculture for wage labor. Most of the islands, however, are so isolated and the cost of shipping is so high that significant future expansion of plantation agriculture in the region is improbable. The mineral-poor geology of the islands means that in most cases a mining economy cannot be developed. Only the island nation of Nauru, with a population of less than 10,000, has an economy based primarily on mining; it possesses some of the world's richest phosphate deposits.

Capitalizing on their tropical scenic beauty, Tahiti, Fiji, and Samoa have developed tourist economies (Fig. 3.23). Cruise lines bring shiploads of foreigners

FIGURE 3.23

Because tourism is an important source of income for several of the Pacific islands, a variety of attractive facilities have been built to accommodate visitors. (Dallas and John Heaton/Stock Boston)

to first-class hotels. Tourism is expanding to other is-lands as well, but most of them are too isolated to share significantly in this means of economic growth. Even where tourism has been developed, it is viewed by many people as a mixed blessing. The contamination of native cultures by Western influence results in in-creasing abandonment of the traditional ways of life, and this in turn causes growing concern to those who wish to safeguard their cultural heritage.

THE ROLE OF CULTURE IN GEOGRAPHY: A SUMMARY

The role of culture, like that of the physical environ-ment, is exceedingly important in geographical stud-ies. Both must be carefully examined if we are to successfully gain an understanding of most spatial var-iations over the surface of the earth. The conduct of human life in all parts of the world involves a complex interaction of people with their habitat—an interaction with culture as the dynamic element. It is through the

medium of culture that people interpret and evaluate their physical environments and determine how to make optimum use of them. As cultures and environ-mental elements vary from place to place, so do the associations of people with their habitats.

Cultural traits, individually and in combination, also have great geographical significance because they are responsible for much of the place-to-place diver-sity evident on the face of the earth. Elements of ma-terial culture—buildings, transportation lines, and ag-ricultural fields—may be more evident on the landscape than religion, language, political ideology, and other components of nonmaterial culture, but all of these cultural traits are important contributors to the world's spatial variety. Furthermore, cultural diffusion is a spatial process that has been responsible for sig-nificantly furthering the development of place-to-place variations in culture. To familiarize students with broad spatial patterns of the world's cultural variety and how it evolved, we devoted much of this chapter to a survey of major culture regions.

KEY TERMS

Culture: The ensemble of learned traits that distinguish individual human groups and their particular ways of life. **90**

Cultural traits: The individual components of a culture that have been acquired through learning. **90**

Cultural group: A society that differs from all others in terms of the unique assortment of cultural traits it possesses. **91**

Ethnic group: A human group that is distinguished by its unique cultural and, in some cases, racial characteris-tics. **91**

Nonmaterial culture: The components of culture that are not material in nature, such as religion and language. **91**

Material culture: The material or physical items, such as clothing, buildings, and crops, produced by humans in conducting their particular way of life. **91**

Acculturation: The adoption by an individual or a cul-tural group of selected traits from a different cultural group. **93**

Assimilation: The absorption of an individual or a cultural group by a different cultural group to the extent that differ-ences in their traits are no longer distinguishable. **93**

Cross-cultural fertilization: The enrichment or im-provement in the culture of two or more groups as they adopt selected traits from one another. **94**

Diffusion: The progressive spread of a phenomenon or idea from a place of origin to other locations on the earth's surface. **94**

Culture hearth: An area where a particular culture has evolved and from which its traits have diffused to other locations. **94**

Agricultural Revolution: A major cultural development, beginning about 10,000 years ago, that involved domesti-cating plants and animals and practicing agriculture for the first time. **95**

Industrial Revolution: A major cultural development, beginning in Europe during the eighteenth century, that consisted of innovations in manufacturing procedures and the invention of machines to make possible the first large-scale production of industrial goods.   **95**

Democratic Revolution: A major cultural development, beginning in Europe two to three centuries ago, that advanced the rights and freedoms of individuals and diminished the authority and special privilege of rulers and aristocrats.   **95**

Paleolithic Period: The Old Stone Age, a period distinguished by human production and use of crude stone tools and survival by hunting, gathering, and fishing.   **95**

Neolithic Period: The New Stone Age, a period distinguished by human production and use of refined stone tools and domestication of plants and animals to initiate farming and herding.   **95**

Culture region: A part of the earth's surface that is defined or delimited on the basis of one or more cultural criteria.   **97**

REVIEW QUESTIONS

1. In the associations of people with their physical environment, what is the role of culture?

2. How is culture acquired by an individual through informal learning? Through formal learning?

3. How do racial traits differ from cultural traits?

4. What are some examples of nonmaterial culture? Of material culture?

5. How is the technology possessed by a society related to its ability to alter the natural environment?

6. What is the difference between *acculturation* and *assimilation*?

7. What is a *culture hearth*? Would you conclude that California has become a modern culture hearth in the United States? Why?

8. According to Carl Sauer, what physical characteristics were possessed by sites where plants were first domesticated and where the practice of agriculture originated?

9. Among the several inventions that ushered in the Industrial Revolution, why is the steam engine often identified as the most important?

10. According to Preston E. James, the Democratic Revolution involves what rights and freedoms of the individual?

11. What are the unifying characteristics of the African culture region?

12. What economic and political problems have slowed the development of modern Africa and contributed to its instability?

13. What were some of the important early developments in the culture hearths of the Islamic culture region?

How did the location of this region contribute to its cultural growth?

14. Traditional economic activity in the Middle East and North Africa has focused on what three types of activities? Why has nomadism been declining in importance? What results have followed development of the region's oil fields?

15. Among the various major conflicts in the Islamic culture region since World War II, why is the conflict between Israel and neighboring countries particularly significant?

16. Why was diffusion of outside cultural traits into most of the Orient slowed? How did early cultural development in the region parallel that of Western civilizations?

17. What have been the most persistent hardships and problems in the Orient? How have the people adapted to them?

18. What developments resulted in a shift of power and influence in Europe from areas in the south to countries facing the Atlantic?

19. How is the European Community serving to strengthen the global importance of the region?

20. How did the Russian Empire's insular position within the Eurasian landmass influence its cultural makeup?

21. What was involved in the recent disintegration of the former Soviet Union and its abandonment of communism? Which former Soviet republics are not included in the Slavic-Russian culture region?

22. How has the Roman Catholic Church become an important cultural institution in Latin America?

23. To what extent have land reform and industrialization progressed in Latin America?

24. Where and by whom were early culture hearths established in Anglo-America? What sort of relationships did European colonists and settlers establish with the native cultures of Anglo-America?

25. Among Anglo-America's various domestic problems and challenges of today, which do you judge to be the most serious? Why?

26. How have Australia and New Zealand managed to retain their British culture since the colonial period? What recent changes might result in significant modification of the culture?

27. What has made possible the establishment of a high standard of living in Australia and New Zealand?

28. What sort of traditional lifestyles were developed by the native people of the Pacific culture region? How have they been altered since discovery of the islands by Europeans? Why is this a concern for many people?

CHAPTER 4

CULTURAL DIVERSITY: LANGUAGES AND RELIGIONS

It is through language that people in every culture are able to share their experiences, concerns, and beliefs, over the past and in the present, and to communicate these to the next generation.

—William A. Haviland

Religious groups often can be identified by their attire. This Moslem woman wears a veil in public as prescribed by her faith.

ifferences among the world's cultures, many claim, are shrinking because of the obliteration of former obstacles to cultural diffusion. The spread of ideas, innovations, technology, production techniques, and many other aspects of culture has become increasingly effective. Great distances, whether over land or water, as well as environmental and human barriers, have been overcome by improvements in modes of travel and communication. The dissemination of information and news by the electronic media is worldwide. Even people in less developed countries who live in isolated villages that lack electricity have battery-powered transistor radios that ensure access to information from other societies. We are reminded regularly that the earth is, in effect, shrinking in size; that a global economy is superseding individual national economies; and that a global community is emerging.

Although trends toward homogeneity are indeed in progress, cultural diversity among the world's people remains the rule. There continue to be striking differences between cultural groups and an amazing assortment of cultural traits that produce complex patterns of human activity and landscape features. Cultures continue to interact with the environment in remarkably different ways. Often the people of these cultures possess certain traits that have served them well for generations, and understandably they are resistant to change. The persistence of cultural diversity ensures many challenges for the geographer who has the task of understanding and explaining differences from place to place on earth. Because of their great significance in contributing to the world's cultural diversity, languages and religions are the focus of this chapter.

LANGUAGE AND CULTURE

➤ It is a common language that is most important in both identifying and perpetuating a specific culture.

Why is language an especially critical element of culture?

For an individual to be considered a member of a particular culture, why is knowledge of the language essential?

The importance of language in the identification and perpetuation of a culture is readily apparent. Language

is the primary vehicle by which ideas, thoughts, beliefs, and experiences are shared and retained within a culture. Language is the means by which a culture sustains its economic, political, and social institutions. Carl Sauer has noted that "any language . . . tends to operate as a cultural cement for those who speak it." The link between a cultural group and its language is so strong that knowledge of the latter is essential if an individual is to fully understand the former. The fact that there are several thousand different languages spoken in the world today, and only a small percentage of speakers are proficient in more than one language, makes it clear that language is a major reason for cultural diversity. It is also a persistent cause of cultural misunderstanding and conflict between cultures.

Language is one of the most obvious ways to distinguish one culture from another (Fig. 4.1). In any cultural group with a common or dominant language, the native speaker is recognized as a member of the group while the individual unfamiliar with the language is identified quickly as an outsider. The native speaker shares the cultural history and collective experiences of the group. Through language each individual has gained insights concerning the group's values, aspirations, beliefs, and perceptions of the outside

FIGURE 4.1
The signs along this street in a Tokyo suburb clearly identify the culture as Japanese. (R. Gabler)

world, all of which are largely unavailable to the outsider who does not speak the language.

Language is more than just a passive key to culture. Both language and culture are interacting constantly with one another and each is a product of the other. The level of vocabulary and the complexity of ideas and knowledge that can be expressed by its language in large part govern the nature of a culture and the ability of that culture to cope with its physical environment. On the other hand, a language is the direct expression of the traits acquired, institutions developed, and experiences shared by members of a cultural group throughout their history. Language and culture are reflections of each other: the richer the culture, the richer the language; and the richer the language, the richer the cultural history and potential for development.

LANGUAGE FAMILIES

➤ Speakers of languages within the Indo-European and Sino-Tibetan language families comprise nearly two-thirds of the world's people.

In what parts of the world do the speakers of these two family groups predominate?

Which language family has the most widespread distribution?

Why is this so?

Although there are thousands of languages or regional variations of major languages, nearly 80 percent of the earth's people speak fewer than thirty languages. It is possible to group these into **language families**, with members of each family thought to have descended from a common parent tongue. The languages within each family group show certain similarities to one another in terms of vocabulary, grammatical structure, and spoken sounds.

Table 4.1 lists some of the major language families and all of the languages within each family group that claim 40 million or more speakers. It is apparent from the table that almost two-thirds of the 5½ billion people in the world speak languages that belong to either the Indo-European or the Sino-Tibetan families. It also is interesting to note that although major languages of the Indo-European group are in use on each of the earth's populated continents, the languages of

the Sino-Tibetan family are spoken by significant numbers of people only in eastern and southern Asia.

The Indo-European Family

The origins of the Indo-European language family have been traced to ancient tribal groups that appear to have lived some 5000 to 6000 years ago in a zone extending from eastern Europe to the area of modern Turkey. As these people subsequently migrated outward, they carried their language with them south and east across the plateau of Iran to India and westward throughout much of Europe (Fig. 4.2). As they settled new areas isolated by great distances from one another, their speech evolved in different ways to form individual languages.

Within linguistic families there are subfamilies of languages that can be grouped more closely because they developed in general proximity to one another and because there are strong similarities in grammar, vocabulary, and sound. Subfamilies of the Indo-European family, for example, include Germanic, represented by English and German; Indic, represented by Hindi, Bengali, Urdu, Punjabi, and Marathi; Romance (Italic), represented by Spanish, Portuguese, French, and Italian; and Slavic, represented by Russian, Ukrainian, and Polish. An example of similarity among languages within a subfamily is the word for "father" as it is expressed in the major Romance languages. "Father" in both Spanish and Italian is *padre*, in Portuguese it is *pai*, and in French it is *père*.

The Sino-Tibetan Family

Although it includes a number of major dialects such as Mandarin, Cantonese, Wu, and Min, each of which is listed as a separate language in Table 4.1, Chinese is spoken by nearly a billion people. Of these dialects, Mandarin or Han Chinese, which originated in the northeastern portion of the country, has been designated the **official language** of the People's Republic of China. It is apparent that Chinese, in one form or another, will long remain the language spoken by more people than any other in the world because of China's large population.

Despite the numerical superiority enjoyed by speakers of Chinese, the Sino-Tibetan language family has not experienced the widespread geographical distribution of the Indo-European family. The explana-

TABLE 4.1   Major Language Families and Individual
Languages with 40 Million or More Speakers
(1993 estimates)

Languages by Family Group	Speakers (in millions)	Main Areas of Use
Indo-European		
English	431	Anglo-America, British Isles, Australia, New Zealand, South Africa, and former British Colonies
Hindi	325	India
Spanish	320	Latin America, Spain, former Spanish Colonies
Russian	289	Russia, former Soviet republics
Bengali	178	Bangladesh, West Bengal (India)
Portuguese	169	Brazil, Portugal, former Portuguese Colonies
German	118	Germany, Austria, Switzerland
French	117	France, Belgium, Switzerland, Quebec (Canada)
Urdu	88	Pakistan
Punjabi	77	Northern India and Pakistan
Italian	63	Italy, Switzerland
Marathi	62	Maharashtra (India)
Ukrainian	44	Ukraine
Polish	42	Poland
Sino-Tibetan		
Mandarin (Chinese)	825	China
Cantonese	61	Southern China
Wu	61	Eastern China
Min	45	Southeastern China, Taiwan
Thai	50	Thailand
Hamito-Semitic		
Arabic	187	Northern Africa, Arab nations of the Middle East
Malayo-Polynesian		
Malay-Indonesian	135	Malaysia, Indonesia
Javanese	55	Java
East Asian		
Japanese	124	Japan
Korean	68	South Korea, North Korea
Vietnamese	54	Vietnam
Dravidian		
Telugu	65	Southern India
Tamil	63	Sri Lanka, Southern India
Altaic-Urallic		
Turkish	53	Turkey

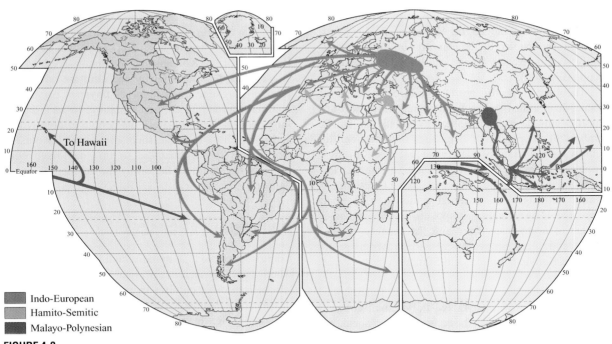

To Hawaii

Indo-European
Hamito-Semitic
Malayo-Polynesian

FIGURE 4.2

The diffusion of language families from the regions in which they originally developed. Individual languages within each family group evolved as migrating tribes settled on lands in which they were isolated by distance and lack of communication with other people.

tion for this is associated closely with the history of the Chinese people. Although there were periods when rulers based in China spread their power and influence over much of central Asia, the Chinese culture was based on a rural, agricultural, and sedentary way of life. The Chinese did not establish overseas colonies, and therefore there was no accompanying spread of the language.

To a large extent the hearthland of Sino-Tibetan languages was isolated from the rest of the world by deserts, mountains, and warlike nomadic tribes to the north and west and by vast seas and equally isolated independent cultures to the east and south. It was only into neighboring Tibet and across the rugged land-bridge of peninsular southeast Asia that Chinese culture and language traits experienced significant diffusion. But as a result, on the broad floodplains of the great river valleys in Myanmar (Burma) and Thailand, regional languages within the Sino-Tibetan family developed in environments similar to those associated with the Chinese language.

Other Language Families

➤ Languages in the Hamito-Semitic and Malayo-Polynesian families are among the most widely distributed in the world.

By what different means did these tongues become spread over such vast areas?

What is the dominant language in each of these two families?

Hamito-Semitic   Hamito-Semitic languages are thought to have originated in southwestern Asia well before recorded history. In fact, an early forerunner of Assyrian from the Semitic subgroup is one of the first languages to have appeared in written form. Today Semitic languages dominate throughout much of arid northern Africa and the Middle East west of Iran, largely because of the association between Arabic and the Islamic religion. The Koran, the chief religious book of Islam, was written in Arabic. As Islam spread westward from its origins on the Arabian peninsula,

Arabic spread with it—often supplanting earlier Hamitic and Semitic languages. However, this ensured that regions occupied by the Hamito-Semitic language family would resist incursions from other language groups (Fig. 4.2).

There are currently about 200 million speakers of Arabic. In contrast, other Semitic languages and all Hamitic languages are spoken by relatively small numbers of people. Such languages include Semitic Hebrew—until recently a language reserved for religious ceremonies but also the official language of Israel—and Amharic, the official language of Ethiopia. Hamitic languages are restricted primarily to Nigeria, where the Hausa tongue is spoken, to the nomadic Berbers of northwest Africa and the Tauregs of the Sahara, and to certain peoples of eastern Africa, principally in Kenya, Ethiopia, and Somalia.

Malayo-Polynesian   One of the most remarkable language families is the Malayo-Polynesian, not because it is represented by large numbers of speakers but because of its widespread geographic distribution across the vast expanses of the Pacific and Indian Oceans. Although probably spoken by only slightly more than 200 million people today, Malayo-Polynesian tongues can be found as far east as Easter Island in the south Pacific, as far west as the island of Madagascar off the coast of Africa, as far south as New Zealand, and as far north as Taiwan off the coast of China.

The original speakers of Malayo-Polynesian languages are assumed to have lived in the peninsular lands of southern Asia where today their languages have been replaced by those of the Sino-Tibetan family. More than 4000 years ago these individuals began to migrate southward through the Malay Peninsula and to the Indonesian Islands (Fig. 4.2). Their further migration throughout the Pacific and Indian Oceans is one of the greatest adventure stories of human history, and their methods of successfully reaching uncharted islands over tremendous expanses of open sea in boats little larger than canoes is one of the most debated mysteries of ocean navigation.

East Asian   The Japanese, Korean, and Vietnamese languages do not comprise a language family. However, each is spoken by significant numbers of people and, although some authorities tend to link them geographically with Sino-Tibetan languages, they are not linguistically similar to each other or to any family

group. Despite the fact that the Japanese incorporated Chinese written characters in their language many centuries ago, their language is independent and so are the languages of the Koreans and Vietnamese.

The explanation of why each culture developed its own language traits involves physical barriers to communication and cultural isolation. In fact, during long periods of their history the people of both Korea and Japan chose to isolate themselves from the outside world, and the Vietnamese to this day have consciously resisted domination by the adjacent Chinese culture.

INDIVIDUAL LANGUAGES

Linguists believe that an individual language develops when a culture occupies a given area in relative isolation from other cultures over a considerable period of time. The language evolves as new collections of sounds—differing in pronunciation, inflection, stress, accent, and tonality—are devised to communicate various aspects of ever more complex social institutions, constantly changing economic conditions, and any significant growth in skills or technology. Another influence in the development of a language is the physical environment occupied by the culture. As an illustration we might compare the vocabulary of Arabic, which developed in the arid Middle East, with the vocabulary of languages spoken by native tribes in the Amazon Basin. In Arabic there are hundreds of words associated with desert life and the camel as the mainstay of a nomadic existence. Yet in Amazon tribal languages there are none.

Diffusion and Distribution

➤ Much of the diffusion of languages to locations well beyond their places of origin can be explained by the expansion of cultures through exploration, trade, and the conquest of new territories.

What languages have been most and least widely diffused?

What factors might bring about changes in the present distribution of languages?

The map in Figure 4.3 indicates the general distribution of native speakers of those individual languages included in the family groups of Table 4.1. The linguistic patterns on this map are the result of a long

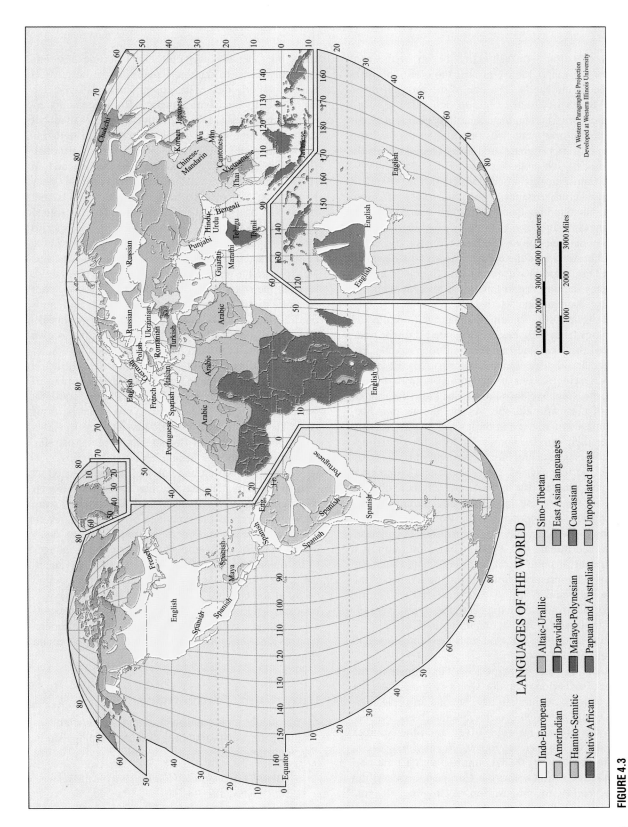

LANGUAGES OF THE WORLD

☐ Indo-European
☐ Amerindian
☐ Hamito-Semitic
☐ Native African
☐ Altaic-Urallic
☐ Dravidian
☐ Malayo-Polynesian
☐ Papuan and Australian
☐ Sino-Tibetan
☐ East Asian languages
☐ Caucasian
☐ Unpopulated areas

A Western Panagraphic Projection
Developed at Western Illinois University

FIGURE 4.3

The current distribution of individuals who are native speakers of major languages. Note how trade, exploration, and conquest have influenced the spread of languages.

history of cultural diffusion that began in the core areas of the major family groups thousands of years ago. (See again Fig. 4.2.) Much of the early diffusion of languages occurred as groups migrated outward from their original language hearth in search of better living conditions, increased opportunities for food and shelter, or a more secure area away from enemies. In some cases, such as that involving the Malayo-Polynesian family group, migration led to the spread of languages great distances from their place of origin and the abandonment of the original hearthland to a different language family. In other cases the language diffusion has been modest, often owing to physical or cultural barriers, and the expanded area now occupied by the family group still retains the linguistic hearth. Examples include Asian languages such as Chinese, Japanese, Korean, and Vietnamese.

As some cultures matured and grew in wealth and technology, they deliberately expanded through trade and territorial conquest. Such activities greatly enhanced cultural diffusion and the spread of certain languages. During the era of the Roman Empire, for example, the Roman legions introduced Latin throughout much of northwest Europe. As the legions marched, the Romans colonized and built cities to provide support for their armies, homes for their provincial administrators, and centers for the growth of trade. Latin became the language of government and commerce, and it was adopted first by the important local citizens and city dwellers and later by many throughout the countryside. Development of the Romance language subfamily, which includes Spanish, Portuguese, French, and Italian, and which is based on Latin, is a direct result of cultural diffusion associated with the Romans. The spread of Arabic throughout much of the Middle East and North Africa was similar. During their period of greatest expansion, the Arabs were efficient traders as well as conquerors and, as their influence spread, they diffused both their language and their religion.

Much of what remains to be explained of the present distribution of major world languages can be traced to the fifteenth century, when European navigators began the great age of exploration and discovery. In their search for gold, silver, and other sources of wealth, and in their attempts to develop new ocean trade routes linking their countries with China and other lands of the Orient, the Europeans opened the ''New World'' to colonization. As Figure 4.3 indicates, the more advanced cultures of European settlers gradually came to dominate many native cultures in the New World during the colonial period.

In North and South America, Romance and Germanic languages supplanted native languages in all but the most remote and inhospitable regions. English is the language of much of North America, although French is spoken by Canadians in Quebec and in smaller areas of the Maritime Provinces of New Brunswick, Nova Scotia, and Prince Edward Island. As a result of the Treaty of Tordesillas (1494), signed by Spain and Portugal, which divided South America into two spheres of influence, the Spanish were able to spread their language to western South America, Mexico, and Central America, and the Portuguese brought their language to the portion of eastern South America that became Brazil. In the islands and lands bordering the Caribbean Sea there currently are speakers of English, Dutch, French, and Spanish who owe their language to the era of European colonization.

Also during later stages of colonization, diffusion of the English language accompanied the growth of the British Empire into the western Pacific, southern Africa, the Indian subcontinent, and other parts of Asia. The modern map of world languages reflects this widespread diffusion of British culture into Australia, New Zealand, and the Republic of South Africa.

In most of Africa, the colonial period reached its peak at a much later date. German and Italian, as well as English, French, Spanish, and Portuguese, were each introduced as the language of administration in one or another colony, but the period of foreign dominance was not sufficiently long for native languages to be replaced permanently. The situation was much the same throughout Asia. As the colonial period ended at the close of World War II, native languages were chosen as official languages by newly independent countries with few exceptions, and European tongues since have filled the role of convenient second languages.

Language Variations

➤ Languages often have been altered in character, producing such variants as dialects and pidgin and creole tongues.

What parts of the United States have the most distinct dialects?

Under what circumstances do pidgin and creole languages develop?

Even in areas in which an individual language has come to predominate, significant regional variations may develop in the use of accents and **dialects**. Although the written language may remain unaltered, the accents and pronunciation of spoken words and phrases may differ to such an extent that the listener from another region may find it difficult to understand the speaker. If you have spent considerable time watching television and listening to the radio, you may have little difficulty understanding the ''broad A'' in the dialect of New Englanders or the ''drawl'' of people from Texas and other southern states, but it is almost certain that you would find the ''cockney'' English in some of London's older neighborhoods as unintelligible as a foreign language.

Both **pidgin** and **creole** serve the purposes of individual languages under certain circumstances. A pidgin language may come into existence when groups from two widely differing cultures establish contact with each other over long periods of time. If there are only a few individuals who are **bilingual**, that is, who speak the languages of both cultures, a third or pidgin language often evolves, usually for the purposes of trade and commerce. A pidgin language contains a limited number of words and simplified grammar. It utilizes the vocabulary of both parent languages but usually it is based primarily on the language of the senior trading partner. Because of the great involvement of European countries in the early years of world exploration and colonialism, pidgin English, French, and Portuguese are the most common pidgin languages. Creole, which can evolve from a pidgin language, is a more fully developed language and may become the native tongue for a culture.

If one language becomes the medium of communication for commercial or administrative purposes over a large area where other languages are the native tongue, this language is termed the **lingua franca**. Swahili, which originally developed as a pidgin language based on several Bantu dialects, is the lingua franca in much of eastern Africa and is a national language of both Kenya and Tanzania. Swahili is considered a creole language also because it began as a pidgin but has since replaced the original language of the culture area. A creole language rarely is written, but as is the case with French Creole in the West Indies

and Louisiana, it can be one of the major elements in distinguishing certain cultures.

ENGLISH AS LINGUA FRANCA

➤ To a major extent, English has become the lingua franca of the world.

By what means did this development come about?

What are advantages and disadvantages for Americans in the use of English as lingua franca?

These days it is a common sight to see Japanese business people and tourists in Germany, the Netherlands, Denmark, and other western European countries. They are talking with local industrial executives, buying and selling manufactured products and agricultural commodities, asking directions of hotel clerks, visiting tourist sites, and conversing with people who speak a variety of European languages. What may come as a surprise at first is that more often than not the language spoken by all the individuals involved is English. When captains of commercial jetliners on international flights contact airport towers throughout the world, the language they speak is English. In countries as diverse as India, Kenya, Korea, Germany, China, and Russia, English is the favored second language and often is taught at each school grade level beginning with children of age 11 or 12.

English has to a great extent become the lingua franca of the industrial and commercial world for several reasons. One reason we have already mentioned was the widespread diffusion of English with formation of the British Empire, on which it was once said that the ''sun never sets.'' (That saying was literally true because at the height of the colonial period the English controlled lands that circled the globe; therefore, the sun was always shining at some place where the British flag was flying.) Throughout the British colonies and wherever British ships sailed, English became the language of government or trade.

The significance of this early distribution of English is apparent in those countries that have adopted the language as their own, but in other former colonies the continued importance of English may not be as clear. India is an excellent example. It is a **polyglot** country, that is, one with citizens who speak a wide variety of native languages (Fig. 4.4). When the British ruled India, English was not only the language of

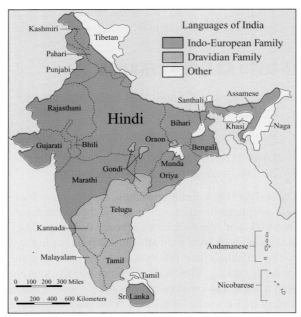

FIGURE 4.4

The distribution of major languages native to the various peoples of India. It is easy to see how the lack of a common language has helped to fragment culturally this country of nearly a billion inhabitants.

government but the language of all those who pursued an education beyond primary school. Hindi, with more native speakers in the core of the subcontinent, also came into more widespread use during the colonial period.

At the time of its independence in 1947, India was faced with a serious dilemma: how to administer a new country without a common language. Hindi was suggested as the official language by the widely respected leader Mahatma Gandhi, but other language groups feared domination by the Hindus if they lost the importance of their own native tongue. Today 15 official languages are recognized in the constitution of India. Hindi remains an important second language for non-native speakers, and English is the lingua franca of external diplomacy and the educated elite. The English language has experienced a similar history in the independent countries of Africa that were formerly British colonies.

Much of the more recent growth of English as lingua franca has been associated with the interna-

tional influence of the United States. During their own period of colonial expansion, Americans carried English to the Philippines and many Pacific islands. Economic colonialism introduced English throughout much of Central America, and United States influence over its southern neighbors made English a favored second language among the well-educated throughout much of South America. At the close of World War II, the United States was the most powerful country in the world, both militarily and economically. Americans possessed a large portion of the world's wealth and consumed a far greater share of the world's commodities than their numbers justified. The United States dominated international commerce; it was advisable to learn English to make it easier to do business with the United States. Americans were recognized leaders in scientific research and technology; it also was essential to learn English to gain access to this wealth of new information and methodology.

The situation is far different today than it was in the 1940s. The economic resurgence of the Western European countries and the rise of Japan and other Asiatic countries as industrial giants and leaders in international commerce have reduced in some ways the influence of the United States. Nevertheless, the United States is still a major trading partner for many of the world's countries. To conduct business with the United States still requires the use of English because few American business people speak the language of another country. And English has become firmly entrenched as lingua franca for much of the developed world.

English as lingua franca has both advantages and disadvantages for Americans. The native speaker usually has a far greater command of a language than the non-native speaker, and the effective use of language is an important tool in negotiations of all kinds, whether industrial, commercial, or diplomatic. Language is also a major key to the diffusion of culture, and significant elements of the cultures of English-speaking peoples, for good or for ill, have been dispersed throughout the world. Whether or not American cultural traits will remain integrated into other cultures remains to be seen, but there is little question that knowledge of the American way of life has been widely diffused along with the English language.

For Americans the major disadvantage of English as lingua franca is that it discourages them from learning a second language—they see little necessity for doing so. Trade deficits continue to mount in the

United States because it is easy for Americans to buy from foreigners who speak their language, but it is more difficult for Americans to sell their products abroad when they do not speak the language of their customers or, because of this language deficiency, do not understand the culture of their customers.

RELIGION AS A CULTURAL TRAIT

➤ Religion has been an important part of human culture since at least the beginning of the earliest civilizations and is a major factor in cultural diversity and conflict.

What were common elements of traditional religions and how did they differ from modern religions?

How have religious differences influenced current world events?

Religion has been a part of culture since humans first banded together to seek food and protect themselves from the forces of nature. Certain natural occurrences—birth, death, the daily movements of the sun, moon, and stars, and cataclysmic environmental changes—were all part of a mysterious and unknown universe that defied human understanding. To cope with these events in their lives, cultural groups developed systems of practices and beliefs that helped them explain the unknown and served to protect them from an often threatening natural environment. Thus **traditional** or **tribal religions** began.

Traditional religions, wherever they developed, had many things in common. Most included the belief that the various elements of nature were occupied by spirits that had the power to control natural events. In these **animistic religions** it usually was possible for all people to communicate with the spirits, although most included certain individuals (a medicine man or *shaman*) who had special powers to influence or intercede with the spirit-filled world (Fig. 4.5). Elaborate feasts and ceremonies often were involved in these early religions, and as most included the concept of life after death, the disposition of the dead had special significance. Magical powers frequently were associated with certain individuals, objects, or locations, and it was believed that the spirits could be influenced and evil avoided by conducting carefully designed rituals or by following special patterns of behavior.

Although some individuals today believe that their religions began with the creation of human life,

FIGURE 4.5

A Native North American medicine man. Within the tribal groups that occupied North America prior to the arrival of Europeans, the medicine man was a figure of power and authority who often commanded as much respect as the tribal chief. (Charles Winters)

cultural historians hold that modern religions evolved from the traditional religions of the past. Whichever is the case, modern religions still provide an explanation for the unknown—for those things that cannot be explained by science or controlled by technology. They also still include ritual and ceremony, recommended moral codes or patterns of behavior, spiritual leaders, and an organized set of principles and beliefs.

Some modern religions, such as Judaism, are **ethnic religions**; that is, they are associated with a particular group of people who share a common cultural heritage and who possess, in addition to religious customs, other common characteristics. Such characteristics may include language, ancestry, national origins,

FIGURE 4.6
These orthodox Jewish men in Israel are examples of people who follow the conservative religious customs of their ancestors. (Mike Abrahams/Network Matrix)

and certain physical features (Fig. 4.6), although this is not always the case. Others are **universalist religions,** which readily include individuals from all ethnic and cultural backgrounds and provide for the expansion of the faith through missionary activities and the conversion of new followers. Examples of universalist religions include Christianity and Islam.

There are other significant differences among modern religions. Some involve worship of a single god (**monotheism**), whereas others embrace multiple gods (**polytheism**). Although religion is a major obstacle to cultural change, some religions are more adaptable than others and have made accommodations to the dynamic nature of societies, especially in the developed world. Certain religions recently have had a growing influence on world affairs, while the influence of others may be waning.

Despite these differences—and because of them—religion today remains a cultural trait of great importance in the lives of the vast majority of the world's people. It permeates and broadly influences all aspects of major world cultures. For some people, religion prescribes their daily, weekly, and annual routine, what food they can eat and when they can eat it, and what clothes they should wear. Through its influ-

ence on a culture's value system, religion can affect a group's economic activities, perception of resources, and attitude toward the physical environment.

Perhaps most important of all, religious differences play a major role in conflict both between and within cultures. Jews oppose Moslems in the Middle East. Bands of Christians and Moslems battle each other and among themselves in Beirut, Lebanon. Irish Catholics oppose Irish Protestants in Belfast, Northern Ireland. Religion helps to separate Islamic Pakistan from Hindu India.

Human geographers study religion because it is a major factor in cultural diversity and an important element in cultural diffusion. In addition, the origins, development, and present distributions of major religions are further examples of the dynamic relationships between humans and the environments they occupy.

MAJOR WORLD RELIGIONS

Excluding surviving examples of traditional or animistic religions in remote areas of the world, there are five important religions that help to structure the activities, attitudes, and beliefs of significant numbers of adherents and indirectly influence the lives of countless other people. These are Judaism, Christianity, Islam, Hinduism, and Buddhism (Table 4.2). The origin, development, and nature of each are linked to earlier religions or animistic practices, and all of the major world religions have been influenced to a greater or lesser degree by one or more of the others.

TABLE 4.2	Major World Religions	
Religion	**Adherents (in millions)**	**Percent of World Total**
Christianity	1,759	33.3
Roman Catholic	996	18.8
Protestant	363	6.9
Orthodox	167	3.2
Islam	935	17.7
Hinduism	705	13.3
Buddhism	303	5.7
Judaism	17	0.3

SOURCE: *The 1990 Encyclopedia Brittanica Book of the Year*

While there are broad relationships among religions, from the perspective of the geographer, the differences may be more important. Religion is a major contributor to cultural diversity, and even when cultures share the same basic religion, divisions within that religion may lead to sharp differences in beliefs and practices and often to conflict between culture groups. The differences, not the similarities, will be most apparent as we examine each major world religion.

Judaism

➤ Although Judaism has a relatively small number of adherents, it has been one of the world's most prominent and widely diffused religions.

How has persecution contributed to the prominence and diffusion of Judaism?

What events have contributed to changes in the distribution of Jews during the twentieth century?

Although Judaism has never numbered more than 20 million adherents, its history is a remarkable story of religious faith and persistence. The origins of Judaism can be traced to Semitic tribes that lived in southwest Asia more than 4000 years ago. In its earliest stages Judaism had strong similarity to other religions of the region's nomadic peoples that included animal sacrifice and the worship of stone idols. Some religious

authorities also believe that such Jewish concepts as an afterlife that includes Heaven and Hell, and one principal god who represents good battling the forces of evil, can be traced to Zoroastrianism, an even earlier religion that existed in the same region.

Throughout its history, Judaism has been a religion characterized by the persecution and migration of its followers. It began to take on its modern monotheistic form after the *exodus*, when Moses delivered the Israelites (Jewish tribes descended from Jacob, also known as Israel) from Egyptian slavery. By about 1000 B.C. the Israelites had successfully invaded Palestine (Canaan), from where they had migrated generations earlier, and established a kingdom there that was dominated by religion.

The rule of the Israelites lasted until early in the sixth century B.C. when the Babylonians invaded Jerusalem and the Jews were forced into exile. Although they were able to return to Palestine some fifty years later, Jews by this time had been dispersed throughout the Mediterranean area (Fig. 4.7). During this period of exile, Judaism was universalist—it accepted converts—and it spread by diffusion with the conversion of non-Jews to the Jewish faith.

Further mass migration of the Jewish people occurred after conflicts between Romans and Jews led to the destruction of Jerusalem in A.D. 70. The persecution of Jews, which increased when the Roman Empire adopted Christianity as its official religion, followed

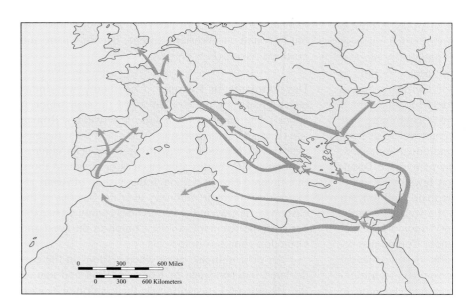

FIGURE 4.7
The diffusion of Judaism throughout the lands bordering the Mediterranean Sea. Much of this early spread of Judaism occurred when the Jews were forced to leave their ancestral home in Jerusalem.

the Jewish people wherever they settled in Europe. Judaism became essentially an ethnic religion that permeated the lives and cultures of its followers and set them apart from their neighbors. During the Middle Ages the unfamiliar customs and uncompromising beliefs of the Jews bred suspicion and fear among outsiders. Either by choice or because of coercion by local authorities, Jews settled in specific neighborhoods or *ghettos* in most European cities.

When the Moors controlled Spain between the tenth and thirteenth centuries, many Jews migrated there because the Moslems were more familiar with their culture and more sympathetic to their religious beliefs than were the Roman Catholics. Diffusion of Judaism continued during medieval times when large numbers of Jews were killed or driven from their homes throughout much of western and southern Europe. As a result, Judaism and Jewish culture spread southeastward as Jews migrated into Turkey and Syria and eastward into Poland and what is now Russia. The refugees often strengthened Jewish communities that had existed in these regions since they were first opened to trade.

As Figure 4.8 indicates, the present distribution of Judaism is far different than that in the Middle Ages. The emigration of Europeans to the Americas in the late nineteenth and early twentieth centuries included large numbers of Jewish people who settled in the major cities of the eastern United States and Latin America. Today about 40 percent of the world's Jewish population lives in the United States; smaller percentages are found in Canada, Argentina, and Brazil.

Although there are sizable populations in France and the United Kingdom, the relatively small numbers of Jews in Europe today can be explained by the *Holocaust*, the systematic murder of nearly 6 million Jews by the Nazi government of Germany during World War II. Many of the survivors fled to the United States or emigrated to Palestine as a continuing part of the **Zionist movement**, an attempt by some Jews to reestablish a country in their traditional homeland. In 1947, when the United Nations recognized Israel, there were more than a half million Jews living in the new country. Today there are more than 3 million. An additional major concentration of the world's 18 million Jews is in the former Soviet Union where approximately 3 million struggled under Communist regimes to practice their religion despite severe governmental restrictions and widespread discrimination. Since the disintegration of the Soviet Union in 1991, however, thousands of Russian Jews have been allowed to emigrate to Israel.

Christianity

> Christianity has the greatest number of adherents and is the most widely distributed of all major world religions.

How is Christianity related to Judaism?

How was the character and distribution of Christianity influenced by developments and events in Europe between classical and modern time?

Judaism, the major world religion with the smallest number of believers, is the parent of Christianity, the religion with the largest number of adherents. The prophet Jesus, who founded Christianity, was a Jew, and the Old Testament, which is the central document of the Jewish faith, is included as part of the Christian Bible. From its beginnings, Christianity has been a universalist faith with a strong missionary component.

After the crucifixion of Jesus, his disciples reported his resurrection and began to spread word of his teachings throughout the Mediterranean world. The apostle Paul was the most effective because he traveled widely through Syria and what are now Turkey and Greece. During the early growth of their religion Christians often were persecuted within the Roman Empire, but during the reign of Emperor Constantine early in the fourth century Christianity became the official state religion. The influence of the Romans assisted the diffusion of Christianity throughout Italy and into Western Europe, Britain, Spain, and northern Africa (Fig. 4.9).

Developments in Europe   Christianity was influenced greatly by the Roman world through which it spread. The empire was balanced between a Roman west and a Greek (Hellenistic) east, and from the earliest days Christianity was divided between congregations that favored Latin services or rites and those that favored Greek. Although the Bishop of Rome attempted to maintain authority over the bishops in the eastern territories, major differences continued to exist between the Roman Catholic Church in the west and Orthodox churches in the east.

An official break came when bishops in the east declared independence of Rome in 1054 and named the Bishop of Constantinople their spiritual leader.

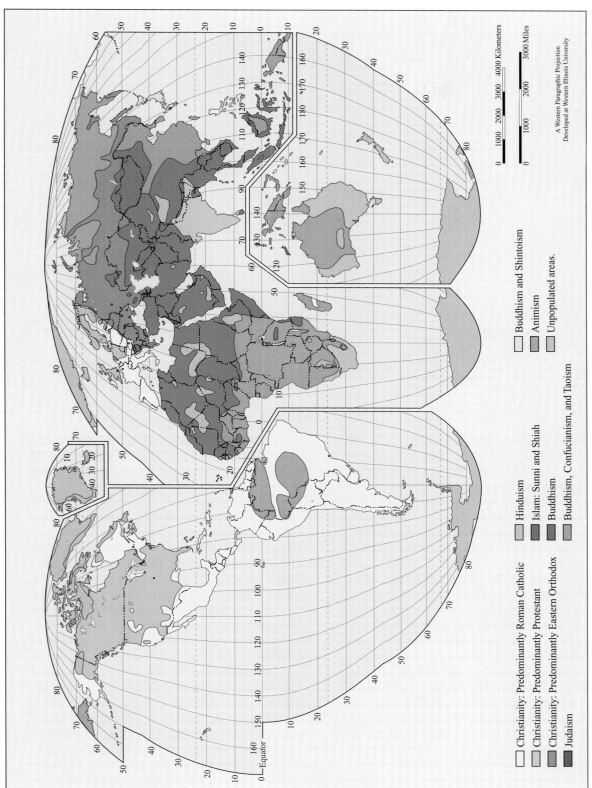

Christianity: Predominantly Roman Catholic
Christianity: Predominantly Protestant
Christianity: Predominantly Eastern Orthodox
Judaism

Hinduism
Islam: Sunni and Shiah
Buddhism
Buddhism, Confucianism, and Taoism

Buddhism and Shintoism
Animism
Unpopulated areas.

1000   2000   3000   4000 Kilometers

1000   2000   3000 Miles

A Western Pangraphic Projection
Developed at Western Illinois University

FIGURE 4.8

World distribution of five major religions. Christianity, Islam, and Judaism have become the most widely distributed. Christianity and Islam have the largest number of adherents and were spread primarily by conquest and conversion. Judaism has the smallest number of adherents and was diffused as a result of persistent oppression and subsequent migration.

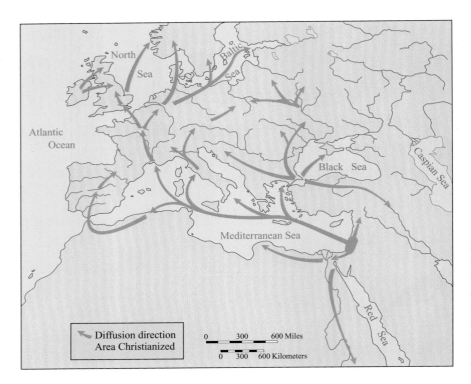

FIGURE 4.9

The spread of Christianity toward the end of the Roman Period. After Christianity was recognized as the official state religion by the Roman Emperor Constantine, it was diffused widely throughout the Roman Empire.

With the fall of Constantinople to the Moslems in the mid-fifteenth century, Christianity suffered a major setback in the Middle East and the Eastern Orthodox churches experienced further fragmentation. In eastern Europe today Orthodox Christianity is represented by what are essentially ethnic churches in Greece, Romania, parts of the former Yugoslavia, Bulgaria, and among various minorities within the former Soviet Union.

Throughout the Middle Ages Christianity continued to gain strength and dominate society in much of Europe. Leaders of the Roman Catholic Church shared power with landowners. Catholic religious orders were founded, cathedrals and monasteries were built, and the church served to stabilize local economies, provide education, preserve knowledge, and tend the sick and the poor (Fig. 4.10). However, further changes were at hand. With the invention of the printing press and the availability of relatively inexpensive written materials, differing opinions and new ideas could spread rapidly. By the early sixteenth century Christian leaders such as Martin Luther and John Calvin had openly challenged the authority and infallibility of the Roman Catholic Church, and the Protestant Reformation had

begun. Religious differences led to open warfare pitting Christian against Christian, and western Europe was divided geographically between Catholic and Protestant.

Introduction to the New World   With the exploration and colonization of the Western Hemisphere by Europeans, Christianity experienced its next major period of diffusion. Spanish, Portuguese, and French Catholics introduced their religion and converted the native inhabitants to Christianity wherever they settled in the New World, and Protestants from England and Holland did the same. The widespread distribution of Christianity illustrated by Figure 4.8 is the result of this diffusion.

The Roman Catholic Church dominates South and Central America and much of the Caribbean. (See *Cultural Landscapes: A Catholic Shrine in Mexico City.*) It also is the major religion of the southwestern United States, southern California, Louisiana, several New England states (due to the nineteenth-century immigration of Irish and southern Europeans), the Canadian province of Quebec, and the far-off Philippines. The majority of those people who live in the remainder of

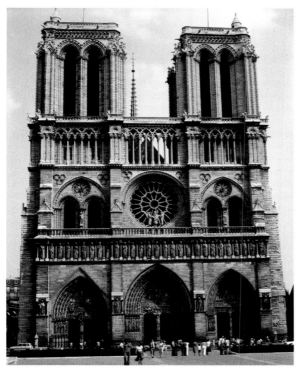

FIGURE 4.10
Notre Dame on the Île de la Cité in Paris. One of the most beautiful cathedrals in Europe, it is symbolic of the significance and influence of Catholic Christianity throughout the Middle Ages. (R. Gabler)

the United States and Canada, the Republic of South Africa, Australia, and New Zealand are Protestants. Of the more than 1.7 billion Christians in the world, it is estimated that nearly 40 percent live in North and South America. Most of the remainder are found in Europe, including western portions of the former Soviet Union. They are divided among those who attend Orthodox churches in the east, Protestant churches to the north, and Roman Catholic churches in central and southern parts of Europe.

Islam

➤ Since its formation in the seventh century, Islam has experienced periods of rapid growth and conflict.

How did Islam expand so rapidly during the first few centuries after its founding?

What are the bases of contemporary Islamic involvement in conflict?

Islam had its origin in the arid regions of southwestern Asia, as did Judaism and Christianity. In fact, Moslems include Jesus, Moses, Abraham, and Noah among their prophets, although Mohammed is considered to be the last and most important interpreter of the Islamic faith. It was Mohammed who was responsible for the *Koran*, a book containing the teachings of Allah (God) as they were revealed to him. Mohammed was born in A.D. 570 in Mecca, in the highlands near the Red Sea coast of the Arabian Peninsula. By the time he had reached middle age, the monotheistic nature of the religion he preached had come into conflict with the animistic beliefs of the Meccans and he was forced to move northward and inland to Medina where he converted many followers and established a power base.

The Spread of Islam   By the time of Mohammed's death in A.D. 632 Moslems had captured Mecca and the Islamic religion had spread throughout the Arabian Peninsula. One reason given by some authorities for the rapid acceptance of Islam was the incorporation into the religion of certain animistic beliefs, including the worship of a black meteorite—the Kaaba—as practiced by the Meccans, and the importance of holy pilgrimages. (See *Cultural Landscapes: Mecca and the Holy Kaaba*.) A second reason is that Islam is a relatively simple, democratic—at least for male aherents—religion. A third reason is that from the outset Islam was associated with military conquest and political control. As Arab armies marched across the desserts of southwest Asia and north Africa, conversion to Islam became a matter of survival for the nomadic tribes.

The diffusion of Arab and Islamic cultural traits continued throughout the seventh and early eighth centuries. Arab control spread northward and eastward into Palestine, Syria, and what is now Turkey, and on into south central Asia. By 732 the Arabs had moved westward to dominate Egypt, much of northern Africa, and Spain before being halted in a decisive battle near Tours in southern France (Fig. 4.11). Additional conquests and extensive trade activities introduced Islam into Persia (Iran), Afghanistan, and throughout the Indus Valley of what is now Pakistan (Fig. 4.12). At the height of Arab power, Moslem influence had reached India, China, Indonesia, and the Philippines.

CULTURAL LANDSCAPES

A Catholic Shrine in Mexico City

Throughout Latin America the Roman Catholic Church is not only a place of worship but also a symbol of the importance of Catholicism in the culture of the region. Indeed, Catholicism is the dominant cultural element in Latin America. The spread of the religion by Iberian missionaries to the indigenous peoples of Latin America was one of the great cultural diffusions of the second millennium A.D. Some aboriginal peoples were forced to accept the church or be killed by the conquistadors, but such pressure to join the Church was not a tactic used by most missionaries. Large numbers of people embraced the Church voluntarily, but not without retaining some of the elements of their old religions. Magnificent places of worship may have made the Roman Catholic Church particularly attractive to the natives. Grand cathedrals were built in all big cities and many smaller ones.

The Basilica of the Virgin of Guadalupe is not a cathedral, but the shrine is the most sacred Christian site in Mexico and draws visitors from all over the country on regular pilgrimages. To visit the shrine, many walk for hundreds of miles and some crawl the last mile on their knees. Compared with Mexico City's splendid cathedral, which also dates to the sixteenth century, the original Basilica is an unimposing church. Built of brick, it is much smaller, and its architecture is of no particular note. Deterioration made the building unsafe, and it was replaced by an adjoining new Basilica in 1976. The sweeping modernistic construction of the new Basilica provides large open vistas for the enormous crowds, but the building lacks the warmth and history of its predecessor, which is now closed. The building itself, however, is not the most important aspect of Guadalupe. Rather, it is the story that goes with the Basilica, the relics it contains, and what it means to Mexican Catholics that are most significant.

Prior to the Spanish Conquest, the hill of the shrine belonged to the Aztec earth goddess, but her temple was destroyed by the Spaniards. Soon thereafter, in 1530, Juan Diego, a native convert to Catholicism, reported that as he was walking across the hill, the dark-skinned Virgin of Guadalupe appeared before him. She asked him to go to the bishop and request that a church be built in her honor on the hill. The suspicious bishop did not react favorably, and the Virgin again appeared to Diego, who was told to pick roses from the hill where only cactus would grow and take them to the bishop. Diego went to the hill and found roses growing there; he picked them, wrapped them in his cloak, and took them to the bishop. When he opened his cloak to the bishop, the roses were gone and on the cloak was the image of the Virgin. The bishop was impressed and ordered that the chapel be built; Juan Diego's miraculous cloak, with the image still intact, was later displayed prominently inside. The Roman Catholic Church recognized the miracle of the Virgin of Guadalupe in 1745, and in 1810, the father of Mexican independence, Miguel Hidalgo, used the picture of the Guadalupe Virgin on his banner of revolution against Spain. Since then she has been the patron saint of Mexico.

The importance of the Basilica of the Virgin of Guadalupe as a feature of the cultural landscape and, by extension, as a representation of the continuing significance of Catholicism in Mexican society, is all the more dramatic in view of the fact that the influence of the Church has been more suppressed in Mexico than in perhaps any other Latin American country. As a result of the Mexican Revolution (1910–1920), the Roman Catholic Church lost its vast landholdings and political influence. Even today, priests and nuns may not teach in schools and are not allowed on the streets in the distinctive garb of their professions. All churches, including the old and new shrines of the Virgin of Guadalupe, belong to the federal government.

The original Basilica of the Virgin of Guadalupe contrasts with the modernistic lines of the adjoining new basilica. (A. R. Longwell)

THOUGHT QUESTIONS

1. How would you explain the fact that many Native Americans throughout the New World voluntarily converted to Christianity?
2. What reasons can you give in support of a suggestion that the Spaniards might have erected a building for Catholic worship where the Basilica of the Virgin of Guadalupe now stands, even without the reported miracle?

3. Why do you think Catholicism remains such a strong element in the Mexican culture despite the official opposition of the Mexican government since the time of the Mexican Revolution?

FIGURE 4.11
La Mesquita in Cordoba, Spain. Originally built as an Islamic mosque, it became a center of Catholic worship after the Moors were driven from Spain. (R. Gabler)

With the growing strength of Christianity and the developing influence of Europeans in trade and commerce, the Arab empire slowly declined. During the eighth century the caliphate, a major center of Islamic authority, had shifted eastward from the Arabian peninsula to Baghdad in present-day Iraq. By the time of the Christian Crusades to regain control of Palestine between the eleventh and thirteenth centuries, Islamic power was centered in Turkey, which is not an Arabic country. Islamic influence reached its peak in the seventeenth century and waned thereafter until there was a resurgence with the expansion of the Ottoman Empire of the Turks prior to World War I. With the end of the war and the destruction of the empire, the historical link between conquest and Islam was broken.

Division and Militancy   As was the case with Christianity, the evolution of Islam has been marked by internal strife and the development of religious sects. The major division separates the *Sunni* sect from the *Shiah* sect. Sunnis, who represent 83 percent of the world's Moslems, historically accepted the religious leadership of the Caliphs, who were Mohammed's followers, and their descendants. The Shiites, who represent almost 16 percent of Moslems, recognize a more direct line of religious authority, beginning with Mohammed and descending through Ali, his son-in-law. The feud between the two sects has been a bitter one and has continued unabated until the present.

Sunnis predominate throughout most of the Islamic world, although Shiites total more than 90 percent of Moslems in Iran and more than 50 percent in Iraq and Bahrein (Fig. 4.8). Shiites tend to be more conservative and militant than Sunnis. Whereas Sunni Moslems respect written Islamic laws that were adopted more than a thousand years ago, Shiite law is based on the religious judgments of the *mullahs* or religious leaders. A major cause of the Iranian revolution in 1978–1979 was the violent reaction of the mullahs and their followers to the modernization and strong Western influences that were rapidly changing their country. Even the Iran–Iraq war of the 1980s, which can be attributed to a struggle for territorial rights and political power, also had a strong religious undercurrent as Iran attempted to export its brand of Islamic militancy to its neighbor.

In recent years Islamic nations and nations with Moslem minorities have been characterized by a wave of fundamental religious fervor and a growing influence of religion on political and governmental affairs. Many believe that the riots in 1988 that killed hundreds of pilgrims in Mecca were instigated by the Shiite Iranians to embarrass the Sunni Saudi Arabians, partially because of the Saudis' strong ties with the Western world. Strong pressure (especially from the poorer classes) to adopt more conservative practices and reject Western values is evident in such diverse countries as Egypt, Bahrain, Pakistan, Indonesia, and even Turkey, which is officially a secular state.

Fundamentalist Moslem societies continue to be male-dominated. Among the persistent religious traditions is a restricted role for women. Seldom do women violate that tradition and engage in a career outside the home. Even the tradition of women using a veil to cover the face in public continues in the most conservative Moslem nations.

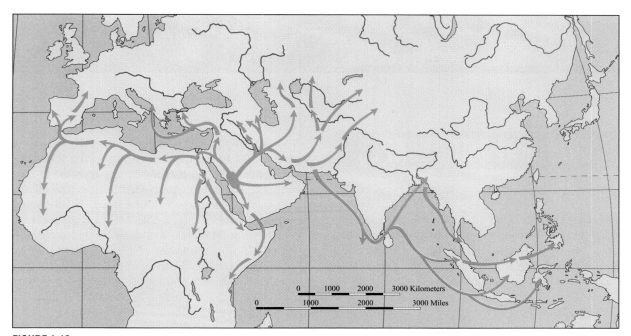

FIGURE 4.12
The diffusion of Islam. As Arab trade, influence, and often conquest spread as far west as northern Africa and Spain and as far east as India, Indonesia, and the Philippines, large numbers of people were introduced and converted to Islam.

Moslem terrorist groups, most often supported by Shiite Iranians, have been responsible for numerous assassinations, bombings, and kidnappings in attempts to influence the policies of governments both inside and outside the Islamic world. Fundamentalist Moslem rebels primarily were responsible for the retreat of the Soviet army from Afghanistan in 1988 and 1989, and within the former Soviet Union itself militant Moslem minorities repeatedly have demonstrated to demand additional freedoms and autonomy. In the world today Islam has become a unifying force among those who oppose modernization, technological change, and nontraditional values associated with the Western world.

Hinduism

➤ Despite its relatively large number of adherents and great diversity, Hinduism is generally dominant only in South Asia.

How did diversity become a distinguishing characteristic of Hinduism?

Why does religion have a particularly great influence on the lives of most Hindus?

In numerous ways Hinduism is not essentially different from the various animistic religions that proceeded it, or from current tribal religions practiced as far distant from its Indian homeland as central Africa. The distinguishing characteristic of Hinduism is its diversity. Each new wave of invaders or settlers who entered the Hindu hearthland along the Indus River in what is now Pakistan brought its own beliefs. Early practices included the worship of many gods, some with human bodies and the heads of animals, as well as a belief in reincarnation and a reverence for all forms of animal life.

When light-skinned Aryan peoples began invading the Indian Peninsula from the northwest in the sixteenth century B.C., they added much to the animism of the dark-skinned Dravidians who occupied most of the subcontinent at that time. They reinforced polytheism and introduced their own religious traditions, new ceremonies and rituals, and a form of ancestor worship. Most significantly, they brought with them

CULTURAL LANDSCAPES

Mecca and the Holy Kaaba

Pilgrimages to holy sites are common aspects of many religions. For the followers of Islam, a once-in-a-life-time pilgrimage (called *hajj*) to the city of Mecca is one of the religion's "five pillars." The first pillar is recognizing only one God (Allah); the second calls for frequent daily prayer. The third pillar calls for giving of alms; the fourth requires fasting during Ramadan, the month when the Koran was first revealed to Mohammed. The pilgrimage to Mecca is the fifth pillar.

As the place where Mohammed, Islam's chief prophet, was born in A.D. 570, Mecca is the most sacred city for Moslems. Mecca is located some 450 miles (725 km) southwest of Riyadh, the capital of Saudi Arabia. It was the focus of major caravan routes from early antiquity and therefore developed into an

The City of Mecca, which has been for many centuries the destination for followers of Islam. The two tall spires are the Prayer Towers of The Great Mosque. The Holy Kaaba, which contains the Black Stone of Mecca (a volcanic rock), is the centerpiece of the Great Mosque. (Mohamed Lounes/Gamma Liaison)

144

important market town. Long before Mohammed's birth, Mecca was a sacred place to a cult of idol worshipers. It now has a population of nearly 500,000, but visitors—the pilgrims—swell the size of the city by hundreds of thousands during major feast days. More than a million pilgrims visit Mecca each year. Most foreign pilgrims arrive in Saudi Arabia at the port of Jidda, on the Red Sea coast about 40 miles (64 km) from Mecca.

The Great Mosque, toward which Moslems in various parts of the world face five times a day when praying, dominates the city of Mecca (see accompanying photo). Dating from the eighth century, it has been enlarged many times and now can accommodate more than 300,000 pilgrims. The centerpiece of the Great Mosque is the Holy Kaaba, a small stone building in the shape of a cube. Built into the eastern wall of the Kaaba is the Black Stone of Mecca, which is kissed by all pilgrims. The entire building is covered by a large embroidered cloth that is changed annually at the season of the pilgrimage. As a part of their ritual, Moslem visitors walk around the Kaaba seven times. It is claimed that the Kaaba was a destination for idol-worshiping Arab pilgrims for several centuries before the establishment of Islam.

The highly structured pattern for the pilgrimage by Moslems was set by Mohammed himself, and it has changed little over the centuries, with the exception of camels being replaced by modern forms of transportation. The pilgrimage is obligatory for every male Moslem once in his life, unless he is financially or otherwise incapable of making the journey. This guarantees the continuing importance of Mecca as a religious center and continuing prosperity for the city's economy, which is based almost entirely on providing food, housing, and other goods and services for the pilgrims.

THOUGHT QUESTIONS

1. What is the purpose of pilgrimages? Why are they important in religions?
2. What are pilgrimage sites for some religions other than Islam? Do any of them involve natural features as opposed to cultural landscape features?
3. Can you think of any other cities that have an economy similar to that of Mecca? Who are the visitors or pilgrims that they serve?

written texts, the *Vedas*, that comprised the collective wisdom or knowledge that supported their religious practices. The Vedas provided an important foundation to the evolving Hindu religion. Centuries later revisions of the Vedas, called the *Upanishads*, reinforced their importance.

The Caste System   As Aryans occupied much of the Indian subcontinent and forced the Dravidian peoples to the south, Hinduism became associated with the development of a highly structured social organization known as the caste system. Hindu society was segregated primarily on the basis of occupation and socioeconomic status. At the uppermost level were the Hindu priests or Brahmans; at the next level were the warriors and nobles who protected the Brahmans; at the third level were the merchants, traders, and large landowners; and at the lowest level were those who toiled in the fields and produced goods with their hands.

Hindus hold that they are born into a caste and remain in that caste throughout their lives, although there are significant numbers of individuals who are outside the system and hence considered "outcastes." Ignored by the castes, these *untouchables*, as they are called, and their descendants are forbidden to participate in Hindu ceremonies, can perform only the most menial tasks, and are relegated to lives of utmost poverty. Although British colonial authorities and (since 1947) the Indian government have attempted to abolish the caste system, the social and economic impact of nearly 3000 years of this aspect of Hindu cultural history is slow to disappear. The destinies of the vast majority of Indians still are determined at birth.

Hinduism Today   Hinduism is the religion of nearly 700 million people in India, and neighboring Nepal is the only other country where Hindus comprise a majority of the population (Fig. 4.8). Yet Hinduism was not always an ethnic religion, as indicated by the ease with which it absorbed the practices of local animistic religions while it spread through the Indian Peninsula and into Southeast Asia where some Hindu beliefs survive in the midst of other religions. In a few of these non-Indian locations, such as the island of Bali in Indonesia, Hinduism remains the dominant religion. Hinduism also is found wherever Indians have migrated in significant numbers. There are a million and a half Hindus in Africa, nearly a million in North America, and more than a half million in both Europe and Latin America.

The impact of religion on the lives of most Hindus is great, especially in India. Frequent religious festivals honor the gods, who are associated with the natural environment on which a predominantly rural and agricultural India must depend. Religious ceremonies, such as marriage, are often elaborate and expensive and may last for several days (Fig. 4.13). A pilgrimage to Benares to bathe in the sacred Ganges River is a goal of many devout Hindus.

Although dietary habits vary widely from one region of India to another, the respect for animal life and the belief in reincarnation in another life form, which are basic to Hinduism, have contributed to restrictions on the eating of meat. In fact, Hindu reverence of the cow has created an ever-increasing economic problem for India. Although cattle are important work animals and provide both milk for human consumption and dung for fuel, in a nation with a rapidly growing population and limited food supplies, there are more than 200 million cows that are protected from slaughter because they are held to be sacred animals. It is predicted

FIGURE 4.13

A traditional marriage ceremony in India. Most marriages in India are still arranged by a professional intermediary who matches the bride and groom with the cooperation of the involved families. After marriage, the bride joins the groom's family and is placed under the supervision of the groom's mother. (J. L. Manaud, S. Elbaz/Odyssey Matrix)

that this number may double by the year 2000 if the animals are permitted to continue competing freely with humans for food.

Buddhism

➤ Although it originated in India, Buddhism found its greatest number of followers in other parts of Asia.

Why did Buddhism become more widely distributed in Asia than Hinduism?

What makes it difficult to determine Buddhism's current number of adherents?

As Hinduism became more restrictive and the caste system evolved, charismatic leaders, usually from the ruling class, led religious reform movements. In this way, just as Christianity grew out of Judaism, Buddhism developed from Hinduism about 500 B.C. The founder of Buddhism, Prince Siddhartha Gautama, derived his title from the village near the present border of India and Nepal where he was born. His doctrines were uncomplicated and appealed to the uneducated rural populations who struggled against a harsh environment for survival. He taught that suffering and death were inevitable but that suffering could be overcome and an enlightened state of peace (nirvana)

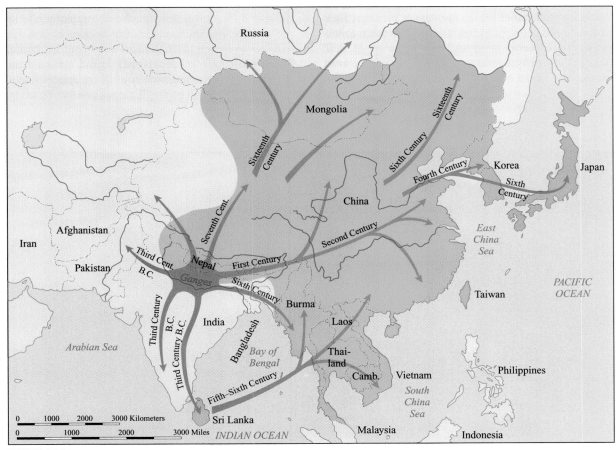

FIGURE 4.14

The diffusion of Buddhism from its origins in northern India. Buddhism became an important universalist religion when the influential King Asoka converted to the Buddhist faith and supported missionary efforts outside India.

could be obtained through personal discipline and meditation.

Gautama, who was also known as Buddha, dispatched some of his followers as missionaries, but the most important diffusion of Buddhism occurred in the third century B.C. At that time Asoka, a powerful and warlike king of northern India, embraced the religion and actively supported missionary work both inside and outside of India. During this period Buddhism diffused as far west as Egypt and north Africa and as far south as the island of Ceylon (Sri Lanka) (Fig. 4.14). Centuries later it spread from Ceylon eastward into Burma (Myanmar), Siam (Thailand), and the Indo-Chinese peninsula. Today Buddhism, along with Christianity and Islam, is one of the three major universalist religions.

At first Buddhists believed that only a chosen few of their number could reach the state of nirvana (*Theravada Buddhism*), but after a few centuries the doctrines were modified to include larger populations within the core of the religion (*Mahayana Buddhism*). Mahayana Buddhism spread slowly along desert and mountain trade routes into Tibet, Mongolia, and northern China and through Siam into southern China. From China there was further diffusion into Korea and Japan (Fig. 4.15).

The greater flexibility of Mahayana Buddhism enhanced its appeal and encouraged local populations to adapt and incorporate its doctrines into their own native philosophies. Buddhism was rapidly disappearing by the ninth century A.D. in its original Indian hearthland, because of persecution by Moslems and its incorporation into Hinduism. However, by then it was firmly linked with regional religions such as Taoism and Confucianism in China and the Korean peninsula, and with Shintoism in Japan. The present distribution of Buddhism, as indicated by Figure 4.8, reflects these developments.

Buddhism provides us with an excellent example of how difficult it is to judge the strength of a religion or to determine the number of its adherents. The significant presence of Buddhism is evident in the cultural landscape of China, Korea, Japan, Thailand, and Burma, and lesser indications of the religion's impact

FIGURE 4.15

Buddhism in Japan. This bronze Buddha in Kamakura, Japan, is reputed to be the largest religious figure made of metal in the world. (R. Gabler)

can be identified in its native India and in the other eight or so countries where Buddhists may be found (Fig. 4.16). However, there are no accurate statistics describing the number of believers in each country and the extent to which they practice the doctrines of their faith. How, for example, does one determine the number of Buddhists in China, where Buddhism is thoroughly blended with earlier doctrines and where a communist government seeks to abolish religion and replace it with economic and political institutions? The most common calculation of the number of Buddhists

FIGURE 4.16
A Buddhist temple in Illinois. The freedom of religion enjoyed in the United States often results in unexpected features in the cultural landscape. (John K. Simmons)

in the world today is approximately 300 million, although the estimates range from 170 to 600 million.

THE IMPORTANCE OF LANGUAGE AND RELIGION

Among those elements that serve to differentiate cultures, language and religion ordinarily are the most prominent. When one culture is distinguished from another, it is the language spoken and the religion practiced by each group that usually are identified as the most important contrasts. The sharing of a common language and religion functions as an incredibly tight bond among the members of a culture. Any attempt to weaken this bond by the substitution of a different language or religion typically encounters hostility and vigorous rejection. Individuals tend to regard their language and religion as their most valued cultural traditions. When those traditions are threatened by change, emotions are aroused and bitter struggle can be expected.

Most scholars undoubtedly would agree that a common language is the most essential possession of a culture. A common language enables the members of a culture to share their ideas, beliefs, experiences, attitudes, goals, and technology. Language makes possible a culture's enrichment and growth as well as the transfer of this culture from one generation to the next. Without a common language, the functioning of a society—the education of its members, its religious services, its economic endeavors, and its exercise of governmental responsibilities—would be ineffective or impossible.

The importance of religion reaches far beyond strictly theologic matters. To varying degrees, religions guide and influence the daily lives of their members. The type of clothing worn, the foods and beverages consumed, the holidays celebrated, the treatment of the ill, the conduct of pilgrimages, and the nature of interpersonal relations are all prescribed for their adherents by one or more of the world's major religions. In many countries (including some with constitutions that require separation of church and state), religion exercises great influence on governmental policies and practices. Cultural landscape features, as we have shown, also often illustrate the importance of religion in world societies.

The paramount role of languages and religions in accounting for differences between cultures, and hence between regions, demands the attention of geographers. These two human traits remain powerful factors in both social and spatial differentiation even though current trends toward cultural similarity around the globe are being identified.

KEY TERMS

Language family A group of related languages that have evolved from a common ancestral tongue. **125**

Official language The language specified by a government to be used for all official or formal communication. **125**

Dialect The spoken variation of a language that is associated with a particular region or socioeconomic group. **131**

Pidgin language Used for communication between speakers of different languages primarily for the purpose of conducting trade, it is a simplified tongue formed by intermixing elements of other languages. **131**

Creole language A language that has evolved from a pidgin or a mixture of other languages. It is a more fully developed language than pidgin. **131**

Bilingual The ability to communicate in two different languages. **131**

Lingua franca A common language used over a wide area by speakers of different tongues, usually for diplomatic or commercial purposes. **131**

Polyglot A country or society in which many different languages are in use. **131**

Traditional (tribal) religions Relatively early and primitive religions that served to explain the unknown and offer protection from threatening natural events. **133**

Animistic religions Primitive religions that involve worship of animals or natural features such as mountains, caves, stones, and trees. **133**

Ethnic religions Associated with a particular ethnic group, these religions do not seek converts outside of the group. **133**

Universalist religions Religions that strive to convert all people and gain universal following. **134**

Monotheism The worship of one god. **134**

Polytheism The worship of many gods. **134**

Zionist movement The effort among Jews to reconstitute a Jewish state in Palestine. **136**

REVIEW QUESTIONS

1. How does cultural diversity pose a challenge for the geographer?

2. What are some examples that illustrate the particularly close relationship between language and the culture of which it is a part?

3. What is a *language family* and *subfamily*? Are there languages that are *not* members of a language family?

4. Why do the Indo-European and Sino-Tibetan family groups have such a large number of speakers? Why is the former family group more widely distributed than the latter?

5. What conditions have influenced the character of individual languages?

6. How did the fact that the Koran was written in Arabic contribute to the diffusion of that language?

7. What and where are the principal exceptions to the dominance of the English language in Anglo-America and the Spanish language in Latin America?

8. In what parts of the former British Empire does English remain the primary language?

9. What are distinguishing characteristics of a *dialect*? What are *pidgin* and *creole* languages?

10. How does a language become a *lingua franca*? What might create the need for a lingua franca? How can the extensive use of English as lingua franca be explained?

11. What do *modern religions* have in common with *traditional religions*? What is an *animistic religion*?

12. How do *ethnic religions* and *universalist religions* differ? What is an example of each?

13. How does religion influence the daily lives of people in different cultures? Where in the world are there current examples of the role of religion in producing conflict both within and between cultures?

14. What led to the dispersion of Jews from the Holy Lands prior to the Middle Ages? How does their current distribution differ from that in the Middle Ages?

15. What historical events led to the fragmentation of Christianity and the widespread diffusion of Christian denominations?

16. How do the *Sunni* and *Shiah* sects of Islam differ? Where are the Shiites most concentrated today?

17. How was Hinduism influenced by the Aryan invasion of India? What aspects of the daily life of its adherents are linked to Hinduism?

18. How did Buddhism come to be more important in eastern and southeastern Asia than in its south Asian hearthland?

CHAPTER 5

GOVERNMENT AND POLITICAL SYSTEMS

*All states, large or small, rich or poor, utilize power in
its various manifestations as an obvious mark of their
importance in the international arena.*

—John E. Kieffer

*A dramatic political event in South Africa was the 1994 election of the first
native African, Nelson Mandela, to the presidency. (Tony Savino/The Image Works)*

olitical systems and governmental institutions, with their distinctive principles and ideologies, are of enormous significance as elements of culture and as contributors to the world's cultural diversity. They are most important among those cultural institutions that provide order and direction to human societies. Governments typically are responsible for establishing and enforcing laws, providing protection and defense, entering into agreements and treaties with other countries, and a great many other activities to promote the security and welfare of their citizens.

Government and political organization evolved as humans came together in societies and acquired their unique complex of cultural traits. Throughout history the critical decisions in a society usually have been made by one all-powerful individual whose title—whether chief, tsar, emperor, khan, or queen—has reflected the individual's lofty status. Such leaders have risen to power with the support of a ruling elite, and their ability to stay in power has depended on their ability to control this political support system. Political systems that effectively provide those who are being governed with an opportunity to choose their own leadership and influence government policy did not begin to emerge until the eighteenth century and have yet to be established in all societies. This development is associated with the Democratic Revolution, which we identified in Chapter 3 as one of the most important cultural changes in human history.

Power is central to the practice of politics, and it is the political system that determines who shall have the power to create laws, implement policies, and interpret regulations. All too often, along with power goes privilege. Throughout history most nations have been characterized by a privileged class, backed by government and often including government officials, that has controlled most of the society's wealth. In contrast, the masses of people seldom have been able to rise above a subsistence level. Such economic disparities affected the availability of education, the rate of adoption of new technologies, and even the attitudes, perceptions, and beliefs of individuals. The misuse of power, associated with privilege and corruption, remains one of the major problems of government in many nations. Most contemporary political systems are structured to prevent the misuse of power, but the problem persists and disagreement continues over which system offers the best solution.

In international affairs the exercise of power also comes into play as individual governments attempt to influence the political ideology, decisions, and actions of others. In general, countries with the greatest economic wealth or military strength are most influential in the international arena. Since the end of World War II the greatest struggle for international influence has been carried out by two ideologically opposed superpowers: the United States and the former Soviet Union. This costly and dangerous contest was ended by the collapse and political fragmentation of the Soviet Union in 1991. Almost immediately after this collapse many political leaders announced the arrival of a "New World Order," in which emerging new powers with different agendas would change the course of future international relations.

GOVERNMENT AND OTHER ELEMENTS OF CULTURE

➤ The close associations among the various cultural traits are well demonstrated by the relationships of government with both language and religion.

How can government affect or be affected by language and religion?

How can differences in language or religion within a country influence governmental stability?

Extremely important interrelationships exist between government and other components of culture; especially significant are the links between government and language and religion. It is government that specifies the language or languages to be used in a nation's schools, in business and commercial activities, and in affairs of state. A nation's government also regulates the extent of its citizens' freedoms, including the freedom of religion. The lack of a common language or the presence of strong religious differences within a nation can lead to internal strife and may even threaten the continued existence of a government or a particular political system.

Language and Government

India provides an outstanding example of the interrelationship between language and government. The constitution of India recognizes 15 major languages, and the national census has identified more than 1600 native tongues or dialects. Such linguistic diversity presents formidable problems for a central government. For a nation to function successfully there must be a sense of national consciousness and a loyalty to a common political system—a sense of **patriotism**—among the people, whatever their cultural or ethnic heritage. Linguistic diversity, however, reinforces regional differences and frustrates efforts to improve communication and create national unity. Furthermore, in India the problem is accentuated by the tendency among speakers of Dravidian languages in the south to fear political control by the more numerous speakers of Hindi in the north. The use of English as a lingua franca is not a solution to the problem, because English is a second language only for the educated elite. The great majority of Indians speak only their native tongue. Today India remains a loose federation of cultural regions that are separated to a significant degree by the lack of a common language.

A different language problem has faced the government of Canada. The problem is directly related to merging the interests and concerns of the French-speaking natives of Quebec with those of the English-speaking peoples in the rest of the nation. Natives of Quebec have insisted on maintaining their French heritage, and consistently they have refused to accept English as their language. Quebec natives have been concerned that if English becomes the only language of education and government, French-Canadian culture would disappear.

The Canadian Parliament passed legislation in 1969 that designated Canada a bilingual nation and required the use of both English and French for all government business. Several years later the Quebec government took legal steps to guarantee that French would continue as the language of the province. Although such actions have helped to preserve French culture in Canada, they may have had the opposite effect on national unity. Today there is a strong movement in Quebec to separate from the remainder of Canada and become an independent nation.

Religion and Government

The strength of the association between religion and government varies widely among the world's nations. The formation of some countries has been based primarily on religion. Such was the case when the Indian

FIGURE 5.1

Government Palace is the seat of civic administration in Vatican City, a tiny but important theocratic country headed by the Pope of the Roman Catholic Church. (Donald Marshall Collection)

subcontinent was divided between Moslem Pakistan and Hindu India. The Republic of Ireland came into existence as a Roman Catholic state. Israel was the product of Jewish Zionism—the struggle to regain Palestine as a homeland for Judaism. Vatican City is a **theocracy**, an independent country where the head of the Church, the Pope, also is the head of state. Figure 5.1 shows the headquarters of civic administration in this tiny but important country. It is obvious that a close link between religion and government also exists in the fundamentalist Islamic nations of the Middle East and in other countries where the government recognizes an official state church. For example, Lutheran Christianity is the official church of Norway and Buddhism is the official religion in Thailand and Myanmar (Burma).

In contrast are nations that insist on complete separation of church and state; even in these cases, however, religion often occupies the attention of government. In the United States school prayer, religious symbols on public property, and government support of parochial schools are recurring issues for courts and legislative bodies. In many countries political officials heed the advice of religious leaders, and political parties have a religious affiliation. Internal religious conflicts pose serious problems for some governments. Catholics and Protestants oppose each other in Northern Ireland, and in India there are periodic outbreaks of violence involving Hindus and other religious groups.

Although atheism was advocated by governments in some of the former communist countries, religion usually persisted in these nations as a strong force that often opposed government policy and pressed for the freedom of citizens to worship as they chose. Among the few remaining communist states, North Korea is the only one that claims to have a totally atheist population. Some scholars have pointed out that communism itself is similar to most religions in that it involves a work ethic, moral code, subordination to central authority, salvation for the masses, and adulation of its leading prophets (Marx and Lenin).

COUNTRY, NATION, STATE, AND NATION-STATE

➤ The world's primary political units commonly are identified as countries, nations, or states, even though definitions of these terms do not coincide.

How does a nation *differ from a* country *or* state*?*

Why do only certain countries qualify as nation-states*?*

Although governmental entities at local and regional levels (e.g., townships, counties, and provinces) have geographical importance, our concern in this chapter is with the world's primary political units, which usually are identified as countries, nations, or states. The use of these terms risks possible misunderstanding, however. To many people, *nation* and *country* are words that have precisely the same meaning; for example, Brazil, Nigeria, and Japan are commonly designated as either nations or countries. (We follow this popular practice and use the two words interchangeably in this book.) To be precise, however, the terms can be distinguished: a **nation** is a group of people, the members of which possess common cultural traits (and in some cases, racial traits) and occupy a particular area. The area inhabited by a nation may extend beyond the boundaries of a single country, however. A good example is Kurdistan, an area occupied by the Kurdish people that lies within five countries (Fig. 5.2). This political division has created horrendous problems for the Kurds. Numbering more than 20 million people, they have been oppressed repeatedly

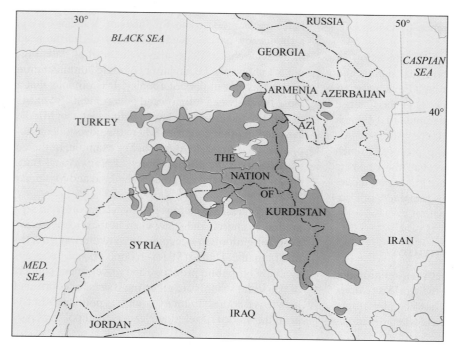

FIGURE 5.2

Kurdistan is a good example of a nation that does not lie within a single state. Rather, it involves parts of five states, some of which have persecuted the Kurds.

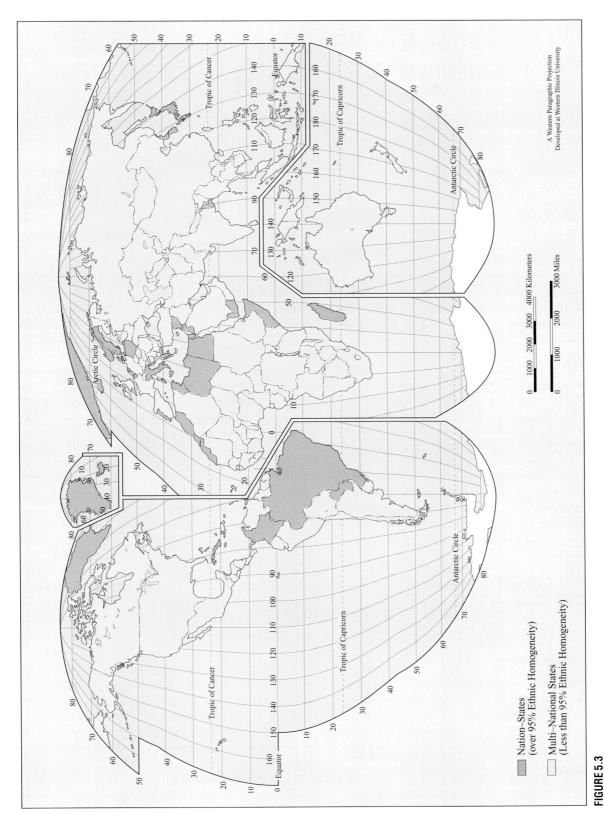

FIGURE 5.3

Political geographers have not agreed on a quantified definition for a nation-state. For the purpose of this map, we have defined a nation-state as a state having more than 95 percent ethnic homogeneity.

Nation–States
(over 95% Ethnic Homogeneity)

Multi–National States
(Less than 95% Ethnic Homogeneity)

A Western Paragraphic Projection
Developed at Western Illinois University

157

by governments that control parts of Kurdistan. In 1988 Iraqi dictator Saddam Hussein's military killed thousands of Kurds with nerve gas, the most dramatic of countless atrocities committed against the people of this divided nation.

A **state** can refer to a political entity that possesses sovereignty over an area delimited by international boundaries. It is, therefore, appropriately used as a synonym for country. Confusion is possible, however, because the word *state* also is applied to regional political units (e.g., the state of Ohio in the United States and the state of Sonora in Mexico) that are subdivisions of countries. Somewhat greater precision of meaning is suggested by **nation-state**, a composite term that is applicable to those cases in which the area occupied by a nation of people coincides with the territory of a political state.

The origin of the nation-state is associated with the political evolution of Europe. During the seventeenth and eighteenth centuries in Europe, for the first time in world history, nationalism became the organizational basis for political states. This led to the replacement of empires and dynastic states, ruled by monarchs who often claimed divine authority, by nation-states. The spread of the nation-state concept to other continents soon followed. Although a nation-state is distinguished by cultural homogeneity, nearly all nation-states include at least small minorities. For the purpose of mapping nation-states in Figure 5.3 (page 157), we have defined them as countries with more than 95 percent ethnic homogeneity. According to that definition, 15 percent of the world's sovereign states qualify as nation-states.

CULTURAL DIVERSITY AND POLITICAL STABILITY

➤ Cultural or ethnic diversity is a potentially powerful centrifugal force that can contribute to a country's political fragmentation.

Which ethnically diverse countries have fragmented in recent years, and what are others that appear to have their unity threatened?

What are possible centripetal forces that might counteract the divisiveness of an ethnically varied population?

The degree of ethnic homogeneity in the world's countries ranges widely (Table 5.1). Although too cultur-

ally diverse to be classified as nation-states in Figure 5.3, a number of European and Asian countries have a level of ethnic homogeneity between 80 and 95 percent. Ethnic homogeneity for the states that were once a part of the Soviet Union ranges from 40 percent (Kazakhstan) to 82 percent (Russia). Many African states, as indicated in Table 5.1, have a low degree of ethnic homogeneity.

The extent of a state's cultural diversity often influences its political stability. Countries in which the citizens comprise a single culturally unified group possess an important stabilizing force. On the other hand, states with culturally diverse populations may suffer serious political instability. As the recent disintegrations of the Soviet Union (1991), Yugoslavia (1991), and Czechoslovakia (1993) have demonstrated, ethnic diversity can be a strong *centrifugal force*—a force that works against unification. The disintegration of Yugoslavia (Fig. 5.4, page 160) provides a worst-case scenario, characterized by civil disorder, international conflict, and unspeakable human rights abuses of one ethnic group by another. The split of Czechoslovakia into the Czech Republic and Slovakia (Fig. 5.5, page 160), on the other hand, was so peaceful and smooth that it became known as the "Velvet Divorce." Although the states that once comprised the Soviet Union are far less culturally diverse than was the Soviet Union itself, the ethnic heterogeneity (Table 5.1) within most of the states will continue to act as a centrifugal force. If such states are to avoid internal conflict, they need a more powerful *centripetal force*—a force that works toward unification—such as a high level of patriotism or favorable economic opportunity for all citizens. Survival of any state, therefore, requires the superiority of centripetal forces over centrifugal forces.

THE SPATIAL EXPRESSION OF POLITICAL UNITS

It is difficult to understate the importance of the world political map (Fig. 5.6, pages 162–163). When geographers and other social scientists insist that all educated people should have a good working knowledge of the nature and location of the world's countries, it is not a casual suggestion or a matter of vested interests. Such knowledge is essential to an understanding of human affairs and global events.

The earth's land surface is divided into a complex assortment of political entities. In addition to independent countries, these include semiautonomous territories, dependencies of other countries, and areas of special sovereignty. The United Nations identifies almost 200 such entities, and as of 1994, 184 were members of the United Nations. Those that are not members are mostly small dependencies. Figure 5.6 identifies all of the world's states insofar as their size and the scale of the map permit. You are encouraged to become familiar with this map and to make frequent reference to it.

Boundaries

➤ Boundaries that separate countries are classified as generic and genetic, with each class composed of several types.

What are some boundary types that have been susceptible to international disputes and conflicts?

Why are geometric boundaries so common in Africa?

TABLE 5.1 Ethnic Homogeneity in Selected Countries

Country	Percent of Homogeneity	Country	Percent of Homogeneity
North Korea	100	Uzbekistan	70
Iceland	100	Turkmenistan	68
Japan	99	Pakistan	66
Morocco	99	Moldova	65
Poland	98	Malaysia	59
Greece	98	Guatemala	55
Libya	97	Tajikistan	55
Haiti	96	Belgium	55
Paraguay	96	Ecuador	55
Finland	94	Iran	51
China	94	Guyana	51
Germany	93	Afghanistan	50
Hungary	92	Laos	48
Sweden	91	Peru	45
Mongolia	90	Ghana	44
Romania	89	Trinidad–Tobago	43
Taiwan	85	The Gambia	42
Vietnam	84	Kazakhstan	40
Israel	83	Ethiopia	40
Russia	82	Senegal	36
United Kingdom	81	Togo	35
Belarus	80	Guinea	35
Zimbabwe	80	Bolivia	30
Bulgaria	80	Cameroon	30
Azerbaijan	78	Sierra Leone	29
Algeria	75	Central African Republic	27
Sri Lanka	74	Canada	25
Spain	73	Côte d'Ivoire	23
Ukraine	73	Kenya	21
Georgia	70	Nigeria	21

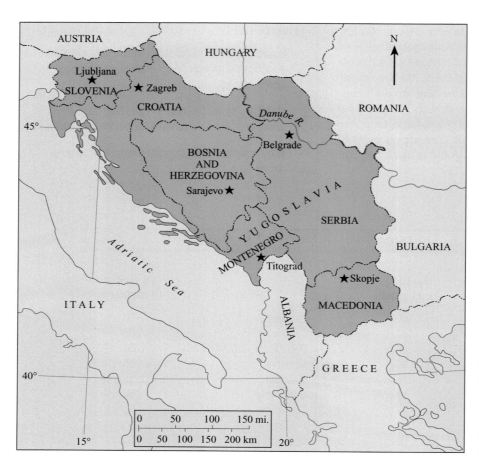

FIGURE 5.4

Ethnic diversity was a strong centrifugal force contributing to the political fragmentation of Yugoslavia in 1991 and to the subsequent civil war and international conflict.

FIGURE 5.5

The split of Czechoslovakia in 1993 into the Czech Republic and Slovakia demonstrated that a state can divide without violent conflict.

Extremely important features on the world political map are the lines representing international boundaries and delimiting the area of sovereignty exercised by each government. International boundaries are not lines but unseen vertical planes that extend both above and below the land surface, separating the airspace of countries above and the mineral rights below. Where these planes intersect the land surface, the boundaries may or may not be demarcated by posts, pillars, fences (Fig. 5.7, page 164), or, in rare cases, walls. Where boundaries cross water bodies, demarcation can be accomplished using buoys. Because it can be a costly undertaking, boundary demarcation often is not carried out between states that have good relations, especially where their boundaries pass through sparsely settled territory.

Political geographers recognize two general classes of boundaries: generic and genetic. **Generic** boundaries—those identified on the basis of their inherent characteristics—consist of four types: (1) natural or physical, (2) ethnographic or cultural, (3) historical, and (4) geometric. **Genetic boundaries**— those identified on the basis of their genesis—also consist of four types: (1) antecedent, (2) subsequent, (3) superimposed, and (4) relict.

Generic Boundaries   The *natural* or *physical boundary* is a generic boundary that follows some feature of the natural landscape. Mountains and water bodies (rivers, lakes, seas) are the natural features that most commonly serve as boundaries. The France–Spain boundary, which follows the divide of the Pyrenees Mountains, is an example of a natural boundary (Figure 5.8a, page 165). The Andean boundary between Chile and Argentina is a similar example. Mountains often separate culture groups and sometimes serve as good strategic boundaries. The seemingly unambiguous nature of alpine boundaries might lead one to believe that they would seldom be the subject of controversy and conflict, but in fact disputes are as common along them as along other types of international boundaries. A boundary dispute between Chile and Argentina raged throughout much of the nineteenth century, despite the use of the Andes as a boundary.

Natural boundaries that follow rivers also are subject to controversy. The states on both sides of a river—say, the United States on the north side and Mexico on the south side of the Rio Grande—must agree on water use rights, navigation rights, bridge and dam construction and maintenance, and what to do about shifts in the course of the river if conflict is to be avoided. Boundaries that follow the shorelines of large lakes and coastlines of seas or oceans may be the best physical boundaries—they are not likely to cause international conflict. Australia, New Zealand, Iceland, and other insular states are, therefore, largely immune to boundary disputes. Maritime (coastline) boundaries are important to a country because they provide access to marine fishing and transportation. *Land-locked countries*, which lack maritime boundaries, such as Bolivia in South America and Zimbabwe in Africa, suffer serious economic handicaps. To engage in export and import activities by sea, for example, they must rely on cooperative neighboring states.

As the name suggests, an *ethnographic* or *cultural boundary* is one that separates two different ethnic or cultural groups. Language, religion, or both may differ on either side of an ethnographic boundary. Following World War I an effort was made in Europe to use cultural boundaries to separate some of the postwar countries. Some ethnographic boundaries follow natural features. For example, language differs on either side of the Pyrenees Mountains (French, Spanish). Figure 5.8b shows a portion of the cultural boundary between the Netherlands and Germany; Dutch is the primary language to the west of it and German to the east. The boundary between Pakistan and India is a notable example of an ethnographic boundary separating religious groups; Islam is the religion of 97 percent of the people of Pakistan, while Hindu is the religion of 83 percent of Indians.

An international boundary that follows an earlier political division is considered a *historical boundary*. Figure 5.8c shows the line separating Ireland and Northern Ireland, one that qualifies as a historical boundary. The boundaries of Switzerland have been stable for such a long period that they also are properly classified as historical boundaries. The portion of the French–German boundary coinciding with that of the old duchy of Alsace is another historical boundary.

A *geometric boundary* usually consists of straight lines that disregard terrain and, very often, cultural patterns as well. Africa abounds with examples of straight-line boundaries created by European colonial powers. Examples from Libya, Egypt, Chad, and the Sudan appear in Figure 5.8d. Although curious and rare, arcs of circles also have been used for boundaries. A number of connecting arcs comprise much of the international boundary between The Gambia and Senegal; The Gambia has the distinction of being the only country in the world whose boundaries consist predominantly of arcs. Geometric boundaries can be suitable in areas of sparse settlement but can lead to conflict when they divide culture groups. Hundreds of ethnic groups in Africa are divided by such international boundaries.

Genetic Boundaries   The *antecedent boundary* is a boundary established prior to the settlement and development of most features of the cultural landscape. The boundary between the United States and Canada is generally considered to be an antecedent boundary. However, because there were some European settlers and fur traders, as well as some indigenous people,

(text continues on page 164)

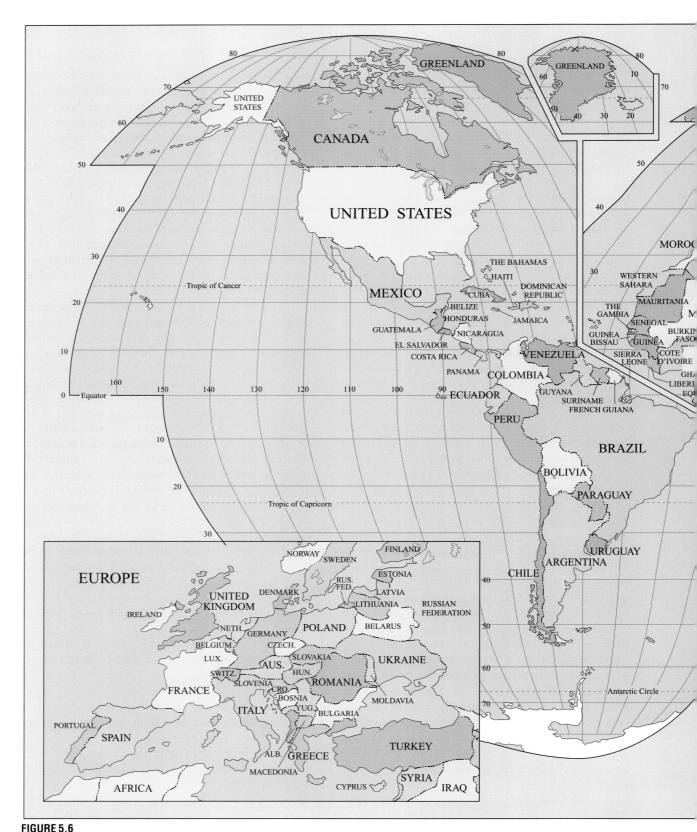

FIGURE 5.6

Knowledge about the location of states relative to each other is essential to an understanding of human affairs and global events, so it is difficult to overstate the importance of the world political map.

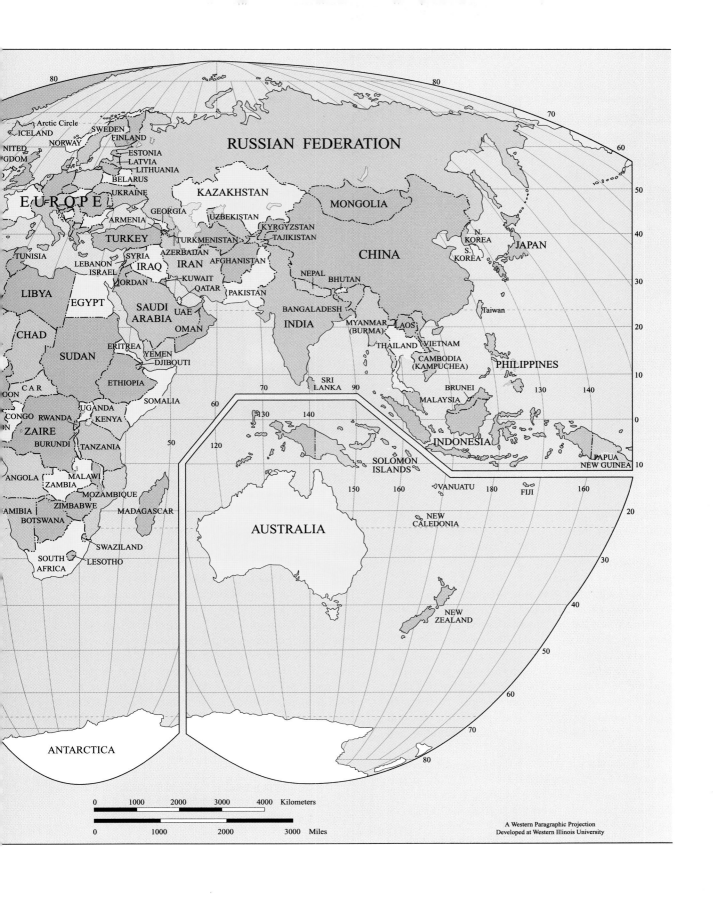

80

80

70

60

Arctic Circle
ICELAND
NORWAY
UNITED
KINGDOM

SWEDEN
FINLAND

RUSSIAN FEDERATION

50

ESTONIA
LATVIA
LITHUANIA
BELARUS

EUROPE

UKRAINE

KAZAKHSTAN

60

GEORGIA

ARMENIA

UZBEKISTAN

MONGOLIA

50

TURKEY

TURKMENISTAN

KYRGYZSTAN
TAJIKISTAN

N.
KOREA
S.
KOREA

JAPAN

40

TUNISIA

SYRIA

AZERBAIJAN

CHINA

LEBANON
ISRAEL

IRAQ

IRAN

AFGHANISTAN

30

JORDAN

KUWAIT
QATAR

NEPAL

BHUTAN

Taiwan

LIBYA

EGYPT

SAUDI
ARABIA

PAKISTAN

UAE

BANGALADESH

20

OMAN

INDIA

MYANMAR
(BURMA)

LAOS

CHAD

THAILAND

VIETNAM

130

140

ERITREA

YEMEN
DJIBOUTI

CAMBODIA
(KAMPUCHEA)

PHILIPPINES

10

SUDAN

C A R

ETHIOPIA

SRI
LANKA

90

BRUNEI

SOMALIA

60

70

MALAYSIA

CAMEROON

UGANDA

50

120

130

140

0

CONGO
GABON

RWANDA

KENYA

INDONESIA

ZAIRE

BURUNDI

TANZANIA

SOLOMON
ISLANDS

PAPUA
NEW GUINEA

10

ANGOLA

MALAWI
ZAMBIA

150

160

VANUATU

180

FIJI

160

MOZAMBIQUE

NAMIBIA

ZIMBABWE

BOTSWANA

MADAGASCAR

NEW
CALEDONIA

20

SOUTH
AFRICA

SWAZILAND
LESOTHO

AUSTRALIA

30

40

NEW
ZEALAND

50

60

70

ANTARCTICA

80

0   1000   2000   3000   4000   Kilometers

0   1000   2000   3000   Miles

A Western Paragraphic Projection
Developed at Western Illinois University

FIGURE 5.7
This fenced portion of the boundary between the United States and Mexico demonstrates that countries often find it necessary to secure their boundaries to restrict unauthorized entry. The entry of "illegal aliens" from Mexico into the United States has been a serious problem between the two countries for years. (Alex Quesada/Matrix)

in much of the area through which the boundary was established by treaties between 1782 and 1846, it is only partially antecedent. The Alaska–Canada boundary, shown in part in Figure 5.9a (page 166), is totally antecedent, as it was fixed by treaty at a time (1825 and 1827) when that area was completely unsettled.

A *subsequent boundary* is one established after (subsequent to) the settlement of an area. Most of the time such a boundary is laid out to minimize potential cultural problems in the area. That is, usually an effort is made to adjust the boundary to ethnographic patterns on the landscape. The India–Pakistan boundary is shown in Figure 5.9b as an example. A new subsequent boundary was created in 1993 by the peaceful split of Czechoslovakia into the Czech Republic and Slovakia.

If a boundary is established after the settlement of an area but with disregard for existing cultural patterns, it is said to be a *superimposed boundary*. The victorious powers in World War II divided Germany with a superimposed boundary that endured for more than four decades before German reunification in 1990. There are numerous superimposed boundaries

in Africa dating from that continent's colonial era. The Angola–Zambia boundary, shown in Figure 5.9c, is an example.

The last of the boundary types in the genetic class is the *relict boundary*. A relict boundary no longer functions as a political boundary, having been eliminated in the development of new political realities in the region. Even so, it may be evident in the landscape as a result of differences in architectural types or other cultural elements on either side of it. Figure 5.9d shows Somalia and the relict boundary that formerly separated British and Italian colonies here. The defunct boundary between the former West and East Germanies is another example of a relict boundary.

Size and Shape

➤ The world's countries exhibit a wide variety of sizes and shapes with corresponding advantages and disadvantages.

What are the potential advantages and disadvantages of a large land area?

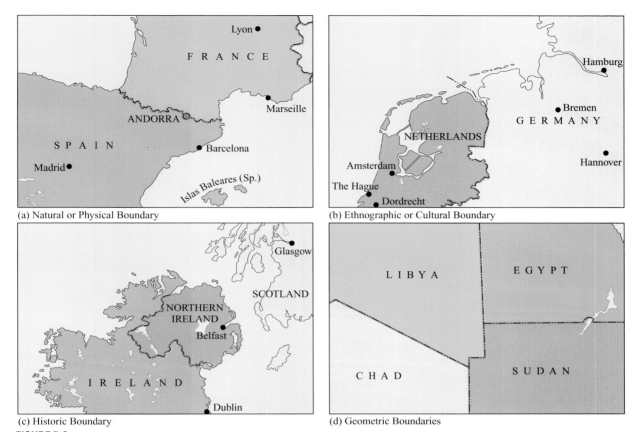

(a) Natural or Physical Boundary

(b) Ethnographic or Cultural Boundary

(c) Historic Boundary

(d) Geometric Boundaries

FIGURE 5.8

Generic boundaries are a group of boundary types identified on the basis of inherent characteristics of the boundaries themselves.

What are the theoretical advantages of a country with a compact shape?

The world political map reveals a wide variety of territorial sizes and shapes among countries. The eight leading countries in terms of size of land area are identified in Table 5.2. Called "giant states" in this table, these countries each have more than a million square miles (2.59 million sq km) in area. These eight giant states comprise about 45 percent of the world's land area and 49 percent of the population. The world political map and Table 5.2 mask many differences among the giant states. The largest in land area (Russia) is six times larger than the smallest (Kazakhstan), but the largest in terms of population (China) has a

TABLE 5.2	The Giant States	
Country	**Area in Square Miles**	**Area in Square Kilometers**
Russia	6,592,850	17,075,481
Canada	3,849,675	9,970,658
China	3,689,630	9,556,142
United States	3,679,245	9,529,245
Brazil	3,286,470	8,511,957
Australia	2,966,200	7,682,458
India	1,266,595	3,280,481
Kazakhstan	1,049,200	2,717,428

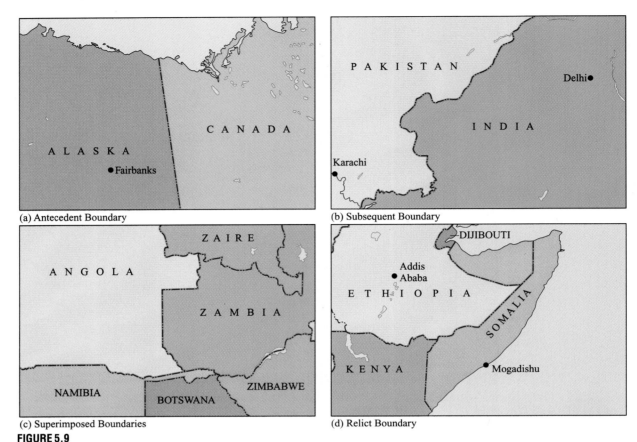

(a) Antecedent Boundary

(b) Subsequent Boundary

(c) Superimposed Boundaries

(d) Relict Boundary

FIGURE 5.9

Genetic boundaries are a group of boundary types identified on the basis of their genesis, that is, when and where they were established relative to the human occupance of the area.

population 70 times greater than that of the smallest (Kazakhstan). There are a number of potential, although not certain, advantages for large states, including the likelihood of abundant and varied natural resources. A large size, on the other hand, also can mean extensive borders to defend and lengthy communication and transportation lines that are costly to build and operate.

At the opposite extreme from the giant states are **microstates.** If a microstate is defined as a state with a land area of less than 1000 square miles (2590 sq km), 27 such political units (14 percent of the world's sovereign states) existed in 1993 (Table 5.3). All of them together comprise only about a hundredth of one percent of the world's land area—a total area about the size of Hawaii. The smallest microstate, Monaco,

has less area than many farms in the United States. Of course the microstates contain only a tiny portion of the world's population, although the sizes of their populations are even more variable than those of the giant states. For example, the population of Singapore is more than 2500 times larger than that of Vatican City, with only about twice the land area.

The functioning and well-being of a state also can be affected by its shape or spatial form. Geographers recognize five types of shapes: (1) compact, (2) prorupt, (3) elongated, (4) fragmented, and (5) perforated. An example of each is shown in Figure 5.10 (page 168). In theory, the perfect shape for a state is a circle, with the capital or principal city located at the center. A circular state would be more advantageous than other shapes because communication, transportation,

TABLE 5.3 The Microstates		
Country	**Square Miles**	**Square Kilometers**
Luxembourg	998.0	2,584.8
Comoros	838.0	2,170.4
Mauritius	790.0	2,046.1
São Tomé and Príncipe	372.0	963.5
Dominica	290.0	751.1
Tonga	270.0	699.3
Micronesia	270.0	699.3
Bahrain	268.0	694.1
Kiribati	266.0	688.9
St. Lucia	238.0	616.4
Singapore	224.0	580.2
Andorra	185.0	479.2
Antigua and Barbuda	171.0	442.9
Seychelles	171.0	442.9
Barbados	166.0	429.9
St. Vincent and the Grenadines	150.0	388.5
Grenada	133.0	344.5
Malta	122.0	316.0
Maldives	115.0	297.9
Vatican City	108.7	281.5
St. Kitts–Nevis	101.0	261.6
Marshall Islands	70.0	181.3
Liechtenstein	62.0	160.6
San Marino	24.0	62.2
Tuvalu	10.0	20.9
Nauru	8.0	20.7
Monaco	0.6	1.6

and defense would be easier to facilitate. No such ideal state exists in reality, of course, but *compact* shapes share some of the advantages of a circular state. Examples of compact states include Uruguay and Ecuador in South America, France and Poland in Europe, Sierra Leone and Côte d'Ivoire in Africa, and Sri Lanka and Cambodia in Asia. The United States was a relatively compact country before Alaska and Hawaii became states. The economic advantages of a compact shape (e.g., reduced costs involved in travel and transportation of goods) and the political advantages (e.g., defense and the unification of outlying

districts with the national core) are not shared by states that have significantly different shapes.

A country that is compact except for a single notable projection or appendage is said to have a *prorupt* shape. States that fit this description include Namibia and Zaire in Africa and Thailand and Myanmar (Burma) in Asia.

If a state has a shape that is very long and narrow, it is said to be *elongated*. The most conspicuously elongated country is Chile, which has a length more than 25 times greater than its narrowest width. Some geographers suggest that in order for a state to be de-

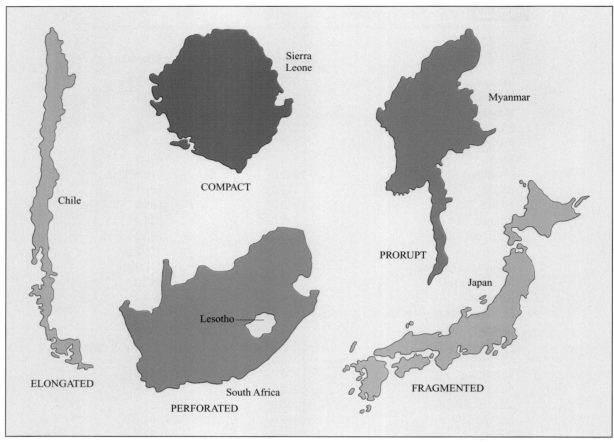

FIGURE 5.10

The spatial forms of states can contribute to their functioning and well-being. Five types of shapes recognized by political geographers are shown here.

scribed as elongated, it should be at least six times as long as its minimum width. Other countries that meet this definition include Panama, Norway, Sweden, Italy, The Gambia, and Togo.

A *fragmented* state is one that consists of two or more areas separated by an international body of water or the territory of one or more other countries. Figure 5.10 shows Japan as an example. Although fragmentation is a centrifugal force that can weaken the unity of a state, the close proximity of the islands of Japan and the nation's well-developed economy minimize this effect. The Philippines, consisting of more than 7000 islands, is so fragmented that transportation and communication links have been difficult to establish, as have other aspects of nation-building. A sovereign state since the dissolution of the Soviet Union, Azer-

baijan (Fig. 5.11) is an example of a country fragmented by land—a projection of Armenian territory— rather than by water.

Finally, a few states are *perforated* by other states. For example, the Republic of South Africa is categorized as perforated because its territory completely surrounds that of the much smaller country of Lesotho (Fig. 5.10). Although small in comparison with the surrounding state, Lesotho nevertheless is far larger than San Marino, a microstate that perforates Italy.

National Cores

> Modern states ordinarily possess a core area that, in terms of most criteria, exceeds the outlying periphery in national importance.

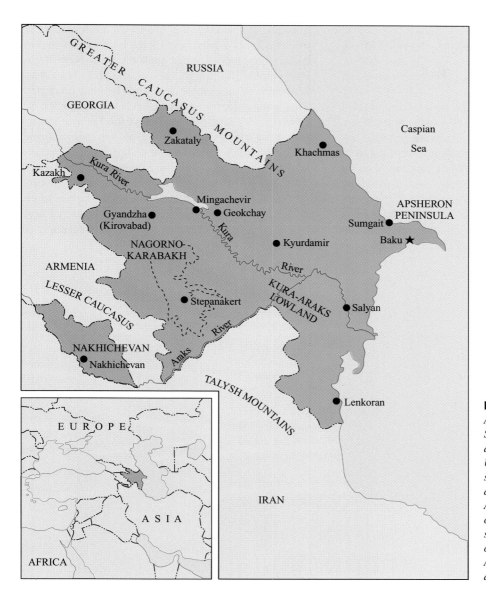

FIGURE 5.11

Azerbaijan, a divided Soviet Socialist Republic prior to the disintegration of the Soviet Union, became a fragmented sovereign state in 1991. Its division by a projection of Armenian territory is a centrifugal force that was significant in the international conflict that raged between Azerbaijan and Armenia during the early 1990s.

What are the usual characteristics of a national core?

How can the unity of a country be threatened by core–periphery relationships or the development of two core areas?

Another significant spatial feature of most modern states is the **national core**, the area in which or around which the state originated and developed. Although growth from a core area has been the normal pattern of evolution by states, we noted earlier that some states were created abruptly by the governments of other countries. Albania, for example, appeared on the map in 1913 because it suited the major powers of Europe to create it. Many African states originated in decisions made by European colonial powers. Even such created states, however, may have or soon develop a core area.

The core often contains the state's major concentration of population, usually including the national capital or the largest city (frequently one and the same). In contrast to the outlying *periphery*, the core is characterized by the country's greatest concentration of economic establishments, transportational infrastructure, cultural variety, wealth, and power. Peripheral areas are less prominent in such characteristics.

France provides one of the best examples of a country with a distinct national core—the Paris Basin, with the city as its nucleus. Switzerland provides another fine example of an old national core. Shown in Figure 5.12, this core was already well-developed by the fourteenth century. Figure 5.12 also reveals how the state expanded from the core area until its present boundaries were established. In Argentina the Pampa region and Buenos Aires constitute the core area; and the lower Nile Valley, including Cairo, is Egypt's na-

tional core. The core area of the United States is not as distinct, but it encompasses the northeastern part of the country and includes such cities as New York, Philadelphia, Baltimore, and Washington, D.C. Two or more core areas have developed in some countries. That is the case, for example, in Canada where the St. Lawrence Valley (Montreal) and the Ontario Peninsula (Toronto) have emerged as separate national cores. Where two cores are in competition, as in Canada, the consequence may be a threat to national unity. More commonly, however, it is the lack of governmental attention to peripheral areas and failure to effectively integrate these areas with the national core that contribute to internal friction and a weakening of state unity.

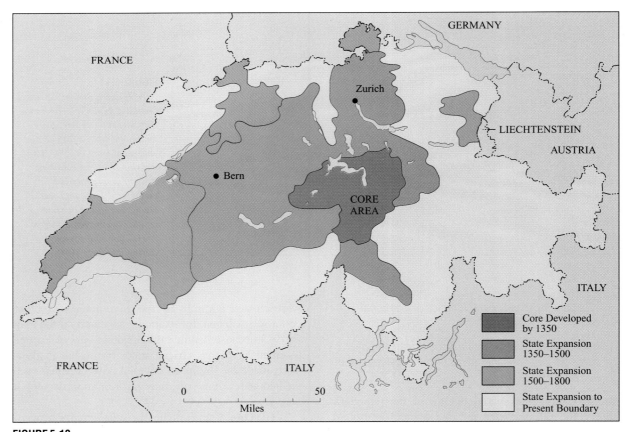

FIGURE 5.12

Switzerland provides one of Europe's best examples of an early national core—a core area that was already well developed by the fourteenth century.

COLONIAL EMPIRES

➤ Empires have been established and dissolved since the time of the earliest human civilizations, but those formed by European colonialism were the most extensive and have had greatest impact on the current world political map.

What is the basis for dividing European colonialism into two stages, and what marked the conclusion of each stage?

Which countries continue to exercise control over the remaining dependent states?

For at least thousands of years human societies have engaged in governmental organization and the extension of political control over outlying areas. In Mesopotamia and other early culture hearths some villages and small cities managed to extend their influence and authority over surrounding territory and people. This process resulted in the first **city-states**, a type of political unit that has survived to the present (although relatively few examples remain). Over time, some city-states were able to expand—often by conquest—the territory under their control and create extensive **empires**. Among many empires established by city-states in ancient times, particularly important were the Greek and Roman empires ruled by the cities of Athens and Rome, respectively. Encompassing the Mediterranean Basin and beyond, these empires had enduring influence of great magnitude on Western civilization. Centuries later the major European states established far more extensive colonial empires and thereby brought their political control and cultural influence to much of the world.

European Colonization

European colonialism began with the Age of Exploration in the late fifteenth century and continued on a large scale until after World War II. It developed in two stages, both of which involved attempts by the imperial nations to exploit resources in foreign lands and gain economic advantages. The first stage took place almost entirely in the Western Hemisphere and was marked by the migration of large numbers of Europeans for the purpose of establishing permanent colonies. Riches from these new territories and subsequent trade with the colonies enabled the European

powers to dominate the world politically, economically, and militarily by the beginning of the nineteenth century.

The first stage of colonialism came to a close and the second stage began as most European colonies in the Americas gained their independence. In addition to the United States, most Latin American countries were governing themselves by 1825. Meanwhile, the European powers were adding to their colonial empires on other continents, especially in tropical regions that were good sources of food and raw materials as well as markets for European manufactured products. The expansion of empires after 1800 was rapid as each colonial power competed with the others—and with the growing imperialism of the United States—to accumulate territory, wealth, and influence. By 1900 virtually all of Africa and large parts of Asia had been claimed by European countries. This second stage of colonialism was different from the first in that the movement of Europeans to colonial areas was mostly temporary and was primarily for the purpose of conducting trade and exercising political control. There was little attempt at permanent settlement except in highland areas of eastern Africa and in southern Africa.

The Transition of Colonies to Independent States

By far the greatest number of countries on the current world political map are the legacy of European colonialism. The reasons for their emergence as independent states are related to world events that ended the two stages of colonial expansion. The first stage ended as the European powers engaged in war among themselves and had less time to devote to their colonies. As control from abroad was relaxed and as reactions to heavy taxation and the colonists' inferior status stirred feelings of nationalism, the colonies declared their independence. The colonies that became the United States were the first to do so, in 1776, and between 1810 and 1825 seventeen other countries in South and Central America became independent states.

The greatest period of nation-building in history occurred when the second stage of European colonialism collapsed at the end of World War II. Waves of nationalism swept Asia and Africa as the remaining colonies demanded self-determination and declared their independence. Between the end of the war and the early 1980s a total of 91 new nations were created from former colonial territories. In 1960 alone, 18 new nations came into existence, 15 of them on the continent of Africa. This dramatic development was not without accompanying bloodshed, unfortunately. The struggle for independence in a number of cases involved military conflict, and often it was followed by civil war as combating groups sought to gain control of the new government. Table 5.4 lists all of the former European colonial dependencies that became sovereign states during the twentieth century—a total of 101 countries.

The Remaining Dependent States

The two major waves of self-determination and nation-building did not bring sovereignty to all of the world's dependencies, however. Table 5.5 identifies 39 countries that are dependent, to a greater or lesser degree, on nine other states. Fifteen of these colonies and territories—38 percent of the total—are dependent on the United Kingdom. Several terms are used by the supervising states to refer to these dependencies. The government of the United Kingdom calls most of its dependencies "colonies." Those dependent on the United States are known as "territories," except Puerto Rico and Northern Mariana Islands, which are called "self-governing commonwealths." The terms "territory" and "self-government" are most often linked to their dependencies by states other than the United States and the United Kingdom.

In all cases the defense and foreign affairs of dependencies are provided by the administering nation. In general the currency of the colony or territory is that of the administering state, but many dependencies are allowed to print their own postage stamps as a means of generating revenue from philatelic sales. The internal as well as the foreign affairs of dependencies may be administered from abroad, but a long-time trend has been toward allowing local self-government. Some colonies and territories are permitted to elect a representative to a legislative body of the "mother country." For example, the U.S. Virgin Islands elects to the U.S. House of Representative a delegate who may vote in committee but not in the House, and French Polynesia elects a deputy and a senator to the French Parliament.

The world's dependencies vary greatly in size and population. Greenland is the largest by far, but most of its land area is covered by an ice cap, and consequently it has only a small population for its size. On the other hand, almost all of the other dependencies are so small in land area that they would be microstates if they were independent. In fact, eight of them are each smaller than 10 square miles (25.9 sq km)—smaller than the area of most medium-sized cities. The British colony of Hong Kong, with more than six million people, has the largest population; the dependency with the second largest population is Puerto Rico with 3.6 million people. (Puerto Rico is the only dependency that could become a U.S. state in the near future; the issue of statehood has been debated in Puerto Rico for many years [Fig. 5.13].) Several colonies have fewer than a thousand inhabitants, and Pitcairn has fewer than a hundred residents.

FIGURE 5.13
Puerto Rico is the only dependency that could conceivably become the fifty-first state of the United States in the near future. The issue of statehood has been debated in Puerto Rico for many years. (Gamma-Liaison © Gary Williams)

TABLE 5.4   Former Colonial Dependencies that
Became States during the Twentieth Century
(Divided by Colonial Power)

State	Year of Dependency Termination
Colonial Power: United Kingdom	
Canada	1931
Iraq	1932
Republic of South Africa	1934
Australia	1942
Jordan	1946
India	1947
New Zealand	1947
Ireland	1948
Israel	1948
Myanmar (Burma)	1948
Sri Lanka	1948
Bhutan	1949
Oman	1951
Egypt	1953
Sudan	1956
Ghana	1957
Cyprus	1960
Nigeria	1960
Somalia (British Somaliland)	1960
Kuwait	1961
Sierra Leone	1961
Tanzania	1961–1962
Jamaica	1962
Trinidad–Tobago	1962
Uganda	1962
Kenya	1963
Malaysia	1963
Malawi	1964
Malta	1964
Zambia	1964
The Gambia	1965
Maldives	1965
Singapore	1965
Guyana	1966
Barbados	1966
Botswana	1966
Lesotho	1966
People's Dem. Republic of Yemen	1967
Mauritius	1968

(table continued on page 174)

| TABLE 5.4 | Former Colonial Dependencies that Became States during the Twentieth Century (Divided by Colonial Power) *(continued)* |

State	Year of Dependency Termination
Colonial Power: United Kingdom	
Swaziland	1968
Fiji	1970
Tonga	1970
Bahrain	1971
Qatar	1971
United Arab Emirates	1971
Bahamas	1973
Grenada	1974
Seychelles	1976
Dominica	1978
Solomon Islands	1978
Tuvalu	1978
Kiribati	1979
St. Lucia	1979
St. Vincent and the Grenadines	1979
Vanuatu	1980
Zimbabwe	1980
Antigua and Barbuda	1981
Belize	1981
St. Kitts–Nevis	1983
Brunei	1984
Colonial Power: France	
Lebanon	1946
Syria	1946
Laos	1953
Cambodia	1954
Vietnam	1954
Morocco	1956
Tunisia	1956
Guinea	1958
Benin	1960
Burkina Faso	1960
Cameroon	1960
Central African Republic	1960
Chad	1960
Congo	1960

TABLE 5.4	Former Colonial Dependencies that Became States during the Twentieth Century (Divided by Colonial Power) *(continued)*

State	Year of Dependency Termination
Colonial Power: France	
Côte d'Ivoire	1960
Gabon	1960
Madagascar	1960
Mali	1960
Mauritania	1960
Niger	1960
Senegal	1960
Togo	1960
Algeria	1962
Comoros	1976
Djibouti	1977
Colonial Power: Portugal	
Guinea-Bissau	1974
Angola	1975
Cape Verde	1975
Mozambique	1975
São Tomé and Príncipe	1975
Colonial Power: Italy	
Ethiopia	1947
Libya	1951
Somalia (Italian Somaliland)	1960
Colonial Power: Belgium	
Zaire	1960
Burundi	1962
Rwanda	1962
Colonial Power: Holland	
Indonesia	1949
Suriname	1975
Colonial Power: Spain	
Equatorial Guinea	1968
Western Sahara (occupied by Morocco)	1976
Colonial Power: Denmark	
Iceland	1944

TABLE 5.5	Dependent Countries of the World (Divided by Administering State)

Colony or Territory	Land Area		Estimated Population, 1994
	Sq mi	(sq km)	
Administering State: United Kingdom			
Anguilla	35	(91)	7,200
Ascension	34	(88)	1,800
Bermuda	21	(54)	62,000
British Virgin Islands	59	(153)	12,500
Cayman Islands	102	(264)	26,000
Channel Islands	75	(194)	152,000
Falkland Islands	4,618	(11,961)	2,200
Gibraltar	3	(8)	31,000
Hong Kong	404	(1,046)	6,100,000
Isle of Man	227	(588)	67,000
Montserrat	32	(83)	12,500
Pitcairn Island	2	(5)	75
St. Helena	47	(122)	6,000
Tristan da Cunha	40	(104)	300
Turks and Caicos Islands	166	(404)	10,000
Administering State: United States			
American Samoa	77	(199)	48,000
Guam	209	(541)	10,000
Johnson Atoll	1	(3)	1,000
Midway Island	3	(8)	500
Northern Mariana Islands	184	(477)	44,000
Palau	192	(497)	15,500
Puerto Rico	3,435	(8,897)	3,650,000
Virgin Islands, U.S.	133	(345)	116,000
Wake Island	3	(8)	300

EMERGENCE OF THE TWENTIETH-CENTURY SUPERPOWERS

➤ By the end of World War II, the United States and the Soviet Union had emerged as two rival superpowers that would dominate world affairs over most of the remainder of the twentieth century.

What were some similarities and differences in the emergence of these two countries as global superpowers?

What were the bases of their strength?

In the quotation at the beginning of this chapter, John E. Kieffer notes that all states exercise power as a mark of their importance in the international arena. In general, the amount of power exerted by a state is determined by one or more of such attributes as its military strength, level of economic development, and demographic size. A country that is able to exert substantial influence in world affairs often is called a *world power*. Most people probably would agree that such countries as the United Kingdom, France, Germany, and Japan are among the current world powers. In contrast are such countries as Haiti, Bolivia, Liechtenstein, Sudan, Swaziland, Madagascar, Mongolia, and

| TABLE 5.5 | Dependent Countries of the World (Divided by Administering State) *(continued)* |

Colony or Territory	Land Area		Estimated Population, 1994
	Sq mi	(sq km)	
Administering State: Australia			
Christmas Island	52	(135)	3,200
Cocos Islands	5	(13)	620
Norfolk Island	14	(36)	2,200
Administering State: France			
French Polynesia	1,545	(4,002)	205,000
New Caledonia	7,335	(18,998)	175,000
Wallis and Futuna Islands	106	(275)	16,000
Administering State: New Zealand			
Cook Islands	93	(241)	19,000
Niue	100	(259)	2,800
Tokelau Islands	4	(10)	1,900
Administering State: Denmark			
Faeroe Islands	540	(1,399)	48,000
Greenland	840,000	(2,175,600)	58,000
Administering State: Netherlands			
Aruba	75	(194)	65,000
Netherlands Antilles	385	(997)	190,000
Administering State: Norway			
Svalbard	23,957	(62,049)	2,000
Administering State: Portugal			
Macao	6	(16)	440,000

Western Samoa that have little power to exercise in the world arena.

During the second half of the twentieth century, world affairs have been most influenced by two *superpowers*—the United States and the Soviet Union. Both countries relied on the strength associated with their huge national territory, large population, and great wealth of resources. Further, both emerged victorious from World War II in 1945 with powerful military machines intact. Over several decades following the war's end, these two great powers—representing different political and economic ideologies—together with their supporting allies, engaged in a tense and costly struggle called the Cold War. In the pages that follow, we will examine the emergence of the two superpowers and their involvement in the Cold War. Also, we will survey the neutral and nonaligned states that sought to avoid involvement in the superpower conflict. Finally, we will focus on the decline of the Soviet superpower, the issues of nuclear disarmament and nuclear proliferation, and the "New World Order" of the post–Cold War era.

Although the United States concluded the nineteenth century as one of the world's largest and most populated countries and a major economic power, its military was anemic and its foreign policy was not well-developed at the time. Soon after the turn of the twentieth century, however, a revived U.S. military intervened in Panama, Cuba, and the Dominican Republic, and dispatched its ships around the world to demonstrate the country's intention to function as a global power. When World War I broke out in 1914, the United States was closely linked, economically and strategically, with Europe. With the war inflicting devastation in various parts of Europe and German submarines threatening international shipping, the United States entered the war in 1917. After the victory of the Allies, the government of the United States was a major participant in the dismantling of the German colonial empire and reorganization of the political map of Europe.

Between the world wars, while the new Soviet Union was taking form, the attention of the United States turned inward with the stock market crash of 1929, the Great Depression, and the economic and social programs of the New Deal. Focused on internal affairs, the country on the eve of World War II was not prepared to exert superpower influence on a global scale. That would soon change, however. The United States entered World War II in 1941 following the attack on Pearl Harbor by Japanese forces. During the war the U.S. government supported research on atomic energy for the purpose of developing a bomb with incredible power for destruction. Soon after the surrender of Germany to the Allies in 1945, the United States delivered a final blow to Japan with an atomic attack on two of its cities. With its military might supplemented by the development of new atomic weapons, the United States was generally recognized as the world's premier superpower at the conclusion of the war.

For the tsarist government of Russia, the early years of the twentieth century were turbulent times that gave little hint of the country's potential for superpower status. There was the disastrous Russo–Japanese War of 1905, in which Russia was defeated by Japan in a conflict over territorial claims, and a popular uprising of workers in 1905 that resulted in the tsar's reluctant agreement for the establishment of an elected legislature. Russia entered World War I because of a defensive pact with Great Britain and France. Ill-equipped to fight a major war, Russia suffered great losses. Meanwhile, rumors of incompetence and treason in high places swept Russia, and in 1917 a spontaneous uprising in the capital overthrew the government. This marked the beginning of the Russian Revolution (1917–1921), during which con-

trol of most of the Russian Empire was taken over by a Soviet communist dictatorship.

As in the United States, the attention of the new Soviet government was focused on internal matters during the period between the world wars. Joseph Stalin emerged as dictator not long after the death in 1924 of V. I. Lenin, called the "father of the Soviet Union." A new constitution adopted in 1936 officially sanctioned the Communist Party, which, under Stalin's direction, had dominated Soviet life. The government gave high priority to education, industrialization, and the collectivization of agriculture. Rapid industrialization during the Stalin era was characterized by emphases on machine tools, heavy equipment, and armaments—emphases that would continue until the final days of the Soviet Union. It was the collectivization of agriculture, however, that was the most conspicuous change in the life of the people. Those who resisted collectivization were ruthlessly crushed by Stalin's military; at least 10 million people died. Including their various "purges" of Soviet society, Stalin and the party under him were responsible for the deaths of about 40 million people, according to reports by Soviet officials in 1990.

Like the United States, the Soviet Union entered World War II in 1941. The consequences of the war, however, were quite different for the Soviet Union than for the United States. The United States lost less than half a million people, nearly all combatants; but the Soviet Union lost about 20 million people, many of them civilians. German forces penetrated deep into Russia, virtually encircling Leningrad and moving to within 30 miles (48 km) of Moscow before retreating because of losses to Soviet troops and the harsh Russian winters. In their westward march to Berlin, which contributed to Germany's defeat in 1945, Soviet forces liberated Eastern Europe, where Soviet influence, and in some cases domination, would continue for decades. Unlike the United States, the Soviet Union did not possess atomic weapons at the conclusion of World War II, but its control over a vast territory that extended from Eastern Europe to the Pacific was enough to qualify for superpower status. (See *The Geographer's Notebook: Mackinder's Heartland Theory and Geopolitics*.)

THE COLD WAR

➤ The Cold War was a competition between the two superpowers for military and technological supremacy as well as international influence.

THE GEOGRAPHER'S NOTEBOOK

Mackinder's Heartland Theory and Geopolitics

When nations and individuals use geographical information and concepts in their efforts to attain political goals, they engage in **geopolitics**. As national governments implement regional and global strategy, participate in international affairs and diplomacy, and deploy their military units in foreign areas, geopolitics typically is involved. Geopolitics should not be confused with political geography, which is concerned with the spatial expression of political entities and events.

The extension of Soviet influence and control over Eastern Europe during World War II caused many government officials and strategists in the West to reexamine the "heartland theory," a geopolitical interpretation of the world posed by Halford J. Mackinder (1861–1947) at the beginning of the century. Some analysts recognized the postwar containment policy of the United States, involving the establishment of military bases on the margins of the Soviet Bloc and the strengthening of relationships with allies in that zone, as strategy influenced by Mackinder's ideas.

Mackinder's heartland theory is one of the best examples of geopolitics. A prominent British geographer and legislator, Mackinder presented his heartland theory in a 1904 article titled "The Geographical Pivot of History" (*Geographical Journal* **23**:421–444) and further expanded it in a book,

Democratic Ideals and Reality, published in 1919 (New York: H. Holt and Co.). He saw the combined Eurasian and African landmasses as "the World Island" and pointed out the enormous importance to the world of the expansion of Tsarist Russia. Much of that country and adjacent parts of central Asia he designated the Heartland of the World Island because of its tremendous wealth of resources and its invulnerable position. The adjacent coastlands, Mackinder said, had always been vulnerable to attacks from the heartland, but the heartland was "the greatest natural fortress on earth." With the frozen Arctic Ocean and mountain ranges and deserts on most of its margins, the heartland was protected from attack by any sea power. The key area in this scenario was East Europe, as indicated in Mackinder's summary of his theory:

> Who rules East Europe commands the Heartland;
> Who rules the Heartland commands the World Island;
> Who rules the World Island commands the World.

With Soviet forces in control of East Europe at the end of World War II, it is understandable why geopoliticians at the time rushed to reexamine Mackinder's ideas.

Although they failed to obliterate Mackinder's theory, critics found several flaws in his ideas. They pointed out that his characterization of the heartland was influenced by the fact that he represented a naval power (Britain at the beginning of the twentieth century). He did not anticipate that aircraft and missiles eventually would be able to strike any part of the heartland and make it vulnerable to attack. Also, he did not foresee the emergence of the United States as a counterbalance to the Soviet Union.

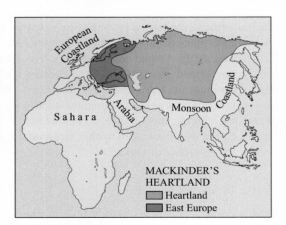

Mackinder's "Heartland" was the part of the World Island that he saw as a great natural fortress. He viewed East Europe as the key area for controlling the Heartland.

THOUGHT QUESTIONS

1. Why do you think Mackinder assigned such importance to East Europe in his theory?
2. Do you feel that Mackinder's theory has any application to the international affairs or strategies of today?
3. What are some current examples of the use of geopolitics in the world?

What was involved in the arms race between the two superpowers?

How did they differ in their technological accomplishments in space?

The term **Cold War** came into popular use soon after World War II to denote the strained relations that developed between the two new superpowers and their allies. Tensions first developed when the Soviet Union set up communist governments in the East European countries it occupied at the war's end. With their political affairs controlled from Moscow, these countries came to be recognized in the West as *satellite states* of the Soviet Union. The United States responded with the Truman Doctrine (1947), offering aid to other nations threatened by the expansion of communism (then Greece and Turkey). Furthermore, the United States in 1948 initiated the Marshall Plan to provide massive U.S. aid to Western European countries with war-shattered economies and thereby strengthen those countries against the threat of communism. The North Atlantic Treaty Organization (NATO) was established in 1949 to provide an effective defense for member countries, including the Western European nations, against any Soviet threat. The Soviets countered in 1955 by establishing with its satellite states a unified military command; the nations whose governments signed the authorizing treaty in Warsaw came to be known in the West as the Warsaw Pact countries.

Soon many countries around the globe aligned themselves with one of the two hostile camps, each led by one of the superpowers. To strengthen their positions, each camp employed diplomatic maneuvering, threats, economic pressure, propaganda, and espionage. To increase the prospect of victory in the event the Cold War turned into World War III, both superpowers heavily invested in military hardware, especially weapons of mass destruction and associated delivery systems.

The Arms Race

Soon after the conclusion of World War II, an *arms race* between the two superpowers began in earnest. Just seven years after the United States used atomic (fission) bombs to bring the war with Japan to a conclusion, it tested its first hydrogen (fusion) bomb. A little more than a year later, in 1953, the Soviet Union tested a thermonuclear bomb, and in 1957 a British

test served notice that a third nation could manufacture fusion weapons of mass destruction. Although nuclear weapons could be delivered to targets by bombers, both the United States and the Soviet Union also perfected missile delivery systems. By 1960 both superpowers possessed intercontinental ballistic missiles (ICBMs). Increasing numbers of ICBMs, deployed in hardened underground silos in the continental interiors, were amassed by the superpowers during the 1960s and 1970s. In the 1980s many of those missiles were equipped with multiple independently targeted reentry vehicles (MIRVs) so that each could strike an assortment of targets. By 1990 more than 100,000 nuclear weapons had been manufactured by the United States and the Soviet Union, and in that year approximately 23,000 of some 50,000 still in existence were deployed and targeted. Of those, the United States had about 12,000 and the Soviet Union had about 11,000. The bulk of each country's nuclear weapons were targeted at those of the other side, but thousands also were aimed at military bases, command centers, "economic targets," and major cities.

Concurrent with the build-up of ground-based missiles was the refinement of other nuclear-weapons delivery systems such as bombers, surface ships, and submarines. In 1990 American B-52 bombers were carrying new radar-elusive cruise missiles equipped with nuclear warheads, and Soviet Bear bombers, also potently armed, were frequently encountered on the fringes of Western airspace. Furthermore, both sides possessed surface ships and submarines equipped with nuclear-armed missiles. In 1990 the Soviet Union had five times as many naval ships and three times as many submarines as the United States, but the U.S. Navy was better armed than its Soviet counterpart with highly accurate nuclear missiles. Furthermore, both superpowers did not neglect to prepare for a "conventional war" during the Cold War. In this arena, the Soviet Union was the leader, with a larger army and a far greater number of tanks.

The Space Race

Both superpowers also invested heavily in what came to be known as the *space race*, the race to become preeminent in the technology necessary to put equipment and people into outer space. The space race began in 1957 when the Soviet Union launched two artificial satellites, Sputnik 1 and Sputnik 2, into orbit around the earth. Although the first tiny satellite

amazed the world, the second—with a live dog included in its 1000-pound (450-kg) payload—was a far
more significant achievement. In the following year
the United States also began launching small satellites
into orbit, and the U.S. Congress established the National Aeronautics and Space Administration (NASA),
which was charged with catching up with the Soviet
Union's space program. Soviet accomplishments in
space continued to capture world attention, however.
In 1959 Soviet scientists launched three unmanned
probes toward the moon; one went into lunar orbit and
transmitted back to earth the first pictures of the far
side of the moon. Anticipating that the Soviets were
planning a human mission to the moon, NASA began
intensive work on its own lunar program. The first
human in space was Soviet cosmonaut Yuri Gagarin
(1934–1968), launched into earth orbit in 1961. Later
that year U.S. astronaut Alan Shepard (b. 1923) made
a suborbital flight, and in 1962 John Glenn (b. 1921)
became the first American to orbit the earth. While the
Soviets focused on other news-making "firsts" (first
woman in space in 1963, first group of three cosmonauts in space in 1964, first person to exit an orbiting
spacecraft in 1965), the United States was training
crews, testing equipment, and working on a powerful new rocket to put astronauts on the moon before
the Soviets could. A target date of 1969 was set for
making the first human footprints on the moon, with
the hope that the Soviets could not accomplish the
feat first.

In July 1969, a lunar module from the Apollo 11
command ship delivered Neil Armstrong and Edwin
Aldrin (Fig. 5.14) to the lunar surface while Michael
Collins remained in lunar orbit in the command ship.
About a year later the best that the Soviets could do
was to land an unmanned, remote-controlled roving
vehicle on the lunar surface. Other missions followed
Apollo 11, and by the end of 1972 twelve Americans
had made footprints on the moon. The conclusion of
the Apollo program in 1972 marked the end of sending
astronauts to the moon in this century. The Soviet
Union never sent cosmonauts to the moon. The governments of both superpowers believed that national
pride and national security were at stake in the space
race, and both may have been too hasty to get to the
moon. Three American astronauts and a larger but un-
disclosed number of Soviet cosmonauts died in test,
launch, or reentry accidents during the Apollo (U.S.
manned lunar mission) and Soyuz (Soviet human-
in-space) programs of the 1960s.

FIGURE 5.14

*American astronaut Edwin E. Aldrin, Jr., poses for a picture
taken by Neil Armstrong during their 1969 "extravehicular
activity" on the surface of the earth's moon. The United
States won the "space race" with the Soviet Union when
Armstrong and Aldrin became the first and second of twelve
Americans who made footprints on the moon between 1969
and 1972. Soviet cosmonauts never reached the moon.
(Photograph provided by NASA)*

The space race changed markedly during the middle and late 1970s and the 1980s. The emphases during
this period were: (1) exploration of the solar system
by American and Soviet remote-controlled space
probes; (2) development of the U.S. Space Shuttle, a
rocket-launched spacecraft designed for crew-guided
reentry; and (3) the construction by Soviet cosmonauts
of circumterrestrial space stations. All three greatly advanced knowledge about the solar system and paved
the way for future space exploration. Figure 5.15
shows the deployment from a NASA Space Shuttle of
a space telescope designed for the peaceful exploration
of the universe. During the 1980s, however, there was
some research by both superpowers on "Star Wars"
technology for possible military use in destroying satellites, spacecraft, launched ICBMs, and earth-based
targets. The dissolution of the Soviet Union ended
Soviet research and reduced the perceived need for
such research by the United States.

FIGURE 5.15
The Hubble Space Telescope being deployed on April 25, 1990, into circumterrestrial orbit from the payload bay of the NASA space shuttle "Discovery"—an example of the peaceful exploration of space after the space race. (Photograph provided by NASA)

Regions of Conflict

➤ Tensions between the two superpowers during the Cold War were accentuated by political and military developments in several regions of the world.

How did the Soviet domination of Eastern Europe elevate superpower tensions?

What brought the superpowers closest to a nuclear war?

In what ways were the respective superpower involvements in Vietnam and Afghanistan similar?

Perhaps it was inevitable that superpower interests would overlap in some regions and produce conflict. Figure 5.16 shows parts of the world in which the superpowers became involved in serious conflicts during the period from 1947 to 1991. Here we will examine some of the more dramatic examples of conflict.

The Cold War began in Europe, we have noted, as a result of the establishment of communist governments in Eastern Europe. Soon the Soviets blocked normal contacts between Eastern Europe and the North Atlantic Treaty Organization (NATO) countries of Western Europe by erecting an "Iron Curtain" that consisted of rigidly controlled international bounda-ries that were in most areas marked by high barbed-wire fences. Even before the establishment of NATO, the Soviets initiated a land blockade in 1948 to hinder Western shipments of goods to West Berlin, an Allied enclave within communist East Germany. The West airlifted food and coal to the besieged city until the blockade was lifted in 1949. The possibility of conflict over West Berlin, however, continued for decades.

Tensions between the superpowers eased as a result of the death of Stalin in 1953 and ensuing "de-Stalinization" measures in the Soviet Union, but the Cold War intensified when the Soviets crushed a Hungarian rebellion in 1956. The construction of the Berlin Wall (Fig. 5.17) by the communists in 1961 further heightened Cold War tensions. Built to halt the embarrassing flow of refugees from East Germany to West Germany, the Berlin Wall quickly became a symbol of communist oppression to those living in the West. Another development was the 1968 invasion of Czechoslovakia by Warsaw Pact forces intent on crushing democratic reforms. Soviet influence also was exerted in Poland in 1981 when workers almost succeeded in toppling the communist government; the military took control of the government, however, and forced the workers' movement underground.

For its part, the United States exercised influence in Europe primarily through economic ties and participation in NATO. During the 1980s the United States furnished NATO with 20 to 25 percent of its air defense, provided nearly all of its nuclear deterrence, and paid about 60 percent of the costs of the alliance. Even in 1992, following the disintegration of the Soviet Union and the Warsaw Pact, the United States still had more than a quarter of a million members of the military stationed in Western Europe.

Figure 5.16 shows three countries in Latin America—Cuba, Nicaragua, and Chile—where the interests of the superpowers clashed during the Cold War. By far the most serious incident occurred in 1962 when the United States discovered that the Soviet Union was constructing missile bases in Cuba. Not willing to tolerate Soviet missiles only 90 miles (233 km) from Florida, the U.S. government issued an ultimatum that the missile bases be dismantled and withdrawn. Because compliance would be humiliating to the Soviets, the world waited for the outcome with apprehension; many experts believe the world was then closer to nuclear war than at any other time in history. Soon after the U.S. ultimatum, however, the Soviet Union backed down and agreed to remove the

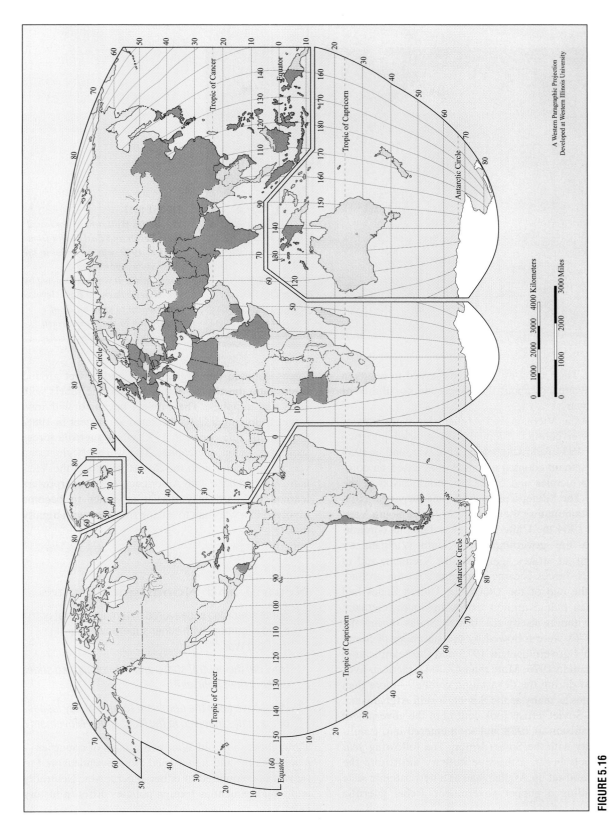

FIGURE 5.16

As the two Cold War superpowers endeavored to exercise influence to their own strategic advantage, conflicts between them became inevitable. This map shows the countries within which one or both superpowers were involved in a conflict.

183

FIGURE 5.17

The Berlin Wall, which separated West Berlin and East Berlin from 1961 to 1989, was a symbol in the West of the oppression of communism. It was constructed by the Soviet-influenced East German government to stem a tide of emigration to the West. (Viesti Associates, Inc. © Joe Viesti)

missiles. The Cuban missile crisis served to heighten public awareness about the dangerous possibility of nuclear war.

In Asia, Vietnam and Afghanistan were sites of superpower conflict. Vietnam was divided into two states in 1954 following a long civil war, and in 1959 North Vietnam adopted a constitution based on communist principles and called for reunification of the country. The Soviet Union and China provided assistance to communist Vietcong guerrillas in South Vietnam. In 1964 the United States escalated its commitment to the government of South Vietnam by launching air strikes against North Vietnam, and in 1965 U.S. forces became combatants on the ground. Before the end of the 1960s, the United States had more than half a million troops in South Vietnam. Troop withdrawals by the United States during the early 1970s were followed by the surrender of South Vietnam's government in 1975 and the reunification of Vietnam in 1976. More than 47,000 American lives were lost during the devastating conflict—more than three times as many as the Soviets lost in Afghanistan.

Pro-Soviet leftists took control of the government of Afghanistan in 1978 and soon entered into a military treaty with the Soviet Union. The following year the Soviets began a massive military airlift into the country and set up Afghanistan as a new satellite state by installing a puppet government. Rebel guerrilla

forces opposed the Afghan army and Soviet ground forces, and the United States assisted the rebels with arms and supplies. The Soviets began to withdraw forces following a U.N.-mediated agreement in 1988. Communist rule ended in 1992 when guerrilla forces took over Kabul, the capital. The war in Afghanistan was as unpopular with the Soviet people as the Vietnam War had been with Americans. Both superpowers learned the hard way that it is easier to become involved in a war than to escape from one with dignity intact.

Neutral and Nonaligned States

➤ Some countries endeavored to remain neutral or to avoid alignment with either superpower during the Cold War.

How did the neutral states and the nonaligned states differ in their policies?

What have been the dominant foreign policy issues of the states involved in the Nonaligned Movement?

Throughout the Cold War, two groups of countries—*neutral states* and *nonaligned states*—endeavored to remain uncommitted to either superpower. Neutrality and nonalignment as foreign policies differ in history and purpose. Neutrality is of European origin and actually predates the Cold War by more than a century; nonalignment originated among the less developed countries and did not emerge as a world movement until long after the start of the Cold War.

Neutrality denotes impartiality and not taking sides. The government of a country may adopt a policy of neutrality in a particular international conflict, or permanent neutrality may become a part of the state's law or the tradition of the people of the country. Permanent neutrality entails a decision by a government—by a people, really—that the state will (1) never start a war, (2) never participate in a war started by other states, (3) never make an obligation that might result in war, and (4) always use every means possible to defend its own territory from outside aggression. Sweden, which has not taken part in a war since 1809, is the prototype of permanent neutrality. Other countries that were neutral states late in the Cold War were Albania, Austria, Cyprus, Finland, Ireland, Malta, Switzerland, Yugoslavia, and the microstates of Andorra, Liechtenstein, Monaco, San Marino, and Vatican City. Their neutrality in no way suggests that they were ideologically or politically indifferent in the Cold War between East and West. Except for Albania, a communist country from 1944 to 1991, they were fully a part of the political system of the free nations of the Western world. Their neutrality meant only that they were committed to the four principles identified previously as defining permanent neutrality. The end of the Cold War did not diminish the desire for permanent neutrality by these states; except for Yugoslavia, which fell apart early in the 1990s, they all retain neutrality as law or tradition.

While the neutral states of Europe are developed countries, the nonaligned states are less developed countries whose governments decided that neutrality was too passive to be constructive in an unstable world and that a more active approach to world peace was needed. The foundations of nonalignment as a policy were laid in the 1950s by the governments of Yugoslavia and India; in adopting this policy they emphasized that nonalignment is an active, positive, and constructive policy striving for collective peace on which to base collective security. The policy of nonalignment quickly spread and became the **Nonaligned Movement** in 1961. By the end of the Cold War approximately 100 nations were members of the Nonaligned Movement. Just as neutrality did not mean that Eu-

ropean neutrals were indifferent to the ideologies, policies, and politics of the superpowers during the Cold War, so it was with the nonaligned states. Many of them, in fact, had very close ties with one of the superpowers.

Three major issues have dominated the foreign policies of the states of the Nonaligned Movement: (1) protest against the Cold War, (2) opposition to colonialism, and (3) economic development of the less developed world. The end of the Cold War eliminated the first issue, although the nonaligned nations no doubt will continue to be concerned with such post–Cold War matters as disarmament and nuclear proliferation. The success of decolonization has virtually ended the second issue, leaving the nonaligned states with little to champion except the self-serving—though just—development of their own economies with assistance from the developed countries. The future of the Nonaligned Movement in the post–Cold War era, however, is uncertain.

Decline of the Soviet Superpower

➣ The decline of the Soviet Union as a world superpower occurred abruptly, and communist control of the country ended in late 1991.

What were important factors that led to this change?

How did the policies of Mikhail Gorbachev contribute to the change?

The Russian-dominated communist elite of the Soviet Union never succeeded in their attempts at Russification—that is integrating the diverse nations of the union into Soviet society. In addition, the malfunctioning of Soviet central planning led to serious economic deficiencies. Transportation problems and the absence of production incentives contributed to inadequate food production. Inefficiency also characterized industrial production because of worker apathy and management corruption. Consumer goods were in short supply; the few manufactured goods available for the consumer market tended to be high-priced and of shoddy construction.

When Mikhail S. Gorbachev became Party General Secretary in 1985, the Soviet Union acquired a leader committed to modernization and reform. In 1987 he introduced a program of economic and social reforms, including expanded freedoms and democra-

FIGURE 5.18
As this political cartoon indicates, the collapse of the Soviet Union at one time seemed unthinkable. The unthinkable became an astonishing reality on Christmas Day, 1991. (Copley News Service)

tization of the political process through *glasnost* (openness) and *perestroika* (economic restructuring), designed to alter the old system. Gorbachev could not do this, however, without alienating virtually every sector of Soviet society, because such dramatic changes could not be accomplished painlessly. *Perestroika* could not keep pace with *glasnost*. People wanted immediate change, and *glasnost* allowed them to say so.

The Moslem areas of Central Asia became a powderkeg in 1990, with frequent cries of "Russians go home." Nationalistic fervor also broke out in the Baltic states, which initiated political moves aimed at achieving eventual sovereignty. Before the end of 1990, almost all of the Soviet republics had declared that their own laws superseded those of the central government. Communist hardliners attempted to overthrow Gorbachev in the summer of 1991 to put an end to the democratic revolution that he had made possible. The failure of the coup hastened the pace of democracy and contributed to the collapse of the Soviet Communist Party, the death of the Soviet empire, the dismantling of the Soviet state, and the devolution of political power to independently governed republics—events that astonished people around the world (Fig. 5.18). On Christmas day, 1991, Mikhail Gorbachev resigned as Soviet president, and the red hammer-and-

sickle flag—symbol of world communism for more than 70 years—was hauled down from the towers of the Kremlin.

THE ISSUE OF NUCLEAR ARSENALS

➤ Controlling the growth of nuclear arsenals and the proliferation of nuclear weapons has been a serious political dilemma.

What progress was made by the two superpowers in reducing the nuclear threat prior to the disintegration of the Soviet Union?

For what reasons are there continuing concerns about nuclear threats to peace and human safety?

We noted earlier that in 1990, as the Soviet Union neared the brink of collapse, the United States and the Soviet Union possessed approximately 50,000 nuclear weapons. Hundreds, perhaps a few thousands, of other nuclear weapons were in the arsenals of the United Kingdom, France, China, and probably South Africa, Israel, Pakistan, and India. For decades the world has been aware that a large-scale nuclear war would cost the lives of scores of millions of people and so devastate the planet that unimaginable suffering would occur for years, perhaps generations. Even so, the chill of the Cold War prevented taking the steps needed to address the threat. The first sign of progress came with the signing of the Nuclear Test Ban Treaty by the United States, Soviet Union, and United Kingdom in 1963. It banned the testing of nuclear weapons in space, above ground, and under water. Four years later the superpowers agreed not to put nuclear weapons into orbit around the earth or anywhere in space.

Despite frequent conflicts of interest as the Cold War continued, it is to their credit that the leaders of both superpowers periodically discussed ways to reduce the escalation of the nuclear threat and occasionally signed a major treaty to effect real progress. During the 1970s the accomplishments primarily were in placing limitations on deployment of antimissile missiles, ICBMs, and submarine-based missiles. During the final decade of the Cold War, however, progress was made in setting the stage for disarmament. In 1987 the superpowers signed the Intermediate-Range Nuclear Forces Treaty (INF) for the elimination of all medium- and short-range nuclear missiles. Just months before the collapse of the Soviet Union, the superpowers agreed on a Strategic Arms Reduction Treaty (START) to reduce their numbers of ICBMs and submarine-based nuclear weapons. After the dissolution of the Soviet Union, the presidents of the United States and Russia agreed not only to abide by START but to increase disarmament further under a new treaty (START II). Even if the provisions of these treaties are fully implemented during the 1990s, however, the United States and Russia will be left with large nuclear arsenals.

At least as frightful as the nuclear arsenals of world powers is the possession of nuclear weapons by the unstable governments of developing countries. Long before making progress in their own disarmament, the superpowers addressed the potential problem of the proliferation of nuclear weapons to other countries. In the Non-Proliferation of Nuclear Weapons Treaty (NPT) of 1968, the United States, Soviet Union, and United Kingdom agreed not to assist nonnuclear nations in obtaining or manufacturing nuclear weapons. France and China did not sign the treaty until 1992. The number of states possessing nuclear weapons increased by three in 1991 with the formation of new countries as the Soviet Union disintegrated. Seeking to ensure the security of its huge arsenal of nuclear weapons following the outbreak of regional violence in 1990, the Soviet government moved tactical nuclear missiles from several republics to Russia. With the break-up of the Soviet Union in 1991, however, ICBMs and nuclear bombs remained in the Ukraine, Belarus, and Kazakhstan, as well as in Russia.

South Africa, which possessed several nuclear devices, signed the NPT in 1992. Its government had decided the previous year to give up nuclear weapons; South Africa thus became the first country in history to relinquish such weapons voluntarily. As of 1993, three major regional states—Israel, Pakistan, and India—had not agreed to the principle of nonproliferation. All three, it is believed, have the capability to deploy nuclear weapons rapidly. Four other countries that had engaged in research for nuclear weapons development during the 1980s have announced since 1990 their decision to abandon such activity; they are Argentina, Brazil, Iraq, and North Korea. Iraq's decision was forced by the United Nations following Iraq's invasion of Kuwait and subsequent defeat in the ensuing Persian Gulf War of 1990–1991. In 1993 North Korea refused to allow international inspectors to examine certain research sites, raising the fear—especially in South Korea and Japan—that the communist and militarist regime in North Korea was pursuing nuclear weapons development despite its announced decision to abandon such activity.

THE NEW WORLD ORDER

➤ The New World Order of the post-Soviet era undoubtedly will confront a variety of problems as well as opportunities to make the world a better place for human life.

Will the anticipated rise of new superpowers be a positive or negative development?

As the twenty-first century approaches, what economic, social, military, environmental, and space challenges are likely to confront the New World Order?

In addition to protecting the peoples of the world from nuclear weapons and shielding their governments from nuclear blackmail, the New World Order of the post-Soviet era will be challenged by a host of other critical problems. These problems are staggering in their collective scope and impact; the United States cannot be expected to solve them singlehandedly (Fig. 5.19). However, other superpowers are emerging, and even

FIGURE 5.19
In the New World Order of the post-Soviet era, the United States generally is considered to be the only superpower. No one nation, of course, can manage the countless crises of today's world. (Copley News Service)

small or developing states can be helpful in the problem-solving process. In addition to the many problems in the post-Soviet world, there also are many opportunities. We will examine briefly some of the problems and opportunities of the 1990s and beyond.

The Emergence of New Superpowers

Both problems and opportunities may be associated with the expected rise of new superpowers, although it must be kept in mind that what is an opportunity for one nation may be a problem for another. The United States already has had to face certain economic problems as a result of the emergence in Japan of an economy with a global reach. The resources and resourcefulness of newly reunified Germany suggest that another economic giant is in the making. Despite the fact that currently neither Japan nor Germany has a world-class military, their economic might and technological know-how provide convincing evidence that they could expand their military capabilities rapidly. Whether they do so or not, some political geographers, foreign affairs specialists, and futurists already are anticipating that in the year 2000 there will be three superpowers—the United States, Japan, and Germany—that together will account for half of the economic activity of the entire world. Russia, we have noted, is still the world's largest country in area and still has one of the world's two largest nuclear arsenals. Without that arsenal, however, Russia would be only a second-rate power. As a consequence, some analysts exclude the country from their list of probable early twenty-first century superpowers. Unlike the adversarial relationship of the two Cold War superpowers, the relationships among the three superpowers of the early twenty-first century generally should be friendly, since no major ideological differences exist among them.

Japan's Asian rivals may be years from superpower status. China is the largest and most populous nation in Asia, but in 1993 its economic output was less than one-eighth that of Japan. In fact, Japan's gross domestic product was well over twice that of China, Taiwan, Hong Kong, India, Indonesia, Thailand, and South Korea *combined*. Of course, with China's possession of nuclear weapons, permanent membership on the United Nations' Security Council, and enormous population, its potential for attaining superpower status is obvious. However, many analysts believe that China will not reach that pinnacle until well after the turn of the twenty-first century, when the capitalist metropolis of Hong Kong—to be turned back over to China in 1997—should be contributing significantly to China's economy.

Global Economic and Social Development

The New World Order and the "peace dividend" resulting from reduced military spending present the opportunity for nations to focus more attention and resources on global economic and social development. During the past two decades the disparity between rich and poor nations has widened; the rich have grown richer while the poor have fallen farther behind. The deterioration of economic conditions has hampered progress in social development, and both have contributed to political strife and military conflict. With the globalization of economies and growing international interdependence, a new approach to economic and social development may be necessary in order for the industrialized nations to maintain their relative prosperity. All too often foreign aid programs in the past were bilateral instruments of the Cold War. The United States, the emerging superpowers (Germany and Japan), and world powers such as France and the United Kingdom, reasonably can expect to shoulder much of the burden of foreign aid in the New World Order. It also is reasonable to expect that more economic and social assistance will be channeled through the United Nations. The Economic and Social Council of the United Nations was weak during the Cold War, but it may emerge as a more important agent of change and progress as the twenty-first century draws closer.

International Conflicts

Over recent decades the Cold War undoubtedly suppressed many potential conflicts that might have erupted without the influence of the superpowers. Even so, warfare was common during the Cold War. Figure 5.20 shows the states that were involved in a war of independence, were invaded by a foreign military, or were afflicted by a civil war during the period 1945–1992. (Many other countries, including the United States, would appear on that map if it also showed states that sent invading or occupying forces into other lands.) Although the end of the Cold War may have diminished the likelihood of a world war, there is evidence that it may have increased the prospect of lesser conflicts. It is not just a coincidence that Yugoslavia was disintegrating, setting the stage for international war, at the same time the Soviet Union was dissolving and other dramatic upheavals were taking

place in Europe. Likewise, the dissolution of the Soviet Union made possible the civil wars that subsequently erupted in some of the former Soviet republics. It is unthinkable that the Soviet government would have allowed such conflicts just a few years earlier.

In spite of the emerging power of Japan and Germany, the United States most certainly will remain the world's greatest power well into the next century. The ability of this superpower to contain regional conflicts or influence their outcome has caused some apprehension among Americans—together with both hope and fear elsewhere in the world—that the United States will become the "world's police." U.S. leadership in crushing Iraqi aggression against Kuwait and in facilitating the distribution of food and combating local warlords in Somalia (Figure 5.21) has contributed to this expectation. In both cases, however, the United States acted with the approval of the Security Council of the United Nations. With China, the world's largest communist country, as a permanent member of the Security Council, such approval of military intervention may not always be possible. It is clear that in the New World Order there likely will be less order, and the task of promoting stability will be far more difficult.

Human Rights Abuses

The world has long experienced the oppression of people and the violation of their human rights by their own governments. In history, the possession of sovereignty led some governments to conclude that how they treated their own people was nobody else's business. In democratic nations the ability of the majority to effect a change in government provides some protection against the violation of the rights of the majority, but this check does not necessarily protect minorities within those states. And people living under totalitarian governments have no protection at all. In 1948, for the first time, the concept of the complete sovereignty of nations was compromised by the United Nations' approval of the Universal Declaration of Human Rights, which gave all people rights that transcend a state's sovereign rights. Still, the Soviet Union and its allies gave only lip service to the declaration; the Soviet government built hundreds of concentration camps for the detention of political prisoners.

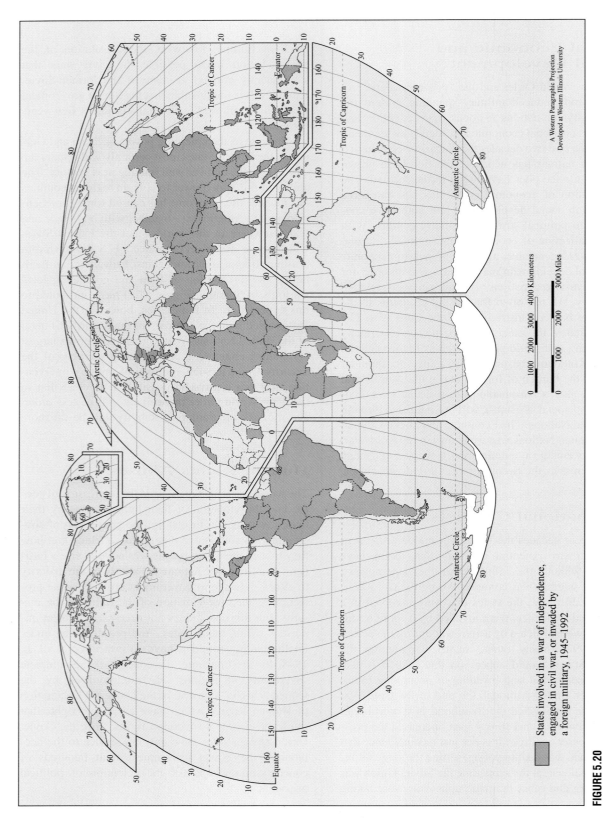

FIGURE 5.20

From 1945 to 1992, a period only slightly longer than the Cold War, numerous countries were involved in wars of independence, were invaded by foreign militaries, or were afflicted by civil wars.

States involved in a war of independence, engaged in civil war, or invaded by a foreign military, 1945–1992

A Western Paragraphic Projection
Developed at Western Illinois University

0 1000 2000 3000 4000 Kilometers

0 1000 2000 3000 Miles

FIGURE 5.21
Food is an important factor in any equation of political power. Late in 1992 the United States sent troops to Somalia to ensure that food relief shipments reached the starving population. The rag-tag armies of rival warlords had been stealing most of the food aid before the U.N. effort. (Jerome Delay/Wide World Photos, Inc.)

Lip service to the protection of human rights continues, while abuses abound. Figure 5.22 identifies for 76 countries the incidence in 1992 of three of the most serious human rights abuses—the torture of political prisoners, the disappearance of people taken into custody, and the execution of prisoners without fair trials. The nations having governments guilty of all three of these indefensible offenses were Brazil, Burundi, Guatemala, India, Iraq, Kuwait, Peru, the Philippines, Rwanda, Sri Lanka, and Turkey. Particularly reprehensible in recent years has been the government of Brazil, which has allowed the targeting of children for human rights abuses. Thousands of street children in large Brazilian cities were murdered during the late 1980s and early 1990s by paramilitary death squads made up, in part, of police officers. Although these murderous groups, funded by business people for the purpose of "cleaning up" their streets and neighborhoods, operated outside the government, the failure of the government to suppress the practice and successfully prosecute those responsible is in itself a human rights abuse. Street children also have been murdered by death squads in Colombia and Guatemala in recent years.

In Myanmar (Burma) the military rulers turned the country into a "secret state of terror" during the late 1980s; during the same period tens of thousands of the opponents of the government of Sri Lanka "disappeared." In 1992 torture was routine in the police stations of Egypt, Turkey, and a number of other nations. China is one of many states in which the government still contends that its human rights abuses are not the concern of the rest of the world; in 1992 that country was holding literally hundreds of thousands of people without charge, according to Amnesty International, the watchdog organization for human rights.

Decreasing tolerance of human rights abuses may become a characteristic of the New World Order, and this may threaten further the age-old doctrine of absolute sovereignty. Evidence for this is seen in sanctions imposed on Iraq by the United Nations before and after the Persian Gulf War. Large-scale atrocities committed against ethnic minorities by the government of Iraq resulted in the establishment of "no-fly zones" (Fig. 5.23) to protect Kurdish people in northern Iraq and Shiite Arabs in southern Iraq from their own government by prohibiting Iraqi aircraft from those areas.

The following table corresponds to Figure 5.22. Dots (•) indicate the offending state is cited for that category.

OFFENDING STATE	Torture of Political Prisoners	Disappearances of People Taken into Custody	Executions Without Fair Trials
Afghanistan	•		
Albania	•		
Algeria	•		
Argentina	•	•	
Austria	•		
Bangladesh	•	•	
Bhutan	•		
Bolivia	•		
Brazil	•	•	•
Burundi	•	•	•
Cambodia	•	•	
Cameroon	•		
Chad	•	•	
Chile	•		
China	•		
Colombia		•	•
Congo		•	
Cuba	•		
Cyprus	•		
Djibouti	•		
Dominican Rep.	•		
Ecuador	•		
Egypt	•		
El Salvador	•	•	
Equatorial Guinea	•		
Gambia	•		
Greece	•		
Guatemala	•	•	•
Guyana	•		
Haiti	•	•	
Honduras		•	•
India	•	•	
Indonesia	•	•	
Iran	•	•	
Iraq	•	•	•
Israel	•		
Italy	•		
Ivory Coast	•		

OFFENDING STATE	Torture of Political Prisoners	Disappearances of People Taken into Custody	Executions Without Fair Trials
Jordan	•		
Kuwait	•	•	•
Lebanon	•		
Lesotho	•		
Liberia	•		
Libya	•	•	
Madagascar	•		
Malawi	•		
Mali	•		
Mauritania	•		
Mexico	•	•	
Morocco	•	•	
Myanmar	•		
Pakistan	•		
Panama	•		
Papua New Guinea	•		
Peru	•	•	•
Philippines	•	•	
Romania	•		
Rwanda	•	•	
Saudi Arabia	•		
Senegal	•		
Sierra Leone	•		
Somalia	•		
South Africa	•		
Spain	•		
Sri Lanka	•	•	
Sudan	•	•	
Syria	•		
Thailand	•	•	
Togo	•		
Tunisia	•		
Turkey	•	•	
Uganda	•		
USSR*	•		
Venezuela	•		
Yugoslavia	•		
Zaire	•		

FIGURE 5.22

* 1992 data unavailable by new states of former USSR. Source: 1992 Annual Report of Amnesty International

Environmental Clean-up

Because environmental crises are treated in the final chapter of this book, we will limit our comments here to the role of the superpowers in contributing to environmental problems and their responsibility in finding solutions to those problems. Before, during, and after the Cold War, all forms of economic activity, especially industrialization, produced serious environmental disruptions in both the East and West. In the Soviet Union and its satellite states, the Cold War emphases on heavy industrialization and militarization account for most of the damage; that is, the govern-

ments bear the primary responsibility. What some environmentalists call *consumption overpopulation*, on the other hand, has produced most of the environmental damage in the West; that is, the people bear the primary responsibility because of their high rate of personal consumption of resources. Another difference between East and West is that the latter began to address environmental problems sooner and in a more serious way. Under the totalitarian regimes of the East, people were unable to influence their governments to reverse the environmental deterioration. In the West, many people had become environmentally aware by the beginning of the 1970s and democratic govern-

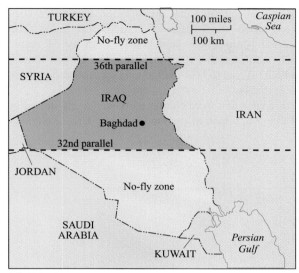

FIGURE 5.23

"No-fly zones" were established by the United Nations to protect Kurds in northern Iraq and Shiite Arabs in southern Iraq from being attacked from the air by their own government.

ments had little choice but to begin addressing pollution problems.

Among the most appalling environmental problems that developed during the Cold War in both East and West are those associated with nuclear weapons. The United States was always more careful than the Soviet Union in protecting citizens from the ill effects of developing and testing nuclear weapons. In the northeastern part of what is now Kazakhstan, the Soviet Union detonated nearly 500 nuclear devices between 1949 and 1989. Many Kazakhs lived close enough to the test site to see the mushroom clouds of the pre-1963 above-ground tests and to suffer the effects of the radiation. An above-normal rate of birth defects and cancer has persisted for years downwind from the now-closed test site. Several other former Soviet republics now must deal with the radiation from improperly stored nuclear wastes. Although more careful than the Soviet Union in the development of its nuclear arsenal, the government of the United States—always seeking to maintain a military edge over the Soviet Union—took unnecessary chances in the processing and storing of radioactive wastes. For

example, weapons contractors were exempt from environmental and safety regulations that governed other industries. Not until 1989 did Washington decide to emphasize environmental and safety concerns in nuclear weapons manufacture, and by that time the Cold War was almost over. To clean up the more than 100 weapons-manufacturing sites in the United States will be extremely expensive and take perhaps three decades.

Public concern and the still unmatched economy of the United States will assure continuing progress in the country's environmental clean-up and environmental protection. If there is indeed a peace dividend resulting from the end of the Cold War, it may contribute to the progress. As some of the former communist states in Eastern Europe work to rejuvenate their economies, they also may be able to seriously address their badly deteriorated environments. Given the magnitude of their environmental problems and their weak economies, the former Soviet republics likely will be able to make only gradual progress in improving the quality of their environments. In contributing to the solution to such global environmental problems as shrinking rainforests, pollution of the oceans, and depletion of the ozone layer, the United States and the emerging superpowers will need to take the lead. At the time of the Rio de Janeiro international Earth Summit in 1992, it was clear that the government of the United States was not ready to assume a leadership role; the government at that time believed it was not in the economic best interest of the country to do so. However, that belief is likely to change during the middle 1990s.

The Frontiers of Space

The end of the Cold War and the space race that was a part of superpower competition in no way diminished the need to expand the frontiers of space. Recognizing the benefits of advancing those frontiers, including spin-off technology for earth-based science and industry, superpowers will continue to explore space. The extent to which Russia will participate during the rest of the 1990s and into the early part of the twenty-first century remains to be seen. Russia was so desperate for foreign exchange earnings in 1992 that there was speculation it would try to sell its earth-orbiting space station. Given the enormity of the economic and social problems in the country, the high cost of space exploration will be criticized by many Russians as a wasteful luxury. On the other hand, continuing involvement in space can provide international prestige that many Russians will value.

Just as its stagnant economy may hinder the space program Russia inherited from the Soviet Union, the huge budget deficit of the United States may slow the aspirations of NASA in space. In 1992 NASA and the executive branch of government were considering a 2019 date for a human mission to Mars, with the construction of an earth-orbiting space station and the return of astronauts to the moon well before that time. At present the technology for a human mission to Mars does not exist, and it is quite likely that the underfunding of NASA projects leading up to such a mission will delay it until later in the twenty-first century. Considering the high cost of putting astronauts on Mars, it is probable that the venture will be an international one involving perhaps several nations. Almost certainly Japan will be involved; the country has been building rockets and launching weather and communications satellites since the early 1980s and is working on a rocket plane, similar to NASA's Space Shuttle, that may debut before the end of the 1990s.

THE UNITED NATIONS

➤ Since the end of World War II, the United Nations has served as a forum for debate and as a means for international action to solve problems of human welfare and disputes between countries.

How have countries of the less-developed world become more powerful within the United Nations during recent decades?

What types of actions has the United Nations taken in its attempts to solve international disputes?

Disastrous losses of life and property during World War I prompted more than 60 nations to join together after the war in the League of Nations, an international organization dedicated to promoting world peace through collective security and peaceful settlement of disputes. The United States never joined the League, and in less than two decades the collective security covenant that was the foundation of the organization had crumbled. The even greater losses of World War II, however, spurred yet another global effort at estab-

lishing an international organization that might succeed where the League of Nations had failed. The United Nations was launched in 1945 by 51 member countries, this time including the United States, which offered to host the United Nations headquarters (Fig. 5.24).

States that were charter members are identified in Table 5.6, which also shows how the United Nations

FIGURE 5.24

The headquarters of the United Nations in New York City is one of the most familiar buildings in the world. The United Nations was launched in 1945 by 51 member-countries, including the United States, which offered to host the organization's headquarters. (© Gamma)

TABLE 5.6	Current Charter Members and Growth of the United Nations

Current Charter Members (1945)

Argentina	El Salvador	Norway
Australia	Ethiopia	Panama
Belarus	France	Paraguay
Belgium	Greece	Peru
Bolivia	Guatemala	Philippines
Brazil	Haiti	Poland
Canada	Honduras	Russia
Chile	India	Saudi Arabia
China	Iran	South Africa
Colombia	Lebanon	Syria
Costa Rica	Liberia	Turkey
Cuba	Luxembourg	United Kingdom
Denmark	Mexico	United States
Dominican Republic	Netherlands	Uruguay
Ecuador	New Zealand	Venezuela
Egypt	Nicaragua	Yugoslavia

States Joining in the Late 1940s

Afghanistan	Myanmar (Burma)	Thailand
Iceland	Pakistan	Yemen
Israel	Sweden	

States Joining in the 1950s

Albania	Indonesia	Morocco
Austria	Ireland	Nepal
Bulgaria	Italy	Portugal
Cambodia	Japan	Romania
Finland	Jordan	Spain
Ghana	Laos	Sri Lanka
Guinea	Libya	Sudan
Hungary	Malaysia	Tunisia

States Joining in the 1960s

Algeria	The Gambia	Niger
Barbados	Guyana	Nigeria
Benin	Jamaica	Rwanda
Botswana	Kenya	Senegal
Burkina Faso	Kuwait	Sierra Leone
Burundi	Lesotho	Singapore
Cameroon	Madagascar	Somalia
Central African Republic	Malawi	Swaziland

(table continued on page 196)

| TABLE 5.6 | Current Charter Members and Growth of the United Nations *(continued)* |

States Joining in the 1960s

Chad	Maldives	Tanzania
Congo	Mali	Togo
Côte d'Ivoire	Malta	Trinidad–Tobago
Cyprus	Mauritania	Uganda
Equatorial Guinea	Mauritius	Zaire
Gabon	Mongolia	Zambia

States Joining in the 1970s

Angola	Fiji	St. Lucia
Bahamas	Germany	Samoa (Western)
Bahrain	Grenada	São Tomé and Príncipe
Bangladesh	Guinea–Bissau	Seychelles
Bhutan	Mozambique	Solomon Islands
Cape Verde	Oman	Suriname
Comoros	Papua New Guinea	United Arab Emirates
Djibouti	Qatar	Vietnam
Dominica		

States Joining in the 1980s

Antigua and Barbuda	St. Kitts–Nevis	Vanuatu
Belize	St. Vincent and Grenadines	Zimbabwe
Brunei		

States Joining in the 1990s

Armenia	Korea, South	Namibia
Azerbaijan	Kyrgyzstan	San Marino
Bosnia and Herzegovina	Latvia	Slovakia
Croatia	Liechtenstein	Slovenia
Czech Republic	Lithuania	Tajikistan
Estonia	Marshall Islands	Turkmenistan
Kazakhstan	Micronesia	Uzbekistan
Korea, North	Moldova	

grew during the decades that followed. The decade of greatest growth was the 1960s, a period of rapid decolonization; all 42 states that joined the United Nations during that period were in the less developed world. This pattern continued during the 1970s and 1980s, further amplifying the voice and increasing the influence of the less developed world in matters of global importance. The slowing of decolonization dur-

ing the 1980s resulted in only seven new U.N. members in that decade, and it is not likely that the 1990s will see many new members except those emerging from the fragmentation of the former Soviet Union and Yugoslavia and the division of Czechoslovakia.

The United Nations has a General Assembly comprised of the representatives of member states. Each country has one vote. More important with regard to international peace and security is the Security Council, made up of 15 members. Ten of those members are representatives from states elected for two-year terms by the General Assembly. The other five occupy permanent seats in the Security Council. These permanent seats are China, France, Russia, the United Kingdom, and the United States. Security Council action requires an affirmative vote by at least nine members, including all of the permanent members. During the Cold War the veto power of permanent members often served to prevent Security Council action. The Security Council directs the various U.N. supervisory forces deployed throughout the world. Fifty-four elected members of the United Nations serve on the Economic and Social Council, which is charged with international economic, social, cultural, educational, health, and related matters. The International Court of Justice (World Court), based in The Hague, Netherlands, is the judicial arm of the United Nations. The Court renders judgments in disputes submitted to it by member states. More than a dozen autonomous agencies have working relationships with the United Nations. Among the better known of these agencies are the Food and Agricultural Organization (FAO), International Bank for Reconstruction and Development (World Bank), the United Nations Children's Fund (UNICEF), and the World Health Organization (WHO).

The United Nations typically is involved in two or three dozen international disputes annually. When a country poses a threat to world peace, the United Nations can impose economic sanctions against it or even intervene with member military forces brought under U.N. command. The U.N. peacekeeping forces helped maintain a ceasefire between India and Pakistan in 1948 and have been deployed in various parts of the Middle East since 1956. They have separated Turks and Greeks in Cyprus since 1964. They moved into Iraq in 1991, into Cambodia and into areas formerly a part of Yugoslavia in 1992, and into Somalia in 1993. Without question, the world has been spared much violence and has avoided many deaths because of the United Nations, and no direct or open warfare has broken out between major powers since 1945. Even so, the existence of the organization was not enough to prevent the loss of many thousands of lives in conflicts and wars involving U.N. members in Korea, Vietnam, the Falkland Islands (Islas Malvinas), Afghanistan, the Middle East, Central America, and Africa.

In the New World Order of the 1990s, the machinery of the United Nations is at the center of international efforts to deal with threats to world peace. It is reasonable to expect that the importance of the United Nations as a facilitator of peace will grow, as will its costs of doing business. Those who welcome an expanding role by the United Nations in the peace process lament that so many member states have hindered the ability of the organization to accomplish its mission by not making timely payments of dues to its headquarters. Lack of adequate funding can significantly impede the work of the United Nations. In 1993 the two states with the largest arrears were the United States and Russia.

KEY TERMS

Patriotism   Loyalty and devotion to one's country or political system.   **155**

Theocracy   A country in which the government is controlled by one or more religious leaders.   **155**

Nation   A group of people occupying a specific area and united by a common cultural or ethnic background.   **156**

State   An area organized as a political unit over which an established government exercises sovereign control.   **158**

Nation-state   A state whose territory coincides with that occupied by a particular nation.   **158**

Generic boundaries   A group of boundary types identified on the basis of inherent characteristics of the boundaries themselves.   **160**

Genetic boundaries   A group of boundary types identified on the basis of their genesis, that is, when and where they were established relative to the human occupance of the area.   **161**

Microstates   Countries distinguished by their unusually small size in land area.   **166**

National core   The area in which a state originated; also, typically it contains the country's greatest population, principal city, and greatest economic development. **169**

City-state A political entity that consists of a city together with the territory under its political control. **171**

Empire An extensive territory or a number of territories and peoples under the control of a single political authority. **171**

Geopolitics The use of geographic information and concepts to attain political goals. **179**

Cold War The competition between the United States and the Soviet Union (together with allies on each side) for military and technological supremacy as well as international influence following World War II. **180**

Neutrality A policy of impartiality, or refusal to support either side of an issue or conflict. Some national governments have a tradition of neutrality, thereby avoiding participation in conflicts or wars. **185**

Nonaligned Movement A joint policy among the nonaligned states to oppose the Cold War and colonialism and to promote economic development in the less developed world. **185**

REVIEW QUESTIONS

1. What are some of the basic responsibilities of governments? In what different ways is power exercised by governments and government officials?

2. How are language and religion closely linked with government in many countries? In what modern countries has the government advocated atheism?

3. How do the terms *nation* and *state* differ in meaning? What qualifies a country to be known as a nation-state?

4. How does cultural diversity in a country often function as a centrifugal force? What factors might serve as more powerful centripetal forces?

5. What is the difference between generic and genetic boundaries? How can boundary types affect the political and economic well-being of countries?

6. How can the size and shape of a country affect its political and economic well-being?

7. What are some of the distinguishing characteristics of a country's national core? Why is the relationship between a country's core and periphery important?

8. What were the similarities and differences between the two stages of European colonialism? What events separated the two stages?

9. What period of history included the creation of the greatest number of new independent nations? What events brought this about?

10. What nations of the world have the greatest number of dependencies? How do dependencies differ in their relationships with their administering nation?

11. What enabled the United States and the Soviet Union to emerge as the world's two great superpowers at the conclusion of World War II?

12. How did the Cold War come about after World War II? Why was the North Atlantic Treaty Organization (NATO) formed in 1949?

13. What was involved in the "arms race" and "space race" between the two superpowers of the Cold War? What were the main accomplishments of the two superpowers in these competitions?

14. What regions of the world were key areas of tension between the two superpower alliances during the Cold War? What events took place in these regions as a part of the Cold War?

15. What principles of foreign policy are followed by neutral states? By nonaligned states? How have the principles of foreign policy of the nonaligned movement changed since it was organized in 1961?

16. What internal conditions and reforms led to the collapse of the Soviet government in 1991?

17. What steps have been taken by the world's nations since 1963 to limit the proliferation of nuclear weapons? To what extent have these measures been successful?

18. What are the major challenges facing the governments of the world in the post-Soviet era? What new superpowers are most likely to emerge?

19. Why might lesser armed conflicts increase in the absence of the Cold War? How has the role of the United States changed in respect to such conflicts?

20. What are some of the common means by which governments continue to violate the human rights of their

citizens? Is there any reason to expect a decrease in human rights abuses in the future?

21. How might the end of the Cold War affect the need to solve environmental problems and the further exploration of space?

22. What factors have limited the ability of the United Nations to live up to the expectations of its founders? Why is it reasonable to expect the peace-keeping role of the United Nations to increase in the future?

A DISCUSSION WITH GRAHAM TOBIN

Dr. Graham Tobin *Even as a teenager, Dr. Graham Tobin was intrigued by the "human side" of geographical disasters such as flooding. He wanted to know, for example, what prompts people to settle on floodplains and why they sometimes ignore flood warnings. His interest in natural hazards developed at an early age, when he was growing up in several flood-prone regions of England.*

Today, Dr. Tobin is a professor of geography and director of the Center for Community and Regional Research at the University of Minnesota, Duluth. Born in 1951, he graduated with honors from the University of Durham in England, where he received an undergraduate degree in geography. His Ph.D. in geography was awarded by the University of Strathclyde, Scotland.

Dr. Tobin is co-author of the book, Human Adjustment to the Flood Hazard, *and he has also completed extensive studies on flooding, wetlands, and managing groundwater resources. Recently he launched a study to determine how individuals were affected by severe flooding in the midwestern United States in 1993. Of*

key interest, Dr. Tobin explains, is "the web of social, cultural, political, economic, and environmental factors" that influence each individual's choice of habitat.

Would you describe what you saw during the great flood of 1993, when you conducted field research?

I have seen quite a large number of floods, but the extent of the devastation that I saw in the midwestern United States in 1993 far surpassed anything that I had ever seen before. At one point, I stood on a bluff overlooking the Missouri Valley, and the whole area was brown, scarred for many miles, from one side of the valley to the other. North of St. Louis, Missouri, was like a huge lake with a few farm houses and trees poking through the water's surface.

The scale of the destruction to agricultural land and urban areas was personally very disturbing. People were shoveling silt and sewage from their homes, throwing away everything they owned. It is very difficult to be a "dispassionate scientist" at times like that. Some regions, such as West Des Moines, Iowa, were flooded more than once. Tama, Iowa, was flooded four times. Chelsea, Iowa, was flooded five times.

The extremely long duration of flooding was also disturbing. In Davenport, Iowa, the Mississippi River reached flood stage on June 11, 1993, then continued to rise until it peaked on July 9. The water was still above flood stage in early August.

Des Moines lost its sewage treatment plant as well as its drinking water supply. Roughly 250,000 people in that community were without running water for 12 days and without drinking water for 19 days. Throughout the Midwest, water resources were polluted as chemicals were washed off farm land and landfills were inundated.

Communities just above St. Louis, such as St. Charles and Chesterfield, really suffered because their levees did not hold. Many people lost everything they owned. Yet these communities are rebuilding.

How widespread was the flooding?

Flooding was extreme throughout the Midwest along the Mississippi River and the Missouri River, as well as their major tributaries, such as the Des Moines River.

On the Missouri River, flooding extended from South Dakota southward through Nebraska, through northeast Kansas, and into Missouri. On the Mississippi River, flooding extended from Minnesota southward through Wisconsin, Iowa, Illinois, and into Missouri.

In St. Paul, Minnesota, the Mississippi reached its crest on June 26, 1993. It did not peak in St. Louis, Missouri, until July 19, 1993. From Davenport, Iowa, to St. Louis, water levels were the highest on record, exceeding those of 1965.

Southern regions of the Mississippi Valley escaped severe flooding, primarily because the Ohio River was not in full spate and did not add substantially to flows on the Mississippi. However, the Mississippi River remained at a high level in Arkansas and Louisiana, but did not exceed previous flood levels.

How many lives were lost and how much property was damaged as a result of the flood?

Unofficial figures suggest that 34 deaths were directly associated with this hazard. Many other fatalities and illnesses may have been indirectly linked to the flood; some people may have suffered heart attacks as flood waters began to rise. At least 26,000 people were evacuated from their homes during the flood.

In terms of monetary losses, the severity of this flood will probably prove to be the greatest on record for the United States. Thus far, at least $8 billion in direct property damage has been reported. An estimated 17,000 square miles of land were flooded, and more than 22,000 houses were damaged.

Why do people settle on floodplains?

In some cases, people have no choice. Houses on the floodplain may be the only houses that these individuals can afford. In other cases, individuals may have lived their entire lives in a particular region, and they may have developed an attachment to the area or to a particular house. Economic incentives to farm more and more land, and the drainage of wetlands for agricultural use, have also promoted more intense use of the floodplain.

Residents of floodplains are periodically going to be damaged by floods. Yet, they enjoy certain benefits associated with living and working in these areas.

Assigning "blame" for flood losses is extremely difficult because of the web of social, cultural, political, economic, and environmental factors which affect an individual's choice of habitat. We cannot say, categorically, that one reason or another precipitated the tragedy. But we can develop strategies for mitigating losses.

Was this natural disaster caused simply by heavy rainfall?

No. The flood was caused by a combination of physical and human processes. Extreme meteorological conditions certainly contributed to the amount of water that was sloshing around. The entire 48 months before the flood were the wettest on record in Iowa, and in July 1993, the state received 10.5 inches of rain. During the summer, Iowa experienced four months of flooding.

But human behavior also plays a part in hazards. Ironically, our attempts to control the river

> "I have seen quite a large number of floods, but the extent of the devastation that I saw in the midwestern United States in 1993 far surpassed anything that I had ever seen before."

and improve drainage may have aggravated the flooding. Draining wetlands for agricultural purposes, for example, can increase property damage downstream. Natural water storage capacity is compromised by this; consequently, more water is transmitted to the river channel, thus raising flood levels.

Furthermore, flood alleviation measures can also exacerbate the flood hazard and promote the unwise use of floodplains. Invariably, the construction of engineering projects, such as levee systems, leads to a false sense of security against flooding that eventually stimulates greater development in flood-prone areas. When large events occur, such as the 1993 flood, that exceed the design standards of the project, then losses can be catastrophic. In addition, levees can alter the river flow and move water rapidly downstream, thus adding to problems in other communities. It is believed that Davenport, Iowa, which has no major structural flood alleviation measure, suffered because of this.

West Des Moines, Iowa, and Hartsburg, Missouri, where flooding was severe.

Flood victims will be asked for details on their flood experience, how long they were dislocated, how much support they received from neighbors, friends, and relatives, and whether their mobility was impaired by flood waters. Our questions will take into account three types of variables that could influence how people dealt with the flood: (1) individual characteristics (such as age and gender); (2) neighborhood characteristics; and (3) urban versus rural characteristics of the region.

We want to know how individuals responded to flood events at the time. We also want to go back a year later and determine the longer-term impacts of flooding. Flood victims received considerable media attention during the event, but after the news media and emergency personnel left, residents had to deal with the devastation on their own.

> "We want to know how individuals responded to flood events at the time. We also want to . . . determine the longer-term impacts of flooding."

You recently launched a survey of flood victims. What do you hope to learn, and what methods will you use?

I hope to determine how flooding affects the physical and mental health of flood victims. My colleagues and I will conduct a fairly lengthy telephone survey of individuals in Des Moines and

Will the flood prompt a reevaluation of structural and nonstructural approaches to loss prevention—from levees to flood insurance?

Authorities are grappling with whether or not to repair or relocate many weakened levees. My guess is that they will probably rebuild most of these structures. After all, urban areas have already been established on floodplains, and we need to protect those communities. It should also be noted that levees have prevented considerable damage from many small floods.

I am sure that nonstructural measures such as the National Flood Insurance program and zoning policies will also be reviewed. Under the National Flood Insurance program, residents of flood-prone regions must have insurance if they obtain a mortgage to buy a house. But if they already own their home, they are exempt from this requirement. Consequently, many flood victims were uninsured.

The Flood Relief Act of 1993 will provide $6.3 billion in federal assistance for flood victims, mainly for immediate relief and repairs rather than any longer-term planning for future events. As we speak, legislators are considering a bill that would provide $105 million to help people move off the floodplains.

How did you become interested in flood hazards?

I was born in the town of Bath, England, which used to flood fairly frequently; that may explain my initial interest in this phenomenon. Later, my family moved to the small village of Standstead Abbotts, about 20 miles north of London. In 1968, this community experienced a major flood. I can re-member standing on High Street and hearing the police warn everybody that the river was going to rise overnight and flood the village. For the most part, people did nothing!

This apparently strange behavior intrigued me. On the one hand, I was impressed by the tremendous power of the water; my main street was under four feet of water. On the other hand, residents and business people reacted too late to take any effective action, and I spent the day helping flood victims. This brings in the human geography and raises many questions. Why do people live in such hazardous locations? How can we explain the behavior of those people? What are the long-term social and economic effects of flooding? And so on. These are the sorts of questions we are investigating in our research.

Will there be job opportunities in the future for students who want to look at human responses to natural hazards?

Yes. The geographer plays a very important role; we must not only examine the physical environment before we can attempt to manage it, but we must also understand what motivates human responses to natural events such as floods, hurricanes, and earthquakes. Information on these responses can be a key to preventing the loss of lives and property.

Central to all study in human geography is the world's human population. In human geography, specific attention may be focused on certain human attributes or particular human activities that enable us to understand better the associations of people with their habitat and differences in the character of places over the earth. For example, in Part 2 of this book we investigated major cultural characteristics of the human population; in Part 4 we will examine various activities that provide a livelihood for the earth's people. It is, however, population itself that is under scrutiny in this part of our book.

The individuals in the accompanying photograph serve to remind us of some important facts about the world's population. First, the human crowding depicted in the photograph is becoming more common-place as world population growth continues at a level not approached in earlier centuries. Many social scientists consider population increase to be the most serious contemporary global problem. At the present rate of increase, world population will double in less than 40 years and thereby greatly intensify demands on our finite resource base. Second, the human cultural and racial diversity evident in the photograph and char-

PART 3

POPULATION

(Alan Carey/The Image Works)

acteristic of much of the world is a consequence of human migrations. Throughout history people have migrated for a variety of reasons to new locations where they often have contributed to human diversity as well as to increases in population numbers. Among contemporary migrants, a large proportion are refugees from environmental disasters, civil wars, or threatening political situations in their homelands. The topic of population growth is the focus for Chapter 6, and human migrations are examined in Chapter 7.

The irregular distribution of population over the earth's surface is the most fundamentally important topic in human geography. While extensive land areas are virtually uninhabited, nearly two-thirds of the world's people are clustered in East Asia, South Asia, and Europe. As we examine the distributional patterns of population in Chapter 8, many details concerning the linkages of land and people in different areas will become evident. Our study of population distribution also will lead us to consider the question of overpopulation in certain parts of the world.

CHAPTER 6

POPULATION GROWTH: THE UPWARD SPIRAL

Population, when unchecked, increases in a geometrical ratio. Subsistence increases only in an arithmetic ratio.

—Thomas Robert Malthus

A Bangladeshi mother and child. Rapid growth in human numbers continues in Bangladesh, the world's most densely populated nation. (Jim Whitmer)

➤ Although the rate of world population growth has been reduced slightly in recent years, nevertheless it remains high enough to pose one of the most serious global problems of our time.

What are some statistics that reflect current population growth?

What are the main concerns of geographers in their uses of demographic data?

Perhaps the most important statistic in the world today is 5,500,000,000—the approximate total human population of the planet earth. This stupendous figure is twice as large as the population total as recently as about 35 years ago. Furthermore, experts project that this figure will double again, barring some form of demographic disaster, in a little more than 40 years. For a variety of reasons, including population control programs implemented in some countries, the rate of increase in human numbers has been reduced somewhat in recent years. Yet the fact remains that even this slightly lower rate of growth is highly alarming; the increase in population continues to be high enough to represent one of the most disturbing global problems of our time. In terms of absolute numbers, world population now is increasing by more than 10,000 each hour, about 250,000 each day, and more than 90,000,000 each year! In several countries a doubling of their current populations could occur in less than 20 years if current growth rates continue.

The ability of the earth to support such enormous numbers of people at even the barest standard of living is in question. Will the resources of the planet and human technological abilities enable an expected population of more than 10 billion to even survive a mere four decades from now? Many population authorities contend that nearly half of the world's present inhabitants suffer periodic food shortages, and as many as 1 billion experience hunger on a daily basis. Frequent newspaper and magazine articles remind us of famine in various parts of the world, while television reports often provide shocking views of the horrors of human starvation occurring in some areas (Fig. 6.1). Plant and animal scientists and experts in food production techniques have been hard at work to find ways of increasing food output for the world's growing population. Nevertheless, many authorities feel that implementa-

FIGURE 6.1
Hunger is a permanent condition for many people in the less developed world. This photograph shows some of the hungry in Dacca, Bangladesh, in line for food. (David Austen Int'l/ Stock Boston)

tion of programs to reduce the rate of growth in human numbers is necessary to avert a demographic disaster.

Although **demography** is the specialized field that studies population, various aspects of population also are essential topics in human geography. Demographers engage in the statistical analysis of population. Geographers often make use of demographic statistics, but their main concerns are the spatial variations in population data and their significance to human–environment relationships. Our focus in this chapter is on change in human numbers. In recent generations that change has been one of alarming growth for the world as a whole, but it has varied significantly from place to place.

THE VITAL VARIABLES

➤ The variables that influence change in a given area's population total are human births, deaths, and migrations.

What is a natural increase in population?

What parts of the world have the highest and lowest natural increases?

An increase in world population occurs when human births exceed deaths for a period of time. However, if we are concerned with the population change in only a single part of the world, human migrations also may be a factor. Although the world as a whole does not gain or lose population through migrations, the population total of an individual region or country can be affected by the net gain or loss of migrants. Nevertheless, the difference between the number of births and deaths is the primary reason for changes in the population totals of nearly all modern countries. Migrations usually are an insignificant factor in national population changes. Most countries today have legal restrictions on the number of immigrants they allow to enter their territory permanently. Migrations were not so rigidly controlled in earlier times, however. During the nineteenth and early twentieth centuries, tens of millions of people participated in international migrations. Most were Europeans who relocated in the New World, especially between the year 1800 and the time of World War I. These migrations obviously had a significant impact on population change in both the sending and receiving countries. We will examine the topic of human migrations separately in the next chapter.

Natural Increase of Population

When population growth is caused by a greater number of births than deaths, it is called a **natural increase**. For the world as a whole, the natural increase of population was 1.6 percent in 1993 (Table 6.1). In that year, Africa, the region with the most rapid growth, had a natural increase of 2.9 percent. At that rate, Africa's population total will double in only 24 years. With a natural increase of 1.9 percent in 1993, Latin America could double its population in the next 36 years if that rate of growth continues. Although these percentages may seem to be quite low, the time needed to double the population at such rates is amazingly brief. This is because of *compounding*, the same principle that enables a small savings deposit in your local bank to grow into a substantial amount by compounding interest over a period of several years. In 1993 the region with the lowest rate of natural increase, 0.2 percent, was Europe. A doubling of Europe's population would require 382 years at that rate. (See *The Geographer's Notebook: Population Doubling Time*.)

Fertility and Mortality

➤ Human fertility and mortality most commonly are represented by crude birth rates and crude death rates.

How might birth and death rates be changed?

How does the range of infant mortality rates compare with that of crude death rates from region to region?

What geographical variations in average life expectancies are evident?

TABLE 6.1	Population Total and Natural Increase for the World and Major Regions: 1993	
Region	**Total Population (millions)**	**Natural Increase (annual percent)**
World	5,506	1.6
Africa	677	2.9
Anglo-America	287	0.8
Asia	3,257	1.7
Europe	513	0.2
Latin America	460	1.9
Oceania	28	1.2
Former Soviet Union[a]	285	0.6

SOURCE: *Population Reference Bureau*

[a]In 1991, the Soviet Union fragmented into 15 separate states, most of which are now members of the Commonwealth of Independent States. The populations of three of those states (Latvia, Lithuania, and Estonia) are included in the total for Europe.

TABLE 6.2	Selected Population Variables for the World and Major Regions: 1993			
Region	Crude Birth Rate	Crude Death Rate	Infant Mortality Rate	Life Expectancy (years)
World	26	9	70	65
Africa	43	14	94	54
Anglo-America	16	8	8	76
Asia	26	9	74	64
Europe	12	10	10	75
Latin America	26	7	49	68
Oceania	19	8	34	73
Former Soviet Union[a]	16	11	28	70

SOURCE: *Population Reference Bureau.*

[a]In 1991, the Soviet Union fragmented into 15 separate states, most of which are now members of the Commonwealth of Independent States. Data for three of those states (Latvia, Lithuania, and Estonia) are included with Europe.

Although more refined measurements of fertility and mortality are possible, **crude birth rates** and **crude death rates** are used most often because they can be calculated easily and they are available for nearly all countries. The crude birth rate is defined as the annual number of births per 1000 population, and the crude death rate is the annual number of deaths per 1000 population. For the world as a whole in 1993, the birth rate was 26 and the death rate was 9 (Table 6.2). From region to region, the range of birth rates is much greater than that of death rates. For 1993, the highest birth rates were in Africa (43), Asia (26), and Latin America (26), and the lowest in Europe (12). The range of death rates in that year ranged from 14 (also in Africa) to 7 (Latin America).

If death rates are lowered further by improvements in sanitation and medical care, a corresponding reduction in birth rates will be required to avoid a greater increase in human numbers. In some parts of the world, as we shall see in following sections of this chapter, lowered birth rates have followed industrial development and urbanization of the population. Also, organized efforts and enforced policies by national governments have reduced birth rates in some countries; an important example is the Chinese government's recent program to force birth rates down in that country, which will be discussed later in this chapter. Efforts to reduce birth rates are thwarted regularly by severe obstacles, however. Traditions, attitudes, and particularly religious beliefs and teachings that oppose restrictions on human reproduction are difficult to overcome. In some societies, for example, the practice of abortion is enmeshed in emotionally charged moral questions (Fig. 6.2).

FIGURE 6.2

The use of abortion as a means of preventing unwanted births is vigorously opposed by many people for moral or religious reasons. This anti-abortion demonstration is in Wichita, Kansas. (Alex Quesada/Matrix)

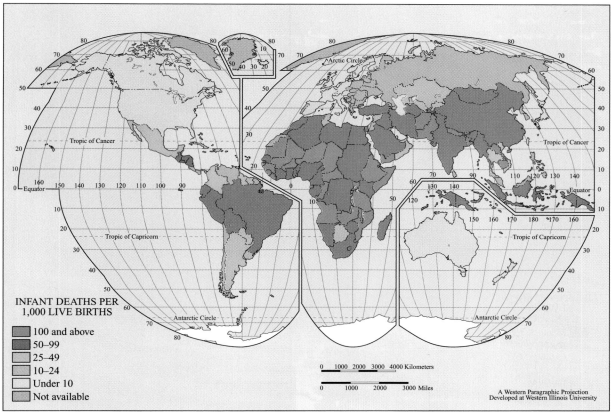

FIGURE 6.3
Infant mortality rates among the world's countries.

Infant Mortality Rates and Average Life Expectancy

Two additional important demographic variables are the **infant mortality rate** and the **average life expectancy** of the population, both of which reflect the available medical care and health conditions of a society. The infant mortality rate is expressed as the number of infant deaths per 1000 live births. For the entire world in 1993, the infant mortality rate was 70. However, it ranged widely, from 94 (Africa) to 8 (Anglo-America) (Table 6.2). Adequate nourishment, good sanitation, and proper medical care are important especially to the survival of infants. In parts of the world in which these are deficient, 10 to 20 percent of the babies fail to reach their first birthday (Fig. 6.3). Parents in such societies tend to have a large number of children in part because they recognize the high risk that one or more will die during infancy. Any reduc-

tion of the infant mortality rate (which also would be reflected in the death rate) naturally will result in greater population growth unless there is a corresponding decrease in the birth rate.

The average life expectancy for all human inhabitants of the earth is now 65 years. Advancements in medicine, the conquest of many diseases, better nutrition, and improvement in general living conditions, particularly in economically developed parts of the world, have enabled people to survive beyond the fourth and fifth decades of their life for the first time in history (Fig. 6.4). Even in poorer parts of the world, notable increases in life expectancy have been attained. Among the major regions, Africa has the shortest life expectancy, but it has risen to 54 years of age. People in other regions can expect to live beyond their sixtieth birthday, and even beyond their seventieth in Oceania, Europe, and Anglo-America. The growing number of elderly people in these societies is creating

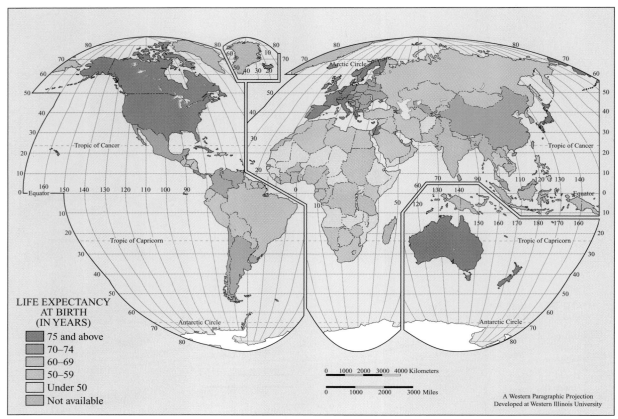

FIGURE 6.4
Life expectancy among the world's countries.

a new set of problems regarding their support and care that we will discuss later in this chapter.

POPULATION GROWTH THROUGH TIME

➢ Considering the span of human history, relatively large population totals for the world are a recent phenomenon.

Why was population growth generally low prior to the nineteenth century?

How was population growth influenced by the Agricultural Revolution?

How was it influenced by the Industrial Revolution?

Prior to 10,000 years ago, the human population of the world probably did not exceed 10 million. Pop-

ulation figures for that long ago, of course, are rough estimates based on archaeological evidence regarding the type of economy then practiced and how many people it could support, as well as the extent and character of the area then inhabited by people. Reasonably accurate census counts in most countries have been initiated only during the past two centuries.

By the time of Christ, the entire world population numbered only slightly more than the present total for the United States (Fig. 6.5). This total reached approximately 500 million by the year 1650, and then doubled over the next 200 years, attaining the milestone figure of 1 billion—about one-fifth of the present total. A population of 2 billion was recorded only 80 years later in 1930. The next addition of a billion to the total required only 30 years. The fourth billion was recorded only 16 years later, in 1976, and 5 billion was reached in 1987. How has this acceler-

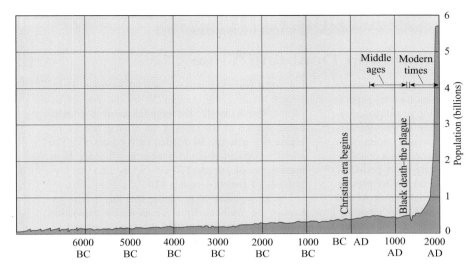

FIGURE 6.5

The world's modern population growth is in striking contrast to that in earlier times.

ating rate of growth come about? What events and developments in human history have facilitated this remarkable increase in human numbers?

Early Population Fluctuations

Throughout all human time prior to the nineteenth century, population growth was erratic and very low by current standards. Even periods of substantial reduction in human numbers was fairly frequent through the Middle Ages. Such events and conditions as plagues, epidemics, undependable food supplies, poor sanitation, inadequate medical treatment, and warfare were common enough throughout all but the most recent centuries of human history to prevent high rates of population increase. Early deaths were so widespread that average life spans were but a fraction of those in modern societies. Improvements in the quality of human life, generally the result of technological developments, were rare prior to the nineteenth century. The few improvements that did occur had far-reaching consequences, however.

The Paleolithic Period   It seems clear that the earliest development to have an important impact on population growth was the Agricultural Revolution, about 10,000 years ago. Prior to that time, during the Paleolithic Period, human food supplies were limited to those that could be obtained by hunting, fishing, and gathering. Considering (1) the variations from place to place and time to time in availability of edible plant

materials and populations of fish and game, and (2) the human skills needed to succeed in hunting and fishing with primitive weapons and devices, it is reasonable to assume that food supplies were highly undependable among Paleolithic people. The acquisition of food for survival probably was a universal occupation and required people to migrate frequently and to live in groups no larger than small bands or tribes.

The Neolithic Period   With the development of crop farming and the herding of livestock, improvement in the dependability and quantity of food supplies and changes in lifestyles followed during the Neolithic Period. It became possible for agriculturalists in some areas to produce food supplies beyond those needed by their immediate families. These surpluses could be used to support other people and free them from the necessity of devoting most of their time and effort to the acquisition of food for survival. Under such circumstances, many people were able to engage in a variety of endeavors that enriched their lives and to gather in substantial clusters of population at specific places—the first embryonic cities in world history. The Agricultural Revolution, therefore, was a major cultural achievement that enabled Neolithic people to live a more varied lifestyle and that reduced one of the obstacles to population growth—a limited and undependable food supply.

During the thousands of years required for the spread of agriculture to all of the inhabited continents, other conditions that restricted population

Population Doubling Time

To illustrate the potential influence of an area's rate of demographic growth on its total population, often reference is made to the population doubling time. A number of the world's countries currently have an annual rate of natural increase so high that, if maintained, it could result in a doubling of their population in an amazingly short period of time. For example, Kenya could double its population in 19 years if its current annual rate of natural increase (3.7 percent) is continued; Zaire's population could double in 21 years at its current 3.3 percent rate of increase; and Nicaragua's population could double in 23 years if it continues its current 3.0 percent rate of growth. On the other hand, Denmark's doubling time would be more than 700 years if that nation maintains its current 0.1 percent rate of natural increase.

The "rule of 70" allows for quick calculation of the number of years needed to double a population at a particular rate of annual increase. It involves dividing the number 70 by the rate of increase. For example, the population of a country could double in 35 years if its annual rate of increase is 2 percent (70 divided by 2 equals 35). The world's population could double in 42 years at its present rate of increase (70 divided by 1.6—the current rate of growth—equals 42).

It is important to recognize that this determination of the doubling time for an area's population involves the assumption that the rate of natural increase will remain constant. Any variation in the rate from time to time, a likely event in any area, will influence the actual doubling time. Furthermore, any change in the population total caused by migrations of people into or out of an area is neglected in this calculation of doubling time. If there is a net gain or loss of population as a consequence of migrations, it too will affect the time necessary for a country's population to double.

The population doubling time for a country is an intriguing statistic, but as discussed earlier, we must remember that it assumes a constant annual rate of natural increase and no loss or gain of population through migration. Of course, no country in the world is likely to fulfill those assumptions over a period of two or more decades. We need to exercise caution, therefore, in using doubling-time figures to anticipate what a country's population total will be in a future year.

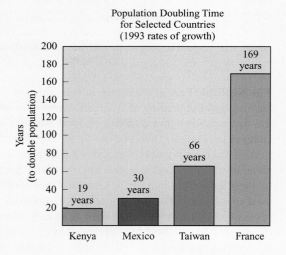

Population Doubling Time
for Selected Countries
(1993 rates of growth)

THOUGHT QUESTIONS

1. In your opinion, what is the principal value of population-doubling-time statistics?
2. What types of future events do you feel could have the greatest influence on the world's population doubling time?

growth—such as poor sanitation, diseases, plagues, and warfare—continued to be important. Human conflicts and epidemics ensured the continuation of high death rates for many centuries. During the Middle Ages, for example, the struggles between groups of Arabs and Christians and the invasions of Europe and China by Asian tribes resulted in the loss of many lives. Bubonic plague was a major cause of early death in Europe through the seventeenth century (Fig. 6.6). Human sacrifices and infanticide were practiced in some societies even into the modern period. By the eighteenth century, Europeans had explored and started colonizing in much of the New World but world population totaled only about 600 to 700 million—about the size of the modern population of Africa.

Modern Population Increases

During the latter part of the eighteenth century another major technological development began, one with a far greater influence on population growth than the Agricultural Revolution. This new development, which first appeared in Great Britain and soon spread to the mainland of Europe, was the Industrial Revolution.

Demographic Impact of the Industrial Revolution
Prior to the Industrial Revolution cities were few in number and most were modest in size, but the establishment of mills and factories in urban places attracted workers from rural areas and stimulated a spiraling growth of cities. As the Industrial Revolution spread to other parts of the world during the nineteenth and twentieth centuries, urbanization of the population quickly followed. Urban life, of course, is vastly different from that in rural areas. The intensive crowding of people, inadequate means of waste disposal, and impure water supplies of the early industrial cities caused discomfort, poor health, and the spread of disease as they continue to do now in many cities of less developed countries.

The quality of life in industrial cities began to improve, however, as authorities established sanitary sewer systems, pure water supplies, schools, and health care facilities. The agglomeration of large numbers of people, in fact, made it more feasible and economical for authorities to provide essential sanitary services, health care, and education in the cities than in the countrysides of industrializing countries. The demographic result that soon followed these improvements was a reduction in death rates and, as a consequence, a sharp increase in population growth. In those countries of the world in which industrialization has occurred, the period following the initial establishment of industry has been characterized by urbanization of the population and an abrupt increase in human numbers brought about by lower death rates.

Revolution in Science and Technology   A revolution in science and technology was associated with the Industrial Revolution and contributed to significant improvements in standards of living. Many people became convinced that science and technology, in fact,

BELZUNCE AMIDST THE PLAGUE-STRICKEN.

FIGURE 6.6
Portrayed here are victims of bubonic plague, one of several checks on population growth during the Middle Ages. (North Wind Picture Archives)

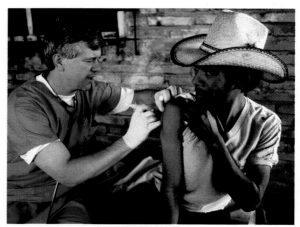

FIGURE 6.7

The control of disease by modern medicine has been an important means of reducing human death rates. In this photograph, a man is being inoculated by a foreign volunteer at a medical clinic in rural Honduras. (Daemmrich/Stock Boston)

could solve most human problems and lead to a better life than was ever before possible. Nations began investing great amounts of their wealth in the training of scientists and the development of technology, confident that the resulting benefits would far exceed the costs.

In the field of medicine the results have been spectacular. Scientific medicine has eased the suffering and provided cures for the ill, developed vaccines to prevent the spread of disease, and taught people how to avoid sickness and lead healthy lives (Fig. 6.7). Feared diseases that took a heavy toll in the past, such as cholera, smallpox, and polio, have been virtually eliminated as a threat to most of the world's population. Infant mortality also has fallen dramatically with improvements in medicine. In the world's industrialized societies that have the benefits of scientific medicine, the lowering of death rates has increased the life expectancy to more than 70 years.

CONTEMPORARY PATTERNS

> Spatial variations in birth and death rates result in the lowest rates of population growth in the world's industrialized nations and the highest rates in the less developed countries.

What are some reasons why birth rates are relatively high in the less developed countries but low in industrialized nations?

Why is the relationship between death rates and levels of economic development less consistent?

What are some factors other than economic development that influence rates of population growth?

The enormous variations from country to country in the contemporary geographic patterns of birth rates, death rates, and rates of population growth become apparent by examining Figures 6.8, 6.9, and 6.10. These three maps also suggest the relationship of birth and death rates to population growth. Keep in mind that these maps show crude birth rates (annual number of births per 1000 population), crude death rates (annual number of deaths per 1000 population), and the natural population increase (annual percentage increase resulting from the excess of births over deaths).

The Geographical Pattern of Birth Rates

Those countries with high birth rates are nearly all in the tropical and subtropical latitudes of Africa, Asia, and Latin America (Fig. 6.8). Africa, with the lowest level of economic development among the major world regions, particularly stands out on the map for its high birth rates. Among Africa's major countries, only one (Tunisia) recorded a crude birth rate below the world average of 26 in 1993; in several of the continent's countries—Angola, Burkina Faso, Côte d'Ivoire, Malawi, Mali, Niger, Somalia, and Uganda—it was 50 or more! Nearly all of the countries along the southern rim of Asia and most of those in the central and northern parts of Latin America also have birth rates well above the world average of 26.

High birth rates clearly are associated with nations that are predominantly agrarian and have attained little industrialization and urbanization. Subsistence agriculture is the most common form of employment, and per capita annual income is very low. For example, all but one (Côte d'Ivoire) of the African countries with a birth rate of 50 or more had a per capita income of less than $500 in 1993. Such societies tend to regard a large number of children as desirable to help work the land and to eventually provide care for elderly parents. In cases in which efforts are made by governmental agencies to reduce birth rates in these countries, widespread poverty and illiteracy are serious obstacles. Contraceptives are likely to be viewed as an unacceptable expense by the poverty-stricken, and printed information on family planning and birth control will be ineffective among the illiterate.

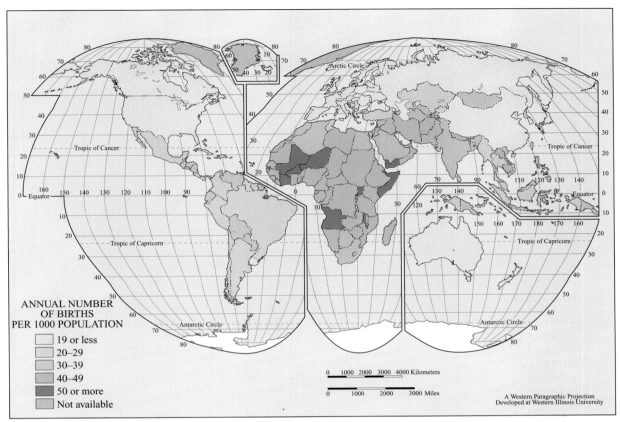

FIGURE 6.8

Crude birth rates among the countries of the world.

Relatively low birth rates, as indicated by Figure 6.8, are characteristic of countries with industrial-urban societies. The United States and Canada, most European nations, the former Soviet Union, South Korea, Japan, Taiwan, Hong Kong, and Australia were the only countries with birth rates of 16 or less in 1993. All have predominantly urban populations and an economy greatly influenced by industrial development. These nations also enjoy relatively high levels of affluence and educational attainment. Large numbers of children are not viewed as an advantage under these socioeconomic conditions. Family planning is understood and accepted, contraceptives are readily available and affordable, and women are often employed outside the home.

The transformation of industrialized countries from earlier rural-agrarian states to their present status was not immediate; in some, such as the European countries, it required a century or more, but others

(notably Japan) managed to accomplish it in only a few decades. It is apparent that a shorter period of time was required by countries that more recently underwent industrialization. It is risky to conclude that more rapid industrialization is a permanent trend, however, with so few countries having made the transition over recent decades. A seemingly safer conclusion is that most of the world's less developed countries will continue to have high birth rates and low levels of economic attainment for many years in the future.

The Geographical Pattern of Death Rates

The continent with the least success in lowering death rates thus far is Africa. For the entire world, the death rate in 1993 was 9 per 1000 population, but in Africa it was 14. As Figure 6.9 indicates, a number of African countries in 1993 had death rates of 20 or more—a

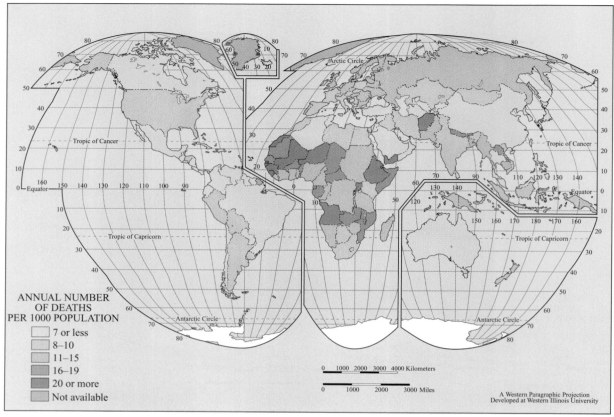

FIGURE 6.9

Crude death rates among the countries of the world.

level that was extremely rare elsewhere in the world. Africa also had the highest infant mortality rate (94) and the shortest life expectancy (54 years) of all major world regions in 1993. The disturbingly common occurrence of death in Africa is largely a consequence of the continent's poverty, inadequate food supplies, poor sanitary conditions, and scarcity of medical care. The death toll among children, who commonly suffer most from poor nourishment and diseases, is particularly depressing (Fig. 6.11). In most countries of Africa, one out of nine infants will not live to mark his or her first birthday. Relatively high death rates, comparable to those of Africa, also are recorded in some of the countries along the southern rim of Asia.

The *age structure* of a nation's population is another factor that impacts on the death rate. Other things being equal, an older population naturally will experience more deaths than a younger population. This explains why death rates are higher in Europe (where 14 percent of the population is 65 years of age or older) than in Latin America (where only 5 percent of the population is 65 years of age older). For the same reason, China also has a relatively low death rate—one that is slightly lower even than that in the United States (7 versus 9).

It is obvious that low death rates are not limited to those countries with elevated levels of economic development. Medical care, including inoculations against disease and treatment for the injured and ill, has spread into many parts of the less developed world with outstanding success in prolonging life. It is clear that a lowering of death rates has been easier to accomplish in modern time than a reduction of birth rates. Africa is the only continent that has yet to experience substantial progress in reducing the occurrence of death and lengthening of life expectancy.

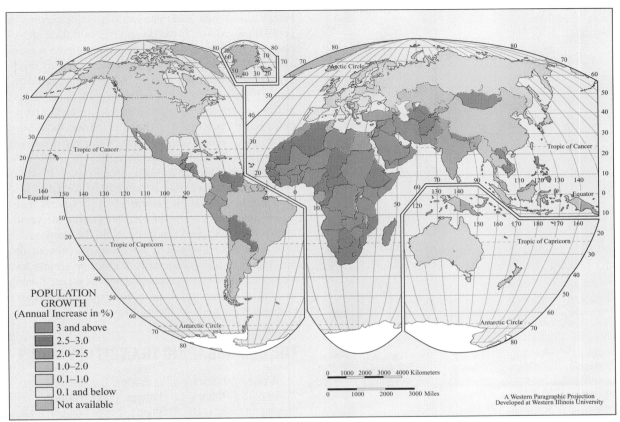

FIGURE 6.10

World patterns of natural population increase.

Judging from post-World War II trends in other less developed regions (eastern Asia and Latin America), we reasonably can expect Africa's death rates soon to begin a downward spiral. Efforts by the United Nations and foreign humanitarian programs of industrialized countries in the near future will bring advanced medical care to those parts of Africa in which diseases, poor health, and complications during childbirth now take a heavy toll on human life.

The Geographical Pattern of Population Growth

As we noted earlier in this chapter, world population presently is increasing at a rate of 1.6 percent annually. However, those countries that are economically developed make only a minor contribution to this growth. As a group, the developed nations have a dem-

ographic growth rate that averages only 0.5 percent annually. The United States and Canada, the countries of Europe (excluding Macedonia and Albania), the former Soviet Union, Japan, Hong Kong, Australia, and Uruguay are the only nations with annual increases of less than 1.0 percent on the map in Figure 6.10, and nearly all of them are among the wealthiest countries in the world. It is the less developed countries—those economically least able to support more people—that are contributing most to the world population explosion. As a group, these countries in 1990 had a growth rate of 2.0 percent annually—about four times that of the developed nations.

Although associations of population growth rates and levels of economic development are generally valid, it should be noted that there are inconsistencies. A prominent example is the wealthy petroleum-exporting countries of the Middle East that continue

FIGURE 6.11
This baby, in the arms of its mother in a refugee camp along the Sudan-Ethiopia border, could easily become a victim of Africa's high infant mortality rate. (Ilene Perlman/Stock Boston)

to have some of the highest rates of population growth in the world. Economic conditions clearly have a major impact on demographic rates, but a number of other factors—for example, religion, education, and cultural traditions—are important, too. Some religions oppose birth control practices, particularly the use of abortion as a method of birth control, and a large number of children is encouraged by attitudes and traditions in some societies. The traditional restrictions in Moslem society on the role of women, essentially requiring that they serve only as homemakers and wives, help account for the high rate of population growth in the Islamic countries of Africa and Asia.

The most alarming condition of demographic growth is in Africa, the continent most dominated by poverty. Here the birth rates are so extremely high that they overcome the world's highest death rates to the

extent that Africa leads the world's major regions in population growth. If the death rates in Africa are reduced in the near future, as we can anticipate reasonably, will the population growth accelerate to levels even greater than the current 2.9 percent annual increase? That result most certainly will occur unless birth rates are reduced. The obstacles to birth rate reductions in societies like those in Africa have been difficult to overcome in the past; whatever success is achieved will require more time, in all probability, than that involved in lowering death rates. It seems inevitable, therefore, that Africa will be forced to deal with future population growth of even greater magnitude than the current spiral. To expect the continent's economy to keep pace with the increase in human numbers, which is necessary to prevent deterioration in living standards that are extremely low already, appears unreasonable. Perhaps recent famine and flights of starving *refugees* from one part of Africa to another are hints of the future.

THE DEMOGRAPHIC TRANSITION MODEL

➢ A *demographic transition model* has been devised to portray theoretical changes through time in a region's birth rate, death rate, and population total.

How are the model's four stages differentiated?

What are the bases for supporting and doubting the global applicability of the model?

Following the early eighteenth century, Western Europe experienced dramatic population changes that accompanied its emergence as the world's first industrialized society. These changes, spanning a period of more than two centuries, involved alterations in birth rates, death rates, and, as a consequence, population totals. Together they constituted a **demographic transition** from the high birth and death rates of the preindustrial era to Western Europe's generally low birth and death rates of the twentieth century. A widely used *demographic transition model* based on this experience in Western Europe has emerged.

The Model's Four Stages

The model recognizes four stages, each of which is distinguished by certain birth and death rates and consequent trends in total population (Fig. 6.12). The central thesis is that as a society progresses from agrarian

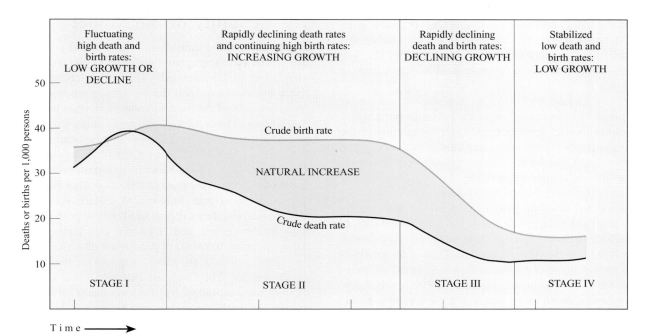

FIGURE 6.12

The Demographic Transition Model.

domination in its preindustrial era to maturity as an industrial-urban state, it will progress through the four stages of the model. Industrialization in Western Europe and a few other areas has been accompanied by improvements in health care and living conditions, by greater educational attainments, and by urbanization and changes in lifestyles, all of which have influenced birth and death rates.

Demographic conditions during preindustrial times are represented in *Stage I* of this model. Preindustrial societies have agrarian-dominated economies, traditional lifestyles, and their people have little or no opportunity to obtain a formal education. In the absence of mechanical devices and implements, working the land requires much labor. It is traditional, and expected, that families will have a large number of children. People usually marry at an early age; married life for a female commonly begins while she is still in her middle-teenage years. Early marriages increase the mother's child-bearing years, and having many children is desirable because the children can help work the land. In some cases, religious beliefs, attitudes about masculinity and fertility, and poor education also contribute to the high birth rates. Under prein-

dustrial conditions, the high birth rates are offset by high death rates, however, and any change in population total is minor or insignificant. Inadequate health care, poor sanitary conditions, diseases and epidemics, undependable food supplies, and even warfare contribute to the high death rates.

Stage II of the demographic transition model is a period of high birth rates, declining death rates, and burgeoning growth of the total population. As modernization of a society gets underway during its early industrial period, death rates begin to decline significantly. Improvements in food supplies, sanitation, and medical care, along with industrial development, are part of the modernization process, and they contribute to longer life expectancy and lower death rates. These changes result in a dramatic increase in total population because birth rates continue to be relatively high during the early industrial period.

In *Stage III* of the model, birth rates begin to decline as the industrialization and modernization of the society progress. Agrarian occupations support fewer people, and an increasing percentage of the population move to urban areas, at the same time attaining greater education and abandoning traditions. Fewer children in the family becomes a desirable and obtainable goal. Although death rates continue to decline during this stage, the reduction in birth rates narrows the gap and total population growth is less rapid than in Stage II.

With full modernization of a society and the attainment of industrial maturity, accompanying social and economic developments foster completion of the demographic transition as depicted in *Stage IV* of the model. At this level of development, very few rural people are needed to work the land and the vast majority (typically two-thirds or more) of the population is located in urban places. Formal education is universal, and a large proportion of women pursue careers outside the home and postpone motherhood or choose not to have children. Birth control materials are available widely, and family planning is accepted and practiced. As a consequence, birth rates fall to levels nearly as low as death rates, and any growth in total population numbers is minor and insignificant. In this stage, **zero population growth** (ZPG) may occur in some societies. Major countries that have reached this stage include most of those in Europe, the United States, Canada, Japan, Australia, and New Zealand.

Most of the less developed countries, which include more than three-fourths of the world's population, are in Stage II of the model, and some have reached Stage III. Over recent decades, these countries have experienced some reduction in their death rates with improvements in disease control and medical care, sanitation, and food supplies. To an important degree, these improvements have been facilitated by humanitarian aid extended by more developed countries and international relief organizations. Food, medical supplies, and the technology to improve the quality of life by such means as establishing a pure water supply have been usual aspects of assistance programs. The results have been an increase in life expectancy (in some cases by twenty years or more), a decrease in death rates, and, of course, a growth in total population because birth rates have remained high. It is ironic that "humanitarian" aid programs, by their success in improving the quality of life in less developed countries, have created more problems associated with the consequent growth in population. It is easier and less controversial to reduce death rates than birth rates, of course. Attitudes, traditions, and religious beliefs can be exceedingly difficult obstacles to overcome in efforts to reduce birth rates.

Applicability of the Model

Is the demographic transition model a useful guide to the world's demographic future? Will the planet's population growth eventually level off as all parts of the world complete their demographic transition and reach Stage IV of the model? Some authorities believe that the model indeed has global application; they support their contention by pointing out how other countries such as the United States, Canada, Australia, and Japan have followed the Western European pattern of completing their demographic transition after becoming modernized and industrially mature societies. Other countries, they suggest, need only to push ahead with modernization and industrial development to solve the problem of world population growth.

Other scholars are more skeptical of the merit of the model. They suggest that the great variety of traditions, attitudes, and socioeconomic practices among the world's societies and the impossibility of industrialization throughout the world make it unlikely that this single model can represent the demographic trends of all nations. These skeptics assert that the model does not accurately reflect what has happened in the less developed countries. Although these countries have the demographic characteristics associated with Stage II and Stage III of the model, the critics argue that their advancement to that level was not brought about by their own industrialization and modernization; instead, they have been the beneficiaries—through aid programs—of other countries in which those developments have occurred.

DEMOGRAPHIC TRENDS: THREE CASE STUDIES

To illustrate some of the contrasts in the demographic trends of the world's nations, we will examine three countries as case studies—Bangladesh, the People's Republic of China, and the United States. Perhaps the worst population problem in the world can be found in poverty-stricken Bangladesh, a relatively new state that in 1993 had an annual natural increase in population of 2.4 percent. China, with the largest population total in the world for thousands of years, has experienced such effective demographic control measures implemented by the government since the early 1970s that its annual rate of natural increase declined to 1.2 percent by 1993. In the United States population growth has declined to a very low level (an annual natural increase of 0.8 percent in 1993), yet early in the twentieth century the country was absorbing an enormous flow of European immigrants and had one of the highest rates of increase in the world. It is obvious that the current demographic situation in each of these countries is vastly different from that in the other two. In terms of the demographic transition model, Bangladesh is most similar to countries in Stage II, China has attained the characteristics of countries in Stage III, and the United States appears to have joined the small group of countries that have reached Stage IV. However, these assignments are subjective because boundaries between the different stages are not defined precisely.

Bangladesh

➤ With one of the world's highest rates of population increase, Bangladesh is representative of countries in Stage II of the demographic transition model.

How is Bangladesh typical of Stage II countries?

What explanations can be given for the continuing high rate of population growth in Bangladesh?

Many authorities feel that the population problem of Bangladesh is more severe than that of any other country, although direct comparisons are difficult to make because each country's situation is unique. In any event, the demographic circumstances in Bangladesh are extremely severe and any significant improvement in the near future seems unlikely. With an area about the size of Wisconsin, Bangladesh is the ninth most populated country in the world, with about 115 million inhabitants. Possessing an average of more than 2000 people per square mile (772 per sq km) Bangladesh is the most densely populated nation (excluding city states) in the world.

Since 1971, when Bangladesh achieved independence from Pakistan, all of the country's heads of state have placed population control as a top priority. A number of outside agencies have joined in the attempt to slow the country's rate of population growth as well. All efforts have had minimal success, however.

Socioeconomic Conditions   The population problem is enmeshed within the prevailing socioeconomic conditions in Bangladesh. The country is extremely poor (the annual gross national product is less than $250 per capita), and it is heavily dependent on agriculture. Ninety percent of the population lives in rural areas, and 80 percent of the labor force is engaged in farming. The people are so crowded on the land that family farms are no more than tiny plots. The average family farm is about two acres (0.8 ha) in size, but nearly 60 percent of the families must survive on one acre (0.4 ha) or less. Machinery and high-yield fertilizers are too expensive for farmers under these circumstances.

As a consequence the farmers view large families as desirable to work the land and obtain the highest production possible. Children also serve as a form of old-age security for parents. Lacking a retirement system or social security program, people must rely on their children for support during their old age. Because Bangladesh has high infant mortality rates (120 infants per 1000 births die within their first year) and high death rates in general, many parents feel it is necessary to have several children to be assured of this support.

Environmental conditions, poor sanitation, inadequate diets, and a shortage of medical personnel contribute to health problems and high death rates. Part of the lower floodplain and most of the delta of the Ganges and Brahmaputra Rivers dominate the territory of Bangladesh. The land is generally flat, low in elevation, and subject to flooding from monsoon rains and storms that move inland from the Bay of Bengal (Fig. 6.13). The floods are an ever-present threat to

FIGURE 6.13
With low delta lands comprising most of its area, Bangladesh is subjected to frequent floods that take a heavy toll of property, life, and food supplies. (Faruque/Gamma)

human life, farm animals, and crops. The water readily becomes polluted and harbors microorganisms and insects that transmit disease, resulting in widespread illness. Poor nutrition also makes the people more susceptible to disease and contributes to poor health. The average person consumes only about 80 percent of the recommended daily minimum number of calories. Because rice is the principle source of food, the intake of protein also is inadequate. Treatment of those who are ill and in poor health is handicapped by a shortage of medical facilities and physicians. Bangladesh has an average of about 1 medical doctor for every 9000 persons. The consequence of this combination of conditions is one of the world's highest death rates and an average life expectancy of only 53 years.

Population Control Efforts   The high level of mortality is offset by even greater birth rates, however, and the alarming growth of population in Bangladesh continues despite government efforts to slow the trend. Those efforts have involved the distribution of condoms and birth control pills, sterilization, and the placement of family-planning counselors throughout the country. (Because of religious convictions— Bangladesh is an Islamic state—abortion is illegal.) The government has been severely criticized for some of its birth control measures and public support is not widespread. More than a million individuals have been sterilized in a controversial program that has raised questions about the use of unsanitary facilities, the urging of people to have unwanted sterilization, and the forced sterilization of some individuals.

The dissemination of information about family planning and birth control procedures is complicated by widespread illiteracy and limited educational attainment. Only one out of five adults can read. The government estimates that 60 percent of eligible children attend primary school, 15 percent attend secondary school, and 4 percent go on to higher education. These figures, however, are assumed to include young people who attend school only part-time during the year as well as full-time students.

The United Nations has estimated conservatively that the population of Bangladesh will grow to 141 million by the year 2000 and will reach 305 million in 2030. In view of present conditions in the country, how can that many more people possibly be supported? The urgency of effective measures to reduce birth rates seems obvious.

China

> China appears to have arrived at Stage III in its demographic transition since the early 1970s.

How has China been able to reduce significantly its rate of population increase?

Why has China's population control program been less successful in rural areas than in the cities?

Because the People's Republic of China is the world's most populated country, its demographic situation is particularly important. In 1987, when the world's population total reached 5 billion, China numbered 1 billion people. However, the country's leaders have implemented one of the most revolutionary family planning programs in modern time. Beginning in the early 1970s, the government initiated policies to encourage couples to delay starting their families and to have fewer children than their parents. Although successful in reducing birth rates, this program was followed in 1979 by a stricter one that encouraged couples to have only one child. Although they have not been uniformly successful throughout the country, the programs resulted in lowering of the average number of births per woman from 5.93 in 1970 to 2.66 in 1979 and 1.94 in 1984.

The Need for Population Control   When the government initiated its programs in the 1970s, the need for population control was obvious in China. An acute housing shortage, particularly in major cities, had been a persistent problem. By tradition, a son is obligated to care for his parents during their old age. As a result, three generations often lived together in a cramped apartment. The government's ability to clothe, feed, and educate the population was a growing concern. The amount of arable land per capita was decreasing with the growth in population. By 1985 the per capita arable land had diminished to only 0.24 acre and was expected to be further reduced to 0.19 acre by the year 2000—about half the world average. This meant that each acre of arable land in China would need to support 5 people at the beginning of the new century, and the pressure on the land would have been even greater if the earlier population trends had continued.

The advance of enormous numbers of young people into their child-bearing years provided further incentive for Chinese leaders to initiate the strict policy of one child per couple in 1979. As more and more of

FIGURE 6.14
One of the consequences of a high birth rate is crowded schoolrooms like this one in China. Governmental policies significantly lowered China's birth rates during the 1980s, however. (Charles and Judy Walker/Liaison Int'l.)

the children of people born during the baby boom of the 1950s and 1960s reached school age, educational facilities became severely strained (Fig. 6.14). In some areas, the ability to educate even one child per couple is questionable because of the shortage of facilities.

The 1979 Population Program   The 1979 program offered a variety of incentives to couples willing to limit their families to one child. Benefits were to begin before the child's birth if the parents signed an agreement to have only one child. The mother would be entitled to as much as six months of paid maternity leave. The couple also was given priority in the allocation of scarce resources, such as housing and milk, and might receive a small cash payment monthly until the child reached a certain age. Placement of the child in a day-care facility and school was another benefit. To further assure compliance, the government also imposed penalties or disincentives for couples that had more than one child. The parents were required to make a cash payment and might lose preferential assignments at work; they also might be passed over for bonuses and be demoted. In addition, the second and subsequent children in the family would not receive priority placement in schools.

China's population program has been more successful in urban centers than in rural areas for several reasons. Local governing units are responsible for the benefits and punishments; ordinarily urban governing units are wealthier and better able to afford the incentives than those in rural areas. The scarcity of adequate housing in the cities also motivates couples to practice birth control. The need for children to care for their elderly parents is diminishing in cities as pensions and old-age benefits become more prevalent. Another reason is the increased availability and knowledge of contraceptive devices in the cities. Although contraceptive devices are used widely throughout the country (nearly three-fourths of all married women of childbearing age use contraception), they are used much less frequently in rural areas.

Many exceptions to the government's policy of one child are allowed. A common one, especially in rural areas, is when the first child is a girl. In Chinese culture (as in others), there continues to be a strong desire for a son to carry on the family name and to care for the elderly in the family. In the stricter days of the one-child policy, the birth of a girl often led to infanticide in order for the parents to have a second child. By granting an exception to the one-child policy in such cases, the governing unit has reduced considerably the incidence of infanticide.

The policy of one child per couple was adopted to slow the birth rate and keep the country's total population from exceeding 1.2 billion by the year 2000. Although that goal will not be met (China reached 1.2 billion in 1990), the policy has had a major impact. From 1982 to 1990 the average family size decreased from 4.41 to 3.96 persons. China will remain the world's most populated country in the near future, but its rate of growth has been reduced significantly.

The United States

➤ Many authorities feel the United States has recently joined the small group of countries that have reached Stage IV and completed their demographic transition.

What evidence suggests that the United States has attained Stage IV?

How has the nature of population growth in the United States differed from that of Bangladesh and China?

The population trend in the United States has included enormous surges and declines in the rate of growth during the country's history. Immigration at times has accounted for a large percentage of the growth. Birth and death rates have fluctuated in response to a great many events and developments, including war, changes in general economic conditions, improvements in medicine and health care, industrialization and urbanization, and public attitudes and practices regarding families and lifestyles. A slowing of rates of growth that got underway during the early 1960s has progressed, and zero population growth for the near future is predicted by many authorities. In contrast to Bangladesh, China, and many other countries, the United States has not adopted a formal governmental policy to regulate its demographic increase (with the exception of immigration, which has been limited by legislative action).

Population Growth Prior to 1920 From colonial time until the 1920s, the natural population growth of the United States was supplemented to an enormous extent by waves of immigrants, for the most part people moving from European areas. The country's territorial growth across the continent provided an abundance of land available for settlement, and the federal government's generosity in distributing land to pioneers at little cost proved to be a great attraction for immigrants from crowded Europe. The discovery of vast stores of natural resources added to the appeal of the United States, as did the country's liberal social policies and labor shortages. Although immigration subsided during the Civil War, the numbers increased for several decades after that conflict and reached a pinnacle between 1900 and 1910 when more than 8 million people arrived from other countries. With industrialization well underway after the Civil War, many immigrants chose to take employment in rapidly growing eastern cities rather than become pioneer farmers or miners in the West. Regardless of whether they settled on the land or in the cities, the immigrants (usually young adults) tended to have more children.

The Demographic Transition after 1920 The decade of the 1920s was an important demographic transition period in the United States. For well over a century, spectacular population growth—boosted by massive immigration—had been underway. The growth had been tempered for brief periods by economic recessions and military conflicts, particularly

TABLE 6.3 Population of the United States: 1790–1990

Year	Census Count	Percent Urban
1790	3,929,214	5
1800	5,308,483	6
1810	7,239,881	7
1820	9,638,453	7
1830	12,866,020	9
1840	17,069,453	11
1850	23,191,876	15
1860	31,443,321	20
1870	39,818,449	26
1880	50,155,783	28
1890	62,947,714	35
1900	75,994,575	40
1910	91,972,266	46
1920	105,710,620	51
1930	122,775,046	56
1940	131,669,275	57
1950	150,697,361	60
1960	179,323,175	69
1970	203,302,031	73
1980	226,545,805	74
1990	248,709,873	74

SOURCE: *U.S. Bureau of the Census.*

the Civil War and World War I, but most years recorded increases between 2.0 and 3.5 percent—one of the highest levels in the world at the time. In 1920, for the first time in history, the nation's population total exceeded 100 million and more than half of this number resided in urban places (Table 6.3).

Significant changes were underway at this time. The country had emerged from World War I as the leading industrial power on earth. The growing dominance of industrial-urban America over agrarian-rural America would be the trend through many decades to come. European immigration, previously unrestricted, also experienced change. Immigration laws passed by Congress in the early 1920s placed a ceiling on the numbers allowed to enter the country and implemented a system of quotas for immigrants according to their nationality. This new legislation reduced dramatically the number of subsequent European immigrants, and the flow was virtually stopped by the *Great Depression* of the 1930s and by World War II. The depression and war also resulted in a substantial decrease in birth rates. Population increase slowed to the lowest rates in the nation's history; between the 1930 and 1940 census counts, the total grew from 123.1 million to 132.2 million—a mere 7.3 percent in ten years. Low population growth continued through the World War II years as well. The war not only stifled immigration, but also shrank birth rates as husbands and wives were separated and marriages were postponed for the duration of the conflict.

Postwar Trends   The termination of the war in 1945 was soon followed by an abrupt increase in birth rates that continued into the following decade and caused a surge in population growth. The now-famous **baby boom** of the postwar period had major social and economic ramifications, including burgeoning enrollments in the nation's schools and colleges from the late 1950s through the early 1970s. Now entering middle age, the "baby boomers," as they have come to be called, have contributed to an increase in the labor force and are expected to place a heavy strain on the social security system and retirement programs in two or three decades. In fact, the nation's social security system already is being stressed by the growing number of elderly people. With death rates generally declining through the past century, approximately 12 percent of the U.S. population is now more than 65 years of age.

The numbers of immigrants also have grown since the end of World War II, and actions by Congress have had an enormous impact on the nature of the immigration. The government's special admission of refugees from areas of political and military disruption, such as Hungary, Cuba, and Southeast Asia, has influenced the character of immigration during the postwar period. Of greater consequence, however, has been the revision in 1965 of the nation's quota-based immigration laws adopted more than 40 years earlier. While Europeans previously were the numerically dominant group entering the country, since the 1960s Latin Americans and Asians, aided by provisions in the new laws, have been the principal immigrant groups (Fig. 6.15). In addition to those legally admitted to the United States, over the past three decades several million other immigrants have entered the country illegally, most by crossing the long border

FIGURE 6.15

The varied origins of current immigrants to the United States are suggested by the participants in this recent naturalization ceremony. (Daemmrich/Stock Boston)

with Mexico. Since the mid-1960s, legal immigrants generally have numbered between 300,000 and 600,000 annually. Although this does not match the annual immigrant flow at the turn of the century, it represents about one-fourth of the current yearly population increase in the United States.

The renewed significance of immigration as a factor in the country's population growth has coincided with plummeting birth rates since 1960, primarily among the Caucasian majority. Reasons for this trend are complex; they include growing urbanization of the population, greater involvement of women in the work force, people marrying later in life, widespread adoption of alternatives to the traditional marriage and family lifestyle, development of the contraceptive pill, and the legal status of abortions. The crude birth rate has declined from 23.7 in 1960 to about 15 or 16 for each year since 1975. Without question, this has been the most significant demographic development in the United States over the past quarter-century, lowering the nation's rate of growth to about 0.8 percent annually. The United States now anticipates only slight change in its total population during the near future.

POPULATION STRUCTURE BY AGE AND SEX

➤ The age structure and sex ratio of a country's population are represented in an illustration called a population pyramid.

How does the shape of a population pyramid reveal important differences in the age structure of less developed and industrial-urban countries?

What are some conditions that may cause an imbalance in a country's sex ratio?

Two revealing characteristics of a country's population are its sex ratio and age structure. A commonly used illustration to portray these characteristics is the **population pyramid**, essentially a compound bar graph that assumes the general shape of a pyramid (Fig. 6.16). Each bar in the pyramid represents the proportion of the population in a specific age range, and the vertical line through the bars divides the population by sex. This illustration can be particularly useful in reflecting a country's demographic history, the impact of migrations, the results of population policies, and several social and economic characteristics associated with population structure.

Age Structure

The *age structure* of a country's population is represented by the general shape of the pyramid. For a typical less developed country, such as Mexico, the population pyramid has an exceedingly wide base because of the high proportion of young people in the population (Fig. 6.16). High birth rates in these countries have resulted in such an abundance of children that those less than 15 years of age usually account for more than 40 percent of the total population; in some countries, the figure is nearly 50 percent! However, countries with industrial-urban societies have relatively low birth rates and much smaller proportions of children in their total population. Adults, including those who attain old age, are represented in greater percentages than in the less developed world societies, which have shorter average life expectancies. The population pyramid for an industrial-urban country, such as Sweden, is therefore narrower at the base, somewhat wider in the middle, and less pointed at the top than one for a less developed country (Fig. 6.16).

The age structure of a society, as represented in a population pyramid, reveals the level of *dependency* in the population. Although there are obvious exceptions, people younger than 15 years of age and older

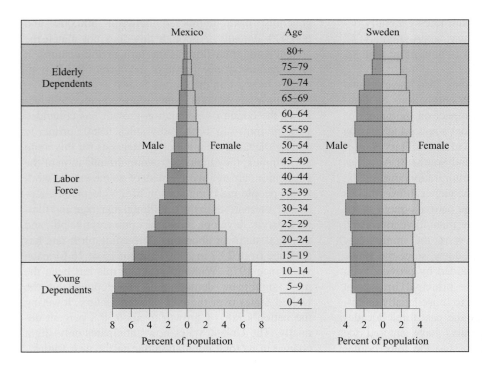

FIGURE 6.16

Population pyramids for Mexico and Sweden.

than 65 years are usually dependent on others (or on society in general) for their well-being and survival. Responsibility for the support and care of the youthful and the elderly rests with those in between who form the economically productive segment of a society. In the poorer parts of the world, the enormous number of children pose a dependency problem of overwhelming magnitude. As Table 6.4 suggests, most countries in Africa and a significant number in Latin America and Asia have more than 40 percent of their population comprised of children less than 15 years old. Because they are consumers of goods and services but are not old enough and mature enough to be producers, these children represent a tremendous economic burden. They need to be adequately fed, clothed, housed, protected, and educated for many years before they attain a level of physical and mental development to be economically productive.

While the proportion of children in the population of the world's industrial-urban countries is much smaller (usually less than 25 percent), elderly people significantly are becoming more numerous. In the United States, more than 25 million people (approxi-

mately 13 percent of the total population) were over 65 years of age in 1993; the "graying of America" has become a common expression of reference to this demographic trend. The increasing size of this dependency group is creating a need for more geriatric programs and health care facilities for the elderly and placing stress on retirement and social security systems (Fig. 6.17).

The ratio of the combined dependency groups (those less than 15 years old combined with those more than 65 years old) to the remainder of the population is called the **dependency ratio**. For example, if a particular country has 32 percent of its population less than 15 years old, 10 percent more than 65 years old, and 58 percent aged 15 through 65, its dependency ratio would be 42:58 or 72.4 percent.

Sex Ratio

In most societies, the population is nearly evenly divided by sex; males and females account for almost equal proportions of the population total. When a population pyramid reveals that the **sex ratio** is not bal-

FIGURE 6.17
At a residential care center for the elderly in Illinois, some of the residents are engaged in a group activity. This facility and its services are representative of many that help care for the growing numbers of elderly people in the United States. (Cynthia Hare)

TABLE 6.4	Dependency Groups, Classified by Major Regions and Selected Countries: 1993

Region Country	Percent of Population	
	Under Age 15	Over Age 64
World	33	6
Africa	45	3
Algeria	44	4
Nigeria	45	3
Kenya	49	2
Zaire	43	3
South Africa	40	4
Asia	33	5
Iran	47	3
India	36	4
Philippines	39	4
China	28	6
Japan	18	13
Latin America	36	5
Mexico	38	4
Cuba	23	9
Brazil	36	5
Peru	38	4
Argentina	30	9
Oceania	26	10
Australia	22	11
New Zealand	23	12
Papua New Guinea	40	3
Former Soviet Union[a]	26	9
Anglo-America	22	12
United States	22	13
Canada	21	12
Europe	20	14
Sweden	19	18
United Kingdom	19	16
France	20	14
Italy	17	14
Poland	25	10

SOURCE: *Population Reference Bureau.*

[a]In 1991, the Soviet Union fragmented into 15 separate states, most of which are now members of the Commonwealth of Independent States. Data for three of those states (Latvia, Lithuania, and Estonia) are included with Europe.

anced, it is an indication that demographically disruptive events have occurred in the area. Where substantial human migrations have taken place, for example, the sex ratio commonly is out of balance. In general, past migrations have involved more males than females. As a consequence, areas of out-migration have been left with a majority of females and places of in-migration have been characterized by more males than females. Frontier areas particularly have been notorious for their shortage of women.

Warfare also has been disruptive to the balance of the sexes. Combat casualties usually take a greater toll on males rather than females. An outstanding modern example is the population of the former Soviet Union in which females accounted for 55 percent and males only 45 percent of the total following the great loss of life during World War II. As a consequence of the shortage of male workers in postwar Soviet society, women necessarily assumed strenuous occupations and professional careers traditionally dominated by men. The agricultural labor force of the country, for example, numbered more women than men, and many Soviet women became physicians and dentists, occupations traditionally dominated by men.

VIEWS ON POPULATION GROWTH

➤ The contrasting interpretations of population growth by Thomas Robert Malthus, Karl Marx, and Ester Boserup reflect the range of views on this controversial topic.

In what ways was Malthus' interpretation of population growth quite pessimistic?

How did Marx see increases in population as potentially advantageous?

How did Boserup's interpretation of population growth differ from that of Malthus?

For centuries people have expressed concern over population levels. Even among scholars in ancient Greece, attention was given to the matter of population. For example, Plato established an optimum population for his ideal city-state, and Aristotle proposed birth control measures to slow population growth and limit poverty. One wonders how they would react to the demographic size of today's metropolitan centers and

nations and to a world population total of 5.5 billion! Since the time of Plato and Aristotle, the issue of population growth has been debated by a great many prominent people and authorities in a variety of fields. The predicted consequences of continued population growth and the suggested remedial measures cover a wide spectrum. To represent this variety, we will present the views on population of three controversial individuals.

Thomas Robert Malthus

Perhaps the most well-known and discussed views on population have been those of Thomas Robert Malthus (1766–1834), a member of the English clergy and professor who studied history, classical languages, and mathematics. After developing an interest in population, he also traveled in various parts of Europe to observe the adaptations of people to their environments and food supplies. In 1798, Malthus published his famous book, *Essays on the Principle of Population*, in which he revealed his theory on population. As indicated in the quotation of Malthus at the beginning of this chapter, the basic premise of the theory is that the world's population grows at a *geometric rate* (2, 4, 8, 16, . . .), doubling every generation, but food production is capable of being increased only at an *arithmetic rate* (1, 2, 3, 4, 5, . . .). The result, Malthus believed, would be mass starvation until population growth was checked and the remaining numbers could be supported by the available food supply. At the time of Malthus' *Essays*, the Industrial Revolution was just beginning in Europe, wealth was concentrated in only a small number of people, agrarian conditions dominated society, the opportunity for economic improvement was very limited, and poverty and hunger were widespread. Given these conditions that Malthus observed around him, his conclusions are understandable.

In explaining past variations in population, Malthus pointed out numerous "checks" on growth, including wars, famines, and epidemics. These checks served to bring the world's population total back in line with food production. If society was to avoid such checks in the future, voluntary measures would have to be adopted to slow the rate of growth. In an 1803 revision of his book, Malthus conceded that people have the ability to recognize the problem of overpopulation and voluntarily slow the rate of increase in their numbers. To reduce birth rates, Malthus urged delayed marriage; he opposed birth control.

As the Industrial Revolution blossomed and population growth in Europe decelerated during the nineteenth and early-twentieth centuries, Malthus' ideas generally were discarded. It was suggested that Malthus' conclusions were questionable because he could not anticipate increases in food production resulting from technological and industrial improvements in agriculture during succeeding generations. Furthermore, his idea that population increases at a geometric rate seemed to be contradicted by the decreases in birth rates underway in Europe following his time. A revival of enthusiasm for Malthus' ideas accompanied the alarming increase in rates of world population growth after World War II, however. Claiming that Malthus' ideas are fundamentally sound and, with slight modification, can be applied to the contemporary world, his supporters have been predicting dire consequences if current rates of population growth are allowed to continue. This school of thought is identified as *neo-Malthusian*.

Karl Marx

The German social philosopher Karl Marx (1818–1883), who was a central figure in the development of modern socialist and communist theory, provided a strikingly different perspective on population growth. Marx interpreted population growth as potentially advantageous and not as the primary cause of poverty and human suffering. The problem of poverty, he said, can be blamed on flaws in the capitalistic system: the exploitation of workers and the unequal distribution of resources (land, capital, and so forth) inherent in a capitalistic society. The solution, in Marx's view, was the adoption of socialism in which the goal is an equal sharing of these resources and the income obtained from economic production among the people. In a socialist society, Marx concluded, population growth would lead to greater production of economic commodities and, as a consequence, a better standard of living for members of society.

Where they have been implemented, the ideas of Marx have not held up very well. As comparisons of the leading socialist and capitalist nations confirm, socialism has not led to superior standards of living in the contemporary world. The two largest socialist nations of the twentieth century, the former Soviet Union and the People's Republic of China, have pro-

vided an interesting commentary on Marx's ideas. After initially embracing Marx's views on population growth, the governments in both countries eventually adopted family planning policies and advocated the use of birth control techniques. Furthermore, the abandonment of Marxist economic policies has been underway in the former Soviet Union since the late 1980s, and even China has adopted capitalistic ventures on a limited scale.

Ester Boserup

In 1965, a noted agricultural economist, Ester Boserup, suggested yet another view of population in her book *The Conditions of Agricultural Growth*. Whereas Malthus saw population growth restricted by agricultural production, Boserup offered the opposing idea that population growth can stimulate greater intensification in agricultural effort and, therefore, greater production of food. Agriculture can be practiced at either a level of low intensity, involving long periods of fallow separating times of cultivation, or progressively higher levels of intensity such as annual cropping and eventually multicropping (the production of two or more crops on a field per year). The greater food needs that accompany population growth are met, according to Boserup, by increases in the intensity of farming. She suggested that it is more realistic to view population growth as a stimulant of agricultural development than to accept the Malthusian interpretation of population growth as being controlled by agricultural output.

As Boserup herself recognized, there are obvious deficiencies in her theory. For example, in a given area the result of intensification in agricultural effort can be deterioration in the soil and consequent reduction, rather than increase, in the amount of food produced. Her interpretation has some validity, however, and it deserves examination as an alternative to the position of Malthus.

POPULATION AND FOOD SUPPLY

➤ The parts of the world with the most severe food deficiencies generally coincide with the regions of highest population growth.

What world regions seem to have both inadequate diets as well as relatively high rates of population growth?

Why is it difficult to determine the adequacy of human diets?

Those parts of the world with the most severe food deficiencies, as we would expect, generally coincide with the regions of highest population growth. The map in Figure 6.18 showing average daily caloric intake suggests the existence of a *world hunger zone* that centers on Africa and extends into southern Asia and parts of Latin America. A calorie is a commonly used measure of energy derived from food. The number of calories required daily to provide minimum nourishment for a person varies according to the gender, size, and lifestyle of the individual. The average female requires fewer calories than the average male; a person of relatively large stature requires more calories than a person of small stature; and a person who leads a strenuous life requires more calories than a person who

is more sedentary. So, 2000 calories a day may be adequate for one person while another may require 3500. With due recognition of these variations, authorities on nutrition have concluded that the worldwide average minimum daily requirement is approximately 2300 calories per person. We might conclude, therefore, that the population of countries on the map in Figure 6.18 with average daily caloric intake of less than 2300 have inadequate diets.

We cannot judge the adequacy of diets by calorie consumption alone, however. Proper nourishment involves a combination of carbohydrates, proteins, fats, vitamins, and minerals. The inadequacy of any one of these elements can lead to physiological underdevelopment or health problems. A common dietary pattern in densely populated areas and less developed countries is over-reliance on grains and other plant-based foods and too little consumption of meat and other

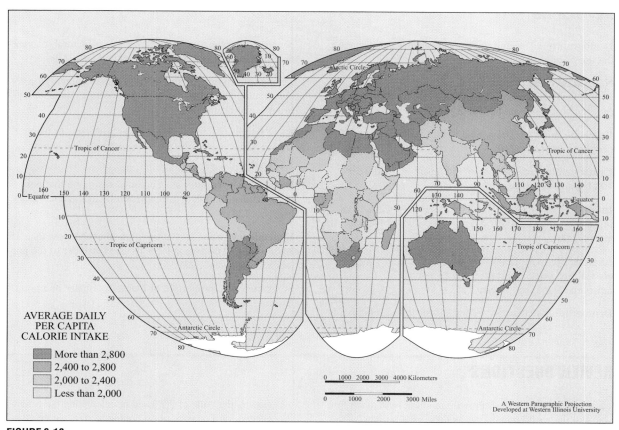

FIGURE 6.18

Levels of nutrition among the countries of the world.

animal-based foods that are rich in protein. Lack of protein in the diet results in retarded growth, susceptibility to certain diseases (such as *kwashiorkor* in children), and the delayed healing of injuries. Meat and milk often are too expensive for poor people to obtain, livestock herding is an extensive form of land use and not practical or possible in heavily populated areas, and some people avoid certain types of meat for religious reasons (such as the avoidance of beef by Hindus and of pork by Moslems). As a result, a large proportion of the world's population consumes inadequate amounts of protein and has a grain-dominated diet that provides an excess of starches. These people are victims of *malnourishment* even though they may have a satisfactory quantity of food and caloric intake.

As world population continues to increase, with a total of more than 10 billion inhabitants on the planet expected in a mere 40 more years, the adequacy of future food supplies becomes an extremely critical question. Does the earth have the capacity to increase food production at a rate comparable to that of population growth? If not, should we anticipate Malthus' scenario of famine and starvation providing a check on population growth? Or dare we hope for human inventiveness—future technological development—to solve the problem and perhaps raise living standards for all of the world's inhabitants? If people conclude that the earth cannot possibly support several billion more humans, will that cause them to accept more willingly birth control techniques to slow the rate of population growth? The answers to such questions are not easy, but the questions cannot be ignored. To deal with them, we need to become as well-informed on the situation as possible, make our best judgment of what will occur, and implement the wisest solutions we are able to devise.

KEY TERMS

Demography The study of human populations through the use of vital statistics. **208**

Natural increase of population The growth in total population as a consequence of the crude death rate being exceeded by the crude birth rate. **209**

Crude birth rate The annual number of births per 1000 people in an area. **210**

Crude death rate The annual numbers of deaths per 1000 people in an area. **210**

Infant mortality rate The annual number of deaths of infants less than one year old per 1000 live births in an area. **211**

Average life expectancy Based on current mortality levels within a population, the average number of years a newborn can expect to live. **211**

Demographic transition The changes through time in a country's birth and death rates and rate of natural increase that in theory accompany its modernization. **220**

Zero population growth (ZPG) The attainment of a stable population total as a consequence of the equalization of birth and death rates. **222**

Baby boom An abrupt increase in birth rates in the United States during the years immediately following World War II. **227**

Population pyramid A compound bar graph that portrays the distribution of a population by age and sex categories. **228**

Dependency ratio The proportion of people less than 15 and more than 64 years of age to the remainder of the population in an area. **229**

Sex ratio The proportion of males to females in a population. **229**

REVIEW QUESTIONS

1. At the present rate of growth, in about how much time will the world population increase approximately equal the number of inhabitants in your hometown?

2. How is the "rule of 70" used in calculating the time needed for a population to double in size? At an annual rate of increase of 2.8 percent, a country's population will double in how many years?

3. What continent has both the highest infant mortality rate and the shortest average life expectancy? How might each of these contribute to high birth rates for this region?

4. About what percentage of the present world population was the estimated total for the world at the beginning of the Agricultural Revolution? At the beginning of the twentieth century? At the beginning of the Christian era?

5. In what major world regions are the birth rates generally above the world average? In what regions are they below the world average? Why do families in agrarian societies often consider large numbers of children an advantage?

6. How can it be that some economically less developed regions have death rates that are as low or lower than those in the industrialized nations?

7. Why is there a good possibility that Africa, which leads the world in rate of population growth currently, will have an even greater rate of increase in the future?

8. What is meant by the conclusion that some societies have attained a *demographic transition*?

9. In the demographic transition model, what are the differences between Stage I and Stage IV? What are the differences between Stage II and Stage III?

10. What is zero population growth (ZPG)? In which stage(s) of the demographic transition model might there be ZPG?

11. Why have efforts by the government of Bangladesh to control the country's population growth been criticized by some people?

12. What tactics were used in China's 1979 program to reduce the country's rate of population increase? To what extent was this program successful? Why was it less effective in rural areas than in cities?

13. In what ways was the decade of the 1920s an important transition period in the population history of the United States? What have been the most significant demographic developments in the United States since 1960?

14. What is indicated about a country when its population pyramid is relatively wide at the base? What is indicated when it is relatively wide in the middle?

15. What problems are posed for a nation when it has a relatively large proportion of its population less than 15 years of age? What problems are posed for a nation when a large proportion is more than 64 years of age?

16. On what bases might Malthus' conclusions regarding population growth be criticized? What is neo-Malthusianism?

17. How did Karl Marx associate population growth and socialism? Have the world's principal socialist countries persistently adhered to Marx's position on population growth?

18. How did Ester Boserup associate population increases and agricultural intensity? What is a deficiency in her theory?

19. As a world average, what is generally considered to be the approximate daily minimum number of calories required per person? What parts of the world fall below this average? What important dietary ingredient is usually lacking in relatively poor, densely populated areas?

CHAPTER 7

HUMAN MIGRATIONS: REARRANGEMENT OF THE WORLD'S PEOPLE

*Give me your tired, your poor, your huddled masses
yearning to breathe free.*

—Inscription on the Statue of Liberty
in New York Harbor

*The Statue of Liberty has welcomed the modern world's greatest proportion
of international immigrants to the United States. (Michael Dwyer/Stock Boston)*

> The migration of large numbers of people through-out history has had a major impact on the world's human geography.

What changes have occurred in areas of human out-migration and in-migration?

How do modern migrations differ from those of earlier time?

The migration of people from one place to another is an extremely important geographical process. Migration obviously results in a re-distribution of population. The present ar-rangement of people over the surface of the earth (the topic of Chapter 8) has been influenced by past mi-grations, some of which have involved several mil-lions of individuals. We can expect other significant migrations and changes in population distribution in the future, but on a much more limited scale because modern countries regulate closely the movement of people across their borders. Migrations also have great geographic importance because they result in changes in the character of both the area of origin and the des-tination of the migrants. Because young adult males tend to be the most common migrants, the age struc-ture of the population and the sex balance are altered in areas of out-migration and in-migration. In addition, migrants introduce their cultural traits—language, re-ligion, technology, methods of using the land and other resources—into areas in which they settle. De-pending on circumstances, these traits eventually may be wholly or partly assimilated or they may become dominant in the new areas. In fact, European migrants over recent centuries have introduced their culture into vast parts of other continents and thereby caused much of the world to become Europeanized in character.

The urge to migrate undoubtedly is a character-istic that humans have possessed throughout their his-tory. Scholars have assembled a great deal of evidence to confirm that migrations of relatively long distance were not unusual even among the earliest humans. An-cient people must have engaged in migrations for a variety of reasons, including the need to acquire food, to escape unfavorable changes in their environment (e.g., floods, droughts, and the eruption of volcanoes), to avoid more powerful enemies, and even to deter-mine what was beyond the horizon. There can be little doubt that wanderlust and curiosity about unknown places have played important roles in the history of human migrations, although more practical motiva-tions are of greater significance.

That human beings are the most widely distrib-uted over the earth's surface of all terrestrial species is a consequence of migrations spanning hundreds of thousands of years. From the area of human origin in Africa, prehistoric people spread into Eurasia prior to the last Ice Age and reached the more distant Ameri-can and Australian land masses about 20,000 to 50,000 years before the present (B.P.). The diffusion of hu-mans over these vast distances obviously required a great span of time (and adjustment to many new en-vironments), but it was accomplished almost entirely by people on foot. Modern migrants have had the ad-vantage of more rapid and efficient modes of travel.

An enormous amount of human ingenuity and ef-fort throughout history has gone into the development and improvement of modes of transportation. From ox carts to jet aircraft, from obscure trails to multilane concrete highways—the improvements through time have resulted in a diminution in the effort, risks, dis-comfort, and time involved in moving from one place to another. In the past, a long-distance migration could be a frightful undertaking and one that could not be reversed easily. Today, at least in modern societies in which there is easy access to safe, comfortable, and rapid modes of transportation, the decision to set out on such a migration can be made much more easily. Transportation improvements also have led to more frequent migrations.

THE GREAT VARIETY OF MIGRATIONS

> Migrations may be classified into a variety of types based on their degree of permanence, the location of destinations, and the motivations of the migrants.

How are permanent and semipermanent migrations distinguished from one another?

How is distance related to international and internal migrations?

What are some of the factors that stimulate migrations?

A problem for anyone who attempts a systematic study of migrations is that they are so extremely varied in character. Migrations may involve individuals or groups of people, relatively short or long distances, and widely differing motivations. Some migrations are seasonal relocations, while others are permanent. Most migrations are undertaken voluntarily, but others have been forced on the participants. To illustrate this variety in somewhat greater detail, we will examine some of the most important ways in which migrations differ.

Seasonal and Permanent Migrations

To differentiate them from other types of human movements, it is customary to define migrations as permanent or semipermanent relocations of people. Thus, a person who undertakes a migration is engaged in moving to a new place of residence. The daily journey between home and work, a weekend trip to visit a relative, and a two-week vacation excursion are examples of human movements that do not qualify as migrations.

Although permanent relocations are most common, many people engage in migrations that involve a seasonal cycle. Good examples are migratory workers and livestock herders (Fig. 7.1). Farm workers who find seasonal employment in harvesting fruit, vegetables, or grain commonly move from one job site to another, following the harvest as it advances (usually poleward) over the course of the season. Livestock herders in some of the world's mountainous areas also migrate seasonally with their animals. Together with their herds, they move upslope in the summer to allow the animals to graze on high alpine meadows and then downslope as winter approaches to find shelter for the livestock in valleys. This ancient practice is known widely by the name **transhumance**. Another example of seasonal migration involves retired people in the United States and Canada who have acquired the nickname of "snowbirds" because they move in winter to southern states like Florida and Arizona to avoid the snow and cold temperatures, then return in summer to their homes in the North.

Refugees—people who flee from what they perceive to be a highly threatening situation in their home areas—often are involved in semipermanent migrations. Their initial moves to other areas are likely to be abrupt and with little or no advance notice. In order to provide at least rudimentary shelter and care while bureaucratic details are worked out for their permanent resettlement, refugees commonly are placed in crude

FIGURE 7.1

Migratory farm workers harvesting broccoli in Fresno County, California. These workers are seasonal migrants, moving from one area to another as the harvest progresses. (Cameramann Int'l., Ltd)

camps or holding facilities. The goal of many refugees is to return to their original homes after conditions have improved or to gain entry to a country that they find particularly attractive. In either case, lengthy delays usually occur and the refugees may spend years or even the remainder of their lives in the "temporary" camp. (See *Cultural Landscapes: The Refugee Camp*.)

Permanent migrations are those undertaken by people who, at the time, do not anticipate a subsequent relocation. In the past, when transportation was more difficult or more expensive, a greater proportion of migrations—particularly those that involved relatively long distances or relocation in another country—were truly permanent than is the case today. Of course, many migrations that are intended to be permanent at the time they are undertaken do not prove to be so; a subsequent change in circumstances, eventual disenchantment with the new location, or the emergence of a new opportunity may stimulate still another move. It is risky to conclude that any migration is permanent prior to the death of the migrant.

International and Internal Migrations

All migrations can be divided into two groups based on whether an international boundary has been crossed. **International migrations**, the movement of people from one country to another, often are migrations involving relatively long distances. (In fact, some

CULTURAL LANDSCAPES

The Refugee Camp

It is difficult to imagine a cultural landscape that exhibits such human despair and suffering as the typical refugee camp. Its inhabitants have been displaced from their homes or even their countries by such events as natural disasters, warfare, or political turmoil. As the accompanying photograph indicates, shelter in refugee camps usually is minimal. When first established, these camps often have no permanent housing, only crude tents. In time, with or without outside assistance, refugees may build for themselves more permanent housing, but even these structures tend to be rather miserable shacks. Services that are found in other human settlements usually are absent. Seldom do refugee camps have running water, and the only toilet facilities are likely to be open latrines. Health care and medical personnel are scarce. No formal education is available to most refugee children. These deplorable conditions are approached only in the slums that flank cities in the less developed world.

In the world today are more than 15 million refugees, with the great majority of them in the less developed countries. Africa, the location of the refugee camp in the photo, particularly has been troubled by refugee problems in recent decades. Political instability has characterized most of Africa since the 1960s. Warfare between opposing political factions and tribal groups has caused at times the flight of refugees by the thousands and even hundreds of thousands across national boundaries in a matter of weeks or months. Also, a persistent drought in the Sahel, a wide semiarid belt just south of the Sahara, has resulted in hundreds of thousands of refugees.

Such a great influx of people—in most cases unwelcome and unwanted in the host country—adversely impacts local and national economies and environments. It is common that the host country is unable to provide enough food and water to meet the needs of the refugee communities, and international aid represents their only hope for survival. When food is donated, often much of it is stolen and sold in local markets, causing agricultural commodity prices to be depressed and disrupting the economy in the host countries. Wood and dung gathering by refugees not only contributes to the barren countryside around their camps, but it also reduces the fuel available for citizens of the host countries.

Without question, the typical refugee camp is one of the most depressing cultural landscapes in the world.

THOUGHT QUESTIONS

1. Are refugee camps always temporary features, or have some been occupied for several decades? Can you identify any that have been inhabited by the same refugee group for more than a generation?
2. Are there any refugee camps or facilities in the United States? If so, how did they become established? What are conditions like in them?
3. Are you aware of any projects to raise funds for the support of refugees in the world? Have you contributed, or would you consider making a contribution, to such a program? Why or why not?

Displaced persons at Camp Nyacyonga near Kigali, Rwanda. (C. Sattlberber/Gamma-Liaison)

international migrations are even intercontinental.) **Internal (domestic) migrations** are conducted within the boundaries of a country and ordinarily are shorter in distance than international or intercontinental migrations. However, in a relatively large country such as the United States an internal migration between, for example, New York and California can extend over far greater distance than many international migrations. Internal migrations commonly are divided into local and interregional movements, roughly based on the distance traveled. Thus, a family's move from a central city to a new home in a nearby suburb would be an example of a local migration, and the transfer of an office worker from a midwestern city to corporate headquarters in New York would be an interregional migration. Although the terms local, interregional, and international migrations imply differences in the length of travel, the distances must be viewed in a relative sense because precise definitions would be unworkable.

The importance of distance in the conduct of migrations was recognized in the latter part of the nineteenth century by a British scholar named E. G. Ravenstein. Among a number of "laws" regarding migrations that Ravenstein formulated, the most commonly cited is that the number of migrants is inversely proportional to the distance traveled. In other words, more people engage in short migrations than in those involving greater distance. This law still applies today, even though transportation has been improved greatly since the time of Ravenstein. The friction of distance is an important influence on human migrations as well as other types of diffusion over the earth's surface.

Ravenstein's law also reflects the principles of *intervening obstacles* and *intervening opportunities*. Between the origin and intended destination of the migrants are often obstacles and opportunities that the migrants initially were unaware of or failed to perceive accurately. Once encountered, these obstacles and opportunities cause migrants to abandon their original plans and settle in a place that is less distant than their intended destination. The obstacles may be environmental features like a desert or a mountain ridge (Fig. 7.2), or they may be of a cultural nature such as travel expenses or restrictive immigration laws. In general, environmental obstacles were more important in the past when modes of travel were more primitive than the motor vehicles and airliners of today. As we shall see in later parts of this chapter, cultural obstacles—particularly immigration laws—have become more significant for twentieth-century migrants. The inter-

FIGURE 7.2
The rugged Sierra Nevada range proved to be an intervening obstacle for many California-bound groups of migrants during the mid-nineteenth century. One of these groups, the Donner party, attempted to cross the mountains too late in the year (1846) and became trapped in deep snow. Many members of the group perished, and those who survived are said to have practiced cannibalism. (Richard Rieck)

vening opportunities for migrants may include employment opportunities, favorable living conditions, and appealing social or political situations. When encountered, any one of them may coax a person to cut short his or her migration.

International migrations are of particular interest in human geography for a number of reasons. (1) They may have an important impact on the population composition and total of both the origin and destination countries. (2) As international migrants transfer their cultural traits to a new land, they may change significantly the culture of the host society. (3) International migrants may also find it necessary to adapt their way of life to a new cultural and environmental milieu. In choosing a place to settle in a new country, however, it is common for migrants to move into a community or neighborhood established by people of the same nationality who migrated earlier or to seek out an area with environmental characteristics similar to those they left behind.

Migrations Classified by Motivation

People who undertake migrations are responding to motivational factors that encourage, sometimes irresistibly, their relocation. Therefore, we might recognize different types of migrations on the basis of their participants' motivations, including escape from repressive political conditions, restrictions on personal freedoms, military conflict, overpopulation, or the desire to be reunited with relatives in another place. Ravenstein and many other authorities have stressed that the greatest number of migrations have been stimulated by economic factors, particularly the opportunity for more rewarding employment. The variety of motivations is great, and we can mention only a few of them.

It has become common to divide migration motivations into **push factors** and **pull factors**. Push factors are those that stimulate a person to leave a place or country. They are conditions (such as scarcity of employment opportunities or political oppression) perceived by an individual as negative, unfavorable, or even intolerable. In contrast, pull factors are those that attract a migrant to a new location. They are conditions or circumstances in the destination that are perceived by the migrant as favorable or attractive. Examples of pull factors are political and religious freedoms, attractive climatic conditions, and a low incidence of crime.

These motivations generally apply to **voluntary migrations** in which the participants are able to exercise a choice regarding their relocation. In contrast are **forced (involuntary) migrations**, which involve people being relocated against their will, such as individuals who are deported from their home country by the government because they are considered to be enemies of the state. Wartime conditions usually bring about massive involuntary migrations. In addition to the relocation of military personnel, civilians are forced to flee combat zones and become refugees. An example of a particularly horrible involuntary migration during World War II was the attempt by Nazi Germany to forcibly transport the Jewish population of Europe to concentration camps, in which eventually 6 million Jews were executed. In past centuries, the slave trade involved the forced migration of 10 to 15 million Africans to the Americas and significantly lowered the population in parts of Africa.

In the remainder of this chapter, we will examine human migrations that have been of major importance because of their scale or their impact on substantial parts of the world. We will not have space to deal with all significant migrations; there have been too many of them. Our approach will involve the examination of prehistoric migrations to learn how people originally spread over all of the inhabited continents. Then we will give attention to major modern migrations, as well as the circumstances and problems associated with them.

PREHISTORIC MIGRATIONS

➤ Prehistoric migrations eventually spread humans from their origins in Africa to all of the earth's continents except Antarctica.

How were prehistoric migrations conducted?

What roles did cultural development and environmental change play in prehistoric migrations?

Most scholars now believe that Africa is where the earliest humans appeared and spread over the landscape. Migrations conducted by early people eventually brought them to all of the other continents except Antarctica (Fig. 7.3). These prehistoric migrations were facilitated by the cultural development of early people, particularly in the skills needed to make tools and weapons and to control and use fire. Environmental changes associated with glaciation during the *Pleistocene Epoch* also were important to the spread of early humans to the more distant continents.

Human Evolution, Cultural Development, and Early Migrations

Anthropologists have found in eastern Africa the skeletal remains and even preserved footprints of hominids (primate mammals) that may have lived in the area as long ago as a million or more years prior to the onset of the Pleistocene. These individuals were bipedal (i.e., they were able to stand upright and move about on two legs), and they had relatively long arms and hands with fingers and an opposing thumb that facilitated grasping and toolmaking. In addition, their brains were relatively large and increased in size as evolution progressed. An early hominid called *Australopithicus* that may have existed as long ago as 4 million years B.P. is believed to have had a brain that averaged about 500 cubic centimeters. However, the brain of *Homo habilis*, a hominid species that lived during the early Pleistocene, averaged a little more than 700 cubic centimeters. (*Homo habilis* appears to have been the first toolmaker among our ancestors.) *Homo erectus*, which descended from *Homo habilis* about 1.6 million years B.P., had a brain nearly twice the size of that of Australopithicus but only about two-

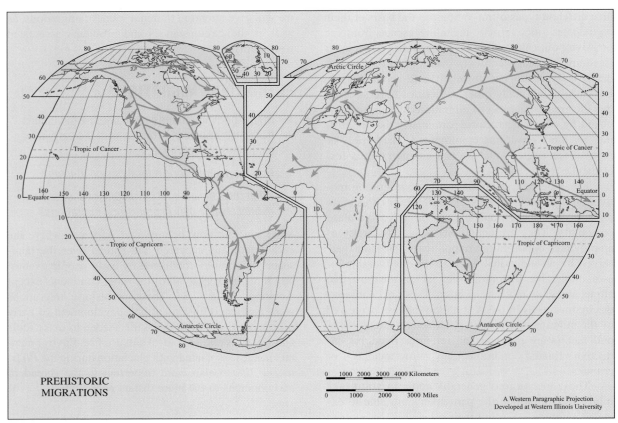

PREHISTORIC
MIGRATIONS

A Western Paragraphic Projection
Developed at Western Illinois University

FIGURE 7.3

Prehistoric people, over hundreds of thousands of years, spread from Africa to Eurasia and eventually to
Australia and the Americas.

thirds the size of that of *Homo sapiens*, the modern human (Fig. 7.4). An early type of *Homo sapiens* was the Neanderthal people, who appeared about 100,000 years B.P. and occupied areas from central Europe to central Asia. By approximately 40,000 years B.P., evolution had reached the point where *Homo sapiens* had attained the brain size and other principal physiological characteristics of the present human population.

The relatively large brain of humans enabled them to communicate in a complex language, to reason, to plan, and to create. By making tools and weapons, early humans were able to use their environments more efficiently and to spread into areas that previously had been uninhabited. The first tools and weapons, made of stone and wood, were replaced by others that were more refined as skills improved over time. The discovery of how to capture or make and use fire was an essential development for the spread of humans

into new lands. Fire not only provided warmth as areas with cold temperatures were occupied, but it could be used to preserve food, to cook food and make it more edible, and to improve efficiency in capturing game. The burning off of old vegetation in an area was found to improve hunting opportunities because grazing animals were attracted by the young and tender plants that appeared following the fire. Also, fire proved to be a means of confining game in a small area to facilitate their capture and of harvesting animals by driving them over cliffs to fall to their deaths.

Homo erectus began venturing from Africa into southern Eurasia about 1 million years ago and, after a prolonged series of migrations, occupied areas between southwestern Europe and southeastern Asia by 700 thousand years B.P. Although *Homo erectus* possessed crude stone tools and may have known how to use fire, it is certain that these people were restricted to the more temperate latitudes of Europe and Asia.

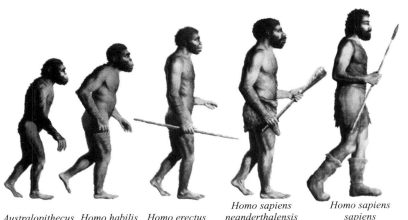

FIGURE 7.4

A comparison of the physical characteristics of selected homonids from over the past few million years.

Australopithecus   Homo habilis   Homo erectus   *Homo sapiens neanderthalensis*   *Homo sapiens sapiens*

However, the later Neanderthal people, who had developed a variety of more sophisticated tools and made wide use of fire, were able to range farther north and probably occupied environments on the margin of the most recent (Wisconsinan or Würm) glacial ice sheet. The alternating advance and retreat of glaciers undoubtedly influenced the area occupied by prehistoric people. It seems certain that as the ice advanced, previously occupied sites had to be abandoned and then were resettled at a later time following glacial melting and retreat.

Environmental Changes and Early Migrations

Among the environmental changes during the glacial and interglacial periods were substantial variations in the level of the world's seas and oceans. The level seems to have been about 300 feet lower during glacial time when a portion of the earth's water supply was locked up in the great ice sheets on the land. Under these conditions, less water was able to flow from the land into the ocean basins and seas to replace that lost by evaporation. The resulting drop in sea level exposed more land around the margins of the continents and created temporary **land bridges** between land masses that were separated at other times by narrow water bodies (Fig. 7.5). Particularly important for the first human migrations to the Americas was a land bridge formed across the Bering Strait that now separates Alaska from the eastern tip of Siberia. Although the spread of prehistoric people from Southeast Asia to Australia required crossing open water, the breadth of these water bodies was diminished by land bridges connecting both mainlands with nearby islands.

The initial migration of prehistoric people from the Asian landmass to the Americas and Australia most likely occurred between 20,000 and 50,000 years B.P. The subsequent spread of people from Alaska to other parts of North America and eventually to the southern tip of South America required a few tens of thousands of years, as did the diffusion of people throughout Australia and the islands of the Pacific.

By the conclusion of the Pleistocene's final glacial period—about 10,000 to 15,000 years ago—humans had migrated successfully to and inhabited all of the earth's major landmasses except Antarctica. For prehistoric people to occupy such a variety of habitats, ranging from tropics to tundra, a number of adaptations and a complex of cultural developments were necessary. Clothing and shelter needs differed from one habitat to another, as did sources of food. Survival in a new environment normally meant that familiar tools and weapons had to be redesigned or new ones invented and that new techniques of hunting, gathering, and preparing food had to be devised. Prehistoric people proved to be highly flexible and skilled in meeting the new demands and challenges as they spread from one environmental setting to another.

The Emergence of Racial Groups

➤ The development of human racial differences is associated with prehistoric migrations.

How are natural selection and genetic drift believed to result in racial differences?

Why is it questionable to classify all humans into only a few specific racial types?

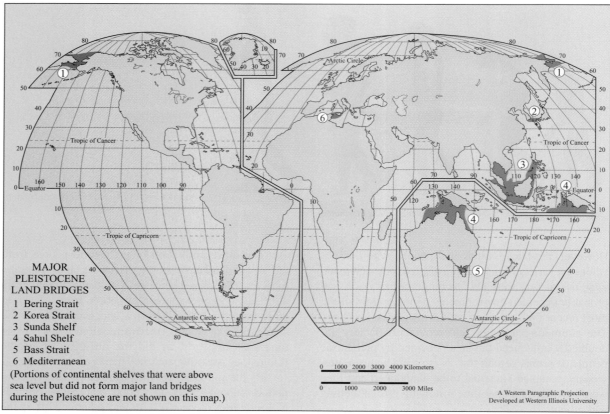

FIGURE 7.5

A lowering of sea level during Pleistocene glaciation formed land bridges that probably facilitated early migrations.

The migration to and prolonged occupance of new environments by humans during the Pleistocene also appear to have resulted in the emergence of distinctive biological characteristics that subsequently have been used to differentiate racial groups. These characteristics, genetically transferred from parents to their children, involve such things as the shape of the head, nose, and lips; character of the hair; color of the eyes and skin; stature; and blood type. Two processes, *natural selection* and *genetic drift*—at work in situations in which relatively isolated groups of people occupied particular environments during the Pleistocene—are believed to be the cause of racial differences. Natural selection assumes that some individuals in the group possessed biological characteristics that equipped them better than others to survive the environmental conditions of their habitat. Over time, these characteristics were inherited by succeeding generations while

other members of the group diminished in relative importance because they were not as well equipped to survive. Genetic drift involves the random or accidental appearance of a biological trait (a mutation) in an individual that, over time, is transferred genetically throughout the group. With genetic drift, the trait may provide absolutely no advantage to the individual in terms of surviving in a particular habitat, however.

By the end of the Pleistocene there had developed contrasting racial types in separated areas of the Old World. The major ones customarily identified and the core areas in which they apparently formed are the *negroid* in tropical Africa, the *caucasoid* in the vicinity of the Caucasus Mountains, and the *mongoloid* in central Asia. Each of these groups commonly is differentiated by a combination of biological traits. However, at least in modern populations, great variations occur in each trait (as in the gradations of "black" and "white" skin color) and many scientists now question the validity of recognizing only negroid, caucasoid, and mongoloid racial types. It is obvious that combinations of racial traits are complex, and it is quite evident that no "pure" races exist in the modern world. What matters most is that all humans belong to the same species, *Homo sapiens*, and have descended from a common source. People everywhere are far more alike than they are different.

HISTORIC MIGRATIONS

➤ During historic time there have occurred numerous major human migrations, each with its own circumstances, motivations, and impact on the involved areas of the world.

What were some of these great movements of people?

What motivated their migrations?

What are the geographically significant results today?

Migrations during the long period between the end of the Pleistocene and modern time generally were associated with conflicts between groups of people, changes in economic systems, deterioration of environmental conditions, and the formation and later disintegration of empires. Before the development of agriculture, the task of acquiring food required a seminomadic lifestyle; people in small bands (probably extended families) roamed the immediate landscape to engage in hunting and gathering. The initiation of crop farming, however, resulted in a gathering of people in areas that possessed fertile soils and abundant water to support agriculture, notably Mesopotamia, the Nile Valley, and northern China's Huang He (Yellow River) Valley. In a similar way, the growth and decline of empires, such as that of the Romans in Europe and the Mediterranean basin and that of the Mongols in Asia and Europe, stimulated migrations—both voluntary and involuntary.

Destructive and threatening environmental events, such as floods, earthquakes, and volcanic eruptions, have been the cause of numerous human migrations. Among environmental phenomena that have stimulated migrations, droughts particularly have been important. Perhaps the most significant examples over the past two thousand years have been the drought-induced flights from Central Asia of livestock grazing groups: Huns in the fourth and fifth centuries, and later the Mongols. Exploiting grassland corridors, these mounted (and therefore highly mobile) groups were able to conquer sedentary people in their path or force them to withdraw to other locations as they spread to the more humid lands of Europe and China. In Europe, a series of migrations resulted as the relocation of one group of people often led to the relocation of another. Collectively, these migrations came to be known as **Völkerwanderung** (literally: folk-wandering).

When the major European nations established colonial empires following Christopher Columbus' crossing of the Atlantic in 1492, there followed massive migrations from the Old to the New World. The Industrial Revolution, initially in western Europe and later in other parts of the world, also stimulated the movement of vast numbers of people from the countryside to towns and cities surrounding mines, mills, and factories. Many millions of people, together with their distinctive cultural attributes, reestablished themselves in new locations—even on different continents—during this period. We are able to characterize these historic migrations with greater precision than earlier migrations because less time has elapsed to obscure the evidence and, in some cases, reasonably reliable records were kept. However, information on certain historic migrations such as the slave trade and refugee movements is highly fragmentary. Our accounts of them, therefore, rely on estimates and consequential evidence.

From the Countryside to the Cities

Over the past two centuries the most common migration throughout the world has involved the movement of people from a rural origin to an urban destination. Rural to urban migrations generally have been stimulated by growing population pressures in the countryside and economic changes brought about by the Industrial Revolution. Western Europe, where the Industrial Revolution began, was the first region to experience rapid urban growth and development of truly large cities as people flowed in from the surrounding countryside. As other parts of the world—North America, Australia, the former Soviet Union, and Japan—became industrialized, their cities also rapidly increased in number and size as they filled with mi-

FIGURE 7.6

On the outskirts of Santo Domingo, Dominican Republic, this squatter settlement is typical of those occupied by many people who migrate from rural areas to urban centers in the less developed world. (R. Gabler)

grants from rural areas. The trend to migrate from rural areas to urban areas has spread most recently to less developed countries in which poverty and population growth in the countryside have driven people to the cities. Unlike the situation in industrial countries in which employment opportunities in the cities for new arrivals were reasonably good, the cities of the less developed world have too few jobs available to absorb successfully the crowds of new migrants. As a consequence, the burgeoning population growth of most of these cities has been accompanied by a corresponding spread of massive slums filled with hopeless, unemployed people. The result is some of the most depressing urban landscapes in the world, which continue to grow as impoverished rural migrants arrive in search of better opportunities (Fig. 7.6). We will give further attention to the migration of rural people to cities in later chapters of this book.

European Migration to the New World

The flow of Europeans to colonial areas and to former colonies in the New World has been a particularly important migration over the past two centuries (Fig.

7.7). About 65 million Europeans participated in this relocation, making it by far the largest intercontinental migration in the history of the world. All parts of Europe contributed to the migration, and nearly every European nationality was involved. People from throughout Europe joined the flow to North America; Spanish and Portuguese settled in Middle and South America, joined later by several other nationalities; British migrants were attracted to parts of Africa (particularly South Africa), Australia, and New Zealand, as well as North America; French settlers moved to northwestern Africa as well as eastern Canada and Indochina; and Italians migrated to parts of northern Africa as well as moving to the Americas in substantial numbers. Other groups involved in this great outflow from Europe included Germans, Scandinavians, Dutch, Belgians, Poles, Hungarians, Russians, and Greeks. These migrants transplanted their religions, languages, technologies, customs, and other cultural traits into the areas they settled, and they overwhelmed the native cultures in the Americas, Australia, and New Zealand.

An especially tragic consequence of European settlement in the New World was the death of millions of native people. Europeans brought with them a number of diseases, such as smallpox, measles, and malaria, that previously were unknown in the New World and against which native people possessed no immunity. The spread of these diseases resulted in a terrible loss of life among the aboriginal inhabitants of the Americas and Australia and New Zealand between the early sixteenth century and the late nineteenth century. Particularly devastated were the large native populations of Latin America. In addition to diseases, other important causes of death among the natives were military campaigns by the Europeans and suicides. A great many natives are said to have committed suicide rather than allow themselves to be subjugated by the Europeans.

The Slave Trade

Finding too few natives to fulfill their need for agricultural laborers in parts of the Americas, European colonists resorted to the forced transportation across the Atlantic of African slaves (Fig. 7.8). Generally accepted estimates place the number of Africans loaded aboard slave ships destined for the Americas at 10 to 15 million. The number who survived the voyage was certainly much smaller. Confined below deck under horribly crowded conditions and without adequate

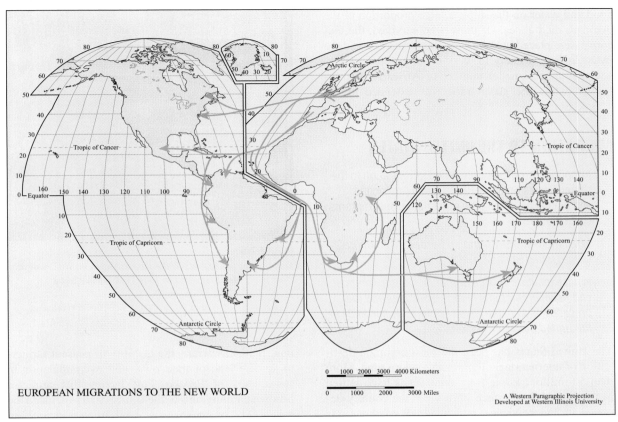

FIGURE 7.7
From 1500 to the early twentieth century about 65 million Europeans migrated to colonial and former colonial areas on the other continents.

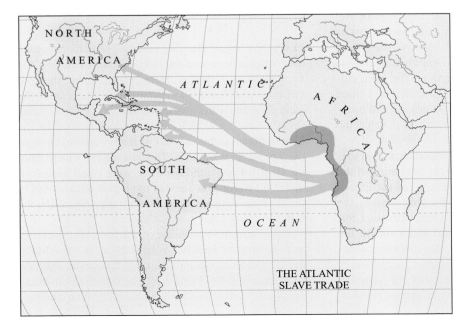

FIGURE 7.8
The slave trade across the Atlantic, mostly during the eighteenth century, led to the resettlement of millions of West Africans in parts of the Americas.

food and water on the ships, a large proportion of the Africans died at sea. Of those who survived, the majority were placed in slavery in South America and the West Indies—usually to work on sugar cane plantations. A much smaller number of Africans were involved when the slave trade was extended to the United States.

MIGRATION TO THE UNITED STATES

➤ Although Europeans dominated immigration to the United States until the 1960s, Latin Americans and Asians have been the most numerous migrants since that time.

What motivations prompted Europeans to migrate to the United States?

What explains the large numbers of Latin American and Asian immigrants in recent decades and the presence of so many illegal immigrants currently in the United States?

The United States has been the most common destination of international migrants in modern time. More than 50 million people from other lands have settled in the United States since 1776 when the country declared its independence, and hundreds of thousands more continue to arrive each year. The majority have been from Europe, but since the 1960s Latin America and Asia have supplied the greatest number. Africa also has been an important source of migrants to the United States, but, as discussed previously, most Africans were brought involuntarily into the country as slaves prior to the early nineteenth century. The American culture has been altered and enriched over time by inputs from each immigrant group. The great cultural variety that is so characteristic of the United States is a reflection of the different origins and backgrounds of immigrants who have helped develop the nation's lands and cities.

Of the 65 million Europeans who relocated in various parts of the New World after the beginning of the nineteenth century, more than half selected the United States as a place to settle (Fig. 7.9). This is easily the greatest single international and intercontinental migration in the history of the world and a record not likely to be broken in the future. This massive abandonment of Europe, primarily by working-class people and peasants, was stimulated by a variety of push factors. These included political and religious persecu-

FIGURE 7.9

Some of the immigrants to the United States in 1907 wait in "the pen" on Ellis Island in New York harbor to be processed. (Culver Pictures, Inc.)

tion, famine, warfare, the inability of peasant farmers to acquire land of their own, and overpopulation in some parts of Europe. Pull factors that attracted European immigrants to the United States included the availability of inexpensive land in vast quantities, opportunity for employment, religious freedom, and democratic government.

Immigration before the Civil War

Europeans began planting colonial settlements along the Atlantic seaboard of North America during the early decades of the seventeenth century, but they did not cross the ocean in substantial numbers until the early decades of the nineteenth century. Prior to 1800, fewer than 2 million Europeans had arrived in the United States and nearly all of them remained east of the Appalachian uplands. The vast majority were from the British Isles, although there were small groups of mainland Europeans such as the Dutch who settled in the Hudson Valley and the Swedes who located in the Delaware Bay area.

Between the beginning of the nineteenth century and the time of the Civil War, Europeans migrated to the United States in numbers that increased dramatically each decade (Table 7.1). The first major increase occurred during the 1830s when more than one-half

TABLE 7.1 Immigration to the United States: 1820–1990	
Years	**Thousands of Immigrants**
1820–1830	152
1831–1840	599
1841–1850	1,713
1851–1860	2,598
1861–1870	2,315
1871–1880	2,812
1881–1890	5,247
1891–1900	3,688
1901–1910	8,795
1911–1920	5,736
1921–1930	4,107
1931–1940	528
1941–1950	1,035
1951–1960	2,515
1961–1970	3,322
1971–1980	4,493
1981–1990	7,338

SOURCE: *U.S. Immigration and Naturalization Service.*

FIGURE 7.10

Immigrants from Europe, together with their possessions, are crowded aboard a ship destined for New York. (Culver Pictures, Inc.)

million arrived, but the flow increased to 1.7 million in the 1840s and nearly 2.6 million in the 1850s. Irish, British, and Germans were the most numerous immigrant groups during this period. In Ireland the very important potato crop was nearly wiped out by a blight in the 1840s, causing a famine that led to the flight of nearly half of the country's population. Many of the Irish who escaped their country's famine at that time chose to relocate in the United States.

Improvements in Transportation Europeans who crossed the Atlantic during the early decades of the nineteenth century usually found passage on sailing vessels that might require as long as six weeks or more to complete the voyage (Fig. 7.10). Often these ships were designed to serve as cargo carriers, and only crude provisions existed for the immigrants crowded on board. Disease spread readily among the passengers and death was not uncommon. During the long voyage, supplies of food and fresh water might become exhausted. Also, storms that might disable or sink the ship were always risks. Under these conditions, the decision to leave Europe for America was not for the timid.

During the middle decades of the nineteenth century the replacement of sailing ships by steamships was well underway, and this greatly reduced the time and risks involved in crossing the ocean. In addition, internal transportation improvements in the United States added to the country's attractiveness to immigrants. The Erie Canal, linking the Hudson River to the Great Lakes, was completed in 1825, and fewer than ten years later steamboats were in service on the lakes to carry passengers and cargo. Thus, at that time it became possible for immigrants and others to follow an all-water route from New York City to the fertile lands and developing cities of the Middle West. Railroad construction also was underway, and by the 1850s a network of tracks was in place in the eastern half of the country. To generate profits, the railroads soon began promoting the Mississippi Valley and areas farther west as places to settle (Fig. 7.11), often sending agents to Europe to spread the message among prospective immigrants. Constructing the rail lines over the countryside also provided a source of em-

BEST FARMING LANDS in the WORLD
FOR·SALE BY THE
ILLINOIS CENTRAL RAILROAD CO.,
In Tracts to suit Purchasers, **AT LOW PRICES.**

THE ILLINOIS CENTRAL RAILROAD COMPANY HAVE FOR SALE,
900,000 ACRES of the best Farming Lands in the Country.

The road extends from Dunleith, in the north-western part of the State, to Cairo, in the extreme southern part, with a branch from Centralia, one hundred and thirteen miles north of Cairo, to Chicago, on the shore of Lake Michigan—altogether a length of 704 miles—and the land which is offered for sale is situated upon either side of the track, in no instance at a greater distance than fifteen miles.

State of Illinois.

The rapid development of Illinois, its steady increase in population and wealth, and its capacity to produce cheap food, are matters for wonder and admiration. The United States Commissioner of Agriculture estimates the amounts of the principal crops of 1864, for the whole country, as follows: Indian corn, 530,581,403 bushels; wheat, 160,695,823 bushels; oats, 176,690,064 bushels; of which the farms of Illinois yielded 138,356,135 bushels of Indian corn; 33,371,173 bushels of wheat; and 24,273,751 bushels of oats—in reality more than one-fourth of the corn, more than one-fifth of the wheat, and almost one-seventh of the oats produced in all the United States.

Grain—Stock Raising.

Pre-eminently the first in the list of grain-exporting States, Illinois is also the great cattle State of the Union. Its fertile prairies are well adapted by nature to the raising of cattle, sheep, horses and mules; and in the important interest of pork packing, it is far in advance of every other State. The seeding of these prairie lands to tame grasses for pasturage or hay, offers to farmers with capital the most profitable results. The hay crop of Illinois in 1864 is estimated at 2,166,725 tons, which is more than half a million tons larger than the crop of any other State, excepting only New York.

Inducements to Settlers.

The attention of persons, whose limited means forbid the purchase of a homestead in the older States, is particularly invited to these lands. Within ten years the Illinois Central Railroad Company has sold 1,400,000 acres, to more than 20,000 actual settlers: and during the last year 264,422 acres—a larger aggregate of sales than in any one year since the opening of the road. The farms are sold in tracts of forty or eighty acres, suited to the settler with limited capital, or in larger tracts, as may be required by the capitalist and stock raiser. The soil is of unsurpassed fertility; the climate is healthy; taxes are low; churches and schools are becoming abundant throughout the length and breadth of the State; and communication with all the great markets is made easy through railroads, canals and rivers.

PRICES AND TERMS OF PAYMENT.

The price of lands varies from $9 to $15 and upwards per acre, and they are sold on short credit, or for cash. A deduction of *ten per cent.* from the short credit price is made to those who buy for cash.

EXAMPLE:

Forty acres at $10 per acre, on credit; the principal one-quarter cash down—balance one, two and three years, at six per cent. interest, in advance, each year.

	INTEREST.	PRINCIPAL.		INTEREST.	PRINCIPAL.
Cash Payment,	$18 00	$100 00	Payment in two years,	$6 00	100 00
Payment in one year,	12 00	100 00	" three years,		100 00

The Same Land may be Purchased for $360 Cash.

Full information on all points, together with maps, showing the exact location of Lands, will be furnished on application, in person or by letter, to

LAND COMMISSIONER, Illinois Central R. R. Co., Chicago, Illinois.

FIGURE 7.11

Advertisements by railroads, such as this one by the Illinois Central Railroad Company, convinced thousands of nineteenth-century immigrants to settle on the frontier of Illinois and areas farther west. (Culver Pictures, Inc.)

ployment for many new European immigrants, an opportunity that particularly attracted Irish laborers.

Attraction of the Frontier   Although the majority of European immigrants found housing and employment in East Coast cities, the rich farmlands of the Mississippi Valley and the timber resources of the Great Lakes region attracted hundreds of thousands of others to the interior. This was frontier territory prior to 1860, and land from the public domain was available for as little as $1.25 per acre. To land-starved Europeans, this opportunity was nearly unbelievable. After establishing themselves on the land or in the new towns of the frontier, many sent letters to friends and relatives back in Europe to urge that they, too, migrate to America. On their receipt, these so-called "America letters" were passed from one eager reader to another and often were printed in local newspapers. The letters usually contained glowing accounts of the land quality, descriptions of accomplishments by settlers, and suggestions for later migrants to facilitate their own trips to the American frontier. It is impossible to determine the precise impact of these letters, but they certainly were an important factor in attracting many European immigrants to the United States.

Slavery in the South   When a great need for rural labor was created by the adoption of tobacco and cotton as money crops in the South during the seventeenth and eighteenth centuries, slavery generally was adopted in the region. As a consequence, about 1 million Africans were brought to port cities of the South and sold as slaves. Most arrived prior to the beginning of the nineteenth century; in 1808, further importation of slaves was prohibited. The practice of slavery in the United States nevertheless continued until the Civil War, with descendants of the original slaves filling the growing need for rural labor in the South. Although most slaves brought to the Americas were from West Africa, they were a culturally diverse group that possessed a variety of languages, customs, and backgrounds.

The Rise and Fall of European Immigration

The American Civil War temporarily slowed the influx of European immigrants during the 1860s, but the numbers increased to new record levels in the 1870s and 1880s (see Table 7.1). Following the war, the farming frontier and the tracks of railroads advanced into the Great Plains. Those who settled on the frontier at that time were able to obtain essentially free land under provisions of the Homestead Act passed by Congress in 1862. By paying only a small fee to register their claim and by making subsequent improvements on the land, pioneers were allowed by the government to obtain title to 160 acres from the public domain. Later legislation increased the allowed claim to 320 and eventually 640 acres. This opportunity to become a landowner on the frontier attracted large numbers of European migrants to the Great Plains. People of a particular European nationality—Swedes, Czechs, Hungarians, Russians, and others—tended to

concentrate in a certain area and thereby form rural ethnic neighborhoods that might extend over several counties in the Great Plains. Many of these neighborhoods, now populated by descendants of the original group, have persisted to the present.

Changes in Origins of European Immigrants   A major change occurred in the origins of Europeans who migrated to the United States during the final decades of the nineteenth century and the early part of the twentieth century. As indicated earlier, people from Ireland, Great Britain, and Germany were the most numerous immigrants in the early part of the nineteenth century. After the Civil War, substantial numbers of Scandinavians also joined the flow across the Atlantic. However, by the 1890s these migrants from western and northern Europe were exceeded in number by ones from southern and eastern Europe, particularly Italy, Austria-Hungary, and Russia, and this pattern continued into the early twentieth century. Contrasts in the two groups came to be quite important. Those from countries in western and northern Europe, where the Industrial Revolution was underway, generally possessed more skills and a better education. The majority were Protestant, and English was the native language of most. The immigrants from southern and eastern Europe tended to be people of rural peasant stock. Most could not speak English, and a smaller proportion of them were members of Protestant denominations.

With the addition of vast numbers of southern and eastern Europeans to the flow, more than 8 million immigrants entered the United States during the first decade of the twentieth century (see Table 7.1). This enormous influx of people was a record never to be approached until the 1980s. The outbreak of World War I caused a major interruption in the movement of Europeans to the United States. Although the end of the war in 1918 allowed a resumption in the flow across the Atlantic, it was a recovery of short duration, as Congress in the 1920s adopted laws to regulate more strictly immigration into the country. The only prior immigration legislation was the Act of 1882, which restricted the entry of immigrants from the Orient into the United States.

Slowing the Flow: Immigration Laws, Depression, and War   Concern over alleged deterioration in the nation's society resulting from the massive influx of southern and eastern European peasants led Congress to incorporate a quota system in immigration laws passed in 1921 and 1924. This new legislation restricted the number of future immigrants from each country to a quota based on the number of people of that nationality who resided in the country in 1890. The laws clearly were discriminatory because they established higher quotas for future immigrants from the countries of western and northern Europe (because people from there were more numerous in the U.S. population in 1890) and lower quotas for those from southern and eastern European nations.

The new laws barely had gone into effect, however, when immigration to the United States was reduced sharply by the Great Depression of the 1930s and virtually ended during the years of World War II. As Table 7.1 indicates, immigrants numbered barely more than 500,000 for the 1930s and 1 million in the 1940s, levels that had been exceeded each decade over the preceding century. When the small numbers of immigrants are coupled with the low birth rates of the Depression and the wartime years, it is easy to understand why U.S. population growth was at a virtual standstill during this period.

With postwar economic recovery underway in the late 1940s and 1950s in the United States, immigration again increased as people fled from areas of Europe devastated by the war and escaped from countries with newly established communist governments. Because the group of migrants included many people with professional backgrounds and scientific training, this flow of Europeans to the United States during the years following World War II became known as a **brain drain** (Fig. 7.12). Although the number of European immigrants increased in this period, the total never reached more than a fraction of that recorded during the early years of the century. Furthermore, Europe's return to political stability and economic prosperity has caused the number of immigrants from that part of the world to dwindle since the 1950s.

New Immigration Laws and the Issue of Illegal Immigrants

The immigration laws of the United States have become much more complex over recent decades. Legislation that allowed Mexicans to enter the country temporarily as seasonal workers, the *Bracero Program*, was terminated in 1964 and was followed by a major revision of the laws governing immigration. New quotas were established in 1965 that allowed 120,000 immigrants from the Western Hemisphere and 170,000 from the Eastern Hemisphere each year. (Quotas for individual countries were abandoned, although a ceiling of 20,000 immigrants per year from any one country was adopted.) Also, preference was given to potential immigrants with relatives in the United States and those with occupational specialties and skills that were scarce in the United States. The total number of immigrants allowed was increased significantly to 714,000 annually for fiscal years 1992–1994 by provisions in the Immigration Act of 1990. This number does not include refugees; their admission to the country is dealt with on a separate basis.

The country's restrictions on immigrant numbers have been exceeded greatly since the 1960s, as millions of people have entered illegally. Most of the illegal immigrants are Mexicans, but there also have been large numbers from countries in Central America and the Caribbean, Taiwan, the Philippines, Iran, and Ireland. Many of these people, mainly Mexicans, enter the United States only temporarily to take jobs on farms during the harvest season (a legal practice for

FIGURE 7.12

Among European professionals who migrated to the United States as part of the brain drain were architects who brought dramatic change to the nation's urban landscape during the second half of the twentieth century. Their influence is reflected in New York City in these rectangular steel and glass skyscrapers, which some refer to as "glass boxes." (Peter Bennett/Viesti Associates, Inc.)

Mexicans while the Bracero Program was in effect). An increasing number of immigrants, however, have taken up residence in the United States in hope that it will be permanent. The exact number of illegal immigrants now in the country is not known; a conservative estimate is 10 to 12 million, but some authorities claim it may be more than 20 million.

Motivations of Illegal Immigrants Although a variety of social and political motivations are involved, it is clear that economic factors have stimulated most illegal immigrants to enter the United States and accept the risk of being apprehended. Deterioration of the Mexican economy during the 1980s and rapid growth of that country's population created massive unemployment. For poverty-stricken Mexicans, the opportunity to obtain jobs is greatly improved by crossing the poorly patrolled 2,000-mile-long boundary that separates the United States from their country (Fig. 7.13). Even if the illegal immigrant is able to obtain only a minimum-wage job in the United States, this income is substantially more than that earned by a typical laborer in Mexico and other less developed countries.

In addition to the lure of possible employment for the poverty-stricken, numerous other factors stimulate migrants to enter the United States without following legal channels. Recent political struggles and guerilla warfare in parts of Central America (particularly El Salvador, Nicaragua, and Panama) have resulted in a stream of refugees northward to the United States. Along the coasts of Florida in recent years there also have arrived numerous small boats crowded with people who are attempting to escape political repression and poverty in some of the Caribbean states, particularly Haiti. Some migrants enter the country illegally simply to rejoin relatives who earlier managed to cross the border undetected. Some Mexican women secretly make their way into the United States before they give birth to ensure that their children will be eligible for U.S. citizenship.

Despite increases in border patrols and surveillance activities, crossing the boundary from Mexico into the United States without detection remains relatively easy. Once inside the United States, it is not difficult for the illegal immigrant to blend into the population because of the heterogeneity of American society. Nevertheless, U.S. immigration authorities recently have apprehended each year about 2 million illegal immigrants, 95 percent of whom have been

FIGURE 7.13
Aliens illegally crossing the border from Mexico into the United States near San Diego, California, in March, 1992. (Inma Sainz de Baranda/Gamma Liaison Network)

Mexican nationals. The consequences for those captured have not been very severe. Most have been detained only a short period, then returned to Mexico where they soon may make another attempt to cross the border. Because it may lead to a deterioration in relationships with Mexico, the U.S. government has hesitated to implement more severe measures.

Reactions to the Issue of Illegal Immigrants U.S. citizens have had mixed reactions to the burgeoning numbers of illegal immigrants. Some see these immigrants as possible threats to national security, as competitors for jobs, as strains on the nation's welfare system, and as agents of change in the basic character of American society. In parts of the country, particularly in the Southwest and in southern Florida, the Spanish language already is more commonly used than English, and many schools now operate as bicultural institutions with instruction carried out in both languages (Fig. 7.14). In the past, other non–English speaking immigrant groups learned the English language and were more or less assimilated into the

FIGURE 7.14

This teacher in a bicultural elementary school classroom in Texas is using both Spanish and English languages in her demonstration. (Bob Daemmrich/Stock Boston)

American culture. The new wave of Hispanic immigrants seems to be in the process of breaking that pattern and forming a bicultural United States.

Many of the country's citizens do not view the illegal immigrants as real threats. They point out that the majority of those immigrants who find work must accept low paying, unattractive jobs such as dishwashers and vegetable harvesters that most U.S. citizens avoid. Further, many believe that the deep religious convictions and strong family ties that many Hispanics and other immigrant groups possess can strengthen American society. Citizens who are sympathetic to the plight of the illegal immigrants point out that the input of earlier immigrants has made the United States a great nation; the country has welcomed immigrants and refugees in the past, as the Statue of Liberty symbolizes, and many believe the country should continue that tradition. By granting these people citizenship and offering them the opportunity to become productive members of its society, the United States can demonstrate to the world its commitment to humanitarian principles.

An important development in the issue of illegal immigrants was the Immigration Reform Act, passed by Congress in 1986. This controversial legislation offered amnesty to illegal immigrants who had been living in the United States since 1981 or earlier if they would register with the government. The number of immigrants seeking amnesty fell considerably below

what officials had expected; only 1.35 million registered before the established deadline. Reasons given include poor communication to the immigrants about the program, the inability of immigrants to provide documented proof that they had been living in the country since before 1982, and the failure of the program to acknowledge that an illegal immigrant household might include some members who are eligible for amnesty and others who are not. More effective solutions obviously are needed to diminish the severity of the problem of illegal immigrants in the United States.

The Dominance of Latin American and Asian Immigrants

Since the 1960s, Europeans have been displaced by Latin Americans and Asians as the most numerous immigrants entering the United States. More than 80 percent of all U.S. immigrants during the 1980s were from Latin America and Asia, up from slightly more than 50 percent in the 1960s (Fig. 7.15). Latin Americans were the leading group for two decades before they were exceeded in number by Asians during the 1980s. Mexico and Cuba have been the countries of origin of most Latin American immigrants, whereas the Philippines and South Korea have supplied the largest numbers of Asians. The number of immigrants from Asia temporarily was swelled by nearly a half-million Vietnamese refugees following the withdrawal of United States forces from Vietnam in 1975. Also, the number of Cuban immigrants increased in 1980 when Fidel Castro allowed 125,000 to participate in the "Mariel Boatlift" to the United States. Other ref-

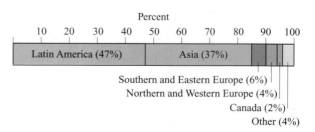

FIGURE 7.15

The origins of legal immigrants to the United States, 1981–90.

ugees from political and military turmoil, as well as poverty in Central America and Haiti, have contributed significantly to the stream of immigrants from Latin America.

Immigrants who have arrived since 1960 are concentrated in California, Texas, New York, and Florida. California has absorbed the largest number of both Asians and Latin Americans, which accounts for much of that state's recent population growth. Among recent immigrants, those from the Caribbean and South America are most numerous in New York. In fact, the community of Puerto Rican immigrants has been prominent in New York for several decades. Because of Puerto Rico's status as a territory of the United States since 1898, migration of people from the island to the mainland has been unrestricted. Florida's recent immigration has been dominated by Cubans. The concentration is in the southern part of the state, particularly Dade County where Miami is located. In addition to their large resident population of immigrants, California and New York have served as the principal gateways for others who have located elsewhere in the country.

The enormous stream of Latin Americans into the United States in recent decades, together with their usually high birth rates, has raised the country's population of Hispanics to more than 20 million (not counting illegal immigrants). This is the largest total for any minority group in the nation except African-Americans. With their high rate of growth, however, Hispanics are expected to exceed African-Americans soon in number and account for one-fourth of the nation's population in less than a decade.

INTERNAL MIGRATION IN THE UNITED STATES

➤ A variety of major internal migrations have been a distinguishing historical and geographical characteristic of the United States.

What internal migration patterns historically have been most persistent?

How can they be explained?

How have movements to the suburbs and to the South reversed earlier migration trends in the United States?

Americans have been among the most mobile people in modern time. The westward movement of the frontier, involving the opening of new land for settlement and the discovery of new resources for exploitation, brought millions of pioneers to areas west of the Appalachians. Often these people, like Daniel Boone, made several moves during their lifetimes as they followed the frontier westward hoping to find greater opportunities than they left behind. The nineteenth-century pioneers made their way to new locations by horse and wagon, river flatboat, steamboat, and railroad. Their twentieth-century counterparts acquired even greater mobility as the automobile and paved roads became common after World War I. Accompanying the improvements in mobility were rapid industrialization and the creation of urban-based jobs that attracted vast numbers of people from the countryside to the cities and eventually to the suburbs. Internal American migrations have become so common that in recent time an average of one out of five people in the United States has moved to a new place of residence each year.

Throughout its history, the United States has experienced two persistent internal migration patterns: a general westward movement of the population and a flow of people from rural areas to the nation's urban centers. We will examine these two trends as well as some recent reorientations in the country's internal migrations.

The Westward Movement

On completing its count of population at the beginning of each decade, the U.S. Census Bureau determines the country's center of population. As Figure 7.16 shows, the center of population has marched steadily westward since 1790 to a location southwest of St. Louis in 1990. This point on the map indicates that half of the population is east of and half west of a line of longitude drawn through the point, and half of the population is north of and half south of a line of latitude drawn through the point.

Attraction to the West The closing of the frontier era in the West near the turn of the twentieth century did not bring to a halt the relocation of Americans in that part of the country. The region's scenery and climate continued to attract easterners, including elderly people looking for an attractive place to spend their retirement years. More important, however, was the

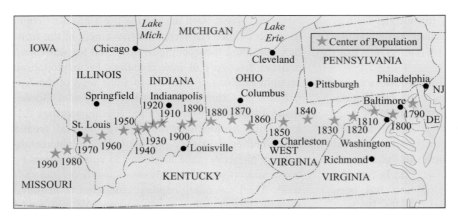

FIGURE 7.16

The persistent westward migration during the history of the United States is reflected in the country's shifting center of population.

lure of jobs associated with the West's economic development. In many locations, the opening of mines, the exploitation of forests, and the expansion of agriculture created new employment opportunities. But even more jobs were opened by the development of industries, primarily on the Pacific Coast. Factories involved in such things as processing, canning, and freezing food; shipbuilding; aircraft manufacturing; the assembly of automobiles; and the production of electronic goods required increasing numbers of workers from eastern regions of the country.

World War II proved to be a major stimulant of migration to the West. Because industries in the east were poorly located to provide military equipment and supplies for the struggle against the Japanese in the Pacific, new manufacturing establishments had to be constructed in the West for that purpose. Workers poured in from the east to operate these facilities, producing basic metals, munitions, ships, and aircraft for the war effort (Fig. 7.17). Also, many thousands of military personnel were temporarily stationed in the West prior to their deployment in the Pacific. After the war, as they returned to civilian life, many of them decided to settle in the West where they had found attractions while in uniform.

Destination California   Since the gold rush to the Sierra Nevada's western foothills in the mid-nineteenth century, California has been the main destination of those who have migrated to the West. For most of its history, the state has been perceived by Americans and others as something of a paradise. Its sunshine, beaches, movie industry, informal lifestyle, acceptance of people with alternative lifestyles and unusual behavior, and willingness to engage in social

experimentation have all been part of the state's mystique. These attributes, individually and in combination, have attracted people to California just as surely as have employment opportunities. About 1.25 million people moved into the state in the 1920s when most

FIGURE 7.17

The labor needs of industries created on the Pacific Coast to manufacture and maintain aircraft and other equipment during World War II attracted many workers from the eastern United States. With so many men in the military, the wartime labor force included a large proportion of women. (FPG International)

of the migrants were from the Middle West, and the number exceeded a million even during the depression decade of the 1930s. The depression-era migrants included many who were fleeing from drought-induced dust bowl conditions in Oklahoma and other states in the Great Plains, such as the "Okies" made famous by John Steinbeck's novel *The Grapes of Wrath*. Industrial expansion stimulated by World War II helped attract 1.5 million new residents to California during the 1940s, and the following decade saw 3 million more enter the state. Immigration slowed substantially for several years following 1965, apparently influenced by growing environmental and social problems such as air pollution, traffic congestion, and racial conflicts. Nevertheless, California at this time displaced New York as the most populated state and recorded nearly 20 million residents in the 1970 census. Since the early 1970s, the number of people entering the state has resumed its upward spiral, but the growth has been mainly because of California's attraction to foreign immigrants.

The Rural to Urban Movement

In a highly urbanized society during the terminal years of the twentieth century, it is difficult to visualize the United States as a predominantly rural nation. Yet that was indeed the character of the country prior to the early 1900s. More than 80 percent of the population was rural before 1850, and it was not until 1920 that the census recorded more urban than rural people in the United States. The proportion of the population who live in places defined as urban by the Census Bureau has increased to about 75 percent at present (Fig. 7.18).

Lure of the Cities The migration of people from the countryside to urban places has been associated closely with industrialization in the past. Jobs created by the development of new industry have attracted workers from farms; furthermore, some of the products of industry have reduced the need for rural labor by mechanization of agricultural operations. In the United States, rapid industrial development was underway during the latter part of the nineteenth and early part of the twentieth centuries, and a massive movement of people from the nation's rural areas to its cities occurred in the same period. The population of some rural areas had started to decline before the end of the 1800s, and by the middle of the twentieth

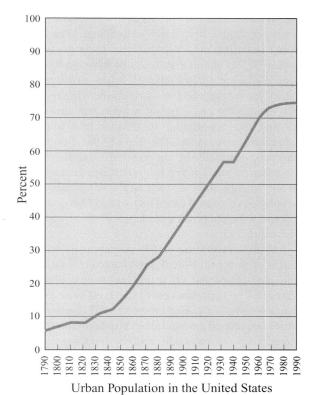

Urban Population in the United States

FIGURE 7.18

The rural-to-urban migration in the United States has contributed to a steady increase in the proportion of people living in the country's urban places.

century some of the predominantly rural states and regions were suffering a population loss.

The attraction of cities included more than just employment opportunities in industry. The clustering of large populations also created jobs in service occupations, and this employment category now provides the majority of American workers with their basic source of income. Cities also lured people from rural settings with their greater educational, recreational, and cultural opportunities. Well-equipped and staffed schools, prestigious colleges and universities, major-league athletic events, concerts, ballet, and theater were important attractions of cities. Some people felt the need to abandon their rural backgrounds and share in the excitement, influence, and power associated with life in the city. By the 1950s the depopulation of rural hamlets and villages led many observers to predict that such small places soon would disappear from the American landscape.

Suburbanization of the Urban Population The common availability of the automobile after World War I in the United States brought about a vast relocation of the nation's metropolitan population from central cities to nearby suburbs. It was no longer necessary for workers to live close to their place of employment in the city. The automobile provided mobility and the opportunity to live in less congested suburban communities. The flight to the suburbs was undertaken initially by the more affluent segment of the urban population, but it soon became characteristic of the middle class as well. As a consequence, the population of central cities increasingly became dominated by the poor, often made up of ethnic and racial minorities.

With acceleration of the migration to suburban places after World War II, the character of metropolitan landscapes and urban life underwent enormous changes. The suburban sprawl involved more than expansion of housing. Even factories, offices, and retail stores abandoned the central cities in favor of suburban industrial parks and malls, thereby reducing the need for suburbanites to commute into the city. The consequent loss of tax revenue by central cities has made it extremely difficult for them to afford needed reconstruction and maintenance of physical facilities as well as social services for their citizens. The decay of the physical city and deterioration in the quality of urban life in the United States during recent decades have been unfortunate trends, difficult to reverse.

In part because of the movement of people to suburban communities, most of the largest central cities in the northeastern United States have suffered a loss of more than 10 percent of their population during the past two decades (Fig. 7.19). A mere generation ago, these cities were counted among the most productive industrial centers in the world. Their subsequent congestion, pollution, budget deficits, racial friction, and crime have contributed to the out-migration of residents and reduced population totals. Another development that helped stimulate the flow of people out of northeastern cities (and the entire northeastern region) has been an industrial depression brought about by foreign competition and escalating production costs. The Northeast's idle and deteriorating factories have earned the region a popular nickname: the Rust Belt.

The migration of urban people to the suburbs was accompanied during the 1970s by a "back to the land" movement that led to a curious reversal in earlier trends. In some parts of the country, rural areas that had been losing population for a half-century or more rather suddenly experienced an increase in their inhabitants, as did some small towns that appeared headed for extinction a couple of decades earlier. The revived small towns usually were ones located close enough to larger cities so that they benefited from the

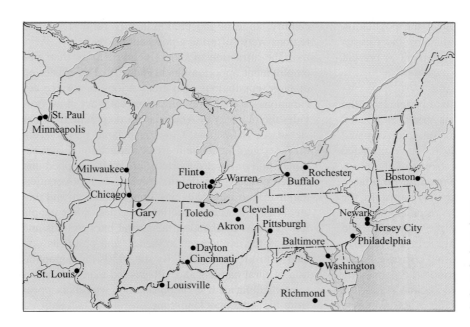

FIGURE 7.19

Most major cities in northeastern United States have experienced a significant population decline during recent decades as many of their citizens have moved to the suburbs and other parts of the country.

flow of people to suburban settings. However, some rural areas located well beyond the commuting zone around central cities also shared in the population growth. The gain in some rural districts could be attributed to economic improvements associated with their development of recreation facilities (e.g., ski slopes and lodges in northern New England). In most areas, though, the increase seems to have been caused by the in-migration of urban people who decided to exchange the problems of congested cities for a simpler and less stressful lifestyle in a relatively remote rural setting. This modest movement back to the land seems to have been a phenomenon generally associated with the social experimentation of the 1970s; it lost its appeal shortly thereafter.

The New Attraction of the South

Perhaps the most significant recent change in the country's internal migration pattern is a reversal of the long-term flow of people out of the South. For most of the twentieth century, the South experienced a net loss of migrants as workers and their families relocated in the cities of the North and West. Generally a rural region, particularly with a large black population engaged in working the land as sharecroppers after the Civil War, the South lagged behind the North in industrial development. The combination of industrial growth stimulated by the two World Wars and a simultaneous decrease in the arrival of immigrant workers from Europe created a severe labor shortage in the North that attracted great throngs of unemployed and underemployed Southerners. The flow involved white southerners from the hill country of Appalachia as well as African-American southerners from the worn-out farmlands of the old Cotton Belt. These people filled the inner cities of the industrial North and West Coast over a period of a half century.

By the 1970s, however, a "New South" had emerged. The relocation of industries from the North to the South, slowly underway since New England textile firms started finding more attractive sites for their mills on the southern Piedmont in the 1920s, suddenly accelerated. The energy shortages of the 1970s dramatically increased the appeal of the "Sunbelt"—the states of the South and Southwest where mild winters translated into lower fuel costs for mills and factories. This development, coupled with other attractions of the South such as relatively low taxes, wages, and

land costs, brought numerous industries to the region and a vast number of jobs to be filled. From towns and cities of the North, crippled by the energy crisis and closed factories, came a virtual army of workers in pursuit of employment in the booming Sunbelt. However, the region's appeal was diminished significantly by the petroleum surpluses of the 1980s that crippled the oil-oriented economies of Texas, Louisiana, and Oklahoma. Nevertheless, the South recorded a net gain of more than 4 million migrants during the 1980s.

An interesting facet of this new flow of migrants to the South is the participation of African-Americans, including many who had abandoned the region as recently as the 1950s and 1960s. Their earlier out-migration had resulted in a majority of African-Americans residing outside the South by the late 1950s. The net increase of the region's African-American population through migration since 1970 has been a surprising development that may soon return the majority to the South again.

MIGRATIONS IN THE OLD WORLD

➤ Major migrations, many of them involuntary, have occurred in Asia and Europe during the twentieth century.

What is surprising about the record of Chinese migration?

Why have major migrations taken place in the Indian subcontinent and Siberia?

What factors have led to major migrations in modern Europe?

We shall turn our attention next to major historic migrations in the Old World and focus particularly on those that have been carried out during the twentieth century. Although some of these have been voluntary movements to areas of greater economic opportunity or lower population density, the majority have been forced migrations and flights of refugees stimulated by wars and political changes.

The Spread of Chinese

In view of the fact that China has been the most populated part of the world for thousands of years, it is astounding that only a tiny proportion of the country's

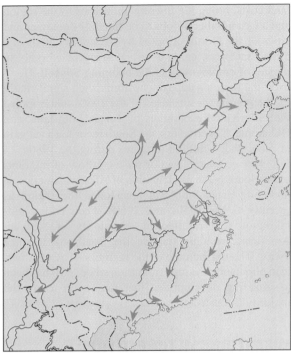

FIGURE 7.20

The pattern of internal migrations in China. Prior to recent generations, the principal migrations were southward to the basins and valleys in central and southern China.

FIGURE 7.21

The Great Wall of China. Constructed during the first millenium B.C. to provide defense against invasions by Mongols, the wall has become a contemporary tourist attraction. (Siyoung Park)

people have engaged in international migrations. Despite devastating earthquakes, storms, and floods; horrible famines; severe population pressure over large areas; and major political upheavals and wars, Chinese migration to other lands amazingly has been limited. Beyond the borders of modern China, only in Southeast Asia are there countries in which Chinese comprise a significant segment of the population.

Prior to the twentieth century, the main Chinese migrations were southward from the culture hearth that formed in the middle and lower valley of the Huang He (Yellow River) some 4500 years ago (Fig. 7.20). To the north and northwest were unattractive cold and dry lands, dominated by militaristic Mongols who lived by grazing livestock. In what proved to be an unsuccessful attempt to protect themselves from invasion by the hostile Mongols, the Chinese constructed an enormous barrier—the Great Wall—during the first millennium B.C. (Fig. 7.21). This amazing

structure, stretching across the landscape of northern China, also served as the general northern limit of settlement by Chinese until modern time. The warmer and better watered lands to the south were more attractive to the agricultural Chinese, and over the centuries they extended their settlements into the valleys along the Yangtze River (Chang Jiang) and eventually into southern China.

Although Chinese first penetrated Southeast Asia much earlier, they did not arrive in substantial numbers until the nineteenth and early twentieth centuries when European colonial powers were engaged in establishing a commercial economy in the region. Where the local labor supply was inadequate, the Europeans imported Chinese workers (as well as others from India) to fulfill their labor needs. Chinese workers therefore helped make possible the development of tin mining and the plantation production of rubber, tea, sugar cane, and other crops in the region. However, many of the Chinese in Southeast Asia eventually made their way into positions in commerce and banking and have come to dominate these facets of the region's economies. In nearly all Southeast Asian countries, Chinese are now a prominent ethnic minority; they comprise 90 percent of Singapore's population.

Chinese migrations beyond Asia generally have been for the purpose of providing needed labor. Only small numbers of people have moved to other continents, the largest coming to the Americas, where somewhat more than half a million Chinese now reside. During the nineteenth century in the western United States, Chinese immigrants commonly were used as laborers in railroad construction and mining operations as well as for domestic workers. The Chinese immigrants in this country are now highly urbanized, and most major U.S. cities contain a Chinese neighborhood or "Chinatown."

The most important twentieth-century migration by Chinese has been northward into sparsely populated Manchuria, an area acquired by China at the end of World War II and now identified as the country's Northeast region. Manchuria was an area of great interest to Russia and Japan as well as China in the early part of the twentieth century. Russia first opened Manchuria to commercial development at the beginning of the century by building a branch of the Trans-Siberian Railroad across the region. Soon the first wave of Chinese migrants—peasant farmers seeking to escape conditions of overcrowding on the densely populated North China Plain—arrived in Manchuria. The government of China strongly encouraged this migration during the 1920s as a means of strengthening its position against invasion by Japan, and by the middle of the decade the stream grew to more than a million immigrants per year. Japan was attracted by the mineral wealth of Manchuria, and in 1931 it was able to establish a puppet government in the region. (The Japanese called this part of the mainland *Manchukuo*.) After a brief interruption, Chinese immigration was resumed in response to the need for labor in the mines and factories operated by the Japanese.

With the defeat of Japan and the end of World War II, China reacquired Manchuria together with its mining and manufacturing complex. Continued development of the industries, mostly in the southern part of the region, has attracted still more migrants and formed a substantial population cluster. It is impossible to determine the total number of Chinese who have relocated in Manchuria during the twentieth century, but about 40 million is a reasonable estimate. Without question, it has been one of the largest migrations in modern time.

The Moslem—Hindu Transfer in South Asia

The separation of Pakistan from India in 1947 led to another of the world's greatest migrations—involving approximately 17 million people—in the years following World War II. Two parts of India where Moslems were concentrated, one on the eastern and another on the western side of the country, became the new nation of Pakistan. This political separation was based primarily on religious factors; it left India even more dominated than it had been before by people of Hindu faith. The new boundaries drawn between the two countries, however, could not separate neatly the Moslems and Hindus because the two groups were intermingled to a degree. As a consequence, nearly 10 million Hindus withdrew from Pakistan's territory and fled to India while about 7 million Moslems moved in the opposite direction from India to Pakistan in the late 1940s (Fig. 7.22).

This exchange of people between the two countries unfortunately was accompanied by a great deal of bloodshed. The political split served to intensify frictions between Hindus and Moslems, and migrants

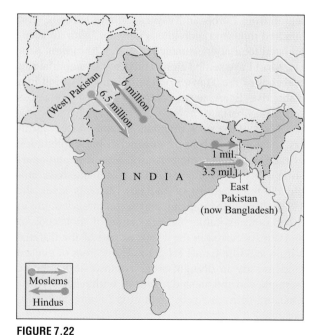

FIGURE 7.22

The migrations of Moslems and Hindus between India and Pakistan following independence.

became targets of hostile crowds as they attempted to flee across the border. Vicious attacks were made by both sides on some groups of migrants of the opposite faith, resulting in a great many injuries and deaths. Bitter feelings between India and Pakistan, based in part on these attacks, have continued to the present time. A later chapter in this conflict occurred in 1971 when East Pakistan staged a civil war and succeeded in breaking away from West Pakistan to become the independent state of Bangladesh. At that time India harbored about 9 million refugees from East Pakistan until they could safely return home after Bangladesh was established.

Russian Expansion into Siberia

Since construction of the Trans-Siberian Railroad near the turn of the twentieth century, Siberia has served as an active settlement frontier for Russia and the former Soviet Union. This vast region came under the control of Moscow when Russian explorers and fur traders crossed the Ural Mountains and made their way eastward to the Pacific Coast during the fifteenth and sixteenth centuries. However, very little settlement took place until completion of the railroad across southern Siberia provided modern accessibility and the opportunity for commercial development. Migration into the region from European Russia soon swelled to several hundred thousand individuals per year, with an accumulated total now estimated at about 20 million people. Most have settled along and near the mainline and branches of the Trans-Siberian railway, resulting in a distinctive linear arrangement of population across southern Siberia.

Most of the early migrants became pioneer farmers and livestock herders in Siberia, but exploitation of the region's enormous natural resources and operation of its new factories and power plants have employed the majority of the new arrivals since the 1930s. The last significant expansion of agriculture in Siberia, necessitating the relocation of thousands of workers, occurred in the 1950s as part of the ill-fated Virgin and Idle Lands Program. Huge areas of unused land, mostly in drought-prone southwestern Siberia, were plowed and planted in wheat. Within a few years, moisture deficiencies brought crop failures and demonstrated that the program was ill-conceived. Many of the workers on these lands returned to European Russia.

The resettlement of Russians in Siberia, where an extremely rigorous climate, isolation, and primitive living conditions must be endured, was not an entirely voluntary migration. To coerce people to participate in the movement, the government used such tactics as appealing to their patriotism and offering bonuses. Far worse was the government's practice of dispatching political opponents, dissidents, and criminals to slave labor camps in Siberia. Joseph Stalin, the Soviet head of state from 1924 until 1953, was notorious for exercising this tactic. This practice was discontinued soon after Stalin's death.

Migrations in Europe

A rather complex assortment of migrations, involving tens of millions of people, has occurred in Europe during modern time. As we have discussed, there have been persistent movements of people from rural areas to the industrializing towns and cities and from areas of relative poverty to districts with better economic conditions. The migration events in Europe during the twentieth century have been compounded by the two World Wars and their aftermaths. Both wars touched off flights of civilians to escape combat zones, and boundary changes at the conclusion of the conflicts caused the relocation of several nationality groups.

World War II was especially disruptive; more than 20 million Europeans were involved in migrations during the struggle, most of them involuntarily. The German military uprooted more than 10 million people from areas that it conquered early in the war and moved them to places where they were forced to work at producing goods for the war effort. Most of the individuals were able to return home at the end of the conflict. However, 6 million European Jews suffered unthinkable tragedies. Over the years of the war, they were killed systematically by the Nazis in isolated concentration camps to which they had been brought from various parts of Europe. This "holocaust" was Nazi leader Adolph Hitler's method of reaching a "final solution to the Jewish question," in other words, to "purify" the Aryan race. Some of the most infamous names to emerge from the war years were Buchenwald, Auschwitz, and Treblinka, three of the largest death camps.

Boundary changes and political developments following the conclusion of the war in 1945 brought still more migrations in Europe. Particularly important boundary shifts resulted in Germany's loss of territory to Poland and, in turn, Poland's loss of its eastern lands to the Soviet Union (Fig. 7.23). Both Germans and Poles fled from their lost territories, with Poles replac-

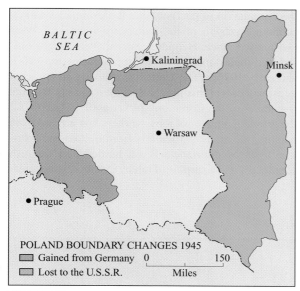

FIGURE 7.23

Changes in the boundaries of Poland at the conclusion of World War II resulted in the relocation of many people.

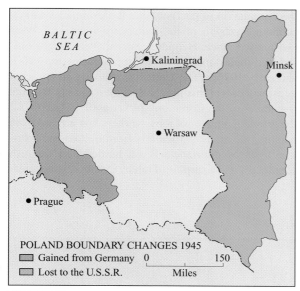
POLAND BOUNDARY CHANGES 1945
Gained from Germany
Lost to the U.S.S.R.

(The sectors of Germany and Berlin occupied by the British, French, and American forces promptly were consolidated into West Germany and West Berlin.) This political split of postwar Europe, including Germany and its principal city of Berlin, into communist and noncommunist segments was followed by an enormous flow of refugees westward across the border. To deter this loss of population to the West, guardposts, electrified fences, and minefields soon were installed on the communist side of the border to form what Winston Churchill dubbed the "Iron Curtain."

East Germany particularly was crippled because nearly 4 million of its people, including many with valuable skills and training, had escaped to the West by the end of 1960. Crossing the boundary in Berlin was relatively easy for refugees, so the city became something of a funnel for those fleeing to the West. However, this situation was changed abruptly and the stream of refugees from Eastern Europe was stopped in 1961 when East Germany constructed the Berlin Wall: the final hole in the Iron Curtain was plugged.

After a generation of containment behind the Iron Curtain, the people of Eastern Europe finally were successful in their challenge to communist authority. Strikes, demonstrations, and economic failures have brought about reforms that were unthinkable as recently as the early 1980s. Among several astounding developments in 1989 were the dismantling of the Iron Curtain and of the Berlin Wall, and the East German government's lifting of travel restrictions on its citizens (Fig. 7.24a and b). Within a matter of weeks,

ing Germans and Russians replacing Poles. The countries of Eastern Europe, which had been liberated from German occupation by the Soviet army, came under the control of communist governments in the immediate postwar period. The same thing happened in East Germany and East Berlin, the parts of defeated Germany that were placed under Soviet occupation at the end of the war by agreement of the Allied Powers.

(a)   (b)

FIGURE 7.24

The Berlin Wall (a) under construction in 1961 and (b) being dismantled in 1989. (UPI/Bettmann)
(S. Ferry/Gamma-Liaison)

more than 200,000 of those people responded by taking refuge in West Germany. The communist government in East Germany soon collapsed, and in 1990 West and East Germany were reunited.

Another major postwar migration in Europe has involved the relocation of several million **guest workers** (Fig. 7.25). This flow of people was in response to labor shortages created by rapid economic expansion in several northwestern European countries, particularly after organization of the European Economic Community (Common Market) in 1958. Stimulated by the elimination of tariffs within the Common Market, economic growth in the member countries of West Germany, France, Belgium, and the Netherlands outstripped their domestic labor supply during the 1960s and early 1970s. (The United Kingdom also attracted guest workers at this time, although it did not become a member of the Common Market until 1973.) To fill the growing number of jobs, workers first arrived from neighboring areas, particularly from Ireland and countries in the Mediterranean Basin, burdened by sluggish economies and a surplus of labor. Eventually this great

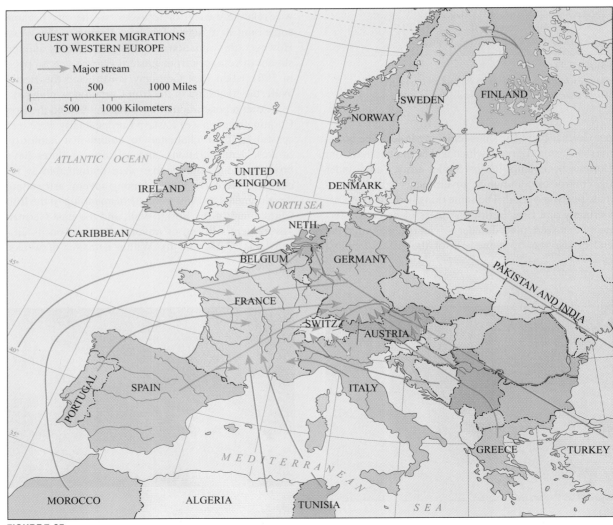

FIGURE 7.25
The migrations of guest workers to countries in northwestern Europe.

influx of guest workers included many from Asia, especially India, Pakistan, and Turkey, and from North Africa.

The settlement of these people in parts of Europe has led to some serious social problems. Young men comprised the bulk of the guest workers, and those with families usually left them behind when they migrated. Most often they regarded their relocation as a temporary measure and expected to return after they accumulated adequate savings or when economic conditions improved at home. However, most workers have remained permanently in the part of Europe where they found employment, living in low-quality housing and forming ethnic neighborhoods in the industrial cities. Some have had their families join them, but others (often after years of separation) have abandoned their wives and children left behind. Another problem has been cultural friction and hostility between local people and guest workers. In Germany, which has attracted several million foreign workers, demonstrations and acts of violence against them have become matters of great national concern (Fig. 7.26).

Israel: The Gathering of Jews

By action of the United Nations, the present country of Israel was created in 1948 to serve as a homeland for the world's Jews. This was accomplished by partitioning the area of Palestine, which had been administered between 1919 and 1948 by the United Kingdom under mandate authority issued by the League of Nations. For quite some time the British had favored

FIGURE 7.26

A 1992 protest in Germany against the terrorist activities directed toward foreign workers by neo-Nazis. (Mike Schroder/Matrix)

the establishment of a homeland for Jews in Palestine and had encouraged Jewish migration to the area even prior to World War II. When the war ended, other world powers—particularly the United States and France—joined with the British in support of the idea, partly in reaction to the horrible slaughter of millions of European Jews in concentration camps operated by Nazi Germany during the war.

After the formation of Israel, immigration of Jews to the new country increased from a trickle to a major stream. At first, European Jews predominated among the immigrants, but eventually the flow included people from the Americas, Africa, and Asia. Even Jews from the Soviet Union and its successor republics, long prevented from emigrating by the communist government, recently have been moving to Israel by the thousands. Many of the immigrants have been highly skilled and well-educated people who have played important roles in developing Israel into a modern state with commercial agriculture based on extensive irrigation, sophisticated industries, and a high standard of living.

In total, more than 2 million Jews have relocated to Israel. Although this number is relatively small in comparison with other international migrations we have examined in this chapter, the consequences of the creation of Israel and the influx of Jewish immigrants have been enormously important. Adjacent to Israel are the Islamic nations of Egypt, Jordan, and Syria, as well as Lebanon (which is approximately three-quarters Islamic and one-quarter Christian), and all have been a threat to Israel's survival. The hostilities between Israel and these countries have included terrorism, guerrilla-style attacks, and periods of total warfare. With its skilled population, industrial strength, and support by the United States, Israel successfully has defended itself and even has captured and occupied parts of the neighboring Arab countries (Fig. 7.27). Its occupation of these lands has further intensified the hostilities.

The conflict has been fueled particularly by bitterness among Palestinian Arabs associated with their withdrawal from lands that became Israeli territory in 1948. (Not all Arabs fled; some chose to remain and live as a minority within Israel.) To provide basic accommodations for those who became refugees, the United Nations established camps in areas on the margin of Israel such as the Gaza Strip and the West Bank. Originally intended to be temporary quarters, these camps now have been occupied for more than 40 years by Palestinian refugees and their descendants. To complicate matters, areas containing the camps were captured by Israel during the war of 1967. Violent demonstrations by inhabitants of the camps and alleged use of excessive force by Israeli soldiers to control the demonstrators have been controversial actions in this extremely sensitive situation.

There are nearly two and one-half million Palestinian refugees in the Middle East region at the present, most are deeply resentful of Israel and cling to the hope that future developments will allow them to return to their original homeland. Dedicated to the recovery of lands controlled by Israel, the Palestine Liberation Organization (PLO) has emerged as a quasi-government for the displaced Palestinians. Negotiations between Israel and the PLO, initiated in 1993, have resulted in the establishment of Palestinian sovereignty over the Gaza Strip and Jericho, a city on the West Bank.

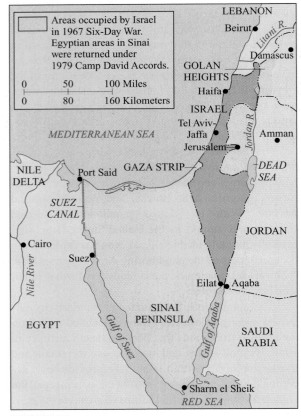

FIGURE 7.27

Areas occupied by Israel in 1967. The Sinai area was returned to Egypt in 1979 as part of the Camp David Accords.

THE MODERN REFUGEE DILEMMA

> The millions of current refugees in various parts of the world represent a serious migration issue that confronts the people of all nations.

Where are the largest numbers of refugees now located?

What circumstances caused them to flee their homelands?

Why should people of all nations be concerned?

Since the time of World War I, the vast majority of the migrants in the world have been refugees—people fleeing from warfare, political oppression, economic chaos, environmental deterioration, or some other threat to their lives or well-being in their homelands. Current refugees, estimated to total more than 15 million, are present in all of the inhabited continents, but they are concentrated especially in Asia and Africa. The United States in recent years has also absorbed a substantial number of Southeast Asian and Latin American refugees. However, as Figure 7.28 and the following list will confirm, these two groups are relatively minor in size.

1. Afghans have comprised the largest group of recent refugees. Civil war and the invasion of their country by Soviet military forces in 1979 to prevent an overthrow of the Marxist government caused nearly 6 million Afghans to flee to neighboring Pakistan and Iran. With the Soviets withdrawing from Afghanistan in 1989 and a coalition of rebel forces gaining control of the government in 1992, many of the refugees began returning home.

2. Palestinians have comprised one of the world's largest refugee groups for nearly a half-century; they currently number nearly 2.5 million. As we described in the previous section, they occupy refugee camps in Israeli-occupied territories and are scattered among Moslem countries of Southwest Asia and North Africa.

3. There are many refugee groups in Africa, including more than 1 million Ethiopians, about one-third of a million Sudanese, and a similar number of Somalians in the eastern Sahara Desert and the adjacent "horn" region of eastern Africa. Severe environmental deterioration along the southern margin of the Sahara, ideological and religious conflict, and civil war are

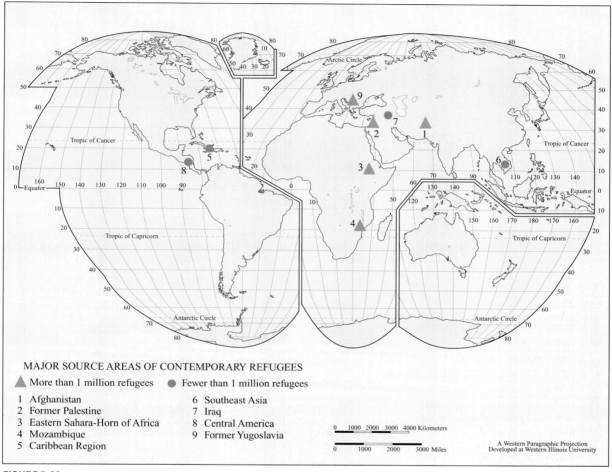

MAJOR SOURCE AREAS OF CONTEMPORARY REFUGEES

▲ More than 1 million refugees ● Fewer than 1 million refugees

1 Afghanistan
2 Former Palestine
3 Eastern Sahara-Horn of Africa
4 Mozambique
5 Caribbean Region

6 Southeast Asia
7 Iraq
8 Central America
9 Former Yugoslavia

0   1000 2000 3000 4000 Kilometers
0   1000 2000 3000 Miles

A Western Paragraphic Projection
Developed at Western Illinois University

FIGURE 7.28
Major source areas of contemporary refugees.

responsible for the terrible refugee situation in these areas. Starvation is routine in the refugee camps of this region.

4. Another major refugee group in Africa is made up of the 1.25 million natives of Mozambique who have fled their country to escape civil war and brutal attacks on citizens. They now occupy primitive camps in neighboring countries (most are in Malawi) and face starvation on a daily basis.

5. Nearly a million Haitians have become refugees from their poverty-stricken and politically unstable country in recent years. Although many have crossed the boundary and made their way into the adjacent Dominican Repub-

lic, nearly half of all Haitian refugees have reached the United States—usually crowded aboard small dilapidated boats that they have managed to sail to Florida. The U.S. government in 1992 initiated a controversial policy of intercepting the boats and returning their passengers to Haiti.

6. In Southeast Asia there are nearly one-half million refugees, mostly from Cambodia but including more than 125,000 from Vietnam. The desperate withdrawal of South Vietnamese from their homeland at the conclusion of the Vietnam War attracted the attention of the world; jammed into pitiful vessels to flee by water, they came to be called **boat people**.

Probably thousands failed to survive the voyages to Hong Kong, the Philippines, and other countries in the vicinity. Nearly all of the Cambodian refugees fled to neighboring Thailand. Their motivation was to escape the massive slaughter of civilians by soldiers of the Pol Pot regime and the invasion of their country by Vietnamese military units. The Vietnamese have withdrawn recently, leaving the future of Cambodia's government in doubt.

7. Perhaps as many as three-quarters of a million Kurdish refugees have been driven out of northern Iraq by Saddam Hussein's military forces since 1990. An ethnic minority in eastern Turkey and northwestern Iran as well as northern Iraq, the Kurds have long sought the establishment of an independent Kurdistan in the region. Their brutal treatment by Saddam Hussein led to a temporary intervention in 1991 by U.S. military forces to protect them from further attack.

8. During the 1980s, military engagements between government and rebel forces in the Central American countries of Nicaragua and El Salvador, as well as widespread poverty in the region, led to the flight of about one-quarter of a million refugees. Although economic conditions remain abysmal, the political and military crises in Central America subsided somewhat by the early 1990s.

9. Much of the world's attention since late 1992 has been focused on the civil war and political fragmentation of Yugoslavia, a former communist state populated by several mutually hostile ethnic groups. By the end of 1993, the estimated number of refugees from hostilities reached 2.5 million. The situation at that time was still volatile and many more refugees were expected to flee. In all likelihood, five or six small independent states eventually will emerge from the disintegration of Yugoslavia.

This list and the information in Figure 7.28 will become out of date quickly. The political, military, and environmental events that lead to flights of refugees occur all too frequently.

From a global standpoint, the human migrations that pose the most serious problems for the present and near future are (1) those involving groups of refugees, and (2) those being carried out by massive numbers of rural people who are relocating in the urban centers of the less developed world. The largest refugee groups, as we have noted, also are mostly concentrated in less developed regions—especially Asia and Africa. In those locations the refugees commonly occupy temporary camps that lack the most basic facilities and are desperately short of food. Developed countries have been willing to accept only a small proportion of the world's refugees as permanent residents and are unlikely to open their borders to significantly greater numbers. Often the refugee camps must rely on the United Nations, religious groups, various welfare agencies, and even individual volunteers for food, shelter, and medical care. Hampered by inadequate funds, too few workers, and sometimes political barriers, these sources of help are unable to fulfill even a fraction of the needs. Living conditions are only slightly better in the urban slums and shantytowns occupied by most rural-to-urban migrants in the countries of the less developed world. We will examine the circumstances of these migrants more closely in Chapter 13.

KEY TERMS

Transhumance   The movement of herders with their livestock to seasonal grazing lands, usually alpine pastures in summer and valley locations in the winter.   **239**

Refugees   People who flee their homelands because of conditions (often political or environmental) that they perceive to be threatening to their personal safety.   **239**

International migrations   Those migrations that involve the crossing of a border separating countries.   **239**

Internal (domestic) migrations   Those migrations conducted within the territory of a single country.   **242**

Push factors   Conditions or circumstances in a place that stimulate a resident to migrate elsewhere.   **243**

Pull factors   Characteristics of a place that attract migrants from other locations.   **243**

Voluntary migrations   Those migrations willingly undertaken by the participants.   **243**

Forced (involuntary) migrations Those migrations conducted by people against their will. **243**

Land bridges Land exposed by the lowering of the sea level during Pleistocene glaciation that then connected areas normally separated by water bodies. Land bridges facilitated migrations by prehistoric peoples. **245**

Völkerwanderung The westward migration of groups from central Asia that displaced people in eastern and central Europe during the early Christian era. **247**

Brain drain The large-scale migration of a society's most educated or talented members. **254**

Guest workers Foreign workers who have immigrated to a more economically developed country for temporary employment. This term is applied most commonly to foreigners who are temporarily employed in the industrialized countries of Europe. **266**

Boat people Refugee groups who have fled their homeland aboard vessels, often poorly equipped and marginally seaworthy. This term has been most often applied to the Vietnamese refugees of the 1970s. **270**

REVIEW QUESTIONS

1. Where is it generally accepted that humans originated? What reasons can be given for why ancient humans migrated to all the continents except Antarctica?

2. In what important ways can migrations be categorized or differentiated from one another? What are some examples of each type of migration?

3. What is the relationship of distance to migration? What factors may intervene to reduce the distance that individuals originally intended to travel when migrating?

4. What examples can you give of "push" and "pull" factors involved in migration? How do involuntary migrations occur?

5. How did the evolution of humans affect migration? What effects did environmental changes have on prehistoric migrations?

6. Which significant historic events prompted major human migrations? What were the motivational factors involved in each?

7. What changes occurred in the migration of Europeans to America between 1800 and 1960? What events influenced immigrant numbers during this extensive time period?

8. Why has the issue of illegal immigrants become so serious in the United States? Why do immigrants attempt to stay in this country illegally, and how do U.S. citizens react to the issue?

9. What areas of the world have been the major sources of migrants to the United States since 1960? Why have migration patterns to the United States changed in recent years?

10. What significant movements have characterized internal migration in the United States since 1800? What motivated these migrations?

11. Which twentieth-century U.S. migration trends can be considered a reversal of earlier migration patterns?

12. Does it seem unusual that only limited international migration of Chinese has occurred? Where are significant numbers of Chinese located outside the country, and what motivated these people to migrate?

13. Why are the Hindu and Moslem migrations on the Indian subcontinent after World War II and the Russian migration to Siberia considered to be either entirely or partially involuntary?

14. What internal migrations have occurred in Europe during the twentieth century? To what extent were each of these migrations voluntary?

15. What distinctive features have characterized Jewish migration to Israel? How have the creation of Israel and the subsequent migration affected world events?

16. Where have refugees been a major concern in recent years? How did these refugee situations come about?

17. Which human migrations comprise the most serious challenge to world leaders now and in the future?

CHAPTER 8

POPULATION DISTRIBUTION: PEOPLE ON THE LAND

In order to understand the relationships between earth and man, the first question to be answered is this: how is population distributed over the surface of the earth?

—Paul Vidal de la Blache

This crowd of bicyclists in Beijing are some of the 1.2 billion people who give China the world's greatest total population. (David Wells/The Image Works)

➤ Familiarity with a world map of population distribution is basic to an understanding of human geography.

In terms of the global arrangement of population, how do the Northern and Southern Hemispheres differ?

How do the New World and Old World continents differ in the number of people they contain?

TABLE 8.1	The 25 Most Populated Countries: 1993	
Rank	Country	Population (millions)
1.	China	1178.5
2.	India	897.4
3.	United States	258.3
4.	Indonesia	187.6
5.	Brazil	152.0
6.	Russia	149.0
7.	Japan	124.8
8.	Pakistan	122.4
9.	Bangladesh	113.9
10.	Nigeria	95.1
11.	Mexico	90.0
12.	Germany	81.1
13.	Vietnam	71.8
14.	Philippines	64.6
15.	Iran	62.8
16.	Turkey	60.7
17.	Egypt	58.3
18.	United Kingdom	58.0
19.	Italy	57.8
20.	France	57.7
21.	Thailand	57.2
22.	Ethiopia	56.7
23.	Ukraine	51.9
24.	South Korea	44.6
25.	Myanmar (Burma)	43.5

SOURCE: *Population Reference Bureau.*

The arrangement of people over the face of the earth is one of the most basic and important aspects of human geography. Differences in population from one location to another can suggest a great deal about the character of places and the lifestyles of their people. Our knowledge of population distribution can help us make sound judgments on a great variety of issues concerning human use of different parts of the world.

If we examine a map of world population, such as the one in Figure 8.1, striking contrasts are apparent. A very general pattern evident on the map is that the Northern Hemisphere contains the vast majority of the world's people. The Southern Hemisphere has much less land area than the Northern Hemisphere, but the difference in population is even greater. There are no clusters of population in the Southern Hemisphere that compare with the largest agglomerations of people in the Northern Hemisphere. The most extreme situation is in Antarctica, the ice and snow covered continent surrounding the South Pole, which has no permanent human inhabitants; only a small number of explorers and members of scientific expeditions have lived in Antarctica on even a temporary basis. If we dismiss Antarctica, the world's most sparsely populated continent is Australia, which is about two-thirds desert and also is in the Southern Hemisphere. As many people reside in the New York City metropolitan area as in all of Australia.

The expression "our crowded planet" is more appropriate for the Northern Hemisphere: it contains more than 90 percent of the earth's 5.5 billion inhabitants. Of the 25 countries with the largest population (Table 8.1), all but Indonesia and Brazil are located entirely in the Northern Hemisphere. Our map of world population shows three enormous clusters of humanity in East Asia, South Asia, and Europe—all contained in the Northern Hemisphere. These three regions, which represent only 7 percent of the earth's land area, account for nearly two-thirds of the world's population.

In contrast are vast parts of the Northern Hemisphere that have very limited populations and some areas of considerable size with absolutely no permanent human inhabitants. In general, these are high-latitude areas that have cold temperatures most of the year and middle- to low-latitude areas with low precipitation amounts. Also characteristic of some sparsely populated areas are poor drainage, rugged terrain, or an isolated location.

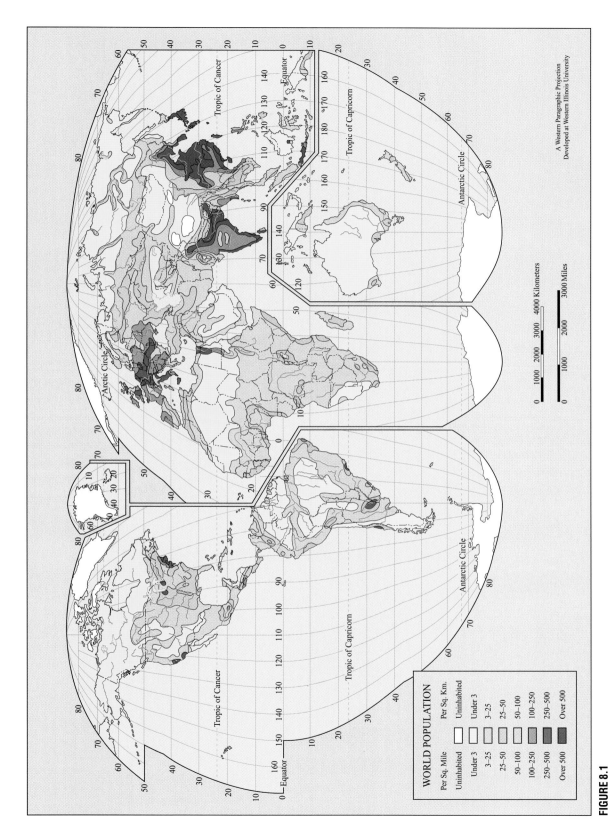

FIGURE 8.1

Distribution of the world's population. How can the great concentrations of people in some areas and the virtual absence of population in other areas be explained?

275

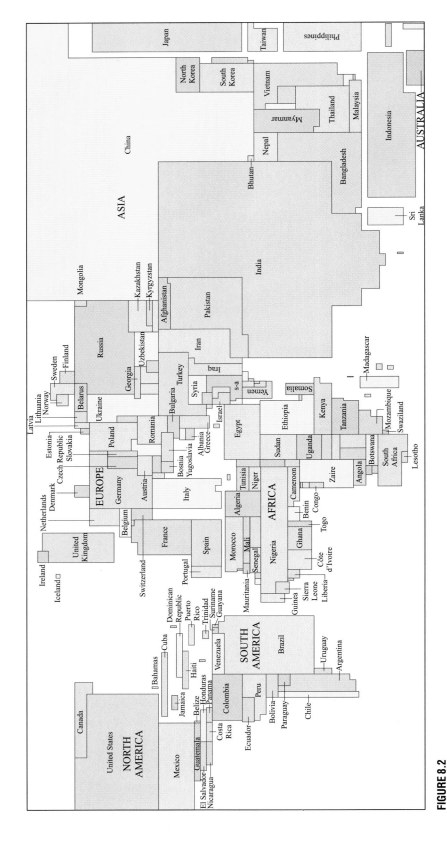

FIGURE 8.2

In this cartogram the size of each country is proportional to its total population.

Another broad pattern of population distribution is evident in Figure 8.2: the populations of the New World continents (North and South America and Australia) are smaller than those of the Old World continents (Asia, Europe, and Africa). This suggests that current population totals are related to the length of time a landmass has been inhabited. However, it should be noted that the most populated continent is Asia, not Africa where humans have existed for the longest period.

The great variation in the distribution of people, with some areas extremely crowded while others are scarcely inhabited, raises many questions. Are environmental conditions, such as climate and landforms, the primary reasons for the uneven distribution of population? What has been the influence of historical events such as migrations and wars on the current arrangement of people over the earth? How important have economic factors been in attracting people to some areas while making them less attracted to others? If vast areas remain sparsely populated, why are people not moving to those areas in significant numbers from the crowded parts of the world? How many people can a given area support without being "overpopulated"? As you proceed through this chapter, it will become apparent that the answers to these questions vary from one part of the world to another; no single answer has worldwide validity.

MEASURING POPULATION DENSITY

➤ Two measurements of population concentration in an area are arithmetic density and physiological density.

How are these two measurements determined?

In what way is the physiological density more significant?

Why is the arithmetic density most commonly used?

In order for us to gauge the degree of concentration of people in an area and to make comparisons from one part of the world to another, we must employ a measurement of population density. Population density is expressed in terms of a certain number of people per unit area, such as 120 people per square kilometer or square mile. The most commonly used types of population density are called **arithmetic density** and **physiological (nutritional) density**.

Arithmetic Density

Because of the ease in calculating the arithmetic density for an area of interest, such as a country or state, it is the type of population density most often encountered. Determining the arithmetic density of a country merely involves dividing the total population by the number of square miles or square kilometers within the boundaries of the country. The result is the number of people per square mile or square kilometer, an average for the country's entire territory. For example, the United States, with an area of 3,680,000 square miles (9,528,000 sq km) and a total population of 258,300,000 in 1993, had an arithmetic density of 73 persons per square mile (28 per sq km) for that year.

Although arithmetic density is a helpful statistic in some ways, it has obvious shortcomings. Because it is a nationwide average, arithmetic density does not reveal place-to-place differences in population concentrations *within* the country. For a large country such as the United States or China in which some areas are heavily populated and others sparsely populated, the arithmetic density therefore has limited value. In a similar way, the arithmetic density of a country that has a large proportion of its population in cities—the most extreme concentration of people in a small area—also has restricted usefulness. For some purposes, it is preferable to omit the urban population and calculate only the rural population density of an area.

Another shortcoming of arithmetic density is that it ignores variations in land quality. The territory of nearly all countries is diverse; some areas may be highly productive, some sterile, and others of intermediate quality. The neglect of variations in the character of land makes the arithmetic density of limited value in deciding if a condition of overpopulation has been reached.

We nevertheless will use arithmetic density figures frequently in this chapter, partly because it is the most readily available measurement of population density for the world's countries. However, we need to keep in mind the limitations of arithmetic density and to recognize that it is likely to better represent the population situation in a small country or area with a relatively uniform distribution of its inhabitants than a large country with great variations in the arrangement of its population.

TABLE 8.2	Arithmetic and Physiological Population Densities for Selected Countries: 1993	
Country	Arithmetic Density (population per sq mi)	Physiological Density (population per sq mi)
Bangladesh	2266	3283
Canada	6	138
China	327	2745
Egypt	152	5894
India	782	1318
Japan	858	6613
United States	70	348

SOURCES: *For arithmetic density: Population Reference Bureau. For physiological density: calculations of the author.*

Physiological Density

A refinement in the measurement of population density can be obtained by using only the *arable* land of a country in calculating its number of people per square mile (or sq km). This statistic, called the physiological (nutritional) density, therefore involves only land that is considered capable of producing food for the population. It is more useful than the arithmetic density in drawing conclusions about the ability of a country to feed its population.

Table 8.2, which provides both arithmetic and physiological densities for a group of selected countries, illustrates how these two measurements might lead to different interpretations of national population situations. For example, Egypt's arithmetic density of 152 people per square mile (59 per sq km) is not particularly outstanding. However, most of the country's area is virtually uninhabited desert. Only about 4 percent of Egypt's territory is arable land, and that is nearly all in the Nile Valley where 95 percent of the population is concentrated. This situation is more clearly reflected in Egypt's extremely high physiological density of 5894 persons per square mile (1456 per sq km).

We need to recognize, however, that the physiological density is not without flaws. Its value is affected by different interpretations of what arable land is; the same quality of land may be considered arable in one society but not in another. Also, different areas of arable land may vary in their productivity of food. In subtropical and tropical areas, for example, it may

be possible to raise two or three crops a year; an area in higher latitudes most likely will be able to produce only a single crop per year. Another point to keep in mind is that a relatively high physiological density of population does not necessarily result in food shortages; a wealthy country, such as Japan, can offset its limited amount of arable land by importing food from foreign sources.

Most of this chapter will focus attention on the spatial arrangement of people and variations in population densities in each of several major regions. Factors and conditions associated with the population patterns and densities also will be examined. To conclude the chapter, we will give consideration to the concept of overpopulation and the issue of human crowding.

EURASIA

➢ Eurasia contains the world's three greatest population clusters.

How does the European cluster differ from the two in Monsoon Asia?

What environmental qualities of Monsoon Asia have been most highly valued by the region's population?

Why have these qualities been most highly valued?

The Old World landmass of Eurasia contains nearly two-thirds of the world's population, most of them in three great clusters located in East Asia, South Asia, and Europe. About half of all humanity is represented by the East and South Asia clusters, which are comprised mostly of rural peasants who live and work on the land. The European cluster, on the other hand, is a highly urbanized population with relatively small numbers of rural people. In addition to these great clusters, smaller areas of Eurasia have high population densities, including parts of Southeast and Southwest Asia. In contrast, vast areas of the Eurasian landmass contain few people and are among the most sparsely populated areas on earth. Place-to-place variations in Eurasian population densities are enormous.

From a demographic standpoint, Monsoon Asia is of supreme importance. Extending eastward from India through the countries of Southeast Asia and northward as far as the Korean Peninsula and Japan, this zone includes both the East and South Asia clusters, which together contain more than two billion inhabitants. The vast majority of these are rural people who live in agricultural villages and depend on the summer monsoon rains to supply water for the crops that provide their sustenance. The agrarian society of this part of the world long ago developed wetland rice as its principal source of food. During the period of its growth from seedling to mature grain, wetland rice is raised on land that must be capable of controlled flooding. Relatively level terrain, large quantities of fresh water (usually from a river or stream), and a moderately long growing season are necessary for wetland rice production. Environments with those qualities have been the most valued areas among people in Monsoon Asia for many centuries and as a consequence are the most densely populated. Areas that are too dry (such as northwestern India) or have a growing season of inadequate length for wetland rice (such as northern China) have attracted far smaller numbers of people.

The level land, available water, and rich soils in the river valleys and deltas have made those areas especially prized in Monsoon Asia, and they are now among the most densely populated lands on earth. By concentrating themselves so heavily in such lowland sites, the people of Monsoon Asia have been especially susceptible to devastation by floods. Rainfall during the summer monsoon period is notoriously erratic; exceptionally heavy rains are not unusual and the result may be extensive flooding of lowland areas. For many centuries floods in Monsoon Asia have been responsible for the loss of a great many human lives—some people have been killed by drowning and others

starved to death because of famines resulting from destroyed rice crops. In recent decades the construction of dams and other water-control structures on the most flood-prone rivers has been a high priority for the governments of countries in Monsoon Asia. These efforts have significantly reduced flood risks in the region.

Another type of construction, apparently going back many centuries, has led to extensive resculpturing of the natural landscape in Monsoon Asia. The demands for level land in areas of rough terrain have been so great that peasants have exerted enormous effort to carve out *terraces* on hillsides and the lower slopes of mountains. Cultivated with great care, these terraces have been important in increasing the ability of Monsoon Asia to support a growing agricultural population (Fig. 8.3).

FIGURE 8.3

Human-constructed terraces, such as these in Thailand, are widespread in Monsoon Asia. They convert sloping land into agriculturally productive areas to help support the region's large population. (J. Lamont)

The East Asian Cluster

➢ East Asia has long been the most populated world region.

What are the most densely populated areas of China, and why are all of them in the eastern part of the country?

How does the location of Japan's population differ from that of all other major countries in Monsoon Asia?

It is believed that East Asia has been the world's most populated major region for many thousands of years—perhaps all but the very earliest span of human history. With a population in 1993 of about 1.4 billion people, East Asia accounts for an enormous segment of all humanity and is rivaled only by South Asia. Agrarian societies have persisted in the region with little change in lifestyles for many centuries, partly because of self-imposed isolation that greatly restricted contact with outside nations. As a consequence, the countries of

East Asia have spent much of the twentieth century attempting to catch up with other parts of the world in technology and modern economic practices. Their efforts have been interrupted by devastating wars and political turmoil. Quickly recovering from its defeat during World War II, Japan has led the way in modernizing its economy by developing manufacturing and trade. Other countries in the region, particularly South Korea and Taiwan, are beginning to follow the same course. China's modernization has lagged behind as internal political struggles and strained relationships with other countries have persisted during its postwar period of communist government.

China Over the long history of China, its population has grown to unprecedented levels. By the end of World War II the country's population totaled more than 500 million, it exceeded 1 billion during the early 1980s, and by 1990 it reached 1.1 billion. (India, the world's second most populated country, has only four-fifths as many people.) As one would expect, China

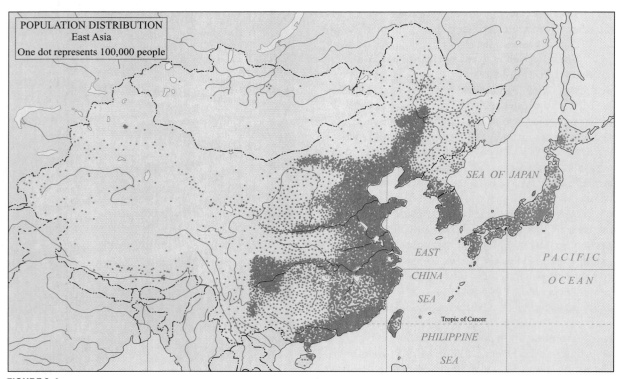

FIGURE 8.4

contains some of the world's most densely populated areas, but it is a large country with an area of 3.7 million square miles (9.6 million sq km) and has an arithmetic density of only 327 persons per square mile (126 per sq km). As Figure 8.4 suggests, about 90 percent of the people live in the eastern third of the country, a humid region sometimes called *China Proper*. The sparsely populated western part of China is arid and mountainous.

Population densities are greatest (more than 3000 people per sq mi or 1200 per sq km in some areas) on the North China Plain, a lowland that has had its soils enriched by silt deposits of the Huang He (Yellow River). Silts carried eastward by the Huang have been distributed extensively over this plain as the river repeatedly has changed its lower course, at times emptying into the sea south of Shandong Peninsula and other times north of the peninsula (presently the case). Farmers have intensively cultivated these rich soils for many centuries, building a network of canals to carry water to their fields. The country's capital city, Beijing, is on the northern margin of this plain.

Farther to the north is Manchuria, to which tens of millions of Chinese have migrated during the twentieth century. Many of these migrants were escaping famines in the overcrowded North China Plain to resettle in the colder and drier environments of Manchuria (now the Northeast Province of China). A result of this massive migration has been an extension into southern Manchuria of the high population densities on the North China Plain.

In the central part of China Proper are three densely populated basins linked by the Chang Jiang (Yangtze River), the country's most important commercial waterway. The uppermost of the three basins is in Sichwan, the most populated province in the country. These basins contain some of China's best ricelands, so they have attracted enormous agricultural populations. Along the river are large urban centers as well, including the great commercial city of Shanghai at the mouth of the Chang Jiang. With a population of 16 million, Shanghai is the largest city in China and one of the biggest in the world.

Other areas with important population concentrations are the valley of the Xi Jiang (Hsi River) in southern China and the lowlands along the East China and South China sea coasts. Human crowding is so intense here that hundreds of thousands of people do not live on the land at all, but instead occupy small houseboats on major rivers along the coasts (Fig. 8.5). The largest city in southern China is Guangzhou at the mouth of the Xi Jiang, but the most impressive urban concentration in this part of the world is Hong Kong where nearly 6 million people occupy an area of only 414 square miles (1072 km). (See *Cultural Landscapes: Hong Kong.*)

Other Regional Concentrations   With nearly 125 million people in 1993, Japan has an exceedingly large population for a country that has only about the same

FIGURE 8.5

These crowded sampans reflect the dense population along the coast of the South China Sea. The boats display New Year's decorations. (Joe Viesti/Viesti Assoc. Inc.)

CULTURAL LANDSCAPES

Hong Kong

The population density of Hong Kong—about 15,000 per square mile (5770 per sq km)—probably is higher than that of any comparable area in the world. The total population of more than 6 million also reflects the colony's enormous demographic growth since the end of World War II when it was inhabited by only one-tenth as many people. Chinese comprise about 98 percent of the present population; among them are many who have fled from communist China. But Hong Kong also has been the destination of tens of thousands of refugees from Vietnam and other parts

Hong Kong's intense population density required the construction of hundreds of blocks of high-rise apartment housing. (Cameramann International, Ltd.)

of Southeast Asia. To house the people, hundreds of blocks of high-rise apartments have been constructed (see the accompanying photographs). However, many people are squatters and occupy rudimentary shacks.

Hong Kong is a British colony that consists of Hong Kong Island, many smaller islands, and the "New Territories" of the Chinese mainland. Its total area encompasses only 380 square miles (984 sq km). Britain claimed Hong Kong Island after its victory over China in the Opium War of 1839–1842. In 1860 Britain gained control over a small peninsula on the mainland, and the New Territories came under British dominion in 1898 through a 99-year lease with China. When this lease expires in 1997, the United Kingdom has agreed to return all of Hong Kong to China. Hong Kong is expected to then become a "special administrative region" of China, with considerable autonomy. Nevertheless, there is widespread apprehension among the inhabitants about what life will be like in Hong Kong under China's control, and many are planning to emigrate before 1997.

Hong Kong's location and natural harbor enabled it to become a major center for trade between the Orient and the West. Cargoes from Western nations were broken into smaller lots for reshipment to destinations in China, Taiwan, the Philippines, and other countries in the region. In turn, goods from these countries were assembled in Hong Kong for shipment to the West. A trade embargo placed on China by the United Nations during the Korean War temporarily interfered with Hong Kong's commercial role, but in the long run it benefited the colony by stimulating the development of industry. Today Hong Kong has a booming manufacturing sector and exports textiles, clothing, shoes, watches, electronic equipment, and many kinds of machinery. Its international trade function is more important than ever before. Both its harbor and international airport are among the busiest in the world. Hong Kong also has become one of the world's major centers of international finance. This fact has led to its unfortunate development as the Pacific's leading center for the laundering of drug money. Also on the dark side are the large numbers of international arms dealers, drug traffickers, and other organized criminals.

Hong Kong's teeming population and great economic significance are reflected in its cultural landscape. In addition to the seemingly countless high-rise apartment buildings are high-rise office buildings, commercial structures, and shopping facilities in which an unbelievable assortment of merchandise and services are for sale. The landscape here is in striking contrast to that in most of Monsoon Asia where rural villages are the typical place of residence.

THOUGHT QUESTIONS

1. Are there any other places in Monsoon Asia that are similar in cultural landscape and economic function to Hong Kong? Under what circumstances did they develop?

2. Why do you think the British decided to transfer control of all of Hong Kong to China in 1997?

3. What changes do you think the Chinese government will bring to Hong Kong after 1997?

TABLE 8.3	Most Populated Countries and Principal Cities in East Asia: 1993		

Country	Population (millions)	Arithmetic Density (population per sq mi)	Principal Cities
China	1178.5	327	Shanghai, Beijing, Tianjin
Japan	124.8	858	Tokyo, Osaka, Yokohama
South Korea	44.6	1170	Seoul, Pusan, Taegu
North Korea	22.6	487	Pyongyang
Taiwan	20.9	1501	Taipei, Kaohsiung

SOURCE: *Population Reference Bureau.*

area as California (Table 8.3). Its arithmetic density is very high—858 people per square mile (331 per sq km). More astounding, however, is its physiological density of 6613 people per square mile (2548 per sq km), which is one of the highest in the world. Only 13 percent of Japan's area is cultivated land.

Among Japan's four main islands (Hokkaido, Honshu, Shikoku, and Kyushu), three are densely populated. The exception is Hokkaido, the northernmost island in the group. Volcanic mountains and hills comprise most of Japan's territory, with plains and other lowlands limited in extent and very crowded. The Kanto Plain, on the eastern side of Honshu, contains the cities of Tokyo and Yokohama and is the most densely populated area of Japan. Other lowlands with outstanding population concentrations and major industrial cities are in southern Honshu and around the shores of the Inland Sea that separates Honshu from Shikoku and Kyushu. With Japan's industrialization and modernization of its economy since World War II, its cities have experienced phenomenal growth. More than three-fourths of the people now live in urban places—a higher proportion than in any other major country in Monsoon Asia. The Tokyo–Yokohama metropolitan area, with about 23 million people, is the world's largest single urban agglomeration.

As in Japan, the Korean Peninsula and the island of Taiwan are rugged hilly and mountainous areas for the most part. Lowlands are restricted in area and very crowded with people. South Korea has somewhat more lowland territory than North Korea and in 1993

exceeded its northern counterpart in total population, 44.6 million to 22.6 million. Taiwan, with 20.9 million people in 1993, is the only other East Asian country that has a sizable population.

The South Asian Cluster

➤ The arrangement of population in South Asia is similar in many respects to that of East Asia.

How and why is the population distribution similar in these two regions?

Where are the most populated areas of India?

How is the population distribution in Pakistan and Bangladesh strikingly different?

In addition to the fact that South Asia and East Asia each contain more than 1 billion people, these two regions share other similarities. Both contain the site of an early civilization that emerged about 4500 years ago, as we described in Chapter 3. Both regions have a long history of peasants in enormous numbers working the land, cultivating rice where environmental conditions allow. Also, a single country is demographically dominant in both regions—China in East Asia and India in South Asia.

No country in South Asia, however, has managed to keep up with the modernization, industrialization, and urbanization of some nations in East Asia over recent decades. The vast majority of people in South Asia continue to be peasant farmers who live in rural

FIGURE 8.6
This family and their dwelling are part of a village near Shantineketan, India. (R. Gabler)

villages and have little contact with the world outside their immediate areas. India, in fact, has been described as a land of villages (Fig. 8.6). In the best agricultural areas the villages are closely spaced, and as a consequence rural population densities are extremely high—more than 2000 people per square mile (800 per sq km) in some instances. There are several large cities, such as Calcutta and Bombay, but each country in South Asia has less than 30 percent of its population located in urban centers. The cities nevertheless are growing rapidly as people stream into them from overpopulated rural areas in search of a means to survive. These migrants place an enormous strain on the urban facilities and institutions, and they often become homeless beggars on the streets of the cities.

India   India's 897 million people, the second largest national population in the world, remain mostly concentrated in the country's lowland areas that offer the best conditions for farming (Fig. 8.7). The broad valley of the Ganges River, which terminates in a complex delta formed by alluvial deposits of the Brahmaputra River as well as those of the Ganges, is India's most populated lowland. Adjacent to the southern slopes of the Himalaya Mountains, which receive exceptionally heavy rainfall during the summer monsoon season, the Ganges Valley is mostly well watered and covered by rich alluvial soils. A long growing season enables farmers in the valley to raise a variety

of crops, but rice is the one most preferred. The Ganges not only provides water for crops, but it is used as well by millions of peasants for washing, drinking, and disposing of sewage. As a consequence, the river that is so important to the daily life of people along its course also often brings them disease and early death.

The other densely populated lowlands of India are fairly narrow plains along the southeastern (Coromandel) and southwestern (Malabar) coasts of the peninsula. Although restricted in width by hilly *escarpments* (the Ghats) toward the interior, these coastal plains have abundant rainfall and long growing seasons for rice and other crops.

The interior of peninsular India, an old eroded plateau, is less productive cropland and less densely populated than the lowland areas. The plateau, known as the Deccan in the south, has rolling to hilly surfaces and highly erratic rainfall during the summer monsoon. The amount of water available for crops may be satisfactory one year and inadequate the next. Even with more drought-resistant crops (such as millet and wheat) substituted for rice, local and regional famines often follow the periods of reduced rainfall. Northwestern India, where annual precipitation is consistently low and desert conditions prevail, is the country's only general area of sparse population.

Pakistan and Bangladesh   Although much smaller than India, both Pakistan and Bangladesh have more

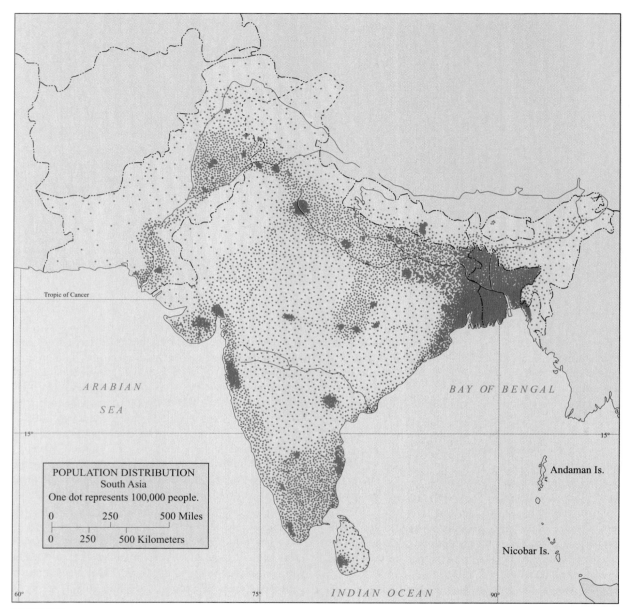

FIGURE 8.7

than 100 million people (Table 8.4) and are in the top ten most populated countries in the world. Environmental problems of a contrasting nature have an impact on the population distribution and widespread poverty of these two nations. Pakistan's territory is predominantly desert; the lack of rainfall largely confines the country's population to the valley of the Indus River where irrigation farming can be carried out. Bangladesh, on the other hand, often suffers from too much rainfall. Occupying the bulk of the Ganges-Brahmaputra delta, the territory of Bangladesh is exceedingly flat and barely above sea level. The normally abundant rain of the summer monsoon provides excessive water, but floods are particularly extensive

TABLE 8.4 Most Populated Countries and Principal Cities in South Asia: 1993

Country	Population (millions)	Arithmetic Density (population per sq mi)	Principal Cities
India	897.4	782	Calcutta, Bombay, Delhi
Pakistan	122.4	411	Karachi, Lahore, Faisalabad
Bangladesh	113.9	2266	Decca
Nepal	20.4	386	Kathmandu
Sri Lanka	17.8	715	Colombo

SOURCE: *Population Reference Bureau.*

when storms (locally called *cyclones*) roar inland from the Bay of Bengal. In this poverty-stricken and very densely populated land, the flooding destroys crops and villages and takes a heavy toll of human life. During severe storms, hundreds of people may be washed into the sea and disappear. The aftermath of a flood brings widespread disease from polluted drinking water and even more death. With such environmental problems and an arithmetic density of more than 2200 per square mile (849 per sq km), Bangladesh is one of the world's most unfortunate countries.

Nepal, in the Himalaya Mountains, and Sri Lanka (formerly Ceylon) off the southern tip of India are the only other countries in South Asia with a significant population. Nepal and Sri Lanka have about 20 million and 18 million inhabitants, respectively.

The European Cluster

➤ The European population cluster is highly urbanized and exhibits exceptionally high densities along an east–west axis.

Why has Europe's population axis become the continent's main area of human concentration?

How do the arrangement and densities of population in Mediterranean Europe contrast with those to the north?

How can most of the population of the Commonwealth of Independent States be considered a part of the European cluster?

Even though Europe has lost tens of millions of emigrants to other parts of the world and several million more people who have been casualties of war during the past two centuries, it remains the world's most densely populated continent. Europe's total population does not approach that of East Asia or South Asia, but its relatively small territorial size helps account for its high density. It is interesting to speculate on what the population situation in Europe might be today if those who migrated to other continents had remained at home and their descendants were added to the total European population; the size of the European cluster might be comparable to those clusters in East and South Asia and widespread poverty might prevail rather than the current high standard of living in Europe. However, the actual number of Europe's inhabitants today is slightly more than 500 million if the population in the European part of the former Soviet Union is omitted. By including it, Europe's total can be placed at about 750 million—or 15 percent of all people in the world.

Although Europe cannot claim the development of a civilization as early as those in North China and the Indus Valley, it is one of the oldest inhabited areas in the world. The European accomplishment that has had particularly great demographic consequence is the Industrial Revolution. We pointed out in Chapter 6 that industrialization has stimulated the growth of cities and led to deceleration of population growth. As the region with the longest industrial history, Europe is now the continent with the greatest concentration of cities and the slowest rate of population increase. The

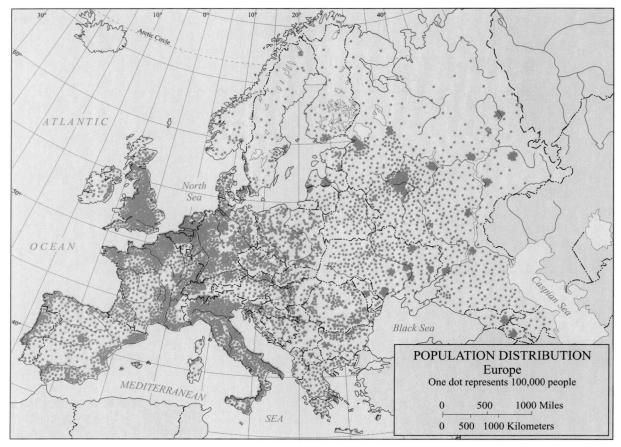

FIGURE 8.8

distribution of population in Europe also has felt the impact of industrialization; areas with industrial resources and places with advantages for the assembly of raw materials and the manufacture and distribution of goods have attracted people in the greatest numbers.

The European Population Axis   Relatively heavy population densities are widespread in Europe, but most prominent is an east–west zone that usually is identified as the **European population axis** (Fig. 8.8). This zone extends from central and southern Great Britain generally eastward through the Netherlands, Belgium, northern France, Germany, Poland, and into southwestern parts of the former Soviet Union. Much of the zone is within the agriculturally productive Great European Plain, but only small numbers of people are farmers here. Instead, the vast majority of the population is located in the numerous towns and cities along the rivers and coasts, in the coal fields, and in the industrial districts of this part of Europe. London,

Manchester, Amsterdam, Rotterdam, Brussels, Essen, Berlin, and Warsaw are a few of the most prominent cities. The North Sea coast, particularly in the vicinity of the mouths of the Rhine and Thames Rivers, is the location of Europe's greatest cities engaged in international trade. The mining and industrial centers are in and near the coal fields of Britain, Germany's Ruhr Valley (Europe's leading mining and manufacturing district in the twentieth century), Upper Silesia in Poland, and other districts along the southern margin of the Great European Plain. In some of the countries associated with the European population axis, arithmetic densities are quite high (Table 8.5). The Netherlands and Belgium (not included in Table 8.5) have the greatest arithmetic densities, with 1164 and 857 people per square mile (449 and 331 per sq km), respectively.

The Mediterranean South   Although some areas have high densities, the Mediterranean lands are not

TABLE 8.5 Most Populated Countries and Principal Cities in Europe: 1993

Country	Population (millions)	Arithmetic Density (population per sq mi)	Principal Cities
Russia[a]	149.0	23	Moscow, St. Petersburg, Gorky
Germany	81.1	601	Berlin, Hamburg, Munich
United Kingdom	58.0	622	London, Birmingham, Glasgow
Italy	57.8	509	Rome, Milan, Naples
France	57.7	272	Paris, Marseille
Ukraine	51.9	223	Kiev, Kharkov
Spain	39.1	203	Madrid, Barcelona
Poland	38.5	327	Warsaw

SOURCE: *Population Reference Bureau.*
[a]Includes Asiatic part.

as prominent a part of the European population cluster as the zone just described. Mostly a rugged and barren region that lacks significant mineral deposits, the Mediterranean South has experienced much rural poverty and retarded industrial development. The region's limited lowlands have the greatest densities, but the more modestly populated uplands—where the potential of the land to support people is much lower—are more severely stressed. Deforestation and soil erosion, underway for centuries on these slopes, are the consequences of excessive human pressure on the environment in parts of Mediterranean Europe (Fig. 8.9).

Italy is the most populated Mediterranean country, with an arithmetic density of about 500 people per square mile (193 per sq km). The valley of the Po River in the northern part of the country contains the greatest concentration of people in all of Mediterranean Europe. With rich alluvial soils, it is a productive farming area and includes the industrial cities of Turin and Milan as well. The Rhone Valley in southeastern France and the eastern coast of Spain are other parts of Mediterranean Europe with relatively dense populations.

FIGURE 8.9

This deforested and eroded landscape in Syros, Greece, is typical of much of Mediterranean Europe. Environmental damage here has significantly lowered the ability of the land to support people. (George Kontakis/Viesti Assoc., Inc.)

The Commonwealth of Independent States The final part of the European population cluster for us to examine is in the Commonwealth of Independent States, comprised of most republics in the former Soviet Union. Although a large part of the Commonwealth's territory is in Asia, more than 80 percent of its population is west of the Ural Mountains and therefore in Europe. The principal concentrations of people are in the central and southwestern parts of European Russia and in the Ukraine, Belarus, and Moldova Republics. This area has less severe climatic conditions than other large parts of the Commonwealth, and it contains most of the farmland as well as valuable mineral resources. The Ukraine Republic, in fact, has the best combination of climate, farmland, and mineral deposits in the Commonwealth. Moscow, St. Petersburg, and Kiev—the three largest cities of the Commonwealth—are included in the European cluster of population.

Tragedy for the population of European Russia has been all too frequent during modern history. Invasions by the armies of Napoleon in the nineteenth century and Hitler in the twentieth century were separated by a major peasant revolt, World War I, and the Bolshevik Revolution. These military conflicts and internal struggles resulted in the death of tens of millions of Russians; World War II took the greatest toll, about 27 million Soviet deaths. Despite such huge losses, the Soviet Union in 1990—the last year of its existence as a country—contained 289 million inhabitants, the third largest population total in the world. About 280 million of those people live in the independent republics that now are members of the Commonwealth. Russia, with nearly 150 million people, is the most populated of the republics.

Other Concentrations in Eurasia

➤ In addition to the world's greatest population clusters, Eurasia contains two other regional population concentrations and vast areas with sparse population.

What factors help explain the population arrangements in Southeast and Southwest Asia?

How has military conflict disrupted populations in both of these regions?

Why does Eurasia have great contrasts in its population densities?

The populations of other parts of Eurasia are overshadowed by the three enormous clusters that we have just described, but the human concentrations in Southeast and Southwest Asia also deserve attention. A lengthy human history marked by early cultural developments and civilizations can be claimed by both regions. Over recent decades, political and military hostilities in both regions have been detrimental to their economic development and costly in terms of human lives.

TABLE 8.6 Most Populated Countries and Principal Cities in Southeast Asia: 1993

Country	Population (millions)	Arithmetic Density (population per sq mi)	Principal Cities
Indonesia	187.6	266	Jakarta, Surabaya, Bandung
Vietnam	71.8	571	Ho Chi Minh City, Hanoi
Philippines	64.6	562	Manila, Quezon City
Thailand	57.2	290	Bangkok
Myanmar (Burma)	43.5	171	Rangoon

SOURCE: *Population Reference Bureau.*

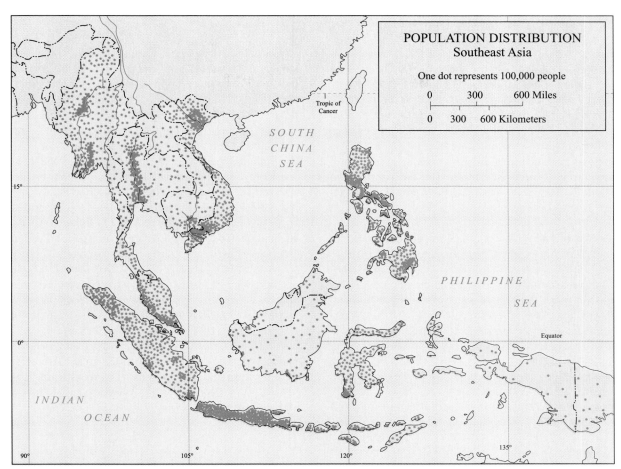

FIGURE 8.10

Southeast Asia The demographic importance of Southeast Asia is diminished by the region's location adjacent to the world's two greatest population clusters in East and South Asia. However, Southeast Asia has about 460 million people and includes the fourth most populated country in the world, Indonesia, which alone is inhabited by nearly 190 million. Each of four other countries in the region—Vietnam, the Philippines, Thailand, and Myanmar (Burma)—contains more than 40 million people (Table 8.6). The population densities in some parts of Southeast Asia are among the highest in the world.

Minerals, especially tin and oil, are important in the region, but agricultural products are the basis of Southeast Asia's economic significance. With emphasis on agriculture, particularly rice farming, the fertile soils of Southeast Asia's river valleys and deltas, coastal plains, and volcanic islands have attracted people in the greatest numbers (Fig. 8.10). The lower valley and delta of the Irrawaddy River in Myanmar, the

deltas of the Chao Phraya in Thailand and the Mekong in Vietnam, coastal lowlands of Vietnam and the southwestern extremity of the Malayan Peninsula, and major lowlands in the Philippine Islands are all areas with high population densities. The most outstanding concentration, however, is on the Indonesian island of Java, where about 120 million people are crowded. This is one of the world's most densely populated areas; parts of the island contain more than 3000 people per square mile (1200 per sq km). The government of Indonesia has attempted to relocate some of Java's inhabitants on other islands that are only modestly populated, but it has had little success.

For much of the twentieth century, Southeast Asia has been involved in conflict that has disrupted the region's economy and population. World War II, struggles with colonial powers (mainly the French and Dutch), internal conflicts and civil wars, and boundary zone invasions by neighbors have been extremely destructive. The involvement of outside powers, including the United States, in the Vietnam War elevated the devastation in that tragic conflict. Preoccupied for decades by these disruptions, Southeast Asia has been unable to reach its potential as a supplier of rice to more populated adjacent regions and as an exporter of minerals and plantation crops to industrial countries. The Vietnam war and subsequent conflicts in the region have taken hundreds of thousands of lives and, as we noted in Chapter 7, stimulated the flight of hundreds of thousands of refugees.

Southwest Asia   With arid climates widespread in Southwest Asia, populations are concentrated in those parts of the region where rainfall amounts are somewhat greater and where water can be obtained for irrigation. Thus the eastern coast of the Mediterranean Sea and the coasts of Turkey, all of which have a Mediterranean climate with seasonal rainfall, and irrigated lands in northern Iran and the lower Mesopotamian Valley stand out on Figure 8.11 with somewhat higher population densities than other parts of the region. The densities in Mesopotamia, however, are very modest compared with those in the Nile Valley in Egypt and the Indus Valley in Pakistan. All three areas are fertile

valleys in general desert settings, among the earliest locations for the development of irrigation agriculture, and the sites of three of the world's earliest civilizations. Yet the modern population densities are substantially lower in Mesopotamia, and scholars have not been able to reach agreement on an explanation.

Iran and Turkey are the most populated countries in Southwest Asia with nearly 63 million and 61 million people, respectively (Table 8.7). Although Turkey has good potential for the development of a diversified economy, Iran's well-being is closely linked to its oil production. The great oil deposits around the Persian Gulf were first tapped early in the twentieth century by wells in Iran, and the country continues to be one of the region's leading producers. However, Iran's economy as well as its population suffered through a revolution in 1978–1979 and a war with neighboring Iraq during the 1980s. These events disrupted the production of oil, and military expenditures drained the national treasury. In addition to the many lives lost during the revolution, the bloody war with Iraq appears to have caused the two sides a combined total of 1 million casualties.

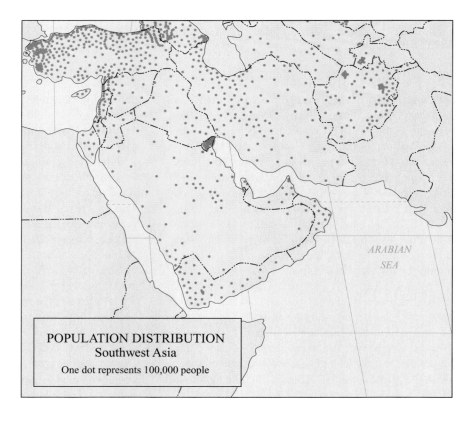

POPULATION DISTRIBUTION
Southwest Asia
One dot represents 100,000 people

ARABIAN
SEA

FIGURE 8.11

TABLE 8.7 Most Populated Countries and Principal Cities in Southwest Asia: 1993			
Country	**Population (millions)**	**Arithmetic Density (population per sq mi)**	**Principal Cities**
Iran	62.8	99	Tehran
Turkey[a]	60.7	207	Istanbul, Ankara
Iraq	19.2	113	Baghdad
Saudi Arabia	17.5	21	Riyadh, Jidda
Afghanistan	17.4	69	Kabul
Syria	13.5	189	Damascus

SOURCE: *Population Reference Bureau.*

[a]Includes European part.

Sparsely Populated Areas

In stark contrast with the regions of high population densities and huge totals in Eurasia are extensive parts of the landmass that contain very few people. In some cases these are areas of rugged mountains, such as the Himalayas, but more generally they are regions with extreme climatic conditions. The thinly populated regions of northern Europe and particularly Siberia are notorious for their long and bitterly cold winters. In addition, the desert areas of central and southwestern Asia have very sparse populations; some sections, such as the southeastern part of the Arabian Desert, are virtually uninhabited.

These areas have been populated sparsely throughout human history but, as we have seen in Chapter 7, twentieth-century migrations have brought millions of new settlers to some locations. Since completion of the Trans-Siberian Railroad early in the century, nearly 20 million Russians have migrated eastward to settle in parts of southern Siberia. Millions of Chinese also have relocated from China Proper to drier areas of the north and west. Nevertheless, Siberia and the arid sections of China are enormous in extent, and these migrations have not been on a large enough scale to alter their character as some of the world's most sparsely populated regions.

ANGLO-AMERICA

The populations of the United States and Canada, the two countries of Anglo-America, display interesting

similarities and contrasts. Both countries have populations of varied ethnic and racial composition, similar lifestyles and high levels of affluence, comparable occupational structures, a high level of urbanization, and low rates of demographic growth. In both countries the population also is unevenly distributed, with concentrations in some areas and vast territories with virtually no people. However, there are differences. The United States is the world's third most populated country with 258 million people, whereas Canada has a total population of only 28 million. This contrast also is evident in the arithmetic density of the two countries: the United States has an average of 73 people per square mile (28 per sq km), but Canada has only 6 per square mile (2 per sq km).

The Northeastern Cluster

➤ The northeastern cluster of population in Anglo-America, like that in Europe, is highly urbanized.

What is the locational pattern of the major cities that dominate this cluster?

What is the composition and extent of Megalopolis?

Where are other conurbations in the region?

The world's greatest population cluster outside of Eurasia is in the northeastern United States and adjacent parts of Canada (Fig. 8.12). This cluster obviously does not compare with the three great clusters of Eurasia in size and antiquity. The Anglo-American cluster, involving about 100 million people, did not orig-

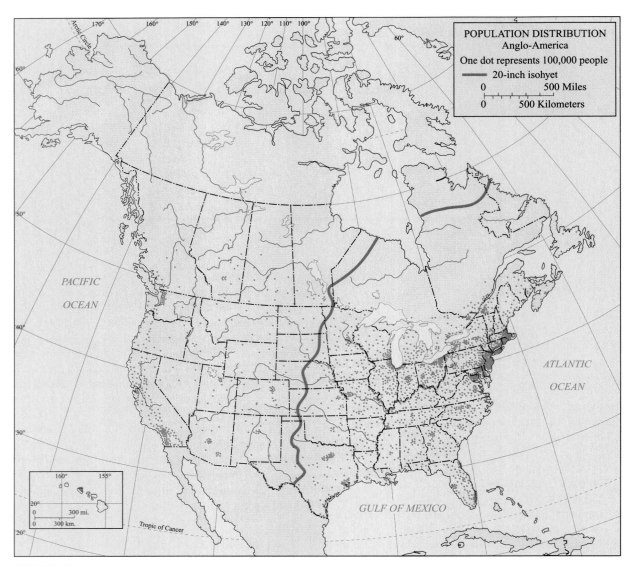

FIGURE 8.12

inate in an early civilization. Origins of the region's dominant culture traits and the people themselves can be traced to Old World areas, particularly Europe. This cluster of population has emerged only since the early part of the nineteenth century; its formation primarily has been in association with the development of industry and commerce on the North American side of the Atlantic. Therefore, it is a highly urbanized population like that in Europe. An enormous assortment of cities and their suburbs—primarily along the Atlantic seaboard, on the shores of the Great Lakes, and adjacent to the principal rivers—dominates the northeastern population cluster.

The concentration of cities and suburbs along the middle Atlantic coast comprises the world's greatest **conurbation**. Metropolitan sprawl in this zone, extending from Massachusetts to the Chesapeake Bay area, has virtually joined together the formerly separated urban centers (Fig. 8.13). In the mid-1950s Jean Gottmann, a French geographer, recognized the importance and unique characteristics of this phenomenal urban complex. He named it **Megalopolis** to convey

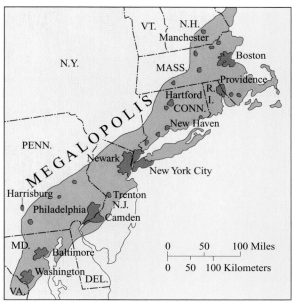

FIGURE 8.13

Megalopolis, the world's greatest conurbation, extends along the Atlantic seaboard of the United States from southern Maine to the Chesapeake Bay.

FIGURE 8.14

The New York metropolitan area, focused on Manhattan Island, is the core of Megalopolis. (J.R. Holland/Stock Boston.)

the conurbation's remarkable scale, and this identification has been in general use ever since. Megalopolis now contains about 45 million people, or nearly 20 percent of the total U.S. population. The principal cities contained within the complex are Boston, New York, Philadelphia, Baltimore, and Washington. The New York metropolitan area (Fig. 8.14), with about 16 million people, is one of the largest in the world.

A few other conurbations, although of far smaller extent, have formed in the area of the northeastern population cluster. They extend (1) from Pittsburgh to Cleveland, (2) from Buffalo to Toronto along the Niagara River and the western shore of Lake Ontario, (3) from Toledo to Detroit, and (4) from Chicago to Milwaukee. The principal cities in each case are among the leading industrial centers in Anglo-America.

Population Contrasts: Eastern and Western United States

➤ The eastern and western United States provide striking contrasts in population densities.

Why has the 100th meridian or the 20-inch isohyet been used as an approximate boundary between these two parts of the country?

How does the population of the West contrast with that of the East?

In terms of population, how is the Pacific Coast an exceptional part of the West?

As we described in Chapter 7, the United States has been characterized throughout its history by a general westward migration of its population. The multiple attractions of land, climate, resources, scenery, and economic opportunities have lured millions of Americans to the West, mostly to the states that border the Pacific Ocean. Nevertheless, about two-thirds of the population remains in the eastern half of the country and most of the western half continues to be sparsely settled. For several decades, geographers have identified the 100th meridian or the 20-inch (50 cm) *isohyet* (line connecting points of equal precipitation) as the approximate boundary between the well-populated East and the sparsely populated West (Fig. 8.12). The significance of this isohyet is that areas to the east, which average more than 20 inches (50 cm) of precipitation annually, are moist enough for successful crop production by standard agricultural practices and therefore are capable of supporting substantial populations. In contrast, most lands west of this line average less than 20 inches (50 cm) of yearly precipitation and are unable to produce crops without irrigation or special dry farming techniques; as a consequence, these lands are less able to support human inhabitants.

The humid eastern half of the United States is indeed one of the world's richest agricultural regions, but its modern population is overwhelmingly urban. Rural population densities seldom exceed 100 people per square mile (40 per sq km), and in most of the region there are fewer than 60 people per square mile (23 per sq km). Cities and their suburbs contain about 80 percent of the population in the eastern United States, and small towns account for most of the rest. Less than 3 percent of the population actually live and work on farms. During most of the twentieth century the region's relatively large population has been associated closely with manufacturing, mining, transportation, trade, government, and other urban-based activities.

The greatest concentration of population and cities, as we have seen, is in the Northeast between the Atlantic coast and the valley of the Mississippi River. However, greater population growth in the South—primarily because of recent migration trends—has narrowed the gap between these two areas. Diversification and revitalization of the South's economy, creating new employment opportunities and attracting job-seekers, have been among the most dramatic regional developments in the United States during the second half of the twentieth century.

Between the 100th meridian and the line of the Sierra Nevada and Cascade Mountains, the West has only a few limited population nodes and very low densities. This region's magnificent scenery and colorful history now attract hordes of temporary tourists, but its aridity and rugged terrain have limited employment opportunities for all but a relatively small number of permanent residents. The main population nodes have developed where adequate water is available to irrigate crops and meet the needs of cities: the Colorado piedmont, including Denver; the Wasatch oasis of Utah, where Salt Lake City is located; and the confluence area of the Gila and Salt Rivers, the site of Phoenix. Otherwise, population densities generally are below 2 persons per square mile (1 per sq km) and much of the land is in national parks and forests, military reservations, and Indian reservations (Fig. 8.15). Mining has been the region's dominant economic sector throughout most of its history, but many of the im-

FIGURE 8.15
This area in northern Arizona reflects the absence of population over vast distances in the western United States. (R. Gabler)

portant mining centers of the past are now only small villages and abandoned ghost towns.

The Exceptional Pacific Coast

Unlike other parts of the West, the Pacific Coast has developed a number of substantial population concentrations. With the exception of southern California, areas west of the Sierra Nevada range and the Cascade Mountains are at least seasonally well watered. Valleys, the largest of which are the Central Valley of California and the Willamette–Puget Sound Lowland in Oregon and Washington, have fertile soils and support moderately dense rural populations. Most people, however, live in major coastal cities that are industrial and commercial centers.

The Pacific Coast has been the destination of most westward migrating Americans for more than a century. Migrants from Mexico and Central America as well as ones from East and Southeast Asia, as we described in Chapter 7, have added significantly to the area's population accumulation. California, the nation's most populated state since the 1960s, has been the West's greatest magnet for migrants since its famous mid-nineteenth-century gold rush. By 1990 the three Pacific Coast states had nearly 37 million inhabitants, or about 15 percent of the national total. Concern about the scale of migration into the area has caused state officials to consider a variety of measures to reduce the influx of people. As a reaction to the crowding, congestion, and other factors, California in fact has experienced a significant out-migration in recent years.

The main population concentrations are in lowlands near and adjacent to the Pacific, although the overflow of major cities has extended development up the slopes of nearby hills and mountains. The greatest single agglomeration of people is in southern California from the vicinity of the Los Angeles Basin to the Mexican border. A Los Angeles–San Diego conurbation has developed here that is the largest on the Pacific Coast. (Los Angeles, in fact, has recently displaced Chicago as the country's second largest city.) Other major population concentrations are in the vicinity of San Francisco Bay and Puget Sound, the two main natural harbors on the coast. In addition to San Francisco, other major cities in the Bay area are Oakland and San Jose. The principal centers on Puget Sound are Seattle and Tacoma.

Canada and the Empty North

➤ Canada's population is concentrated in a few separated areas along the country's southern margin.

What are the most populated areas in Canada and how are they separated from one another?

How have Canada's population characteristics created major problems for the country?

The most striking feature of Canada's population arrangement is the concentration of people along the southern margin of the country (Fig. 8.12). Ninety percent of all Canadians live within 200 miles of the border with the United States. To the north of this narrow zone is one of the world's most extensive areas of sparse population, which also involves Alaska. Densities of fewer than 2 persons per square mile (1 per sq km) are typical here, and some areas virtually are uninhabited. This pattern suggests that Canadians have chosen to live as far as possible from the rigorous environment of the continent's northern reaches.

Even along Canada's southern margin are long stretches of sparsely occupied land that separate areas of concentrated population. The northward extension of the Appalachian Mountains isolates several nodes of people along the Atlantic Coast from the well-populated St. Lawrence Valley. The southward projection of the thinly peopled Canadian (Laurentian) Shield into the upper Great Lakes region forms a gap of nearly 1000 miles between the population concentrations of the Ontario Peninsula and the Prairie Provinces (Manitoba, Saskatchewan, and Alberta). Farther west, the sparsely inhabited Rocky Mountain zone isolates the population nodes, including Vancouver, in southern British Columbia from the Prairie Provinces.

The two main concentrations of Canadians are in the Ontario Peninsula (adjacent to Lakes Huron, Erie, and Ontario) and the valley of the St. Lawrence River. These two areas are among Canada's best agricultural districts, but more important, they are highly industrialized and contain major urban centers. Montreal is the dominant city of the St. Lawrence Valley, and Toronto is the main one in the Ontario Peninsula. Although no thinly inhabited zone is located between these two areas, they nevertheless are separated effectively by serious cultural differences. French Canadians are most concentrated in the St. Lawrence Valley, and English-speaking Canadians dominate the Ontario Peninsula.

These characteristics of Canada's population are at the heart of two major problems for the country. The problem of developing and populating the vast areas of the North is one that the country is not likely to overcome in the near future. The affluence and lack of serious crowding in the South more than offset any motivations for significant numbers of people to relocate in the North. The second problem, unification of the geographically and culturally separated population concentrations in the South, has been particularly challenging for Canada. Establishing transportation links between the widely separated concentrations has been difficult and costly, and little progress has been made in reducing the cultural gap between the French- and English-speaking segments of the population.

LATIN AMERICA

➤ Latin America's racially and ethnically diverse population exhibits a distinctive distributional pattern.

To what extent are Brazil and Mexico the demographic giants of the region?

What factors have contributed to the coastal and highland population concentrations in Latin America?

To what extent is the concentration of population in a core area a common pattern among Latin American countries?

The population composition tends to be highly varied in New World areas, and this is especially true of Latin America. Probably 20 to 30 million native Americans (sometimes called Amerindians) occupied this region immediately prior to European colonization; most were concentrated in two areas, (1) the central and northern Andes Mountains, and (2) central and southern Mexico and adjacent parts of Middle America, where their ancestors had developed advanced civilizations hundreds of years earlier (Fig. 8.16). The earliest European colonists were Spaniards and Portuguese. The Spaniards were attracted to the areas of large native populations in the Andes and Middle America, whereas the Portuguese settled in Brazil. In subsequent generations, new settlers arrived in Latin America from several other European countries. Another element in the modern population mix is the de-

scendants of African slaves brought to Latin America. Asians also are represented, as people from Japan, India, and other countries have participated in twentieth-century migrations to Latin America. The intermingling of these groups has led to intermarriage and offspring of mixed blood. Particularly numerous in the modern population are people of mixed Amerindian and European blood, called **mestizos**.

An important facet of the current population distribution in Latin America is the location of concentrations of major racial and ethnic groups. Amerindians, for example, remain dominant in parts of Middle America, the Andes Mountains, and isolated interior areas of South America. Europeans are widely scattered, but they dominate the populations of the middle-latitude countries in southern South America. People of African ancestry are concentrated along the tropical coasts of eastern and northern South America and the islands of the West Indies. Nearly all of the population of Haiti is black, the most complete domination of a Latin American country by a single group.

Brazil and Mexico: The Two Giants

Among the countries of Latin America, Brazil and Mexico are demographically dominant (Table 8.8). These two nations account for more than half of the 460 million people in Latin America. Brazil, with 152 million inhabitants, has a greater population than that of the other South American countries combined. The total of 90 million people in Mexico exceeds the combined population of the remaining countries in Middle America.

In both countries, the population is highly concentrated in a core area that contains the two largest cities. Southeastern Brazil has a huge cluster of people, including the country's two biggest urban centers—Rio de Janeiro and São Paulo. South-central Mexico, the focal area of the Aztec Indian civilization, is that country's national core. It contains Mexico City, now the largest urban center in the Western Hemisphere, and Guadalajara, the second largest Mexican city. Population growth in both national cores currently is enormous, largely because their cities are swelling with migrants from rural areas.

Because Brazil and Mexico also have vast areas that are sparsely inhabited, their arithmetic densities of 47 and 122 people per square mile (18 and 47 per sq km), respectively, are not impressive. Brazil's huge

FIGURE 8.16
These women in the Yucatan Peninsula of Mexico are full-blooded native Americans. Their ancestors formed the Maya civilization of pre-Columbian time. (R. Gabler)

TABLE 8.8	Most Populated Countries and Principal Cities in Latin America: 1993		
Country	**Population (millions)**	**Arithmetic Density (population per sq mi)**	**Principal Cities**
Brazil	152.0	47	São Paulo, Rio de Janeiro, Belo Horizonte
Mexico	90.0	122	Mexico City, Guadalajara, Monterrey
Colombia	34.9	87	Bogotá, Medellín
Argentina	33.5	32	Buenos Aires
Peru	22.9	46	Lima
Venezuela	20.7	61	Caracas

SOURCE: *Population Reference Bureau.*

Amazon Basin is mostly a rainy tropical area that remains very thinly populated despite long-term efforts by the government to promote its settlement. Northern Mexico, largely a desert area, has an equally sparse population. However, border towns in northern Mexico have been growing rapidly because of economic advantages associated with being adjacent to the United States.

The Coastal and Highland Concentrations

The general pattern of South America's population arrangement features concentrations along the coasts and in the highland areas (Fig. 8.17). In part, this pattern is related to the fact that the majority of the continent is in tropical latitudes where lowlands are usually hot and at least seasonally humid. These uncomfortable climatic conditions are tempered somewhat in coastal locations where the land is periodically cooled by breezes from over the ocean. Cooler conditions are even more pronounced in highland areas. For every increase in elevation of 1000 feet, there is an average temperature decrease of 3.6°F (6.6°C per 1000 m). In the tropical mountains between about 2000 and 6000 feet (600 and 1800 m) above sea level, temperatures are so moderate that Latin Americans refer to this zone as the *tierra templada* (temperate land).

Densities of population usually are greater in this zone than in the one below (from sea level to about 2000 feet or 600 meters), called the *tierra caliente* (hot land), and in the zone above (from above 6000 to 11,000 feet or 1800 to 3300 meters in elevation), called the *tierra fría* (cool land).

Highland basins in the Andes Mountains of western South America and the mountains of Middle America also have attracted clusters of population because of their fertile soils (Fig. 8.18). These mountains include volcanoes that, during periods of activity, have filled basins with mineral-rich basalt and ash. Over time, this volcanic material has weathered and enriched the soils. The basins and valleys also have benefited from the accumulation of alluvial soil materials that have washed down the slopes of adjacent mountains. In addition to rural population concentrations in such areas, the Latin American highlands also contain major cities such as La Paz, Quito, Bogotá, and Mexico City that commonly are more than 6000 feet (1888 m) above sea level. People who are unaccustomed to such high elevations usually discover that the reduced oxygen supply causes them to be short of breath after only slight physical exertion.

The concentration of population along and near the coast also reflects Latin America's traditional economic role as a supplier of raw materials and agricultural products for the industrialized countries of

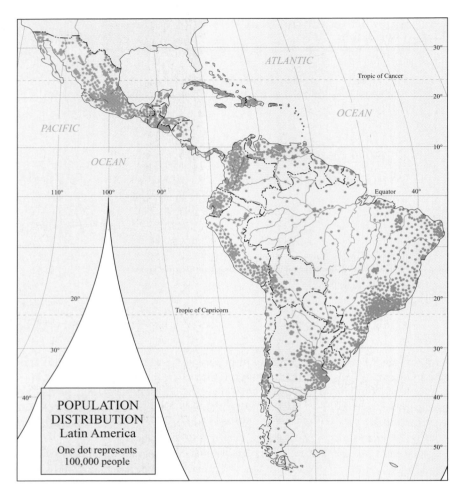

POPULATION
DISTRIBUTION
Latin America
One dot represents
100,000 people

FIGURE 8.17

Europe and North America. Because most of the region's commodities have been destined for export from its harbors, it made economic sense to avoid locating production facilities in distant or inaccessible parts of the interior. Thus, plantations, ranches, mines, and other economic operations were developed as near as possible to the harbors or along railroads and rivers that connected them with the harbors. The employment opportunities that these facilities offer have tended to discourage people from moving into the interior.

National Cores and Empty Areas

Most countries in Latin America share a common arrangement of their population. They have a single population agglomeration that is centered on one or two major cities, with the remainder of their territory sparsely inhabited. The well-populated area serves as the national core while the sparsely occupied areas include the country's border zone that is adjacent to foreign territory. The national wealth and political influence are concentrated in the core while the outlying areas are poorly developed and politically neglected. Of course, there are exceptions to such generalizations, but they identify geographically and historically persistent patterns in Latin America. Among the major countries that possess these characteristics are Brazil and Mexico (which we described earlier), Venezuela, Argentina, and Chile.

In Venezuela, the well-populated core overlooks the Caribbean Coast between the oil-producing Lake Maracaibo Basin and the mouth of the Orinoco River.

FIGURE 8.18

A cluster of population at 8,000 feet (2,450 m) in the Andes Mountains of Bolivia. (Cameramann International, Ltd.)

Caracas, an impressive modern capital city, is the focal center of the core. In contrast with the core area, where plantations and oil fields generate the main sources of national wealth, the interior is mostly a tropical grassland (the *Llanos*) that is thinly populated and generally used for cattle grazing.

The core of Argentina is the Pampa, an agriculturally productive area in the eastern part of the country that raises massive amounts of wheat, corn, and cattle for export. Buenos Aires, on the coast of the Río de la Plata, is the national capital and urban nucleus of the core. Sparsely populated outlying areas are arid Patagonia to the south, the Andes Mountains to the west, and the isolated Gran Chaco to the north.

The central part of Chile, including the city of Santiago, is that country's well-populated national core. Called the Vale of Chile, this area has a mild Mediterranean climate and productive farm lands. The northern one-third of elongated Chile is dominated by the extremely dry Atacama Desert; the southern one-third is part of the rugged Andes and has a fjorded coastline. Both are sparsely populated.

AFRICA

> Although the continent of Africa is second only to Asia in total population, it has few areas with high concentrations of people.

What factors account for the relatively few large concentrations of population in Africa?

What accounts for the major concentrations in Nigeria and Egypt?

Africa became known as the "Dark Continent" by Europeans because their explorations of the interior were delayed so long by physical barriers. Crossing the vast arid zone of the Sahara was extremely risky, and penetrating the continent from the sea was difficult because of falls and rapids on the rivers and dense vegetation along the equatorial coasts. Curiosity and interest in the resources and native inhabitants of tropical Africa extended over many centuries before the explorations and colonization activities of Europeans were essentially completed during the early part of the twentieth century.

The population of Africa experienced both losses and gains following European contact. The most significant result was that Europeans reduced the population by implementing a slave trade that grew, as described in Chapter 7, to massive proportions during the seventeenth and early part of the eighteenth centuries. It is estimated that 10 to 15 million people were removed from West Africa to be transported across the Atlantic and enslaved on the plantations of Latin America and the southern United States. On a much smaller scale, Europeans added to the population of Africa by settling in selected parts of the continent. Middle latitude areas of southern Africa attracted the most Europeans, but significant numbers also settled along parts of the Mediterranean Coast and on fertile farmlands in eastern Africa. As the African countries acquired their independence, mostly since World War II, many people of European ancestry fled the continent. Now only about 2 percent of Africa's population is of European origin, and most of them are in the Republic of South Africa.

Africa's total population of about 677 million is second only to that of Asia, yet the continent has very few large concentrations of people. As Figure 8.19 reveals, the population is spread over the landscape in moderate densities except for the sparsely occupied deserts and a few areas with high concentrations. This pattern reflects both the environmental character of Africa and the pre-industrial nature of the economy.

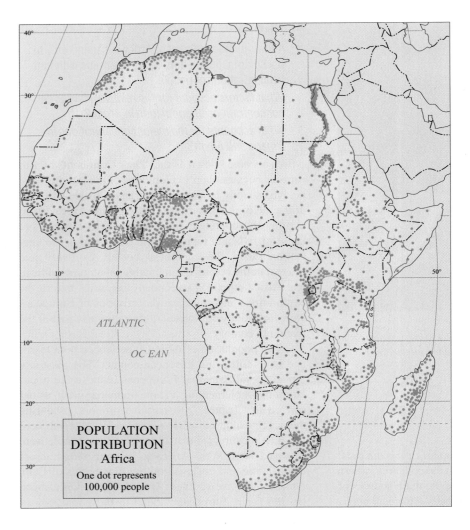

POPULATION
DISTRIBUTION
Africa

One dot represents
100,000 people

ATLANTIC

OC EAN

FIGURE 8.19

Roles of the Environment and Economy

Although Africa and Latin America are both largely tropical in location and share a high rate of population growth, the two regions have a number of striking contrasts. The geologic structure of Africa is dominated by an enormous ancient plateau that usually terminates near the coastline of the continent in a steep escarpment. Therefore, broad coastal lowlands where population might concentrate are rare in Africa, and no hot, humid, and sparsely populated interior lowland on the scale of the Amazon Basin exists. Africa also lacks a rugged mountain chain that, like the Andes, spans the length of the continent and offers numerous sites for population to concentrate in cooler elevations.

The only extensive highlands are the Atlas Mountains along the northwest coast, the Drakensberg Mountains along the southeast coast, and the East African Highlands. In eastern Africa volcanic cones rise, singly and in clusters, several thousand feet above the general plateau surface. The well-known Mt. Kilimanjaro and Mt. Kenya both exceed 17,000 feet (5100 m) above sea level and are major tourist attractions. Nearby basins with fertile soils derived from volcanic ash and basalt have important population concentrations (Fig. 8.20). Another prominent feature of the highland zone in East Africa is a series of elongated and steep-sided valleys (called *rift valleys*) that are partially filled by lakes. These water bodies, as well as Lake Victoria, which occupies a broad basin, also

FIGURE 8.20

A native agricultural settlement in eastern Africa. (Donald Marshall Collection)

have attracted small clusters of population to their shores. Sites in the rift valley zone of East Africa are where anthropologists, notably members of the Leakey family, have found the oldest known skeletal remains and other evidence of the earth's earliest human inhabitants.

With the exception of Australia, Africa has a greater proportion of its territory in desert than any other continent. Much of southwestern Africa is covered by the Kalahari Desert, but it is merely a fraction of the size of the Sahara in the north. The deserts are Africa's most sparsely populated regions; some fairly extensive areas are even uninhabited. Livestock herders and, in the Kalahari, nomadic hunters are widely scattered over these dry lands. However, water is available in a number of scattered areas for oasis development and the support of concentrations of crop farmers. The largest of these is the Nile Valley, which we will examine later in this chapter.

Although the European colonists developed plantations and commercial farms, opened mines, and constructed commercial facilities, the great majority of Africans continue to be subsistence farmers. In the tropical areas south of the Sahara, their villages are spread over the land in a manner that produces low to moderate population densities. The better farmlands generally have higher densities, and areas with dense rainforests or poor soils are inhabited by fewer people.

Africa has few major cities, and in some countries less than 20 percent of the population is urban. The principal exception is the Republic of South Africa, which has more than a million inhabitants in each of three cities—Capetown, Johannesburg, and Durban. South Africa has the most diversified economy and the highest level of industrialization in all of Africa.

The Nigerian and Nile Valley Concentrations

With the modern political fragmentation of Africa into some 50 countries, most national population totals are not very impressive. Nigeria, home to about 95 million people, is the continent's most populated country (Table 8.9). Egypt ranks second with slightly more than 58 million inhabitants, although its Nile River Valley is one of the most densely populated areas in the world. Most African countries have fewer than 30 million inhabitants, but we must keep in mind that Africa's rate of demographic growth is very high and that most countries will double their population totals in 20 to 30 years, if present growth trends continue.

Nigeria's population is most concentrated in the country's coastal zone, including the lower valley and broad delta of the Niger River. Lagos, the largest Nigerian city, also is located in this zone. This clustering of people along the coast was encouraged during colonial times by the development of facilities to produce and ship tropical farm products and minerals to European markets. Rapid exploitation of oil deposits in the Niger delta since the 1970s has helped diversify the economy and has provided greater economic motivation for the clustering of population along the coast. Population concentrations in the interior of the country are based more on traditional native livelihoods of subsistence agriculture and livestock herding. Contrasts in lifestyles and cultural differences between coastal and interior groups of people have been difficult obstacles for the political unification of modern Nigeria.

In Egypt there is a striking transition from the Nile Valley to the barren desert on both sides that is vividly portrayed in Figure 8.21. The desert is so arid that it is avoided by most forms of life, including humans. The valley, however, is a crowded strip of green irrigated fields, villages, and cities; it is one of the most intensively used and densely populated areas imaginable. Although it averages only seven miles in width, the Nile Valley contains 95 percent of the 58 million inhabitants of Egypt. Population densities in the valley

TABLE 8.9 Most Populated Countries and Principal Cities in Africa: 1993

Country	Population (millions)	Arithmetic Density (population per sq mi)	Principal Cities
Nigeria	95.1	270	Lagos, Ibadan
Egypt	58.3	152	Cairo, Alexandria
Ethiopia	56.7	133	Addis Ababa
Zaire	41.2	47	Kinshasa
South Africa	39.0	83	Johannesburg
Morocco	28.0	162	Casablanca
Tanzania	27.8	81	Dar-es-Salaam
Kenya	27.7	126	Nairobi
Sudan	27.4	30	Khartoum
Algeria	27.3	30	Algiers

SOURCE: *Population Reference Bureau.*

FIGURE 8.21
Viewed from aloft, the irrigated farmlands of the Nile Valley in Egypt contrast sharply with the barren lands of the adjacent desert. (Robert Caputo/Stock Boston)

are enormous—more than 5000 persons per square mile (1900 per sq km)! Furthermore, if the present rate of population growth in Egypt is maintained, it will result in a doubling of the total in only 30 years. Given its poor economic status and its rapid population growth, the ability of Egypt to adequately support and feed its people in the future is highly doubtful.

AUSTRALIA

➤ Among the inhabited continents, Australia is the most sparsely populated.

How have historical events and environmental conditions contributed to Australia's low population total?

What parts of Australia and which of the nearby islands are most populated?

Australia is easily the most thinly populated of the world's inhabited continents. With an area of nearly 3 million square miles (7.5 million sq km), it has a total of only 18 million people and an arithmetic density of 6 persons per square mile (2 per sq km). Of course, most of the continent has a dry climate; as we noted at the beginning of this chapter, about two-thirds of Australia is desert. Nevertheless, there are some fertile

farmlands and rich mineral deposits that have enabled Australia's people to develop a diversified economy and enjoy a high standard of living.

Australia, as well as neighboring New Zealand, became thoroughly Europeanized as the British colonized these lands following the arrival of explorer James Cook in 1770. From 1778 through 1848, the British brought groups of convicts from Europe, using remote Australia as a penal colony. Other immigrants from Britain and eventually various parts of the world helped increase the population and expand the settled areas to their present extents. In the meantime, Australia's original inhabitants—the Aborigines—have declined in number from about 300,000 at the beginning of the colonial period to fewer than 225,000 today.

The impact of moisture on the settlement pattern of Australia clearly is evident on the map of population (Fig. 8.22). The central and western parts of the country, dominated by desert conditions, are scarcely inhabited (Fig. 8.23). The vast majority of Australians live in the eastern and southeastern coastal zone where rainfall amounts are more than 20 inches (50 cm) per year. Melbourne and Sydney, Australia's two principal cities, are included in this zone. The only other area with even a slight concentration of population is the southwestern corner of the country where there is a Mediterranean climate with seasonal rainfall.

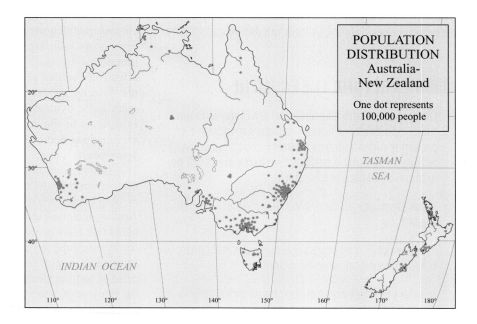

FIGURE 8.22

FIGURE 8.23
The arid and sparsely populated Outback of Australia. The prominent feature in the photo is Ayers Rock, an erosional remnant. (J. Lamont)

In the vicinity of Australia, only Papua New Guinea and New Zealand have significant population totals. Each of these countries, however, has fewer than 4 million people. The entire realm of Oceania, including all neighboring islands together with Australia, possesses only 28 million inhabitants.

REGIONS BEYOND THE ECUMENE

➤ Current and future technological developments may make it possible for human numbers to increase in presently uninhabited or sparsely populated areas of the world, but it is unlikely that these areas will be extensively settled in the future.

What are major obstacles to the settlement of such areas?

What areas of little population show the least promise for future demographic growth?

In which of these areas is population most likely to expand?

Humans have occupied each of the earth's continents (except Antarctica) for at least several tens of thousands of years, and during that long period they consistently have avoided certain types of regions as places to settle in significant numbers. Our survey of current population distribution confirms that these regions are still largely beyond the **ecumene**, a term introduced by early Greek scholars to identify the effectively settled portion of the world. Reasons for the scarcity of population in certain environments seem quite evident, but we must be cautious about exceptions to the rule and the possibility of current explanations being diminished by future cultural developments.

The regions most avoided by people are those with environmental conditions that make the practice of crop agriculture extremely difficult or impossible. Arid regions that are too dry and polar and subarctic lands that have growing seasons of inadequate length for crops are the most extensive parts of the world with little or no population (Fig. 8.24). In addition, some areas of rugged mountainous terrain and some parts of the rainy tropics are clearly beyond the ecumene. We also can identify areas that are largely unpopulated because they have poor drainage or unproductive soils, but usually these are parts of larger regions with other limitations. This facet of world population distribution is rational if we keep in mind that the basic distributional pattern was established prior to the industrial period and that the vast majority of the world's people continue to make their livelihood by farming. Even in countries that have become highly industrialized and now have only a small proportion of their people engaged in agriculture, there has been little alteration of the earlier pattern of population distribution.

It is obvious that cultural developments have made it possible for regions with environmental limitations to support more people than in the past, at least in certain locations. The discovery and exploitation of oil resources in the deserts of Southwest Asia and North Africa, the construction of facilities such as the Aswan High Dam to expand irrigation in desert areas,

and the establishment along some desert coasts of desalinization plants to derive fresh water from seawater are examples of developments that have increased population numbers in parts of the world's arid lands. In a similar way, the implementation of mining activities and the construction of transportation lines in polar and subarctic areas have attracted new settlers. In Siberia, for example, a small agglomeration of people in the mining district of the Kuznets Basin and a narrow ribbon of population along the Trans-Siberian Railroad have appeared only since the development of these two entities during the present century. Some parts of the world's most difficult environments have even been converted into tourist attractions, thereby improving their ability to support a permanent population that serves the needs of tourists. It would be foolish indeed to ignore the likelihood that similar developments in the future will expand the ecumene.

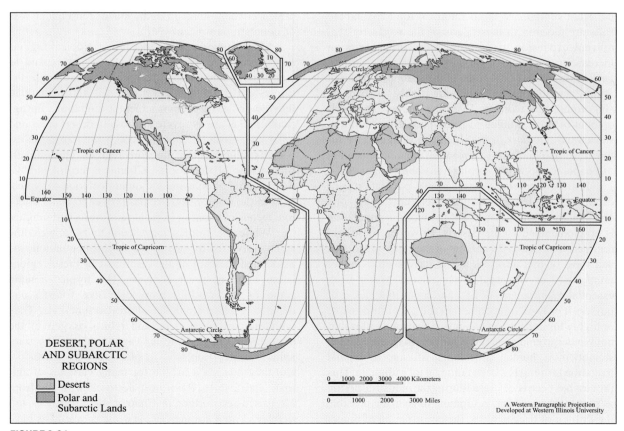

FIGURE 8.24

The world's least populated lands are in desert, polar, and subarctic regions.

An even greater mistake, however, would be to anticipate that major regions now beyond the ecumene will be settled extensively in the future. These areas simply involve obstacles to human comfort and economic gain—primarily in the form of extreme environmental conditions—that seem to be permanently unacceptable to nearly all people. As a matter of fact, some thinly populated regions have been experiencing an out-migration as their few inhabitants learn about easier lifestyles in neighboring areas with less rigorous environments. As a consequence, these regions may contain an even smaller population in the future than they do now. The regions that seem most likely to remain largely beyond the ecumene are the polar and subarctic lands and the deserts of the world.

The polar and subarctic regions encompass about 26 percent of the land area on earth but presently contain less than 1 percent of the world's population. Their potential for agricultural development is very poor. Scientists may be successful in shortening the growing season required for some crops, but the yearly period of subfreezing temperatures is too long and the soils are too thin in these parts of the world for significant expansion of farming. More probable is an increase in exploitation of natural resources, particularly the minerals and forests, in these regions. Modern mining and logging, however, are highly mechanized and require few workers. Even the large-scale development of oil has failed to bring people to Alaska in substantial numbers. It is difficult to imagine any future developments that will result in a major relocation of people to the world's polar and subarctic lands.

Primarily because of exceptional population concentrations in a few irrigation districts, notably Egypt's Nile Valley, about 6 percent of the world's population is now contained within deserts. However, these arid regions cover nearly 20 percent of the earth's land area and most of this territory, as we have seen, is either uninhabited or very sparsely populated. Water is an essential requirement for life, and areas that lack it or possess it only in scanty amounts are either impossible or highly limited human habitats. The capture of water, both underground and on the surface, in desert areas to support more human and animal life and to expand irrigation farming has been going on for millennia. This process has been accelerated during the industrial period as new technology and equipment have made possible the drilling of deeper wells, the construction of bigger dams and reservoirs, and the digging of more extensive canals and ditches to distribute water.

As a consequence, the limited fresh water supplies in deserts have become thoroughly exploited. In some areas, groundwater has been exhausted and surface streams and rivers are being used to their full potential. Obtaining greater amounts of water in dry lands is becoming physically impossible or prohibitively expensive. Artificial rainmaking (cloud seeding) is seldom feasible in desert areas because the air contains so little moisture to begin with. Converting salt water from the sea into fresh water for consumption and irrigation is technically possible but still very expensive. Even where adequate wealth is available to build and operate desalinization plants, the processed water is limited in quantity and too scarce to distribute away from the coast. In summary, the prospects for increasing water supplies in the world's deserts are not good, and major increases of population in these regions therefore are not likely. As a matter of fact, deserts have been growing in extent in some parts of the world, particularly Africa and Asia, as areas marginal to them have experienced persistent drought and a consequent loss of population in recent years.

Many authorities feel that humid tropical regions are where the ecumene is most likely to expand as world population growth continues. Although the tropics are in many ways a difficult human habitat, they do not possess environmental limitations for agriculture that are as severe as those in desert areas and polar and subarctic lands. Indeed, some crops are especially suited to the moisture regimes and uninterrupted heat of the tropics. Chemical fertilizers have the potential of delaying the rapid depletion of typical soils in the tropics, and fire has proven to be an effective means of clearing tropical rainforests and jungles.

While the tropics may seem to be a welcome safety-valve for the world's growing population, the associated clearing of the rainforest in these regions is an issue of great concern. The tropics contain some of the world's most extensive forests, and these trees serve a number of critical functions. They withdraw carbon dioxide and return oxygen to the atmosphere, they add water vapor to the air by transpiration, they hold soil in place to reduce erosion, and they provide a habitat for many varieties of animals and insects. Rainforest destruction in the tropics (discussed further in Chapter 14) already is underway at an alarming rate, and many scientists have predicted dire consequences for the earth and its inhabitants if this trend continues. Nevertheless, further clearing of the rainforests probably will be unavoidable if the tropics experience increasing population densities.

OVERPOPULATION AND HUMAN CROWDING

➤ The term "overpopulation" defies definition; it is extremely difficult to determine if an area of the world is overpopulated.

Why is overpopulation such an elusive concept?

What factors must be taken into consideration when making a judgment concerning overpopulation?

Areas of severe human crowding that have been examined in this chapter commonly are said to be suffering from overpopulation. Certainly many people would agree that parts of China, the Ganges Valley, Bangladesh, Java, central Mexico, the Nile Valley, and perhaps a number of other areas have an excessive population. Some might even contend that the world as a whole is now overpopulated. But what *is* overpopulation, and how can we determine when it has been reached in a particular area? Can certain criteria be used to define overpopulation throughout the world?

We may be tempted to conclude that overpopulation has been reached in an area when a significant proportion of the people must endure a less than acceptable standard of living. But what proportion is "significant"? And how do we determine what is an "acceptable" standard of living? A standard that is acceptable to one group of people may be unacceptable to another. Even the meaning of "standard of living" is obscure. Diet obviously is an essential element of a people's standard of living; however, the adequacy of a particular diet varies not only from group to group but also from one individual to another.

Another approach might be for us to determine a certain density of population that represents the threshold of overpopulation. However, if we are to make a judgment on whether a certain density, say 500 people per square mile (200 per sq km), represents a condition of overpopulation in a particular area, we must have information about the **human carrying capacity** of the land and the culture of the people. An area's human carrying capacity (i.e., the maximum number of people that can be supported at a standard of living that is acceptable to them) is influenced by the agricultural potential of the land and the resources available. (The greater the amount of food that can be produced and the larger the quantity of resources, the more people that can be supported.) In addition, we also must take into consideration the technological level of the people and the type of economy practiced in determining the carrying capacity. If the population has a low level of technology and a simple economy like subsistence farming (Fig. 8.25), it may not utilize the available resources fully and attain potential production levels. In that case, the carrying capacity would be limited more by cultural factors than by physical shortcomings of the land. However, Japan is an example of an area in which the carrying capacity is high because the level of technology and the complex economy are able to overcome the scarcity of domestic resources and the low agricultural potential of the land. To use a particular population density as a definition of overpopulation throughout the world obviously is impossible. Although an average of 500 people per square mile (200 per sq km) easily can be supported at a high standard of living in some areas, the same density may be marked by widespread poverty and inadequate diets in other parts of the world.

Overpopulation clearly is a subjective concept; it cannot be precisely defined or accurately measured. As we make judgments about overpopulation, we must keep in mind that each area has a unique combination of conditions and we must avoid extending our conclusions to other areas that may seem similar.

FIGURE 8.25

A subsistence farmer in India prepares his land for planting. The low level of technology exhibited here is one of several factors that can restrict the human carrying capacity of an area. (R. Gabler)

KEY TERMS

Arithmetic density A measurement of population density expressed as the average number of people per unit area (sq mi or sq km) for the total area of a country or state. **277**

Physiological density A measurement of population density expressed as the average number of people per unit area (sq mi or sq km) of arable land in a country or state. Also known as nutritional density. **277**

European population axis The most extensive zone of relatively high population densities in Europe. It extends in a general west–east pattern from southern Britain to western Russia. **288**

Conurbation A continuous urbanized zone that has been formed by the horizontal growth of cities and their suburbs. **293**

Megalopolis A particularly extensive conurbation that extends from southern Maine to the shores of Chesapeake Bay along the East Coast of the United States. **293**

Mestizo A person whose ancestors were both Amerindian and European. Mestizos are the most prevalent individuals in extensive parts of Latin America. **298**

Ecumene The effectively settled or populated parts of the earth. **305**

Human carrying capacity The maximum number of people that an area theoretically can support at an acceptable standard of living. **307**

REVIEW QUESTIONS

1. Where are the major population clusters located on a map of world population? Why is such a large percentage of the world's people located in the Northern Hemisphere?

2. What measurement of population density is most widely used? How is physiological density more revealing than arithmetic density of population?

3. What three major population clusters are located in Eurasia? What physical and historical (human) factors help to explain the growth of each of the three?

4. Which country has the greatest number of people in East Asia? What other East Asian countries have large populations? How is the population distributed within these countries?

5. What are the major similarities and differences in a comparison of the East Asian and South Asian population clusters? What factors influence the distribution of people in South Asia? Which countries have the most people?

6. What demographic characteristics are most closely associated with the European population cluster? Where are most of the people of Europe concentrated? What explains the differences in population densities between the European population axis and the Mediterranean South?

7. What percentage of the former Soviet Union's population is located in Europe? How can this be explained?

8. What circumstances have contributed to significant population concentrations in Southeast Asia? What circumstances have contributed to significant population concentrations in Southwest Asia? Which countries have large populations in each of the two regions?

9. What environmental conditions explain the sparsely settled areas of Eurasia?

10. What similarities are evident in a comparison of the populations of the United States and Canada? Why is there such disparity in total population and in population density between the two countries?

11. What is a *conurbation*? What major cities are included in the conurbation called *Megalopolis*? Where are other developing conurbations in North America?

12. What explains the striking population contrasts between the eastern and western United States? In the western United States, how is the Pacific Coast an exceptional area?

13. Where do most of the people of Canada live? What problems for Canada can be traced to the nature and distribution of the country's population?

14. What are the major racial and ethnic groups of Latin America? Where does each group tend to be dominant?

15. What two countries account for the majority of people in Latin America? Where are the people in these two countries concentrated? What climate and landform characteristics are associated with the general distribution of Latin America's population?

16. What common arrangement of population is shared by many Latin American countries? How has this characteristic affected the distribution of wealth and political influence of people living in these countries?

17. What roles do the physical environment and the nature of the economy play in explaining the distribution of Africa's population? Which two African countries have the greatest population and where are the people concentrated in these countries?

18. What single characteristic of Australia is most closely associated with the arrangement of the country's population?

19. What is meant by the *ecumene*? What major obstacles will discourage significant expansion of the ecumene in the near future?

20. Why is it difficult to designate a particular area of the world as overpopulated? What characteristics of an area must be considered when making a judgment regarding overpopulation?

A CONVERSATION WITH JOHN BONGAARTS, DIRECTOR OF RESEARCH, THE POPULATION COUNCIL

"There is not enough food for today," Dr. Paul R. Ehrlich
wrote in his landmark book, The Population Bomb.
"How much there will be tomorrow is open to debate."

John Bongaarts *(front) leads a workshop in Thailand.*

As a graduate student in the late 1960s, John Bongaarts was so inspired by Paul Erlich's urgent words that he prepared a doctoral dissertation on the role of high birth rates in global population trends. Since then, he has sustained a distinguished career in demographic research. Currently, he serves as vice president and director of the Research Division of The Population Council, located in New York City.

Born in 1945, Dr. Bongaarts grew up in Holland, where he received an undergraduate degree in systems analysis from Eindhoven Institute of Technology, The Netherlands. He earned his Ph.D. in physiology and biomedical engineering in 1972 at the University of Illinois Medical Center. Dr. Bongaarts joined the staff of The Population Council in 1973, after completing postdoctoral studies at the Johns Hopkins School of Hygiene and Public Health under a fellowship provided by the National Institutes of Health.

Renowned for his analysis of global population projections, he is co-editor of four books, including *Family Demography: Methods and Their Applications.* He is a member of the Royal Dutch Academy of Sciences and the Johns Hopkins Society of Scholars. In 1986, he received the prestigious Mindel Shep Award for research excellence from the Population Association of America.

The Population Council was formed in 1952, in response to startling world population projections by the Population Division of the United Nations. What are the functions of your organization?

The Population Council is an international, non-profit scientific organization that undertakes research in three key areas: (1) biomedical research to develop contraceptives; (2) social-sciences research addressing the causes and consequences of population growth; and (3) reproductive-health research.

Our work focuses primarily on population problems in the developing world. The organization's long-range goal is to bring about a more sustainable, equitable balance between people and available resources.

> "More people were added to the global population after 1950 than in all of history before that time."

You develop models to show how specific policies might slow population growth. Does your research often require travel to foreign countries?

Yes, I travel a great deal! For example, I recently stayed on the volcanic island of Bali, in Indonesia, where I attended a conference. While I was there, I made a side trip to visit clinics that provide family planning services.

Indonesia has one of the most effective family planning programs in the world. Women are counseled carefully about all available methods of contraception. (The large majority of women in Bali use oral contraceptives or intrauterine devices.) Although Indonesia is still a relatively poor country, it has achieved a sustainable rate of population growth, with fewer than three births per woman.

Bali is very densely populated. It was interesting for me to see firsthand how that population has made use of its available resources. Rice terraces enable farmers to grow food on fairly steep slopes. They have extremely fertile soils, which support multiple crops each year. The region is a wonderful example of how human ingenuity can accommodate a large population, given scarce natural resources.

The island is also a case study in how a traditionally agricultural society can make the transition to a more service-oriented economy. The tourist industry in Bali is booming. Many people who are no longer needed in agriculture are providing tourist services in hotels, restaurants, and shops.

Will the world's population continue to increase substantially in the future?

Yes. In the year 1800, the world's population stood at 1 billion individuals. By 1950, global population had increased to 2.5 billion. Worldwide population in 1993 was 5.5 billion, with roughly three-fourths living in less developed regions. More people were added to the global population after 1950 than in all of history before that time.

According to projections prepared by the United Nations and the World Bank, the population in the developing regions of Africa, Asia, and Latin America will increase from 4.5 billion in 1995 to 8.6 billion in 2050, and to 10.2 billion in 2100.

Why do you think it is so important to limit population growth?

Rapid population growth is a substantial hindrance to social and economic development, and it strains our environmental resources.

In many sub-Saharan African countries, for example, the population grows at a rate of 3 to 4 percent every year. Governments in those countries struggle to build an adequate number of schools for all the children being born, to train teachers and doctors, and to build new transportation infrastructures, housing, and health-care facilities. These countries have to invest a large proportion of their income simply to keep pace with population demands. To grow, they would need to invest at a much higher rate, and that would be very difficult.

Our environmental resources are increasingly under pressure because of rapid population growth. This is particularly true in the world's most densely populated regions, including South Asia and the Middle East. Rapidly growing metropolitan areas such as Mexico City are becoming almost unlivable because of the proliferation of slums, traffic, smog, and other social, economic, and environmental problems. All of these problems are partly attributable to unchecked population growth.

Is better family planning the answer to rapid population growth?

Family planning programs throughout the world clearly provide contraceptive products and services needed by many, many people. Over 100 million women have an unmet need for contraception. One of every six married women living in less developed countries outside China do not wish to become pregnant, yet they are not using contraception, often because it is unavailable to them.

My research has shown that preventing all unwanted births in the less developed world would decrease the projected population size in 2050 by 1.1 billion individuals, or by 1.9 billion in 2100. Unfortunately, family planning programs are still very weak in many less developed regions.

But family planning alone will not slow population growth to zero because women in many regions want more than two children. Women in Africa, for instance, often want five or six children. In addition to providing stronger family planning, societies should strive to reduce the demand for very large families, and address the phenomenon of "population momentum" (the tendency of a youthful population to increase even after birth rates have stabilized).

Why do people often want many children? How can societies encourage smaller families?

Children are valuable in less developed regions because they provide labor for largely agricultural societies. They also provide "old-age security" for their parents. People want to be sure that they have a surviving son—and preferably more than one son—to take care of them in their old age.

Also, children are not very costly in many less developed countries. They must be fed and clothed, but governments do not make the large investments in education that we encounter in the more developed nations.

Governments could adjust the costs associated with large families through programs that encourage human development. An emphasis on better education, for example, is one of the most powerful ways to bring about social development and to provide a better livelihood for the next generation. Requiring children to attend school increases the cost of raising a child because parents must invest in books and uniforms, and because children who are in school cannot provide farm labor. At the same time, girls who stay in school longer are less likely to begin their families at a very young age, and they are more likely to achieve higher socioeconomic status. Improving the status of women is key to providing roles for them outside of motherhood.

High infant mortality is another important issue that must be addressed to reduce the demand for births. In many countries, one of every five children dies in childhood. That is a powerful reason to continue childbearing; parents feel they must have children to offset the expected loss of other children.

If families could reduce the average number of children that they have to two, they could cut the future population size by 0.6 billion in 2050, or by 1 billion in 2100.

In addition to better family planning and a reduction in the demand for births, you believe that societies could take action to slow "population momentum." Please explain this concept.

Population momentum is the tendency of populations to continue growing even when most families in the region have only two children. If families limited themselves to two children, we would still see the world's population grow to over 7 billion. This is because most of the world's population is still very young. In Africa, nearly half of the population is under the age of 15. As all of these young boys and girls become parents, they will stimulate population growth again.

We can offset population momentum, in part, by delaying the average age of childbearing. If, instead of having a first child in their late teens, women wait until they are older and permit more time to pass between the birth of each subsequent child, the population momentum would be slowed. If we could raise the average age of marriage by five years, then population momentum could be reduced by 1 billion people over the next century.

Perhaps even more important, we should continue to address adolescent sexuality and reproductive behavior through stronger educational efforts. When adolescents become sexually active, unfortunately, they often do not use contraceptives, or they use them sporadically. Preventing teen pregnancies is essential for slowing population momentum.

A third way to arrest population momentum and motivate a woman to delay her first birth is to emphasize education at the secondary level. The longer a young woman stays in school, the older she probably will be when she has her first child.

What methods do you use to predict population trends?

I use software tools that provide standard population projections. These are accessible to anyone with a personal computer. Let's say that I want to illustrate the effectiveness of family planning programs by projecting the potential consequences of preventing unwanted pregnancies. I start with a standard reference projection provided by an information source such as the World Bank. Next, I apply additional information to that projection, such as the number of women who say they do not want children, yet use no contraception. I determine how many births could be prevented if those women *did* have access to contraception. Then I project current population figures to reflect the lower fertility rate.

Will jobs be available in the future for human geographers who want to study world population trends?

In my opinion, there will be a substantial number of jobs for geographers and other researchers who want to analyze population issues. For example, a variety of institutions (for example, universities, government statistical offices, and marketing departments of companies) collect and analyze demographic data. There is also a large family planning service industry providing couples with information about and access to contraceptives. I also see an increase in jobs that help us better understand our environment and how it relates to the number of people in the world, and the distribution of that population—whether they live in rural or urban areas, in developed or less developed countries.

Representations of traditional farming and modern industry serve to remind us of the enormous contrast in economic development that divides the world's nations into categories of poor and rich. This division is an issue of great significance in the contemporary world and poses a serious threat to global stability. In fact, the issue has been increasing in severity because the "wealth gap" separating these two groups of countries has widened with the passage of time.

The economies of about four-fifths of the world's countries (containing three-fourths of the world's population) are dominated by farming and other types of primary production. These are the economically less developed nations, and most suffer extreme poverty. The great majority of the people in these nations live in rural areas and have inadequate diets, health care, and educational opportunities. Many rely on subsistence agriculture for their livelihood and have little or no involvement in commercial activities. These nations tend to be tradition-bound and resistant to change. Whatever success they may have in raising their economic output is usually offset by their high rates of population growth.

The world's relatively developed countries, by contrast, are industrial and commercial powers that possess considerable wealth. They rely heavily on ad-

PART 4

ECONOMIC DEVELOPMENT AND LIVELIHOODS

(Bob Stern The Image Works)

vanced technology to improve their production efficiency. Their labor force is largely engaged in secondary (manufacturing) and tertiary (service) occupations; only small percentages are farmers. Most citizens of these nations live in urban centers and enjoy a wide assortment of consumer goods and social advantages that are uncommon in the rest of the world. With relatively low rates of population growth, these countries have made substantial progress in raising standards of living.

Part IV of this book is devoted to the issue of economic development and to those economic and related social characteristics that divide the world into less developed and developed countries. After a survey of the world's economic contrasts in Chapter 9, we examine the process and ingredients of economic development. The distinctive livelihoods and social characteristics of the less developed countries are the focus of Chapter 10, while those of the developed countries are scrutinized in Chapter 11. An important feature of the latter two chapters is a consideration of the role of women in the economies of the two groups of countries.

ECONOMIC DEVELOPMENT: THE RICH AND THE POOR

Throughout the world . . . traditional societies are in the throes of the "revolution of rising expectations" as their peoples seek to achieve the higher living standards that Western contact and influence have demonstrated is possible.

—D. W. Fryer

The level of development of industry and services is a revealing difference between the rich and poor nations of the world. (Telegraph Color Library/FPG International)

➤ One of the strongest challenges facing present and future generations is the great contrast between the economically rich and economically poor nations of the world.

What are some obvious examples of this contrast?

What are some of the underlying causes of the tremendous gap between the rich and the poor?

What individual exceptions often are evident within both rich and poor nations?

More than three-fourths of the world's people reside in countries that are economically poor. These nations have been unable to keep pace with other parts of the world in economic development, and the bulk of their populations must endure poverty in some form on a daily basis. Insufficient employment and incomes, inadequate diets and housing, and limited access to medical care and education are some of the distinguishing characteristics of human life in the world's poor coun-

tries (Fig. 9.1). The economies here are dominated by traditional ways of making a living, particularly farming, and any fundamental change in economic procedures is implemented slowly and may be resisted vigorously. Advanced technology generally is unavailable, human and animal muscle power is relied on heavily because of limited mechanization, and funds for capital investment in economic improvements are scarce. Hopes are dim for significantly better living standards in the future, partly because the typically high rates of population growth offset any increases in the production of commodities.

In striking contrast are the economically wealthy nations of the world, such as the United States, Germany, and Japan. The great majority of the people in these countries have at least adequate food, clothing, housing, and medical care, and many are able to enjoy an abundance of material goods and recreational opportunities. Education is nearly universal in the wealthy countries, and many individuals even have access to college and university instruction. Gainful occupations are abundant, and only very small percentages of those in the labor force must endure unemployment or underemployment. Worker productivity tends to be quite high because of widespread mechanization and the adaptation of technology to economic tasks. Emphasis is placed on increasing production efficiency, and experimentation with new procedures for raising production rates is common. Funds necessary for economic improvements and expansion generally are available. The wealthy countries have highly diversified economies, with agriculture only a minor source of employment; most jobs are in urban-based activities, especially in services and manufacturing. The population, therefore, is highly urbanized, and rates of demographic growth are relatively low. To ensure economic expansion, the wealthy countries are increasing their participation in international trade to obtain raw materials and tap markets for their products in foreign areas.

While generalizing about the world's rich and poor nations, we need to remember that there are important exceptions. Even the wealthiest countries possess pockets of poverty and groups of people, usually minorities, who have been unable to share in the affluence of the society at large. Likewise, the world's poorest nations typically have a small number of wealthy people, an elite group that commonly includes the major landowners, military and religious leaders,

FIGURE 9.1

The difficult life of these inhabitants of a fishing village in India's Orissa State is comparable to that of many people in the world's poor countries. (R. Gabler)

and those who hold positions of political power. Often poor countries also contain an impressive city (usually the capital) with extravagant public facilities. This city may suggest national prosperity to uninformed visitors, but in reality it only masks the prevailing poverty of the country.

THE WEALTH GAP AND INDUSTRIALIZATION

➤ The economic differences between wealthy and poor nations are almost always associated with modern industrialization in the former and the lack of such development in the latter.

Why is industrialization so important to economic growth?

Why are some nations heavily industrialized and others not?

Is the eventual major industrialization of all nations a probability?

Societies and nations undoubtedly have been separated by a wealth gap for millennia, but the gap has widened steadily in recent generations as economic development in the wealthy countries generally has progressed more rapidly than that in the poor countries. In other words, as the rich have become richer in modern time, the poor have fallen farther behind because of their inability to keep pace. This trend was accentuated by the industrialization of national economies, beginning in Europe and North America during the eighteenth and nineteenth centuries. From these original areas, industrialization later spread to Australia, the former Soviet Union, Japan, and a few other areas. Some analysts of the global economy have interpreted this pattern as a **core–periphery relationship**. That is, the original industrialized areas on the margin of the North Atlantic Ocean represent the *core* from which this new complex economy has been spreading into areas on its *periphery*.

Involving the use of inanimate sources of power and machinery to perform tasks, industrialization makes possible an enormous improvement in the efficiency of workers and great increases in the volume of goods produced (Fig. 9.2). Corresponding increases in the income of workers expand the market potential for goods and services and make available surplus

FIGURE 9.2
Workers on the assembly line of a Nissan automobile factory in Barcelona, Spain. The proportion of the labor force employed in industry is a major criterion in distinguishing between rich and poor countries. (Alex Quesada/Matrix)

funds for individuals to place in savings. Invested savings provide capital to finance further economic expansion. In this way, industrial economies become considerably more diversified than preindustrial ones.

The motivation among poor countries to initiate industrialization is understandably strong. In the modern world, it is the industrialized countries that possess the enviable combination of wealth, military strength, and political influence; in addition, their industrial lifestyle has aided in bringing their population growth under control. In poor countries, however, the process of industrialization faces severe obstacles. Scarcities of capital and technology, poor transportation systems, limited domestic markets, and a shortage of experienced workers and managerial personnel are some of the major handicaps that must be overcome. Nevertheless, industrialization continues to spread into new areas, and some nations (e.g., Taiwan and South Korea) that were poor in the recent past are now in the process of joining the industrial elite. Many firms in the older industrialized areas have aided this process by establishing branch factories in poor nations to take advantage of their low labor costs. Mexico, for ex-

FIGURE 9.3
Workers at the gate of a Chrysler factory in Toluca, Mexico. Such investment by Chrysler and other foreign corporations has significantly bolstered the economy of Mexico. (Steven Starr/Stock Boston)

ample, has benefited enormously from the establishment in its territory of manufacturing and assembly plants by U.S. corporations (Fig. 9.3).

Will industrialization eventually transform all parts of the world and essentially eliminate the current wealth gap? That scenario would seem to be impossible; the earth's resources cannot support industrialization on that scale, and the accompanying degradation of environments would be intolerable. The diffusion of industry already may be slowing, particularly because of growing competition for markets, the depletion of resources, and accelerating costs of energy. If the spread of industrialization is coming to an end, how *will* the wealth gap be reduced? What measures or reforms can be implemented? To continue with a minority of the world's population enjoying the advantages of life in wealthy industrial societies while the majority fall ever farther behind because they live in preindustrial countries is a serious threat to world stability. As the poor become increasingly aware of how they are disadvantaged by the growing inequality

in distribution of the world's wealth, the potential for massive disruption is increased.

Economic development obviously is a continuum along which some countries have progressed farther than others. Nevertheless, it is fairly easy and commonplace to divide the world's nations into two groups: the rich and the poor (Fig. 9.4). This classification may be arbitrary and highly generalized, but it probably represents the most significant current division of the world's nations.

THE TERMINOLOGY TANGLE

➢ Although it is obvious that great differences exist among the nations of the world, there is considerable disagreement about the terminology used to identify nations representing various levels of wealth and economic development.

Why is it so difficult to classify nations into major groups or categories?

What are the advantages of classifying countries as developed or less developed?

For a number of years, authorities have searched for acceptable and appropriate names for the two groups of countries we have been discussing. Our identification of wealthy and poor nations is based solely on their relative economic conditions. We recognize that many economically poor countries may be rich in other respects, such as their traditions and cultural heritage.

Developed and *underdeveloped* are other terms often used to differentiate countries on the basis of their economic condition. However, many scholars have urged that the word *underdeveloped* be avoided because of the risk that it may be interpreted as involving more than just economic status and therefore convey an unintended negative image of a country. More acceptable titles in their view are *developing countries* or *less developed countries*. Also, some people have suggested *emerging countries* as another alternative.

The names *First World*, *Second World*, and *Third World* are commonly used (particularly in the popular media) to identify groups of countries on the basis of their economic status and ideology. In this scheme, the economically advanced capitalist countries comprise

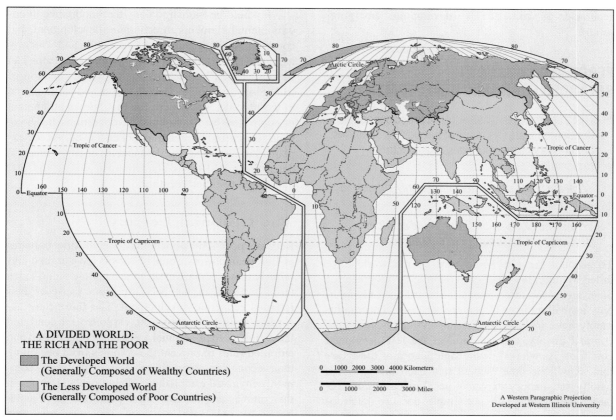

FIGURE 9.4

The division of the world into rich countries and poor countries. Within each group there is, of course, considerable variation among the countries in their degree of wealth or poverty. The greatest contrast, however, is between the two groups.

the First World; the communist or socialist countries with a centrally planned economy form the Second World; and the remaining countries, all of which are economically poor, are grouped as the Third World. This classification, however, is marred by some obvious inconsistencies. For example, on the basis of their level of economic development alone, some of the Second World countries are quite similar to those in the Third World group.

The terms *North* and *South* also have been employed to identify the more developed and less developed groups of countries, respectively. These designations are based on the general global position of the less developed countries to the south of most of the economically advanced nations (Fig. 9.4). The eco-

nomically advanced nations are mostly—but not entirely—located north of latitude 30° in the Northern Hemisphere. The overgeneralization involved in using expressions such as the *Developed North* and the *Less Developed South* is apparent when we recall that Australia and New Zealand, two of the world's most economically advanced countries, are in the Southern Hemisphere.

The terms that we have chosen for general use in this textbook are the developed countries and the less developed countries. This coincides with what appears to be the prevailing practices in current academic circles. The alternative terms for the less developed countries seem flawed because they may be interpreted as prejudicial (underdeveloped) or they may convey inaccuracies in some cases (developing, emerging, south).

PERCEIVED CAUSES OF RETARDED ECONOMIC DEVELOPMENT

➢ There are multiple reasons for retarded economic development among many of the world's countries, but no single cause provides a satisfactory explanation.

What are some of the more commonly suggested explanations?

Why is the explanation for retarded economic development of a country so complicated?

To account for why some parts of the world have failed to attain the level of economic development of other areas, too often people have assigned blame to only a small number of perceived causes. These commonly have included environmental deficiencies, the colonial history, and isolation of the less developed countries. As we review the significance of these factors, it will become evident that each one is not a wholly satisfactory explanation. The reasons for retarded development are not simple, because the problem itself is complex.

Environmental Deficiencies

The level of economic development in a country obviously can be influenced by environmental conditions. Fertile soils, nearly level terrain, a lengthy growing season, adequate water supplies, and an abundance and variety of natural resources clearly are valuable environmental attributes from an economic standpoint. For industrialization, the presence of metallic ores and energy resources is particularly important. Possession of an enormous amount of fertile land and a vast quantity of natural resources unquestionably facilitated development of the United States into an economic power. But does a scarcity or absence of one or more of these environmental attributes doom a country to poverty? Despite a paucity of good agricultural land and a lack of natural resources, Japan has become one of the world's most economically advanced nations. Switzerland and Norway, both mountainous countries with a scarcity of agricultural land and mineral resources, are two other examples of wealthy countries that have overcome severe environmental limitations.

It would be foolish to deny the importance of environmental elements in economic development, but countries such as Japan, Switzerland, and Norway have demonstrated that environmental handicaps can be surmounted by such means as the application of technology, economic specialization, and participation in world trade. The conclusion that human attainment is controlled by environmental conditions has long been recognized by geographers as flawed. As we explained in Chapter 1, the deficiencies of environmental determinism led to its abandonment during the first half of the twentieth century.

The Colonial Legacy

Because most of the poor countries are former colonies of European powers, some observers have argued vigorously that colonialism or, to use a more value-laden term, imperialism, has been the prime cause of their retarded economic development. The Europeans, according to this interpretation, exploited the land and the people of their colonial areas and even devised and enforced rules to prevent the colonies from becoming their economic competitors. The exploitation commonly involved establishing plantations and mines in the colonies and forcing native people to serve as laborers for only meager wages. The Europeans then used the minerals and other raw materials obtained from the colonies to expand industrial production at home, and they further improved their standard of living with food and fibers imported from their colonial plantations. Furthermore, the Europeans created a captive market for their surplus industrial production by (1) forbidding their colonies from developing competing industries, and (2) by requiring that their colonies trade only with them.

Even after obtaining political independence, most former colonies have been unable to change significantly their economic relationships with their former mother countries. They have continued in their role as suppliers of agricultural products and minerals, with their well-being highly dependent on economic conditions, trends, and decisions in the former mother country. Thus, economic colonialism has tended to persist despite the termination of political colonialism.

These negative aspects of colonialism can be confirmed easily with numerous examples, but is this the full story? Would the former colonies be farther advanced in their development had they not been colonies brought under the control of the European powers? Perhaps not, in the opinion of some analysts. The Europeans typically brought political stability, administrative expertise, capital, and technology to their colonies. They established a variety of new economic enterprises, and built railroads, other transportation facilities, hospitals, and schools. Without such priming of their economies by the Europeans, it is reasonable to assume that the former colonies might be even less developed than they are today. In fact, some of the world's wealthiest countries at present—including the United States, Canada, Australia, and New Zealand—are former colonies. To conclude that colonialism has been the principal cause of limited economic development in large segments of the world obviously is open to much doubt.

Isolation

Another argument is that isolation has prevented economic growth in some areas. Isolation may be the result of location in a remote area, as in the case of Paraguay in South America or Mongolia in Asia. A country's landlocked position in the interior of a continent or its separation from other areas by rugged mountains, swamplands, or other environmental obstacles may also contribute to its isolation. Furthermore, some countries in the past have isolated themselves voluntarily by withdrawing from interaction with other parts of the world for political or cultural reasons. In any case, the isolation commonly is interpreted as an economic handicap because it restricts opportunity to participate in international trade and to benefit from the diffusion of ideas and procedures that can facilitate economic growth. Figuratively speaking, backwater areas are viewed as unable to keep up with those parts of the world that are in the mainstream.

This argument seems both logical and supportable by a number of example areas (including Paraguay and Mongolia) that appear to be handicapped by their isolation, but there are troublesome questions about it. How can Australia and New Zealand, both separated by great distance from the world's main centers of economic innovation and development, be among the world's most prosperous countries? Considering the relatively remote location of Japan from other major economic centers, how has it managed to attain such a high level of development? Furthermore, if accessibility is so important, why is most of the Middle East—long recognized as one of the world's great crossroads regions—so poorly developed?

The prosperity of Auckland, New Zealand, is suggested by this view of the city's waterfront. A former British colony, New Zealand has attained a high level of economic development despite its remote location and scarcity of natural resources. (Dallas and John Heaton/Stock Boston)

There always will be some areas that, for economic purposes, are less favorably located than others. However, with transportation improvements, the ongoing elimination of political and trade barriers, and the trend toward an economy that is global in scope, the importance of isolation as an economic handicap is diminishing rapidly. Certainly no part of the world is now as isolated as it may have been in the past, and we reasonably can expect continued reduction of isolation in the future.

MEASUREMENTS AND INDICATORS

➤ The measurement and comparison of economic development among countries of the world is a complex process that produces results of varying accuracy and reliability.

What are some of the most widely used indicators of economic development?

What are some of the advantages and disadvantages of each?

Comparing and contrasting the nations of the world in terms of each one's degree of economic health is not a simple matter. Wealth and poverty have many facets and are not defined easily. As we have noted in Chapter 6, a certain standard of living may be satisfactory in one society but unacceptable in another. Even within a single country such as the United States, the definition of poverty is arbitrary and the subject of much disagreement. No single criterion satisfactorily measures economic health. Even if one did, we would have to use it with caution in making international comparisons and contrasts because of inconsistencies and variations from country to country in the collection of data. The best approach is to use a combination of criteria, flawed though each may be, and form a composite characterization of national economic levels.

For our purposes we will examine (1) gross national product per capita, (2) economic structure, (3) energy consumption, and (4) certain demographic and social indicators of variation in economic development around the world. This combination of criteria commonly is considered to have the best diagnostic value, although other indicators (e.g., the production of basic metals and participation in commerce) have merit as well.

TABLE 9.1	GNP Per Capita for Selected Countries: 1990–1991 *(in U.S. dollars)*

Country	Amount
Japan	26,920
Sweden	25,490
United States	22,560
Canada	21,250
France	20,600
United Kingdom	16,750
Australia	16,590
Saudi Arabia	7070
South Korea	6340
Brazil	2920
Mexico	2870
Indonesia	610
China	370
India	330
Nigeria	290
Zaire	220
Bangladesh	220

SOURCE: *Population Reference Bureau.*

Gross National Product

The single measurement generally considered to best reflect the level of national economic development is the **gross national product** (GNP). This statistic is calculated simply by adding together the value of all goods produced and economic services rendered in a country during a given year. For international comparisons and contrasts, it is helpful to determine the GNP on a per-capita basis to eliminate differences between countries attributable to population size. If we were to rely simply on total GNP, one might gain the erroneous impression that India, for example, has a healthier economy than Denmark's. It is fortunate that GNP data are available for nearly all of the world's countries.

The annual GNP per capita for some countries exceeds $10,000 (Table 9.1), suggesting great wealth and a high level of economic development. For the most part, these are modern states with highly diversified economies—such as the United States, Germany, Japan, and Australia (Fig. 9.5). However, this group also includes some countries in the Middle East

that have greatly enriched themselves by exporting oil to major industrial nations. In their case, a high ranking in per capita GNP does not reflect a well-developed, diversified economy. In fact, the wealth of these countries is subject to abrupt fluctuations with variations in the price of oil, and the duration of this wealth undoubtedly will be determined largely by how long their oil reserves last.

At the opposite end of the scale are countries with an annual per capita GNP of less than $500 (Table 9.1). As examination of Figure 9.5 will confirm, these nations most notably are concentrated in Africa and southern and southeastern Asia. Their populations are engaged largely in subsistence economic activities, producing commodities for their own consumption and survival. Industry and commerce typically are limited in development. There can be no question that severe poverty is widespread in these countries, but conditions generally are not as bad as the extremely low per capita GNP figures suggest. The reason is that commodities produced for subsistence never become a part of the commercial economy and therefore their

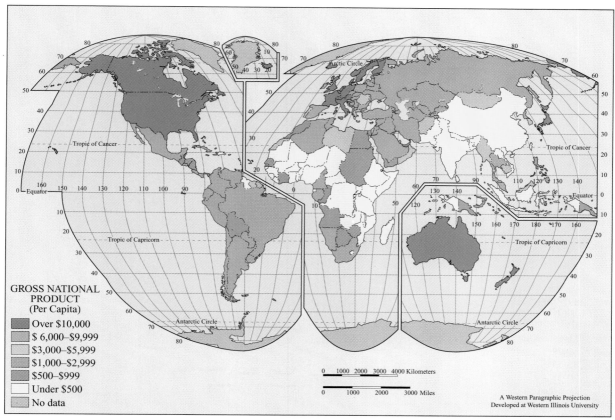

FIGURE 9.5

Per capita gross national product (GNP) for the world's countries. The per capita GNP is commonly used to compare the level of economic development among countries.

value goes unrecorded and escapes inclusion in calculations of the GNP. This is an important deficiency of the GNP as a measurement of national economic development.

Economic Structure

A nation's level of economic development also is suggested by the proportion of its labor force engaged in each sector of the economy. The three most commonly recognized sectors are called primary, secondary, and tertiary.

The Primary Sector   The primary sector involves the exploitation of natural resources, such as soil, vegetation, minerals, and wildlife. The use of land to produce crops and livestock as well as the extraction of

materials of value that exist in nature (e.g., iron ore, petroleum, timber, and fish) are classified as **primary economic activities**. Agriculture is usually the dominant primary economic activity, but in some cases mining, logging, fishing, hunting, or gathering may be important. The primary sector, particularly agriculture, usually occupies the greatest proportion of the labor force in the less developed countries, whereas it is only a minor source of employment in the developed countries.

Figure 9.6, a map of employment in agriculture, illustrates that the nations with less than one-fifth of their labor forces in agriculture are among the world's most developed. By mechanizing their farming operations, these countries have greatly reduced the number of workers needed to produce crops and livestock. Most prominent among these countries on the map are

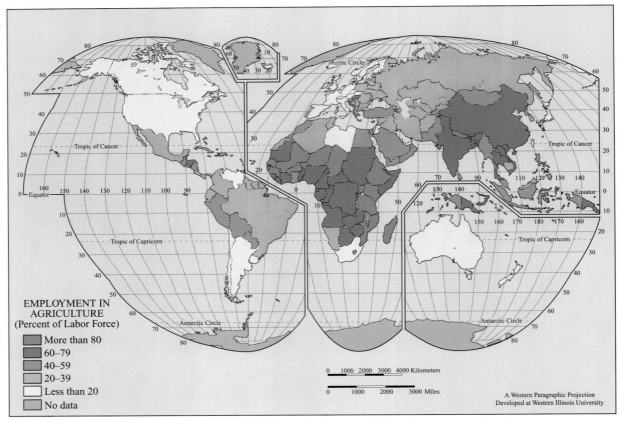

FIGURE 9.6

Employment in agriculture in the world's countries. Farming typically occupies the largest proportion of the workers in poor countries, but only small percentages of the labor force are employed on farms in the wealthy nations.

the United States, Canada, Japan, Australia, and several European nations, all of which have less than 10 percent of their labor forces in agriculture. (In the United States, the figure is now less than 3 percent.) On the other hand, most of the countries of Africa and Asia as well as a few in Latin America have more than half of their workers engaged in farming. The scarcity of agricultural machinery in these areas requires much human labor to produce the farm commodities.

The Secondary Sector The **secondary economic activities** involve the refining, processing, and fabrication of raw materials into products of greater value. All manufacturing processes, therefore, are secondary activities. In manufacturing, the value of raw materials is increased by converting them into another form. The

process may be as simple as converting wheat grain into flour, or it may be relatively complicated as in the assembly of component parts into a motor vehicle. The manufacturing of goods may be carried on by a single worker in a home workshop (a so-called cottage industry), or it may involve mass production in a huge factory with hundreds or thousands of workers engaged in highly specialized tasks on an assembly line. In either case, the individuals are engaged in a secondary economic activity.

The economically advanced nations tend to have a greater proportion of their labor force engaged in manufacturing than do the less developed countries. However, manufacturing employs no more than one-third of the workers in the most advanced countries and the percentage has tended to decline with further

(a)

(b)

(c)

The three economic sectors: (a) Agricultural activities, such as this harvest of sugar cane in Brazil, are representative of the primary sector. (b) Manufacturing, including the assembly of TV sets in this factory in Malaysia, constitutes the secondary sector. (c) Service activities, such as the financial services conducted on Wall Street in New York City, form the tertiary sector. (Cameramann Int'l., Ltd.; Karen Kasmauski/Matrix; Stacy Pick/Stock Boston)

development. Improvements in efficiency and the continuing substitution of machinery, including robots, for human labor have reduced the need for workers in modern manufacturing enterprises.

The Tertiary Sector   Tertiary economic activities involve the performance of services that have value to individual customers or clients or to society as a whole. Services, in this case, include wholesale and retail sales, maintenance and repair, personal care, governmental functions, the exercise of legal actions, and instructional activities. Thus, clerks, janitors, automobile mechanics, computer programmers, legislators, and members of the legal, medical, and teaching professions are all examples of those employed in the tertiary sector of an economy.

In the world's most advanced countries, the greatest proportion of the labor force is now employed in the tertiary sector. More than 65 percent (two-thirds) of the workers in the United States, for example, now fill service occupations, and the number is steadily increasing. The growth in importance of the tertiary sector has prompted some authorities to suggest that the United States has moved into a post-industrial phase in its economic evolution. In countries with poorly developed economies, on the other hand, employment in service occupations remains much smaller than that in the primary sector.

Among the numerous service activities, one that has burgeoned in importance during recent years in advanced countries as a result of the widespread use of computers is the processing of data and other information. Some sources have even gone so far as to classify information processing as the *quaternary sector* of an economy. However, we have chosen to restrict our characterization of economic structure to the traditional three sectors and include information processing as a tertiary activity.

Energy Consumption

The amount of energy consumed by a nation is another commonly used indicator of economic development. Because mechanization, industrialization, and high standards of living are based on the input of energy, the more economically advanced countries consume the bulk of the world's fuels and other sources of inanimate power. The United States has had a particularly great appetite; with only about 5 percent of the world's population, it has regularly accounted for approximately one-third of all energy consumed in the world. To facilitate comparison of countries, we have included a map (Fig. 9.7) showing per-capita consumption of all forms of commercial energy converted into equivalents of petroleum. World patterns of energy consumption are quite similar to those of GNP (Fig. 9.5). The United States, Canada, most of the European countries, the Commonwealth of Independent States, Australia, and New Zealand are all relatively large consumers. In addition, some of the Middle Eastern producers of oil also rank high as consumers. At the other extreme, very low energy consumption char-

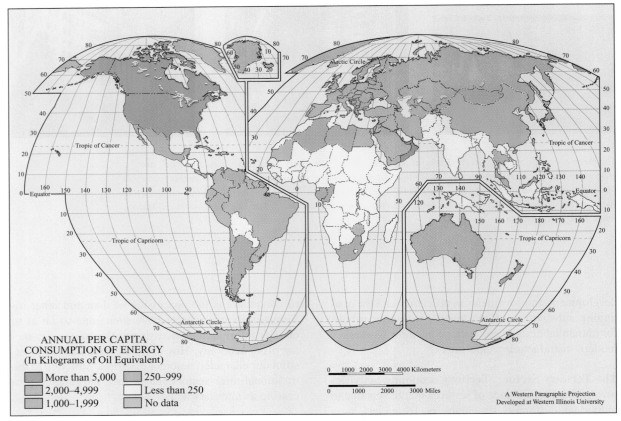

FIGURE 9.7

Energy consumption in the world's countries. There is a striking contrast between the world's rich and poor countries in the consumption of commercial energy.

acterizes most of the countries of Africa and South and Southeast Asia. A few parts of Latin America also are quite low consumers of energy.

The world's less developed countries not only consume much smaller amounts of energy per capita than the highly developed countries, they also must rely on cheaper and less efficient forms of energy. Fossil fuels (primarily oil, natural gas, and coal), water power, and nuclear energy are the forms most commonly used in the industrialized countries. These sources of energy are usually unavailable or too expensive for most people in the rest of the world. The alternatives for them are fuelwood, charcoal, kerosene, animal dung, and muscle power (Fig. 9.8). In the tropics, the great demand for wood as fuel and as the raw material for charcoal is one of the causes of the rapid deforestation currently underway in those regions.

FIGURE 9.8

An important source of fuel in India is dried animal dung. In the foreground of this photo are dung "patties" that have been placed in the sun to dry before they are burned as fuel. (R. Gabler)

Although our map of energy consumption is a good indicator of spatial variations in economic development, we need to exercise some caution in using it for that purpose. Like the map of per capita GNP, it tends to exaggerate the differences between the economically advanced countries and poor countries. Energy use in poor countries is somewhat more than the amount indicated on the map because such things as wood and dung are gathered and burned as fuel without being measured and recorded. Another factor that contributes to the exaggeration is the general location of the industrialized countries in the middle latitudes, where seasonal temperature extremes stimulate elevated levels of energy consumption.

Demographic and Social Indicators

The world's economically advanced and less developed countries also are differentiated by many demographic and social characteristics. As we emphasized in Chapter 6, population growth is very modest in industrial-urban societies but it is most rapid in those parts of the world that have attained the least economic development. In the latter areas, which are predominantly agrarian and rural in character, improvements in average living standards are difficult to attain because increases in economic production are offset by population growth. Another demographic pattern we noted in Chapter 6 is that birth rates tend to be highest in the less developed countries. As a consequence those parts of the world have a high proportion of their population—40 percent or more—comprised of children less than 15 years of age. The large size of this group of dependents, youngsters who are not yet members of the labor force, is a heavy economic burden for the less developed countries. Children under the age of 15 usually account for less than one-fourth of the population in the economically advanced countries. Thus, a greater proportion of the population in these countries is in the labor force—an important economic advantage.

One of the most basic differences between the less developed and advanced countries involves the physical well-being of their populations. In Chapter 6, we called attention to the general malnourishment of people in poor countries and, in some cases, even severe famine. Diets are particularly deficient in much of Africa and parts of southern Asia. People also need access to medical care in order to maintain good health,

but physicians, nurses, hospitals, and clinics are in short supply in the less developed countries. A map showing the average ratio of persons per physician (Fig. 9.9) is helpful in understanding the differences in availability of medical care. In the more developed countries there are no more than 1000 people per physician, but the ratio is significantly higher in most of the less developed countries. Poor economies usually result in poor health among the population, and workers who suffer from poor health are usually poor producers of economic goods—an unfortunate cycle in the world's less developed countries.

Education is another important indicator of a country's level of economic development. In poor societies, even the most elementary schooling may be viewed as an unaffordable luxury. Universal education of children through their adolescent years is common only in the world's most advanced countries. To become literate—to acquire the skills of reading and writing—is the most basic educational attainment. Nevertheless, as Figure 9.10 indicates, it is common for less than half of the adult population to be literate in less developed countries, particularly those in Africa and southern Asia. Of course, a poorly educated person—particularly one who is illiterate—is less capable of aiding the economic progress of his or her country than one who is better trained. Furthermore, with the rapidly growing role of technology in the performance of economic tasks, education is an increasingly essential tool of the work force.

GEOGRAPHIC PATTERNS OF DEVELOPMENT

➤ Examination of a map showing the economic development of the world's countries reveals that, with a few important exceptions, both the poor and wealthy countries are grouped together in a few geographic regions.

Which regions contain the majority of less developed countries?

Which regions contain the majority of developed countries?

Which countries currently are experiencing the greatest change in their economies?

From our examination of the combination of indicators in the preceding section, we are able to detect impor-

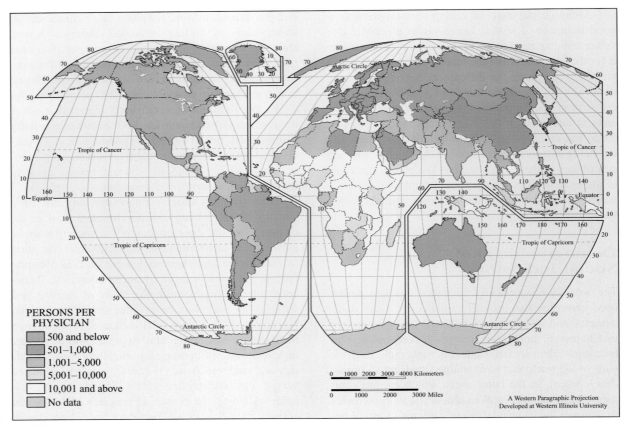

FIGURE 9.9

Average number of persons per physician in the world's countries. The scarcity of physicians and medical facilities is one of the distinguishing characteristics of the less developed countries.

tant variations in the geographic patterns of economic development. The simple division of the world into rich (developed) countries and poor (less developed) countries, as shown on the map in Figure 9.4, is helpful in identifying general patterns, but we can recognize now that there are significant variations within those two categories. In this section we will summarize briefly major regional and national differences in economic development. Details on the economies of the less developed and more developed regions will be presented in the two chapters that follow.

The Less Developed Regions

Our indicators suggest that most of the countries of Africa and several in Asia represent the lowest level of economic attainment in the world. Human poverty

is particularly widespread in Africa, although that continent possesses considerable resources. The lack of technology and capital have been major obstacles to economic development in Africa, but its most difficult economic problems revolve around the extremely high birth rates and rates of population growth in nearly every country. Other important detractions from economic growth have been political instability and internal strife during the relatively short period that most African countries have been independent. (As we pointed out in Chapter 5, European colonial powers held political control over most of the continent until after World War II.) Areas with such problems and uncertainties are usually not considered attractive places for foreign investments.

The people in nearly all African countries are mostly rural agriculturalists, have very little formal ed-

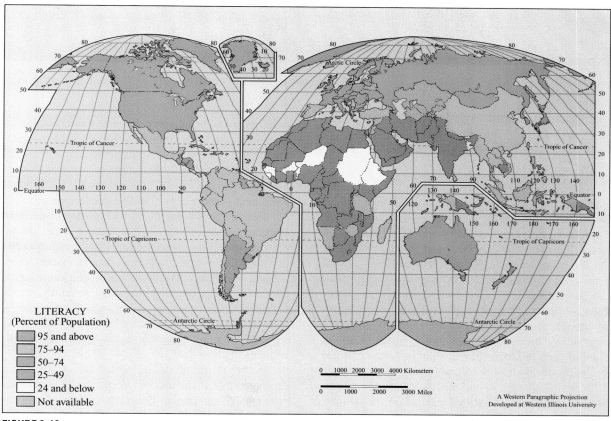

FIGURE 9.10

Literacy in the countries of the world. The ability of adults to read and write is generally more common in the developed countries than in the less developed countries.

ucation, suffer from inadequate diets and health care, and generate very little income. Subsistence farming is widespread, and there is relatively little participation in the money economy. (See *Cultural Landscapes: The Periodic Market.*) In many areas crop farmers must contend with tropical soils that are quickly depleted and eroded when placed in cultivation, and herders have problems in the form of livestock diseases and overused grazing lands. The few African farm products and minerals that can be marketed in foreign areas are mostly subject to great fluctuations in demand and prices. Some examples are cotton, coffee, copper, and oil.

A notable exception is the Republic of South Africa, which has been able to diversify its economy and attain a much higher level of development than that in other parts of the continent. Balanced development of

agriculture, mining, and manufacturing has made possible an impressive national economy, but the prosperity has not been shared by the majority of South Africans. The wealth has been controlled by the white population minority, and racial conflict threatens to cripple the country's economy.

Along the southern perimeter of Asia from the Mediterranean coast in the west to the Pacific coast in the east is a broad zone in which economic conditions are almost as poor as those of Africa. Important exceptions are Israel (in which a modern economy has been established since the country's formation in 1948), the oil-rich countries bordering the Persian Gulf, the commercial nodes of Singapore and Hong Kong, and the rapidly industrializing states of Taiwan and South Korea. Otherwise, generally low levels of economic attainment prevail, with particularly

CULTURAL LANDSCAPES

The Periodic Market

A traditional element of the cultural landscape in most countries of the less developed world is the periodic market. These markets usually are established in villages, but they also may be found in other locations. As the name implies, the periodic market is a place where, on days determined by a market cycle, goods can be purchased or bartered. The market cycle usually ranges from two to twelve days, varying from country to country and according to the size of the village. It is typically shorter for larger villages and longer for smaller ones. A small village might have an eight-day cycle, for example, with its market day on the 1st, 9th, 17th, and 25th days of the month. People with items to offer arrive in time for market day. Some may move with their merchandise from market to market by truck or bus, but many walk to market and carry their goods on their heads or backs.

In some cases, merchants from large urban centers bring manufactured goods to sell at periodic markets, but the usual merchandise consists of agricultural produce, fowl and other small animals, and handicraft items from the local area. Sellers commonly set out their products for display on the open ground, although the more successful may erect a canvas shelter for their goods. Little or no organization of the marketplace is evident. Sometimes merchandise is grouped by type in the larger markets, but random placement is more typical in the smaller ones.

Few purchases are made with money at periodic markets, because the economic status of most participants is near the subsistence level and they have little or no available cash. As a consequence, market transactions usually involve bartering. A chicken may be traded for a large bundle of firewood, several yams for a dipper of dried peas, or a young goat for a basket of peanuts and a stalk of bananas. Prolonged haggling is involved in such exchanges as each person attempts to strike the best deal.

Although the periodic market has a significant economic role in the less developed world, it also has great social importance. The market is a popular gathering place for people to visit with friends and relatives, to share news and gossip, and to exchange views on such matters as government and religion. It is a place for children to play and for young women and men to meet. Dancers and other entertainers may visit the marketplace to perform before an audience. For those who gather at the site, market day is an exciting social occasion as well as an economic event.

A periodic market in South Korea. Although farm products typically are most common, a wide assortment of commodities usually are available at periodic markets. (Siyoung Park)

THOUGHT QUESTIONS

1. How might a periodic market in Korea differ from one in tropical Africa?
2. For consumers and producers of goods in rural areas of the less developed world, what are possible advantages of the periodic market as a medium for economic transactions? Can you think of any disadvantages?
3. Is there anything comparable in the United States to a periodic market? If so, how is it comparable?

A camp of cattle herders in Sudan. Overgrazing has seriously damaged vegetation and land in much of Africa. The result has been a decrease in the size of herds and less food available to support the herders. (Robert Caputo/Stock Boston)

FIGURE 9.11
The depth of poverty in Haiti is suggested by the conditions in this photograph. (Frederic Savariau/Gamma Liaison)

wretched conditions in overcrowded and flood-prone Bangladesh. Burdened by enormous populations, China and India also have stunning poverty. The economy in each country relies heavily on agriculture, and worker productivity is low (especially in India). Both have important resources, however, and are attempting to acquire the technology to modernize their economies. In recent years the communist government in China has been relaxing its Marxist principles and allowing a limited return of capitalism in hopes of improving economic output.

The rapid escalation of oil prices on the world market following 1973 brought an enormous increase in national income to the Persian Gulf countries as well as to Libya in North Africa. This newly acquired wealth is reflected in relatively high per capita GNP figures for these nations. A large part of the wealth, however, is absorbed by huge military costs in this strife-torn region. Also, even the most basic necessities of life—water, food, and shelter—are very expensive in these countries, largely because they are dominated by an arid climate. For example, in order to have an adequate supply of fresh water, some of the Persian Gulf countries must go to the great expense of operating desalinization plants to process sea water. Thus, a number of economic problems perforate the veneer of wealth in these countries; the greatest threat

is any interruption in their sale of oil at relatively high prices to the rest of the world.

Political hostilities and military conflicts in recent decades have affected nearly the entire southern periphery of Asia, disrupting economies and draining the natural and human resources of the zone. Peace and stability must be reestablished in the region before significant improvement in living standards can be accomplished.

Latin America also is one of the less developed regions, but its poverty is not quite as severe as that in most of Africa and the southern perimeter of Asia. It is difficult to imagine worse economic conditions than those in countries such as Bolivia and Haiti (Fig. 9.11), but most of Latin America is not so wretchedly poor. The region has struggled with a great many economic problems and obstacles to development, including political corruption and frequent revolutions that have toppled governments, a high rate of population increase, over-reliance on a small number of export products that are subject to great fluctuations in prices, and astronomical levels of inflation. One of the most persistent basic problems in the region has been the need for land reform. From colonial time to the present, in most parts of Latin America a small number of landlords have controlled nearly all of the best land. The great masses of rural people therefore have been denied the opportunity to own the land on which they work, a situation that has contributed to low production efficiency. Only in a few Latin American countries, notably Mexico, has the government successfully expropriated land from the landlords and redistributed it among the peasant farmers.

The economy of Latin America has been influenced greatly by the United States and, to a lesser degree, European countries. Access to the affluent and huge markets in the United States and European countries, as well as to investments by firms from those areas in Latin American enterprises, have assisted the region's development. For some of the countries located relatively close to the United States, income from U.S. tourists and from smuggling illegal drugs into the United States also has become very important to their economies.

Brazil and Mexico, with developing manufacturing to supplement mining and agricultural production, have had the most important economies in Latin America in modern time (Fig. 9.12). Now their economic well-being, like that of many less developed

FIGURE 9.12
Brazil's enormous steel mill at Volta Redonda is indicative of that country's industrial progress. (Ellis Herwig/Stock Boston)

countries, is being threatened by their inability to repay huge loans obtained from international agencies and banks in the United States and Europe in order to finance production expansion. Faced with national bankruptcy, these countries desperately have been attempting to renegotiate their loans or obtain approval for only partial repayment. Mexico's participation with the United States and Canada in the North American Free Trade Association (NAFTA) is expected to provide an important stimulus to the country's economic future.

The More Developed Regions

The United States and Canada together form the largest region of high economic development in the world. These two countries have economies that are closely intertwined, enjoy exceedingly high living standards, and lead the world in most indicators of development. They are particularly notable in terms of having a very high proportion of their labor force employed in the tertiary sector of their economies. The United States is the greatest producer of agricultural commodities in the world and also leads in agricultural exports. Although many of its manufacturing firms have been crippled by foreign competition, the United States continues to be the world's leading industrial power.

Despite such impressive credentials, this region has begun to experience a number of troubling economic problems. After nearly a century of leading the world, the United States and Canada now must deal with a diminished resource base and environmental deterioration. Some of the major farming areas, particularly the Great Plains and the U.S. South, have suffered severe soil erosion; the once enormous high-grade iron ore deposits of the Lake Superior district have become depleted; about 40 percent of all oil consumed in the United States must now be imported; and acid rain from air polluted by midwestern industries is killing forests in eastern Canada and the United States. High industrial production costs in the two countries, caused by such factors as expensive raw materials and labor, pollution control requirements, and aging factories and machinery, have given foreign manufacturers an important edge in the competition for markets. With its huge appetite for foreign imports, the United States became the world's leading debtor nation during the 1980s, after being the top creditor in previous years.

CULTURAL LANDSCAPES

The Channel Tunnel

Because it mostly is hidden beneath the sea, the recently completed Channel Tunnel is a relatively inconspicuous feature of the European cultural landscape. Sometimes called the Eurotunnel or the Chunnel, it connects Britain and France under the waters of the English Channel and is expected to revolutionize the transportation geography of Europe.

The most ambitious construction project ever undertaken in Europe, the $17 billion venture was long in coming. The French, who built the monumental Suez Canal and seem fascinated by big projects, had been urging the British to cooperate in constructing an under-the-channel tunnel for almost 200 years. A French proposal in 1802 called for a candlelit tunnel through which horse-drawn vehicles would pass, but construction technology for a project of such magnitude did not exist at the time. Other proposals followed before one actually was initiated from both France and Britain in 1882. Some 2 miles (3.2 km) of this tunnel were completed before the British, fearful of military invasion from France through the tunnel, terminated the project. Other plans were foiled by the hostilities of World Wars I and II. Serious consideration again was given to a channel tunnel during the 1960s, and new construction was begun in 1974. The British government curtailed that start in less than a year. Close political ties between the United Kingdom and France in the mid-1980s led to an agreement to consider bids for a privately constructed tunnel. In 1986 a consortium of companies was awarded the project. Now called Eurotunnel, the consortium was given the right not only to build the tunnel but to operate it for 55 years.

At least 11 gargantuan tunnel-boring machines, each the length of two football fields, were used in the project. Some worked eastward from Dover, England, while others bored westward from Calais, France.

Thirty-one miles (50 km) separate the two places. The design of the project actually includes three tunnels, all lying as much as 300 feet (91 m) under the sea. From center to center, two rail tunnels lie almost 100 feet (30 m) apart, and between them is a smaller service tunnel that connects with the rail tunnels every 1230 feet (375 m). The service tunnel was connected from both sides of the Channel, although not completed, in 1990. Both rail tunnels were connected in 1991, and work on the subterranean infrastructure continued until the complex opened in 1994.

Oversized, high-speed trains transport people, cars, trucks, and buses through the tunnels. During peak hours, trains depart every quarter hour. As many as 10,000 people use the trains during busy hours. The Eurotunnel consortium expects almost 14 million people to have used its services during the first year, with that number increasing each year for at least a decade. Furthermore, it is expected that the trains will move some 6 to 7 million tons of freight annually.

The French have been operating high-speed (168 mph, 270 km/h) supertrains since 1981, and they introduced one in 1988 that is designed for speeds of 186 mph (300 km/h). High-speed railways also were in use or under development by 1990 in other busy European transportation corridors. However, to the consternation of the French—who outnumber British Eurotunnel investors by four to one—Britain has been slow to develop high-speed rail links to the Channel Tunnel. At least during the tunnel's early years of use, the rail trip between London and Paris may average three hours instead of the two-and-a-quarter hours that would have been possible had the British kept pace with other European countries in the development of high-speed trains. Their delay is a result of the government's decision that projects related to the Channel Tunnel must pay for themselves by extra revenue generated and not be a drain on public revenues. Even if the London–Paris connection is slower than technology permits, certainly the new Channel Tunnel is one of the most exciting European developments of the modern period.

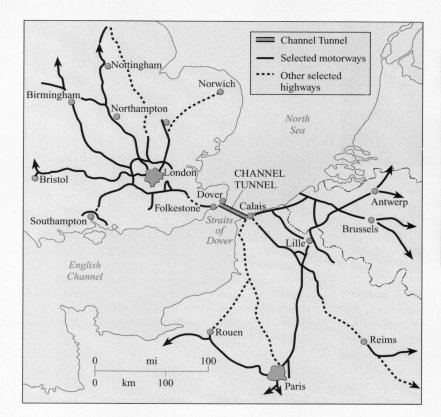

Connecting France and Britain beneath the waters of the English Channel, the Channel Tunnel was opened in 1994. The facility accommodates trains that carry passengers, cars, trucks, and buses. (Gamma Liaison)

THOUGHT QUESTIONS

1. Had the Channel Tunnel been completed in 1964 instead of 1994, how might it have affected European economic integration?

2. Suppose that a group of German corporations offered the Eurotunnel consortium $30 billion for its 55-year rights to operate the tunnel—a considerable return on its invest-

ments. If you were a member of the Eurotunnel consortium's decision-making board, what would be your position on the offer? If you were a member of the United Kingdom's Parliament, would you oppose or support the German proposal and offer? Why or why not?

One of the penalties of economic development in the United States has been acid-rain damage to some of the nation's forests. The dead trees in this photo are a result of acid rain on the slopes of Mt. Mitchell, North Carolina. (Judy Canty/ Stock Boston)

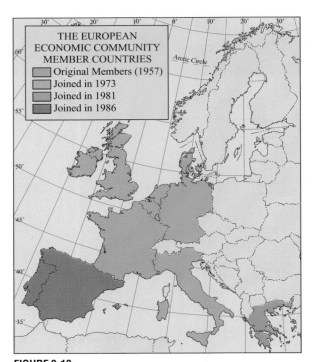

THE EUROPEAN ECONOMIC COMMUNITY MEMBER COUNTRIES
Original Members (1957)
Joined in 1973
Joined in 1981
Joined in 1986

FIGURE 9.13
The European Economic Community expanded from six original members in 1957 to twelve as other countries joined the organization during the 1970s and 1980s. The next countries expected to become members are Norway, Sweden, Finland, and Austria.

For most of the past few centuries, the economy of Europe has been the world's most advanced. Acquiring colonial possessions following explorations and discoveries in the New World gave an early boost to Europe's economy. After the Industrial Revolution and general modernization of their economies, the countries of western Europe were the first to attain high living standards. With fewer resources, eastern and southern Europe lagged behind in industrialization and have not reached such high levels of development to this day. Western Europe, however, remained the region of highest development until the United States emerged as the world's dominant economic power early in the twentieth century.

A number of twentieth century events, particularly the two devastating world wars and the loss of colonial possessions, caused temporary setbacks in Europe's economic development. The continent also has been handicapped by its intricate political fragmentation, ethnic frictions, and the infamous *Iron Curtain* established to isolate communist Eastern Europe from the West following World War II.

Economic problems caused by the political fragmentation of Europe, notably the uneven distribution of resources and tariff barriers to the movement of commodities across international boundaries, have

been reduced greatly since formation of the multinational **European Economic Community** (EEC) in 1957. The original six member countries (the former West Germany, the Netherlands, Belgium, Luxembourg, France, and Italy) experienced major rejuvenation of their economies during the 1960s and early 1970s as they adopted cooperative measures and removed restrictions to the flow of materials and workers among each other. Their successes stimulated Denmark, the United Kingdom, and Ireland to join the EEC in 1973 and Greece, Spain, and Portugal during the 1980s, bringing the total membership to twelve (Fig. 9.13). These countries have made remarkable progress in abandoning old nationalistic and ethnic frictions to join together in a cooperative movement that has enabled them to become one of the most advanced economic units in the world.

In Eastern Europe, however, economic growth has been slow since World War II. These nations had

FIGURE 9.18
A scene in rural Mexico. The use of animal muscle power and hand-made tools is typical of Rostow's Stage I (Traditional Societies). (R. Gabler)

cedures and techniques from generation to generation (Fig. 9.18). Any changes are rare and may even be feared. Power in the society resides in the landed aristocracy—those few people who possess large landholdings and obtain enough income to enjoy a luxurious lifestyle. They are able to spend their surplus wealth on luxury items rather than invest it in means to increase production because peasant labor is available and cheap. Politicians and bureaucrats are likely to be members of the aristocracy or indebted to them; as a consequence, governmental action to initiate change in the economic system seldom occurs. A rigid class or caste system also is typical of traditional societies and restricts the opportunity of peasants to improve their socioeconomic status.

Stage II: The Preconditions for Take-Off   Because resistance to change is so great in traditional societies, establishing the preconditions for take-off ordinarily requires a great deal of time. This stage involves the beginnings of economic diversification (so that agriculture is no longer the dominant activity), initial improvements in efficiency of production, and changes in the society's attitudes and goals. A very important

change is the emergence of a desire for higher living standards. The abandonment of traditional methods is set in motion, and social restrictions on production improvements are eroded. These changes may be initiated by an elite group within the society or introduced by a power from outside the region or country. In general, this stage is a transition period leading to sustained economic growth.

Stage III: The Take-Off   In the modernization of an economy, this stage is most critical. Rostow described the take-off as "that decisive interval in the history of a society when growth becomes its normal condition." The sustained growth is fostered particularly by increases in capital investment to a level that exceeds the rate of population growth. Thus, the society must include entrepreneurs who are willing to invest their profits in additional growth, although some of the capital may be obtained from foreign sources. Political policies and social attitudes must support economic growth for the take-off to be implemented. At least one high-growth industry is established in this stage, and demands are created for other manufactured products. In essence, the take-off represents the beginning of the industrial period.

Stage IV: The Drive to Maturity   In this stage, industrialization continues to expand, with one industry after another in the lead. Capital investment remains high—exceeding the rate of population growth—and modern technology is extended into all sectors of the economy. With mechanization in agriculture reducing the need for rural labor and with the growth of manufacturing and service occupations in the cities, a dramatic urbanization of the population is carried out. Participation in the global economy is important for a country in this stage, with exports used to pay for imports of industrial raw materials and technology. The drive to maturity is a complex process and therefore may require a number of decades to complete. When maturity is attained, the economy is highly diversified and technology is integral to all sectors.

Stage V: High Mass Consumption   This stage is distinguished by primary emphases on consumer goods and services in the leading sectors of the economy. With high per capita income, a large proportion of the population enjoys purchases of items beyond the basic necessities. Rostow suggested that the auto-

FIGURE 9.19
*Rush-hour traffic in New York City. The automobile is
symbolic of Rostow's Stage V (High Mass Consumption).
(John Lei/Stock Boston)*

mobile is symbolic of this stage (Fig. 9.19). People
employed in the services and highly skilled industrial
workers form the bulk of the labor force. As a consequence, the population is highly urbanized. The
abundance of wealth generated by the economy in this
stage allows for generous allocations to social welfare
programs and national defense.

Rostow felt that his five stages would apply to
every region, nation, or society and that they are experienced in order as economic development occurs.
Locational, environmental, or cultural differences
from place to place have no impact, in his judgment,
on the model's applicability.

Critiques of the Models

Although models such as those of Carol and Rostow
have been enormously popular means of portraying
and analyzing the development process, critics have
identified several apparent flaws in them and have
questioned their value. In general, the development
process is too complex to be distilled into such simplified models, according to some. Authors of the
models also have been criticized for basing their stages
on European development experience; in other parts

of the world, it is claimed, development must follow
a different course because of different historical, cultural, and environmental circumstances in these areas.
Therefore, it is misleading to suggest that every area
or society must progress through each of the stages in
order. It is not difficult, in fact, to identify areas in
which a stage was bypassed as a low-level native economy was replaced by a much more advanced economy
introduced from the outside. Many of the former
colonies of European powers are examples of this
sequence.

The models also are criticized because basically
they are descriptive and have little analytical value.
They are weak in terms of identifying a critical event
or occurrence that marks precisely the transition from
one stage to the next. As a result, some critics have
suggested that the concept of stages should be replaced
by the idea that economic development is a continuous
process. Despite their flaws, models such as the two
just described are likely to continue in use because
many people consider them to be effective means of
representing in simplified steps the essentials of economic development.

CAPITALIST AND COMMUNIST ECONOMIC MODELS

➤ One of the major global episodes of the twentieth
century has been the competition between the
opposing economic systems of capitalism and
communism.

*What are the major characteristics of a capitalist
society?*

*What are the major characteristics of a communist
society?*

Which system has emerged as more effective?

*What is the evidence that one is more effective than
the other?*

Economic development in the twentieth century has
been intricately linked with the opposing ideologies of
capitalism and communism. We noted in Chapter 5
that, as part of their global struggle for influence since
World War II, the communist Soviet Union and the
capitalist powers of Western Europe and the United
States have promoted the adoption of their respective
economic policies and agendas by less developed
nations. Of course, this struggle also has included con-

trasting social and political systems, and in a few areas such as Korea, Vietnam, and Nicaragua it even involved bitter military conflict.

Capitalism has deep roots in European history, but it became particularly important in association with the dramatic social and economic changes that accompanied the Industrial Revolution. Central elements of capitalism are private ownership of property and the means of production, individual initiative, the profit motive, and competition. The European countries spread or reinforced the capitalist system throughout most parts of the world during the nineteenth and early twentieth centuries.

The modern communist challenge to capitalism came about when the ideas of the German philosopher Karl Marx were implemented in the Soviet Union following the country's Bolshevik Revolution of 1917. Marx was critical of capitalism and saw in that system an inevitable conflict between the *proletariat*, or working class, and the wealthy. In his view, capitalism led to exploitation of laborers to the benefit of the moneyed class—a relationship that ought to be ended by the creation of a classless, socialist society. Under the leadership of V. I. Lenin and his successor, Joseph Stalin, the Soviet Union set out to establish a Marxist society and economy, one in which private ownership of property was eliminated and all facets of the economy were planned and regulated by the government.

By the time of World War II, the Soviet government had expropriated virtually all privately owned land, production facilities, and other property, and it had initiated a series of economic plans that particularly emphasized the growth of heavy industry. Convinced of the superiority of communism and enthused by the emergence of his country as an industrial giant, Soviet Premier Nikita Khruschev (1894–1971) in the mid-1950s boasted to the capitalist powers (particularly the United States): "We will bury you."

Following World War II, communist governments gained control of a number of other countries—the East European states, mainland China, Mongolia, North Korea, North Vietnam, and Cuba—and reorganized their economies along the lines of the Soviet model. (In addition, several other nations have become socialist to a limited degree and some have had temporary Marxist governments. A few, such as India, have adopted what they considered the best aspects of both capitalist and communist systems.) In these new communist states, implementing Marxist principles had varying economic results. Perhaps the most im-

These household appliances offered for sale in Guandong Province illustrate the prosperity associated with the permission of limited capitalism by China's government. (Forrest Anderson/Gamma Liaison)

pressive accomplishment was in China where chronic famines were overcome and self-sufficiency in food supplies was approached. More commonly, however, the new system led to economic stagnation or decline.

By the 1980s, the economies of most communist nations around the world were in shambles and deficiencies in the system were clearly evident. Massive bureaucracy, emphasis on quantity rather than quality in the production of commodities, the low priority assigned to consumer goods, artificially established prices, and poor motivation among workers were flaws that could no longer be ignored. In contrast to the prosperity in capitalist Western Europe, the poor economic conditions in the Eastern European countries contributed to the abandonment of communism by most of these countries during the late 1980s and early 1990s. In China, the communist government has allowed a limited return of capitalism in the form of private operation of certain economic enterprises and the use of profit incentives. In the Soviet Union President Mikhail Gorbachev implemented *perestroika*—a reorganization program that involved decentralization of planning, privatization of some production operations, and transition to a market economy. By the end of 1991, the communist Soviet Union had ceased to exist and the country's long experiment with a Marxist economy was finished.

With these astounding changes and accompanying appeals to the major capitalist countries by leaders of communist and former communist states for assistance in rebuilding their economies, it appears that the long-standing competition between the two systems is evaporating rapidly. Whatever strategies for economic development are implemented in the years ahead, it seems unlikely that they will incorporate traditional Marxist principles.

AUTARKY VERSUS INTERNATIONAL TRADE

➤ The countries most successful in improving their economic status have chosen to specialize in production and engage in international trade rather than follow a policy of autarky.

What is autarky and why have some nations chosen to implement it?

Why is specialization and trade perceived as a better policy than autarky?

To strengthen their economies, many nations have experimented with programs to promote self-sufficiency in modern times. Their prime objective has been to avoid the expense and risks of relying on foreign imports. The usual strategy is to diversify the national economy or promote the production of commodities to substitute for ones that have been imported in the past—a practice commonly known as **import substitution**. Economic independence can offer freedom from fluctuations in the quantity and price of goods available on the world market, and it can be a source of security during wartime.

Autarky (the practice of national self-sufficiency) now is regarded widely to be economically unsound, however. No country possesses the resources and abilities needed to turn out the great variety of goods required if it is to attain a modern economy. Inefficiencies and high production costs are inherent in the practice of autarky. The countries most successful in improving their economic status recently have relied heavily on world trade. The program they have followed often is articulated succinctly as "specialize in what you do best and import the rest." Production specialization allows for greater efficiency and reduced costs, which in turn improves the likelihood of profitable sales in the world marketplace. With these profits, a country can then purchase from foreign suppliers at relatively low cost the goods that it is unable to produce efficiently at home. Participation in the global market therefore appears to offer greater prospects for improved living standards and national economic growth than the alternative practice of autarky.

CRITICAL COMPONENTS OF DEVELOPMENT

➤ There are several significant elements in the development process, each one of which influences the status of a country's economy.

Which are the major elements?

How does the nature of each affect the status of a country's economic development?

Why is there no reliable path each less developed country can follow as it seeks economic growth and development?

As we have noted, economic development is a complicated process that intricately links human societies with their habitats. We will examine five elements that are especially critical in the development process: natural resources, human resources, capital, technology, and cultural infrastructure. As we shall see, the status of each is partly responsible for the current level of any nation's economy, and any economic expansion will require some alteration or change in one or more of the critical elements.

Natural Resources

Any component of the physical environment is identified as a natural resource if (1) it is perceived by people as being useful or having value, and (2) it can be exploited by available technology. Therefore, the list of natural resources in an area is subject to constant change. People of the most simple culture with limited technology are likely to value as important natural resources such things as wild game, fish, vegetation, and water but place no value on iron ore, petroleum, and uranium. The latter items are natural resources only to people of relatively complex cultures who have developed a need for them and the technology to make use of them. The number of natural resources in most areas generally is increasing because the culture of the people is becoming more complex. However, the number of natural resources also can be reduced by their depletion.

Resources are extremely varied in character, but they can be grouped into three categories. **Renewable resources** are capable of being replenished. Soils as well as biotic resources such as forests, fish, and game are renewable. A renewable resource may be depleted in an area, but it is capable of being reestablished either by natural processes or human action. On the other hand, **nonrenewable resources** are incapable of being replenished within a practical period of time. Mineral ores and fuels, such as iron ore, copper, coal, and petroleum, are the principal examples. Although these resources are formed by natural processes, the time required is so lengthy that their exploitation, for all practical purposes, leads to permanent depletion. We are able to postpone the depletion of nonrenewable resources only by discovering previously unknown reserves and by developing the technology to economically use lower-grade deposits. The third category, **flow resources,** includes flowing water, tides, winds, and solar radiation. All of these resources are potential sources of energy that are not depleted with use. Nevertheless, they must be used as they flow past a particular location or their potential value as a resource at that time is lost.

Because nearly all resources are distributed unevenly around the world, some countries and regions are more richly endowed than others (Fig. 9.20). The Middle East contains more than half of the world's known oil deposits but few other resources of significance. The former Soviet republics, the United States, and China possess about two-thirds of the world's coal, while Latin America and Africa have only very small deposits. Iron ore is rather widely distributed, but it is scarce in the Middle East and most of Africa. Although no area is totally lacking in resources, it also is true that no country is completely self-sufficient. Furthermore, any country that makes significant strides in economic development will require a greater quantity and variety of resources, and in all probability will become increasingly dependent on foreign sources for its needs.

Possession of a rich resource base and the knowledge and means of exploiting it obviously give a country an important advantage for economic development. In its development, the United States has benefited greatly from its vast resource wealth, as did the former Soviet Union. (Before its disintegration, the Soviet Union was the most nearly self-sufficient of all industrialized countries in terms of amount and variety of resources.) It is equally evident that a country is handicapped when it has a scarcity of resources within its territory, but this is a problem that can be overcome. As Japan and a few other countries have demonstrated, a high level of economic development can be attained by purchasing resources in the world marketplace to offset shortages at home. National economies that are based on imported rather than domestic resources are at somewhat greater risk, however. The outbreak of war as well as political and economic events can be severe threats to countries that must rely on imports.

It is ironic that some of the world's poorest countries are well endowed with important resources. Nigeria and Mexico, for example, have major petroleum deposits; Zambia has tremendous quantities of copper; Bolivia contains the main tin deposits in the western hemisphere; and Brazil and several other tropical countries have vast forests. For a great variety of reasons the poor countries have been unable to take advantage of their resource bases to significantly improve their economic conditions. In some cases, the resources have not been exploited fully because of a lack of technology, capital, or markets. The less developed countries also commonly find it difficult to produce, process, and market resources at prices that are competitive with those in the developed countries. The developed countries are likely to have more modern and therefore less costly production procedures and transportation options (Fig. 9.21). In addition, there has been a long history of outside powers exploiting the resources of less developed countries for their own benefit, taking advantage of the colonial status or the economic weakness of those countries.

Human Resources

To make an economy operate, people are needed in some number both as a labor force and as a market. The market within a country may grow somewhat as the population increases, but market expansion is linked more closely with the success of the labor force in increasing its income and, as a result, its ability to purchase commodities. The world's greatest markets are not in China and India, the most populated countries, but rather in the United States, Western Europe, and Japan, where there are large numbers of well-paid workers who are also affluent consumers. A typical worker in Germany may have 20 or 30 times the amount of income to spend on consumer goods as the typical laborer in India. A strong and growing market is an important stimulant for economic expansion.

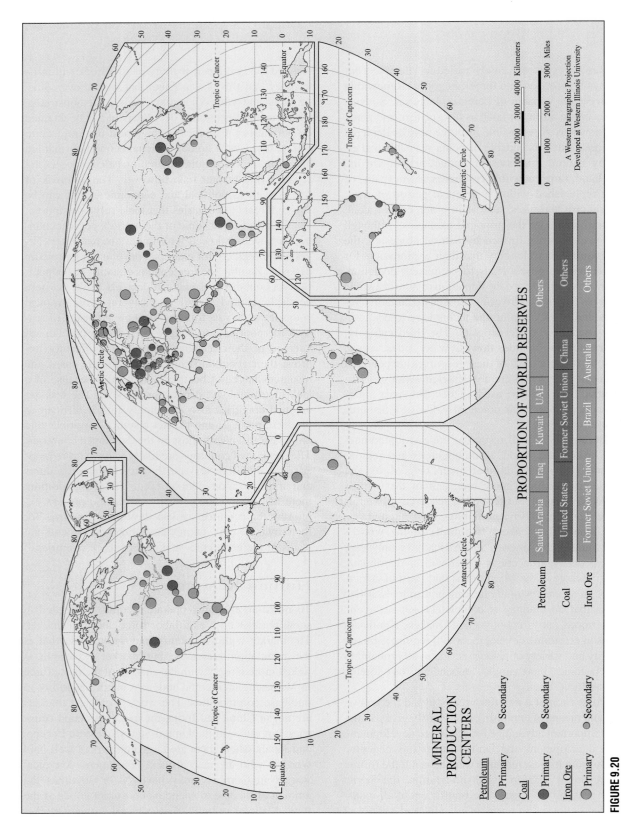

MINERAL PRODUCTION CENTERS

Petroleum
- Primary
- Secondary

Coal
- Primary
- Secondary

Iron Ore
- Primary
- Secondary

PROPORTION OF WORLD RESERVES

Petroleum	Saudi Arabia	Iraq	Kuwait	UAE	Others

Coal	United States	Former Soviet Union	China	Others

Iron Ore	Former Soviet Union	Brazil	Australia	Others

A Western Paragraphic Projection
Developed at Western Illinois University

0   1000   2000   3000   4000 Kilometers

0   1000   2000   3000 Miles

FIGURE 9.20

Coal, oil, and iron ore, the world's three major mineral resources. Possession of or access to these minerals is critical to the economic development of any nation.

FIGURE 9.21
Processing facilities for copper ore from the Chiquicamata mine in Chile. Although a less developed country, Chile possesses the world's greatest copper deposits. (Rob Crandall/Stock Boston)

FIGURE 9.22
Japan's human resources. Workers on an assembly line at the Matsushita Electric Company, Osaka, Japan. (Cameramann Int'l., Ltd.)

A large labor force may be an economic advantage for a nation, particularly if the workers are well educated, skilled, disciplined, and motivated. A large number of workers of poor quality may be a cheap labor supply; however, they most likely will be inefficient as well. A labor force characterized by low productivity and low income is a severe obstacle for economic expansion. On the other hand, as Japan has demonstrated over recent decades, a labor force of high quality can be the foundation for national economic development and help overcome such obstacles to growth as a shortage of natural resources (Fig. 9.22).

The population of a nation can be its most valuable resource. Like other resources, however, it may be used in ways that fall far short of its potential. For example, in many societies and some religious groups there are rigid class (or caste) structures and traditional gender roles that prevent full utilization of the population's skills and abilities. When an individual's economic role is restricted on the basis of gender or placement in a certain class or caste at birth, a terrible waste of human potential is the result. A well-known example that we described in Chapter 4 is India's caste system (a central part of the Hindu religion), which traditionally has limited job options to those relegated to the caste into which a person is born. In much of Africa and the Arab Middle East, women have been assigned low status in society and a highly restricted economic role. Certain tasks typically are associated with gender by inflexible socioeconomic systems throughout the developing world. Even in the most advanced countries—including the United States—the lifting of restrictions on the economic role of women has been only a recent development. The idea of "men's work" and "women's work" is deeply ingrained and difficult to obliterate in modern as well as traditional societies. In addition, employment opportunities often are limited for racial, ethnic, and religious minority groups. Such restrictions on the potential economic contributions of segments of societies obviously are detrimental to development.

Capital

Any economic improvement in a society requires the expenditure of capital in some form. Whether establishing a new mine to tap a mineral deposit, a new power plant to generate electricity, a new fertilizer plant to increase agricultural production, or a new road to improve transportation, capital is essential. Among the more advanced countries, the funds required for a needed economic improvement usually are not difficult to obtain. However, capital typically is scarce in poor countries, and lack thereof is often an obstacle to important economic expansion.

Capital is created within a country usually from the profits earned by firms and from the savings of workers. Governmental regulations, involving such things as price controls and the availability of commodities for purchase by workers, can have an important impact on capital accumulation. In poor countries, where many people are merely subsistence workers and where production efficiency is low and profits are slim, capital accumulation is extremely difficult (Fig. 9.23). High inflation rates, another common characteristic of poor countries, discourage savings; people prefer to spend their money on goods and services before its value is eroded by inflation. High rates of population growth also make capital accumulation difficult; workers with numerous children to support are not likely to have surplus money to commit to savings.

The scarcity of domestic capital has caused less developed countries to solicit funds from external sources, usually international agencies or the more economically advanced countries (Table 9.2). Loans obtained from these sources, often at high rates of interest, must be repaid on schedule. Many of the less developed countries have found it difficult or even impossible to meet repayment schedules on their loans. The solvency of these countries is threatened by the enormous payments needed to service their debts. Some government officials now are pleading to have part or all of their country's indebtedness forgiven by lenders as the only means of avoiding national bankruptcy. The chances for other loans in the future are diminished of course by the inability to meet obligations to earlier creditors. Poor countries also have obtained "gift capital" as part of the foreign aid programs of some of the wealthy nations. The problem for the recipient is that foreign aid usually comes with strings attached. The donor typically provides the aid not out of pure generosity, but with an agreement that the recipient country will reciprocate with a political, military, or economic favor. In some cases, capital is given with the understanding that it will be spent only on goods and services available from the donor nation. It is apparent that the better alternative for a less developed country is to avoid external sources of capital and strive to accumulate it within its domestic economy.

FIGURE 9.23

The World Bank headquarters in Washington, D.C. The World Bank provides loans for economic development projects in less developed countries. (Frank Fisher/Gamma Liaison)

TABLE 9.2	External Debt of Selected Less Developed Countries: 1990 *(in millions of U.S. dollars)*

Country	Amount
Brazil	116,173
Mexico	96,810
India	70,115
Indonesia	67,908
Argentina	61,144
China	52,555
Turkey	49,149
Egypt	39,885
Nigeria	36,068
South Korea	34,014
Venezuela	33,305
Philippines	30,456
Algeria	26,806
Thailand	25,868

SOURCE: *The World Bank.*

Leaders in some countries with limited capital to invest in economic growth have been attracted to **growth pole theory.** According to this theory, if the limited capital is invested in selected urban centers (growth poles), the resulting economic improvement at these points eventually will radiate outward into the surrounding countryside. Where it has been implemented in less developed countries, growth pole theory generally has failed to improve economic conditions in the countryside. The usual result of investment in urban centers has been the migration to those places of rural people in search of jobs, thereby compounding the problem of rapid urban growth in the less developed countries.

Technology

To further economic development, technology is of extreme importance because of its potential for greatly increasing production efficiency. Technology involves the application of science and engineering to solve problems and perform tasks. Even Paleolithic societies possessed limited technology, devising crude stone tools to improve their efficiency in acquiring food. More recently, the application of technology has brought about such astounding developments as the Industrial Revolution, jet engines, and nuclear energy. In the contemporary world, there are enormous differences in the level of technology possessed by societies. Some small groups that are isolated from outside contacts and have no opportunity for formal education, such as tribes of Amerindians in the upper Amazon Basin, continue to possess only Stone Age technology. At the other extreme are nations in which high technology in such form as computers and robots has a great impact on daily life.

An important aspect of technology is its mobility. Once a discovery or invention is made, it tends to diffuse from the originating center to increasingly remote areas. Even when attempts have been made to prevent the spread of technology, such as that associated with the atomic bomb following World War II, these attempts almost always have failed. Studies of the diffusion of technology have identified the relative importance of distance and interpersonal contacts; the barrier of distance is diminished when contacts between people are more frequent. For people to acquire technology from an outside source, they must be willing and able to absorb it. If they are resistant to change or poorly educated, the transfer of ideas or information

FIGURE 9.24
The application of technology in a less developed country: The Tata-Timken bearing factory in Jamshedpur, India. (R. Gabler)

will be slowed. For countries that have been late in developing, the mobility of technology is an advantage of a sort. At little expense they are able to obtain technology developed earlier by the advanced countries at great cost in effort, money, and time (Fig. 9.24).

The advantages of the newest technology are nearly always restricted to the economically advanced nations, however. They are more likely to possess the scientists and engineers and can more easily afford the expenditures needed to create new technology. This enables them to set the pace in production efficiency and output of the most sophisticated products. Less developed countries are caught in the seemingly unending problem of catching up. If they fail, the consequence is that they fall farther behind in production efficiency, thus widening the economic gap between them and their more advanced competitors.

The Cultural Infrastructure

A society's economic advancement can be encouraged greatly by certain aspects of its culture. Survival stimulates people to produce enough to meet their basic needs, but they must be motivated to produce beyond subsistence levels for economic improvement to occur. They must become aware of and place value on higher living standards, and they must acquire a will to progress toward higher economic goals. If their culture places a high value on education; encourages innovation, change, and progress; and offers potential

FIGURE 9.25
These elementary school students in Costa Rica are learning to use a computer in their work. Such emphasis on education is an important measure in fostering eventual economic development. (Ed Lallo/Liaison Int'l.)

rewards for entrepreneurs willing to take risks in business and commerce, the prospects for economic growth are greatly improved. It is extremely important for the society to encourage individual initiative and avoid socioeconomic restrictions based on traditional gender roles and racial, ethnic, and religious prejudices.

The less developed nations typically are tradition-bound and highly resistant to change in any form. Production methods as well as personal attitudes and objectives remain the same for generations (Fig. 9.25). Anything new is looked on with suspicion and fear. Survival is the principal goal in life for most members of the society. Higher economic goals are either unknown or viewed as unobtainable. Motivations for individual improvement are either weak or do not exist. Because opposition to change is so great, it is exceed-

ingly difficult to revise the cultural infrastructure. National leaders, in advocating or implementing change, must have strong convictions and be willing to risk the loss of their personal power or influence for the eventual improvement of their countries.

THE UNCERTAIN PATH TO DEVELOPMENT

Because economic development is such a highly complicated process, the path for less developed countries to follow in striving to attain higher living standards is uncertain. There is not widespread agreement among authorities—even those with similar ideologies—on the best strategies for promoting economic growth. We have suggested the importance of natural resources, human resources, sources of capital, technology, and the cultural infrastructure, but development strategies also must deal with such varied matters as population growth, the system of land ownership, taxation, the education and health care systems, the transportation and communication infrastructure, and trade policy. The task is compounded by the fact that each country's circumstances are unique, and therefore no single scenario for economic improvement can possibly be successful throughout the less developed world. Furthermore, the potential success of any development strategy is impossible without governmental stability and the absence of military conflict.

Despite the complexity and uncertainty involved, a reduction in the scale and extent of poverty in the world is a challenge that must be accepted. Humanitarian reasons alone are adequate to assign highest priority to this task, but future stability of the world's community of nations also is at stake. The current chasm between the poor and the rich will not be tolerated indefinitely.

KEY TERMS

Core–periphery relationship The association or interaction between a more highly developed core area and less developed peripheral areas. **321**

Gross national product The total value of all goods produced and services provided annually within a country. **326**

Primary economic activities Such economic pursuits as

agriculture, fishing, forestry, and mining that involve the exploitation of natural resources. **327**

Secondary economic activities Manufacturing activities that consist of processing raw materials into a finished product of higher value. **328**

Tertiary economic activities Service activities such as retail sales, teaching, governmental work, and mechanical repair. **329**

European Economic Community   An organization formed in Western Europe in 1958 to promote free trade among member countries and eventually bring about their complete economic integration.   **340**

Council for Mutual Economic Assistance   An organization that once linked the former Soviet Union and its Eastern European satellite states to promote their mutual economic status.   **341**

Import substitution   The practice by a country of avoiding the importation of needed goods by producing identical or similar products itself, even if it is ill-suited to do so.   **348**

Autarky   The practice of self-sufficiency by a country.   **348**

Renewable resources   Resources such as soil and timber that can replenish themselves or return to their original state after being exploited. Their use normally does not involve the risk of their total exhaustion.   **349**

Nonrenewable resources   Resources such as mineral ores and fuels that exist in finite amounts and are subject to total exhaustion when exploited.   **349**

Flow resources   Resources such as flowing water, wind, and solar radiation that must be used at a particular time and at a particular location or their potential is lost.   **349**

Growth pole theory   A theory that economic development, when stimulated in selected (usually urban) centers, will spread subsequently to surrounding areas.   **353**

REVIEW QUESTIONS

1. What are the major characteristics of societies in the economically poor countries of the world that distinguish them from the economically wealthy countries?

2. How has industrialization or its absence affected the differences in standards of living among the countries of the world?

3. What terms are used commonly to identify the economically rich and poor nations of the world? Why are the terms "developed" and "less developed" countries preferable to others that have been suggested?

4. What are some of the possible causes for retarded economic development in a less developed country? Why does no single cause satisfactorily explain retarded economic development?

5. What is meant by *gross national product*? What other criteria are used commonly to measure the level of a country's economic development so that it may be compared with other countries?

6. What major nations are commonly highest and lowest on a scale of economic development when judged on the basis of multiple criteria?

7. In which regions of the world are located those countries with the lowest level of economic development? What problems in each region most seriously restrict economic growth?

8. What regions of the world are occupied by developed countries? What historical events and recent changes in each region have had major effects on economic development?

9. What are the five stages of development proposed by Hans Carol? What are the five stages proposed by Walter Rostow? What are the main characteristics of each stage?

10. What are the advantages and disadvantages of economic development models?

11. What are the main features of capitalist and communist economic models? Which model is being adopted at an increasing rate? Why is this occurring?

12. What is meant by *import substitution*? What is meant by *autarky*? Why is autarky considered to be economically unsound?

13. Why are the natural resources of an area subject to constant change? How do renewable, nonrenewable, and flow resources differ from one another? What are examples of each type of resource?

14. How does each of the following help to determine the current level of a country's economy: natural resources; human resources; capital; technology; cultural infrastructure?

15. What components of economic development, other than the five listed in Question 14, might also be considered when planning development strategies for a particular country?

16. Why is it so difficult to reach agreement regarding which development strategy holds the greatest promise for the less developed countries of the world?

CHAPTER 10

SOCIETIES AND LIVELIHOODS IN THE LESS DEVELOPED WORLD

There is nothing perfectly secure but poverty.

—Henry Wadsworth Longfellow

Children comprise a large segment of the population and are valued for their labor in countries of the less developed world. (Rajesh Vora/The Image Works)

The general survey of the characteristics and processes of economic development provided in Chapter 9 supplies the background necessary for a more in-depth examination of societies and livelihoods in the less developed countries and the developed countries. The geography of the intertwined social conditions and economic systems that prevail in the less developed countries is considered in this chapter, while that of the developed countries is examined in Chapter 11. The countries in each group are identified in Figure 9.4 of Chapter 9. It is unfortunate that the less developed countries outnumber the developed countries four to one. More than three-fourths of the world's population reside in the world's countries classified as less developed.

CHARACTERISTICS OF TRADITIONAL AGRARIAN SOCIETIES

➤ Nearly all of the world's less developed countries have traditional agrarian societies with high rates of population growth and widespread poverty.

How do birth rates and death rates compare in these societies?

Within individual countries in the less developed world, how is the wealth distributed?

Traditional agrarian societies prevail in nearly all of the less developed countries. They are classified as agrarian because most people depend directly on agriculture for their livelihood, and they are considered traditional because the modernization that transformed the developed countries has wrought much less change within them. The major characteristics of traditional agrarian societies can be grouped into four categories: (1) population; (2) income; (3) economies and land tenure; and (4) social conditions.

Population Characteristics

The populations of traditional agrarian societies and less developed countries in general are predominantly rural. That is, they reside in a dispersed distribution on the land and in rural villages and hamlets. It is not uncommon for 7 or 8 out of 10 people to live in rural areas. Most people in these societies are members of farm families. Their labors are devoted primarily to activities associated with the production of livestock and crops. Large families are considered desirable to

help work the land and eventually to help care for aging parents.

These factors, together with traditions and religious beliefs, result in high birth rates. Nearly all of the less developed countries have high birth rates. Death rates, historically high in the less developed world, have been reduced significantly in recent decades and remain high only in Africa. Higher birth rates than death rates in most less developed countries produce in those countries a high rate of population growth—a rate four times that of the developed nations. Despite high death rates in Africa, birth rates are so very high in many of that continent's countries that demographic growth is spiraling at an alarming rate. The same is true of several Asian nations. In Chapter 6 we described Bangladesh as a country facing an uncertain future because of rapid population growth. Many other less developed countries are confronted with similar problems.

Income Characteristics and the Urban Poor

The most characteristic aspect of income in traditional agrarian societies is its short supply. Poverty is rampant. While per capita income in some developed nations exceeds $10,000 per year, in most less developed countries the average person earns less than $500 per year. Haiti, Ethiopia, and Bangladesh are arguably the poorest countries in Latin America, Africa, and Asia, respectively.

Another characteristic of the wealth in the less developed world is its uneven distribution within individual countries. An income disparity between the "haves" and "have-nots" also exists in developed countries, but the problem tends to be much worse in traditional agricultural societies. In many less developed countries, fewer than 5 percent of the population own more than half the land. Agrarian reform in recent decades has reduced the gap between the rich and poor in the control of land, but the gap in the control of national wealth has continued. Most of the families that were wealthy before land reform remain wealthy, and most families that were poor before agrarian reform remain poor. In many countries, in fact, the gap between the rich and poor has widened in recent years.

Although there are some wealthy people in even the poorest nations, in general a shortage of capital prevails in traditional agrarian societies. This leads to international debt as poor countries acquire credit to finance internal improvements and to buy such necessities as food and petroleum. International debt has become a problem of crisis proportion for many less developed countries. Some nations no longer can pay even the interest on their foreign debt.

Often poor people from rural areas move to cities in hope of finding a better life. Some of them find what they are searching for, but most discover that urban poverty is at least as grinding as rural poverty. Most rural-to-urban migrants are forced to take up residence in squalid shantytowns on the outskirts of the city because they lack the financial resources or credit to establish themselves in better neighborhoods. These urban slums generally lack potable water, proper sanitary facilities, and easy access to schools and health clinics. Without job experience for industrial and service occupations, the residents of these slums usually are unable to obtain employment sufficient to enable them to buy adequate food and other necessities. In their old homes in the countryside, they could at least produce some of their own food and gather firewood for heating and cooking.

Even so, the lure of the city may be great. Cities are regarded as places of excitement and opportunity, even by prospective migrants who have realistic expectations of the stark realities that probably await them. The magnetic attraction of big cities is especially strong in Latin America, where the population is now predominantly urban.

Economies and Land Tenure

➤ Traditionally, most of the land—and the best land—in the less developed world has been owned by few of the people, leaving little land—generally the less desirable land—for the majority of landowners.

What are latifundia *and* minifundia*?*

What causes the fragmentation of landholdings? Why is this a problem?

As noted in Chapter 9, the less developed countries have economies that are based largely on primary production—mining, forestry, fishing, and agriculture. Mining, forestry and fishing are less significant than agriculture but are nevertheless important to the economies of many nations. For example, Bolivia and Malaysia export tin, and chromium exports bolster the economy of Zimbabwe. The export of logs to Japan

brought badly needed foreign exchange earnings to Indonesia during the period of 1960–1990. Commercial fishing has become important to the economy of Chile. But even in these countries there are far more farmers than people engaged in mining, forestry, and fishing. Figure 9.6 in Chapter 9, a map of employment in agriculture, shows that in most of the less developed countries more than half of the labor force is engaged in farming. Seven out of every 10 members of the labor force in Bangladesh and Haiti are employed in farming, and 8 out of 10 laborers in Ethiopia are farmers or herders. The production of crops for sale or barter plays an important role in traditional agrarian societies, but the emphasis is on the production of subsistence crops. Much human labor is involved because poverty and small landholdings preclude the ownership of agricultural machinery by most farm families.

Agriculture is greatly affected by land tenure. The terms **latifundia** and **minifundia** apply to land tenure systems in Latin America, but similar systems exist in India and Southeast Asia (Fig. 10.1). Large estates with a strong commercial orientation are *latifundia* (singular: *latifundium*). Small holdings with an emphasis on subsistence agriculture are *minifundia* (singular: *minifundium*).

The large estates, called *haciendas* in most of Latin America, traditionally have been owned for generations by wealthy families. Plantations, which have many characteristics in common with *haciendas*, usually are owned by corporations, primarily major international corporations. Agricultural production on large estates is based on the employment by the landowners of large numbers of landless, often illiterate, workers, usually at low wages. Often these workers are bound to the estate by debt to the company store; they cannot leave in search of a better life because of their debt, and the estate owner sometimes sees to it that they remain in debt. *Hacienda* owners traditionally have lived in a mansion on the estate, but increasingly they are city dwellers and absentee landlords. Some *haciendas* and plantations produce several cash crops, but monoculture (the cultivation of a single crop) is more common.

A considerable proportion of the agricultural population of the less developed countries live hand-to-mouth in a mere subsistence state. These people have little contact with foreign commerce and exchange. Some are small farmers who cultivate their own land, but others are *sharecroppers*—farmers who cultivate

(a)   (b)

FIGURE 10.1a and b

*In Latin America there is a striking contrast between large estates (latifundia) and small landholdings
(minifundia) because they often exist side by side. Rural people who serve as laborers on an estate to produce
a commercial crop such as coffee (a) often live and raise subsistence crops on a small adjacent parcel of land
(b). (Rob Crandall/Stock Boston; Eric A. Wessman/Stock Boston)*

a parcel of someone else's land and pay a portion of their crops as rent. The small properties of both are known in Latin America as *minifundia*. Fragmentation of landholdings is a characteristic of *minifundia*; subdivided through inheritance, properties become smaller and smaller. *Latifundia* tend to dominate the best land, leaving the more marginal areas for *minifundia*. The small farmers and sharecroppers are disadvantaged, therefore, not only in the size of their farms but in the quality of their land.

Indebtedness is a problem for most tenant farmers and many small farmers who own their own land. They often cannot afford hybrid seed, fertilizers, and pesticides. Agricultural techniques used by them are mostly traditional, and crop yields tend to be low.

Social Conditions

➤ Common social problems in the less developed world are hunger, disease, poor medical and educational services, cultural conflicts, and the oppression of women.

What diseases are most common in the less developed countries?

How do these countries compare with the United States in terms of medical and educational services?

In what ways are women in many less developed countries more oppressed than women in the United States?

Because of poverty, the internal wealth gap, scarcity of investment capital, the weaknesses of the agrarian economy, and the high population growth rates in the less developed countries, various social problems result. These include hunger, disease, poor medical and educational services, and internal cultural conflicts. In addition to these problems, women are restricted to inferior roles in many less developed countries.

Hunger People who cannot cultivate or buy enough food for good health are hungry often and suffer from *undernutrition* (inadequate calorie intake). Good health also requires that people consume food containing the proper balance of protein, carbohydrates, fats, vitamins, and minerals. Poor people in the less developed world seldom have a balanced diet; they usually live mostly on low-protein, high-starch foods derived from grains such as wheat, rice, or corn. As a result, they often suffer from *malnutrition*, or deficiencies of protein and other nutrients. Probably half of the approximately 4 billion people in the less developed world suffer from undernutrition. Hundreds of thousands to several million people starve to death each year, but most fatal victims of malnutrition die as a result of disease that has attacked their weakened bodies. Each year 20 to 40 million people—half of them children less than 6 years old—die prematurely from malnutrition and otherwise nonfatal diseases. The inadequacy of potable water supplies adds to the death toll. While some of the world's wealthy people drink costly bottled water from France, almost 2 billion of the world's poor people drink and bathe in water contaminated with deadly parasites and pathogens.

Disease   Manifold diseases afflict a large proportion of the population of most less developed nations. *Diarrhea* alone kills millions of people annually, most of them children. *Marasmus*, caused by calorie and protein deficiency, affects millions and also causes large numbers of deaths, especially among children. It produces bloated abdomens, emaciated limbs, and shriveled skin, often depicted in the media coverage of famine in Africa. *Kwashiorkor*, another nutritional deficiency disease, most often afflicts children 1 to 3 years old. Caused by protein deficiency, it results in swollen abdomens, hair loss, diarrhea, and stunted growth. Other diseases related to inadequate diets abound. Half of the women and children and 10 percent of the men of tropical Latin America, Africa, and Asia suffer from *iron-deficiency anemia*, which drains the strength of its victims. In the mountainous areas of the tropics, iodine deficiency causes large numbers of people to suffer *goiter*, an abnormal enlargement of the thyroid gland that often leads to deafness.

Many other diseases are not related to diet but are more deadly because of the poor nutrition common in the less developed countries. *Schistosomiasis*, caused by a worm carried by a snail host, is a painful, incurable, and often fatal disease that affects about 200 million people around the world. Its victims become too weak to work, and almost a million of them die each year. *Malaria* and *yellow fever*, transmitted by mosquitoes, have been serious diseases for generations and still have not been eradicated. *Sleeping sickness*, transmitted by the tsetse fly, afflicts millions of people in Africa. Other common diseases in the less developed world are *tuberculosis, pneumonia, leprosy, influenza, venereal diseases,* and *plague*. Recently *AIDS* has spread so extensively in Africa that it amounts to a new and deadly plague.

Medical and Educational Services   Because of poverty, most of the less developed countries are unable to provide adequate social services to their people, especially to those who live in rural areas. Medical and educational services are deficient by standards deemed acceptable in the developed world. Some developed nations spend 300 times more on health care per person than many poor countries. In fact, the pitiful annual expenditures per citizen for health care in some

FIGURE 10.2

A health clinic in Thailand. In most of the less developed world, health care is deficient because of poverty or ill-conceived government priorities. (Matthew Naythons/Stock Boston)

less developed nations would be barely sufficient to buy a bottle of aspirin in the industrial world. The high death rates in the less developed countries are in large measure a result of the inadequacy of medical facilities (Fig. 10.2) and the shortage of medical professionals. While in the United States the ratio of population to hospital beds in 1993 was about 200:1, the corresponding ratio in the Republic of Togo was 1000:1; in Paraguay it was 1300:1; and in Myanmar (Burma) it was 1400:1. The shortage of hospital beds and the inability of poverty-stricken people to pay for adequate medical services result in many births in less developed countries being unattended by health professionals, thereby increasing infant mortality. For example, less than half of all births are attended by health personnel in Ecuador, El Salvador, Haiti, India, Pakistan, Papua New Guinea, Peru, and most African nations. The shortage of physicians in the less developed countries even exceeds the deficiency of hospital beds. While in the United States the ratio of population to doctors in 1993 was about 500:1, the corresponding ratio in Guyana was 5000:1; in Senegal it was 13,000:1; and in Nepal it was 20,000:1. Rapid rates of population growth keep the ratio of population to physicians high. Exacerbating the problem is the fact that many foreign medical students who receive their training in the United States or Europe do not return to their native countries to practice.

Educational services are usually better than medical services in the less developed world, but generally they are inadequate. Primary and secondary education are compulsory and almost universal in developed countries, but in many less developed countries only a minority of school-age children attend school regularly. Despite six years of compulsory education as a legal concept, in Guatemala only four out of ten school-age children attended school regularly in 1990. Education receives more emphasis in some nations than in others. In the African country of Gabon, for example, nearly 100 percent of school-age children attended primary school in 1993. Mexico and North Korea have compulsory education for 10 and 11 years, respectively, and the majority of school-age children attend school faithfully.

The degree of emphasis placed on formal education in turn influences literacy rates. In general, the less developed world is far less literate than the developed world. Among the countries in which the literacy rate is below 30 percent are Ethiopia, Haiti, India, Liberia, Malawi, Mali, and Pakistan. The African nation of Mali may have the dubious distinction of being the least literate country in the world; only about 13 percent of its people could read and write in 1993. However, illiteracy is not widespread in all less developed countries. Nine out of ten adults in Mexico, for example, can read and write, and almost every adult in North Korea is literate.

Internal Diversity   A certain amount of cultural diversity exists in all countries. Cultural heterogeneity *can* be a good thing, adding to the richness of a nation's heritage. Often, however, cultural plurality leads to social conflict. Most examples of such conflict occur in the less developed world, but developed countries also provide examples of *plural societies* having disparate interests.

Africa is the continent with the greatest cultural diversity and the largest number of resulting conflicts. Contributing to the problems that would exist anyway because of the complex cultural plurality are the in-

ternational boundaries, most of which are related to nineteenth-century colonial activities of various European states. We noted in earlier chapters that the establishment of these boundaries was accomplished with scant attention to the diversity of ethnic, linguistic, and religious associations on which they were imposed. Potential conflicts were suppressed to a large degree by the colonial powers, but following independence much violence and bloodshed resulted as tribes clashed and states engaged in boundary disputes. Since the independence of the African nations, several millions of people have been displaced from their homelands; as described in Chapter 7, many people are still refugees.

The Oppression of Women   In the developed countries, including the United States, women continue to struggle to obtain equal rights with men, and most people believe that inequalities still persist. Nevertheless, women in the developed countries have made great strides toward equality. By contrast, women have not been able to emerge from conditions of overwhelming oppression in a great many countries of the less developed world.

Discrimination against girls begins even before birth in some nations. *Amniocentesis*, a genetic test designed to screen for birth defects, is being used currently in India and China to determine the gender of the unborn so that parents can choose to abort female fetuses (Fig. 10.3). In some Asian abortion clinics, unborn females are far more likely to be aborted than male fetuses.

If discrimination against girls does not begin before birth, it is likely to begin immediately after in most less developed countries. Studies confirm that in countries in which the preference for boys is strong, girls receive less food and inferior medical care. In rural Bangladesh, for example, malnutrition is four times more common among girls than boys. When they become ill, girls are much less likely than boys to receive medical attention in some Asian countries. Hospitals and clinics often treat 20 times as many boys as girls. This discrimination shows up in the mortality statistics for girls and women. In some Asian nations the proportion of women in the population has been declining for almost a century. The relatively low proportion of females to males in the populations of India and China is striking when compared with the situation in Australia (Table 10.1).

Girls in the less developed countries also are much less likely than boys to receive an education.

FIGURE 10.3

In China billboards serve to remind young couples of the government's "one child" policy—an attempt to drastically reduce the country's rate of population growth. Because the preference for a son remains widespread among Chinese, particularly in rural areas, couples often choose to have an abortion of the first fetus if it is determined to be that of a girl. (Forrest Anderson/Gamma Liaison)

Especially at the secondary level, the education of girls is deficient; in many countries, in fact, it is almost entirely lacking. This sex discrimination in education results in greater illiteracy among females than males.

One of the most appalling forms of mistreatment based on sex is genital mutilation, known euphemistically as female circumcision. Probably more than 100 million women have been subjected to this practice in central Africa, the Persian Gulf area, Malaysia, and Indonesia. In at least a dozen countries more than a third of the girls and women have endured genital mutilation. The purpose of the surgery is to guarantee the virginity of a bride by either eliminating the pleas-

ure of sexual intercourse or making it physically impossible for the female to experience intercourse without additional surgery just before marriage. As a consequence, there are two degrees of severity of the mutilation. In both forms there are often medical complications as well as much pain, and many girls die. African men who maintain that female circumcision is an important cultural tradition are criticized by human rights activists who insist that there is nothing inherently African about barbarous cruelty. Yet because so many men will not marry uncircumcised women, girls continue to submit themselves to genital surgery.

The corruption of the concept of *dowry* gives rise to another form of abuse of women on the Indian subcontinent. Dowry refers to the material goods that the bride's parents must give to the groom as part of the marriage settlement. Once a gesture of love, dowry has become a financial burden to the parents of unwed daughters—another reason female babies may be unwelcome. Some husbands view dowry as a way to gain wealth. If promised money or goods are not delivered after the marriage, the wife may be tormented until she ends her life by suicide, freeing the husband to seek another dowry. Sometimes the wife is murdered, often by being doused with kerosene and set afire. Attributed to "kitchen accident" by the murderers, the practice has come to be known as "dowry death" or "bride burning." In some parts of India, the incidence of death by "accidental burns" among young women is 10 times greater than in most less developed countries.

Most wife abuse in the less developed world is in the form of battery, and studies indicate that wife-beating is far more common in many less developed countries than in most developed countries. In some countries it is estimated that more than half of all

TABLE 10.1 Population by Gender in Selected Countries, 1990				
	Male		**Female**	
	Total (in 000)	Percent	Total (in 000)	Percent
India	437,330	51.6	408,861	48.4
China	593,633	51.5	559,837	48.5
Australia	8,531	49.9	8,555	50.1

SOURCE: *United Nations, 1992*

married women have been physically abused by their husbands.

The oppression of women has major economic implications. Discrimination and violence against women undermine the goals of governments in less developed countries for social and economic development. The monumental problems confronting the less developed world cannot be met without the full participation of women. Yet women cannot fully participate if they are undereducated, undernourished, denied adequate health care, and scarred by psychological abuse and physical violence.

SUBSISTENCE LIVELIHOODS

➤ Livelihoods based on subsistence activities other than cultivation are more prevalent in the less developed countries than in the developed world. These activities include gathering, hunting, fishing, and pastoral nomadism.

Where are there groups who still practice these activities, and why are their numbers steadily declining?

How does the livelihood of pastoral nomads differ from that of other groups?

In Chapter 9 we described *primary economic activity* as involving the exploitation of natural resources such as soil, vegetation, minerals, and wildlife. Subsistence economies are linked to part of the primary sector—the part that aims primarily at satisfying the food and other material requirements for a people's survival, as opposed to production of cash crops or raw materials for sale. Agriculture is the dominant primary activity in most parts of the world, and in the less developed countries most farmers devote a large part of their labors to subsistence agriculture. We will conclude this section by examining the nature of both primitive and intensive forms of subsistence agriculture. We will first survey nonagricultural economic activities.

Gathering, Hunting, and Fishing

The most ancient forms of subsistence activity are gathering, hunting, and fishing. They predate the origins of agriculture by at least 2 million years. Before people became effective in hunting and fishing, they practiced *gathering*, the lowest order of economic activity. They subsisted on the fruits, nuts, berries, roots, leaves, and fibers that they collected from trees, shrubs, and smaller plants. Their gathering was an *extensive activity*, meaning that it required a great deal of land area per person.

Subsistence gathering survives today only in isolated areas, and only a few thousand people currently practice this form of livelihood—a number that shrinks every year with the encroachment of "civilization." These people belong to tribal groups and still lead simple lives, despite their awareness of such strange things as jet aircraft and helicopters. They reside in the Amazon Basin, portions of central Africa, parts of Southeast Asia, and some islands of the East Indies and South Pacific (Fig. 10.4).

Hunting and fishing were other Paleolithic (Old Stone Age) forms of subsistence activity that survived and persist today. Although the earliest humans presumably were gatherers only, the technology for successful hunting and fishing developed during the Paleolithic. This technology included the invention of wood and stone weapons, snares, fishhooks, and nets, and the use of poisons in fishing and fire in driving game. The development of the new technology enabled people to move into high-latitude areas where gathering could not have provided sufficient food for subsistence. In other areas hunting and fishing did not necessarily replace gathering. In many societies men became hunters and fishers while women continued to devote much of their time to gathering plant foods.

Hunting and fishing, like gathering, are extensive activities, and the movement of game and fish resulted in the migration of the early hunters and fishers. Life was sedentary only in places where game and fish supplies were abundant throughout the year. Archaeological evidence indicates that most societies suffered periodic famine. Some groups practiced infanticide (killing of newborns) to keep the population in line with available food supplies.

Primitive hunters and fishers today live in the same tropical areas identified earlier as supporting primitive gatherers and in the cold lands of northernmost North America and Eurasia (Fig. 10.4). Livelihood in the high latitudes is based almost entirely on animal life, especially caribou and musk ox from the land; fish, seals, and walrus from the seas; birds from the air; and eggs robbed from nests. Typical of the people of this realm are the North American Eskimos (called *Inuit*) (Fig. 10.5), who are especially skilled hunters.

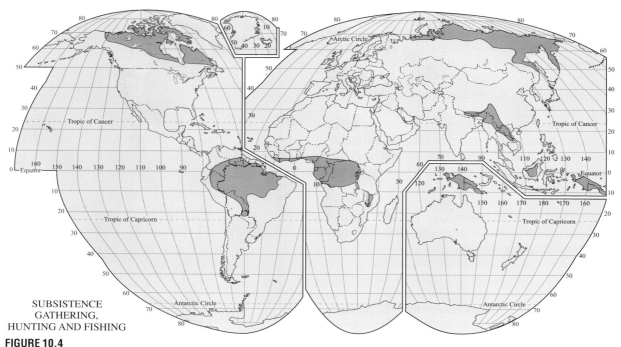

FIGURE 10.4

Gathering, hunting, and fishing are the oldest forms of subsistence activity. Only a fraction of 1 percent of the world's population depend for their livelihood on these primitive types of primary activity.

FIGURE 10.5

The Inuit, or Eskimo, people of the northern reaches of North America earn their livelihoods by fishing and hunting. Their ancient lifestyle has been altered significantly by modern civilization; hunting, for example, often is done using snowmobiles for transportation. (Lionel Delevingne/Stock Boston)

The Inuit developed a remarkable set of implements and variety of clothing and shelter to help them survive the severe winters of the tundra. Women spent much time sewing clothes from the skins of caribou, seal, polar bear, and other animals. Men devoted most of their time to hunting and fishing. However, contact with outsiders has brought many changes to Inuit life. The women still sew, but many use sewing machines; the men still hunt, but many do so from snowmobiles. Practically all Inuit now live in prefabricated housing built by the government in widely separated villages along the Arctic Sea and Hudson Bay. Many Inuit people live in poverty, and in fact are poorer than their ancestors.

Pastoral Nomadism

Pastoral nomadism is a more advanced form of livelihood than primitive gathering, hunting, and fishing because it involves the nurturing of the resource (cattle, sheep, goats, camels, caribou, reindeer, and yaks) to maintain and increase the supply. Nevertheless, it is the simplest form of *pastoralism*, an economic activity that is inherently very extensive. *Pastoral* comes from *pastor*, which is an old English word for *shepherd*. A *nomad* is a wanderer. **Pastoral nomadism**, therefore, involves the herding of grazing animals by nomads.

This type of livelihood was not possible before the domestication of grazing animals, one of the developments that ushered in the Neolithic Period (New Stone Age). The domestication of livestock animals began with sheep about 11,000 years ago; the pig was domesticated about 8500 years ago; and domestic cattle appeared about 7000 years ago. The domestication of these animals seems to have centered in the humid area north of Mesopotamia.

The economic needs of nomadic herders are met primarily by their herds. The animals supply food (milk, cheese, and—only on rare occasions—meat), materials for clothing (fibers and skins), shelter (skins for tents), fuel (dung), and tools (bones). In return, the herd animals require only food (native grass), water, and protection from predators. Because of depletion of the available grass and sometimes the shortage of water, nomads must move their herds often—weekly or even daily in some cases. When the herds are moved, the families of the herders relocate. The small community—a hamlet of tents, actually—is moved perhaps dozens of times a year (Fig. 10.6).

The size and composition of herds vary a great deal among pastoral nomads. Livestock are generally owned by families, and families are grouped into tribes. The migratory unit, however, is usually smaller than a tribe. In the Middle East, each migratory unit consists of 5 or 6 families. Each family requires 25 to 50 goats or sheep or 10 to 25 camels for bare subsistence. Wealth and prestige usually are related to the size of a family's herd.

The largest zone of nomadic herding stretches across northern Africa, the Arabian peninsula, and into central Asia (Fig. 10.7). Approximately 15 million pastoralists live here. This area includes some of the world's largest deserts and sizable areas of semiarid steppe. In the deserts, camels are the most common grazing animals. Sheep and goats predominate in the drier portions of the steppes, and cattle are numerous in the rainier margins of the steppes. An extended drought in the African Sahel (the grasslands immediately south of the Sahara Desert) from the late 1960s to the late 1980s resulted in the death of hundreds of

FIGURE 10.6

Camel, cattle, and sheep nomads at a watering point in the Sudanese Sahel. The man standing in the foreground is Mustapha Khogali, a geographer from the University of Khartoum, Sudan. (Frederick Bein)

thousands of animals. Many of the nomads of the Sahel also starved; others fled to population centers in hopes of finding food relief until conditions enabled them to return to herding.

Pastoral nomadism occurs not only in the dry lands of Africa and Asia but in the cold lands of northern Eurasia and a smaller region in Alaska and northwestern Canada (Fig. 10.7). The grazing animals here, reindeer and caribou, subsist on the scant tundra vegetation. The herders drive the animals poleward in the summer when tundra plants germinate and mature, and then equatorward when the cold winter ends the short growing season in the northern tundra.

Primitive herding, like primitive gathering, hunting, and fishing, is an economic activity that is being practiced by fewer and fewer people. Commercial livestock ranching has encroached into areas formerly used by nomads. The development of modern transportation has reduced the need for camel breeding and the caravan trade. Some central governments, such as those of Saudi Arabia and the former Soviet Union, have endeavored to settle nomads and give them a sedentary and "better" life. Other nomads have been lured from the deserts and steppes by the opportunity

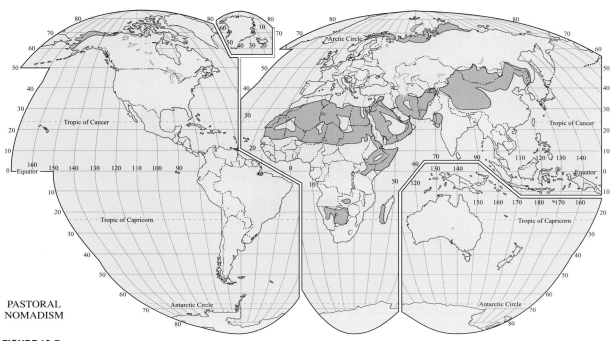

FIGURE 10.7

Approximately 15 million nomadic herders live in the largest zone of pastoral nomadism, which stretches across northern Africa, the Arabian Peninsula, and into Central Asia.

of wage-labor in the oil fields of the Middle East. The last stronghold of nomadism is the Mongolian People's Republic, where as recently as 1980 more than half the population consisted of nomadic Mongols. Even here in the homeland of Genghis Khan, however, nomadism declined during the 1980s as foreign aid from the Soviet Union and various eastern European countries encouraged the development of agriculture and industry.

Shifting Cultivation and Intensive Subsistence Agriculture

➤ Other subsistence livelihoods are based on cultivation, both shifting cultivation and intensive subsistence agriculture. The latter is found in only a small number of countries, but these countries include a large portion of the world's population.

What is shifting cultivation and where is it practiced?

What accounts for the large outputs of rice per unit of land in wet paddy farming?

In the wet tropical environments of the world, the most common use of the land is an ancient rudimentary form of subsistence agriculture usually identified as **shifting cultivation**. Centuries ago, shifting cultivation was practiced much more widely. Today, however, it is confined to rainy areas in the low latitudes, such as parts of Middle and South America (particularly the basin of the Amazon River), central Africa, and certain mainland and island areas of Southeast Asia. To some extent, plantations and sedentary farms have displaced shifting cultivation from coastal zones in the tropics. In total, the remaining areas in which shifting cultivation is practiced in scattered localities amounts to about one-fourth of the world's land surface (Fig. 10.8), but the land area actually under cultivation in any given year is a very small portion of that amount. Although population densities are generally low in these areas, the total population—particularly in Africa—is increasing. It is estimated that more than 200 million people are supported by shifting cultivation.

Shifting cultivation is conducted by small groups of people, commonly extended families or tribes, who

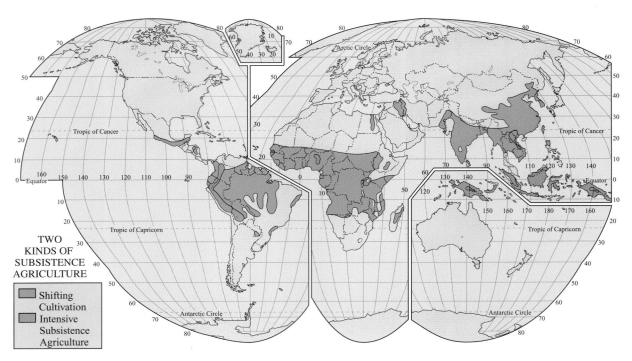

FIGURE 10.8

*Two very different kinds of subsistence agriculture—shifting cultivation and intensive subsistence
agriculture—are shown on this map. Only some 200 million people are supported by the former, but
the latter provides the livelihood for over 3 billion people.*

reside in villages and who share the nearby land. The
site of the village is usually along a stream or river,
which serves as a source of fish, the domestic water
supply, and a means of waste disposal. Structures in
the village are made of local materials and are seldom
built to survive for an extended period. The entire village may be relocated when the soil productivity in
the immediate area is diminished, the accumulation of
garbage and waste becomes intolerable, or damage is
caused by the flooding of a nearby stream or river.
Population growth in the village also may lead to abandonment of the old site by some or all of the inhabitants and the reestablishment of one or more new villages in other locations. With these prospects, it is not
rational for shifting cultivators to construct houses and
other buildings for a lifetime of use.

Shifting cultivation is an adaptation to conditions
of the tropical environment that is made possible by
low population densities and the absence of competitors for use of the land. As a first step, it involves the
establishment of a clearing in the tropical vegetation—

jungle, brush, and rainforest containing trees of enormous size. Usually equipped with only simple tools
such as the machete and ax, the farmers have learned
to use fire as a means of reducing the labor expended
in clearing land. After large trees are killed by cutting
a girdle through their bark and smaller plants are cut
down and assembled in piles, fire is set to the dead
vegetation. (This method of land clearing has given
rise to the use of "slash-and-burn agriculture" as an
alternative title to shifting cultivation.) From the van-
tage point of an aircraft over tropical forests, it often
is possible to see several columns of smoke from the
fires employed in land clearing. The ash remaining
from the burned vegetation has value as temporary
fertilizer for the first crops raised in the clearing. Tree
stumps and trunks that survive the burning are merely
ignored; their removal is unnecessary because shifting
cultivation does not involve plowing the land and
planting crops in neat rows. In this system, farmers
plant seeds in low mounds of soil formed with a hoe
or in a hole punched in the surface with a pointed stick.

Environmentalists generally consider shifting cultivation to be an ecologically sound form of land use, since the forest quickly reclaims abandoned clearings.

The subsistence agriculture of large portions of southern and eastern Asia contrasts sharply with the rather extensive primitive farming practices of other portions of the tropics and subtropics. It is termed **intensive subsistence agriculture** because it involves large labor inputs and high yields per unit of land. Despite the high output of farm commodities per hectare (or acre), however, usually little surplus is produced because of the vast food requirements of the dense populations of the areas where intensive subsistence agriculture is practiced. These areas are identified in Figure 10.8. The relatively small number of countries in which intensive subsistence agriculture is common contain about two-thirds of the total world population. That fact testifies to the tremendous importance of this category of agriculture. There are two types of intensive subsistence agriculture. One is dominated by wet paddy rice and the other by the production of other crops such as wheat, maize, millet, soybeans, sugarcane, root crops, and vegetables.

Wet Paddy Rice   Rice is the most distinctive and most important product of intensive subsistence farming in the monsoon lands of southern Asia. Although much *dry* rice (or *upland* rice) is produced in areas that cannot be irrigated, greater yields occur with *wet* rice, which is grown in *paddy* fields (Fig. 10.9). Paddies are fields that can be flooded and on which the water can be retained. They have been recessed below the surrounding land by excavation or formed on terraces by damming the margins. Most paddies of both types were created centuries ago with the investment of countless hours of human labor. The typical Asian rice paddy is less than a hectare (even less than an acre) in size.

Water requirements for wet rice are high, and the monsoon rains of southern Asia are abundant during the warm season. Large portions of this area receive more than 60 inches (152 cm) of precipitation annually. By contrast, Chicago averages 33 inches (84 cm) of precipitation annually. Even the monsoon rains may provide too little water for paddy rice, however, and many paddies are designed to be flooded by river water.

Winter is the dry season in the monsoon lands and the time to repair the irrigation and drainage channels

FIGURE 10.9
Paddy rice fields in Thailand. The highest yields in intensive subsistence agriculture occur with ''wet rice'' production in paddies. Paddy rice cultivation is common in the lowlands of southeastern Asia. (J. Lamont)

and the banks of earth that serve to impound water. The first rains soften the soil, which is usually plowed by the indispensable water buffalo. Meanwhile, rice seedlings are being grown in manure-fertilized seedbeds. As transplanting time approaches, the paddy is flooded to the requisite depth. In some areas the rice seedlings are transplanted into neat rows in the saturated soil beneath the water, but in others the placement of the plants is indiscriminate. Women do more than their share of this backbreaking work; in fact, in some cultures the transplanting of rice is considered the responsibility of women. Men help with the hoeing and harvesting operations. Harvesting is done by hand with a sickle, and thrashing is also usually a manual operation. At all stages of production, wet rice farming is labor-intensive. Small farm machinery, now common in Japan and China, is slow in spreading throughout monsoon Asia because of the poverty of the area; the subsistence nature of agriculture means that little cash is generated.

Wet paddy farming produces large outputs of rice per unit of land not only because of the intensity of labor required but also because of multiple cropping. Two, three, and—in a few very favorable locations—

even four crops of rice can be produced in a single year. In areas in which only one crop of rice can be raised, the fields are normally used in the dry season for the production of other crops, often vegetables.

Dry-Field Agriculture Because of terrain, soil and moisture conditions and length of growing season, it is not practical or profitable to grow paddy rice in many parts of the monsoon world, and in these areas other crops are cultivated. Crop yields are not as high as in multiple-crop farming of rice, but both the subsistence nature of agriculture and the labor-intensive approach to farming are as typical of nonpaddy (*dry-field*) as paddy cultivation. The two systems also have in common very small field size and farm size. Many farmers in India cultivate farms smaller than 2 acres (0.8 ha) in size. Finally, the lack of mechanization is as common in dry-field as in paddy agriculture; human and animal power accomplish most of the work.

In intensive dry-field agriculture, no crop is dominant in the farm economy. In moister areas, upland rice and corn are almost universal. With decreasing precipitation, corn is replaced by wheat and, in still drier environments, by many varieties of millet and sorghum. However, these crops are seldom used in a monoculture, as in wet-rice farming. Instead, they are rotated and interspersed with other crops, such as soybeans, sugarcane, root crops, and vegetables.

COMMERCIAL AGRICULTURE

➤ Emphasis is placed on production of agricultural commodities for the marketplace in commercial agriculture, which includes livestock ranching, plantation agriculture, and small farming.

Of these three kinds of agriculture, which is the most intensive?

The most extensive?

Why has there been a great expansion of cash-crop farming in the less developed world during the twentieth century?

Commercial agriculture, as the term implies, places emphasis on production of agricultural commodities for the marketplace. Those people engaged in this primary economic activity may or may not produce food for their own consumption. Most small farmers engaged primarily in commercial agriculture also grow some subsistence crops, but most plantations are strictly commercial operations. Commercial agriculture can be subdivided into three very different types of activity: livestock ranching, plantation agriculture, and small farming.

Livestock Ranching

Livestock ranching, also called commercial grazing, typically occurs the greatest distance from market of any form of commercial agriculture. This is because it is a very extensive form of economic activity that requires relatively little labor and supports relatively few people per unit of land. The basis of livestock ranching is natural grasslands—the prairie, short grass, and steppe regions of the middle latitudes and the savanna grasslands of tropical latitudes. Figure 10.10 identifies six major regions in which commercial grazing is practiced; all continents except Europe and Antarctica have a large region within which livestock ranching is the major agricultural activity. Half of the regions shown in Figure 10.10 lie primarily in developed nations and will be considered in Chapter 11. A dozen Latin American and African nations have grazing lands important to their economies.

Of the five countries having the largest number of cattle, three are less developed countries: India, Brazil, and China. In India and China cattle are a constituent of other agricultural systems, so no livestock ranching area for those countries appears in Figure 10.10. India has more cattle than any other nation, but these animals are not slaughtered for food because of religious considerations. Brazil has vast areas of savanna grasslands that enable it to support the world's second largest number of cattle. Savanna grasses are poor in nutrients, however, because of the poverty of tropical soils, and Brazilian cattle generally do not match the quality of those produced in the middle latitudes.

As with cattle, three of the world's largest producers of sheep and goats are less developed countries: China, India, and Turkey. Sheep and goats are three times as numerous as cattle in Turkey; China has twice as many of the smaller livestock as cattle; and India has almost as many sheep and goats as cattle. Worldwide, sheep are the second most common livestock animal, and goats rank third in total numbers. Sheep are raised for meat and wool; goats are kept for milk, meat, and mohair.

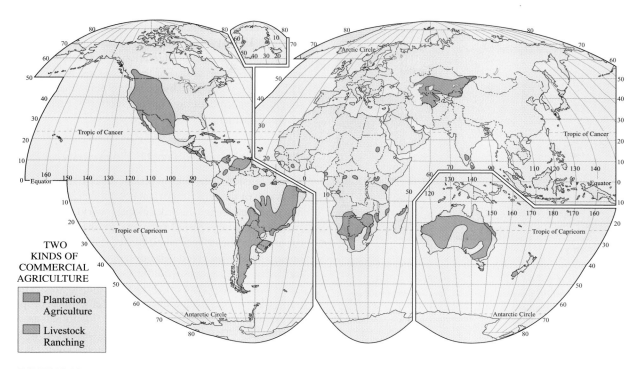

FIGURE 10.10

Unlike each other in most regards, livestock ranching and plantation agriculture are both commercial activities.

Plantation Agriculture

While livestock ranching is as extensive in the developed world as in less developed countries, **plantation agriculture** is almost totally limited to the less developed world. Tropical plantation farming is one of the most distinctive and oldest types of large-scale specialized agriculture. It began centuries ago following the colonization of the humid tropical portions of the Americas, but its development has taken place largely during the past 100 years. Because of the intensity of the operations and the high yields possible with tropical crops, relatively little land is required. Only about 10 percent of the world's cropland occurs on plantations (Fig. 10.10).

Individual plantations are rather large holdings, ranging from about 200 acres (81 ha) to 120,000 acres (48,580 ha). The size of the holding, the high cost of infrastructure development, and the expense of cropland inputs (fertilizers, herbicides, and insecticides) limit the ownership of plantations primarily to large corporations. Most of these corporations are owned by

stockholders in the United States, Europe, and Japan—major destinations of the commodities produced on the plantations. The administrative and technical staffs of the plantation involve both men and women—although traditionally more men are employed—usually from the developed country that hosts the headquarters of the corporation. The laborers, most of whom are unskilled, are recruited from local or nearby districts (Fig. 10.11).

The plantations are organized on an efficient basis, and much of the work is done by hand. The principal farm implements continue to be the hoe and the machete, even though mechanization has been increased greatly in recent decades. The comfortable living conditions of the managerial staff contrast sharply with the living quarters of the laborers. The corporation pays high salaries to management personnel to attract them to jobs in the usually remote areas of the less developed world. The wages paid to the local laborers ordinarily are very low by comparison to those of unskilled wage laborers in the nation of the corporation's origin. By local standards, however, these

FIGURE 10.11

This photo was taken on a tea plantation in India. Although most people in the less developed countries earn their livelihood from agriculture, relatively few are employed on plantations. (R. Gabler)

wages tend to be competitive and, in some cases, very good.

Plantations exist on every continent possessing a tropical climate. They have the longest history in Latin America. Following the opening of the Suez Canal in 1869, large plantations were established in Asia. Africa was the last region of the tropics to experience plantation development—late in the nineteenth century. In all three major regions a large number of commercial crops are grown. Some are *tree crops* (coffee, tea, cacao, rubber, coconuts, palm oil); others are *field crops* (sugarcane, bananas, henequen, sisal); and still others are *annual crops* (tobacco, peanuts, cotton, jute). The leading plantation commodities in terms of weight exported and the leading exporting nations are sugar (Cuba), palm oil (Malaysia), rubber (Malaysia), and bananas (Ecuador). Lower on the list of terms of weight but very high-value plantation commodities are three beverage crops: coffee (Brazil), cacao (Côte d'Ivoire), and tea (India).

There are risks involved in any agricultural enterprise, and one of the risks in plantation agriculture is that world prices of tropical crops are very volatile. When prices are depressed, workers often are laid off or required to work for lower wages. Sometimes plantations fail; in the financial interests of stockholders, corporations will not operate an unprofitable plantation indefinitely. There also are setbacks resulting from insects and plant diseases associated with monocultures. Finally, there may be unfortunate environmental consequences of plantation agriculture, such as accelerated soil erosion. For those reasons, many tropical nations, while not discouraging plantations, have sought ways to encourage the production of cash crops by small farmers.

The Role of Small Farmers

The expansion of cash crop production by small farmers is one of the most important economic changes that has occurred in the less developed world during the twentieth century. **Small farmers** are those who own (or lease) and cultivate small farms. Although there is no universally accepted definition of the size of a small farm, few geographers would disagree that most small farms are smaller than 50 acres (20.2 ha) in size. The term *small holding* often is used to refer to these properties, and the small farmer is also identified as a *smallholder*. The great expansion of cash crop production by small farmers in the twentieth century has been the result of (1) a shift of production by many farmers from subsistence crops to cash crops, and (2) a significant increase in the number of small holdings created through agrarian reform implemented by the government specifically for the purpose of involvement in the export economy.

Economically and socially, the production of cash crops by small farmers has much to commend it. A small farm requires little capital investment, and the smallholder has few fixed costs. It is easier for the small farmer than the plantation to interplant crops and to harvest field crops or annual crops while waiting for a tree crop to mature to productivity. When commodity prices sag on the world market, the small farmer usually can survive quite well by growing subsistence crops. Also there are no laborers to lay off, because the typical small farm is a family operation. Smallholders suffer the greatest disadvantage in the cultivation of crops that require large seasonal labor inputs or elaborate and costly processing—crops such as sugarcane, tea, and sisal.

Whatever crops they produce, small farmers often encounter difficulties in getting their harvested crops processed or sold. Until about 1960 they had to deal with foreign export firms. Because their commodities usually did not match the quality of plantation-produced crops, often they did not receive a good price; sometimes they were even cheated. In the 1960s, the governments of many nations began creating agricultural marketing boards to supervise the export trade in farm commodities. The record of these marketing boards has not been good, however. They are as likely to favor the middleman as the farmer. Many of them are characterized by a management that is inept, corrupt, or both, and few of them are popular with farmers. This problem has not been alleviated by land development and the Green Revolution.

LAND DEVELOPMENT AND THE GREEN REVOLUTION

➤ Two major approaches by governments in addressing agrarian problems are land development and the Green Revolution. Neither has been entirely successful.

What is land development, and why has it yielded disappointing results?

What has been the greatest success of the Green Revolution?

Why have so many farmers failed to benefit from the technology of the Green Revolution?

To help solve some of their agrarian problems, less developed countries have turned to *land development* and the *Green Revolution*. Land development and the Green Revolution are endeavors to improve the quality of life of many people in the less developed world. The two concepts overlap so much that it is difficult to distinguish them in some cases, but that may not be important. What is important is the extent to which they succeed, independently or together, in providing a better life for people.

The Disappointing Results of Land Development

Land development involves the relocation of people to an area that has been set aside and "developed," usually by the central government, for their permanent settlement. The primary objectives are usually to redistribute population, to develop the region, to provide land for the landless, and to develop agriculture. Serious problems have been associated with land development throughout its history. We will comment here on seven such problems: (1) the high costs of land development; (2) the inadequacy of the infrastructure

often provided to the settlers; (3) lack of nonfarm employment; (4) landholding consolidation; (5) conflicts between neighbors; (6) ecological problems; and (7) landholding abandonment. After briefly surveying these problems, we will examine their causes.

Land development is a very expensive undertaking. Forests may have to be cleared, and in some areas drainage and irrigation canals have to be constructed. Roads, houses, and public buildings such as schools and administrative headquarters have to be built. During the 1980s the cost of settling one landless family on a small holding in a new land development scheme in a less developed country ranged between $5000 and $50,000. The high cost of development makes it very unlikely that a settlement project can become profitable in terms of return on invested capital.

Despite the huge investments, the infrastructure provided to the settlers may be inadequate to make life in the project attractive to settlers. In some of the land development schemes in Guyana, for example, settlers were granted farmland and a houselot but no house or credit. The construction of housing was the top priority of settlers, but without credit many of them were able to build only miserable shacks (Fig. 10.12). In hun-

FIGURE 10.12
This shack was built by a settler in a Guyanese land development project to provide shelter for his family. The formerly landless peasant family had been granted a small parcel of land by the government but no credit or other assistance for housing. (J. Vining)

dreds of settlement projects throughout the less developed world, high development costs have precluded the early provision of schools and health centers. Some settlers have waited for years for promised schools.

The lack of nonfarm income has been a serious problem in the majority of settlement projects. Agriculture is characterized by slack seasons during which farmers often seek nonfarm income, but the remote locations of most land development schemes restrict the opportunity of finding supplemental income. Consequently, underemployment is typical.

Agrarian reform usually includes as one of its purposes an increase in the number of landholders, and granting land in new settlement projects to the landless is a way of accomplishing this. Postdevelopment landholding consolidation, however, works against that goal and has become a serious problem in many projects. Most colonists are required to live on their land for a number of years before receiving title to their holding. Once they receive a land title, many settlers sell their land, often to another local farmer. This process returns some people to landlessness and wage labor while increasing the farm size of the most successful farmers.

Conflict between neighbors has been a problem in some settlement projects. When a project is settled by people of two or more cultural groups with a history of conflict, disputes between neighbors can be expected. Besides internal conflicts, tensions between settlers and indigenous populations may lead to serious difficulties. Such tensions may build if settlers are perceived to have larger landholdings and better provision of social services or to be encroaching on land traditionally farmed by the local community.

Ecological problems contribute to the failure of some land development projects. The improper control of water in settlement schemes established on land that must be drained or irrigated can produce drought conditions or flooding and bring misery to the settlers. Soil damage can result from the use of earth-moving equipment during land development. On sloping land, deforestation can produce soil erosion.

The final problem common in land development schemes is landholding abandonment. The quality of life in most projects does not equal that in the former core areas of a country. Disappointed in their often unrealistically high expectations, settlers may abandon their landholdings and seek better opportunities elsewhere.

Worldwide data are not available on the number of land development projects that have been undertaken during the twentieth century, their total area, and their aggregate population. It is clear, however, that there have been several thousands of such ventures, involving millions of hectares of land and several millions of people. Land development obviously has been a major endeavor by governments in the less developed world. But, despite the hundreds of millions of dollars that have been invested—mostly since the 1960s—planned land settlement has not lived up to expectations. This approach to development so far has made no more than a modest contribution to the solution of the problems of population distribution, unemployment, and poverty. Few land development projects have achieved their stated objectives; most have lapsed into stagnation.

Three major requirements for successful land development are (1) suitable land; (2) a sizeable amount of money; and (3) a suitable human (labor) resource. Most of the countries that have attempted land development have had suitable land, but future colonization must be based more and more on increasingly marginal lands. Money is always in short supply in the less developed countries, and as the costs of land development continue to increase, the pace of new project development can be expected to decelerate. The labor resource historically has been underutilized because of inadequate allocation of other resources or suppressive institutional systems that fail to provide incentives for increased production. It remains to be seen whether governments will come to grips with this problem.

Despite their limited success, land settlement programs are popular in much of the less developed world, mainly because they are politically expedient and create less opposition than other agrarian reform measures. The evidence, however, indicates that land development alone cannot be expected to solve agrarian problems.

Successes and Failures in the Green Revolution

The **Green Revolution** is a term coined in the 1960s to describe increased output obtained from improved, high-yielding varieties of wheat and rice developed by plant breeding research programs in Mexico and the Philippines. The term has since been generalized to refer to any system of scientific agriculture based on a combination of some, although not necessarily all, of the following: (1) biotechnology, including genetic engineering, to produce high-yield crop varieties; (2) increased mechanization; (3) expanded use of fertilizers; (4) application of pesticides; (5) irrigation; (6) the use of agricultural cooperatives; (7) expanded agricultural extension for farmer training in the new technology; (8) improved marketing assistance; and (9) more short-term credit for farmers. Since the 1960s the most important of these factors in expanding crop production have been the new hybrid crop varieties and the greater use of fertilizers.

The greatest success of the Green Revolution has been a quantum leap in food production per unit area of land in many countries. The nations that have benefited most are identified in Figure 10.13. Nearly 90 percent of the increase in world grain output in the 1960s and about 70 percent of that in the 1970s were the result of the Green Revolution. During the 1980s some 80 percent of the increased production of grains could be attributed to the Green Revolution. Likewise,

80 percent of the increased production projected for the 1990s is expected to result from the new technology. World wheat production more than doubled between 1965 and 1985, and world rice production increased by 75 percent during the same period. The greatest increases in wheat production occurred in Bangladesh, China, India, and Pakistan, and the largest increases in rice production were in Indonesia, Pakistan, and North Korea.

Bangladesh is a good example of the beneficial effects of the Green Revolution. When that country became independent in 1971, some experts believed that the problem of producing sufficient food for more than 90 million people on an area of land smaller than that of Illinois was hopeless, especially because of the frequency of natural disasters associated with floods and storms. The introduction of the new agricultural technology, however, enabled Bangladesh to increase its rice production by half and its wheat output by ten times within a dozen years of independence. Despite the very high birth rate and the high incidence of nat-

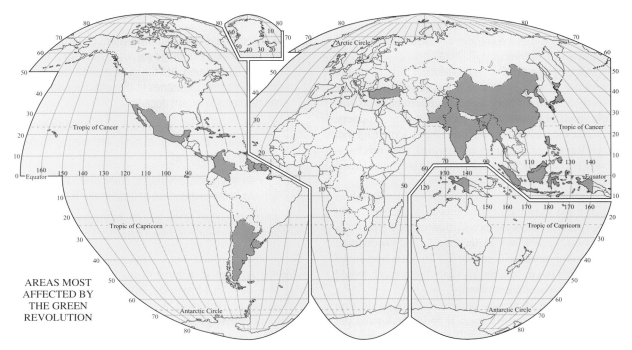

FIGURE 10.13

The Green Revolution, which produced a quantum leap in world grain production during the 1960s through the 1980s, was most effective in the areas emphasized on this map. Unfortunately, Africa did not benefit greatly from Green Revolution technology during that period, and Latin America did not show nearly as much progress as Asia did.

ural disasters, the Green Revolution has permitted this nation to feed its people as well in the 1980s as it did in the 1970s. Bangladesh remains one of the world's most chronically destitute countries, but without the Green Revolution famine would have claimed many more lives during the past two decades.

The Green Revolution has provided appreciable optimism throughout the less developed world. The new technology has given many poor nations hope that someday they may be able to overcome the problems of poverty, hunger, and malnutrition.

Despite such successes and widespread optimism about the Green Revolution and what it might be able to accomplish, not all farmers in the less developed countries have benefited from the new technology. Where overall crop production has been expanded by the Green Revolution, many farmers have not participated because of what some experts have referred to as the "class bias" of the new agricultural technology. Technology of the Green Revolution involves large amounts of chemical fertilizers and, usually, pesticides—agricultural inputs that are expensive. Wealthy landowners can afford such inputs, and many small, well-established farmers can buy them on credit. Poor and landless peasants, however, are unable to secure credit to obtain these resources because they lack sufficient assets to serve as collateral.

Not only has the Green Revolution failed to benefit millions of small farmers, it has contributed to the poverty of some. Many large landholders, who formerly had assigned small farms to sharecroppers, withdrew their land from tenants after discovering that Green Revolution techniques, coupled with mechanization, allowed them to cultivate all their land themselves with the help of seasonal labor.

Another problem with the Green Revolution is that in many countries the emphasis of the new technology has been on the production of cash crops for the export market, not on increased food production. Poor nations need cash to pay for imports and make foreign debt payments, but feeding their people would seem to deserve greater priority.

Impressive increases in world food production disguise the fact that the average food production per person declined between 1950 and 1990 in almost a third of the less developed countries. Figure 10.13 shows that most of Africa and Latin America have not been helped greatly by the Green Revolution. Africa was self-sufficient in food until the 1960s, but at the very time when the new technology was beginning to

increase agricultural outputs in Asia, per capita food production in Africa began to decline. The new hybrid crops were best suited to lowland and irrigated farms and did not do well on the poorer upland soils and semiarid parts of Africa. Some of the "improved" crops introduced to Africa did not cook well or taste good. Most of the new varieties were developed for maximum yields when heavily fertilized and were not bred for resistance to drought, disease, or pests. African farmers discovered that without fertilizers and pesticides, the new "high yielding" varieties did not produce as much as traditional varieties. Women, who grow much of the continent's food, largely were neglected when agencies introduced Green Revolution technology to Africa.

Lessons have been learned from the failures of the past, and the Green Revolution can be expected to expand successfully in more countries in Africa and Latin America. The projected role of biotechnology in the agriculture of the less developed world will be examined later in this chapter.

NONAGRICULTURAL LIVELIHOODS

➤ Many less developed countries derive a large portion of their foreign exchange earnings from forestry, fishing, and mining, but the relative importance of these extractive industries in the world economy has declined in recent decades.

From the standpoint of providing a livelihood for people, how do forestry, fishing, and mining compare with agriculture?

Why do many less developed countries have a high ranking in the production of timber and fish?

Which countries in the less developed world are leading producers of fossil fuels?

Subsistence farming and commercial agriculture provide the livelihood of most of the rural population of the less developed world. From the standpoint of providing a livelihood for people, other forms of economic activity—forestry, fishing, mining, manufacturing, and service—are far less important. Nevertheless, a great many less developed countries derive a large portion of their foreign exchange earnings from some of these activities, and no survey of employment in the poorer nations is complete without an examination of these industries.

Forestry, Fishing, and Mining

Forestry, fishing, and mining are **extractive industries**—that is, they are activities by which people extract natural resources from the biosphere and lithosphere. In general, the relative importance of these activities in the world economy of the twentieth century has declined as manufacturing and service activities have become more prominent.

Forestry   Forestry includes all those activities associated with the use and management of forests. In the tropical world, forests are used extensively by gatherers who collect nuts, sap, and bark that can be used for food or sold. Gathering, the simplest form of livelihood, was considered earlier in this chapter. The gathering of fuelwood for use in domestic cooking and heating is a necessary subsistence activity in much of the less developed world. The shortage of fuelwood is a problem of crisis proportions in more than three dozen countries (Fig. 10.14).

Cutting trees for lumber or pulpwood (for the manufacture of paper) may be termed *timbering*. Most of the timber that is cut in the less developed countries is exported to the developed nations. Japan is by far the world's leading importer of unmilled logs, and the United States is the leading importer of milled wood and pulpwood. Some of the less developed countries are among the world's leading producers and exporters of wood. Heading the list of exporters of unmilled logs is Malaysia, which accounts for about a third of total exports. Indonesia, Côte d'Ivoire, and Gabon also are among the world's five leading exporters of unprocessed logs. There are no less developed countries on the list of leading exporters of milled wood, and Brazil is the only less developed nation among the five major exporters of pulpwood.

Tropical forests are characterized by a large number of species of trees per unit land area, and this causes a problem in harvesting timber for export. *Selective cutting* (cutting trees here and there) rather than *clear cutting* (harvesting all of the trees in a given area) is the preferred method of harvest, given the heterogeneity of species. The greatest demand is for such high-value woods as mahogany, teak, ebony, cedar, and balsa. Some environmental damage results from

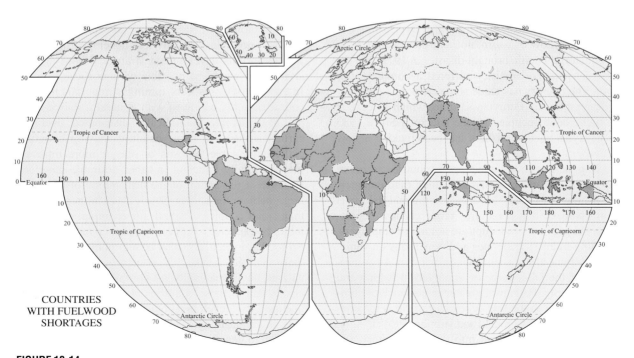

FIGURE 10.14

The principal domestic heating and cooking fuel in the less developed world is fuelwood (firewood), which now is in short supply in many of the less developed countries.

the selective cutting of these and other woods, but this commercial logging is not the most serious threat to the rainforest. (Tropical deforestation is examined in Chapter 14.)

Fishing Millions of people in the less developed world provide food for their families and gain some income from fishing. Their catch is not counted in commercial fishing statistics, however, because most of it is eaten or sold in the local village. Of the 17 nations that each harvested more than a million metric tons of commercial fish annually during the late 1980s, 10 were less developed countries. Although none of these nations came close to the huge harvests of fish taken by Japan and the former Soviet Union, more than half of the world's commercial catch during the 1980s was harvested by the less developed countries. Leading the list of less developed countries in terms of fish harvest, in order, are Chile, China, and Peru.

Peru's position as a commercial fishing nation has declined sharply since 1972. In the late 1960s Peru surpassed Japan to become the world's leading producer of fish. Peru at that time was harvesting mostly anchovies from the nutrient-rich waters off its coast. Fishery officials ignored the warnings of the United Nations Food and Agriculture Organization that the annual catch was exceeding the yield. Overfishing and temporary inflow of warm, nutrient-poor waters from the equatorial Pacific brought disaster in 1972, and the Peruvian anchovy industry suffered a complete collapse. The country has made some economic recovery by harvesting the Peruvian sardine, which took over the niche once occupied by the anchovy. Since 1983 the Peruvian anchovy fishery has been making a slow recovery.

In general, the less developed countries are more important to world commercial fishing than commercial fishing is to them. Modern commercial fishing is so mechanized that it requires relatively few people, so the fishing boats and ships are not major employers. A fishing industry generates additional jobs on shore, but still there are no countries in which a large proportion of the labor force is employed in fishing and fish processing. Perhaps a greater importance of commercial fishing in the less developed world is the contribution it makes to local food supplies.

During the 1990s and into the next century, the U.N. Food and Agriculture Organization expects that the major increase in demand for fish will come from developing countries, mainly because of rapidly in-

creasing populations in many of those nations. Much of this increased demand cannot be met by existing fishing areas. Four methods have been proposed by the United Nations Food and Agriculture Organization for increasing the supplies of fish for human consumption: (1) expanding **aquaculture**—the intensive production of aquatic species in confined areas; (2) expanding the market for squid, octopus, and other nonconventional species; (3) developing a market for undesirable fish species that usually are discarded at sea; and (4) switching some of the fish sold as animal feed into the market for human consumption. Aquaculture, especially, shows much promise. It is already a major source of animal protein for the poor in many less developed countries, particularly in Asia. Almost three-fourths of the world's annual aquaculture harvest comes from the less developed countries. China alone accounts for almost half of this harvest. (See *Cultural Landscapes: Aquaculture Ponds in China.*)

Mining Like forestry and fishing, mining is an extractive enterprise that does not represent a major source of livelihood. The number of miners and oil field workers is relatively small, even in many countries in which the products of mineral extraction account for a large part of foreign exchange earnings. Foreign capital earned from mineral exports, however, makes it possible for many less developed nations to pursue various development strategies more aggressively than would be possible without those exports. In that and other respects, mining is important in those countries richly endowed with mineral resources.

Minerals are sporadically distributed over the earth's surface, so some countries having commercially exploitable deposits of one or more minerals may be totally deficient in other desirable minerals. Because of the nature of the distribution of minerals, large nations tend to possess greater mineral wealth than small countries. Brazil, for example, reasonably might be expected to have more mineral resources than Sri Lanka; indeed, Brazil *is* better endowed with minerals than Sri Lanka. Of course, some developing nations have practically no commercial mineral deposits, and in those countries mining is of no consequence. Less developed countries with abundant minerals of great strategic value, by contrast, are in a good position to benefit from the exhausting supplies in the developed world.

Iron makes up about 95 percent by weight, of the metals extracted from the earth each year. Production patterns have changed markedly in recent decades. Historically, Europe and the United States dominated iron mining, and for more than two decades before its disintegration in 1991 the Soviet Union was by far the leading producer. Other nations, including less developed countries, have expanded greatly their output in recent years. Four of the world's ten leading producers are less developed countries: Brazil, China, India, and Venezuela. Possessing the world's largest high-grade reserves, Brazil also is the leading exporter.

The mining of bauxite, the ore of aluminum, also is important to the economies of a number of developing nations. Most of the ore extraction occurs in countries that are not major manufacturers of aluminum, hence most of the product enters the export trade. Bauxite is the major export commodity of the small countries of Guinea, Guyana, and Jamaica. Brazil is a major producer and exporter, but that country is so well endowed with minerals and other resources that bauxite mining and exporting are a less important source of employment and foreign exchange earnings than in the smaller nations mentioned.

The third mineral that is a part of the mainstay of the metals industry is copper, important because it is a good conductor of electricity. Less developed nations are even better represented in the production of copper than of iron ore and bauxite. Chile, Zaire, Zambia, Peru, and Mexico, together with five developed nations, comprise the top ten copper producers. Chile heads the list, accounting for a greater output than the United States, which ranks second in copper production. Chile's Chuquicamata copper district (Fig. 10.15) may contain more ore reserves than any other deposit in the world, so copper mining and exporting will contribute significantly to the Chilean economy for decades to come.

Fossil fuels—coal, petroleum, and natural gas—are the minerals that provide most of the energy consumed in the developed world, but they also are important in less developed countries—all of which use them and some of which produce them.

Coal is the world's most abundant fossil fuel; vast deposits will remain long after global supplies of petroleum and natural gas are exhausted. A less developed country, China, is the world's leading producer of coal, having recently surpassed the annual output of the former Soviet Union and the United States. China's preeminent position likely will continue, since that country's government has announced that it plans

FIGURE 10.15

The Chuquicamata copper mine in Chile lies in what may be the world's largest reserve of copper. Because of its high degree of mechanization, mining is an extractive economic enterprise that provides a livelihood for only a relatively small part of the labor force, even in Chile. (Rob Crandall/ Stock Boston)

to double production between 1987 and 2000. India, South Africa, and North Korea also rank among the world's top ten producers of coal, although coal generally is in short supply in the less developed countries.

Petroleum is the most important commodity in international trade today. Therefore, nations that are well endowed with commercial deposits have a distinct economic advantage over those lacking oil supplies. Developing nations with fragile economies and no domestic oil deposits scarcely can afford the price of oil imports. Nevertheless, the demand for petroleum is worldwide and, unfortunately, there are relatively few suppliers and no known vast untapped reserves. Almost two-thirds of the world's proven oil reserves are in just five Persian Gulf countries—Saudi Arabia, Kuwait, Iran, Iraq, and the United Arab Emirates. All are less developed countries, despite their oil wealth, because they have not yet acquired other characteristics of full development. One of these countries, Saudi Arabia, possesses one-quarter of all known world re-

CULTURAL LANDSCAPES

Aquaculture Ponds in China

Conspicuous features of the cultural landscape in eastern China are thousands of small ponds and other artificial water bodies used for the practice of aquaculture. An intriguing method of food production, aquaculture involves the "cultivation" of animals and plants in controlled water bodies. The most common and rapidly growing form of aquaculture in China and elsewhere is fish farming. Many of the ponds now used for fish farming in China are former rice paddies. Although aquaculture also involves raising fish in pens in rivers, most production in China is from small ponds such as those in the accompanying photo.

China leads all the world's nations in fish farming, with an annual production of more than 4 million metric tons. Japan ranks second, but most of the other leading producers are less developed countries. Because it enables surprisingly large quantities of food to be produced in limited areas, aquaculture is an attractive alternative to traditional types of crop farming and animal herding in these countries. In addition, fish are an important source of protein in the diets of the citizens of less developed countries. People in the less developed countries usually are not able to fulfill their need for protein with food derived from other animals; meat is expensive and consumption of certain types is forbidden in some cultures (notably beef in Hindu and pork in Moslem cultures).

Aquaculture in China has ancient origins, dating back more than 3000 years. The practice has expanded greatly since the 1950s, and continuing growth is expected. Already, fish farming in ponds on the outskirts of large cities is contributing significantly to the food requirements of the urban population. Several factors have encouraged increases in the production of fish by aquaculture in China. They include the country's overexploitation of fish in the shallow waters of its continental shelf, its underdevelopment of a deep sea fishing fleet, and damage to freshwater fishing resources by its construction of sluices and dams on rivers.

Chinese aquaculture involves production of more than 200 species of freshwater fish, ten of which are important commercial species, as well as several aquatic plant foods such as lotus roots and water chestnuts. Carp is the most important fish. The improvement of breeding techniques in recent years has included the artificial incubation of carp.

Another recent improvement in the industry has been the construction of processing plants for fish food in China. Prior to the 1980s China had to import fish food. Continuing growth of aquaculture will require future expansion of cold-storage and fish-processing facilities. Projected expansion of the industry points to the fact that China will continue to be the world leader in aquaculture throughout the 1990s, although fish farming is rapidly growing in other areas (including the United States).

Some of the numerous aquaculture ponds in China. The high yield of fish, usually carp, from such ponds has helped fulfill the food requirements for China's huge population. (Siyoung Park)

THOUGHT QUESTIONS

1. Why do you think aquaculture is more important in China than in northern Europe?
2. Why is aquaculture becoming increasingly important in China?
3. Do you think that aquaculture might have even greater importance in China if that country had a free market economy? Why or why not?

serves of petroleum. Persian Gulf oil production patterns were disrupted in 1991 by a war following the invasion of Kuwait by Iraq. Hundreds of Kuwait's oil wells were blown up and set on fire by the Iraqi army. Iraq's production was curtailed by international sanctions and the massive destruction of its transportation infrastructure by the armed forces of the United States and other members of the United Nations coalition.

Seven of the top ten oil producers are less developed countries. Saudi Arabia is the leading producer among the less developed countries and is the top-ranked exporter of oil (Fig. 10.16). Besides the other

Persian Gulf nations, less developed countries that are major producers of petroleum are Mexico, China, Venezuela, Nigeria, and Indonesia. Most of these countries have attempted to use foreign exchange earnings from oil exports to develop their economies.

The third fossil fuel is natural gas, the major source of energy for the heating of homes and commercial buildings in the United States and many other developed nations. During the 1970s and 1980s, proven reserves of natural gas doubled, and now they have about the same energy content as the proven reserves of crude petroleum. Geologists expect to find even more gas deposits, especially in less developed countries that have not been explored widely for this resource. Already a number of less developed nations are important producers, however. These include Algeria, Argentina, Indonesia, and Venezuela. Iran has very large reserves but is not yet a major producer.

Manufacturing and Service Industries

➤ Manufacturing and service industries are still in their infancy in most of the less developed world.

In which of the less developed countries is the manufacturing sector of the economy best developed?

In addition to being smaller, how does the service sector of the economy in the less developed countries differ from that in the developed countries?

This section will be brief because manufacturing and service industries are still in their infancy in most less developed countries. These sectors of national economies are growing, however, and because these activities are characteristic of developed economies, the developing nations are especially interested in their continued growth. Promoting manufacturing, especially light manufacturing, is a major element in the development strategy of most of the less developed countries. Advancing the service sector, particularly government services and transportation, likewise ranks high in development priorities.

FIGURE 10.16
A petroleum installation in Saudi Arabia, the world's leading exporter of oil. Revenues from petroleum sales afford Saudi Arabia and other Persian Gulf nations an opportunity to channel capital into development of other areas of their national economy. (Paul Lowe, Network Matrix)

Manufacturing Although less developed countries are superficially similar, they differ greatly in their economic and industrial structures. The differences are often as great as those existing between the less developed countries and the developed countries. Differences in location, size, resource base, and population all influence the level of—and the potential for—industrial development. Large countries with abundant resources and large populations have been most successful in developing the industrial sector of their economies, of course. It is not surprising, therefore, that Brazil, Argentina, Mexico, and India have gross domestic products in which a fairly large proportion is the result of manufacturing activities. It is also not surprising that small countries such as Bhutan, Burundi, the Gambia, and the Solomon Islands have little manufacturing.

After World War II the diffusion of manufacturing activity to less developed countries was a process that began to alter global patterns of economic activity. Pioneering this process of internationalization of manufacturing was the textile industry. The manufacture of other consumer necessities, such as apparel and footwear, began moving to less developed countries during the 1960s and 1970s to take advantage of the lower labor costs available there. More capital-intensive goods followed in the 1980s. Some of the nations that benefited most already have become developed nations. Other developing nations that are currently benefiting from rapid industrialization are called **newly industrializing countries** (NICs) by economic geographers. Mexico, Brazil, and Argentina are examples of NICs.

Small-scale enterprises numerically are very important in the manufacturing sector of all types of economy but are particularly so in most less developed countries. Small-scale manufacturing is characterized by (1) relative ease of entry; (2) reliance on local resources; (3) family ownership; (4) labor-intensive and traditional technology; (5) fewer than 50 employees; and (6) unregulated and competitive markets. Typical light manufacturing includes food processing, brewing, bottling, rubber processing, weaving, soap manufacturing, leather processing, brick-making, and furniture-making. All less developed countries have factories devoted to some of these activities.

Small-scale manufacturing is conducted by local entrepreneurs, the national government, and *multinational corporations* (corporations owning or controlling assets in two or more countries). The role of the multinational corporation has been important in introducing industrial technology to less developed countries. Local entrepreneurs have been adept at borrowing imported technology to build their own businesses and corporations, which are usually focused on the

FIGURE 10.17
Workers in this Chinese factory assemble diesel engines for fishing boats. China is one of the world's most rapidly industrializing less developed countries. (Siyoung Park)

production of consumer goods. Government-owned enterprises, on the other hand, have been concentrated primarily in heavy, capital-intensive industries.

Figure 11.21 in Chapter 11 shows the manufacturing regions of the world. The concentration of major regions in developed nations of the Northern Hemisphere is conspicuous, as is the absence of such regions in the less developed world. Minor regions of manufacturing occur in a number of developing areas, however. Noteworthy for including such regions are China, India, Mexico, Brazil, and Argentina. Brazil and China rank among the world's ten leading producers of steel. At least ten less developed countries have automobile assembly plants operated by multinational corporations, and China and India operate domestically owned automobile plants. China also manufactures locomotives, train cars, ships, and fishing boats (Fig. 10.17); Brazil is a leading producer of ships and military vehicles.

The Service Sector

The *service sector* of an economy includes those activities associated with government, education, transportation, communications, banking, insurance, wholesaling, and retailing. These activities are concentrated in or emanate from cities. The service sectors

CULTURAL LANDSCAPES

The Tourist Landscape of French Polynesia

Many parts of the less developed world have come to rely quite heavily on tourism as a supplement to their traditional economic activities. For tourists from such relatively affluent regions as Western Europe, Anglo-America, and Japan, the attractions of these areas are likely to be environmental attributes—especially scenic or climatic—historic sites, or certain cultural practices of the people. Where tourism has emerged as an important element in the economy of less developed countries, that fact is clearly evident on the landscape by the presence of such features as resort hotels, fine restaurants, and modern transportation facilities. The image of luxury conveyed by these landscapes, of course, is in great contrast to the low level of economic development evident in most other parts of the typical less developed country.

Many people who share the daily stresses of fast-paced life in an urban-industrial society perceive a South Pacific island with rugged mountains, blue lagoons, sandy beaches, and coconut palms swaying gently in a warm tropical breeze as the ultimate setting for rest and relaxation. Tahiti and Bora-Bora in French Polynesia fit that image perfectly, as the accompanying photograph confirms, and their cultural landscape reflects the importance of tourism in their economy.

The 115 islands of French Polynesia are distributed over 1.5 million square miles (3.9 million sq km) of ocean in five archipelagoes, but they total only about 1500 square miles (4000 sq km) of land area. Most of the islands remain virtual paradises with white sand and black sand beaches, forested volcanic peaks, and a benign climate, although the French have devastated a few of them with tests of nuclear devices and radioactive fallout. Tahiti was claimed by the French in 1768, and all of the islands were organized into a single colony in 1903. French Polynesia became an overseas department of France in 1946 and later attained the status of an overseas territory with the right to have a locally elected government. Large numbers of natives died from exposure to diseases brought by the Europeans during the nineteenth and early twentieth centuries. The combined population of the islands presently is about 200,000, and nearly 80 percent continue to be of Polynesian descent. More than two-thirds of the people live in Tahiti, which is the site of the capital city, Papeete. Tahitian and French are the official languages, but English also is common in Tahiti and a few other islands where tourism is significant.

Coconut products and mother-of-pearl continue to be major exports of French Polynesia, but the main imports—tourists from the developed world—now are far more important to the economy and have had a great impact on the cultural landscape. Tahiti's international airport is served by frequent connections with the west coast of the United States and Canada, Hawaii, Europe, Australia, New Zealand, Japan, and other countries in Asia. Cruise lines based in North America, Europe, and Japan regularly bring tourists to Tahiti and several of the other islands. Luxury passenger liners and yachts share Papeete's busy harbor with international cargo freighters and ships carrying copra (dried coconut meat that yields coconut oil). Tahiti now has at least four first-class hotels and a number of smaller hotels. Tourist accommodations also are available in private homes and campgrounds.

The tourist orientation of the local economy is evident in the assortment of available activities. Golf, tennis, yachting, fishing, and horseback riding are all readily available to visitors. More adventuresome tourists may travel to Tahiti's inland mountains, waterfalls, and valleys by four-wheel drive vehicle or helicopter. Shopping also is tourist-oriented, emphasizing Polynesian fashion, handicrafts, and jewelry; South Seas black pearls set in 18-karat-gold designs are popular with wealthier tourists. Small French restaurants and hotel dining rooms specializing in Continental and Tahitian cuisine have expensive menus

As this scene in Bora Bora indicates, some parts of the less developed world are able to profit from their scenery and tropical environment through tourism. In addition to beaches, the tourist landscapes in these areas usually include modern hotels, restaurants, golf courses, tennis courts, and shopping facilities. (Robert J. Sager)

that attest to their tourist orientation. Papeete is a vibrant town after dark, and the sidewalk bars are active even during the week. Several nightclubs feature Polynesian shows.

This high development of tourism enables French Polynesia to have a much higher standard of living, on average, than that in most other Pacific islands. A large proportion of the people of Tahiti have occupations related directly or indirectly to tourism. These jobs typically provide wages that exceed those obtained by picking coconuts or working in a copra plant. Most of the tourist-related jobs are in Tahiti, however, and do not significantly benefit the people of other islands. As a consequence, harvesting coconuts and fishing in the lagoons continue to be the major economic endeavors of most people on the other islands of French Polynesia.

THOUGHT QUESTIONS

1. Do you feel that the quality of life for the majority of inhabitants in French Polynesia is better today than it was before the introduction of commercial tourism? Why?
2. What will be the likely results if tourism continues to expand in Tahiti for an extended period of time?
3. Why do you suppose that French Polynesia remains an overseas territory of France when so many other colonial areas have long ago declared their complete independence?

FIGURE 10.18
Retail activity is more informally organized in the less developed countries than in the developed world. The Bangkok shop owner (right background) has a permanent store specializing in plasticware, but the women selling vegetables in the foreground have the flexibility of easy relocation of their traditional vending operation. (Donald Marshall Collection)

of developed and less developed nations differ because of some of the fundamental differences between the two groups of countries. In general, the service sector in the economies of less developed countries is not nearly as well developed as it is in the developed countries. The urban nature of service activities and the rural character of the populations of many less developed nations is a dichotomy that helps to explain the weakness of their service sector. Although the service sector tends to be smaller in less developed economies, it is no less integral to the functioning of urban places in the poorer nations of the world. Because of underemployment, personal services (maid service, shoeshining, gardening, and so forth) represent a larger proportion of the service sector in less developed countries.

Finance and insurance are especially weak segments of the service sector of the less developed world. (Most people have no money to invest and never own a life or health insurance policy.) However, many services provided by central governments are rather well developed. For example, although the rate of literacy is still low in many less developed countries, considerable emphasis is placed on education. Since other aspects of development are linked to transportation, the governments of countries with major un-

developed areas usually devote a great deal of attention and resources to expanding and improving the transportation network. Wholesaling as a service activity is relatively poorly developed, and retailing is quite different than in the developed world. More of the labor force is involved in retailing in less developed countries than in the developed countries, although the organization of retail activity is much more informal (Fig. 10.18). The clerical class is relatively small. More goods are sold by peddlers, vendors, street hawkers, and artisans than by supermarkets and department stores.

THE ILLICIT NARCOTICS INDUSTRY

➤ The production, distribution, and sale of illegal narcotics is a major problem in the world, yet this activity is an important source of employment and income in a number of less developed countries.

What are the principal illegal narcotics and where are the major centers of their production?

Why is it so difficult to halt, or even slow, the international trade in illegal narcotics?

The production, distribution, and sale of illegal narcotics is a $100-billion-a-year industry that, to a greater or lesser degree, affects people in every country in the world. The primary production of most narcotic substances takes place in less developed countries; for that reason, we discuss the industry in this chapter. Drug consumption is global, but the United States represents the largest market. There may be more than a million drug addicts in the United States and perhaps another 20 million people who engage in "recreational" drug use. Every day hundreds of people from all sectors of society move from recreational use to addiction. The story is the same in Europe, where there are more than a million frequent drug users. Less developed nations also are consumers as well as producers of illicit drugs. The incidence of addiction in Pakistan, for example, far exceeds that in the United States as a percentage of total population.

Marijuana

Marijuana, an unrefined drug made from the leaves and other parts of the *Cannabis sativa* plant, is smoked by the users as a cigarette or in a pipe. Many users—and others who do not use the drug—defend its alleged benefits and call for its legalization, despite sci-

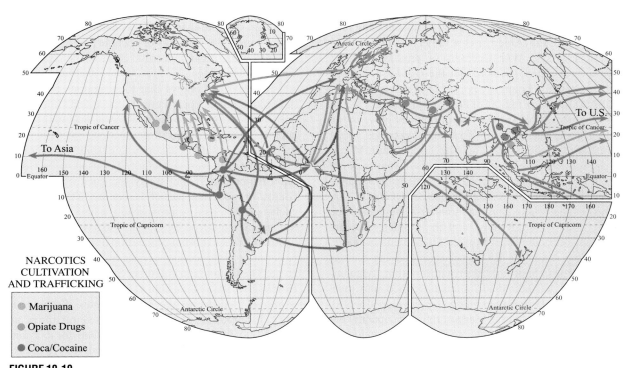

FIGURE 10.19

Illicit narcotics are produced primarily in the less developed world, but the major markets lie in the developed countries—especially the United States.

entific evidence of long-term deleterious effects to the health of habitual users.

The production of marijuana occurs primarily in Latin America. The major producers are Mexico, Guatemala, Costa Rica, Colombia, and Cuba. In the Old World only Thailand is a large producer. These production centers are shown in Figure 10.19, which also identifies the supply routes. Note on this map that the United States is the destination of most marijuana. Although most of the marijuana consumed in the United States is supplied by less developed nations, production in the United States increased dramatically during the 1980s. By 1990 at least 25 percent of the marijuana consumed in the United States was produced domestically—much of it in elaborate indoor growing operations with heat lamps, sprinklers, and automatic fertilizing systems.

Heroin/Opium

The opium poppy (*Papaver somniferum*) was cultivated in the Middle East at least 6000 years ago and spread from there to India and Southeast Asia. In the eighteenth century Great Britain granted the East India Company a monopoly on the Indian poppy industry, and in the nineteenth century Britain fought two "Opium Wars" with China for the right to sell Indian opium in China. Opium-eating was not uncommon in India, but smoking was the preferred method of opium use in China and Southeast Asia. In 1806, well before the first Opium War, a German pharmacist poured liquid ammonia over opium and produced morphine, a potent pain-killing drug. It was not until 1874 that a British research chemist boiled down some morphine to produce the first heroin. Commercial production began in 1898, and by 1924 there were some 200,000 heroin addicts in the United States alone. Heroin can be used in different ways—sniffed, smoked, or injected—but injection became the usual method. Because of the seriousness of the problem of heroin addiction, Congress banned the import and manufacture of the drug in the United States in 1924. Heroin is so addictive that about 95 percent of the world's nations ban its use even for medical purposes.

Where there is demand for a high-value product, however, laws alone do not suffice to prevent its production. The opium poppy is grown primarily in southern Asia and Latin America (Fig. 10.19). Some of the Asian centers of production are ancient, but production in Latin America is a rather recent development. Two Old World centers of production stand out—the *Golden Triangle* and the *Golden Crescent*. The Golden Triangle is a 150,000-square-mile (388,500-sq-km) region of forested highlands where field after field of yellow opium poppies glow in the bright mountain sunlight. This area comprises northern Laos, northern Thailand, and northeastern Myanmar (Burma). The Golden Crescent is in southwestern Asia and is a crescent-shaped region made up of northern Pakistan, most of Afghanistan, and central Iran. The Golden Triangle produces about 70 percent of the total illicit opium supply, and the Golden Crescent probably accounts for another 20 percent or more. Myanmar heads the list of opium-producing nations and supplies about a third of world output. Afghanistan ranks second. Most opium is refined into morphine or heroin before export to the developed world. Myanmar has the world's largest refining capacity, but Bangkok in Thailand is the center of most major export deals. Figure 10.19 shows the main trafficking routes for opiate drugs. The United States is the leading importer, although the relative demand for heroin declined during the 1980s as a booming demand developed for cocaine. A new demand is occurring in the 1990s, however, as the smoking of heroin gains popularity in response to the risk of AIDS from needle use.

Cocaine

In the world of illicit narcotics, cocaine is king. Tens of millions of people worldwide sniff it, smoke it, or inject it. It brings them pleasure, unbounded energy, eventual misery, and sometimes death. Cocaine is derived from the leaves of the coca shrub (*Erythroxylum coca*), which grows in the valleys and on the slopes of the Andes Mountains. For at least 3500 years Andean people have chewed coca leaves. The alkaloid compound now called cocaine was first isolated from coca in the mid-1800s. Sigmund Freud once considered cocaine to be a godsend for treating morphine addicts; Coca-Cola was a cocaine-based soft drink before its manufacturer switched to caffeine in about 1900. Today it is illegal in most countries to produce or possess cocaine, except for prescribed medical use. The skyrocketing demand for cocaine in the United States and other developed nations during the 1980s, however, resulted in greatly expanded production of

the drug. Despite efforts in the developed world to educate people to the risks of cocaine use, demand for it is unabated. Organized crime controls the supply, as with all illicit drugs.

Figure 10.19 shows that three nations dominate the production of coca: Peru, Bolivia, and Colombia. Peru is the largest producer of coca, accounting for about 60 percent of world production, but Bolivia is the quintessential coca country, despite its second-ranked position in total output. Tin used to be Bolivia's major export, but today the coca industry accounts for more than half of the country's total foreign exchange earnings. Approximately a half-million Bolivians are employed by that industry (Figure 10.20). Colombia ranks third in production of coca leaves, but it is the world's leading refiner and exporter of cocaine. The Colombian and other South American drug cartels also are responsible for the manufacture and export of "crack" to the United States. Crack is a smokable cocaine distillate that is several times as potent and more quickly addictive than the cocaine powder from which it is manufactured. (Much crack, however, is not imported but is manufactured in laboratories in the United States from imported co-

FIGURE 10.20

Engaged in drying coca leaves as an early step in the production of cocaine, these two people are among several hundred thousand Bolivians who earn at least part of their income in the cocaine industry. (Nesley Bocxe/Photo Researchers)

caine.) Figure 10.19 shows the major routes for the movement of cocaine. Some of the cocaine sent to Africa and Europe is destined for the United States but uses transshipments in order to reduce the possibility of detection.

The "War" on Drugs

The war on drugs is an international effort, conducted primarily by national governments, to suppress the production, marketing, and consumption of illicit drugs. Most of the money for the war on drugs is provided by the governments of developed nations, especially the United States, but much of it is spent in the less developed countries that are the major drug producers. Increasing amounts of foreign aid are tied to programs aimed at reducing the production of drugs. For example, in 1990 Bolivia received $35 million in military aid as part of the antidrug program of the United States. In return the Bolivian military was actively engaged in destroying fields of coca.

In the late 1980s the war on drugs in Colombia became a real war—the Medellin cartel was using extreme violence to crush all attempts to stop the flow of cocaine. In a supreme gesture of arrogance, the cartel offered in 1988 to pay off Colombia's $15 billion foreign debt in exchange for a pardon. By 1991, however, the Colombian government had won its long war with the Medellin cartel; however, the Cali cartel, headquartered in Colombia's third largest city, has since emerged as the world's major cocaine distributor.

A dramatic episode in the drug war occurred late in 1989 with the invasion of Panama by U.S. military forces. The Panamanian dictator General Manuel Noriega had been using his country's banks to launder money for Colombian drug rings, and he had been indicted by a U.S. court. (See *The Geographer's Notebook: Drug Money Laundering*.) The general surrendered early in 1990 and was taken to the United States to stand trial. He was found guilty of drug and racketeering crimes in 1992.

The long international boundary between the United States and Mexico presents a major challenge to both countries as they seek to control illegal activities in the border area. Vast quantities of drugs enter the United States across that border, so considerable emphasis in the war on drugs has been focused in that area. On occasion relations between Mexico and the United States have been strained because of differ-

ences of opinion regarding the enforcement of drug laws. A testimony to the determination of drug lords to pursue their illegal activities at any cost was the discovery in 1990 of a sophisticated tunnel under the international boundary between Agua Prieta, Mexico, and Douglas, Arizona. The 100-yard-long, 30-foot-deep concrete tunnel had been constructed clandestinely at an estimated cost of $1 to 2 million. One end of the tunnel terminated under a hydraulic-controlled pool table; law enforcement officials described it as "like something from a James Bond movie."

The war on drugs is carried out domestically as well as internationally, as the governments of most developed nations seek to protect their citizens from the evils associated with drug dealing and drug abuse. The price of conducting the war on drugs is high, but greater is the cost of not protecting people from drug criminals and the poison with which they destroy lives.

PROSPECTS FOR THE LESS DEVELOPED COUNTRIES

➤ Despite the Green Revolution and numerous other programs to foster development, the prospects remain poor for significant improvement in the economies of most less developed countries.

Why is this so?

Why are there major shortages of food in some areas of the world and large surpluses in others?

How has international debt affected development in the less developed countries?

Perhaps the wisest thing that one can say about the future is that it is unknown. Although we cannot know what the future holds for the less developed world, current trends can be used to project some of its more likely prospects. Few development specialists are very optimistic about that future, however.

The Malthusian theory of geometric population growth versus arithmetic increase in food production was presented in Chapter 6, as was the Marxist philosophy that population growth leads to a higher standard of living, and the Boserup thesis that population growth continually spurs increased food production. The dramatic recent decline of communism was based in part on the fact that Marxist economic philosophy, as applied, did not work very well. The chief limitation of the Boserup thesis may be that increased agricul-

Drug Money Laundering

Individuals and groups who obtain large sums of money through their involvement in the illegal drug business commonly launder those funds to conceal their sources and amounts. The laundering of drug money is a runaway global industry that almost certainly amounts to tens of billions of dollars annually. The process usually involves moving the money through various banks and other financial agencies in different countries. Drug dealers in the United States, aware that departing air travelers are rarely searched, may take money out of the country in their luggage. Large shipments may be flown out on private planes or packed in seagoing freight containers, which are almost never inspected carefully. The next step is depositing the money in a foreign bank. From that point the laundering operation becomes intentionally complicated to make any discovery of the original source of the funds more difficult.

Let us look at a hypothetical example of an American drug dealer to illustrate the scheme's complexity. A Paris banker in whose bank the drug money is deposited sets up a dummy corporation in Rotterdam for the client and transfers cash to the bank's Rotterdam branch. The client controls the

new Dutch "corporation" through a newly created trust company set up by the Paris banker in the Netherlands Antilles. The client's identity as owner of the trust company is protected by the island's impenetrable secrecy laws. The Antilles branch of the Paris bank then "lends" the client his own money held in Rotterdam. If the client subsequently is questioned about the source of his wealth, he can point to his loan from a respected international bank. This and similar laundering schemes depend on the collaboration, or sometimes just the negligence, of bankers and other money-handlers who can use electronic-funds networks to shuffle assets quickly from one place to another.

---

tural output, produced by population growth, can lead to deterioration of the soil resource and eventually to *reduced* food production. What about the Malthusian theory? Although long discredited by the effects of agricultural improvements that accompanied the Industrial Revolution, the theory has been embraced by many physical and social scientists during the latter part of the twentieth century. These *neo-Malthusians*, most of whom correctly could be described as conservationists or environmentalists, are worried that if present trends continue, the world will become more crowded and more polluted, and many resources will be depleted or degraded. They believe also that this will lead to greater political and economic turmoil and increase the threat of war.

Members of an opposing group are called *cornucopians*, most of whom are economists. Named for the cornucopia, the horn of plenty—a symbol for abundance—cornucopians believe that technological advances will more than keep pace with population growth and will produce a future in which people will be healthier, will live longer, and will have greater material prosperity. The cornucopian view may have greater applicability to the developed than to the less developed world, since the magnitude of the problems faced by the less developed countries makes it very difficult for most development specialists to imagine a future of prosperity for many of these countries. Two of these monumental problems—the food shortage and the debt crisis—are addressed briefly.

Efforts to stop money laundering schemes have had little success. For many years Swiss banks have provided secret numbered accounts that have served as havens for the assets of criminals and dictators. In 1990, however, Switzerland began cooperating in the prosecution of money launderers. Luxembourg has declared money laundering a criminal offense but at the same time has fortified its banking secrecy laws, which help make laundering schemes possible.

Dozens of countries, many in the less developed world, now have banking systems that knowingly participate in money laundering. The center of activity has shifted to the Pacific where havens of financial secrecy have multiplied on such remote islands as Nauru and Palau. Citizens of Vanuatu (for-merly New Hebrides) have found that profits from international finance beats coconut farming. In Port Vila, the capital, it is not unusual for a $100 million transaction between international banks to take place on a given day. The premier money laundering center of the Pacific, however, is Hong Kong.

THOUGHT QUESTIONS

1. Can you identify other people, in addition to drug dealers, who engage in money laundering? For what reasons do they launder their funds?
2. Why do you think the Pacific Basin has become the center for laundering activities? Is this shift possibly associated with locational changes in other activities?

A view of Willemstad, the capital of Curaçao (Netherlands Antilles). Individuals engaged in laundering drug money often choose to move the funds through financial institutions in the Netherlands Antilles because they legally are able to conceal their identity. (Gale Zucker/ Stock Boston)

The Food Shortage

Not all geographers agree that a food shortage exists in the world, but the problem is real enough to the millions of people who starve to death every year. If all of the food produced in the world were apportioned equally among all of the world's people, no one would suffer hunger. In that regard, there is not a food shortage but rather a food distribution problem. In a politically and economically complex world, however, who can expect realistically that the distribution problem will ever be resolved? While several developed nations are having to deal with the "problem" of surplus agricultural production, many less developed countries face the much more serious matter of food shortages: over 1 billion people in the world are malnourished.

Agriculture is the mainstay of the economies of most less developed nations, but in some countries it has not been able to keep pace with the rapid population growth. Land development, which has opened new areas to farming and provided new farms to millions of landless people, has helped, but most of the projects have been plagued with problems. Agrarian reform in established farming districts has redistributed land without, in many cases, producing significant increases in food production. The Green Revolution has resulted in huge increases in crop yields in many developing nations but has failed to benefit the poorest farmers and too often has focused on cash crops rather than subsistence crops.

Certainly the Green Revolution has been the most exciting and significant development in the modernization of agriculture, especially in Asia. Without it, many countries already would have lost the battle to have enough food available for their rapidly growing populations. Additional benefits will accrue as the Green Revolution reaches areas in Latin America and Africa previously unaffected by it, but neo-Malthusians are not optimistic about its ability to feed a hungry world. Cornucopians expect biotechnology to greatly expand the importance of the Green Revolution. Genetic engineering, the most fundamental of the new biological techniques, already has moved forward in the livestock industry, because more is known about the basic cell processes of animals than of plants. The "father" of the Green Revolution, the American Norman Borlaug (Fig. 10.21)—a scientist who received the Nobel Peace Prize for his work in developing high-yield wheat—has little expectation that major gains in crop yields can be achieved soon as a result of biotechnology. He has stated that he never expected the Green Revolution to be a final solution to the world's food problem. It was designed instead to give nations a period of 20 or 30 years during which they could work to bring their population growth under control. Many nations did not do so; quite a few did not even try.

In many parts of the less developed world, the supply of agricultural land is threatened by various kinds of degradation, and this makes the ability of people in many nations to feed themselves in the future all the more uncertain. Water and wind erosion are reducing soil productivity in some areas, and salinization in irrigated areas is ruining soil for crop plants. In some semiarid environments in which livestock ranching is the principal economic activity, desertification is turning steppe grasslands into deserts (Fig. 10.22). About 60 percent of the world's semiarid rangelands have experienced at least some desertification because of overgrazing and drought. The expansion of cattle ranching through the clearing of tropical rainforests is causing environmental degradation and benefiting few in the less developed countries because most of the beef is exported.

The Debt Crisis

When the developing nations set out to modernize their economies in the 1950s and 1960s, their financial systems comprised mainly foreign-owned commercial banks. Governments sought to remodel their financial resources in keeping with their development strategies. New financial institutions were set up to provide funding at low interest rates to certain enterprises in various sectors of the economy. The governments themselves borrowed heavily from domestic and foreign banks to finance deficits and the needs of government-owned industries and government-sponsored development projects. In some nations this contributed to high rates of inflation.

By the 1970s many less developed nations were heavily indebted and found it increasingly difficult to obtain credit from foreign banks at favorable interest rates. A large proportion of the debt being incurred was for the purchase of armaments rather than for development projects. (During the period 1970–1990, less developed nations increased their military budgets

FIGURE 10.21

Norman Borlaug, the father of the Green Revolution. An American agronomist, Borlaug was awarded the Nobel Peace Prize in 1970 for his work in developing high-yielding grains. By introducing such grains into demographically stressed nations, Borlaug's goal was to give these countries a period of 20 to 30 years to bring their rate of population growth under control. (E. Schuh/Gamma Liaison)

fivefold.) By 1982 it was all but impossible for heavily indebted nations to borrow from foreign banks. An international recession in the early 1980s reduced the ability of many countries to pay the interest on foreign debt. Hundreds of banks in the less developed countries became insolvent (their liabilities exceeded their assets) during the 1980s. Some economists, in fact, describe the 1980s as "the lost decade" for the poor nations of the world because of the developmental setbacks of the period. In 1990 the debt load of the less developed countries was a crushing $1.3 trillion and the United States, the creditor of most of that debt, was seeking ways to assist the debtor nations with debt reduction.

The huge amount of current debt and the inability of many developing nations to pay even the interest on their foreign debt indicate the unlikelihood of much flow of new capital to most less developed countries during the next decade or two. This has important and unfortunate implications for the progress of development in many less developed nations.

What *is* the most serious problem confronting the less developed world? The food shortage? The debt crisis? Or some other problem not examined in this chapter? The answer varies, of course, from country to country and with the interests and concerns of the politician, academic scholar, or other expert who answers the question. It is sufficient to conclude that the less developed countries will suffer critical problems and face monumental challenges in the years ahead. The degree to which they overcome their problems and make the correct choices in development strategies will have global significance.

FIGURE 10.22
These Bagara cattle nomads wait out the dry season in the Sudanese Sahel, a part of the drought-ravaged Sahel region on the southern margin of the Sahara. Desertification has been a serious problem here during much of the 1980s and into the 1990s. (Frederick Bein)

KEY TERMS

Latifundia Landholdings of unusually large size, such as estates and plantations. Where latifundia exist, only a small number of people own most of the land. **359**

Minifundia Landholdings of unusually small size, often too small to adequately support a family. **359**

Pastoral nomadism An ancient form of livestock herding most commonly practiced by wandering tribes and bands in Old World dry lands. Frequent movement is required to locate adequate pasture land for the livestock. **366**

Shifting cultivation A type of subsistence crop farming, now most common in tropical rainforest regions, that involves the clearing and temporary cultivation of an area until its soil is depleted (usually within a few years). The area is then abandoned as the clearing and cultivation activities are shifted to a new location. **367**

Intensive subsistence agriculture Subsistence farming that is distinctive in terms of large labor input and high yields per unit of land. It is most common in densely populated areas of Asia. **369**

Commercial agriculture The production of agricultural commodities primarily for sale in the marketplace rather than for providing subsistence. **370**

Livestock ranching The grazing of livestock for commercial purposes, usually on a relatively large landholding. **370**

Plantation agriculture The use of a relatively large landholding, commonly in a tropical or subtropical area, to produce a commercial crop such as sugar cane, cotton, or coffee. **371**

Small farmers Individuals who cultivate only relatively small- or modest-sized landholdings. **372**

Land development Any program or scheme, usually designed and implemented by a national government, to develop and settle people on land in a frontier zone. **373**

Green Revolution A major increase in food grain production in parts of the less developed world, made possible by the development of high-yielding hybrids and the application of agricultural chemicals. **374**

Extractive industries Economic activities that involve extracting natural resources from the physical environment. Important examples are forestry, fishing, and mining. **377**

Aquaculture The production and harvesting of fish and other marine organisms in confined water bodies. **378**

Newly industrializing countries (NICs) Countries in the less developed world that are undergoing significant development of their industrial economy. **383**

REVIEW QUESTIONS

1. What proportion of the world's population live in the less developed countries?

2. What is a sharecropper? What does a sharecropper have in common with a smallholder? How do the two differ?

3. What are marasmus, kwashiorkor, and iron-deficiency anemia, and to what extent do they adversely affect people in the less developed world?

4. How does literacy in Mali and Mexico compare? What are some other countries with very low rates of literacy?

5. How are male and female children treated differently in parts of the less developed world? How are women often abused or oppressed in some of the less developed countries? What are some economic implications of the oppression of women?

6. What Paleolithic forms of subsistence activity survive today in the less developed world? Where are they practiced?

7. When and where were the major livestock animals domesticated?

8. What are the factors usually responsible for the "shift" in shifting cultivation?

9. How do the roles of men and women usually differ in wet-paddy rice production?

10. How does dry-field crop production in southeastern Asia differ from wet paddy rice production? How are the two systems similar?

11. Who owns most tropical plantations? From where do the managerial staffs usually come? Who provides most of the labor for planting, cultivating, and harvesting?

12. Why do small farmers often encounter difficulties in getting their harvested crops processed or sold?

13. What are some of the problems that have caused land development to fail to achieve its potential in the less developed countries?

14. Which three less developed countries have the most successful fishing fleets? Why did the Peruvian anchovy industry collapse in 1972?

15. What is the major mineral export of Guinea? Chile? Brazil? Kuwait?

16. Why do Brazil and India have better developed manufacturing sectors than Burundi and Bhutan?

17. Why are finance and insurance especially weak segments in the service sector of economies in the less developed countries?

18. Where are the "Golden Triangle" and "Golden Crescent," and what is their chief export?

19. What are major obstacles for the less developed countries as they attempt to improve their economic situation and the quality of life for their people?

CHAPTER 11

SOCIETIES AND LIVELIHOODS IN THE DEVELOPED WORLD

*Wealth is the application of mind to nature;
and the art of getting rich consists not in industry,
much less in saving, but in a better order,
a timeliness, in being at the right spot.*

—Ralph Waldo Emerson

*An American woman astronaut repairs the Hubble telescope: Such images
exemplify the strong emphasis developed countries place on technology.
(NASA)*

nly about one-fifth of the world's countries are classified as developed, and less than one-fourth of the world's population resides in those countries. Economically, however, the developed nations have an importance that far exceeds their small number and small proportion of the world's population. In Chapter 9, Figure 9.4, we have identified the developed countries.

The developed countries properly might be considered to have *modern industrial societies*, as opposed to the traditional agrarian societies of most less developed countries. They are modern in that they have been transformed from the traditional societies they once were by the greater use of mechanization, the use of more energy, and the adoption of new methods of production. They are all more or less industrial, and the most advanced countries are even moving to a post-industrial stage in which there is a greater emphasis on service professions and less concentration on manufacturing.

FIGURE 11.1
Brussels, capital of Belgium, the world's most urbanized nation. Ninety-seven percent of the people in Belgium live in cities. (Martin Rogers/Stock Boston)

CHARACTERISTICS OF MODERN INDUSTRIAL SOCIETIES

➤ Basic differences between the developed world and the less developed world are revealed in their population and economic characteristics.

How do the developed countries differ from the less developed countries in terms of their urbanization and birth and death rates?

How do they differ in terms of personal income and economic structure?

The distinguishing features of modern industrial societies can be grouped into four categories: (1) population characteristics; (2) income; (3) land tenure and economic systems; and (4) social conditions.

Population Characteristics

The populations of modern industrial societies tend to be more urban than those of traditional agrarian societies. As the economy of a country develops, new job opportunities arise, and a large proportion of those are factory jobs in cities. At the same time, the mechanization and increasing productivity of agriculture diminishes the need for many farmers. The economic development of a nation, therefore, usually involves a rural-to-urban migration. By 1993 the world population was 42 percent urban and 58 percent rural. The developed country with the most urbanized population is Belgium, in which 97 percent of the population lived in towns and cities in 1993 (Fig. 11.1). More than two-thirds of the population is urban in most developed countries (Table 11.1).

The populations of the developed countries also are characterized by low birth rates, low death rates, and low rates of population growth (Chapter 6). The crude birth rate (annual births per 1000 population) averages 26 for the world as a whole, but it is much less than that in the developed world. The crude birth rate is lowest in Europe, where it averages 12; it is less than 10 in some European countries. In the United States it is 16, and in Japan it is 10. As well as low birth rates, there are low death rates in developed nations, in large part the result of good diets and high-quality health care. The average life expectancy at birth in many African countries is less than 50 years, but in most developed nations it is more than 70 years. In the United States it is 75 years, and in Japan it is 79 years. A third characteristic of the populations of the developed countries is their overall low rates of growth. Although the world population is growing at a rate of 1.6 percent annually, the developed countries have population growth rates that average only 0.4 percent per year. These figures suggest that economic conditions have a major impact on demographic rates.

Income

Wealth generally is in short supply in the less developed world, but in the developed world it is relatively plentiful. Poor people and "pockets of poverty" (concentrations of low-income people) are part of every developed country, but poverty is not nearly as prevalent as in the less developed countries. Even many of the poor people in the developed countries own an automobile or television set and would not be considered poor by the standards of the less developed world. Most people in the less developed countries earn less than $500 annually, but income per capita in a number of developed nations exceeds $10,000 per year (Table 11.2).

TABLE 11.2	The Ten Countries with Highest Average Per Capita Annual Incomes: 1991
United States	$22,470
Switzerland	$21,700
Luxembourg	$20,200
Canada	$19,400
Japan	$19,100
Denmark	$17,700
Sweden	$17,200
Norway	$17,100
Iceland	$16,300
Germany	$14,600

SOURCE: *World Almanac, 1994.*

TABLE 11.1	Urban Population in Selected Developed Countries: 1993	

Country	Percent of Total Population
Belgium	97
United Kingdom	90
Netherlands	89
Australia	85
Denmark	85
Germany	85
New Zealand	84
Sweden	83
Spain	78
Canada	77
Japan	77
United States	75
Russia	74
France	73
Norway	72
Bulgaria	68
Italy	68
Hungary	62
Poland	62
Austria	54

SOURCE: *Population Reference Bureau.*

Associated with the high incomes of the developed countries are high levels of personal consumption. In addition to luxury items possessed only by the wealthy in the less developed countries, the people of developed countries often have insurance policies and savings accounts or other investments. The middle class is not well developed in most of the less developed world, but modern industrial societies have a large middle class; in fact, most of the people in the developed countries consider themselves to be members of the middle class (Fig. 11.2). The upper class

FIGURE 11.2

A middle class suburban neighborhood in Amsterdam, the Netherlands. Most people in the developed world consider themselves members of the middle class. (R. Gabler)

also is larger in the developed countries than in the less developed countries. In 1990 the world had more than 150 billionaires; some were Persian Gulf oil magnates, but the great majority resided in and made—or inherited—their fortunes in developed nations. There may have been as many as 2 million millionaires in the world in 1990, and again the greatest number of them by far lived in developed countries.

Land Tenure and Economic Systems

Although control of most of the land by few of the people is fairly common in the less developed world, it is not characteristic of the developed world. There are, of course, some very large, privately owned properties in many of the developed nations. In the United States and Australia, for example, some farms consist of thousands of acres and some ranches measure tens of thousands of acres. These are the exception, not the rule. Millions of farmers in developed countries, however, own farms of more modest size. In Japan and some of the European countries, most of the farms are quite small, often less than 25 acres (10 ha). In the United States and Canada, however, family farms consisting of 400 acres (135 ha) are common.

Agriculture and the other forms of primary economic activity (mining, forestry, fishing) are not as important to total economic productivity in the developed world as in the less developed countries. In the United States and Japan, for example, less than 3 percent of the gross national product (GNP) comes from agriculture. In both countries, industrial production is at least 12 times as important and service activities at least 20 times as important as agriculture in terms of their proportion of the GNP. Manufacturing and service activities, weak in less developed economies, prevail in the developed world. The most typical occupation in Bangladesh and Haiti is farming; the most typical occupation in the United States and the United Kingdom is in such services as teaching, working in a bank, selling insurance, or working in a government office. There is much greater variety in the economies of the developed countries.

Social Conditions

➤ Although numerous problems still exist, social conditions in the developed countries are far better than those found in less developed countries.

What factors have contributed to these better conditions?

In what major social areas are the developed countries more advanced than the less developed countries?

Because of the low population growth rates, general prosperity, large middle class, and availability of investment capital, social conditions in the developed world involve fewer serious problems than in the less developed world. Hunger is not a widespread problem that restricts productive human activity, and disease is controlled to the extent that scientific knowledge permits in a well-developed health care system. Great emphasis is placed on education. Women, still oppressed in much of the less developed world, are assuming more diversified roles in society in general and in the workplace in particular.

Health Tropical conditions yield a great variety of living organisms, including many that transmit disease; however, most developed nations lie in the middle latitudes and consequently do not have to deal with many of the diseases that afflict people in tropical countries. Diarrhea, which kills millions of people annually in the tropics, is a relatively minor health nuisance in the developed countries of the middle latitudes. Because of better nutrition, such diseases as marasmus, kwashiorkor, iron-deficiency anemia, and goiter are not major afflictions in modern industrial societies. Other diseases that are far more prevalent and more deadly in less developed countries than in developed countries are schistosomiasis, malaria, yellow fever, sleeping sickness, tuberculosis, pneumonia, leprosy, influenza, venereal diseases, and plague. AIDS is deadly wherever it occurs, but its victims in the developed countries have a longer life expectancy.

Not only are developed countries relatively free of some of the world's human diseases, they are better prepared than the less developed countries to deal with health problems. The developed countries generally have far more health facilities, hospital beds, nurses, and physicians. The availability of hospital beds and health professionals makes it possible for practically all births in developed countries to take place in hospitals (Fig. 11.3), whereas more than half of the births in many poor countries are not attended by health personnel. This is one reason why infant mortality rates are lower in the developed countries.

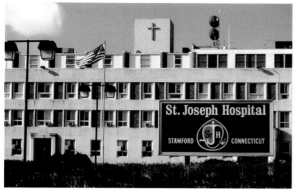

FIGURE 11.3

A hospital in Stamford, Connecticut. High-quality health care is far more available in the developed countries than in the less developed countries. (Cameramann Int'l)

FIGURE 11.4

A building on the campus of the University of Konstanz in Germany. Higher education is much more available in the developed than the less developed world. (R. Gabler)

Education   Modern industrial societies have more money per capita than traditional agrarian societies to spend on education. As a result, education receives a higher priority in developed countries than in most of the less developed countries. Primary and secondary education are compulsory and almost universal in developed countries; as a consequence, practically the entire adult population in these nations is literate. It is in higher education, however, that the developed world is particularly prominent. Whereas most less developed countries are striving to provide universal pre-collegiate education for their youth, a large proportion of the young adults in the developed countries are enrolled in postsecondary technical schools, community and junior colleges, and universities (Fig. 11.4). The United States alone has more than 1400 four-year institutions of higher learning and more than 1000 two-year colleges. Some less developed countries have only a single university.

The Rise of Women   Women have made tremendous strides in recent decades toward equality with male members of society in most of the developed nations of the world. Much of this progress has been the result of a worldwide **women's movement** that has championed the rights of women to equal treatment with men under law and in the workplace. As a result of the successes of the women's movement, the idea that women must be responsible for traditionally "female"

activities such as housekeeping and child rearing is now obsolete in most developed countries. That does not mean, of course, that equality has been fully attained in the developed countries and that it is no longer necessary to be concerned about women's rights.

In some developed countries more than half of the women now work outside the home. The proportion of women in the workforce of developed nations has increased steadily in recent years. For example, in 1940 only about one-fourth of the women in the United States were employed, but in 1990 more than half were working outside the home. The U.S. female labor force share is well above the average for the world, but even higher proportions exist in Eastern Europe and some of the former Soviet Republics.

Changes also have been taking place in the kinds of work women perform in the labor force. Women traditionally were concentrated in low-skilled, repetitive work without formal responsibility and with far fewer prospects of promotion and advancement than their male colleagues. To a great degree, this pattern continues. Most secretaries, sewing machine operators, teachers, and nurses are still women. Nine out of ten bank tellers, child care workers, dental hygienists, receptionists, and telephone operators in the United States are women. At the same time, no more than 1 out of 20 engineers, airplane pilots, construction workers, miners, heavy equipment operators, surveyors,

FIGURE 11.5
During the decade 1970–1980, women in the labor force of the United States made considerable progress in moving into occupations formerly dominated by men. The pace of the movement of women into administrative positions increased during the following decade. (Stacy Pick/Stock Boston)

cartographers, loggers, truck drivers, or company executives are women. Job segregation on the basis of gender, however, has diminished significantly in the United States over recent decades.

Between 1960 and 1970, an inflow of men into traditionally female-dominated professions and of women into male-dominated professions produced a modest drop in the segregation index. A more dramatic decrease occurred between 1970 and 1980 as women made notable progress in precisely those professional occupations that were most male-dominated in 1970. With the exception of physicists and astronomers, their numbers increased in all fields in which they had been low in 1970. There were sizable increases in many executive, administrative, and managerial occupations filled by women during this same period (Fig. 11.5). The move of women into occupations traditionally dominated by men continued at a rapid pace during the 1980s and 1990s. Even if this rapid pace of change continues, however, it will take more than three-quarters of a century for women in the United States to represent half of the labor force in occupations now dominated by men. Such parity may never be achieved in some occupations.

Occupational segregation contributes to the "earnings gap," about which much has been written in a

number of Western developed nations. In 1990, for every dollar made by an average year-round, full-time male worker in the United States, an average women made only $0.70. Pooling of women in "pink collar" occupations through choice, convention, or training has led to overcrowding in these occupations and, as a consequence, to lower wages and limited potential for advancement. Income generated by the female labor force—concentrated in low-paying occupations such as secretary, waitress, cashier, nurse, and hairdresser—cannot compare, on the average, with income derived by men traditionally employed in higher paying jobs. Components of tenure—attachment to the labor force and seniority—are additional factors related to the earnings gap. Women's family responsibilities have led to breaks in work history and less work experience, measures of labor-force attachment. Because of the lateness of their mass entry into the labor force, women generally have lower seniority than men. Even taking such variables into consideration, however, there is still a portion of unequal wages that can be attributed directly to discrimination. One approach by the women's movement to this discrimination has been the concept of equal pay for equal work. The concept recently has been replaced by equal pay for comparable work, a comparison across occupations. Until women receive equal pay for comparable work, and until other forms of discrimination against women have been wiped out, the need for the women's movement will continue.

LIVELIHOODS ON THE LAND AND WATER

Manufacturing and service activities dominate the economies of developed nations, and relatively few people in these countries are employed in primary activities (agriculture, forestry, fishing, and mining). Even so, it is necessary for us to examine briefly livelihoods on the land (agriculture, forestry, and mining) and water (fishing) to avoid implying that these activities are without significance in the developed countries. No geographer would question the role of these activities in influencing human lifestyles and affecting cultural landscapes in the developed world.

Commercial Agriculture

➤ Subsistence agriculture is inconsequential in developed countries. However, three major categories of commercial agriculture exist: herding (ranching and dairy farming), mixed farming, and commercial crop production (cash grain farming and specialty crop farming).

What are the distinctive characteristics of each category?

In which countries is each category most concentrated?

While most farmers in the less developed world engage primarily in subsistence agriculture, very few farmers in the developed world do so. Most farmers in the developed countries have gardens and produce a portion of their own food requirements, but the land they till is cultivated almost entirely for the production of cash crops. The modern farmer is a self-employed businessperson who closely monitors fluctuations in the prices of commodities in local agricultural markets. Farmers tend to be interested, as well, in national and international developments that may have implications for the pricing of farm products. Commercial agriculture in the developed world takes many forms, which may be generalized and categorized into *commercial herding, mixed farming,* and *commercial crop production.*

Commercial Herding Animal husbandry (the management of domesticated animals for economic gain) is the primary concern of commercial herders, who usually tend cattle or sheep. The nature of a livestock-based local economy depends on the density of the human population, the available supply of animal feed, and the possibilities for alternate agricultural enterprises. In Chapter 10 we considered nomadic herding and livestock ranching in the less developed countries. Nomadic herding rarely is practiced in developed nations, but livestock ranching is the prevailing economic activity across large portions of many developed countries. A second form of commercial herding found in almost all developed nations, at least to a small degree, is dairy farming.

In the subhumid and semiarid midlatitude grasslands where rainfall is too meager to permit crop production, livestock ranching is the prevalent agricultural activity. The *carrying capacity* (ability of the land, per unit area, to support livestock) is low, so ranches tend to be very large properties, usually from 2000 acres (810 ha) to 100,000 acres (40,486 ha). Like nomadic herding, livestock ranching is an extensive land use; that is, the value of the output and the number of people supported are low per unit area of land. Un-

like nomadic herding, livestock ranching is sedentary and is a relatively recent form of economic enterprise. Although nomadic herding has survived from ancient times, livestock ranching is only about 200 years old.

Figure 10.10 identifies the major world regions in which livestock ranching is practiced. Half of the six major areas shown on that map are contained in less developed countries; these are discussed in Chapter 10. The three sizable areas in developed nations are the western United States, Kazakhstan, and most of Australia. In total numbers of cattle, the United States is the third-ranked nation, behind two less developed countries—India and Brazil. Australia is far down on the list of cattle producers, but it remains in the top ten. However, Australia is the third-ranked producer of sheep and goats, behind China and India. The ranchers of Australia have 12 times as many sheep and goats as the ranchers of the United States (Fig. 11.6).

It is important to note, however, that in a number of developed nations, most of the livestock are not found on the ranches in the natural rangeland. In fact, only about a tenth of the world's cattle and only about a third of the sheep and goats are kept on ranches. The vast majority of livestock are raised in more humid areas as a part of agricultural systems other than ranch-

FIGURE 11.6
A sheep ranch in Australia. Ranching is far more important in the economy of Australia than in that of most developed countries, but even there it provides relatively little livelihood because of its extensive nature. (W.P. Fleming/Viesti Assoc. Inc.)

ing. Only about 1 percent of the people who earn their living from agriculture are ranchers, and that tiny percentage is expected to decline during the 1990s and into the next century.

Most ranches do not engage in *transhumance,* but the practice is employed often enough that it warrants identification and comment. Transhumance is the transfer of livestock from one range to another, usually in response to seasonal changes (see Chapter 7). The ranch headquarters is not abandoned in transhumance; that is, the entire ranch family usually does not participate in the livestock drives. Much of the labor often is done by hired cattle drivers or sheepherders. In the United States, transhumance is practiced in the Rocky Mountains, the Sierra Nevadas, the Cascades, and the ranges of the Great Basin. Cattle generally are moved shorter distances than sheep. Although transhumance traditionally has involved driving herds "on the hoof," modern transportation (railroads and trucks) enables the long-distance movement of livestock to seasonal ranges. Some sheep herds in the western United States are transported hundreds of miles during the course of a year.

Dairy farming is a far more intensive activity than livestock ranching, both in terms of land use and labor inputs. Less land is required per head of dairy cattle because well-managed pastures of domesticated grasses provide the forage, not wild grasses on natural ranges. Dairy farming is a labor-intensive activity primarily because of the large amount of care required by dairy cows; they must be milked twice a day. Dairying also is a more capital-intensive enterprise than ranching. Elaborate buildings and expensive machinery are required. Bulk milk cooling equipment and storage tanks alone can cost hundreds of thousands of dollars. Dairy farms, therefore, have very high market values for their size (Fig. 11.7).

Because milk is a perishable commodity, traditionally it has been produced in close proximity to major markets. (See *The Geographer's Notebook: Von Thünen's Model of Rural Land Use.*) Most large cities have a *milkshed,* the surrounding local area within which dairy farms are located. Where large cities are close together, as in the northeastern United States, individual milksheds usually have merged into larger milk-producing districts. In the modern era of dairying, the use of refrigerated tank trucks has made it possible to produce milk at greater distances from market. In general, however, the greater the distance of a dairy farm from a major market, the more likely the

FIGURE 11.7
A modern dairy farm in Nova Scotia, Canada. Dairying is one of the most labor-intensive forms of agriculture. (J. Vining)

milk will be used for making butter or cheese—higher valued products that can better absorb the cost of transportation. Wisconsin is far from the major eastern markets, and as a consequence about 95 percent of the state's milk production is processed into butter and cheese—predominantly cheese. In Pennsylvania, about 95 percent of the milk is marketed in fluid form.

The developed nations produce more than twice as much milk as the less developed countries, and all of the world's major dairy regions are in the developed countries. One of these regions is in the northeastern United States and southeastern Canada; a second extends across the United Kingdom, northern Europe, Belarus, and into Russia; and a third consists of southeastern Australia and the North Island of New Zealand. The United States is the world's leading milk producer, but the economy of New Zealand is more closely tied to dairying. Dairy products account for nearly one-third of New Zealand's exports.

Mixed Farming   An agricultural system in which farmers derive income from both livestock and crop production is called **mixed farming**. Mixed farming, therefore, can be considered a form of agriculture intermediate between commercial herding and commer-

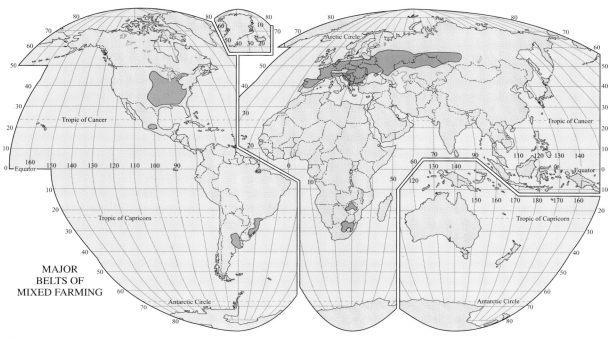

FIGURE 11.8

In mixed farming, both livestock and crop production contribute to the livelihoods of farmers. The Corn Belt of the United States is one of the most productive mixed-farming regions in the world.

cial crop production. Most crops are grown for sale and as feed for animals that also are sold. Mixed farming is practiced in areas comprising about one-third of the area of the United States, in most of central and northern Europe, and in a wide belt across the former Soviet Union (Fig. 11.8). The **U.S. Corn Belt** provides an excellent example of mixed farming.

The Corn Belt is an agricultural region that extends across the Midwest from Ohio to Nebraska. By far the greater part of the region consists of irregular and smooth plains that have soils ranging from good to excellent in natural fertility. The rich soils combine with adequate moisture and proper length of the growing season to make this area ideal for the production of corn. The same conditions are equally ideal for soybeans, but corn is the more traditional crop. The Corn Belt is one of the world's premier *breadbaskets* (major food-producing districts), accounting for a greater output of foods and feeds than any other area of comparable size in the world.

In the United States as a whole, corn occupies about a fourth of all harvested cropland, but in the

Corn Belt it often exceeds 50 percent. It is an attractive crop for farmers to grow because of its effectiveness in fattening cattle and hogs. Because there is a close correlation between hog raising and corn production, most of the nation's hogs are in the Corn Belt. Iowa and Illinois, the first- and second-ranked states in corn output, are also the first- and second-ranked states in the number of hogs produced. Iowa produces one-fourth of the nation's pork, more than twice as much as any other state. Beef cattle also commonly are found on Corn Belt farms. In fact, cash receipts from the sale of cattle exceed those from corn sales. Because the cattle were fattened on corn, however, the *value* of the corn produced in the Corn Belt, if not the cash receipts, is greater than the value of the beef produced.

Another reason corn is an attractive crop for farmers to grow in this area is the high yields that can be obtained. Corn yields in Iowa and Illinois, which usually range between 110 and 140 bushels per acre, exceed those in nearly all other areas. Soybeans produce only about half that yield per acre, but often this commodity's price is twice that of corn. As a consequence,

Von Thünen's Model of Rural Land Use

Johann Heinrich von Thünen (1783–1850), a German estate owner, in 1826 devised a geographical model that helps to explain the influence of distance on land use in the rural area surrounding a market town or village. He developed the model after observing that lands having apparently identical physical properties were used for different purposes. Von Thünen deduced that the uses of parcels of land are a function of the differing values placed upon seemingly identical lands. He concluded that those differing values reflect the cost of overcoming the distance separating a given land unit from the market center. The greater the distance, the higher the production cost to the farmer, because transportation costs have to be added to other production expenses.

To illustrate this principle, von Thünen conceived an "isolated state," a hypothetical area removed from outside influence. In his model of the isolated state, portrayed in the accompanying illustration, the only variable influencing land use is distance from the single market in the area. He assumed uniform terrain (a plain), uniform soil fertility, and uniform climate. In addition, he assumed a homogeneous population engaged in a commercial farm economy, each farmer striving for the highest possible returns from his operation. Given the assumed uniformities, the zones of land use would appear as concentric circles around the market center. Each larger circle would represent a more extensive form of economic activity than the

nearest smaller circle. The most intensive agriculture, therefore, would be practiced closest to the market, and the least intensive (most extensive) would be farthest away.

The zone closest to the market, as indicated in the illustration, specifically would be used for the production of perishable commodities like milk and vegetables because of the necessity of getting them to market quickly. A woodland occupies the second closest zone to the market in von Thünen's model, a fact that might seem surprising to those examining the model today. However, a market center required large quantities of wood for fuel and building material in von Thünen's time. Being heavy and costly to transport, wood ideally was obtained from a forested zone relatively close to a center of population. Beyond the forest is a zone of moderately intensive cultivation involving a rotation of crops. The next largest circle of land is devoted in alternate years to crop production and pasture. Surrounding that zone is another that reflects a still less intensive land use: the medieval three-field system in which land divided into three fields is alternately cultivated, used for pasture, and allowed to lie fallow. The least intensive land use, permanent grazing, occurs in the most distant zone.

Von Thünen's isolated state, now more than a century and a half old, continues to be significant in geography. As the earliest attempt to model spatial patterns, von Thünen's work inspired the development of more recent models that have furthered our

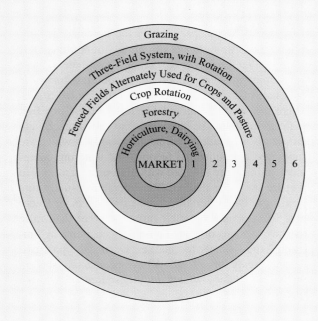

MARKET 1 2 3 4 5 6

Horticulture, Dairying

Forestry

Crop Rotation

Fenced Fields Alternately Used for Crops and Pasture

Three-Field System, with Rotation

Grazing

The Von Thünen Land Use Model

understanding of variables that influence the arrangement of phenomena over the earth's surface. Furthermore, the von Thünen model is not entirely out of date. Although the character of modern agriculture, transportation, and life in general makes some aspects of the model inapplicable to the pattern of today's rural land use, a number of studies by geographers have confirmed that the basic idea remains sound. The cost of transportation, a reflection of distance, continues to be a key factor in the type of use made of rural land.

THOUGHT QUESTIONS

1. How do you think the arrangement of land use zones would be changed by the addition of a second market center in von Thünen's isolated state?

2. What would happen to the pattern of the zones if the single market center was located on a river that provided less expensive transportation than the overland movement of products?

3. Why do you think von Thünen's model might better reflect current patterns in the less developed countries than those in the developed countries?

FIGURE 11.9
Corn (right) and soybeans (left) are the most important crops on this eastern Indiana farm and on most other farms in the Corn Belt. (J. Vining)

soybeans also are an attractive crop—one that has made a rapidly increasing impact on American and world agriculture in recent decades. Soybean oil, pressed from the beans, is a vegetable oil for which there is a large world market, and the soybean meal left over from oil extraction is itself a nutritious animal feed. About two-thirds of the soybeans produced in the United States are grown in the Corn Belt, the rest mostly in the southeastern states. Although the term "Corn Belt" is not likely to be replaced, "Corn and Soybean Belt" would be a more accurate name. Because of the productivity of this region, the United

States leads the world in total output of both corn and soybeans (Fig. 11.9).

Most Corn Belt farmers have livestock, but only a fraction of them specialize in the fattening or "finishing" of large numbers of animals in confinements (pens) called *feedlots* (Fig. 11.10). Nevertheless, these operations are very important, accounting for more than half of the cattle marketed in the United States. There are several hundred feedlots in the Corn Belt with more than 10,000 cattle or hogs each and thousands of smaller feedlots. In these lots, which are supported by automated feeding and watering equipment, animals are fattened with high-protein rations to prepare them for market. The operators usually buy yearling calves, often from western ranchers, or feeder pigs from other Corn Belt farmers, rather than raise their own calves or pigs. Thus they specialize in "finishing" the animals for market. During the past two decades many large feedlots have been established in the Great Plains—closer to the source of western feeder livestock.

Commercial Crop Production

Whereas mixed farming involves an emphasis on the production of both crops and livestock, the livestock component largely is missing in *commercial crop production*. Two very different types of agriculture make up this major category: grain farming and the production of specialty commodities. The goal of both is to produce the largest quantity of salable commodities at the lowest possible costs, maximizing profits for the producers.

The major world regions of **commercial grain farming** (also known as *cash grain farming*) are shown in Figure 11.11. All of these areas lie between 30 and 55 degrees of latitude, so commercial grain farming is another middle latitude agricultural system. Countries having sizable areas devoted to cash grain farming include the United States, Canada, Argentina, Australia, and four former Soviet republics—Russia, Ukraine, Uzbekistan, and Kazakhstan. We will focus on commercial grain farming in North America.

Cash grain farmers are highly specialized. They usually select a single grain—wheat, most often—to serve as the main source of income. Most of them depart from a monoculture only to rotate crops for the purpose of soil protection, soil enrichment, and insect or disease control. Except for some tropical plantations—and excluding livestock ranches—cash grain

FIGURE 11.10
A feedlot on a Corn Belt farm. Most Corn Belt farmers do not fatten (or "finish") their livestock for market; rather, they sell young animals to feedlot operators. (R. Gabler)

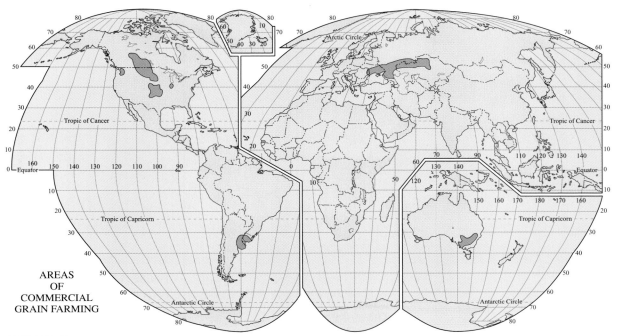

FIGURE 11.11

Commerical grain farming (or ''cash grain farming'') is, like mixed farming, a middle-latitude agricultural system. The major areas of production are shown here.

farms are the largest farms on earth. Most of the privately owned grain farms in the United States and Canada range from 500 to 2000 acres (202 to 810 ha) in size. No form of agriculture is more highly mechanized than cash grain farming. A high degree of mechanization is necessary because grain farming is practiced primarily in subhumid areas, where yields tend to be low and where a farmer can make a living only by working a large holding. The farming methods, therefore, are extensive, meaning that the human labor inputs per unit of land are small.

North America contains three major wheat producing districts, shown in Figure 11.12: (1) the Spring Wheat Belt; (2) the Winter Wheat Belt; and (3) the Palouse district. Spring wheat generally is planted in areas in which winter wheat cannot be produced because of the severity of the winter. Planted as early as possible in the spring, it matures quickly and is harvested in the late summer or early fall. Most U.S. production is in the states of Montana, North Dakota, South Dakota, and Minnesota. The rest of the North American Spring Wheat Belt lies in three Canadian

provinces: Alberta, Manitoba, and Saskatchewan. Winter wheat is planted in lower latitudes in which winters are not as severe. The winter wheat belt of North America lies primarily in Colorado, Nebraska, Kansas, Oklahoma, and Texas. The crop is planted in the fall, lies dormant through the winter, and shoots up rapidly in the spring. It is harvested in late spring or early summer. Both winter and spring wheats are produced in the Palouse district of Washington and Oregon, and a large portion of the production is consumed in the Pacific Northwest.

A less developed nation, China, leads the world in wheat production, but that production is by means of intensive subsistence agriculture, not cash grain farming. Wheat is the major grain crop produced in Russia, Ukraine, Uzbekistan, and Kazakhstan, and—as in China—production is for domestic consumption. The United States, unlike China and the former Soviet Republics, is a major exporter; no other nation exports more wheat than the United States.

Cash crop production that is focused on other than the major food crops (mostly grains) may be

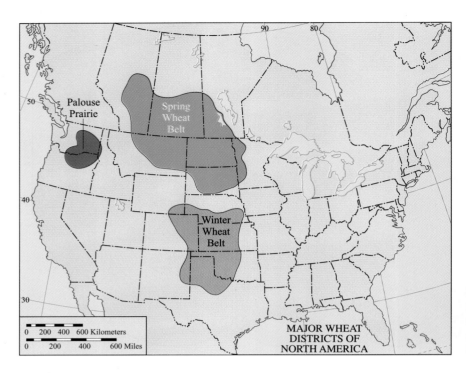

FIGURE 11.12
North America has three major wheat-producing regions. The United States is the world's leading exporter of wheat.

termed **specialty agriculture**. Specialty crops include cotton, tobacco, citrus, grapes, other fruits, nuts, and vegetables.

A number of specialty crops are associated with **Mediterranean agriculture**, which includes the production of small grains and livestock animals as well as specialty commodities. This particular mixture of activities appropriately could be considered a form of mixed farming because of the animal husbandry involved, but here we will focus on the crops within the context of specialty agriculture. Because the Mediterranean Basin is where this agriculture is most widespread (Fig. 11.13), "Mediterranean" is the name given to this agricultural type wherever it is practiced in the world.

The hot dry summers and mild moist winters of Mediterranean climate provide ideal conditions for the production of grapes, olives, figs, citrus, and other specialty crops. There is a striking correlation between the global distribution of grape production and Mediterranean climate; in almost every area of Mediterranean climate, grapes are an important specialty crop and wine manufacture is common. The leading producer of grapes is Spain. About 90 percent of U.S. grape and wine production comes from California, which has a large area of Mediterranean climate. Al-

though grape cultivation has spread to most regions of Mediterranean climate, olive production has remained concentrated in the Mediterranean Basin, which accounts for about 90 percent of world output. Spain, again, is the leading producer. The olive's ability to withstand summer drought and to grow on poor soils has made it of fundamental importance in Mediterranean agriculture since classical times.

Citrus crops—primarily oranges, grapefruit, and lemons—represent one of the most commercialized forms of Mediterranean agriculture, but they also are produced in other subtropical climatic areas. Florida, which has a mostly humid subtropical climate, produces far more citrus than California. Largely on the basis of production in central Florida, the United States long led the world in output of citrus, but Brazil surpassed the United States in the mid-1980s when severe winters temporarily crippled the Florida citrus industry.

Cotton and tobacco are other specialty crops that can be grown in both Mediterranean and other subtropical climates. Cotton farming had its greatest expansion in the United States only after the invention of the cotton gin in 1793. By the middle of the nineteenth century, a Cotton Belt had developed in the subtropical southeastern states; corn and other subsistence

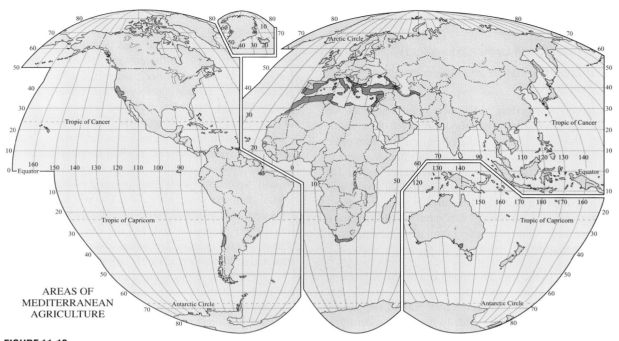

FIGURE 11.13

The Mediterranean Sea gave its name to Mediterranean agriculture, which is common in most of the countries bordering that body of water. The same agricultural system prevails in areas elsewhere in the world having a Mediterranean-type climate.

crops were produced here, but cotton dominated the rural landscape. By the end of the 1930s, soil erosion in the hilly cotton districts had become severe, and a major insect infestation (boll weevil) and various cultural factors contributed to the breakdown of the Cotton Belt. Some cotton plantations remain in the lower Mississippi Valley and in the Blackland Prairie of east central Texas, which are now the major areas of cotton cultivation in the Southeast. In addition, irrigated cotton is produced in western Texas and the southern portions of New Mexico, Arizona, and California. By far, Texas produces more cotton than any other state in the United States.

Irrigated cotton also is produced in the former Soviet republics of Turkmenistan, Uzbekistan, and Kyrgyzstan. Since the late 1960s those republics collectively have grown more cotton than the United States, but the United States remains the world's major exporter.

Tobacco is a specialty crop for which there is a continuing strong demand despite compelling evidence that it threatens consumers with serious health hazards. Of the developed nations that produce tobacco, the United States has the largest acreage under cultivation, but a less developed country, China, produces about twice as much tobacco as the United States. For two centuries, Virginia and Maryland were the great tobacco producers among U.S. states, but by 1990 North Carolina ranked first and Kentucky second. The United States produced more than a billion pounds of tobacco in 1990. In this country tobacco output is guided by complex federal policies involving production allotments, price supports, and marketing controls. Federal support of tobacco production has come under increasing criticism in recent years, but the tobacco industry has a powerful lobby in Washington, D.C., that works to protect the interests of the tobacco farmer and others involved in the industry.

Forestry, Fishing, and Mining

➤ Forestry, fishing, and mining contribute in significant ways to manufacturing industries in the developed world.

Which nations are preeminent in importing logs for their lumber industry?

In catching fish for their food-processing industry?

In importing iron ore and coal for their steel industry?

Relatively few people in the developed countries, we have seen, earn their livelihood directly from agriculture. The same is true of the other primary economic activities—forestry, fishing, and mining. These extractive enterprises, however, contribute in significant ways to such manufacturing industries as wood and pulp processing (lumber, furniture, paper), fish processing (canning, freezing, fish meal manufacturing), and ore and metals processing (smelting, casting, rolling, fabricating).

Forestry   In the less developed world, the harvesting of fuelwood is an important subsistence activity, but fuelwood plays an inconsequential role in the economies of the developed world. In the middle latitudes, where most of the developed nations lie, forestry means the management and use of trees for the production of industrial wood (lumber and plywood). Timbering in the middle latitudes provides approximately 80 percent of the world's industrial wood. The leading producer of roundwood (logs) is the United States. Canada and several of the former Soviet republics also are important producers of roundwood.

About one-fifth of the earth's land surface is forested, and a little more than half of this forested area is in the middle latitudes. The greater output of industrial timber from these temperate forests (80 percent) than from tropical forests (20 percent) is the result of their closer proximity to market. Most industrial wood is consumed in industrialized nations; tropical forests are remote from most major consuming countries. Because forests are so widespread over the planet and wood is a low-value commodity relative to its bulk, only a small proportion is traded internationally. Nevertheless, world trade in wood products amounted to about $50 billion in 1990, and wood was the third most valuable primary commodity in world trade after petroleum and natural gas. Developed nations dominate not only production but imports of roundwood. Japan is the leading importer of unmilled logs for lumber, and the United States is the major importer of lumber and pulpwood.

Since the early part of the seventeenth century, the United States has lost more than 40 percent of its

original forested area. Since 1925, however, the country's forested area has remained nearly the same—about one-third of the land area. Some three-fourths of this forest land is in the eastern half of the nation. Little of it is "virgin timber"; nearly all is "secondary growth." The remaining forests are mostly in the Rocky Mountain and Pacific Coast regions, and some of this timber is still "old-growth" (Fig. 11.14). Almost 60 percent of the commercial forest land of the United States is owned by several million farmers and other small landowners. Seldom are these small, privately owned "woodlots" well managed, and a large proportion of them are never harvested. The rest of the country's commercial forests are owned by local, state, and federal governments and by the forest industries. These forests usually are better managed and more productive than most privately owned forest holdings.

There is some question as to whether the demand for timber in the United States during the next few decades can be met without greatly increasing imports. Forest depletion is already taking its toll in some areas. For example, annual harvests from the Pacific Coast region have exceeded annual growth since 1952. Some of the forests of the Northeast are suffering from the effects of acid rain. Forest damage caused by acid rain and air pollution also is a problem in Canada and Europe. In Chapter 14 we will examine this problem in greater detail.

FIGURE 11.14

The logging of old-growth ("virgin") timber in the Pacific Northwest of the United States provided a livelihood for relatively few people even before environmental concerns for the endangered northern spotted owl led to government action that ended some harvest operations. (R. Gabler)

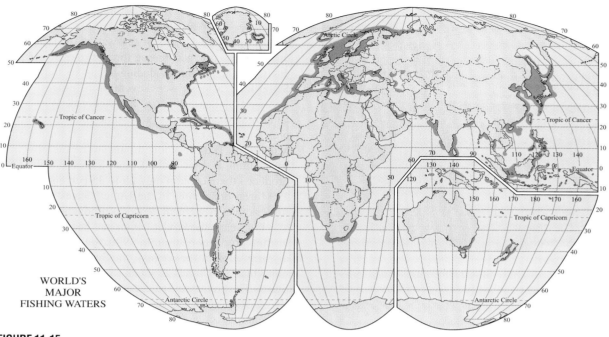

FIGURE 11.15

Commercial fishing, common in the areas indicated on this map, is such a mechanized industry that it provides a livelihood for less than 1 percent of the labor force of the developed world.

Commercial Fishing The major commercial fishing waters of the world are shown in Figure 11.15. The United States, Europe, and several former Soviet republics are conspicuously well endowed with fishing resources. The United States and Russia, in addition to their off-shore fishing waters, possess frontage on large inland lakes and seas that provide additional fishing resources—the Great Lakes in the United States and the Black Sea and Caspian Sea in Russia. The oceans supply about 87 percent of the annual commercial catch, while the rest is taken from inland waters. The proximity of the world's major fishing waters to continental coastlines is notable in Figure 11.15. Almost all of the marine catch is taken from the plankton-rich waters over the shallowly submerged continental shelves. At the same time, the largest portion of the oceans is nutrient-poor and supports relatively little marine life—a fact that has led some writers to describe the deep seas as vast watery deserts.

Most commercial fishing is a corporate affair. Thousands of small, privately owned boats still operate in all major fishing waters, but corporation-owned fishing fleets—including huge factory ships—are be-

coming increasingly dominant in the industry. Today's fishing fleets are highly modernized (Fig. 11.16). They use helicopters, aerial photography, sonar, radar, temperature measurement, and other procedures to find schools of fish. Once the fish are taken by means of sophisticated netting systems, often they are frozen or canned at sea in the factory ships. Commercial fishing boats consume huge amounts of diesel fuel and gasoline, and a large amount of total operating costs is for fuel. That fact helps to explain the high price of seafood.

Japan is the world's leading fishing nation. Japanese fleets harvested more than 10 million metric tons of fish in 1990. The United States ranks second. Russia, Norway, and Denmark are the only other developed nations among the world's ten leading fishing countries.

Between 1950 and 1970 the annual world commercial fish catch more than tripled—an increase larger than that of any other human food source. This increase led to unwarranted optimism about the ability of the seas to support a rapidly growing world population. In fact, the per capita world fish catch declined

FIGURE 11.16

A Japanese corporation–owned driftnet fishing ship. Japan is the world's leading fishing nation. (Payne/Liaison)

between 1970 and 1990 in spite of a slight increase in the total annual harvest. Because of overfishing and water pollution, it is expected that by the year 2000 the per capita fish catch will be back to the 1960 level.

Mining   Both metallic minerals and fossil fuels, we have seen, are sporadically distributed over the earth's surface. As a consequence, some nations are well endowed with one or more minerals but are totally deficient in others, and large countries tend to be more self-sufficient than small ones. The United States became a powerful nation in part because of its rich mineral endowment; its mineral wealth is in large measure the result of its large size.

Developed nations have industries that require as raw materials a large number of metallic minerals. There is an industrial use for every metallic mineral found in the earth's crust, but the "big three"—iron ore, bauxite, and copper ore—are the mainstays of the metals industry.

Concentrations of iron (iron ore) are plentiful in the earth's crust, but the metal is never found in quantity in a reasonably pure state. Large deposits in the United States once had an iron content of more than 50 percent, and some of the deposits of Brazil contain ores having more than 60 percent iron. Very little iron

ore mined today contains more than 25 percent iron, however.

In 1950 the United States was the leading producer of iron ore, accounting for a third of world production. The major producing areas in the United States then, as now, were several iron "ranges" south and west of Lake Superior in Michigan, Wisconsin, and Minnesota. The most accessible and highest grade ores were part of the Mesabi Range of northeastern Minnesota. The Mesabi continues to be the principal iron mining district in the United States, but the ores produced there contain only 25 to 35 percent iron. By 1990 iron ore output in the United States accounted for less than 10 percent of world production.

For years, the Soviet Union had been the world's leading producer of iron. In 1990, the year before the disintegration of the country, the Soviet Union mined more than four times as much iron ore as the United States. The Soviet equivalent of the Mesabi Range was Krivoi Rog, then and now the major iron district of Ukraine. Russia's Kursk Magnetic Anomaly (KMA), southeast of Moscow, contains at least twice and perhaps 10 times the amount of recoverable reserves of iron as the Krivoi Rog reserves. Although the KMA, at the present rate of production, could supply all of Russia's requirements for more than 150 years, the country also possesses additional vast deposits farther east near the cities of Magnitogorsk and Chelyabinsk in the Ural Mountains and in its border area with Mongolia (near the city of Novokuznetsk). These huge reserves ensure that Russia will be a leading producer of iron ore for a long time. A third former Soviet republic well endowed with iron reserves is Kazakhstan; its great iron field is located near the city of Karaganda.

After steel (a product of iron ore), aluminum is the most important structural metal, and the distribution of its principal ore, bauxite, is of great significance. By far, the leading producer of bauxite is Australia, which exports most of its output to the United States, Europe, and Japan. Half a dozen multinational corporations dominate the production of bauxite and aluminum in both developed and less developed nations. Although generally well endowed with mineral resources, the United States and Russia lack high-grade bauxite deposits. The United States is the preeminent importer of bauxite. Russia, which mines medium-grade deposits in the south-central part of the country, is not a major importer.

Important primarily because it is a good conductor of electricity, copper also is one of the "big three" of the metals industry. The world pattern of production has not changed significantly in recent decades. As we noted in Chapter 10, a less developed country, Chile, is the world's leading producer of copper ore, but the United States is not far behind. Third-ranked Canada produces less than half as much copper ore as the United States.

Copper deposits in the United States lie mostly in the West. Arizona produces more copper than any other state, but the largest single copper mine in the country is at Bingham, Utah. The Bingham mine (Fig. 11.17) has operated continuously since 1865. The ores lie near the surface, permitting inexpensive open-pit mining and the use of lower-quality ores. (Money saved through inexpensive surface mining enables the company to spend more on processing poorer ores.)

The fossil fuels (coal, oil, and natural gas) are much more important in the developed countries than in the less developed countries. This is because industrialized economies are more completely dependent on them for energy than are traditional agrarian economies in which human and animal power still represent a sizable portion of total energy expenditures. The production of fossil fuels in the less developed countries was examined in Chapter 10. Here we will survey their production in the developed world.

Coal, an organically derived sedimentary rock, served as the principal energy source of the Industrial Revolution in Europe. Coal has a relatively widespread distribution in the earth's crust. However, nearly all of the world's *major* coal fields occur in the Northern Hemisphere. A country is more likely to have exploitable deposits of coal than of oil or natural gas. Unfortunately, most of Latin America, Africa, and Oceania are deficient in coal. The world's leading coal producer, China, is a less developed country. Among developed nations, the United States and Russia mine the most coal and possess the largest reserves. Like China, these two countries have enough coal reserves to last two or three centuries at current levels of consumption (or at least a century, assuming a 2 percent annual increase in consumption). Two other former Soviet republics that have major coal fields are Ukraine and Kazakhstan.

The United States, historically the leading producer and exporter of coal, was surpassed in the mid-1980s by China as a producer and by Australia as an

FIGURE 11.17
An aerial photograph of the Bingham Copper Mine in Utah, the largest open-pit mine in the United States. (U.S. Department of Agriculture, ASCS Western Aerial Photo Lab)

exporter. Still, there are vast reserves of coal in the United States that probably will last for centuries.

Figure 11.18 shows the distribution of four types of coal deposits in the United States. *Anthracite,* the hardest form of coal, is found in the folded and faulted geologic structures of the ridges and valleys of Pennsylvania and, to a lesser degree, in Virginia. However, anthracite accounts for only 2 percent of the U.S. coal reserves. (Anthracite is also rare worldwide; the only other nation with commercial deposits is the United Kingdom.) Some 45 percent of U.S. coal reserves consist of high-sulfur *bituminous* coal with a high fuel value. This kind of coal is found mostly in the midwestern and east-central parts of the nation. Illinois contains more high-grade bituminous coal than any other state. Most of the country's low-sulfur *subbituminous* and *lignite* coals lie in the West. Subbituminous coal is less energy-rich than bituminous, and lignite is a soft brown coal of even poorer quality.

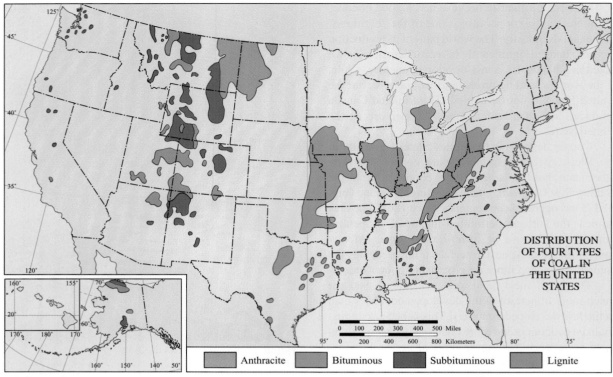

FIGURE 11.18

Although the United States historically has been the leading producer and exporter of coal, China now produces more and Australia exports more coal than the United States. The four types of coal deposits found in the United States are mapped here.

Subbituminous coal is widely distributed in the West, but lignite is limited mostly to Montana and the Dakotas. Because of its low quality, there is presently no well-developed market for lignite. About fifty-five percent of U.S. coal reserves lie west of the Mississippi River. Although only one-third of the nation's output is from these deposits, the production of coal in the West increased eightfold between 1970 and 1990. The demand for low-sulfur coal will result in expanded mining of western beds, despite their great distance from the major markets in the eastern part of the country.

About 60 percent of the coal mined in the United States comes from surface (open-pit) mines, with approximately 40 percent obtained from underground sources. The principal consumers of coal are electric utility companies. In 1990 they consumed about 85 percent of the country's coal production.

Petroleum is one of the world's most unevenly distributed resources. Among the 10 leading producers of petroleum, only 3 are developed nations: Russia, the United States, and the United Kingdom. Almost two-thirds of proven reserves are in just 5 Persian Gulf countries, and most of the rest occurs in 15 other nations. More than 150 countries, therefore, are almost totally lacking in domestic supplies of petroleum. Because so many countries possess little or no oil, and with some of the major producers being even larger consumers, there are large-scale exports from nations having surpluses. The United States, Japan, and western European countries are major importers of petroleum.

Oil was discovered in the United States near Titusville, Pennsylvania, north of Pittsburgh, in 1859; the first Russian oil well was drilled in 1863 near the Black Sea. Pennsylvania dominated U.S. oil produc-

FIGURE 11.19

In the United States, the production of petroleum in the Midcontinent oil field began in 1889 and continues to be important more than a century later, despite the development of other important fields along the Gulf Coast, in California, and in Alaska. This photograph shows the towers of an oil refinery in the Gulf Coast field. (George Craig/Liaison Int'l)

tion until about the turn of the century; the first major Soviet oil field at Baku, in what is now the country of Azerbaijan, dominated the Soviet Union's production until the 1950s. Early in this century, especially after World War I, rapid growth in the manufacture of automobiles, trucks, buses, tractors, and aircraft increased the demand for gasoline and the need to open new oil fields. In the United States, commercial production in the Midcontinent field (Fig. 11.19), which had begun in 1889, was greatly expanded, and by 1920 Oklahoma was the leading state in oil output. The Gulf Coast field became an important producer by 1920, as did the California field. The Soviet Union opened a "second Baku," the Volga-Urals field, which eclipsed Baku in production in the mid-1950s and was eclipsed itself in the 1970s by the West Siberian field. In 1990 the West Siberian field accounted for almost two-thirds of Soviet production. In 1992 several of the former Soviet republics possessed producing oilfields, but Russia's production capacity still represented about three-fourths of the Soviet Union's in 1990. The Midcontinent and Gulf Coast fields were still of major importance in the oil industry of the United States in 1992, but by that time Alaska's North Slope field had made significant gains. (See *Cultural Landscapes: The Alaska Oil Pipeline.*)

The third fossil fuel, *natural gas,* is a mixture of 50 to 90 percent methane gas and smaller amounts of heavier gases, such as propane and butane. Some natural gas occurs in geologic domes above deposits of crude oil, while other gas deposits are not associated with petroleum. When a deposit is tapped and developed, the propane and butane are removed as *liquefied petroleum gas* and the rest of the gas, mostly methane, is cleaned and transported, usually by pipeline, to consumers. By means of extreme refrigeration, natural gas can be converted into *liquefied natural gas* and transported in railroad tank cars or tanker ships.

The United States and some of the republics of the former Soviet Union are by far the largest producers of natural gas. The use of this resource emerged only recently because of the inherent difficulty and cost of delivering natural gas to market. The United States developed its Oklahoma and Texas gas fields after World War II, and most industries and home heating were converted from coal and oil to natural gas during the 1950s and 1960s. The Soviet Union began a similar transition during the 1980s.

Of the former Soviet republics, Russia possesses the largest reserves of natural gas. In fact, Russia's West Siberian oil field contains two-thirds of the 1990 proven reserves of the former Soviet Union. Its large reserves enable Russia to be the world's leading exporter of gas; most exports go by pipeline to Europe. Turkmenistan and perhaps Ukraine also have gas reserves larger than those of the United States. The reserves in the United States may become exhausted soon after the year 2000. Known reserves throughout the world, in fact, will not last long—no more than a few decades.

CULTURAL LANDSCAPES

The Alaskan Oil Pipeline

The emergence of Alaska as a major producer of oil was made possible by construction of a pipeline across the north–south breadth of the state during the 1970s. With a length of 800 miles (1280 km) and a diameter of 48 inches (122 cm), the pipeline is capable of delivering 2 million barrels of oil per day to the port of Valdez on Prince William Sound. The pipeline is a remarkable feature of Alaska's cultural landscape, and one that has been the object of much controversy.

After years of exploratory drilling, the oil deposits of Alaska's North Slope (the area between the Brooks Range and the Arctic Coast) were first tapped in 1968 at Prudhoe Bay. When efforts to reach the new oil field by tanker ship through ice-choked Arctic waters proved to be impractical, it was concluded that a pipeline to an ice-free port on Alaska's southern coast would be the only feasible means of transporting the oil to markets. When plans for the pipeline were revealed, environmentalists objected to it so strenuously that the project was delayed several years.

The Alaskan Pipeline. (Liaison International)

face and flood the immediate area. Another concern was that a pipeline above the surface of the earth would interrupt the migrations of caribou and other animals important to the subsistence of native populations. Perhaps the most disturbing risk posed by critics concerned Alaska's relatively frequent earthquakes. Should the pipeline be ruptured by an earthquake, a massive oil spill undoubtedly would result.

These environmental risks of the pipeline project were pushed aside, however, as a crisis in world oil supplies followed the 1973 boycott imposed by Arab producers. A consortium of oil companies began construction in 1974 and completed the pipeline three years later. At times, more than 20,000 workers were engaged in the construction, working 12 hours a day and 7 days a week in severe weather and over extremely difficult terrain. Alaska's oil production by 1980 was exceeded only by that of Texas among the nation's producing states.

The only major environmental disaster associated with the transportation of Alaskan oil to market ironically involved a tanker ship rather than the pipeline. With so much attention focused on pipeline-related risks, the possibility of an off-shore accident was given little attention. In March 1989, the tanker *Exxon Valdez* ran aground on a reef and lost its cargo of crude oil into the waters of Prince William Sound. Tens of thousands of marine animals were killed, and attempts to clean up the polluted coastline required several months of work. It was the worst oil spill in the history of the United States. The pipeline itself, however, has been in operation for more than a decade and a half without a major environmental mishap.

Environmentalists provided a number of reasons for their opposition to the pipeline. Construction activities, they pointed out, would endanger some of Alaska's fragile ecosystems. In high-latitude environments, the natural restoration of damaged ecosystems may require many years. Because the oil would need to be heated to facilitate its flow through the pipeline, there was the possibility of melting the adjacent *permafrost*. A common phenomenon in Arctic and subpolar areas, permafrost is a permanently frozen subsurface layer of soil and rock. Any hole melted in it may allow pressurized groundwater to reach the sur-

THOUGHT QUESTIONS

1. Do you feel that the case of the Alaskan pipeline indicates that environmentalists are unnecessarily pessimistic about such projects? Why or why not?

2. In the long term, is Alaska likely to be better or worse off as a consequence of the exploitation of its oil resource? In what ways?

LIVELIHOODS IN THE FACTORIES

Having examined the ways that people in the developed countries earn their living from primary economic activities, we are ready to examine livelihood activities in the factories of the developed world. The first factories we will consider are those engaged in the generation of electrical energy—a logical continuation of the preceding discussion of fossil fuel energy sources. Then we will turn to manufacturing activities and focus particularly on the iron and steel industry and high-technology industries.

Producing Electrical Energy

➤ Developed countries generate and consume far more electricity than less developed countries. In descending order of importance in the method of generation in the United States, the major sources are thermoelectric, nuclear electric, and hydroelectric.

What are the advantages and disadvantages of each source of electricity?

Even though there are more than four times as many less developed countries as developed countries, the latter generate and consume more electrical energy. Variations exist within both groups of nations in the principal ways that electricity is generated. There are three ways that have become conventional: (1) generation by hydroelectric plants; (2) generation by thermoelectric plants using fossil fuels; and (3) generation by nuclear power plants. The "hydro" in "hydroelectricity" refers to water, and water—unlike fossil fuels and other combustible materials—has no capacity within itself to produce energy. The kinetic energy of *moving* water, however, can be converted into electricity by means of turbines and generators. The movement is downward and usually vertical; that is, *falling* water is directed through turbines to drive electrical generators. Turbines may be installed at the bottom of waterfalls, but almost all hydroelectricity is produced by the fall of water over (or through) dams.

Hydropower supplies about 20 percent of electricity worldwide—less than coal but more than nuclear energy. North America produces more hydroelectricity than any other world region. In 1990 the United States and Canada accounted for almost 30 percent of global production. The North American hydropower plant with the largest capacity is at Grand Coulee Dam, a 550-foot (167.6 m) dam on the Columbia River in Washington. Russia has even larger hydroelectric plants in operation. Hydropower is especially important in Japan, a nation that has developed almost 100 percent of its water power potential. The largest share of unexploited hydropower capacity is in the less developed countries. In the United States, Japan, and many other developed countries, hydropower's share of total generation of electricity has been declining in recent years because of increasing production from other sources.

Although less physically spectacular than hydro installations, *thermoelectric* (or *thermal power*) plants are immensely more important in most developed countries and many less developed countries as well. Advantages of thermal power stations over hydroelectric plants include lower cost of installation and the fact that there are fewer physical controls over their location. For the operation of the steam turbines used in thermoelectric plants, a large and continuous supply of water is necessary, so thermal power plants are located on the banks of rivers or shores of lakes. The United States is the world's leading producer of thermoelectricity. The generation of thermal power in this country exceeds hydropower output by more than eight times. The high operating costs are a major disadvantage of thermal power plants. Water is not *consumed* in a hydroelectric plant, but fuel must be consumed to generate electricity in a thermoelectric plant. A second disadvantage is pollution. The burning of fuel at a thermoelectric plant creates air pollution, and the hot water produced in the process can adversely affect the ecology of the body of water into which it is discharged. Another disadvantage is that the *cleanest* fuels, natural gas and petroleum, are in relatively short supply and will become increasingly costly in the years ahead. However, the earth's crust yields abundant supplies of coal, which serves as the predominant fuel in thermal power stations.

The United States is the world's leading producer and user of nuclear electric power, although nuclear energy represents a larger proportion of total energy production in France—11 percent in the United States, 33 percent in France (Fig. 11.20). Nuclear power accounts for more than twice as much electricity output as hydropower in the United States, but thermoelectric plants supply almost four times more electricity than nuclear-powered plants. In 1990 the United States had 108 operating nuclear power plants, almost twice as many as the Soviet Union (56) or France (55). The fourth through fifth ranked nations were the United Kingdom (40) and Japan (38). Nuclear power represents high technology, so plants are concentrated in the developed countries; relatively few less developed countries have such plants.

In 1990 there were 416 nuclear reactors worldwide, and they were producing about 17 percent of the world's electricity and less than 5 percent of total inanimate energy (that is, energy from inanimate sources). Between 1990 and 2010, the proportion of total energy produced by nuclear power probably will decline because of the retirement of aging plants.

Because radioactive substances can cause cancer in humans and animals, and can contaminate the environment for years, nuclear power production has the potential for more serious accidents than other forms of energy production. Possibly the worst nuclear accident in history occurred in the southern Ural Mountains of the Soviet Union in 1957. Just what happened was never revealed by the Soviet Union, but it is clear that the accident involved nuclear production for weapons, not electrical energy, and it is known that about 30 towns and villages disappeared from Soviet maps—communities evidently evacuated and abandoned. The worst accident in the history of U.S. commercial nuclear power happened at the Three Mile Island power plant near Harrisburg, Pennsylvania, in 1979. No one died in the accident, but 144,000 people were evacuated and possible long-term health effects are still being debated. The most devastating accident in the history of commercial power production was the massive explosion that occurred in one of the reactors at the Chernobyl power plant near the Soviet city of Kiev in 1986. About 135,000 people were evacuated. Within four years about 50 people had died from radiation exposure, and tens of thousands of people probably will die prematurely because of exposure to Chernobyl radiation.

The Chernobyl disaster further eroded public support for nuclear power worldwide—support that already had been waning for several years. Since 1975 more than 100 orders for new nuclear plants in the United States have been canceled—some because of public concern about possible accidents, others because of the incredibly high costs of installation. In 1990, however, 11 years after Three Mile Island and four years after Chernobyl, polls showed that the majority of U.S. citizens favored continuing development of commercial nuclear power. This new attitude re-

FIGURE 11.20

A nuclear power plant in France. Nuclear electric power, as a proportion of total energy production, is far more important in France than in the United States. However, the United States has almost twice as many nuclear power plants. (Mark Antman/Stock Boston)

flected public recognition of the seriousness of air pollution and acid rain, unfortunate by-products of thermoelectric power generation.

The Nature and Distribution of Manufacturing

➤ The degree to which a nation becomes industrialized depends on its location, history, raw materials, and human resources.

How is the industrialization of a country influenced by each of these factors?

What are the major factors that account for the location of industry?

At one time manufacturing meant making something by hand with the aid of a few tools and no external power. Indeed, the word "manufacturing" was derived from Latin words for "hand" (*manus*) and "making" (*factura*). A general term applied to such simple manufacturing is *primitive household industry*. As early technologies evolved, humans learned to harness water power with waterwheels and wind power with windmills. This technology made possible what has been termed *simple-powered household industry*. Both primitive household industry and simple-powered household industry—perhaps with more modern power sources—are still practiced today. Their products are termed *handicrafts*. Although strong consumer interest in handicraft items continues in the developed countries, household industries represent only a minuscule portion of total manufacturing in the developed world. In the less developed countries, however, handicraft items account for a large portion of total manufacturing. *Community workshop industry* also is important in the less developed countries. Following the development of simple-powered household industry, further technological advances and the specialization of labor made this form of community enterprise possible. Increased output of manufactured goods was the result. All three of these simple approaches to manufacturing were used in the early civilizations and prevailed until the time of the Industrial Revolution.

Manufacturing includes all those activities humans employ to (1) assemble raw materials in an establishment, whether cottage workshop or factory

building; (2) upgrade the usefulness of the raw materials by changing their form; and (3) ship the more valuable resulting commodities to other places. The focal point of modern manufacturing is the factory, the link between source regions for raw materials and market regions in which the manufactured products are consumed.

Most developed nations would not be developed without the industrial sectors of their economies. The degree to which a nation becomes industrialized depends on its location, history, raw materials, and human resources. An isolated location typically has been a liability to a country's development of manufacturing. The endowment of natural resources is of obvious importance. In general, history reveals that the larger a country, the more likely it is to possess the raw materials on which manufacturing industries might be based. Their large sizes provided abundant natural resources for the United States and Russia. Small countries such as Taiwan and the Netherlands have far fewer domestic natural resources, but they have developed industry on the basis of their human resources—the final factor that influences the progress

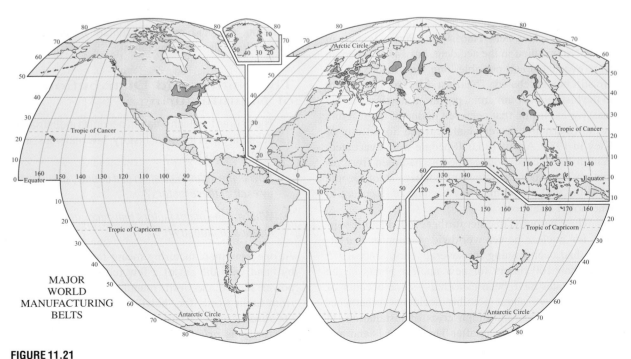

MAJOR WORLD MANUFACTURING BELTS

FIGURE 11.21

The major manufacturing districts of the world are predominantly in the developed countries. The degree of industrialization is one of the greatest differences between the developed countries and the less developed countries.

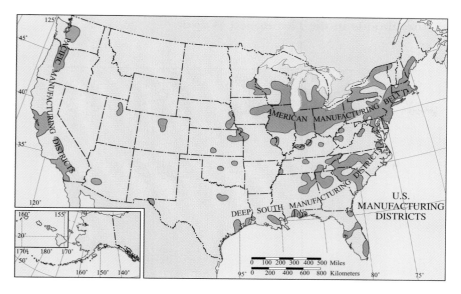

FIGURE 11.22

The United States has one large manufacturing belt made up of more than a dozen smaller manufacturing districts in the Northeast, with more recently developed belts in the South and West.

of industrialization. Regardless of the supply of locally based raw materials, industrialization will not take place unless there are entrepreneurs, managers, and laborers of sufficient skill to develop it. Japan provides perhaps the best example of a nation that has become highly industrialized more on the basis of human resources than of domestic natural resources.

Manufacturing is more capital intensive in the developed countries than in the less developed countries. The commodities manufactured and consumed in technologically advanced economies involve high percentages of finished metals, fabricated metal products, chemicals, and electronics. Although there is *some* manufacturing of transportation equipment in the less developed world, many developed nations have factories that produce a wide range of goods in this category—automobiles, trucks, buses, railroad cars and engines, boats and ships, and aircraft. Since World War II, space-age technology has emerged in the developed countries, and several developed nations now produce rockets, spacecraft, and computers—all modern examples of capital-intensive manufacturing.

A good measure of the success of a country as an industrial nation is the value of its exports of manufactured goods. Despite some exceptions, it can be inferred that a country that is exporting manufactured goods retains a sufficient number of such products to satisfy domestic requirements. (The best example of an exception was the Soviet Union, which for decades exported manufactured goods to Cuba, various countries in Eastern Europe, and other nations despite great shortages of such goods at home.) For most of the period between World War II and the 1980s, the

United States was the leading exporter of manufactured goods, but in 1990 both West Germany and Japan exported a greater value of such products. The value of U.S. exports of manufactured goods in 1990 was about $200 billion; Japan's exports exceeded this amount by 12 percent and West Germany's exports were 32 percent higher. Other countries among the world's ten leading exporters of manufactured products in 1990, in order, were France, Italy, the United Kingdom, Belgium, Canada, the Netherlands, and South Korea.

Specialists in the geography of manufacturing are particularly interested in the distribution of manufacturing activity. They have observed that the distribution of factories is generally influenced by five **industrial location factors**: raw material, power, labor, transportation, and market. Because there are very few areas with a flat land surface, uniform resources, uniform climate, and uniform population distribution, it is not surprising that industrial activities are concentrated in regions or zones. Even highly industrialized nations like the United States and Russia have vast areas of agricultural land, forested land, and wilderness areas in which little or no manufacturing activity occurs. The very existence of other forms of land use means that manufacturing is an economic activity that is concentrated. The regions or zones in which the concentration of industrialization is notable are sometimes described as **manufacturing belts** (Fig. 11.21). The United States has one large manufacturing belt made up of more than a dozen smaller manufacturing districts; other important manufacturing zones occur elsewhere in the country (Fig. 11.22). The former Soviet republics have several manufacturing belts (Fig.

FIGURE 11.23

The republics that constituted the Soviet Union until 1991 contain several manufacturing belts.

11.23), as does Europe (Fig. 11.24). The industrial zones of Japan (Fig. 11.25) have almost merged into one great manufacturing belt as that country has grown to become an industrial giant. Manufacturing districts of lesser importance exist in other parts of the developed and less developed world.

The Iron and Steel Industry

➤ Although other industries are of major importance in the developed countries, none is as basic to economic development as the manufacture of iron and steel.

Why is iron and steel considered the basic industry?

Which countries are the leading iron and steel producers?

What factors determine the location of this industry?

The iron and steel industry is of unparalleled importance to the manufacturing sector of the economies of the developed world. Iron and steel are the foundation of modern machines, equipment, and tools. So basic is the manufacture of iron and steel to economic life that it long was used as an index to general business activity. (By the 1980s this function had shifted to more knowledge-intensive industries such as computers and other high-technology activities.)

The iron and steel industry is primarily a processing industry. Its products—girders, plates, sheets, rods, wires, and rails—are the processed raw materials of industries that produce complex finished products. Some corporations that manufacture iron and steel, however, also have extensive business interests in related activities, such as shipbuilding or bridge building.

The essential raw material for the iron and steel industry is iron ore, but other ingredients also are nec-

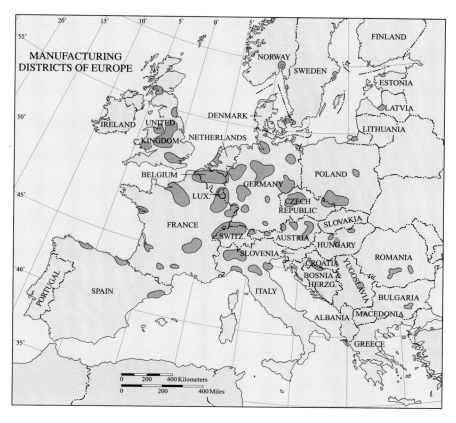

MANUFACTURING
DISTRICTS OF EUROPE

FIGURE 11.24

*A number of important
manufacturing districts have
developed in Europe, the region
where the Industrial Revolution
began.*

essary. Coke (a by-product of coal) and limestone are heated with iron ore in a furnace to make steel by removing excess carbon from the mix. To the resulting steel, one or more *ferroalloys* (such as nickel or tungsten) are added to its molten form to give it the qualities required for its ultimate use. Great quantities of water are necessary to flush through the jackets of the furnaces to keep them from melting during the process.

The ideal site for iron and steel mills has in its immediate area abundant deposits of iron ore, coal, and limestone, plus plenty of water and major buyers of iron and unfabricated steel. Nature and the distribution of economic activity seldom provide perfect industrial locations, however. More often than not, iron and steel mills are situated closer to markets for their goods than to sources of raw materials. The greater importance of the market as a locational factor is seen in the example of Baltimore, Maryland, which, with none of the three major raw materials, was able to develop a bigger iron and steel industry than Bir-

mingham, Alabama, which has nearby supplies of iron ore, limestone, and coal.

World iron and steel production peaked in 1974, and has since declined. The start of the decline coincided with a major international energy crisis associated with restrictions in the export of Middle East oil. The iron and steel industry had enjoyed a boom period for two decades prior to 1974 despite some problems that began in the 1960s in some producing areas. Those problems included the failure to keep production costs in check and, particularly in the United States and Western Europe, the failure to adopt new technology. By the early 1970s major consumers had amassed large stockpiles of steel to protect themselves in the event of strikes or other supply problems in the industry. When the energy crisis developed, they cut back on orders and operated from inventories on hand. This prompted steel producers to cut prices, which reduced profits. A severe recession in the iron and steel industry resulted. Hardest hit was Great Britain, which had pioneered the industry. Other European producers

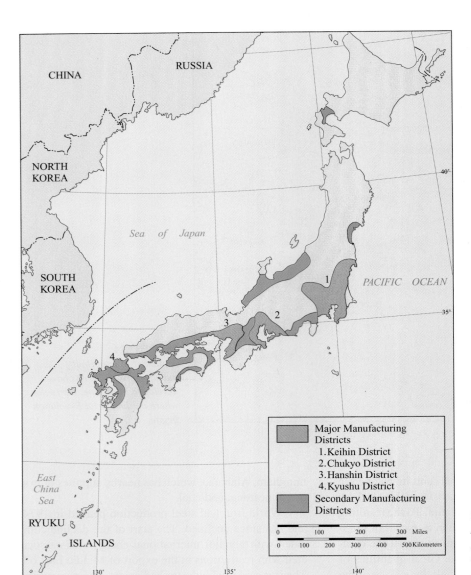

FIGURE 11.25

As Japan became an industrial giant, its many manufacturing districts almost merged into one giant manufacturing belt.

suffered to a greater degree than did Japan and the United States.

On the eve of the dissolution of the Soviet Union in 1991, that country was by far the world's leading producer of iron and steel. For several years Soviet production had averaged about 160 million metric tons of crude steel annually—about 60 percent more than second-ranked Japan and 70 percent more than third-ranked United States. It is not yet clear what effect independence and instability will have on industrial production in the former Soviet republics. Russia possesses more than half of the former Soviet Union's

steel-making capacity, but the new republic may not be able to out-produce Japan or even the United States. Ukraine has numerous steelworks with a capacity that may permit it a place among the world's top ten producers. Kazakhstan has steelworks at Karaganda, but its steel production will be minor compared with that of Russia or Ukraine. Other developed countries that are major producers of steel are Germany, Italy, France, and Poland. Great Britain no longer ranks in the top ten.

While stagnation has characterized much of the world's iron and steel industry in recent years, several

This steel bridge in Trenton, New Jersey, reflects an earlier time when the city's steel industry and export business were more prosperous than they have been since the 1960s. (Trentonian Collection/ Trenton Public Library)

less developed countries have experienced such growth that they are now among the major producers. China is the leading producer in the less developed world, but it is not yet an exporter. Brazil and South Korea, also among the world's leading producers, have become major exporters of steel. Brazil's iron ore deposits are so rich that the country's future as a producer and exporter probably is assured, even though coking coal has to be imported. South Korea has to import both iron ore and coking coal for its industry, but nevertheless has become the world's newest major exporter.

Pittsburgh, Pennsylvania, was the first city to become prominent in the U.S. iron and steel industry. By the middle of the nineteenth century, the excellent coking properties of Pittsburgh coal and the discovery of small local deposits of iron ore had laid the foundations for the establishment of the industry there. For more than half a century following the end of the Civil War, Pittsburgh dominated the industry. By the early part of the twentieth century, however, the Midwest had become the major market for steel, in large part because of the concentration of the automobile industry in Detroit. The first large iron and steel mill went into operation in Chicago, Illinois, in 1911, and the industry began its development on the shore of Lake Erie (Detroit, Michigan; Cleveland, Ohio; and Buffalo, New York) soon thereafter. During the period between World Wars I and II, the middle Atlantic seaboard (Bethlehem, Pennsylvania; Trenton, New Jersey; Baltimore, Maryland) became an attractive area for steelmaking. World War II generated such a huge

demand for steel that the industry grew rapidly in all producing areas and expanded into new regions.

When recession hit the iron and steel industry in the 1970s, U.S. producers began a retrenchment, although they did not fare as badly as producers in Western Europe. Like British and European concerns, U.S. steel manufacturers had not aggressively adopted efficient new technologies during the 1960s, despite their overcapacity to produce. Overcapacity itself was a problem when the energy crisis prompted the recession, because there was too much steel and there were

The recession in the iron and steel industry of the United States following the 1960s led to the closing of this mill in Pennsylvania and many others in the Northeast. (Cary Wolinsky/Stock Boston)

too few buyers. In 1970 the United States produced more than 130 million tons of steel. By 1975 production was down to 116 million tons, and a decade later it was less than 90 million tons. During the same period, 1975–1985, employment in the industry declined by more than half, from more than 350,000 to about 150,000 jobs. Despite some improvements during the 1980s, in part associated with Japanese investments in the U.S. iron and steel industry, overcapacity and technological backwardness still characterized the industry at the beginning of the 1990s. After losing billions of dollars in the early and middle 1980s, however, the industry became profitable again by 1990 as a result of reduction in production costs. The challenge for the rest of the 1990s will be to try to achieve the high efficiency standards of the steel industry of Japan, now the leading exporter. Steel analysts, however, are uncertain about the future performance of U.S. steelmakers relative to those of Japan and South Korea.

High-Tech Industries

➤ Highly developed countries have high-tech industries that create products in the forefront of science.

Which industries might properly be described as high-tech?

What has been their relationship to the history of space exploration?

Which two developed countries are most rapidly advancing the frontiers of high technology at present?

Modern industries that place a great deal of emphasis on research and development (R&D) include in their workforces a high proportion of scientists and engineers, and create products in the forefront of science are identified as **high-tech industries**. High technology is "space-age" technology because it is associated closely with the development of space exploration. The human desire to understand the universe put artificial satellites in orbit, sent spacecraft to the outer limits of the solar system and beyond, and put humans on the moon—all of which required a higher order of technology than existed before the late 1950s. The desire for better military preparedness during the Cold War also spurred the development of new technology, which was required to launch and aim intelligence satellites and to target warheads accurately.

In addition to accomplishing extraordinary space feats and contributing to frightening military capabilities, high technology resulted in many benefits to mankind as inventions developed for space and military applications were adapted to more mundane uses. Digital electronics, for example, have been applied to everything from microwave ovens to automobile speedometers, and laser technology has found uses in such disparate areas as delicate surgeries and commercial security systems. Although one is tempted to be frustrated with the glitches and hassles computers offer, it is difficult to imagine life without them. Computers are able to accomplish certain work tasks millions of times faster than a human can. There are other high-tech industries, such as the aerospace industry and biotechnology, but we will focus on computers and the semiconductors on which computers and other modern electronic equipment are based. Like other high-tech enterprises, the computer industry is limited largely to the most highly developed economies, especially those of the United States, Western Europe, and Japan.

The era of microelectronics began with the introduction of the transistor in 1948. In the early 1950s two U.S. companies, Remington Rand and International Business Machines (IBM), were marketing commercial mainframe data-processing computers. By 1960, IBM, which had introduced faster transistor technology the previous year, was the clear leader in the computer field. IBM's dominance of the large-computer industry would continue into the 1990s. In 1990 about two-thirds of the mainframe computers sold worldwide were IBMs. The large size of IBM and the location of its headquarters (Fig. 11.26) in a suburb of New York City gives the state of New York dominance among U.S. states in the manufacture of mainframe computers. Very costly research programs are underway in the United States and Japan to develop supercomputers possessing artificial intelligence—the ability of computers to program themselves and make logical, knowledge-based inferences. Already there are mainframe computers that can carry out an astronomical 100 million operations per second.

Intermediate in size and capability are minicomputers, used primarily for administrative and management applications and inventory control in industry. Although New York leads in the manufacture of mainframe computers, the U.S. minicomputer industry is concentrated in Massachusetts, especially in the Bos-

FIGURE 11.26

The headquarters of IBM, the giant American firm that has dominated the history of computers and semiconductors. (Gamma Liaison)

The emergence of Silicon Valley in California as a center of high-tech industries has been accompanied by a boom in new construction and massive traffic congestion. (Frank Wing/ Stock Boston)

ton metropolitan area. The industry has close R&D ties to the Massachusetts Institute of Technology. No single manufacturer dominates the minicomputer industry as IBM does with mainframes.

The computers familiar to most people today are microcomputers, or personal computers, such as the IBM-PC and the Apple Macintosh. During the 1970s microcomputers were used primarily by industries, large businesses, and government agencies, but by the 1980s they had become so inexpensive that a substantial school, small business, and home market developed. In 1985 the microcomputers surpassed the mainframes in the value of units sold. More than a dozen major manufacturers share the market. Among the most highly respected microcomputers are those made by IBM, a fact that has resulted in the marketing of hardware and software by many other manufacturers that are advertised as being "IBM compatible."

Closely tied to the computer industry is the semiconductor industry. Without semiconductors, computers would have no memory. The computer industry provides the market for about half of the semiconductors sold. Numerous other products, however, also require the memory storage that semiconductors can provide—products such as automobile electronics, digital watches, calculators, cash registers, automatic tellers, industrial robots, and even electronic toys. A semiconductor is a tiny silicon "chip" on which an integrated circuit of diodes, resistors, transistors, and capacitors are manufactured. The assembly of these

microelectronic components requires exacting quality control in a facility free of dust and other contaminants.

The semiconductor industry of the United States was born in *Silicon Valley*, a name popularly given to Santa Clara County in California. The Valley includes more than a dozen cities, including Palo Alto—the home of Stanford University—and San Jose, noted for its high-tech workforce. Scores of high-technology companies are sprinkled throughout Santa Clara County. They include not only manufacturers of semiconductors but companies that make computers, peripheral equipment (such as disk drives, modems, and printers), military electronics, and aerospace equipment. The rapid growth of Silicon Valley raised local housing prices so greatly that decentralization of the industry began early in the 1980s into other parts of California and neighboring states. During the same period the semiconductor industry of Japan was experiencing phenomenal growth.

Catching up with the U.S. electronics industry was established as Japanese government policy in the late 1950s, and IBM, specifically, became the major target of the electronics industry of Japan. The government, which controlled bank lending, allocated Japan's then-scarce capital to companies it chose as its champions in this computer race. In the early 1970s, the computer war became a semiconductor war. The government organized major electronics companies into consortia charged with research aimed at leapfrogging the United States in the manufacture of semi-conductors.

By 1979 U.S. companies could not satisfy the large domestic and European demand for chips, and Japan stepped in with semiconductors of very high quality. Supported and backed by their government, Japanese companies started "dumping" chips on the U.S. market—selling them below cost in an effort to capture customers. To the Japanese this was good business, but dumping is illegal in the United States, and in 1980 U.S. producers threatened lawsuits. It was not possible, however, for the U.S. companies to compete successfully. They were mostly small companies far more dependent on semiconductors as a percentage of total business than the Japanese corporations. They also lacked the government backing that manufacturers in Japan enjoyed. By several measures, including total investment in the industry and R&D spending, Japan surpassed the United States in 1984.

Perhaps expecting to duplicate what the Japanese government had done in the late 1950s, the federal government of the United States in 1988 formed a consortium with 14 domestic manufacturers of semiconductors to take the steps necessary to assure that the United States would remain a world leader in chip technology. Spurred by the fact that the United States had been "losing its chips" for many years, this consortium—the Semiconductor Manufacturing Technology Institute (Sematech)—set about arranging research financing for the flagging but still-important industry. In 1990, however, Japan was investing twice as much in semiconductor R&D.

LIVELIHOODS IN SERVICE ACTIVITIES

➤ The service sector is far more important in the economy of developed countries than it is in that of less developed countries.

What are tertiary activities?

What is their relationship to central places?

In Chapter 10 we defined the *service sector* of an economy as including those activities associated with government, education, transportation, communications, banking, insurance, wholesaling, retailing, and similar services. Furthermore, we noted that the service sector of the economies of less developed countries lags far behind that of developed countries. The various activities of the service sector are *tertiary activities*. That

Law enforcement is one of many service activities that make up the tertiary sector of an economy. (Natsuko Utsumi/ Gamma Liaison)

is, they are economic pursuits that do not qualify as primary activities (the harvesting of naturally produced commodities) or as secondary activities (the conversion of raw materials into commodities of higher value). Each tertiary activity is a spatial variable that can be mapped and studied independently. There is a tendency, however, for service activities to agglomerate. Barber shops, law offices, clothing stores, post offices, libraries, dry cleaning establishments, and parking garages all tend to be located in the same general areas. Specifically, tertiary activities are functions of *central places*, or agglomerations of population. The larger the central place, the greater the number of service activities available. A hamlet may have only one business—a gasoline station, for example. A metropolis, on the other hand, may contain thousands of service establishments. Although service activities tend to agglomerate, the economic life of central places usually does not consist solely of such enterprises. Primary and secondary economic activities, especially secondary activities, also are important in many communities. We will examine two service activities—government and international trade—as examples of the significance of tertiary activities in the economies of the developed nations of the world.

Government

➤ Government at all levels is a major industry and most often the largest employer in both the developed and less developed countries.

In what areas of the economy in developed countries is government involved?

Where is much of the government employment located?

In the developed countries, what role does government often play in transportation, agriculture, industry, and energy production?

One of the largest industries—and for a long time, the most rapidly growing—is government. In economies at all levels of development the central government is usually the largest employer by far. Government employment rolls are particularly large in nations considered "welfare states"—countries having well-developed government programs of social assistance, such as Australia, New Zealand, and the Scandinavian countries. In some countries more than a fourth of all civilian employees work for the central government. In the United States the share of government employment is considerably lower; even so, in 1990 about 3 million people, including military personnel (or about 2 million, excluding people in the military), were on the payroll of the U.S. government. Only a small proportion of total government employment in the United States and other developed countries is involved directly in the administration of bureaus and agencies. By far the larger share consists of postal workers, health personnel, law enforcement agents, inspectors, park rangers, educators, and workers in other areas of central government responsibility.

The apparent tendency of central governments to enlarge the number and variety of their activities is the subject of **Wagner's Law**, formulated as early as 1876 by a German economist. This theory holds that the encroachments of the state will progressively reduce the field of private economic activity. It could be argued that the nineteenth-century *laissez-faire* (the policy of nonintervention by government in economic affairs) was just an interlude, and Wagner's Law is the normal process by which governments operate. Excluding what happened in centrally planned economies during most of the twentieth century, it is easy to provide examples of burgeoning government bureaucracies in capitalist economies. The government of the United States, for example, enlarged its areas of responsibility dramatically following the 1932 election of President Franklin D. Roosevelt (1882–1945). It is doubtful, however, that expansion of the scope of state interest in free-market economies has materially

reduced the scope for private enterprise. For the most part, new services provided by government are those for which the expectation of return on capital is too low to be attractive to private enterprise.

The distribution of tertiary activities reflects the general distribution of population, but this is not true of the service activities provided by central governments. Except for post offices and other agency offices that cater to local populations, the service activities of national governments tend to be highly centralized with a large proportion usually concentrated in the national capital. In many nations, the capital is not only the center of government activity but also the largest city and major center of commercial and industrial enterprise. This is true, for example, of most of the capitals of Europe. In other developed countries, government is the principal activity of the capital, which may not be the largest city and may have little industry. The United States and Australia are two examples. Both of these capitals, Washington, D.C., and Canberra (Fig. 11.27), have relatively little industry, and a large proportion of the workforce in both is employed by the government. Although there are some good reasons for the concentration of government, excessive centralization also can result in problems.

The functions of central governments are manifold and are likely to involve a broad range of eco-

FIGURE 11.27
Canberra, the capital of Australia. This city, like Washington, DC, has little industry, and a large proportion of the labor force is employed in government. (Peter Menzel/Stock Boston)

nomic enterprises. For example, a central government may assume responsibilities regarding transportation and freight rates, agricultural production and marketing, industrial production, and the generation and sale of energy.

One of the first areas of the domestic economy in which both the United States and Canadian governments became involved was the regulation of transport and, especially, of the freight rates charged by canal and riverboat lines and railroads. As their nineteenth-century frontiers expanded westward, it was considered important by the governments of these countries to protect the interests of the people and the state against unfair business practices. The United States created the Interstate Commerce Commission in 1887, and 15 years later the Canadian government established a Board of Railway Commissioners. These agencies endeavored to prevent monopolies and ensure efficient service. As time went by, government regulation was extended to new modes of transport—pipelines and airlines. This trend was reversed in the late 1970s and 1980s, when deregulation became the U.S. government's approach not only to transportation but also to communications. The withdrawal of certain government restrictions on railroads reflected the fact that the nation's railroads were no longer a powerful force that had to be controlled, but a weakened industry that needed assistance.

CONRAIL trains in the railyards at Rochester, New York. CONRAIL was a result of railroad deregulation by the federal government in 1976; the nation's railroads were no longer a powerful business that had to be controlled, but a weakened industry that needed assistance. (Tom Pollak/Gamma Liaison)

Almost every national government assumes some responsibility for overseeing the production and marketing of agricultural commodities. The large-scale nineteenth-century disposal of public lands in the United States and Canada was, in part, for the purpose of facilitating the agricultural development of those nations. The U.S. Department of Agriculture (USDA) was established in 1862, the same year that Congress passed the Homestead Act. From these beginnings, government involvement in agriculture expanded to experimental farms, on-farm assistance, and the publication of a vast array of literature to aid farmers. During the economic depression of the 1930s, the governments of the United States and Canada sought to rescue farmers by means of various schemes, including direct payments to farmers to plant particular crops. Quotas were imposed on the amount of land farmers could use for certain crops, and farmers were guaranteed minimum prices for crops cultivated on assigned acreage. This approach was intended to reduce surpluses that Anglo-American farmers had been producing. Surpluses continued to pile up, however, because of a rise in agricultural productivity; that is, farmers were producing more commodities on less land. Large-scale overproduction during the 1950s led to adoption of the "soil bank"; the government paid farmers to take land out of production. The U.S. Food Security Act of 1985 provided an ambitious and very successful new program that offered government payments to farmers for retiring highly erodible land. Since the 1930s, therefore, the governments of the United States and Canada have been very much involved in agriculture.

Central governments get involved not only in primary production but also in secondary production, through control and protection. Controls are viewed by governments as necessary to prevent monopolies and to protect workers and consumers. Both the United States and Canada have antitrust legislation to prevent monopolies that would not serve the public interest. Both countries also have legislation regarding health and safety standards in factories, and regulations about product safety. Likewise, both nations have environmental laws that place certain restrictions on manufacturing industries. The most important impact of government on industry, however, may be its role as a customer. The U.S. Department of Defense alone purchases goods and services valued at more than $200 billion a year.

In addition to their self-appointed responsibilities in regulating transportation, agriculture, and industry, governments are involved in the production and marketing of energy. In 1990 neither the United States nor Canada had a comprehensive energy policy, but the governments of both were regulating various energy industries. Oil and natural gas have been regulated for many years. Central goverment taxes on gasoline provide revenues that can be used by the government for highway construction. Numerous government regulations affect the coal industry. For example, coal cannot be mined by the open-pit method without subsequent land reclamation (filling the pit, replacing the soil, and planting vegetation) by the coal company. Such laws are in the public interest, so most people agree that their government is performing a public service in passing and enforcing them.

Subnational governments also engage in service activities. In large countries subnational governments are those that operate at the state (or provincial) level and at the local level. The state is the highest order of subnational government in the United States, and the province is the highest order of subnational government in Canada. Governments at this level often have responsibilities in highway construction, law enforcement, and education. In the United States, for example, almost every state has a highway department, state police, and one or more state universities. State support of precollegiate education also is common. Local governments operate at one or more levels, depending on the political organization of a country. Most U.S. states are subdivided into counties, each of which has its own government. One community in each county typically serves as the *county seat*, the focus of governmental activities at the county level. Those activities usually include road maintenance, law enforcement, and education. Local schools in the United States are primarily the responsibility of the county in which they are located. Except for some hamlets and some small villages, most communities have local governments, and the number of their functions increases with the size of the community. Some villages may have no paid employees except the mayor, whose responsibilities are so few that he or she may receive only a token salary. Large cities, on the other hand, may have thousands of people on their payrolls. Garbage collecting, fire fighting, and police work are common government occupations at the local level in towns and cities.

International Trade

➤ International trade is a tertiary activity of great significance that throughout history has involved the dominant civilizations and countries of the world.

What elements of a country's economy are involved in the conduct of international trade?

What nations are the world's leading importers and exporters?

No nation, we have seen, is self-sufficient in all of the requirements of modern life. Some countries lack critical raw materials. Others are unable to satisfy their own requirements in agricultural commodities, and many countries do not have sufficient energy resources to meet their needs. International trade, therefore, is of such significance that it is worth being singled out for special consideration as a tertiary activity. It is a service activity that is performed by producers, transportation carriers, and governments. Without producers, there would be nothing to export and import; producers are very much involved in the arrangements that lead to exports. Without the transportation industry, goods would not move from areas of surpluses to areas of need. Without governments, there would be international commerce, but it would be unregulated and not always in the public interest.

International trade dates to the earliest civilizations, but even in prehistoric times the exchange of

International trade, a major tertiary activity, is the lifeblood of most national economies. The shipping underway here is at "Worldport," the port of Los Angeles. (Jean-Marc Giboux/ Gamma Liaison)

goods between tribes was common. Long-distance trade was carried on by caravan over desert routes, notably between the ancient civilizations of Mesopotamia and Egypt. The Phoenicians, operating from the eastern shores of the Mediterranean Sea, were the first people to develop a seaborne trade with supplementary overland routes. They became the great merchant sailors of the ancient world, dominating Mediterranean trade for a thousand years. Later the Greeks introduced the use of money into commerce, which until then was conducted by barter. The Romans were not seafarers, but their commerce expanded greatly following their conquest of Greece. For the first time, large quantities of high-bulk, low-value goods (such as grain) were moved long distances to satisfy the requirements of Rome. International trade stagnated during the Middle Ages, even though it was during this period that modern banking and bookkeeping methods were developed in Venice and other Italian cities.

The great discoveries of fifteenth- and sixteenth-century voyages of exploration opened new areas for international commerce. Spain, Portugal, England, France, and Holland acquired and colonized vast tracts of territory around the world. This colonialism facilitated **mercantilism**, an economic policy that prevailed in Europe from the sixteenth through eighteenth centuries. Under mercantilism, government control was exercised over industry and trade in accordance with the theory that national strength is increased by a preponderance of exports over imports. In particular, European powers were interested in importing precious metals and raw materials from their colonies and exporting finished goods to them. Mercantilism was followed by the *free-trade system* in the nineteenth century. Free trade meant that governments were involved in commerce only to the extent of assuring free markets. The revival of mercantilist philosophy, or *neomercantilism*, began early in the twentieth century as governments began clamping new controls on trade to protect their own national interests.

World War I and, particularly, World War II greatly affected the character, distribution, and volume of international trade. The major defeated nations—Germany, Italy, and Japan—were virtually eliminated from world trade for a short while after World War II. The former West Germany eventually achieved an important position in world markets during the 1950s and Japan in the 1960s. The positions of the victor nations also changed. The United States rose to the leading position in international trade, and Great Britain lost its long-standing lead. France also declined as an international economic force.

Western Europe and Anglo-America now account for about two-thirds of the world's international trade. Of the ten leading nations in value of imports, all but Japan are included in those two world regions. Of the ten leading exporting nations, by value, only Japan and Hong Kong are not part of them.

At the start of the 1990s, the United States was the world's largest importer of goods by far; the value of U.S. imports in 1990 was close to half a trillion dollars. The imported goods included machinery and transportation equipment (45 percent of total imports), other manufactured products (30 percent), fossil fuels (9 percent), food and livestock (5 percent), chemicals (5 percent), and other items (6 percent). Other nations importing over $100 billion (U.S.) worth of goods in 1990 were, in descending order, Germany, the United Kingdom, Japan, and Italy. Petroleum was high on the import list of all of those countries.

The United States is no longer the world's number one exporter of goods. That position was occupied by Germany in 1990, but third-ranked Japan was rapidly catching up with Germany and the United States (in second place). Other countries exporting goods with total values in excess of $100 billion (U.S.) were France, the United Kingdom, and Italy.

Goods exported by the United States in 1990 included machinery and transportation equipment (44 percent), chemicals (10 percent), food and livestock (9 percent), crude materials other than fuels (9 percent), other manufactured goods (7 percent), mineral fuels (3 percent), and other items (18 percent). The ten major industrial suppliers of U.S. exports in 1990 were, in descending order, General Motors, Ford, Boeing, General Electric, IBM, Chrysler, DuPont, McDonnell Douglas, and Caterpillar. Agricultural commodities do not rank high among U.S. exports, but their total value more than doubled during the 1980s, in part because of the sale of grain to the Soviet Union.

The biggest success story in international trade in recent years is that of Japan. A major element of that country's spectacular economic accomplishment has been its international trade. By protecting its domestic markets while flooding the world market with high-quality products, Japan has maintained a favorable balance of trade; that is, the value of its exports exceeds that of its imports. As Japan developed a healthy trade balance, that of the United States slipped to the point that by 1990 U.S. imports greatly exceeded exports.

PROSPECTS FOR
THE DEVELOPED COUNTRIES

➤ The future for developed countries is far brighter than that faced by the less developed countries, but serious problems confront the developed world.

What are some problems of the developed world, and what can be done to alleviate them?

To what extent do each of these problems affect the United States?

In examining the prospects for the future of the less developed countries it is difficult for us to be optimistic because of the magnitude of some of the problems confronting the people of the developing world. Serious problems also exist in the developed world, and some of them are examined in this section. Such problems have the potential, if worsened sufficiently, to send economies into tailspins and cripple national and international orders. However, the people of the developed countries possess the physical and human resources to nullify the effect of these problems and, in some cases, to turn them into opportunities. Whether or not they will use their resources successfully to overcome their problems remains to be seen. Cornucopians, most of whom are economists, as we have mentioned, are those who believe that technological advances will more than keep pace with population growth and will lead to a future in which people will be healthier, live longer, and have greater material prosperity. We indicated that the cornucopian view may have greater applicability to the developed than to the less developed world. Not all scholars, however, are as optimistic as the cornucopians.

The Rusting of
Industrial Heartlands

In order to maximize immediate profits by getting the most out of infrastructure that is already in place and already paid for, some industries avoid investments in the latest technology. Competitors, often in other countries, who do invest in technologically advanced production facilities eventually are more successful in the marketplace. Old plants and sometimes even entire industrial districts cease to be competitive and begin to suffer. Plants may close and unemployment results. Outmoded equipment not sold for scrap rusts in place. "Rust Belts" develop in older industrial cores whose

factories have not kept abreast of new developments. The best example may be the iron and steel industry of the United States and Western Europe, which declined with the rise of the iron and steel industry in Japan and South Korea, where more efficient technologies were adopted. Besides the conservatism of management—their slowness to invest in more efficient production facilities—an industrial area may decline for other reasons. The old producing area may lose its resource advantage, for example, as local resources are exhausted. Also, labor may be much cheaper in the new producing areas. Whatever the reason or combination of reasons, old industrial heartlands often develop into Rust Belts. Portions of the U.S. Manufacturing Belt, several industrial districts in Great Britain and Germany, and other old manufacturing regions have become Rust Belts.

Associated with shrinking employment in manufacturing, especially in heavy industry, has been an expansion of the service sector of the economies of many long-industrialized countries. That is, there are fewer blue-collar jobs and more white-collar jobs in these countries. The term **post-industrial society** has been used to describe such countries. There are many unanswered questions about the future of post-industrial societies. Will they be able to maintain their industrial importance with lightly staffed, highly automated factories? Can they provide an adequate supply of exports to support a healthy balance of international trade? Can service jobs be expanded rapidly enough to supply adequate employment in the face of declining industrial employment? Can service jobs provide sufficient income to support those who hold them? The answers to these questions will go far toward determining the future of many Western democracies.

Financial Systems in Distress

At the beginning of the 1990s, national financial systems were in an unfortunate state of serious distress. In the less developed nations, the principal problem was foreign debt, a difficulty examined in earlier chapters. In the developed world, serious financial problems were manifold, but indebtedness was foremost among them. The governments of the developed countries take in vast sums of money, mostly in the form of taxes, but they have a way of spending more than they receive from their citizens; in other words, they indulge in deficit spending. For the most part, these countries become indebted the same way that people do—by buying on credit and borrowing money. During the 1980s, deficit spending in the United States amounted to an average of more than $200 billion annually. In 1990 the U.S. national debt exceeded $3 trillion, or more than $12,000 per capita. The interest on the national debt accounted for more than 20 percent of the federal budget in 1990. Many other developed nations also were suffering the consequences of serious debt as the 1990s began, but none was as afflicted by debt as the United States.

The United States had another serious financial problem during the 1980s and into the 1990s. More than 1100 savings and loan associations were closed or merged during the 1980s, mostly because of mismanagement. At the beginning of the 1990s, hundreds of others were insolvent (i.e., their obligations exceeded their assets). In 1989 Congress passed legislation to rescue the savings and loan industry. The bill Congress passed provided $166 billion over ten years to close or merge savings and loan associations. By 1992 it was clear that the total cost of rescuing and restructuring the industry might be as much as a trillion dollars over 50 years, most of which would be paid by taxpayers. The savings and loan crisis made it all the more difficult for the United States to overcome its problem of national debt.

Cultural Plurality

Although cultural heterogeneity can be a good thing, adding to the richness of a nation's heritage, it also can lead to social conflict. Most such conflicts occur in the less developed world, but the developed world also provides examples of *plural societies* with disparate interests that sometimes lead to turmoil. The United States, Canada, and the former Soviet Union provide good examples.

The large cities of the United States particularly reflect the country's plural society. New York City's population is about 55 percent white, 24 percent black, and 20 percent Hispanic. The population of Atlanta is approximately 67 percent black, 32 percent white, and 1 percent Hispanic. Miami's population is about 44 percent white, 38 percent Hispanic, and 17 percent black. Large Asian minorities live in Honolulu, Los Angeles, San Francisco, and New York City. In part because of the civil rights movement led and inspired by Martin Luther King, Jr. (1929–1968), much progress was made in unifying the people of the United States. More than two decades after his tragic

murder, however, unfortunate incidents of racial and ethnic discord still occur in this country. Although people disagree about whether these incidents threaten the foundation of American society, most people agree that they are intolerable. The 1990s can be a decade during which the citizens of the United States can help make King's dream come true, or it can be a decade of worsening difficulties. The outcome will depend on the willingness of individuals to abandon racial prejudice and show respect for fellow Americans and, indeed, for all people.

Canada presents a dramatic example of cultural dualism that has led to conflict. As we noted in Chapter 4, more than two-thirds of the people in Quebec speak French as their preferred language. Quebec is the only Canadian province in which French speakers predominate and control the provincial government. In the neighboring province of Ontario, by contrast, more than three-fourths of the people speak English as their first language. These language and other cultural differences have resulted in major political frictions. Dissatisfaction among French Canadians arose after World War II, and soon developed into open hostility, because Quebec's population began to decline as a percentage of Canada's total population, and this decline was perceived as a threat to the French culture and heritage of the region. In the 1960s a separatist political party developed in Quebec and grew rapidly. The Quebec Party advocated the secession from Canada of an independent Quebec, and in 1976 the party achieved power within the provincial government. Although the separatist party has not maintained uninterrupted control of the provincial government, the separatist movement is still alive and well (Fig. 11.28). The central government has made certain concessions to Quebec, and these have weakened the position of the government in dealing with similar demands from other provinces. The end of this cultural-political struggle probably has not been reached, but fortunately this is a struggle that can be resolved peacefully, if not quickly, and there is little likelihood of armed conflict.

Armed conflict is not altogether unlikely, however, in the clash of cultures in the former Soviet Union. During the Cold War, government leaders in the Soviet Union often pointed out the racial problems of the United States, when in fact the Soviet Union was beset with cultural conflicts of perhaps far greater magnitude. In Chapter 5 we discussed the factors that led to the break-up of the Soviet Union. In general,

FIGURE 11.28
Proud of their heritage, many French-Canadians in Quebec Province favor independence from the rest of Canada. (Gamma Liaison)

the new republics are each more culturally homogeneous than was the Soviet Union. Still, considerable cultural plurality remains in several, especially in Russia. Cultural complexities, coupled with severe economic problems, virtually ensure continuing difficulties in this region for the rest of the century. By 1993 civil war already was raging in Georgia and Tajikistan, and an international conflict had erupted between Armenia and Azerbaijan.

Converting to a Peaceful Economy

The major reason that the United States had such a huge national debt and the people of the former Soviet Union are deprived of many of the amenities of life found in most developed countries is that both countries during the Cold War invested such large portions of their national budgets in defense. The Cold War that gripped the planet for almost half a century began to thaw in 1989, the year that witnessed the demolition of the Berlin Wall. Within months of that historic event, most of the countries of Eastern Europe rejected communism—possibly because of the Soviet Union's venture into *glasnost* and *perestroika*. As a result of arms control and disarmament treaties, the United States and the Soviet Union were destroying major weapons systems in 1990. These events presented a remarkable opportunity to redirect priorities. Government leaders in both the United States and the Soviet Union took steps to scale down military spending.

Then, late in 1991, the break-up of the Soviet Union further enhanced the possibility of decreased militarism.

Converting a great deal of society's productive wealth from military to civilian use is an ambitious undertaking. Government leaders attempting it realize that changing world events can thwart their efforts. For example, as the U.S. Congress was endeavoring to rein in military spending in 1990, Iraqi strongman Saddam Hussein sent an army of tanks rolling into Kuwait, initiating the Persian Gulf War of 1991. Massive U.S. military spending was involved in Operation Desert Shield (to prevent additional Iraqi expansionism) and Operation Desert Storm (to force the Iraqi military to withdraw from Kuwait). Converting to peaceful economies, however, should present no insurmountable problems. The major barriers are not technical but political, ranging from the power and agendas of vested interests to the widespread misconception that military spending makes good economic sense. Local economic hardships cannot be avoided and already have been experienced. The closing of U.S. military bases (Fig. 11.29) adversely affects the economies of nearby communities. Some of the former Soviet republics, which long faced a crippling housing shortage, cannot provide adequate shelter for former military personnel who have returned to civilian life.

The conversion from military to peaceful economies can become an instrument of social transforma-

FIGURE 11.29
Military vehicles at Fort Hood, Texas. Fort Hood was one of many military bases in the United States that faced downsizing in the early 1990s. (Daemmrich/Stock Boston)

tion and economic renewal. By freeing resources and providing a planning mechanism for their alternative use, conversion can be an essential component of attempts to reverse industrial decay and revitalize the civilian economy. There is no question that the world's armies and military industries will remain large, and no doubt wars will occur in the future as they have for the entire history of humankind. It is hoped, however, that the 1990s will be a decade in which progress can be made in channeling resources into social and economic revitalization and environmental restoration.

KEY TERMS

Women's movement   A loosely coordinated effort to protect the rights and improve the status of women.   **401**

Animal husbandry   The raising of and caring for domesticated animals as an economic activity.   **403**

Mixed farming   A type of farming in which both crops and livestock are raised.   **404**

U.S. Corn Belt   A highly productive agricultural region of the United States that emphasizes the production of grain crops, especially corn and soybeans, and livestock.   **405**

Commercial grain farming   A type of farming typically devoted to the large-scale production of a single grain crop for sale. Also known as cash grain farming.   **408**

Specialty agriculture   A type of commercial farming focused on production of specialty crops rather than major food grains.   **410**

Mediterranean agriculture   A variant of specialty agriculture that is distinguished by a combination of crops raised in all regions of Mediterranean climate.   **410**

Industrial location factors   An assortment of factors that influence where manufacturing establishments are located.   **423**

Manufacturing belts   Zones or regions containing high concentrations of manufacturing activities.   **423**

High-tech industries   Those industries engaged in the development and manufacture of the most technically sophisticated industrial products, such as computers and robots.   **428**

Wagner's Law   A theory, promulgated by a German economist named Adolph Wagner, that governments progressively assume responsibility for the economic welfare of their citizens and thereby diminish the role of the private sector.   **431**

Mercantilism   An economic policy of the major trading nations in Europe during the sixteenth through eighteenth centuries. It was based on the theory that national strength is attained by increasing exports of finished goods and imports of raw materials and precious metals.   **434**

Post-industrial society   A stage of development reached by a society or country when service activities exceed manufacturing in economic importance and as a source of employment.   **435**

REVIEW QUESTIONS

1. What are some of the major differences between modern industrial societies and traditional agrarian societies?

2. To what extent has the women's movement brought change in the developed countries? Why do many people of both sexes feel that the women's movement still has important work to do?

3. What is animal husbandry? What is the carrying capacity of land? What is a milkshed?

4. What is mixed farming, and how is the U.S. Corn Belt a good example of this kind of agriculture?

5. What is the difference between winter wheat and spring wheat? Which is raised in each of the three major wheat-producing districts of North America?

6. What metal ores are the "big three"—the mainstay of the metals industry? Which developed countries are the leading producers of each?

7. Why are highly industrialized countries more dependent on petroleum than the less developed countries? Which three developed countries are among the world's ten leading producers of oil?

8. Which developed nation is the world's leading producer of nuclear electric power? Approximately how many nuclear power plants are in that country? How many exist in the world?

9. In what ways does manufacturing in the developed world differ from manufacturing in the less developed countries?

10. How is the iron and steel industry of "unparalleled importance" to the manufacturing economies of the developed world?

11. What factors help explain the decline in the world's iron and steel industry after 1974?

12. Where is Silicon Valley, and why is it important?

13. How do Wagner's Law and *laissez-faire* relate to the role of governments in providing services?

14. What are the roles of subnational governments in the service sector of developed economies?

15. What is neomercantilism?

16. What do the cornucopians believe about the future of the world?

17. Why do Rust Belts develop in industrial heartlands?

18. What are post-industrial societies, and why do they face uncertain futures?

19. What is the "savings and loan crisis" in the United States? What caused it? How has it affected deficit spending?

AN INTERVIEW WITH STEVEN P. NORMAN, PEACE CORPS VOLUNTEER

Steven P. Norman *While serving as a Peace Corps volunteer from 1991 to 1993, geographer Steven P. Norman worked with rural farmers in Costa Rica, Central America, to discourage deforestation and promote sustainable land uses. By providing technical assistance for seed selection, planting, and pesticide use, he helped prevent further stress to Costa Rica's environment.*

Born May 10, 1965, Mr. Norman spent his childhood on a farm near the small town of Liberty, Pennsylvania. In 1991, he earned a master's degree in geography from Western Illinois University, Macomb. His graduate thesis traced changes in the forest cover of McDonough County, Illinois.

In addition to his service in the Peace Corps, Mr. Norman has served as a forestry intern for the Pennsylvania Bureau of Forestry and as a soil conservation intern for the U.S. Soil Conservation Service. Most

What prompted you to join the Peace Corps?

After finishing my graduate thesis, I needed a break from academia. I had always wanted to know about other places and to experience other cultures in the world. Working for the Peace Corps allowed me to immerse myself in another culture in a relatively safe way, because the Peace Corps provides insurance, survival money, and other support.

I had seen Peace Corps advertisements, but I did not have any close friends who had been in the program. Ultimately, it was the reputation of the Peace Corps that prompted me to consider it. When the Peace Corps assigned me to work with Costa Rican farmers, I drew on my experiences from growing up on a farm.

Your Peace Corps training involved three months of classroom and field instruction in Spanish, forestry techniques, and cross-cultural adaptation skills. Tell me about that experience.

Some people thought the training was very rigorous. Personally, I loved living in a foreign culture where virtually no one spoke English. From the time I was very young, I wanted to learn another language, and the Peace Corps provides top-of-the-line language instruction.

During the training period, I lived with a middle-class Spanish-speaking family. The four children ranged in age from 5 to 18, and I shared a

recently, he worked as a cartographer for the North-central Pennsylvania Conservancy, where he prepared maps for analysis of wetland conservation strategies.

room with one of the teenagers. It was the most wonderful family in the world! They opened up to me right away, giving me complete access to their home and to their lives.

They were extremely clean people, but a funny thing happened on my first day with them. A door of the house had been left open because the mother was cooking and the kitchen was hot. While the mother had her back turned, a chicken walked right into the house, jumped onto the stove, and proceeded to eat rice straight from the pot! Soon the pot, rice, and chicken were on the floor. Although the mother was horrified, we all laughed about it later.

After I had completed my training, I moved to the Osa Peninsula of Costa Rica to begin my assignment. For the first seven months, I stayed with a young cattle farmer and his wife and small child. Later, I used palm fronds and palm thatch to build myself a little hut in the woods, next to the Golfo Dulce Forest Reserve, surrounding Corcovado National Park.

Please describe the region where you worked.

Costa Rica is located in Central America, between Panama and Nicaragua. It is a small, mountainous country, about the size of West Virginia. The region is geologically active, with a number of volcanoes that rumble and shoot ash. Earthquakes are quite common.

In Costa Rica, the land's elevation ranges from sea level to 12,500 feet within a very short distance. Farmers grow coffee, beans, and corn on these steep slopes. Because the region receives so much rainfall, serious soil erosion results when the nat-

> "I had always wanted to know about other places and to experience other cultures in the world. Working for the Peace Corps allowed me to immerse myself in another culture in a relatively safe way, because the Peace Corps provides insurance, survival money, and other support."

ural forest is cleared.

The Osa Peninsula is covered by classic rainforest that receives about 15 feet of rain each year. The climate is marked by a short dry season, followed by heavy rainfall. On the peninsula, the Golfo Dulce Forest Reserve was established adjacent to the Corcovado National Park to protect it.

How have settlement and land-use patterns contributed to environmental problems on Osa Peninsula?

Because the Osa Peninsula is bordered by water on three sides, settlement on it was limited for many years, but in the late 1970s, a road was built, making the region more accessible. Soon, poor farmers who had nowhere else to go decided to move there, and they began to clear the land.

Yet it was still difficult to get timber from the peninsula to markets on the mainland. Consequently, most of the region's finest woods were simply cut and burned where they fell. Quite often, land that was cleared became sterile and useless in a few years because of infertile soil, steep slopes, and heavy rainfall.

In the mid-1980s, lumbering operations began to target the virgin forests of the Osa Peninsula. Every year, more and more trees are cut under a government plan to manage the forests. Unfortunately, the management plan does not stop deforestation, because farmers are motivated by short-term economic factors to keep increasing their crop land.

The forests of the Osa Peninsula are being impoverished. Farmers and lumbermen are taking too many valuable trees, without leaving enough seed trees behind.

You worked for the Costa Rican National Forestry Department and members of a rural farmers' union. What were you trying to accomplish?

I helped farmers establish small tree plantations. Although a plantation is less ecologically valuable than the forest, it can produce a lot of wood in only about 30 years. As the price of wood in Costa Rica increases year by year, these plantations will take pressure off the remaining forest. A tree plantation is sustainable, and it provides the farmer with a long-term investment.

My farmers' union had a terrible reputation for cutting and burning trees in the forest reserve. Many of these farmers had uncertain land titles and were hostile toward the government. Since their land could be taken from them at any time, they wanted a quick cash return for their timber. They did not think about the longer-term impacts of clear-cutting, such as soil erosion and the loss of valuable resources for the future. They also rarely made efficient use of the wood they cut.

The tree-planting program was supported by the Netherlands, as a "debt for nature swap." Because the government of The Netherlands is concerned about global deforestation, it established the tree-planting program as a way for Costa Rica to repay its national debt.

Were you ever in any danger because of the farmers' hostility toward government management efforts?

The farmers who had agreed to participate in the program were more willing to accept my help and work with me. Fortunately, I did not have to work with *all* the farmers. Some of them were openly hostile toward me. I was actually called a spy and other names by a few farmers!

I tried not to come across as someone sent from America to tell them what to do. The first challenge for any development worker is to listen and learn from the native people. You cannot walk in and say, "You have to do this." It is important to understand people's problems first.

We were able to overcome some apprehension by focusing on indigenous tree species, rather than exotic trees. Farmers knew the value of these native trees. They would have been far less interested in planting exotics.

Was the tree-planting program successful?

A great deal of planting was accomplished the first year. Our progress stalled in its second year, unfortunately, because of a disagreement between the farmers and the government.

In Costa Rica, you cannot cut a tree without permission from the government. That is the government's way of controlling deforestation. Farmers wanted the government to give them permission to cut their trees and sell them for lumber, in exchange for tree planting. The government said the farmers could not have tree-cutting permits unless they could demonstrate land ownership.

Many farmers on the Osa Peninsula just claim their land, without having a solid title to it. They still have, however, a legitimate right to the use of their land. The government, meanwhile, is under intense international pressure to preserve the forest. Yet, the government is not willing to pay the farmers for their land, or to help them relocate.

In addition to the tree-planting program, you also prepared a Spanish guide to help farmers better manage endangered trees on their land. Tell me about that.

The tropical forest is home to so much biodiversity. On a single hectare of land where I worked in Costa Rica, you can find 160 different tree species. In most regions of the United States, by comparison, you might find 5 to 20 different types of trees on that much land.

Some trees in Costa Rica are commonly used for fence posts, lumber, and even medicine. These trees are the most threatened in the forest. Often, the farmers were surprised to learn that these trees were so rare. I provided alternatives and suggested cutting only when the trees exist in sufficient numbers to regenerate.

On the Osa Peninsula, many farmers still own some virgin forest. Many endangered species can be saved. Sadly, some trees are so rare that I predict they will be gone very soon.

Why is biodiversity so important?

It is incredibly important to maintain the intricate systems of wildlife and plants that exist in every region of the planet. Such biodiversity is valuable to society. For example, useful plant chemicals that could yield cures for diseases are disappearing from tropical forests every day.

The harpy eagle has disappeared from Costa Rica because we destroyed too much of its habitat. Now that we have lost these birds from the forest, it is hard to bring them back.

Would you recommend Peace Corps service to others?

Yes, although the Peace Corps is not for everyone. It is hard work! The Peace Corps can be a wonderful experience for those who have just completed school, but it is not a long-term career for most people. It is a stepping stone.

The Peace Corps changed my life. I am much more appreciative of the things we take for granted here, and I will always cherish the good friends I made in Costa Rica. When I become a teacher, I hope to share my Peace Corps experiences with my students to help them learn what the rest of the world is like. Maybe in the process, they will better understand their own culture.

An ominous trend over recent decades has been the spread of rapid urban growth from industrialized regions to countries in a preindustrial stage of development. As a consequence, the time is near when a majority of the world's population will reside in urban settlements. Driven by the gathering of migrants from rural areas, the unprecedented growth of cities in the less developed world has produced an assortment of critical problems—squalid living conditions, severe crowding, high levels of unemployment, lack of basic human services, and many others—that beg for solution. Some of these problems are painfully evident in the accompanying photograph.

The settlements created by people in occupying the earth are challenging objects of study in human geography. Of course, they are extremely varied in size and complexity. Although some are dispersed—such as scattered farmsteads occupied by single families—others are nucleated agricultural villages, towns of substantially greater size and diversity, and highly complex cities that may contain millions of inhabitants. In every case, however, the human settlement is a prominent feature of the cultural landscape and a reflection of its environmental setting and the culture history of its inhabitants. Each settlement also has a functional role that links it with the surrounding countryside and with other settlements.

For most of the time since formation of the earliest human civilizations, the vast majority of people have lived in settlements no larger than villages. Even today

PART 5

HUMAN SETTLEMENTS

(McGlynn/The Image Works)

villages are a common settlement type, and in predominantly agrarian countries and regions they continue to house the majority of people and provide essential economic functions. Because villages are the most important type of rural settlement, they are the principal focus of Chapter 12.

Urban centers were of modest size and were relatively few in number until the Industrial Revolution. In countries where it occurred, industrial development attracted people from the countryside to fill new jobs in the cities and led to a great increase in the number and size of urban centers. By early in the twentieth century, cities accounted for the majority of the population in several industrial countries. As indicated at the beginning of this essay, the rapid growth of cities

more recently has shifted to other parts of the world that have yet to attain a high level of economic development. In most of these countries, excessive population and limited economic opportunity in the countryside have motivated rural people to relocate to towns and cities. Lacking a corresponding increase in jobs to support their burgeoning populations, these urban centers have become some of the most distressed places in the world. In Chapter 13 we examine the trends in world urbanization as well as spatial attributes and functional characteristics of cities, the most complex of all human settlements.

CHAPTER 12

RURAL SETTLEMENT: FARMS AND VILLAGES

Village life is embedded in the primary association of birth and place, blood and soil.

—Lewis Mumford

The inhabitants of rural settlements such as villages and farms continue to account for more than half of the world's population. (Photonica)

One well-known geographer has observed that most settlements "just seem to happen" and that in general we still know little about their existence and why they change through time. Nevertheless, we will endeavor to shed some light on a subject of tremendous importance in human geography—the settlement of people on the land. Although humans can alter the physical environment in other ways, the transformation of natural landscapes into cultural landscapes is accomplished most dramatically where people *settle* on the land. Settlements, therefore, are central to all of human geography.

Not all human groups are tied closely to a particular point on the land. Some are engaged in *nomadism*, the wandering lifestyle described in Chapter 10. Unlike nomads, most of the world's peoples are tied to specific places. That is, they are *sedentary*. Sedentary populations create relatively long-lasting patterns and structures of material culture (land division, drainage and irrigation facilities, streets, buildings, cemeteries, etc.) that can be observed and compared as essential elements in understanding the cultural landscape. Such observations and comparisons are important parts of the work of specialists in settlement geography.

DIFFERENTIATING RURAL AND URBAN SETTLEMENTS

➤ Although no sharp distinction between rural and urban can be made, a traditional separation of these two settlement types is based on their economic functions.

What is the essence of this traditional separation?

On what aspects of the cultural landscape does the geography of rural settlement focus?

Some settlement geographers are interested in rural settlements and others concentrate their attention on urban settlements. The distinction between rural and urban is a relative one; no sharp line divides rural folk from city dwellers. In terms of size, what would be considered a village in one country might be a town in a second country and a city in a third—no international agreement establishes size boundaries between settlement types. A traditional distinction is that the people in rural settlements earn their livelihoods directly from the land—that is, from primary production—whereas the people in urban settlements usually are engaged in secondary and tertiary activities. Even

that distinction, however, has been weakened during the twentieth century.

The geography of rural settlement focuses on three separate aspects of the cultural landscape: (1) the *settlement pattern*, or distribution of farms and other settlement units; (2) the *field pattern*, or the forms resulting from the human division of the land for productive use; and (3) *house and farmstead types*, including the architecture and building materials. Although some information about field patterns and house and farmstead types is presented in this chapter, the emphasis is on rural settlement patterns and their temporal (time-to-time) and spatial (place-to-place) variations.

Throughout the world, the single most common form of human settlement is the village. Towns and cities are far fewer in number than villages, and the number of people who are dispersed on the land in isolated farmsteads is far smaller than the number of residents of villages. About half of the world's population lives in rural settlements, and the vast majority of them reside in the world's approximately 2 million villages.

CLASSIFICATION OF RURAL SETTLEMENT

➤ The great variety of rural settlements is illustrated by the different ways they may be classified.

What types of rural settlements are differentiated on the basis of size?

What types are differentiated on the basis of function?

Settlements can be classified on the basis of size, function, and structure. The use of these factors in the classification of rural settlements is presented in this section.

Classification by Size

Using population data, it would seem to be an easy matter to classify settlements on the basis of size. Indeed, it *would* be easy if everyone agreed on the names of the settlement categories and the number of inhabitants representing the boundaries between the categories. Unfortunately, such agreement has not been accomplished. Even if settlement specialists could agree on the boundaries, the boundaries would be arbitrary. Nevertheless, some useful observations can be made.

A British classification that is said to work well for rural settlements in the United Kingdom consists of four categories: (1) *isolated dwellings*, with 1 to 10 people; (2) *hamlets*, with 11 to 100 people; (3) *small villages*, with 101 to 500 people; and (4) *large villages*, with 501 to 2000 people. Larger places in that scheme are classified as towns and cities, and these places are urban, not rural. In the United States, however, urban settlements are considered to have no fewer than 2500 residents, and some settlement specialists consider all smaller places to be villages. Others distinguish hamlets from villages. A modern dictionary of human geography states that hamlets have 100 to 200 inhabitants, while villages have 500 to 2500; the gap between the two size categories suggests a deficiency in this simple, two-class scheme.

Whether hamlets have 100 or fewer residents, as in the British classification, or 200 or fewer, as in the simple American classification, it is clear that they are very small rural places. Whether villages may have as many as 2000 or 2500 inhabitants, few would question their rural character.

Classification by Function

Rural settlements also can be classified on the basis of their primary function (Table 12.1). "Why is this hamlet here?" and "What do the people in this village do?" are questions related to the functions of rural places. Although settlement specialists have not adopted a classification that is generally used in the field of settlement geography, we will identify seven types of rural settlements in terms of primary function. All will be described as "villages" for the sake of uniformity, but most of them also occur as hamlets.

Farm villages are rural settlements in which the farmers live "in town" rather than in houses situated on the land they farm. The concept of the farm village may seem strange to many people in the United States, where most farmers live on the land they cultivate and are separated from the houses of neighbors. In most of the world, however, farm houses tend to be clustered into villages. This is especially true in preindustrial societies, but farm villages continue to be common in many developed countries. We will examine later the factors that have favored the development of isolated farmsteads in the rural areas of the United States and farm villages in the rural districts of most of the world.

Although farm villages are more common than any of the other types of rural settlements based on primary production, three other types are included in the classification presented. One of these is the *mining village*, located at or near the site of a mining operation (Fig. 12.1a). Economically exploitable deposits of minerals are distributed sporadically over the earth's surface, and their occurrences naturally control the development of settlements based on their extractions. Also, the size of the deposit may determine the size of the community in which the miners reside. Large-scale mining operations may even support the existence of urban settlements. The names of mining villages

TABLE 12.1 Types of Rural Settlements by Function	
Type	**Characteristic Livelihoods of Residents**
Farming village	Field agriculture, gardening, herding, agricultural commodity processing
Mining village	Mining, concentration of ore, transportation of ore
Fishing village	Fishing, fish processing
Logging village	Logging, transportation of logs, sawmilling
Administration village	Jobs associated with the business of government
Residential village	Varied. The community provides a "bedroom function" for people who may have many occupations
Market village	Retail and service occupations

(a)   (b)   (c)

FIGURE 12.1

(a) A view of Calico, California, a mining village in the Mojave Desert. Calico originated as a silver-mining center in the late nineteenth century. (N. Archbold) (b) Peggy's Cove, Nova Scotia, is probably the most photographed fishing village in the world. (J. Vining) (c) St. Simeon, a logging village in Canada's Quebec Province, is surrounded by forests in this view. (P. Quittemelle/Stock Boston)

sometimes reflect the resource on which they are based. Examples include Copperfield, which overlooks the Bingham Canyon copper mine in Utah, and Carbon Hill, located near open-pit coal mines in eastern Illinois.

Fishing villages also are based on an extractive industry and are common in coastal and lakefront areas having an abundant fishing resource offshore (Fig. 12.1b). A few villages have even been named for a fish; an example is Salmon Bay in Quebec.

The remaining type of village based on an extractive industry is the *logging village*, located within or adjacent to a large stand of harvestable timber (Fig. 12.1c). "Lumber camps" are temporary hamlets, but there are in the Pacific Northwest of the United States and elsewhere in the world many permanent villages in which most people in the work force are employed by the timber industry.

Other rural settlements have little or no connection to extractive industries. From medieval times *administrative villages* have been established for the purpose of supporting the business of government. In the United States most county seats began as rural settlements. Some modern Native American settlements in this country also might be classified as administrative villages.

Many rural communities, especially those near large cities, may be classed as *residential villages*. Their chief function is to provide homes for people who commute to work in neighboring cities. Such settlements are said to serve a "bedroom function." They are more characteristic of developed than less developed countries.

The seventh type of community in our functional classification of rural settlements is the *market village*. Because villages are small, they have relatively few business establishments compared to towns and cities, but the businesses they do contain (grocery store, general store, gasoline station, etc.) are of great importance to their residents and to people who live nearby. Many of the villages of the United States are market villages to a considerable degree (Fig. 12.2).

We have not exhausted the possibilities. Many military bases, prisons, and leper colonies, for example, are village-sized communities. The vast majority of the world's villages, however, fit into the seven types of rural settlements just presented.

Classification by Structure

➤ In terms of structure, rural settlements can be divided into two broad groups—dispersed settlement and nucleated settlement.

What are the distinctive characteristics of dispersed settlement?

What are the distinctive characteristics of nucleated settlement?

FIGURE 12.2
Part of the business district of Winterset, Iowa, a typical market village in the United States. (Charles Nes/Gamma Liaison)

Rural settlement in different parts of the world displays a fascinating variety of forms, but it is convenient to distinguish two broad groups—dispersed settlement and nucleated settlement.

Dispersed Settlement   In areas where houses are scattered widely across the land and not clustered into hamlets or villages, a **dispersed settlement** pattern is said to exist. The settlement unit usually is composed of a single-family dwelling—a farm or ranch house, most often—together with one or more barns and sheds. The fields, pastures, and other land from which the family earns its living stretch out from the isolated settlement. The degree of isolation varies widely, sometimes within the same country. In the humid farming districts of the United States, farmsteads often are no more than a quarter of a mile (0.4 km) apart, whereas in the dry lands of the Southwest, ranches may be separated by many miles. In dispersed settlement each farm or ranch serves as a settlement unit by itself, not as a portion of a larger settlement unit.

Nucleated Settlement   In areas where houses and other buildings are clustered or agglomerated, a **nucleated settlement** pattern exists. That is, nucleated settlement consists of hamlets, villages, and larger nonrural communities. Nucleated is an older form of settlement than dispersed, and it is characteristic of more countries than dispersed settlement. The nature of the aggregation of buildings varies from settlement to settlement. In some hamlets and villages, buildings appear to be arranged randomly, so that there is no appearance of orderliness. Others are constructed using geometric shapes. We will examine the shapes of nucleated rural settlements later in this chapter.

LAND DIVISION SYSTEMS AND RURAL SETTLEMENT

➤ Land division systems used in the United States fall into two broad categories: irregular surveys and rectangular surveys.

How does the irregular "metes and bounds" system work, and where was it applied in the United States?

Where was land surveyed into "long lots"?

What are the essentials of the U.S. public lands survey system?

Whether rural settlement is dispersed or nucleated, one of the most important factors in the permanent location of people on the land is the system of land division used. To avoid conflicts with neighbors, individuals must know where their land ends and that of others begins. In the same way, the people of a communal village must know the limits of the land associated with the village. This makes desirable some generally accepted method of identifying land boundaries. Real property survey systems were developed to meet this need for order in matters pertaining to land ownership. Two broad categories of land surveys are irregular surveys and rectangular surveys.

Irregular Surveys

An irregular survey either avoids the use of a uniform rectilinear grid or modifies an overall grid pattern to conform to the configuration of the landscape. The irregular survey pattern, therefore, is more or less unregulated. Even so, there may be well-established rules for the establishment of such irregular patterns.

Metes and Bounds   The **metes and bounds** system of survey was brought to North America by early colonists, although there were pre-Columbian antecedents. Certainly, many Native American farmers knew, centuries ago, precisely the limits of lands associated with their kinship groups and tribes. Indigenous peoples in other parts of the world similarly possessed principles of territoriality. Metes and bounds survey, however, unlike word-of-mouth traditions about land division, is based on established principles, and the results are recorded and often established on maps.

These principles, like those of oral land traditions, are ancient. The Egyptians first used land survey about 5000 years ago, and the Babylonians about 4500 years ago. Although the methods they used are not known, both civilizations were capable of exceptional accuracy in measurements. Before the settlement of Canaan by the Israelites, that country was subdivided by a team of ten surveyors, the Jewish historian Josephus reported. Again, no details are known. Perhaps the metes and bounds survey technique was used in all three of these areas, although it is possible that an "irregular rectangular" system was used.

Metes and bounds surveys consist of land description employing landmarks, directions, and distances. An example of an ancient metes and bounds description (Fig. 12.3) might be stated this way: "Commencing at the mouth of Hermit's Cave, thence due south a distance of 1820 feet to the north bank of Crystal Creek, thence west along the creek to the beginning of the rapids, thence north 800 feet to the giant boulder, thence northeast to the mouth of Hermit's Cave." By citing direction to the nearest second (of a minute of a degree) and distance to the nearest hundredth of a foot, the metes and bounds survey system can be used to locate precisely a parcel of land. The biggest problem with this system is the impermanence of landmarks. Hermit's Cave may collapse, and Crystal Creek may change its course. An iron post set to mark the corner of a property may be stolen or may rust away. This problem with changing landmarks can lead to legal disputes.

Figure 12.4 shows the extent of areas in the United States with different survey systems. The metes and bounds survey extends from Maine to Georgia and reaches west almost to the Mississippi River in Kentucky and Tennessee. Smaller areas occur in the lower Mississippi Valley and along portions of the California coast.

Long Lots The **long-lot** system of survey is a more or less irregular one in which the landholding units are very elongated in order for a large number of owners to have access to a valuable and limited resource. Most often the resource is frontage on a body of water, but it might be frontage on a road or access to a forest.

Long lots are common in the hills and marshes of western and central Europe. The first long lots in Eu-

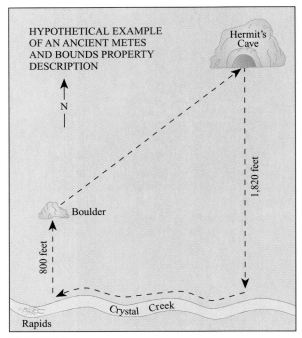

FIGURE 12.3

This hypothetical description illustrates the ancient metes and bounds system of delimiting property: "Commencing at the mouth of Hermit's Cave, thence due south a distance of 1820 feet to the north bank of Crystal Creek, thence west along the creek to the beginning of the rapids, thence north 800 feet to the giant boulder, thence to the mouth of Hermit's Cave."

rope may have originated in the Netherlands in the tenth century A.D. The European long lots in areas of level terrain tend to have straight boundaries, but in hill lands property lines are often irregular and only slightly parallel.

The long-lot concept was introduced to the New World by Europeans. Examples can be found in Argentina, Brazil, Canada, and the United States. Long lots in the United States are characteristic of French-settled areas in Louisiana, Missouri, Illinois, Indiana, Wisconsin, and Michigan (Fig. 12.4). A French-settled area of the Mississippi River delta divided into long lots is shown in Figure 12.5. Notice that the lots are not uniform in length or width, and note how the lots were modified into triangles to accommodate a bend in the river.

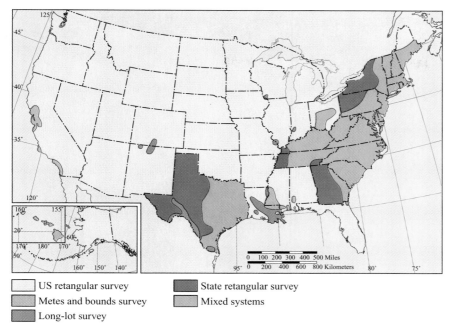

FIGURE 12.4

Land survey systems of the United States. The real property survey systems mapped here, and a few other types employed elsewhere in the world, were developed to meet the need for order in matters pertaining to land ownership.

☐ US retangular survey

☐ Metes and bounds survey

☐ Long-lot survey

☐ State retangular survey

☐ Mixed systems

Rectangular Surveys

A rectangular survey is one that uses coordinate boundary lines—lines that cross each other at right angles, producing land units that are square or rectangular. This survey concept predates that of long lots but probably is not as ancient as metes and bounds.

The Roman Centuriatio   The Roman system of rectangular survey had antecedents in the Po Valley of Northern Italy, where the Etruscans evidently divided at least portions of their domain into square and rectangular parcels. The orderly Roman system, or **centuriatio**, however, was applied primarily to colonial territories bordering the Mediterranean Sea. When the empire was expanded through diplomacy or conquest, often the "new land" was surveyed according to the provisions of the *centuriatio*.

The centuriation system involved the subdivision of the landscape into 132-acre (53.4 ha) plots, each a *centuria*. Each plot was square, measuring approximately 776 yards (705 m) long on each side. The boundary lines bore no relationship to the concepts of latitude and longitude. Roman roads tended to be straight, since they were built along the boundary lines between farms. With respect to rural settlement patterns, the most important consequence of centuriation

was its encouragement of dispersed settlement. In some areas surveyed by the Romans, the square properties remain, but the passage of two millennia has erased all surface traces of the *centuriatio* in most lands once a part of the Roman Empire. Modern remote sensing techniques, however, reveal abundant subsurface evidence of the ancient patterns.

U.S. Public Lands System   Thomas Jefferson, as chairman of a congressional committee charged with the task of devising a uniform method of land division for the Northwest Territory, proposed that it be divided into square blocks of 10 by 10 miles (16 by 16 km), each block subdivided into 100 parcels of one square mile (2.59 sq km) each. Jefferson may have been inspired by the Roman *centuriatio*, or he may have drawn his idea from the rectangular system used in the Netherlands for lands reclaimed from the sea.

When Congress passed the Land Ordinance of 1785, it accepted the proposal for a land division system based on grid lines laid out according to the cardinal points of the compass. Land was to be divided into parcels based on selected north–south lines called *principal meridians* and east–west lines called *base lines* (Fig. 12.6a). For Jefferson's 100-square-mile (259 sq km) blocks, however, Congress substituted 36-square-mile **townships** six miles (9.7 km) on each

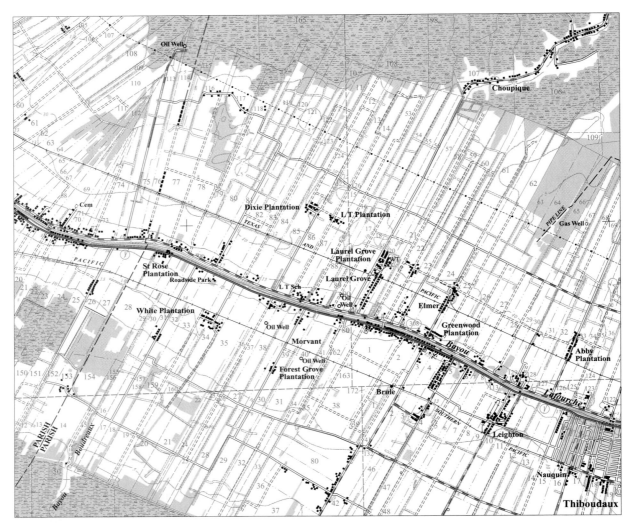

FIGURE 12.5
Natural levees along a Mississippi delta distributary divided into French long lots. (Thibodaux, Louisiana;
scale 1:62,500; contour interval 5 feet; U.S. Geological Survey)

side—a change more in keeping with the New England townships familiar to the lawmakers. The townships would be divided into 36 numbered sections, each 1 mile square (2.59 sq km) or 640 acres (259 ha) in area (Fig. 12.6b). Each section could be further subdivided into square or rectangular parcels of various sizes. Figure 12.4 shows the vast portion of the United States to which the new system of land division was applied as settlement advanced.

State Rectangular Surveys   Similar rectangular surveys that were not a part of the federal survey system are found in portions of the original 13 colonies. These surveys were used in western New York, northwestern Pennsylvania, western Georgia, portions of Tennessee and Kentucky, and most of western Texas (Fig. 12.4). In most of these areas, individual rectangular schemes for surveying unallotted frontier lands were developed around 1800 by state agencies or land companies

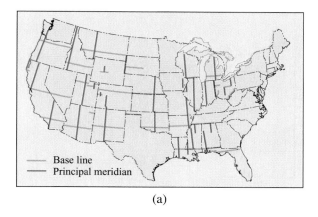

(a)

FIGURE 12.6

(a) Principal meridians and base lines of the United States Public Lands Survey System, also called the township and range system. All properties surveyed according to this system are located with respect to the intersection of a principal meridian and base line. (b) Method of locating property according to the Public Lands Survey System. A township consists of 36 sections, each of which is one square mile (2.59 sq km) in area. Each section can be subdivided into quarter-sections, and they in turn can be similarly subdivided.

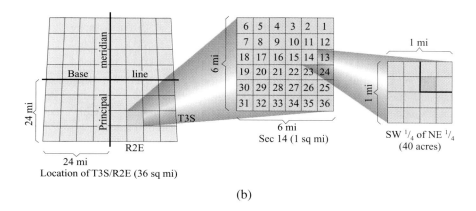

(b)

within the states. They were based on the concepts of the federal system.

DISPERSED RURAL SETTLEMENT

A dispersed settlement pattern, we have seen, occurs when houses are widely scattered across the land rather than being nucleated into hamlets or villages. Settlement geographers often speak of dispersed settlers as living "on the land." We will examine the factors contributing to dispersal, the problems associated with living on the land, dispersed settlement in Europe and the United States, and the changes that are taking place in the American farmstead.

Factors Favoring Dispersal

➤ Eight factors that contribute to the development of a dispersed settlement pattern can be identified.

What are these eight factors and how does each influence the rural settlement pattern?

What are problems inherent in dispersed settlement?

Figure 12.7 identifies eight factors that contribute to the development of a dispersed pattern of rural settlement. *Rectangular survey*, the first factor indicated, encourages settlement on the land by its very nature, while at the same time providing no impediment to nucleated settlement. The geometry of rectangular survey influences the structure of the rural road network, the organization of fields and farmsteads, and the structure of rural administrative units. Note in Figure 12.8 the dispersed distribution of rural houses in an area surveyed by the township-and-range (U.S. rectangular survey) system.

The second and third factors in Figure 12.7 are *harsh* and *favorable environments*. Why should these

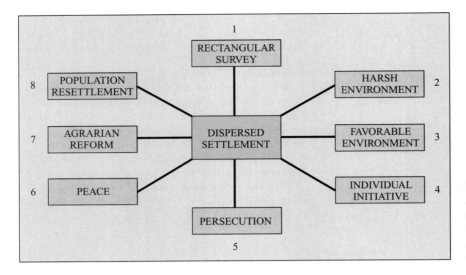

FIGURE 12.7

Eight factors favoring dispersed settlement. Both physical and cultural factors are significant in explaining why people live "on the land."

environmental extremes both favor dispersed settlement? Landscapes in which human activities are limited by difficult terrain, unpleasant climate, or unproductive soil are usually lands that must be used extensively rather than intensively. Extensive land use, such as livestock ranching, requires a lot of land to support a person or a family. Much of this land might be too far from home if one lived in a village; so dispersed settlement becomes more desirable. At the same time, favorable environments in which the land use might be of a more intensive nature also support dispersed settlement. For example, in areas where soils are uniformly fertile over a large area and where water supplies are virtually ubiquitous, dispersed settlement

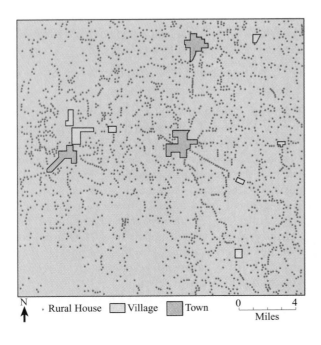

FIGURE 12.8

Settlement pattern in Orange County, Indiana. Three towns and seven villages comprise the nucleated settlements, but the distribution of dispersed rural houses is perhaps the most striking thing about the county's settlement geography. Most of these dwellings are not farmhouses; they were constructed for owners who are not farmers. The large number of them is evidence of a continuing preference by many Americans for the privacy allowed by dispersed settlement. The houses arranged diagonal to the grid lines of the survey system are along major roads. Rugged terrain and the public ownership of recreational lands in the southwestern part of the county account for the sparse distribution of houses in that area.

will be attractive. In such instances, people will not be restricted to a small area by shortages of good soil and water, conditions that favor nucleation.

In individual cases of a family's settlement on the land, factors identified in Figure 12.7 as *individual initiative* and *persecution* may have had a role to play. The desire of pioneers to "get away from it all" is a well-known theme in the literature of frontier settlement. Getting away from it all may mean escaping religious or ethnic persecution, or it may be a matter of putting oneself outside the jurisdiction of laws with which one disagrees. In most cases, however, relocating is for the purpose of achieving a higher standard of living in an area where the physical and cultural environment is judged to offer greater opportunity. A certain amount of risk is always involved, so relocating involves individual initiative.

Because defense against enemies has been a good reason for the agglomeration of settlement from ancient times, it stands to reason that uninterrupted *peace* in an area is a factor that would facilitate the dispersal of settlement. This is especially true with advancements in communications and transportation. With good communications and good roads, even settlers in remote districts might feel that they would have time to retreat to the greater safety of defended positions in the event of a collapse of peace.

The next two factors in Figure 12.7, *agrarian reform* and *population resettlement*, may or may not be related in particular ventures. Agrarian reform is usually the effort by a national government to provide cultivable or grazing land to landless people, often after nationalizing—confiscating or purchasing—tracts of land from large landholders. The parcels of land granted or sold at low cost to the new settlers may be scattered over a large area. The distance of the new landholder's property from the nearest village may encourage the establishment of a farmstead on the holding. In many reform projects, the settler is expected to build a house, often with government financial assistance, on his or her property. Some agrarian reform projects, therefore, by the very nature of their provisions, encourage or require dispersed settlement. Population resettlement is often, although not necessarily, a part of agrarian reform. It is not involved when the landless people who live in a village and who work for the owner of the surrounding land are granted landholdings in the nationalized estate lands but continue to live in the village. Population resettlement, when

carried out by a national government, may be based on motives other than reforming agriculture. It might be a way of reducing urban unemployment, for example, or settling a remote area in order to establish de facto control of territory.

Problems of Farm Dispersal

We already have noted that sometimes there are certain risks involved in living on the land. In times of political upheaval, international stress, or rural brigandage, lack of security may be a problem for dispersed settlers. People living on the land do not have the strength in numbers enjoyed by residents of nucleated settlements. The high cost of transportation is another problem with dispersed settlement. Road construction is expensive. So is the cost of providing public utilities to settlers whose farmsteads or ranches are scattered over the landscape. Also, it is more difficult to provide quality health care and educational services to dispersed settlers than to those living in nucleated settlements. The distance of dispersed farmers from farm supply sources and farm commodity markets increases the cost of operations. In some agrarian societies, farmers who live on the land may be less able than those in agricultural villages to acquire additional farm labor in periods of peak labor requirements.

For some individuals, especially for settlers in pioneer areas, an additional problem is loneliness. When people from farm villages become dispersed settlers, sometimes because of government-sponsored resettlement schemes, loneliness can become a real problem—one that has contributed to the failure of many settlement projects in various parts of the world.

DISPERSED SETTLEMENT IN EUROPE

➤ The farm village and dispersed settlement are both common features of the European landscape, although rural settlement in Europe is primarily nucleated.

When and for what reasons have both primary and secondary dispersals occurred in Europe?

How and why has enclosure been involved?

Two types of processes have been recognized in the evolution of dispersed rural settlement: primary dispersal and secondary dispersal. Primary dispersal occurs during the initial phase of the settlement of a territory as individual pioneer settlers venture into a "new land." Secondary dispersal, occurring much later, involves the spread of settlement across the "old land" from existing nucleations. In some areas it is easy to determine which process accounts for the dispersed settlement observed on the landscape. In other areas a distinction is not easy to make; the results of both processes frequently exist side by side. In Europe both primary and secondary dispersal have occurred, the primary preceding the secondary by many centuries. As in most of Asia and Latin America, rural settlement in Europe primarily is nucleated, although secondary dispersal during recent centuries has reduced the proportion of the rural population that resides in farm villages.

The primary dispersal of rural population in Europe occurred both in prehistoric and historic times. Because early dispersed settlement left a more obscure archaeological record than early nucleated settlement, less is known about it, even though European villages were very small and dispersed settlement was common. The rather uniformly productive landscapes of Europe facilitated the dispersal of early agricultural populations. After the Roman conquest, villages grew larger and the proportion of people living in nucleated settlements eventually exceeded that of people residing on the land.

Secondary dispersal of European rural population has been mostly a late medieval and modern development. The disintegration of feudalism was a major factor in moving people out of agricultural villages; as peasants became free, they tended to move away from the estates of their former landlords. Later, during the fifteenth to nineteenth centuries, the European **enclosure movement** relocated large numbers of people from villages to the countryside.

Enclosure is a term that applies to (1) termination of *the commons*, land owned by all the people of a community; (2) the consolidation of small, fragmented properties into landholdings of sufficient size to support a farm family and allow for the production of surplus commodities; and (3) allocation of the new holdings to farm families. This kind of land tenure reorganization took place in portions of Scandinavia, Britain, western Germany, France, Belgium, and Italy. In the Scandinavian countries, governmental decrees issued in the late 1700s and early 1800s led to the abolition of fragmented holdings and brought about the dispersal of the majority of the rural population.

The enclosure movement in Great Britain spanned several centuries, but it peaked between 1750 and 1850. The government transformed the rural landscape by consolidating the small, fragmented properties that had resulted largely from land subdivision associated with inheritance practices. To accomplish this, some people were forced to give up their claims to small holdings. Because the enclosure movement overlapped the Industrial Revolution, many displaced villagers were able to move to urban settlements and become factory workers. In the cities many displaced farmers worked long hours for low wages, lived in slums, and were afflicted by disease and misery.

Greater agricultural efficiency resulted from the consolidated farms, since the farmers who remained did not have to waste time moving farm implements from one discontiguous field to another. A great many of the farmers moved from the villages to new farmsteads on their land—a case of secondary dispersal. As a consequence, the isolated farmstead, rare in medieval England, is now a common feature of the English landscape.

The Italian government in the 1920s and 1930s undertook a program of creating dispersed farmsteads in the southern part of that country. This program, which continued into the 1960s, was based on the need to develop a more labor-intensive system of agriculture to absorb the surplus agricultural labor and increase production. By 1965 more than 40,000 new farm dwellings had been constructed under this government program, most of which were scattered across the rural landscape—a striking example of the restructuring of rural settlement.

The current trend in most of Europe is toward the gradual elimination of the farm village and its replacement by dispersed farmsteads, a process that may take centuries. The greater agricultural efficiency allowed by dispersed rural settlements is preferable to the conditions that earlier encouraged the formation of villages.

DISPERSED SETTLEMENT IN THE UNITED STATES

➤ Dispersed settlement is most common today in Anglo-America and some of the other lands in the New World that were colonized by Europeans.

What factors in the New World encourage dispersed settlement?

What features of the rural landscape in the United States resulted from governmental policies regarding the disposal of public lands?

Although dispersed settlement is becoming increasingly important in Europe and other parts of the Old World, it is in some of the lands colonized by European nations that this form of rural settlement is most conspicuous. These areas include the United States, Canada, Australia, New Zealand, and southern Africa. Most of the United States was surveyed after 1785, we noted earlier, according to the provisions of a new rectangular system. The method of survey and the ways that the federal government chose to dispose of the public lands were instrumental in producing a dispersed pattern of rural settlement throughout most of the country.

The federal government acquired its vast areas of public domain from cessions by the original states and from purchases and virtual confiscations of lands claimed by foreign governments. Long before this phase of land acquisition concluded, the government set about transferring ownership to individuals. There were two reasons for this: (1) the belief that a democracy is best established in a nation in which most of the land is privately owned by the people; and (2) the possession by the government of much land but little money in a time when funds were needed for building a nation.

Initially, land was sold by the township at $2.00 per acre ($4.94 per ha), and most of the sales were to land companies and other speculators. In 1804 the government began selling 160-acre (65-ha) quarter-section parcels, and eventually the quarter-section came to be considered by lawmakers as the ideal farm size, even though it proved to be not at all ideal in some parts of the country. The price later was lowered to $1.25 an acre ($3.09 per ha). The ultimate price reduction came with the important Homestead Act of 1862, which made essentially free land available.

Application forms for homesteads in the United States. Under provisions of the Homestead Act, it was amazingly simple for a person to acquire a 160-acre farm from the public domain. (Culver Pictures)

There was only a filing fee of $10.00 necessary to establish ownership of a 160-acre homestead by a farm family who resided on the land for five years. Other federal legislation made it possible for individuals to acquire, virtually without cost, 480 acres (194 ha) of forest land or 640 acres (259 ha) of desert land. In addition to transferring land directly to individuals, the government granted vast tracts of land (1) to territories and states to support schools and for other public purposes and (2) to railroad and canal companies in order to encourage the development of transportation facilities.

The historic disposal of the public domain into the hands of speculators, squatters, and bona fide settlers was a major step that has had long-term effects on American society. The very distribution of people today was greatly influenced by it. Since the quarter-section was long considered the most desirable size of a farm, the allocation of 160-acre (65-ha) properties meant that there were originally four families per square mile—a score or so of persons. Four homes to the square mile and about four schools to the township provided the simple general pattern for much of the rural Midwest.

This pattern became best displayed on the smooth upland prairies, where the roads faithfully followed the section lines and property lines and therefore ran either north–south or east–west. The farmsteads themselves were strung along the roads of the grid in a dispersed fashion; seldom did farmers cluster their farmsteads at the four corners where sections met. Notice that in the portion of the topographic map in Figure 12.9 there is not a single crossroads at the corners of four sections where more than one farmhouse is situated. This map was selected because of the notable cultural feature near its center—Homestead National Monument of America, commemorating the importance of the Homestead Act of 1862 and the fact that the first land claimed under its provisions is located here.

Dispersed living, therefore, became the American norm during the eighteenth and nineteenth centuries. Farmers lived "in the country" and "went to town" for business and pleasure. The economy, from the beginning, was based on marketing products, but it also involved a high degree of self-sufficiency. The satisfaction people found in independence and self-sufficiency compensated for the isolation. Despite the isolation of dispersed living, American farm families were always

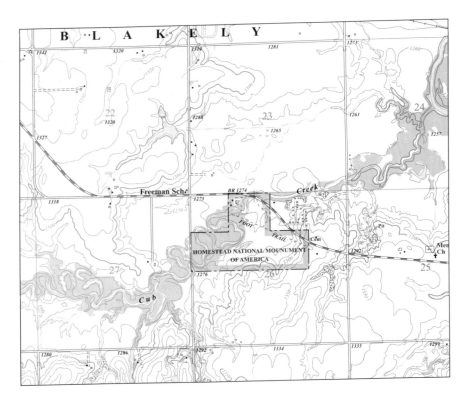

FIGURE 12.9

An area of predominantly dispersed settlement in Nebraska. (Beatrice West, Nebraska; scale 1:24,000; contour interval 10 feet; United States Geological Survey)

a part of a larger community. The country school, country church, and nearest market and supply center all had roles to play in this sense of community.

THE CHANGING CHARACTER OF THE AMERICAN FARMSTEAD

➤ Mechanization of agriculture in the United States during the twentieth century changed the character of the American farmstead and resulted in a rural-to-urban migration. Counter-urbanization, however, has recently brought people back to the land.

How has the American farm changed since the 1930s?

What has caused counter-urbanization?

The rural America of yesteryear is not the rural America of today. Most of the small country schools were consolidated decades ago. Most of the country churches are gone. Relatively few farmers, in fact, remain on the rural landscapes. In the United States, as in virtually all parts of the world, people have been leaving the countryside to move to towns and cities. The mechanization of agriculture enabled individual farmers to increase their productivity greatly, resulting in the need for fewer farmers. Opportunities in manufacturing and service industries persuaded many farmers to leave the land and adopt new lifestyles in the cities or suburbs. In 1935 there were almost 7 million farms in the United States; by 1990 there were only about 2 million.

Accompanying the reduction in the number of American farms has been an increase in the size of those farms. Typical farms, we have seen, were originally 160 acres (65 ha) in size; many were much smaller. A process of enlargement began almost immediately after farmers gained title to their lands. By 1990 the average farm comprised about 450 acres (182 ha). In contrast to small farms, large farms commonly (1) are owned by farmers who rely less on off-farm income; (2) are more capital-intensive; (3) rely more heavily on wage labor; (4) have higher fixed costs; (5) are more bureaucratic in their organization; (6) receive more federal government support; (7) are major beneficiaries of tax loopholes; and (8) use the latest agricultural technology.

The decline in farm population that accompanied the growth of farm size resulted in many abandoned

FIGURE 12.10
Derelict farm houses like this one are evidence of the dramatic decline in farm population in the United States over the past half-century. (J. Vining)

farmsteads. A section of land that once supported four farms may have only one or two farms today. The sight of deserted farmsteads on country roads, their derelict houses and barns sagging, their lanes overgrown by brush, is common in the United States (Fig. 12.10). Farmstead abandonment has not altered the pattern of rural population distribution, however. The vast majority of farm families still reside on the land in a dispersed pattern (Fig. 12.11), but there are just not as many of them.

Counter-urbanization, a trend that emerged during the 1970s, has increased the size of the rural population in some parts of the United States, however. For many years people have been moving out of cities and into suburbs. The new trend involves people moving from both cities and suburbs into the country. Factors contributing to this movement include low-cost rural housing resulting from farm abandonment, reduced commuting time because of new expressways and rapid transit, and disenchantment with traditional urban and suburban lifestyles. The back-to-the-land movement is contributing to dispersed rural settlement in areas within commuting distance of many cities.

FIGURE 12.11
Unlike farmers in many parts of the world who live in villages, most farmers in the United States live "on the land" in isolated farmsteads like the one in this photograph.
(J. Vining)

NUCLEATED RURAL SETTLEMENT

The bulk of the world's rural population lives in hamlets and villages, not dispersed across the countryside. Most people have ancestral origins that go back to a village community. Not only is the small nucleated community the traditional settlement form in most countries, it is a cultural characteristic that has had a powerful influence on the development of many societies. Here we will examine the characteristics of nucleated rural settlement, beginning with the factors that help account for the agglomeration of people in the rural landscape.

Factors Favoring Nucleation

➤ Eight factors that contribute to the development of nucleated settlement can be identified.

What are these factors and how does each influence nucleated settlement patterns?

What are some of the problems of nucleated settlement?

Earlier we considered eight factors that contribute to the dispersal of rural population. Figure 12.12 identifies eight factors that favor the development of clustered settlement.

The first is a *harsh environment*. Groups of people may be better able to cope than individual families with the uncooperative or unpleasant realities of a harsh environment. In a very cold land, such as Siberia, communal living might better enable people to deal with the severe winters, whereas solitary life in such an environment would be more risky. In a rainforest, the communal efforts of tribal life might better deal with the rainforest vegetation and poor soils than the individual efforts of the isolated family. Terrain is another environmental factor that may contribute to the aggregation of people. In areas of rugged terrain, people usually settle in the small valleys and hollows; the limited extent of this more favorable land encourages the concentration of settlement. Water is also an environmental factor significant in affecting settlement patterns. Both too little water (dry lands) and too much water (flood-prone lands) may be influential in concentrating people into local areas having optimal water availability.

Defense, the second factor in Figure 12.12, historically has been a major reason for the agglomeration of settlement and continues to be important in areas of cultural instability and conflict. The use of defensive locations for rural settlement is perhaps nowhere better demonstrated than in the United Kingdom. Across the British Isles are scattered thousands of **hillforts**, the remains of small settlements of the Iron Age (800–0 B.C.) and the Roman period (A.D. 0–400). Most of them occupy hilltop locations and display the relics of fortifications built of earth, stone, or timber. The central aim of the development of those sites was to provide a safe haven—a place secure from attack by unfriendly neighbors or invading armies. The hillforts, usually called "forts" today, were not military garrisons but were built to protect residents who spent most of their time in the normal activities of agriculture and manufacturing (Fig. 12.13). Similar hillforts occur throughout Europe.

Religion is the next factor in Figure 12.12. Some of the earliest permanent settlements were established, totally or in part, to serve religious purposes. In the nineteenth and twentieth centuries thousands of farm villages were formed by organized religious groups in various parts of the world. Many were founded by religious cult leaders and their followers. One of the

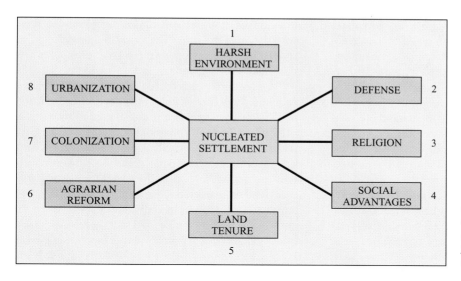

FIGURE 12.12

Eight factors that favor the development of nucleated settlement. All but one of the factors identified here are cultural.

more recent and tragic examples was Jonestown in Guyana, a socialist commune that was only four years old in 1978 when more than 900 people were murdered or forced to commit suicide by the fanatic cult leader of the village.

Dispersed settlement cannot provide the *social advantages* of village life. In a nucleated settlement it is easier to provide educational services and health care. It is also easier to organize social clubs and co-operative societies in villages. For the village dweller loneliness is not the problem that it can become for the isolated farmer.

Certain *land tenure* systems and methods of organizing labor lend themselves more than others to a nucleated pattern. Medieval European farming, with its emphasis on communal field labor, clearly favored nucleation. Certain modern farming systems, such as some of those established for ideological reasons in the Soviet Union, China, and Israel, have required nucleated settlement and communal labor. The long-time thrust of the Soviet government in collective farming perpetuated and emphasized the nucleated pattern of rural settlement that had characterized Russia even before the Bolshevik Revolution of 1917.

Agrarian reform, as we have seen, is large-scale government-sponsored change in the institutional setting of rural society and agriculture. It involves not only land reform (changing the land tenure), but also the establishment of rural settlement patterns and government support for agricultural and social programs. The enormous economic and social gap between wealthy landowners on the one hand and struggling masses of small farmers and landless workers on the other has been one factor that has caused the governments of some less developed countries to initiate agrarian reform measures. In some cases this has involved the nationalization of large estates and redis-

FIGURE 12.13

Burrough Hill is the site of an Iron Age hillfort in Great Britain. Hillforts were small settlements designed for defense, dating to the first millennium B.C. (R. Gabler)

tribution of the land in small holdings to individual farmers. Although this process can result in dispersed settlement, as was noted in our examination of Figure 12.7, often it produces new nucleated settlements. For example, many new agricultural villages called **ejidos** came into existence after 1917 as a result of agrarian reform in Mexico. Population resettlement, therefore, is often a major aspect of agrarian reform.

The movement of people from one place to another and their resettlement in new farm villages may also be the result of *colonization*, the seventh factor in Figure 12.12. The term is not used here in the sense of pursuing a policy of colonialism; instead, it refers to the organized settlement of a new area, usually as a result of a government program implemented in a more or less isolated part of the country. The availability of public land has prompted many developing countries to adopt population relocation schemes bearing such labels as land colonization, resettlement, transmigration, or land development. They have been presented by proponents (primarily government officials) as potentially tidy solutions to a number of problems, including curbing unemployment, providing land for the landless, reducing population pressures in the core area, and increasing agricultural production. The settlers may be dispersed on the land or granted a building site or a house in a new village. Some governments have experimented with both patterns. Whatever the settlement pattern used, colonization schemes are costly undertakings. Despite the hundreds of millions of dollars that have been spent on them, their results have not been very encouraging. If not complete failures, they have given settlement officials cause for concern in almost all parts of the world. Thousands of new villages have come into existence because of government-sponsored resettlement projects; hundreds of them have been abandoned completely for reasons described in Chapter 10.

The final factor in Figure 12.12 is *urbanization*. In developed countries, as urban centers grow, nearby villages often grow into towns and nearby hamlets may grow into villages. It is not unusual, as well, for new hamlets to spring up as a result of counter-urbanization.

Problems of Nucleated Settlements

Many people, especially those accustomed to life in urban centers, associate a variety of problems with nucleated rural settlements. These problems diminish the

attraction of villages and undoubtedly inhibit their prospects for growth. The vast majority can be grouped into three categories: (1) isolation, (2) limited goods and services, and (3) lack of freedom.

Villages often are viewed as remote and isolated places of small size in the "boondocks." Indeed, the small size of villages is a disadvantage to those who prefer the cultural offerings and excitement of the city. Also, because of their small size, villages present limited opportunities for social contacts. However, villages are not as isolated as dispersed farmsteads; villagers tend to characterize the inhabitants of dispersed farmsteads as living in the boondocks.

Villages are not able to offer nearly as many goods and services as urban places, and people who prefer urban life may consider this to be a disadvantage of smaller-than-urban places. However, people who live on dispersed farmsteads may be able to obtain most of the goods and services they need in the nearest village and may not think of the village as being disadvantaged.

Lack of personal freedom may be viewed as a problem in villages by both dispersed populations and urban dwellers. People who live on the land usually enjoy their independence and their freedom to do whatever they like on their own land; it would "cramp their style," some believe, to live in a nucleated settlement. Those who favor urban living may also feel that freedoms are limited in villages. Among the masses of humanity who make up a city, one can find a certain amount of anonymity, freedom from social pressure, and tolerance of a wide variety of views and lifestyles. In a village, everyone might know everyone else, and there might be social pressure to conform to the local mores. Those often are perceived disadvantages of village life, even though such stereotyping is unfair, no doubt, to many villages.

THE EARLIEST VILLAGES

Remarkably little is known about the earliest human settlements, and the limited record is the subject of academic controversy. It is clear, however, that early *Homo sapiens* were not settled people. As small groups of hunters and gatherers, they did not remain in one place long enough to make much of an impact on the land. During the early and middle Paleolithic (Old Stone Age), some 50,000 to 100,000 years ago, favored dwelling places were natural shelters, such as caves and canyon overhangs, and even these habita-

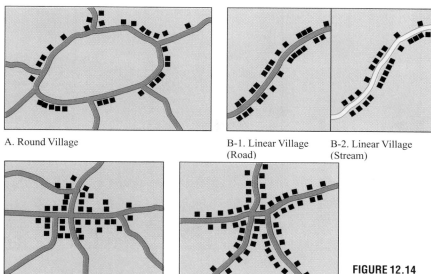

A. Round Village

B-1. Linear Village (Road)

B-2. Linear Village (Stream)

C. Cluster Village

D. Star Village

FIGURE 12.14

Some typical medieval European village types that have persisted in the landscape.

tions seldom were occupied year round. Later in the Paleolithic, improvements in hunting and gathering economies enabled greater permanence of dwelling sites; there is archeological evidence of hut construction in this period. These were the precursors of the village, but there was no long-term habitation.

Beginning about 10,000 years ago was a period during which people possessed better tools and practiced a subsistence economy that served as a transition between food gathering and settled agriculture. Plant and animal domestication made it possible for people to establish permanent agricultural villages in some areas. In portions of southwestern Asia, farming communities had become common by 7000 B.C. Even before 8000 B.C. cereal-cultivating farmers lived in Palestine in villages composed of oval or round huts. Farming also developed early in China, and from about 7000 B.C. it spawned an increase in rural settlement. In Mesoamerica, a comparable development—without animal domestication—took place, several thousands of years later. Sedentary agriculture spread from southwestern Asia to southern and central Europe during the early Neolithic period (New Stone Age). It is generally accepted that the first substantial farming activity associated with permanent settlement in Britain dates to about 5000 B.C.

Prehistoric communities, as a rule, were very small—hamlets and villages. In most of these prehistoric settlements, houses were probably distributed in a disorderly scattering, but in others the dwellings were arranged in an orderly fashion along streets.

EUROPEAN VILLAGES FROM THE MIDDLE AGES TO THE TWENTIETH CENTURY

➤ Villages remained the home of most Europeans until the middle of the nineteenth century, even though the village to a great extent was a product of the Middle Ages.

What led to the development of different village types or forms in Europe?

What explains the decline of European villages in this century?

In Europe the characteristic settlements of the early medieval period were hamlets, although there were also many villages. The stagnation of urban life after the fall of Rome resulted in an urban-to-rural migration that fostered the growth of villages, especially those associated with castles and monasteries. Invasions of "barbarians" from the north and east led to the increasing construction of walls and moats around larger villages and towns. The estates of nobles were called *feuds*, so the land tenure system, in which peasant farmers worked the fields of the estate owner in exchange for protection, is called the *feudal system.*

Because a great many European villages share common patterns, it is useful to examine some of the types recognized by settlement geographers. Figure 12.14 shows several types that were common in the Middle Ages and that persist, in some areas, in more or less recognizable forms today.

FIGURE 12.15
A view of the village green and adjacent houses of a contemporary round village, East Witton, in England. Round villages were widespread in medieval England and Germany. (R. Gabler)

FIGURE 12.16
A linear village in East Anglia, England. Linear villages are common throughout Europe and around the world. (R. Gabler)

Round villages, particularly common in Germany and Britain, consisted of houses fronting a road around a circular or almond-shaped *village green* (Fig. 12.15). The village green was used for sporting events, periodic markets, or as an enclosure for livestock.

Linear villages are common throughout Europe and around the world. Some linear physical or cultural feature prompts this type of village development. The physical features include rivers, long narrow river terraces, very narrow valleys, and lines of springs. Cultural features that often encourage linear village development include roads, railroads, and canals. Roads probably account for the largest number of linear villages; in fact, these settlements are often called *street villages* (Fig. 12.16).

In the *cluster village*, the arrangement of the houses is almost random, although a majority of the dwellings may be located along the roadways. There is greater adherence of the settlement pattern to the transportation network in a *star village*, which results from the configuration of the road system. Cluster villages can be seen throughout Europe, and star villages occur in parts of northern and western Europe.

Hamlets and villages were still being created in Europe during the twelfth and thirteenth centuries, though the period of growth in rural settlement was about to suffer some setbacks. The countryside was filling up. The best lands had already been claimed by the nobility and the church. Some villages located on marginal lands were already shrinking before the Black Death plague began in 1349. By the time the

plague ran its course, hundreds of villages across Europe had been largely depopulated, and many disappeared completely.

The Black Death was accompanied and followed by an economic depression of great magnitude and considerable duration. A collapse of prices for agricultural commodities contributed to a rural-to-urban population migration. In some areas, such as Britain, a large-scale shift from cultivation of crops to sheep raising contributed to rural depopulation because fewer workers were required. The changing demographic and economic patterns of the late Middle Ages brought about the elimination of nearly one-quarter of the villages in England. In some districts in Germany, 80 percent of the villages disappeared.

The Middle Ages conventionally are thought of as the dominant period for the European village, but in fact the population remained predominantly rural until the middle decades of the nineteenth century, and the village remained the home of most people until that time.

The Thirty Years War, which began in 1618, and another major economic depression reduced the number of villages during the seventeenth century. Government-sponsored enclosure, described earlier, also caused desertion of many villages as people moved to dispersed farmsteads. New growth in old farm villages, however, occurred during the eighteenth century—"the golden century of farming." Higher farm commodity prices prompted estate owners to make way for more farm land by clearing forests and draining wet lands; many new villages resulted. This process continued during the nineteenth century as Europe's population continued to grow. However, while new farming lands were being created, the enclosure movement in the old agricultural districts continued to take people out of villages and settle them on the land.

Early in the twentieth century World War I altered many existing social and economic institutions in Europe and was a key event in the collapse of the estate system on which many villages from the previous centuries were based. The estates in eastern Europe that managed to survive World War I were seized by communist governments after World War II, and collectivization of farmland in the region helped to perpetuate nucleated rural settlement. In western Europe the farm villages have been dying for much of the present century. The very basis on which the village flourished for thousands of years—agriculture and crafts—no longer plays a serious role in the life of most rural communities. The industrialization of agriculture has meant that (1) relatively few farmers are needed; and (2) most farm headquarters are on the land, not in the village. Also, the improvement of transportation has reduced the role of the village as a market and supply center.

The departure of farmers from the villages of western Europe has resulted in stagnation or desertion of many villages. Others, especially those within easy commuting distance of the larger cities, have been able to change their functions and survive, even prosper. Most of these have become bedroom communities from which people commute to work in the city. The recent urban-to-rural migration trend has caused many villages to grow into towns and cities.

Europe, therefore, provides numerous examples of villages that have ceased to exist as units of nucleated rural settlement for two very different reasons: (1) they have lost population until they are no longer villages; or (2) they have gained population until they are no longer villages. Still, many thousands of villages remain across Europe.

VILLAGES IN THE UNITED STATES

From the earliest days of prehistoric native settlement to the last decade of the twentieth century, the village has been an important form of settlement in the United States. With about three-fourths of the nation's population now residing in urban places, it may be tempt-

ing to think of the rural village as a quaint anomaly, undeserving of serious study. Villages, however, are considerably more numerous than cities and, as local government units and residential communities, they play an important role in our settlement complex. Three groups of villages, each with many variations in details, are examined here: (1) the Native American village; (2) the utopian village; and (3) the "typical" American village.

Native American Villages

➤ A variety of both dispersed and nucleated settlements were established by Native Americans in pre-Columbian time.

Why were different types of native settlements developed?

Which type was occupied by the greatest number of inhabitants?

How did Native American settlements differ from region to region in North America?

Prior to the arrival of Europeans in America, both rural and urban settlements existed in parts of what is now the United States. The rural settlements were both dispersed and nucleated, since some Native Americans preferred to live on the land while others favored communal life. Dispersed settlement was more hazardous in times of conflict between tribes, so there was a tendency during those times for dispersed families to retreat to the greater safety of nucleated settlements. The extent of dispersed settlement, therefore, varied not only from place to place but also over relatively short periods of time. Because dispersed settlement leaves a more obscure archaeological record than nucleated settlement, archaeologists tend to focus their studies on the latter. One classification system of nucleated pre-Columbian native settlements includes seven types: (1) camps; (2) villages; (3) towns; (4) ceremonial centers; (5) village clusters; (6) town clusters; and (7) town-ceremonial centers.

Camps were impermanent and usually occupied no more than 1 acre (0.4 ha) of land. Their significance as temporary settlement units varied regionally and temporally. For example, their number diminished in the southeastern portion of what is now the United States from about the beginning of the Christian era. In northeastern New England, however, they were common until the period for which a written record exists.

A *village* typically covered several acres and may have had only a few to perhaps as many as a few hundred dwellings. In many instances "a village plan" provided an orderly arrangement of houses, while in others an apparently random placement of dwellings prevailed. In terms of the total population housed, the village was more important than the smaller camp and the larger town. *Towns* were the largest individual communities. Some of the prehistoric aboriginal towns covered hundreds of acres and included many hundreds of houses.

Ceremonial centers constitute the fourth settlement type. Like Native American towns, they will be mentioned only briefly in this chapter, but for a different reason; while towns are too large to constitute rural settlements, ceremonial centers were not intended for permanent human habitation. Instead, they served religious purposes primarily, including interment of the dead in many cases. Ceremonial centers sometimes formed the foci of surrounding rural settlement, but the centers themselves are not examined here.

Village clusters, a fifth type of Native American settlement, were particularly common. Neighboring villages were so closely related culturally that constant contact between them and probable participation in a common sociopolitical organization are indicated. Very often clustered villages shared a common ceremonial center. The other two types in the classification—*town clusters* and *town-ceremonial centers*—were not rural in character.

Most Native Americans who were hunters and gatherers and those whose livelihoods were based on fishing were not sedentary people; their subsistence activity required them to move frequently. Some, however, were able to reside in more or less permanent villages in areas that provided an abundance of game, fish, or wild plant foods. This was true, for example, of some of the early Native American groups in Alaska and salmon-fishing tribes of the Columbia Plateau. Permanent villages in most areas were established by people with closer ties to the land—in other words, farmers. The characteristics of these villages and the structures they contained varied greatly from region to region.

Excavation was involved in the construction of some village buildings. In the small native villages of Alaska, the randomly arranged *lodges* were partially dug into the ground, roofed with beams and poles, hung with mats, and provided with an entry. Semisub-terranean earthen lodges, including substantial communal structures, made up some of the villages of the Pacific Northwest. The earliest agricultural villages in the Southwest consisted of *pit houses*, structures built of adobe over pits dug into the shallow desert soil. Adobe was a common building material in the Southwest. Later some tribes in this area constructed residences entirely underground.

Perhaps the best-known prehistoric village ruins in the Southwest today are those at Mesa Verde, a national park in Colorado. *Cliff dwellings* were constructed here during and after the twelfth century by people whose economy was based primarily on agriculture. Large natural overhangs, or rockshelters, allowed the construction of complexes such as Cliff Palace (Fig. 12.17), which contained more than 200 rooms. Equally spectacular are the remains of some of the villages in Chaco Canyon in New Mexico. The most impressive is Pueblo Bonito (Fig. 12.18), a D-shaped communal village consisting of a single complex, sandstone-block structure that covered 2.5 acres (6.2 ha), contained more than 800 rooms, and had a population that once exceeded 1200. About 125 planned villages in the Chaco system flourished during the period A.D. 950–1300.

FIGURE 12.17
Cliff Palace at Mesa Verde, Colorado. Natural overhangs called rockshelters facilitated the construction of dwellings here during and after the twelfth century. (Norbert Archbold)

FIGURE 12.18
Pueblo Bonito in Chaco Canyon, New Mexico. With at least 800 rooms, Pueblo Bonito was the largest "apartment building" of North American antiquity.

Although excavation preceded or was a part of the construction of semisubterranean and subterranean housing in some areas, in other districts structures were built atop human-made plateaus. Native Americans who constructed ceremonial or burial mounds are called *mound builders*, and they include the Hopewell and Mississippian cultures of the Mississippi River drainage basin. The Hopewell people constituted a well-organized, village-based culture in which surplus human and material resources were used in the construction of elaborate earthen walls around treasure-laden burial mounds. Because such structures required much labor, villages were situated nearby. Conspicuous consumption is a continuing theme in Hopewell archaeological sites, a testimony of a well-to-do people whose culture flourished during the period 100 B.C. to A.D. 300.

Cultural deterioration followed Hopewellian prosperity, but after a few centuries the Mississippian culture complex began to emerge in the same areas—the drainage basin of the Mississippi River and its tributaries—and also in the Southeast. This predominantly agricultural complex showed its greatest growth during the period A.D. 700–1200. Large villages were in existence by A.D. 1000 with subsidiary farming communities nearby. An outstanding feature in many areas of Mississippian culture was the earthen temple

mound on which the major community buildings were placed. Houses were made of wood and mud, and floor plans were generally rectangular. Some villages were walled with timber palisades for protection. A recently excavated example of a walled Mississippian village is Orendorf (Fig. 12.19), located in central Illinois.

Native Americans who lived in the forests of the Northeast also favored palisaded walls around their communities for protection from their enemies. By A.D. 1000 the Iroquois of New England and New York had developed farm villages consisting of multifamily dwellings. With passing centuries, as the population increased, the villages became larger and more numerous. The multifamily houses typically were close together, arranged in orderly rows, and surrounded by a log wall (Fig. 12.20).

The European settlement of the eastern part of the country resulted in conflicts with the natives that caused many of them to migrate westward voluntarily. In addition, European diseases killed many natives. An unknown but great number of Native American villages in the East, therefore, had disappeared even before the Indian Removal Act of 1830. This forced relocation of perhaps 100,000 Native Americans between 1830 and 1840 resulted in the elimination of a few hundred additional eastern villages. By 1890, when the U.S. Cavalry murdered more than 200 of

FIGURE 12.19
Orendorf, a walled Mississippian village in Illinois. (Upper Mississippi Valley Archaeological Research Foundation)

Sitting Bull's people at Wounded Knee, South Dakota, most Native Americans had been moved to reservations.

In 1990 there were about 1.5 million Native Americans in the United States—probably a larger number than at any time in history or prehistory. The great majority of these people lived in five states: California, Oklahoma, Arizona, New Mexico, and North Carolina. Approximately half of them lived in urban

places where many had undergone assimilation into the larger society. The other half were rural dwellers, some living in villages, others on dispersed farms and ranches. The villages are primarily within or near reservations (Fig. 12.21) or in places where former reservations existed.

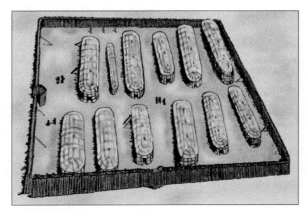

FIGURE 12.20
Typical fortified Iroquoian village, A.D. c. 1600. The families that lived in each multifamily dwelling probably were connected by kinship.

FIGURE 12.21
Many native Americans today live in poverty, some dispersed on farms and ranches, others in villages such as this one near Santa Fe, New Mexico. The majority of native Americans in the United States live in the Southwest. (Nita Winter)

Utopian Villages

➤ Villages founded by "utopian" groups have contributed to the variety of settlements established in the United States.

What motivations were involved in the establishment of these utopian settlements?

What factors contributed to their early successes?

What often led to the failure of these groups or to alterations of their original goals?

The adjective "utopian" means "excellent, but existing only in fancy or theory." The term has been adopted by settlement geographers to describe communities founded for the purpose of achieving some person's or group's idea of excellence. More often than not, the settlers in utopian communities shared a common religious faith, and the desire for freedom to practice their faith without outside interference was a strong motive in the founding of most of those settlements.

Puritan Settlements in New England   Puritanism in America generally is understood to mean the early Congregationalism of New England. The colonists were a selected people with a strong clerical leadership, and their purpose was to accomplish in America that which they had been prevented from accomplishing in Europe; by the power of their example they hoped to force a desired reformation of the Anglican Church in England. They did not expect America to be Utopia, for they had no illusions that founding colonies in a new land would be easy. The religious zeal of the Puritans, however, and the role of religion in the establishment and functioning of their colonies make it proper to classify the early Puritan settlements as utopian villages. (Later some of them—Putney, Vermont, and Wallingford, Connecticut, for example—grew to become towns and cities.)

Seventeenth-century agrarian colonies in New England were group efforts at land development. The English Crown had granted extensive lands to trading companies, and in turn they gave out "towns" or "townships," which usually ranged from 50 to 100 square miles (129 to 259 sq km), to groups of immigrant colonists. Many of the communities founded on those undeveloped tracts of land were planned nucleated villages, typically located near the center of the land grant. House lots usually ranged from a ¼ acre (0.1 ha) to 2 acres (0.8 ha) in size—large enough for

a dwelling, a few outbuildings, and a small garden. In addition to the area subdivided into house lots was one or a few larger tracts of farm lots, where the settlers raised most of their food. These individually assigned fields were of identical size in some communities but varied in size in others; equality more or less characterized the assignment of land. In some New England towns (townships) in which a serious effort was made at equitable land distribution, each family received several strips of ground in each farmland block, which assured that each family had shares of different types and qualities of land. Also, there were **common lands**, or simply *commons*, consisting of one or more large parcels set aside for common grazing. Likewise, forest land usually was held in common. However, not every Puritan settlement in early New England was an American version of an English parish, and many of them did not have land patterns similar to those in late medieval England. Many Puritans, in fact, adopted a dispersed pattern of population distribution and farming from the early colonial period. Variations in settlement patterns existed in different parts of New England, and there were many colonists throughout the region who were not among the religious zealots.

The New England nucleated settlement, usually led by a Puritan church leader, satisfied the religious, educational, and other social needs of the people. There was an additional advantage: defense against attacks by Native Americans. Eventually, the threat of such attacks subsided and the village populations grew—two facts that encouraged population dispersal from the original centers of settlement. When no more land was available in and around a village, a new village might be launched nearby. The withdrawal or pacification of the Native Americans, however, made the frontier an attractive alternative for the more venturesome families. Increasingly, large blocks of land were acquired by land companies that were more interested in subdivision and quick resale than in dealing with English congregations of would-be settlers. Land availability and growing dissention in the Puritan church, as well as increasing safety from attacks by natives, encouraged pioneering and expanded the dispersed pattern of rural settlement that would prevail eventually in most of the lands of the United States.

With time the Puritan was transformed into the Yankee, but not before imparting to America the principles of liberty from arbitrary power, checks and balances to government, morality, and the ethic of hard work. (The principal of religious freedom also has

FIGURE 12.22
These restored buildings from the Puritan era are part of the cultural landscape of Portsmouth, New Hampshire.
(F. Clarkson)

been attributed to the Puritans, but in fact they favored religious freedom only for themselves and expelled from their communities those who dared to disagree with their doctrines.) The New England landscape today displays only remnants of the old Puritan settlements (Fig. 12.22).

Yankee and Immigrant Colonies in the Midwest
Many of the Yankee and foreign immigrant settlements founded on the midwestern frontier were utopian villages. *Yankee colonies* were pioneer settlements established by descendants of the New England Puritans who participated in the general westward migration of pioneers from the Northeast during the early nineteenth century. Most of these colonies were products of one or both of two movements in the Northeast that reached their zenith in the mid-1830s: the Congregational-Presbyterian "Great Revival" and a land speculation craze of greater magnitude than the country had ever experienced before in its history.

The Great Revival was a religious movement that began in New York in 1825 and spread to other parts of the Northeast. The major issues of the movement were temperance, antislavery, and anti-Catholicism, the last being particularly important in the decision to plant colonies in the Midwest. New Protestant settlements, it was reasoned, would help counteract the "Catholic threat" resulting from foreign immigration to the Mississippi Valley. Widespread land speculation was the second motivation for Yankee colonization schemes in the Midwest. National prosperity,

cheap land, increasing availability of loans, and the improvement of transportation were essential factors in the speculation movement.

The Yankee colonies can be divided into two categories: (1) those consisting of part or all of a church congregation, usually Congregational or Presbyterian, transplanted to the frontier from some northeastern state; and (2) those sponsored by a land company or association that functioned primarily to facilitate the settlement process. As a rule, the religious colonies were more thoroughly organized than the others.

The settler in the typical Yankee colony received a town lot in a central village, plus a block of farmland near the village. In some colonies the settler also received a wood lot, but in others the forest land was used in common. The typical Yankee village included a church and a school. Soon after their founding, some colonies were able to establish a grist mill or saw mill. Probably it was assumed by the founders of most Yankee colonies that the farmers would live in the villages, as had many of their ancestors in New England. In a large proportion of these settlements, however, farmers never built a house on their town lot but instead established a farmstead on their farm ground. The village in Yankee colonies usually served only as a market and supply center, not as a utopian community of farmers. The colonies in which most of the people were members of a single congregation were more likely to be utopian settlements.

Immigrant colonies also were likely to exist for a time as utopian villages. Several dozen immigrant colonies were founded in the Midwest by Canadian, English, Scottish, French, German, Swiss, Swedish, and Norwegian groups. Although there were exceptions, the immigrant colonies favored nucleated settlement and close social ties, and some involved communal land ownership and communal labor. In general, these were rigidly organized communal groups with highly centralized leadership. In many cases a single individual provided the inspiration and direction for the development of immigrant colonies. One such man was Eric Janson, founder of a Swedish immigrant colony in Illinois.

The growing liberalism and the perceived laxity of morals within the Established Church of Sweden during the early decades of the nineteenth century led to efforts by fundamentalist groups to reform the church. When the church began persecuting a large group of fundamentalists led by Eric Janson, he grew increasingly fanatical, claiming to be a God-sent prophet. His followers, who became known as Jansonists, increased in number to about 4000. Janson convinced many of them to join him in seeking religious freedom in the United States. In 1846 Janson and some of his followers established in northwestern Illinois a new colony, which they called Bishop Hill after Janson's birthplace in Sweden. Between 1846 and 1854, some 1500 Jansonists emigrated to Bishop Hill.

The village never contained a population of 1500 people, however, because there were many deaths during the early years and periodic abandonment of the sect by disillusioned individuals and families. Throughout most of the 14-year history of Bishop Hill

as a communal society, its population ranged between 400 and 800. Janson sent out 12 "apostles" to proselytize among the Americans, but their efforts brought few converts to Jansonism.

Bishop Hill was laid out on a grid pattern but with blocks of different sizes (Fig. 12.23). A village park was established near the center, and most of the major buildings were constructed within a distance of two blocks from it. The colony grain mill, cemetery, warehouses, and orchards were located around the margins of the village. Domestic life, like everything else, was communal. Most of the people lived in dormitories. The largest housing unit was a three-story brick building containing 96 rooms—the "Big Brick" dormitory (Fig. 12.24). The Jansonists produced subsistence crops, flax, and broom corn. They manufactured bricks, wagons, farm implements, harnesses, textiles, and brooms. A great variety of goods were available at the general store, and travelers were boarded at the colony's hotel.

Janson died in 1850, before the colony achieved its greatest development and prosperity. After functioning for 14 years as a communal society, the Bishop Hill colony was dissolved formally during the period 1860–1862. Contributing factors were (1) a decline in the colonists' religious fervor; (2) a growing aware-

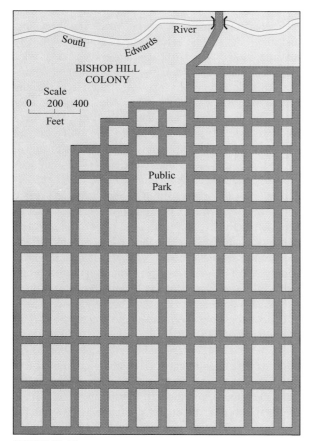

FIGURE 12.23

The layout of Bishop Hill, a utopian community in Illinois. Bishop Hill was established by a Swedish religious group that practiced a communal lifestyle from 1846 to 1852.

FIGURE 12.24

The "Big Brick" dormitory of the Bishop Hill Colony contained 96 rooms (one family per room) with a common dining area on the ground floor. The building was destroyed by fire in 1928. (Bishop Hill Heritage Association)

ness of the opportunities and rewards associated with individual endeavor; (3) increasing dissatisfaction with those who provided the leadership after the prophet's death; and (4) mounting financial setbacks after a nationwide depression in 1857. The subdivision of the common property among the colonists in 1861 and 1862 marked the death of the utopian community.

The Typical American Village

➤ The typical American village differs significantly from rural villages in most of the world.

How does the American village differ from its counterpart elsewhere?

How has the typical American village changed during the twentieth century?

In the United States villages can be defined as communities of fewer than 2500 people. Very small villages are called hamlets. As we noted early in this chapter, there has been no general agreement on a population size to serve as the boundary between a village and a hamlet.

For thousands of years in some parts of the world and hundreds of years in others, the typical village was an agrarian community. Farmers lived in the village and worked land nearby. That pattern continues to prevail in hundreds of thousands of villages around the world, even though rural population dispersal has been a modern trend in many countries. What is typical of rural settlement in most of the world is not typical in the United States, however. The Puritan colonies and most other utopian settlements were farm communities, but good examples of agrarian villages are few and far between in the United States today. Since late in the colonial period, the typical American village has been a trade center, not a settlement of farm families. Most American farmers have lived on the land or "in the country." The typical American village (Fig. 12.25) historically has been the market and supply center for farmers and others, as well as a residential center for nonfarm rural population. (See *Cultural Landscapes: The Midwest Livestock Auction.*)

Until the late eighteenth century, European settlement in the United States was limited to a narrow strip of land, no more than 200 miles wide, along the eastern seaboard. The economy was predominantly agrarian, and there were many farm villages—old Puritan

villages in the North and villages on plantations in the South. By the beginning of the nineteenth century, settlement had begun its westward expansion into the vast areas acquired by the federal government, and new states were coming into existence.

Since most farmers on the frontier took up residence on the land, the founding of villages was left to others. From the beginning, most of the communities established in the new territories were created by private promoters on land secured through the government's land-grant programs. The land distributed by the federal government previously had been surveyed according to the official rectilinear survey system, so perhaps it was natural that promoters seeking to develop new communities preferred a grid-pattern layout of blocks and roads. In determining the site for a new settlement, the founder usually gave consideration to at least a few of the locational factors identified in Figure 12.12. When good sites were chosen, villages prospered as residential, market, and supply centers and grew into towns; better situated towns eventually became cities. When the organizers made a poor choice of site, the community failed to attain significant size, and many disappeared. In some cases, the choice of site was good, but changing conditions later made the community less attractive. For example, a settlement developed on the route of a proposed rail line often failed when the railway route was changed.

Nineteenth- and early-twentieth-century villages typically included a school, one or more churches, several retail stores, a blacksmith's shop, a doctor's office and perhaps a dentist's office and mortuary, a mill or some other facility to process the major cash crop of the area, sometimes a jail, and often a bank. If the community served as county seat, it had a court house; county seat villages, however, usually grew to urban size. By the early part of the twentieth century, there was usually a gasoline station. The larger the village, of course, the more services and the greater the variety of goods available.

Country and village were interdependent. By a tradition that may go back to the town markets of Europe, Saturday was the day for "going to town" to transact business and to visit. Returning to the village the next morning to attend church was a ritual for many. Retired farmers sometimes abandoned the land to settle in the community.

The rural American village eventually changed because of the industrialization of agriculture and

FIGURE 12.25

A "typical" American village. Villages traditionally have been market and supply centers for farmers as well as residential centers for nonfarm rural populations. (Dean Abramson/ Stock Boston)

other forms of primary production, growing urbanization, improvements in transportation, and advances in communications. Fewer farmers were needed. Those who continued to farm were no longer dependent on the nearest village as a market or supply center. Business in the village stores slumped, and some stores went out of business. The local bank often failed. The doctor, dentist, and mortician moved to a larger town. The village took on an appearance of stagnation. Out-migration of young people left the village with an older population than in earlier times.

For decades such changes have led to predictions that nucleated rural settlements are doomed, and yet there were more villages in 1990 than in 1910. The much larger total population of 1990 made this possible, despite the trend toward increasing urbanization during the period 1910–1990. Many villages did disappear during that eight-decade period. Most of them were communities that had never achieved much size. There is compelling evidence that a village of 200 people is far more likely to gradually become deserted than one of 1000 people. Furthermore, there is some evidence that a population of about 300 may be a critical threshold for a village. That is, communities with a smaller population are less likely to grow and more likely to shrink than one with a population of more than 300.

Another factor that seems to contribute to the growth of villages is inertia. There are many exceptions, but in general larger villages—the ones most likely to prosper and grow—tend to be older than smaller ones. Most of the nation's larger villages existed in the nineteenth century, grew rapidly before 1910, but grew slowly in most decades since that time. During the 1970s the process of counter-urbanization, described earlier, began to move people out of urban areas and into the countryside. The trend of former city-dwellers taking up residence in nucleated rural settlements has contributed to **nonmetropolitan turnaround**, a cessation of decline for many villages and the rapid growth of others. This transition of the American village in the 1970s and 1980s was a remarkable one with important implications for the present and future role of the village in the settlement geography of the nation.

The character and make-up of villages is different in the 1990s than in earlier decades. The prophets of doom who predicted the death of the village failed to consider the adaptability of rural people and the potential attractiveness of rural living. Even as many villages were losing services, families who had lived there for generations were determined to accept change, if necessary, in order to perpetuate their communities. They welcomed new neighbors who were

CULTURAL LANDSCAPES

The Midwest Livestock Auction

A distinctive aspect of the cultural landscape in the rural Midwest of the United States is the livestock auction. These auctions usually are located in the region's hamlets and villages, where their presence is marked by large sale barns. Both cattle and hogs, as we pointed out in Chapter 11, are important elements in the mixed farming economy of the Corn Belt. Although most livestock produced by Midwestern hog and cattle farmers are sold privately and do not pass through auction barns, the livestock auction has long been an important enterprise in the region.

Livestock and other auctions in the United States have antecedents in Europe. During the colonial period, trade auctions were held in several European countries to dispose of products from the colonies. These auctions provided an exceptionally rapid and effective means of disposing of perishable commodities. The Dutch may have introduced auctions to the American colonies; the first evidently was held in New Amsterdam (New York) in 1662. There is no record of the first American livestock auction, but it may have occurred as early as the seventeenth century.

Livestock auctions in the Midwest date to the first half of the nineteenth century, although the first permanent livestock auction barns were not established until early in the 1900s. There were no livestock auction barns in Illinois in 1900; by 1937 there were 140. The number of sale barns in Illinois declined steadily

The Hersman Livestock Auction barn on sale day.

after 1937, and today there are only about 40. Other states in the Midwest have experienced a similar reduction in number of their livestock auction barns during the past half-century. In some parts of the Midwest this decrease has been related to diminishing numbers of livestock as farmers switched from mixed crop and livestock farming to cash grain farming. Many smaller sale barns went out of business because they could not compete successfully with larger auctions having lower costs per animal sold. Also, better highways and more efficient trucks enabled producers to transport livestock greater distances to market, thereby reducing the need for local auctions.

The Hersman Livestock Auction barn, shown in the accompanying photo, is located near the tiny community of Hersman, Illinois. Despite its association with a hamlet that lacks even a post office or gasoline station, the sale barn is one of the ten busiest in the state. On sale day (Tuesday) its huge parking lot is crowded. Like many auction barns, it includes a restaurant that is a popular gathering place for area farm-

ers throughout the week. Thus, livestock auction barns serve an important social function in addition to their economic role in the rural Midwest.

Livestock auctions operate in much the same way as other auctions. Auctioneers who own sale barns or who are employed by sale barn owners represent the sellers, and the auction company receives a percentage of the receipts. The potential buyers, most of whom are farmers or the representatives of slaughter houses and meat-packing companies, are assigned bidding numbers. The sale goes to the highest bidder and is recorded by bidding number. The auction barn has a sales area, similar to a small arena, in which livestock are displayed for prospective buyers. Animals are sold individually or in small lots. The largest portion of the sale barn is subdivided into small holding pens in which animals are kept prior to being herded into the sales arena and where they can be inspected by potential buyers. Following the sale they are returned to the pens to await being loaded into the trucks and trailers of the buyers.

THOUGHT QUESTIONS

1. What do you think would happen to the Hersman Livestock Auction if most of the farmers within 40 miles of Hersman would switch from mixed farming to cash grain farming?

2. If the Hersman Livestock Auction should close its restaurant, would the volume of livestock sold by the business likely be affected? Why or why not?

3. The Hersman Livestock Auction barn is adjacent to a state highway, three miles from a U.S. highway. If Hersman were located instead within three miles of an access ramp to an interstate highway, would the livestock auction's volume of business likely be affected? Why or why not?

moving out from the city and suburbs. Villages closest to the suburbs of large cities increasingly became residential in character.

By the 1980s, however, it was not necessary for a great many workers to commute from outlying villages to the city because so many manufacturing jobs by that decade had moved beyond the suburbs to small-town America. Firms seeking good sites for branch plants had located there so they could have the pick of the local labor force and not have to rely on usually more expensive urban labor. This has contributed to the good economic health of numerous villages across the country.

The residential function of the typical American village is evidenced by the fact that only about 15 percent of the employed people who live there are actually working in the community. Villages have qualities that make them attractive places for many workers and retired persons to live. Compared to large cities, they are viewed by many as quiet, friendly, clean, safe, uncongested, and slower-paced. Those are among the factors that help to account for the nonmetropolitan turnaround.

KEY TERMS

Dispersed settlement The settlement of people on the land in scattered farmsteads. **451**

Nucleated settlement Any human settlement, ranging in size from a hamlet to a major metropolis, in which the houses and other buildings are in close proximity or highly concentrated. **451**

Metes and bounds A land survey system in which natural features such as trees, boulders, and water bodies are used to establish property boundaries. **451**

Long lot A relatively long and narrow parcel of land, usually with one end of the property adjacent to a river or road. In North America, long lots are found in areas originally settled by the French. **452**

Centuriatio An orderly survey system, involving rectangular units of land, used by the Romans in classical time. **453**

Townships Units of land in the United States that were surveyed according to provisions in the Land Ordinance of 1785. An ideal township is square and contains 36 sections, each of which is a square mile in area. **453**

Enclosure movement In western Europe following the Middle Ages, the enclosure movement involved consolidating land into individual farms and the relocation of rural people to those farms. **458**

Hillforts Small hilltop settlements with fortifications dating from the Iron Age in western Europe. **462**

Ejidos In Mexico, agricultural villages that control the surrounding land. As part of Mexico's agrarian reform program, the village allocates land for use by its inhabitants but retains ownership of the land. **464**

Common lands Parcels of land reserved for use by all citizens. In colonial New England, certain grazing areas and wood lots were set aside as common lands to be used by all inhabitants. **471**

Nonmetropolitan turnaround A reversal of the population decline in some rural settlements in the United States during the 1970s and 1980s. **475**

REVIEW QUESTIONS

1. Why is it that the concept of the farm village seems unfamiliar to many people in the United States?

2. What do mining villages, fishing villages, and logging villages have in common?

3. What are Old World antecedents of the modern metes and bounds survey?

4. What is the purpose of the long-lot survey system?

5. How are both harsh environments and favorable environments conducive to dispersed settlement?

6. What are some of the problems that may be associated with dispersed settlement?

7. What was the European enclosure movement?

8. Besides their sizes, how do large farms differ from small farms in the United States today?

9. What are some of the problems that may be associated with nucleated settlement?

10. When and in which areas did the earliest farming communities develop?

11. What were some common types of medieval European villages?

12. How was nucleated settlement in Europe affected by the following: Black Death; a shift in some areas from crop cultivation to sheep raising; the "golden century of farming"; World War I; the communist takeover of eastern Europe after World War II; and the industrialization of agriculture?

13. What is significant about Cliff Palace and Pueblo Bonito?

14. What were early Puritan settlements in New England like?

15. What factors facilitated the establishment of Yankee colonies in the U.S. Midwest?

16. What were the origins of settlers in immigrant colonies in the U.S. Midwest?

17. What was the typical American village like in the early twentieth century? How was this community affected later by the industrialization of agriculture, increasing industrialization in general, improvements in transportation, and advances in communication?

18. What is nonmetropolitan turnaround? What factors have contributed to it?

CHAPTER 13

CITIES AND URBANIZATION: PATTERNS AND TRENDS

Cities have always been the fireplaces of civilization, whence light and heat radiated out into the dark, cold world.

—Theodore Parker

Large cities typically are places of ethnic heterogeneity. This Chicago resident's hat reflects pride in her African heritage. (The Image Works)

Although the majority of the world's people have lived in rural settings throughout history, urban places have existed for more than five millennia, and their growth in both number and size has been spectacular since the Industrial Revolution. Industrialization has been a powerful force in attracting rural people into cities by creating a need for many workers and by generally improving the quality of life. Nearly half of all people in the world now live in urban centers, and the proportion continues to increase each year. In most industrialized countries more than 65 percent of the population is urban, and in some the level even exeeds 80 percent. Recently a new era in world urbanization has become evident, marked by a surge in the urban growth rates of preindustrial countries. If this new trend continues, and we have every reason to expect that it will, in the near future the level of urbanization will no longer represent a significant difference between industrial and preindustrial nations. Indeed, many of the Latin American countries already have more than 65 percent of their populations in cities.

Urban settlements encompass both towns of modest size and major cities that may contain many millions of inhabitants. In a few areas of the world, the close spacing and horizontal growth of cities have resulted in the formation of virtually continuous built-up zones or urban regions containing tens of millions of people. Urban settlements differ from their rural counterparts in a number of ways, most obviously in their greater size and functional complexity. Another significant distinction is that most employed residents of urban centers are engaged in tertiary (service activities) and secondary (manufacturing) occupations, whereas rural people usually support themselves by primary economic activities (mainly agriculture). However, it is not easy to arrive at a precise differentiation between urban and rural places.

Urban centers exist only because they are most efficient in providing functions that a society feels are needed. In addition to serving as places of residence for many people, towns and cities commonly possess such functions as trade and commerce, manufacturing, public administration, and personal services. The number and mix of functions vary enormously from one center to another because they are influenced by several variables, including the size of the urban center, the nature of the surrounding area, and the nation's level of economic development. The functions of a town or city are available to its inhabitants as well as to people in a surrounding trade area. The extent of a trade area is usually proportional to the size of its associated central place (urban center), but there also may be other influencing factors. The trade area of a large and functionally complex city may be so extensive that it crosses international boundaries and reaches beyond oceans.

In this chapter, after discussion of perceptions and definitions of urban places and examination of locational characteristics of urban centers, our focus will be on urbanization. We will trace the origin and spread of cities, study the trends and patterns of urban growth, and examine the contemporary spatial patterns of urbanization. In the latter part of the chapter we will consider urban functions and the internal structure of cities.

WHAT IS AN URBAN PLACE?

➤ Cities are highly complex entities with many important functions, and as a consequence they exert enormous influence on a society.

In what ways do cities exhibit wealth and power on one hand and poverty and hopelessness on the other?

How do individual perceptions of cities differ?

Theodore Parker's quotation at the beginning of this chapter suggests that cities commonly have been identified as the catalysts of civilization. They are the places of greatest economic importance in each nation, they contain the most notable cultural features and institutions, and they are where the society's most powerful and prominent individuals usually choose to reside. As the main centers of government, finance, education, manufacturing, and commerce, the cities of a nation exert enormous influence on its entire population. The cities are where each society's most important plans are formulated and its most important decisions are made.

Without question, urban centers are the most complex features constructed by societies on the surface of the earth. They are places where people and buildings are highly concentrated, with an impressive assortment of multistory buildings—magnificent skyscrapers in some cases—that usually give identity to

FIGURE 13.1

Approaching downtown Atlanta. Nearly all major cities are distinguished by a unique assortment of multistory buildings in their downtown area. The high value of land in a city's downtown area makes vertical construction more economical than horizontal construction. (John Elk III/Stock Boston)

a central commercial core or ''downtown'' area (Fig. 13.1). These buildings serve an assortment of purposes: many house retail and service establishments; others are hotels and apartment complexes; and some are office buildings. The headquarters of major corporations usually are housed in downtown buildings of the larger cities. Transportation routes converge on urban centers, and traffic on city streets and highways often is congested. All urban places have residential districts and neighborhoods as well as a central business district, but larger cities also contain an assortment of other special-function areas including industrial zones, commercial strips along important streets and highways, warehousing districts, shopping malls, and parks and other recreational areas. With their intensity of land use, cities also are areas where the natural landscape has been most completely obliterated. Furthermore, cities are major sources of environmental pollution, particularly air, water, and noise pollution.

Urban Contrasts

Contrasts abound in urban centers. Every positive attribute appears to be offset by a negative characteristic. Cities may be the focal point of great wealth, but their population includes many people who are destitute and disturbing numbers of homeless people. In contrast to the luxury apartment complexes of the wealthy are the neighborhoods of the poor in which housing quality often can be appalling. Differences in the lifestyles of society's rich and poor are evident everywhere, but the magnitude of these differences always seems greatest in cities. Few urban scenes are as depressing as those of street beggars in Calcutta and the dilapidated housing in the slums of New York City.

Most of us have vivid perceptions of urban places, but even our perceptions reveal great contrasts. To some people a city is exciting and attractive, a place with interesting and stimulating people and many appealing cultural facilities, recreational activities, and employment opportunities. Others perceive cities as dirty and dangerous, with despicable litter and graffiti, prostitutes, drug addicts and dealers, and crime so common that it is unsafe to be on the streets at night. The crime, congestion, pollution, and complexity of the city cause some people to view life there as intolerable. In contrast, others consider living anyplace else an unacceptably boring and dull experience.

In the final analysis it appears that the positive perceptions of urban places overpower the negative ones. That conclusion is supported by the persistent migration of rural people to urban places and the growth of urban populations around the globe. Urbanization clearly is a powerful universal current. In some Western nations, however, the migration of people from major cities to surrounding suburbs and smaller towns has resulted in a recent population decrease for certain cities.

Delimitations and Definitions

➤ Definitions and terms that identify and delimit urban places are arbitrary and inconsistently used from country to country.

Why are there differences in how countries define "urban?"

What criteria must be met for a place to qualify as urban in the United States?

What is a Metropolitan Statistical Area?

It would seem to be a simple task to separate by definition urban places from the generally open space of

rural areas, but in fact definitions in use are inconsistent and quite arbitrary. For international comparisons of urbanization, it would be ideal if each country used the same definition. That is not the case, however. Each country has adopted a definition of "urban" that seems to fit its demographic and spatial circumstances. For example, in Canada, where population is sparse and distances are vast, the definition of "urban" requires a minimum of only 1000 people in a nucleated settlement. In contrast, crowded Japan uses a minimum of 30,000 people in its definition of urban. In the United States the definition of urban long used by the U.S. Census Bureau requires that a community be incorporated and have a minimum population of 2500. The arbitrariness of the U.S. definition is evident. Some towns with fewer than 2500 people may engage only in urban functions, yet they are classified by the census as rural. Likewise, a suburban community of

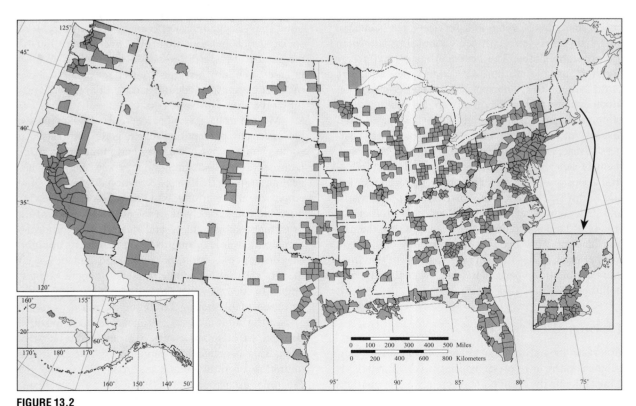

FIGURE 13.2
The Metropolitan Statistical Areas in the United States. According to the 1990 census, a population of at least one million is contained in each of 39 MSAs.

10,000 or 15,000 people fails to qualify as urban if it is unincorporated.

Methods of delimiting the spatial extent of urban places are equally troublesome. Perhaps the most obvious method is to use the municipal boundary, or corporate limits, of incorporated communities. This boundary marks the extent of the *legal city*—the area over which the municipal government exercises legal authority. From time to time, the legal city may increase its area by the *annexation* of a neighboring tract that is built up and meets certain criteria. Often the municipal boundary fails to enclose all of the adjacent built-up areas, however. As a consequence, we also can identify a *physical city* that usually is of greater extent than the legal city. As a matter of fact, the physical city may include one or more adjacent suburbs that have been incorporated and are themselves legal cities. The complex formed by a relatively large *central city* and surrounding towns and suburbs—both incorporated and unincorporated—that are functionally linked to the central city commonly is called an *urbanized area*.

In the United States, urbanized areas have long been officially recognized and defined by the U.S. Census Bureau. The term **Metropolitan Statistical Area** (MSA) is now used by the U.S. Census Bureau for these units, replacing the earlier title of *Standard Metropolitan Statistical Area* (SMSA). Each MSA coincides with the area of a county or a group of contiguous counties that contains a central city of at least 50,000 or an urbanized area of at least 50,000 and a total metropolitan population of at least 100,000. Nearly 300 MSAs now exist in the United States (Fig. 13.2). The most controversial aspect of MSAs is the use of county boundaries in their delimitations. Counties within MSAs usually contain more land used for rural than urban purposes.

Conurbation is another title commonly used for certain urbanized areas. It customarily is applied to an urban complex in which neighboring cities and towns have become physically linked by means of their horizontal growth. No official definition has been formulated, but conurbation is a name that connotes a closely knit cluster of urban centers. As we noted in Chapter 8, the world's largest and best known conurbation is Megalopolis, the highly urbanized portion of the U.S. Atlantic Coast that extends from southern New England to the vicinity of Chesapeake Bay. In a later section of this chapter, we will identify several other major conurbations in the world.

LOCATIONAL CHARACTERISTICS OF URBAN CENTERS

In our effort to understand urban settlements, we must search for answers to a number of important questions. For example, why were urban settlements founded at particular places? Why have cities had different rates of growth? Why have some urban centers specialized in a particular function while others have focused on different functions? A variety of factors will be involved in the answer to such questions, but the importance of location will certainly be stressed by a geographer. In discussing locational characteristics pertinent to towns and cities, we have chosen to group them under site and situation.

Site Characteristics

➤ The characteristics or qualities of individual sites have had great influence on where urban centers were established and how they developed.

What characteristics of their sites have been particularly important for urban places?

How can the spatial arrangement of cities be explained by site characteristics?

How can the characteristics of a city's site change from positive to negative over time?

An urban center's **site** concerns characteristics of the specific area it occupies. In the founding of human settlements, a variety of site characteristics were important. In cases where there was reason to be concerned about a possible raid or attack on the settlement, sites were chosen that offered a measure of protection or an advantage for defense. For that reason, peninsulas and islands were favored sites for early cities. Both Venice and Paris, for example, were founded on islands to take advantage of protection offered by the surrounding water. The Île de la Cité in the Seine River is now famous as the original site of Paris (Fig. 13.3). Many other prominent cities occupy sites on hills or other elevated ground because these locations were originally chosen with defense in mind. Settlement sites on elevated land also were often chosen because they had better natural drainage than lowland areas and therefore were considered to be places where people would be less likely to suffer from diseases. An example from classical time is Rome, which

FIGURE 13.3

The original site of Paris was an island—the Île de la Cité—in the Seine River. Prominent structures on the island are the Cathedral of Notre Dame and the Palace of Justice. (R. Gabler)

was constructed on a group of hills to avoid the nearby malaria-infested Pontine Marshes.

Sites that offer access to water have been especially important locations for towns and cities. Fresh water for domestic consumption is necessary, of course, to sustain all human communities. The importance of fresh water is particularly evident in arid areas; in the founding of desert settlements no other site characteristic approaches the availability of water in significance. Even in humid areas, the origin and viability of countless towns and cities are related to the accessibility of water at their sites. The industrialization, elevation of living standards, and population growth of modern cities have greatly increased their thirst for water and thereby accentuated the importance of this site factor. Los Angeles and Phoenix are two major cities in the United States that now face threatening deficiencies in their water supplies, but many other urban centers share this problem.

Access to water also has been extremely important to towns and cities for transportation and the opportunity to carry out trade. Prior to the development of road and railroad networks, sites adjacent to navigable water were crucial to the economic survival and growth of urban centers. Examination of an appropriate map or globe will confirm that most of the world's major cities occupy coastal and riverside sites, and nearly all cities of substantial size in the United States are adjacent to navigable water bodies. Three of the most notable waterside urban sites in the United States are those of New York City at the mouth of the Hudson River; Pittsburgh at the junction of the Monongahela, Allegheny, and Ohio Rivers; and San Francisco on the peninsula between the Pacific Ocean and San Francisco Bay. The head of navigation on rivers also has been a common site for the establishment of cities. Well-known examples in the United States are the *Fall Line* sites of Washington, D.C.; Richmond, Virginia; Columbia, South Carolina; and Columbus, Georgia (Fig. 13.4). The Fall Line is the edge of the Appalachian Piedmont where upstream navigation of rivers is terminated by rapids and falls as the flow of these streams proceeds toward the lower Coastal Plain. In addition to being the starting point for downstream shipping, the head of navigation also forces the transfer of interior-bound cargo from boats for further shipment by other means, thereby creating a commercial opportunity for any city at that site.

Sites adjacent to roads and railroads, particularly where these routes intersect one another or a navigable water body, also commonly have been chosen for the establishment of towns and cities. In western states such as North Dakota, the influence of railroads and highways on the location of urban communities is clearly evident in Figure 13.5. With no navigable rivers present, access to land transportation is of para-

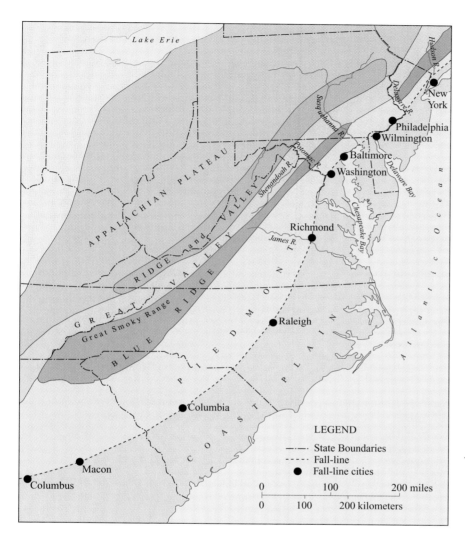

FIGURE 13.4

Fall Line cities in the eastern United States. The falls and rapids on rivers descending from the Appalachian Piedmont to the Coastal Plain interrupted water transportation and thereby created a commercial opportunity for cities founded on those sites.

mount importance. Those settlements not founded on sites adjacent to railroads and important roads soon withered. Threatened more recently are towns that have been bypassed by new highways and those on railroads that have discontinued service.

For some cities, even the geological character of their sites has had important ramifications. For example, the massive and stable bedrock of Manhattan Island has facilitated the construction of enormous skyscraper buildings in New York City. On the other hand, cities built on earthquake-prone sites, such as Los Angeles (Fig. 13.6), or where the surface has tended to subside, as it has in Venice, have suffered

serious and sometimes tragic consequences. In addition, air pollution problems can be accentuated by the landform character of an urban site. A prominent example is the air pollution of Mexico City, a problem intensified by the city's location in a basin that hinders dispersal of the pollutants.

Site characteristics and their significance are not necessarily permanent. An initial attribute of an urban site can be elevated or reduced in importance or even eliminated by such things as environmental changes, the application of new technology, growth and development of the city, or simply historical change. A site that was valued for defensive reasons hundreds or

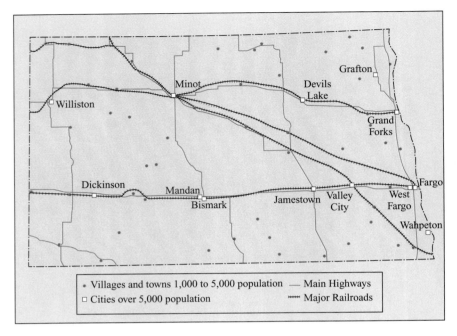

FIGURE 13.5

A site that provides access to transportation lines is essential to the viability of urban settlements. Only the major highways and railroads of North Dakota are represented on this map, but their influence on the establishment and development of urban centers is readily apparent.

thousands of years ago may provide no comparable advantage for the modern city. Many towns and cities originally founded on sites adjacent to navigable waterways are now inaccessible by water as a result of the shrinkage of seas and lakes and changes in the course of rivers. Also, the significance of a site on a

FIGURE 13.6

The sites of some cities pose certain environmental risks. Some of the destruction from the 1994 earthquake in the San Fernando Valley in southern California is shown in this photograph. (Spencer Grant/Stock Boston)

navigable waterway is reduced as a city's land and air transportation linkages are developed.

Situation Characteristics

➤ An urban center's economic character or functional role commonly is influenced by its situation or regional setting.

How does a city's situation differ from its site as a locational and economic factor?

How can the character of a city's situation change over time?

In contrast to the *local* attributes of site, a town or city's **situation** is its *regional* setting. In Chapter 1 we introduced the concept of situation and identified it as the relative location of a place. The relative location, or regional setting, of an urban center is commonly a major factor in its economic character or functional role. From the surrounding region or a nearby area, a city may have the opportunity to obtain a natural resource or agricultural commodity for processing. The region may contain people who are potential customers for the city's goods and services. If the city has a central location within a particular market area or a strategic location relative to a transportation corridor, it may have the opportunity to become a distribution or transportation center.

To illustrate the significance of situation, let us consider some examples. Bombay was able to exploit its situation adjacent to the vast cotton-growing area in western India and become a major textile manufacturing center. Birmingham, situated in England's coal-rich Midlands region, became one of the earliest centers of heavy industry. Situated in the central part of South Africa's gold-mining Witwatersrand district, Johannesburg developed into the modern world's leading center for processing and trading gold. Houston, situated near the productive oil fields of the Texas Gulf Coast in the United States, evolved into an enormous refinery center as well as an administrative capital for the petroleum industry. Surrounded by the bituminous coal fields of Pennsylvania, Pittsburgh was able to assemble the fuel for blast furnaces economically and thereby develop into a major iron and steel manufacturing center. Adjacent to the productive Corn Belt, Chicago became a major manufacturer of agricultural implements as well as a processing center for the livestock and grains raised on the region's farms. In addition, the establishment of Chicago as a great railroad center was related to its situation—a central position in the Middle West and a location near the southern end of Lake Michigan. The lake, of course, was a barrier that forced the channeling of east–west railroads around its southern end and into the lap of Chicago (Fig. 13.7).

Over time, the situation of a city can change for the better or worse as events unfold. The discovery of a valuable nearby mineral deposit or development of a recreational lake in the vicinity may improve a city's situation in terms of providing opportunity for economic growth. On the other hand, a city situated in an agricultural region can be adversely affected by drought or any weather event detrimental to farming operations. In the same way, the depletion of a natural resource in a surrounding or nearby region can seriously reduce a city's situational advantages. The characteristics of each urban center's situation are dynamic and require adaptation as change occurs.

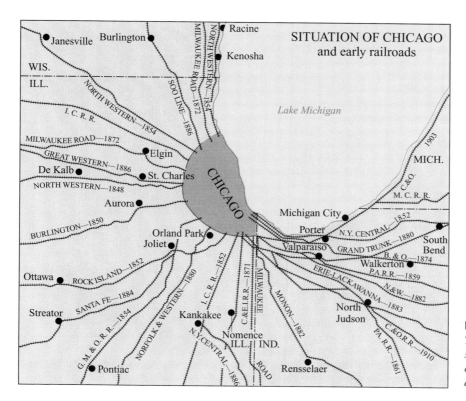

FIGURE 13.7

The situation of Chicago near the southern end of Lake Michigan contributed to its early development as a railroad center.

THE ORIGIN AND SPREAD OF URBAN SETTLEMENTS

➤ The development of agriculture and the accumulation of surplus food supplies led to the emergence of the earliest urban centers in Mesopotamia and other early civilization hearths.

How was formation of the first cities dependent on agricultural development?

Approximately when did the first cities appear in the various civilization hearths?

How did the earliest cities in the Americas differ from those in the Old World?

The gathering of people into urban settlements was not possible prior to the domestication of plants and the early development of agriculture at the beginning of Neolithic time. As we have described in previous chapters, Paleolithic people most likely were semi-nomadic, moving frequently in their unending search for edible wild plants and animals in order to survive. Their need to migrate prevented their agglomeration in substantial numbers at a particular place on a permanent basis. The developments that interrupted Paleolithic lifestyles and made possible the formation of the world's earliest embryonic cities were the discovery of crop farming procedures and the assembly by agriculturalists of surplus food supplies. After the first domestication of plants about 10,000 years ago, a few thousand years passed before early farmers became numerous enough and productive enough to meet the food requirements of even small urban settlements.

The Earliest Cities and Civilization Hearths

Archaeological evidence has established that the world's first urban centers were formed in several major river valleys in Asia and northeastern Africa. These areas were the *hearths* for the earliest human civilizations (refer to Fig. 3.4), and the embryonic cities that developed here were part of several major cultural advancements that marked the beginning of civilizations. Although established much later, the first urban centers in the Americas were components of early Amerindian civilizations.

The conditions necessary for the formation of urban centers were reached first in Mesopotamia. The cultivation of crops at an early date spread from nearby uplands into this fertile valley watered by the Tigris and Euphrates Rivers. The consequent production of surplus food by Mesopotamian farmers enabled some of the population to gather in agglomerated settlements and engage in a variety of other activities. Remains of the oldest known cities, including Ur, Erech, and Nineveh, have been discovered there (Fig. 13.8). They appear to have been founded about 5000 to 7000 years ago. By modern standards, the early Mesopotamian cities were quite small; they probably contained no more than 10,000 people. Nevertheless, they were an important development in human history and were essential to the emergence of the world's first civilization.

After those in Mesopotamia, cities emerged next in the lower Nile Valley, the Indus Valley, and the middle Huang Valley—other centers of early human civilizations—about 4500 to 5500 years ago. These areas are remarkably similar to Mesopotamia in general environmental character; all are fertile lowlands, well supplied with water from major rivers, and have moderate to long warm seasons for plant growth. In each case, crop production was established at an early date and supported the formation of agglomerated settlements. Is it possible that the practice of farming and

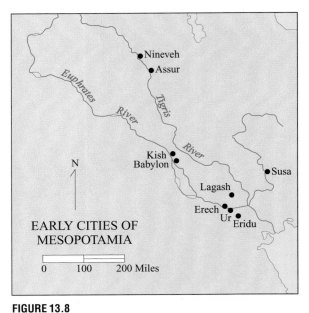

FIGURE 13.8

Some of the world's first urban centers were established more than 5000 years ago in Mesopotamia.

the idea of urban settlements were introduced into these areas from Mesopotamia by traders and travelers? Some scholars believe that there is adequate evidence of prehistoric contacts between Mesopotamia and these other centers to make a strong argument for such diffusion. Others, however, maintain that these widely separated areas originated agriculture, cities, and other elements of civilization independently, without outside influence.

The pre-Columbian native civilizations of the Americas also formed cities based on their development of crop agriculture, although these civilizations and their cities emerged at a much later date than those in the Old World. They seem to have first appeared little more than 2000 years ago, but some of the cities clearly are much younger. The Inca civilization and its cities controlled a vast empire in the Andes Mountains of South America. Cuzco, the Inca capital, was elaborately constructed and included monumental buildings. Nearby was Machu Picchu, an Inca fortress city so inaccessible in the mountains that its spectacular ruins were not discovered until 1911 (Fig. 13.9). In Meso-America there were two concentrations of early cities: one in Yucatán and adjacent areas that contained the Maya civilization, and another in south-central Mexico where in pre-Columbian time a succession of native civilizations, culminating in that of

FIGURE 13.9
The ruins of Machu Picchu, a fortress city of the Inca civilization in the Andes Mountains, escaped discovery until 1911. (Rob Crandall/Stock Boston)

the Aztecs, had developed. Maize and a host of other plants were domesticated in this region by natives and provided food for these civilizations. The cities of Meso-American civilizations appear to have been less numerous but more extensive in area than those of the Old World civilizations.

Functions and Features of the Earliest Cities

➤ Although the earliest cities were small, they performed several important functions for their populations and for people in the surrounding areas.

What were the most essential functions of these cities?

What structures or physical features of early cities were related to their main function?

How and why were early cities associated with the diffusion of ideas and materials over vast distances?

Founded in these several widely separated areas of the earth, over a period of thousands of years, the earliest cities were not as unlike in character as one might anticipate. For the most part, they were small agglomerations of people; each probably numbered no more than a few thousand. They served as collection centers for food produced by agriculturalists in their vicinity. The food supplies—mostly grain—were stored for later distribution to the city's inhabitants as needed, and some may have been carried over long distances by traders. Early cities also provided administrative organization and other important services, including defense and religious ceremonies, for people in the area around them as well as for their own inhabitants. The administrative role appears to have been particularly important in the early cities of China. The bond between early cities and people in their surrounding countrysides often became so strong that de facto city-states were formed.

Among the functions of ancient cities, perhaps none was more important than religious rituals and ceremonies. Priests or religious authorities often were the most important and powerful individuals in the cities and exercised a great deal of influence. They often held the status of god-kings and not only performed rituals and ceremonies but also collected tributes and taxes and controlled the distribution of food. Religious structures such as temples and the palaces and tombs of priests usually were placed on elevated

FIGURE 13.10

Among several known pyramids erected by early Amerindian civilizations is this one in the Mayan city of Chichén Itzá. (R. Gabler)

ground to be the most prominent features of the early cities. In Mesopotamia's early cities the most prominent structure was the *ziggurat*, a tower constructed like a pyramid with a shrine at the top. Pyramids built for religious purposes also dominated the cities of native civilizations in Meso-America (Fig. 13.10). Some scholars have maintained that the similarity of these pyramids and those of the Nile Valley civilization is solid proof that such designs and ideas were carried to the Americas from the Old World by ancient sailors who succeeded in crossing the intervening ocean in prehistoric time.

Early cities were important also because they could provide defense from raids or attacks by enemies. This function undoubtedly attracted threatened people from the countryside and contributed to growth of the cities. To aid soldiers in providing protection, it was common for enclosing palisades or a wall with watchtowers to be constructed around the city. The soldiers also might serve to collect tribute or taxes from people under the jurisdiction of the city. Military officers, like priests, were powerful and important people—members of the elite in early urban societies.

Of necessity, the earliest cities were centers of commercial activity. No city, ancient or modern, can survive without commerce; at the very least, urban populations must obtain most or all of their food from areas outside the city. In turn, materials and products from the earliest cities seem to have been carried by traders to distant markets up to hundreds and even thousands of miles away. Much more than material goods was involved in the exchange function of early cities, however.

Traders, travelers, and even invaders also brought ideas, methods, techniques, and skills. This served as a catalyst for a great variety of achievements, including the perfection of new means of measurement and record keeping, the development of metallurgy, and new scientific and philosophic concepts. For the first time in history, people in the early cities began to devote their attention and effort to specialized tasks or endeavors. Thus, a division of labor developed—a crucial occurrence in the emergence of a civilization.

With growth in their functional complexity, Mesopotamian cities became the first important centers for the spread of ideas and the distribution of products. Scholars have long debated the extent of ancient Mesopotamia's contacts and influence; it may well have involved most of the breadth of Eurasia as well as parts of Africa. Other Old World areas where early cities emerged also benefited from the infusion of ideas by outsiders and developed civilizations, but at a later time than Mesopotamia.

Mohenjo-Daro, one of the early cities of the Indus Valley civilization, has been of particular interest to geographers because it seems to have been the earliest urban settlement to incorporate a grid pattern in its internal arrangement. Other early cities appear to have grown in a rather haphazard manner, resulting in little or no internal regularity. For the development of Mohenjo-Daro to adhere to the square and rectangular components of a grid suggests the presence of an authority to execute an urban plan. The idea of a **grid pattern town** seems to have diffused from here to various parts of India and westward to the Near East, the Mediterranean Basin, and Western Europe over the span of several millennia. During the colonial period, Europeans carried the plan to the New World where they commonly employed it when founding new settlements. The grid pattern formed by perpendicular north–south and east–west streets and square or rectangular blocks of consistent size is now a nearly ubiquitous characteristic of nucleated settlements in most parts of North America.

Early Cities in the Mediterranean Basin and Europe

➤ From the time of classical Greece and Rome, cities in the Mediterranean Basin and Europe played major roles in the establishment and operation of empires and colonial networks.

What was the character and role of cities during the Greek and Roman eras?

What was their character and role during the Medieval period?

What was the impact of colonialism on existing cities in Europe and in colonial areas?

From southwestern Asia the idea of urban communities and plans for the arrangement of cities spread to the Mediterranean area and southern Europe some 3000 to 5000 years ago. The Phoenicians, remarkable early traders from the eastern shore of the Mediterranean, were particularly instrumental in the early phase of this diffusion. Most effective in building cities, however, were the Greeks and Romans of classical time.

Greek and Roman Cities   From the island of Crete the building of cities by the Greeks progressed to their mainland core area and eventually throughout their empire around the Mediterranean and eastward to the shores of the Black Sea. In turn, the Romans picked up where the Greeks left off and spread urbanization further by establishing cities in extensive parts of Europe north of the Alps. The Greek and Roman cities served as trading centers, but they also were centers of authority and a means of exercising control over the territory and people within their empires.

In some ways Greek cities were similar to those of the Mesopotamian and Indus Valley civilizations. For example, they were surrounded by walls that allowed entry only by means of gates; they contained granaries, temples, and palaces; and they were centered on a prominent citadel or *acropolis* built on the most elevated ground (Fig. 13.11). Also, some Greek cities were designed to conform to a grid pattern in their internal arrangement. At the same time, distinctive characteristics of Greek culture were incorporated in the structure of their cities and the architectural style of their buildings. The fondness of the ancient Greeks for symmetry and beauty and their thoughtful planning

FIGURE 13.11
The acropolis in Athens, Greece. In classical Greece, the acropolis of most cities served defensive or religious purposes. (Eleni Mylonas/Viesti Assoc.)

are readily apparent even today in the ruins of their early cities.

Throughout their empire, extending north of the Alps as far as the British Isles and eastward to the Black Sea coast, the Romans established hundreds of new urban settlements ranging from small outposts and forts in marginal locations to provincial capitals that exercised administrative control over sizable areas. To their inheritance of Greek urban planning and design, the Romans added engineering skill and attention to practical matters. They built excellent aqueducts and roads to serve their network of towns and cities and systematically divided these centers internally into functional areas or blocks. Thus certain parts of the Roman city were set aside for such purposes as the marketplace, the public forum, workshops, and, of course, housing. Presiding over the entire complex was Rome itself, the imperial capital. At the height of its power, Rome probably contained several hundred thousand inhabitants and was the largest city in the world.

Prior to the disintegration of the Roman Empire, urbanization in Europe reached a peak that would not be matched for more than a thousand years. The decline of Rome during the fifth century A.D., hastened by invasions of tribes from the east and disruption of trade in the empire, led to the abandonment of a great many urban centers. The unity of the empire was shattered, replaced by the territorial fragmentation and predominantly rural life of the early Medieval period. The limited number of European cities that managed to survive were well fortified or strategically located for the conduct of long-distance trade. They were like tiny islands in a threatening sea, left to their own devices as they struggled to survive physically, economically, and intellectually.

Moslem Cities In contrast to the urban decline in Europe during the Middle Ages, cities such as Baghdad, Constantinople, Damascus, Cairo, and Alexandria in the neighboring Moslem world continued to thrive and grow. These centers had become the repositories of Greek and Roman knowledge and technology to which Moslem scholars made important additions of ideas and discoveries. The Middle Ages was the period of ascension for Moslem culture and these cities were the cores of development, superseding their European counterparts in vitality and size. From their hearth in the Middle East, Moslems extended their control over North Africa and even penetrated into the Iberian and Balkan peninsulas of Europe. European challenges to Moslem domination of this

vast area commenced with the Crusades to the eastern Mediterranean Holy Lands between the eleventh and fourteenth centuries.

Revitalization of European Cities As Europeans scored successes in their struggles against the Moslems, as they reopened interregional trading routes, and as they rediscovered the fund of Greek and Roman accomplishments, their cities revived. Renewed as centers of mercantilism, administrative authority, and intellectual ferment, the cities of Europe attained increasing importance. Major centers bustled with trade, assembling an assortment of goods from as far away as tropical Africa and the Orient. Many cities outgrew the enclosing walls on which they had relied for defense during earlier Medieval time and attained new population records (Fig. 13.12). Paris probably contained about 250,000 inhabitants by the fifteenth century; although much smaller, London nevertheless was an important city of about 50,000 people. In addition, Venice, Genoa, Vienna, Prague, and many other cities were centers of growing vitality as Europe positioned itself for a long period of exploration and discovery, conquest, and colonization.

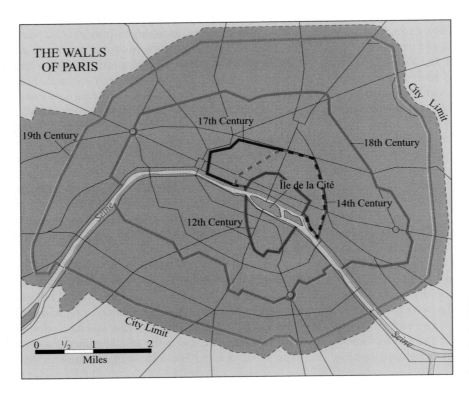

FIGURE 13.12

The walls of Paris. Growth of the city in earlier centuries required construction of new walls at an ever-greater distance from the center.

Colonization and Urban Development

From the fifteenth through the nineteenth centuries, the extension of European colonial control over the Americas, Australia, Africa, and parts of Asia had a major impact on the spread and development of cities. To whatever functions the native cities served, the Europeans usually added administration and trade. Furthermore, if native cities were inadequate in number for the purposes of the Europeans or absent from sites that they considered important, new cities were established. In fact, along the Atlantic seaboard of colonial North America all cities were of European creation because the sparse population of natives had formed only small villages. Most often in colonial areas the European-built cities were established along the coast so they could serve as ports for the exchange of products between colony and mother country. In some cases the Europeans established new cities adjacent to native cities if the latter could not be readily adapted to their purposes. New Delhi, built by the British adjacent to Old Delhi in India, is a notable example. Urban population growth in the colonies was a result of both European immigration and an influx of native people to meet the labor needs created by new European-established functions. (In many cases, the Europeans forced or coerced natives to move from the countryside into cities where labor was needed.)

Urban landscapes in colonial areas were dramatically transformed by European introduction of new functions, city plans, architecture, and other cultural elements. Like the Romans in earlier times, the Europeans used colonial cities as nodes from which they exercised their authority and control. Therefore, forts, military barracks, cannon emplacements, and a prominent headquarters or mansion for the European governor appeared as new features in colonial cities (Fig. 13.13). The colonial power often introduced the urban grid pattern, sometimes superimposing it on native cities with a different internal structure. The arrival of Europeans usually was followed by an increase in the architectural variety and the functional elements and zones of colonial cities—the imprint of European control and activity.

The establishment of trade between colony and mother country, of course, was a great stimulant to growth in commercial activity and population among such colonial port cities as Calcutta, Bombay, Rangoon, Capetown, and New York, but it also invigorated their European counterparts. London, Liverpool, Amsterdam, Hamburg, Lisbon, Barcelona, and other European ports blossomed as ships arrived from the colonies with such products as precious metals, spices, foodstuffs, fibers, tobacco, and wood. Millions of Europeans—another form of ''cargo''—bound for various parts of the New World also had an important impact on many of the European and colonial port cities.

ACCELERATING URBANIZATION

Despite many developments over several thousand years, the proportion of the world population living in cities remained quite small until the nineteenth century. From a current perspective, it seems amazing that no more than 3 to 4 percent of the people in the world lived in urban places up to the time of the Industrial Revolution. Only a few functions were performed by preindustrial cities, however, and the ability of these cities to support a large population was limited. As a rule, living conditions in cities were quite poor prior to the nineteenth century. The problems of providing

FIGURE 13.13

A surviving British mansion from the colonial period is in the foreground of this view of present-day Calcutta. (R. Gabler)

pure water and disposing of sewage had not been satisfactorily solved, and as a consequence widespread disease was common among the crowded population. (Many cities in the less developed world continue to struggle with these problems today.) Europe was the most urbanized continent in 1800, but only a few countries—the United Kingdom, France, the Netherlands, Belgium, and Portugal—had more than 10 percent of their populations in towns and cities. London, the largest European city, still had fewer than a million people in 1800, and Paris contained about 600,000.

Impact of the Industrial Revolution

➤ The accelerated growth of cities and the rapid urbanization of rural populations have been direct results of the Industrial Revolution.

What changes associated with the Industrial Revolution stimulated urban growth?

How has urban growth progressed since 1800 in Europe?

Stimulated by the Industrial Revolution, a dramatic increase in urban population began near the turn of the nineteenth century and has continued to the present. As Table 13.1 indicates, the percentage of the world's population living in urban areas has approximately doubled every 50 years since 1800. A majority of the world's people soon will be urban dwellers—a situation that never before has been approached.

The mechanization of economic production and application of technology to various human endeavors brought striking changes in lifestyles and changes in the location of employment, which led to a rearrangement of population from rural areas to towns and cities. In agricultural areas, mechanization and technology reduced the need for rural laborers. In cities and towns, jobs were created by the establishment of factories and mines. These changes brought about an increasing flow of migrants from rural areas to urban centers, which supplemented the natural population growth in cities and towns. In addition, it was not uncommon for entire new towns to be formed by migrants who gathered around factories and mines established at rural sites.

Urban growth also was greatly stimulated by improvements in transportation that accompanied industrialization and the modernization of economies. Boats, ships, and railroads powered by steam engines

TABLE 13.1 Urban Population of the World: 1800–1990

Year	Percent Urban
1800	4
1850	7
1900	14
1950	29
1960	34
1970	38
1980	41
1990	47

SOURCE: *United Nations.*

and, somewhat later, motor vehicles and aircraft powered by internal combustion engines were invented and perfected. Put into service, these new modes of transportation strengthened the commercial ties of cities with their trade areas and vastly increased the distance over which trade could be routinely conducted. Greater trade meant more income and jobs for cities and consequent increases in their populations.

The initial impact was felt first in Great Britain, where the Industrial Revolution began during the latter part of the eighteenth century. The subsequent growth of British cities was stunning. In 1800, London—with 959,000 inhabitants—was by far the largest British city; no other urban center in the country contained as many as 200,000 people. In 1850, fifty years later, London's population had grown to 2.4 million, five other cities exceeded 200,000, and England and Wales had become the first areas in world history to have more than half of their populations classified as urban. With the exception of London, the early British cities that experienced most rapid growth were in the coalfields because coal was the initial critical raw material of the Industrial Revolution (Fig. 13.14).

Similar results followed the diffusion of industrialization to the European mainland and North America during the nineteenth century. In 1800 Paris was the only city on the European mainland with as many as 500,000 people, but by the end of the century five cities (Paris, Berlin, Vienna, St. Petersburg, and Moscow) exceeded 1 million in population. Also, Germany joined Britain as the only nation with a greater urban than rural population before 1900.

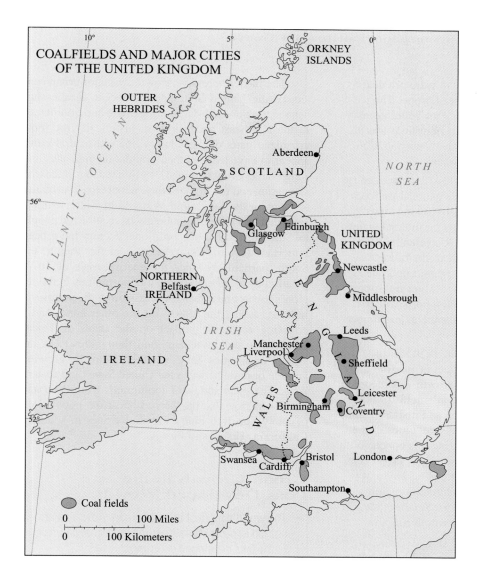

COALFIELDS AND MAJOR CITIES
OF THE UNITED KINGDOM

FIGURE 13.14

As confirmed by this map, most major British cities have a close geographical association with coalfields. London is the major exception.

Metropolitan Development in the United States

➤ Temporal and spatial patterns of metropolitan evolution in the United States have been influenced by developments in technology, industrialization, and transportation.

How did urban growth and development progress in the United States during the four epochs specified by John Borchert?

What factors account for the recent acceleration of urban growth in the Sun Belt?

The population of the United States was 75 percent rural in 1790 (the year of the first U.S. census), but an urban majority was attained by 1920. New York be-

came the first U.S. city to record 1 million inhabitants in 1880; only twenty years later, its population was nearly 3.5 million.

The influences of developments in technology, industrialization, and transportation on metropolitan evolution in the United States have been emphasized in a study conducted by John Borchert, an American geographer. Borchert analyzed the country's urban growth and development during four epochs, each of which he characterized by a different level of technological attainment:

1. *The Sail-Wagon Epoch*, 1790–1830, during which nearly all urban centers were limited to the Atlantic Coast and nearby internal waterways. The largest cities—Boston, New York, and Philadelphia—had only small domestic

497

hinterlands or trade areas and were oriented primarily toward the sea and Europe. The struggle between these cities for better access to the interior was underway, but little was accomplished, primarily because transportation was poorly developed and slow.

2. *The Iron Horse Epoch*, 1830–1870, marked by the establishment of a crude national railroad network. Most of the fastest-growing cities during this epoch were ports on internal waterways in the Midwest (e.g., Cleveland, Detroit, Chicago, and St. Louis) where the railroads converged. Although of growing importance, railroads only complemented water transportation during this epoch, linking ports with neighboring farmlands and mineral and timber producing areas.

3. *The Steel-Rail Epoch*, 1870–1920, distinguished by rapid development of the iron and steel industry. Substantial growth was recorded by cities in or near the nation's fields of high-grade bituminous coal, such as Pittsburgh, and by the emerging major industrial cities of the Northeast and Midwest during this epoch. With improved accessibility by rail, new urban centers developed in the important agricultural districts of the West and in areas containing mineral and timber resources. Smaller cities registered their greatest growth during this time.

4. *The Auto-Air-Amenity Epoch*, 1920–present, characterized by the impact on the nation's metropolitan complex of highway and air transportation expansion as well as increasingly important amenities. Improved transportation has made possible the dispersal of people to suburbs and satellite cities, with the growth of central cities slowed or reversed as a consequence. The search for amenities has created not only burgeoning suburbs but booming Sun Belt urban centers in the South and Southwest.

Borchert also recognized that the magnitude of growth and the spread of urbanization in the United States have been influenced by other factors, some of which transcend these epochs. Westward expansion of the settled area, for example, was underway during the first three epochs, and foreign immigration has boosted urban growth throughout the nation's history.

The most impressive growth by major urban centers of the United States during recent decades has been in the Sun Belt states of the South and Southwest. In the Northeast and Midwest, historically the most urbanized parts of the country, the old central cities appear to have reached their population pinnacles and some have even declined, victimized by industrial stagnation and the flight of their people to suburbs and to cities in the South and West. Mild winter climate and other amenities undoubtedly have attracted people to Sun Belt cities, but additional factors have been important as well. The relocation of factories to the South, particularly since the energy crisis of 1973, greatly improved employment opportunities in the region's towns and cities. (A recession in the petroleum industry during the 1980s, on the other hand, had a crippling economic impact on the states of Texas, Oklahoma, and Louisiana, and their cities.) On the West Coast, cities have benefited from the growing volume of trade between the United States and eastern Asia. The great influx of immigrants from Asia and Latin America also has helped boost the populations of many Sun Belt cities, especially ones in southern California, Texas, and Florida.

Urban Growth in the Less Developed World

➤ The world's highest rates of urban growth have shifted in recent time from the industrial countries to the less developed countries.

How do the circumstances and consequences of high urban growth rates in these two groups of countries differ?

In the less developed countries, why are rural people migrating to the cities in vast numbers?

In an amazing trend that has emerged over the second half of the twentieth century, urban growth in the less developed world has forged ahead of that in the industrialized countries. Between 1950 and 1985 the urban population of the industrialized countries nearly doubled, increasing from 450 to 840 million, but in the less developed countries it quadrupled as their collective total of urban dwellers mushroomed from 285 million to 1.15 billion. Because more than three-fourths of the world's people live in less developed countries, it is perhaps not surprising that their *absolute* urban population substantially exceeds that of the industrialized countries. What is particularly impressive is that the less developed countries now have a much higher *rate* of urban population growth than their industrialized counterparts. Two very important differences in the urbanization of the industrialized and less developed countries are apparent. First, the relatively high urban growth rates of the industrialized countries were not as abrupt as they have been in the less developed countries. Second, rapid urban growth in the industrial countries was accompanied by expansion of manufacturing and the creation of a great many urban jobs, whereas that generally has not been the case in the less developed countries. As a consequence, urbanization in the less developed world has resulted in more acute social and economic problems than it did in the industrialized countries.

Future urban growth rates are expected to be greatest in Africa, the continent that currently has the least-urbanized population and the lowest level of economic development. According to United Nations projections, the urban population of Africa will double between the years 1985 and 2000. The largest absolute increase in urban population, however, will be in Asia where the cities are expected to gain another 500 million people during the same period. Asia's massive total population will result in a greater absolute gain than in other regions that have a higher rate of urbanization.

Accelerating urbanization in the less developed countries is becoming evident in the sizes and ranking of the world's largest cities. As Table 13.2 indicates, in 1960 only three (Shanghai, Beijing, and Buenos Aires) of the world's ten largest cities were in less developed countries. By the year 2000 it is expected that all but two (Tokyo and New York) of the ten largest cities will be in less developed countries. In that year Mexico City is projected to be the largest with nearly 25 million inhabitants, although it contained only one-fifth that number in 1960. The United Nations has estimated that the less developed world will have 18 cities with more than 10 million people by the year 2000, whereas in 1960 only Shanghai was that large. Furthermore, the United Nations expects that by the year 2025 there will be 135 cities with more than 4 million inhabitants—114 of which will be in less developed countries.

In addition to relatively high rates of natural population increase, major cities in most of the less developed world are being swollen by massive migrations from rural areas and smaller towns. Limited areas of good agricultural land, the persistence of traditional farming practices, and ever-increasing demographic growth have resulted in widespread poverty in rural areas. For the surplus rural population, moving to a city offers the only hope of improving living conditions short of emigrating to a foreign country. (The

TABLE 13.2 The World's Ten Largest Cities: 1960 and 2000 (population of urbanized area, in millions)

	1960			2000[a]	
Rank	City	Population	Rank	City	Population
1.	New York	14.2	1.	Mexico City	24.4
2.	London	10.7	2.	São Paulo	23.6
3.	Tokyo	10.7	3.	Tokyo	21.3
4.	Shanghai	10.7	4.	New York	16.1
5.	Ruhr–Rhein	8.7	5.	Calcutta	15.9
6.	Beijing	7.3	6.	Bombay	15.4
7.	Paris	7.2	7.	Shanghai	14.7
8.	Buenos Aires	6.9	8.	Tehran	13.7
9.	Los Angeles	6.6	9.	Jakarta	13.3
10.	Moscow	6.3	10.	Buenos Aires	13.1

SOURCE: *United Nations Development Programme,* Human Development Report 1990.
[a]Projected figures.

latter, however, is not a realistic alternative for most of the rural poor because of legal restrictions and the costs involved.) It is ironic that improvements in rural areas, such as the consolidation of tiny parcels of land into larger and possibly profitable units, the mechanization of farming operations, and the upgrading of roads, result in an even greater scale of migration to the cities. Fewer farming units mean reduced opportunity for farmers, mechanization means reduced need for labor on farms, and road improvement facilitates migration to cities.

The migrants commonly perceive the cities as places with better opportunities for employment and improved living conditions. Also, some view cities as more interesting places to live, places where they can participate in exciting activities or at least observe them. Governments in the less developed world usually reserve for their largest cities the few capital improvements they are able to afford, and any major industries that exist are almost always in the principal urban centers. As a consequence, some employment opportunities in construction and manufacturing are available, but the jobs, particularly in construction, often are only temporary. The national capital, which in the less developed countries usually is the largest city as well, has the added attractions of jobs associated with the political bureaucracy and excitement linked to political events. Of course, each country's largest markets and principal cultural, educational, and recreational facilities also are in the main cities and represent other attractions for migrants.

The vast majority of rural-to-urban migrants in the less developed countries, however, have inadequate skills and experience for urban-based jobs and little notion of the competition for those jobs prior to their arrival in the cities. Typically they end up as additions to the burgeoning slums of the cities, either unemployed or able to find only temporary work at the most menial tasks. Many, including large numbers of children, survive by combing through garbage dumps, begging, and stealing.

Although urban landscapes throughout the world exhibit slums and dreary quarters inhabited by the poor, few are as extensive and have such depth of poverty as those in the rapidly growing cities of the less developed world. Usually unable to afford housing within the city itself, the people often form **squatter settlements** on unused land adjacent to the city. Various names are given to these settlements around the world, including *favelas* in Brazil, *bidonvilles* in parts of Africa, and *bustees* in India. Their location on the

FIGURE 13.15
Squatter settlements, occupied largely by recent rural migrants, have evolved on the margins of major cities in the less developed world. The one in this photograph is adjacent to Caracas, Venezuela. (Camermann Int'l., Ltd.)

margin of cities is about the only thing they share with suburbs in the industrialized world. They usually lack the most basic human services, including pure water supplies and the means of disposing of sewage; their housing is the most rudimentary imaginable (Fig. 13.15); and disease is routine. It is difficult to imagine a more hopeless situation, yet the migrants continue to arrive. Already more than half the population of many cities in the less developed world live in slums and squatter settlements.

Burgeoning Suburbs

➤ The horizontal spread of cities is a worldwide phenomenon, but the character of urban places has changed most dramatically in the industrial countries with growth of their suburbs during the twentieth century.

Why has suburban growth in the United States generally exceeded that in other industrial countries?

What problems have been created by the growth of suburbs in the United States?

What measures have been attempted to reverse them?

An important facet of modern urbanization in both the less developed world and the industrialized world has been the astounding growth of suburbs on the periphery of the cities. The shacks and poverty-stricken populations that are so common on the outskirts of cities in the less developed world clearly do not fit our usual impression of a suburb, however. In most industrial societies, particularly the United States, a suburb is characterized by relatively new single-family houses (often with attached garages for the ubiquitous automobiles) on large and attractively landscaped lots, inhabited by members of the middle and upper classes. The typical residents of these suburbs are urban families who have chosen to live here to avoid aspects of the nearby city that they consider negative—residential crowding, high taxes, poor schools, high crime rates, racial conflict, pollution, and so on. For some, residence in a suburb is a matter of prestige, an indication that they have attained a relatively high economic status.

The emergence of suburbs as major residential areas in industrial societies may be viewed as a consequence of change in the relative strength of *centripetal* and *centrifugal urban forces*. In the past, centripetal forces were dominant, attracting people and businesses toward the center of the city. As we have seen, the core of the city offered the greatest accessibility, an attribute that was extremely critical when transportation was limited. Stores, offices, and factories needed to be in a central location where they could be reached by an adequate number of workers and customers in order to operate and make a profit. Urban residents likewise had no choice but to live as close as possible to places where they worked and shopped. With growing acquisition of private automobiles during the twentieth century, however, this situation drastically changed. Personal mobility was vastly improved with the automobile, and the centripetal forces were overcome by centrifugal forces—the attractions of the suburbs. One could enjoy life in the suburbs and, in a private car, commute to the workplace, stores, and other attractions in the city.

In the United States, a large country with much available space and with a tradition of little governmental interference in private ventures, suburbs have been built over landscapes as far away as tens of miles from the nearest central city (Fig. 13.16). It is not uncommon, particularly along major roads and high-

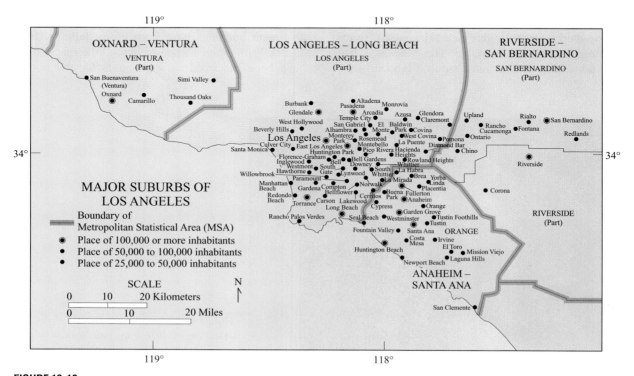

FIGURE 13.16

The many suburbs of Los Angeles have sprawled over much of the area within 60 miles of the city.

ways, for the suburbs of one city to become physically linked with those of another. More than half of the U.S. population now lives in suburbs. In most other industrial nations, suburbanization has not progressed to such a great extent. Less available land for development and more stringent governmental regulations on horizontal urban growth are the usual reasons.

In the most recent major rearrangement of urban land uses in the United States, factories, warehouses, stores, and offices have followed the population to suburban sites. Originally residential communities for urban workers, suburbs now are the sites of industrial parks, shopping malls, and office complexes. Even hospitals, museums, theaters, sports arenas and stadiums, and other specialized facilities have joined the trend and moved to the suburbs. Some suburbs thus have become multifunction communities, greatly reducing the need for their residents and those of less developed nearby suburbs to commute to the central city. In a striking reversal of the usual commuting pattern, it is becoming increasingly common for less affluent city residents to travel daily to suburban job sites.

Suburbanization has had noticeable devastating consequences for central cities in the United States. The economic and cultural importance of cities has been eroded by the movement of people and facilities to the suburbs. Once thriving central business districts are struggling to remain viable. The cities have had their population growth rates reduced (and in some cases even reversed). Perhaps most serious, however, has been the abandonment of the cities by such a large proportion of their middle and upper classes, leaving behind the poor (mostly racial and ethnic minorities) and the ongoing need for public services—police and fire protection, refuse collection, day care, education, counseling, and recreation. The growing cost of these services, together with the loss of potential tax income from relocation of the more affluent classes and businesses to the suburbs, has created a grave budget crisis for most central cities. City officials for many years have appealed to the federal government for greater financial assistance, stressing that the country should not stand by while its great urban centers crumble. Federal aid, however, has not been increased adequately to stem the urban decay; in fact, the extent of the federal government's obligations to the nation's cities has become a hot political issue.

A variety of specific remedial measures have been attempted to rejuvenate the cities and reverse their deterioration. Both publicly and privately financed urban renewal projects have been implemented in nearly all major cities. Some have involved the construction of public facilities such as convention centers and museums, but the most controversial usually have been housing projects. Most authorities now agree that public housing projects with closely grouped multistory apartment buildings have been costly failures (Fig. 13.17). With too many people in too little space (they have been described as warehouses for the poor),

FIGURE 13.17
Multistory public housing units such as these in Chicago generally have suffered from overcrowding and crime. (Cameramann Int'l., Ltd.)

drugs, vandalism, and other crime have been rampant. Even the private conversion of older buildings into high-quality housing for the affluent has been controversial. Known as **gentrification**, this process forces out the poor who previously occupied the buildings and creates a new housing dilemma. As far as reversing the flow of the middle and upper classes to the suburbs, the establishment of luxury apartments, condominiums, and other high-quality housing in the cities apparently has had little consequence; the suburbs continue their steady growth.

THE URBAN HIERARCHY

➤ The hierarchy of nucleated settlements in a country or region exhibits a number of relatively consistent patterns and relationships.

How does the rank–size rule apply to the urban hierarchy?

What is a primate city?

To what extent is a primate city a consistent element of the urban hierarchy from country to country?

In most areas of substantial extent, such as that of a country, the assortment of agglomerated human settlements on the landscape comprises a hierarchy. That is, when the settlements are ranked by their population size, functional complexity, or related measurement, they tend to form recognizable classes or groups ranging in order from the smallest and least complex to the largest and most complex. Geographers have examined various aspects of the urban hierarchy and its character in different parts of the world. Typically, the lowest-order grouping is formed by the smallest settlements, each of which is characterized by only a few functions and serves as a market center for trade areas of the most limited extent. These small settlements are more numerous than those in any other group, however. Proceeding up the hierarchy, the settlements in each higher-order group are fewer in number, are larger in population, have a greater assortment of functions, and serve a more extensive trade area than those in the group below. A particular settlement can move up or down in the hierarchy as it gains or loses population and changes in functional character through time. We will have more to say about the hierarchy of urban functions in a later part of this chapter.

The Rank–Size Rule

An interesting theoretical correlation between the rank of places in the urban hierarchy and their population sizes is called the **rank–size rule**. According to this theory, when the urban settlements in a country or similar area are ranked by population total, the population of each place as a proportion of that of the largest city will generally correspond to its ranking. That is, the second-ranked city will be about one-half the size of the largest, the third-ranked will be about one-third the size, the fourth-ranked will be about one-fourth the size, and so on. This correlation is nicely illustrated when the cities of an appropriate country are plotted on a logarithmic graph, as has been done in Figure 13.18.

The rank–size rule has been found to be most applicable to developed countries of substantial areal size. The populations of the largest cities in a sample of developed countries given in Table 13.3 show a close match between theory and reality. Cities in less developed countries listed in the table show a substantial departure from the rank–size rule, however. These countries appear to have an immature urban hierarchy—often one in which the biggest city is inordinately large compared with other urban areas in the country.

Primate Cities

The tendency of many countries to have their urban hierarchy dominated by a single large city was pointed out in 1939 by an American geographer, Mark Jefferson. **Primate city** was the name suggested by Jefferson for such places. The primate city typically has a population that is several times larger than that of the second-largest city and is clearly the leading economic, political, cultural, and educational center of its country. It attracts the most talented, skilled, and ambitious segments of the society as well as less gifted masses. There are many obvious examples of primate cities in the less developed world, such as Mexico City in Mexico, Buenos Aires in Argentina, Cairo in Egypt, and Manila in the Philippines. Although there are several exceptions, such as Paris in France and Stockholm in Sweden, a single city is not usually so dominant in the urban hierarchy of most industrialized countries. Even some of the less developed countries—notably those with a large area and population such as China, India, and Brazil—lack a primate city.

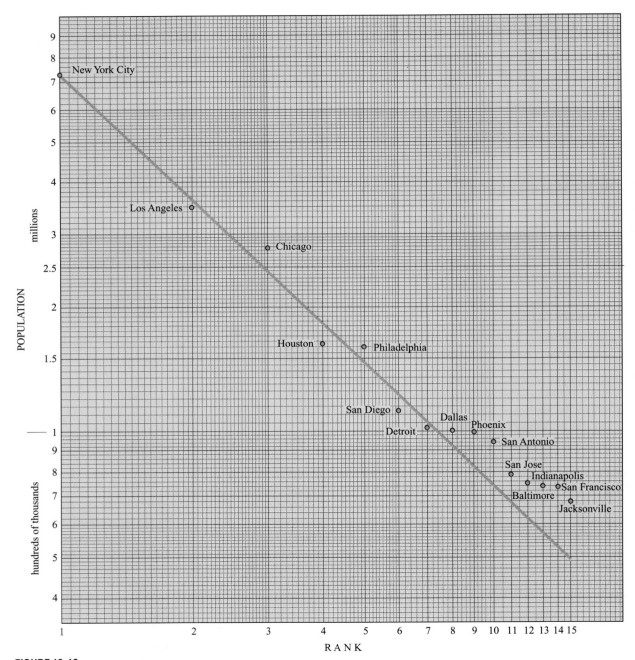

FIGURE 13.18

The rank and size of the 15 largest cities in the United States, plotted on a logarithmic graph. If the cities perfectly conformed to the rank–size rule, they would be located on the diagonal line when plotted.

TABLE 13.3   The Largest Cities in Selected Countries
(population in thousands)

Developed Countries		Less Developed Countries	
Cities	Population	Cities	Population
Belgium (1988 est.)		Iran (1986)	
Brussels	970	Tehran	6022
Antwerp	479	Mashad	1466
Ghent	233	Esfahan	1001
Charleroi	209		
Germany (1991 est.)		Mauritania (1987 est.)	
Berlin	3000	Nouakchott	400
Hamburg	1600	Nouadhibou	70
Munich	1300	Kaedi	22
Cologne	946		
Switzerland (1989)		Peru (1989 est.)	
Zurich	346	Lima	5659
Basel	171	Arequipa	612
Geneva	161	Callao	574

Descriptions of the primate city often emphasize that it is most representative of the nation's character or that it is the essence of the nation's society. Differences are vast, however, between the primate city and other settlements, particularly in less developed countries. While rural areas and small communities often are relatively isolated and traditional, the primate city is usually the most progressive, cosmopolitan, and modern entity of the nation. It normally has the best transportation ties with the outside world and, even in the poorest countries, some manufacturing facilities. Such contrasts need to be kept in mind while considering the accuracy of claims that the primate city is representative of the larger society.

SPATIAL PATTERNS OF URBANIZATION

➤ The degree of urbanization is most closely related to the level of economic development in most parts of the world.

What are the exceptions to this relationship?

Urbanization is most advanced in which parts of the industrial world?

In which parts of the less developed world is urbanization most advanced?

A world map of current levels of urbanization (Fig. 13.19) is a valuable instrument that we can use to help confirm and summarize points made in earlier sections. Also, we can gather ideas from it on where there is the most potential for future urbanization. As we attempt to interpret the spatial patterns on this map, we will first consider some factors responsible for the patterns and then examine urbanization in both industrialized and less developed regions.

Influencing Factors

To understand the place-to-place differences in urbanization depicted on Figure 13.19 we first must remember that there are inconsistencies from country to country in how "urban" is defined. Until an international definition is adopted and data are gathered on that basis, this problem is unavoidable. Fortunately, it is responsible for only minor variations; other factors are far more important in accounting for the differences from country to country.

The character of a country's economy, as we have noted earlier, is a particularly important factor in the urbanization of its population. It stands to reason that countries with less developed economies in which most people work at agrarian tasks should be less urbanized than those with modern industrialized econ-

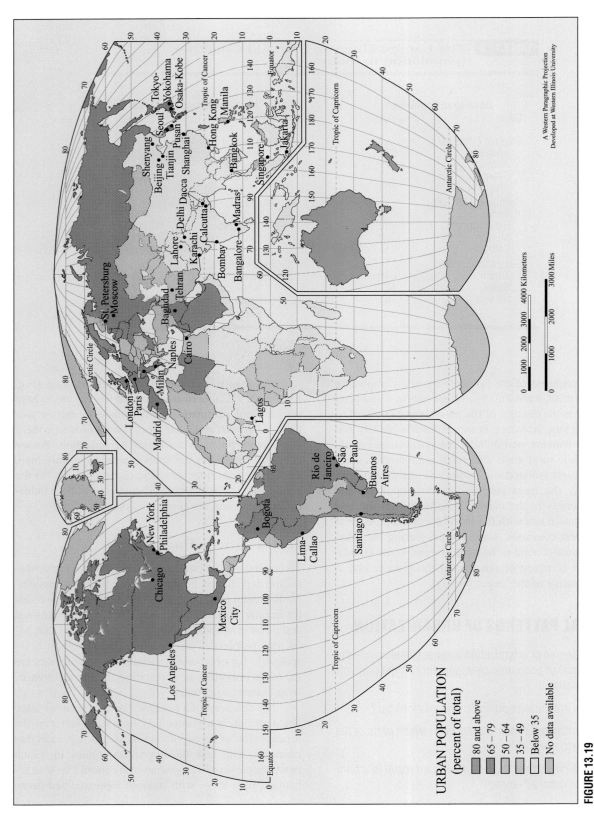

FIGURE 13.19

Levels of urbanization among the countries of the world. The least urbanized countries generally have attained the lowest degree of economic development.

URBAN POPULATION
(percent of total)

- 80 and above
- 65 – 79
- 50 – 64
- 35 – 49
- Below 35
- No data available

A Western Paragraphic Projection
Developed at Western Illinois University

omies. Indeed, such agrarian countries as Cambodia, Bangladesh, Afghanistan, Ethiopia, Kenya, and Uganda have extremely low urban percentages—less than 20 percent of their total population. Figure 13.19 shows low levels of urbanization in most of Africa and Monsoon Asia, regions in which retarded economic development is widespread. By contrast, the highly industrialized areas of Anglo-America, Western Europe, Japan, and Australia all have more than 70 percent of their population in urban places.

Factors other than the level of economic development of a country also must be taken into account, however. The relatively high urban percentages in much of Latin America and some countries in the Middle East are a case in point; these are not areas with well-developed industrial economies. In some countries it appears that a great majority of the people live in cities because the rural environment is too harsh to support much of an agriculture-based population. The climate may be excessively arid or tropical, the terrain may be too rugged, or productive soils may be absent, yet the country may be able to support an urban population on the basis of such economic activities as mineral production and processing, commerce, and tourism. The relatively high levels of urbanization in some countries also may reflect domination by the primate city in those societies. In comparison with rural areas and smaller communities, the primate city in those cases usually is viewed by the people as such an economically and socially advantageous place to live that it now accounts for a large proportion of the total population. In addition, there are a few modern city-states such as Singapore and Hong Kong in which the city contains all or nearly all of the total population.

Urban Patterns in the Industrial World

The importance of an industrial economy as an urbanizing influence is clearly confirmed by Figure 13.19. The most urbanized major regions and countries—Australia, western Europe, Anglo-America, Japan, and some parts of the former Soviet Union—also are the most industrialized.

It may seem surprising that Australia is the most urbanized continent (Table 13.4). Vast areas of extreme aridity have made most of Australia unable to support a significant rural population. Settled and developed by British colonists, manufacturing and service activities have come to dominate the continent's

TABLE 13.4 Urban Population of Major World Regions: 1990	
Region	**Percentage Urban**
Australia	86
Europe	75
Anglo-America	74
Latin America	69
Soviet Union[a]	66
Africa	31
Asia	29

SOURCE: *Population Reference Bureau.*
[a]In 1991, the Soviet Union fragmented into 15 separate states, most of which are now members of the Commonwealth of Independent States.

economy and encourage urbanization. Although 86 percent of Australia's people live in urban places, the continent has a small total population and few large cities. Sydney, Melbourne, Brisbane, Perth, and Adelaide are the only cities that exceed 1 million in population. Nearby New Zealand, with a colonial history similar to that of Australia, is nearly as urbanized, with 84 percent of its population in urban places.

As the first area to experience the Industrial Revolution, Europe became the earliest continental area with a predominantly urban population and still is ranked highly (see Table 13.4). Many European countries now have more than three-fourths of their population in urban places and in some (Belgium, Denmark, Germany, the Netherlands, Spain, Luxembourg, and the United Kingdom) the proportion equals or exceeds 85 percent. The lowest percentages of urban dwellers generally are shared by countries in the eastern part of the continent, where industrialization has been slower to develop.

The greatest clusters of cities, or conurbations, in Europe are on the island of Great Britain and in the middle and lower parts of the Rhine Valley (Fig. 13.20). The largest conurbation, with somewhat more than 20 million people, is formed by London and neighboring cities in southeastern England. London alone has 7 million inhabitants and is one of the world's premier cities; in the early nineteenth century it became the first city in history to attain a population of 1 million. Other British conurbations are in the Mid-

FIGURE 13.20

The major cities of Europe. Note the areas where urban centers are clustered into conurbations.

lands (including Birmingham, Leeds, and Sheffield), Lancashire (Liverpool), southern Wales, northeastern England (Newcastle), and central Scotland (Glasgow and Edinburgh). Across the English Channel in the Netherlands, Amsterdam, Rotterdam, and The Hague are included in a thoroughly planned conurbation called *Randstad Holland*. Planners in the Netherlands are attempting to guide the growth of these three cities so that the Randstad (meaning "ring-city") will be one of the world's most liveable urban environments. The Ruhr–Rhine conurbation in Germany is a cluster of industrial cities (including Essen, Dusseldorf, Dortmund, and Cologne) centered on the coal resource of the Ruhr Valley and accessible to the transportation offered by the Rhine River. A few other less populated conurbations have developed in such areas as the Po Valley in northern Italy and Upper Silesia in Poland, but the remaining large cities in Europe virtually stand alone. These include Moscow, St. Petersburg, and Kiev (the largest cities in Russia and Ukraine) as well as Madrid, Berlin, Rome, Paris, Budapest, Bucharest, Barcelona, and Warsaw.

In Anglo-America, the United States and Canada have similar high levels of urbanization—about three-fourths of their populations. In both countries the urban population first exceeded the rural in the early part of the present century and the gap has widened steadily. Not all cities have shared in the growth, however. As we described earlier, several major cities in the northeastern United States have lost population during recent years. People apparently have fled from these cities for such reasons as shrinking employment opportunities (especially in manufacturing); concern about personal safety and crime, racial frictions, deteriorating educational systems, and traffic congestion; and the attractions of suburban life. The abandonment of central cities in favor of neighboring suburbs has resulted in a greater degree of suburban sprawl in the United States and Canada than in any other major part of the world. The enormous horizontal growth of urban developments has often linked neighboring cities, forming continuous built-up zones of great extent. Megalopolis, stretching along the Atlantic seaboard from southern New England to the shores of Chesapeake Bay, is the most outstanding example (Fig. 13.21).

Containing more than 40 million people, Megalopolis is the world's premier urban region. It includes the central cities of New York, Philadelphia, Boston, Baltimore, and Washington, D.C., plus many smaller cities and towns and countless suburban communities. New York City, in the very middle of Megalopolis and the nation's leading manufacturing, commercial, and financial center, is clearly the focus of the region. In terms of its population size and economic importance, Megalopolis is superior to any other conurbation in the world.

The United States and Canada have several other highly urbanized zones in which expanding suburbs around closely spaced central cities pose the potential for additional Megalopolis-like developments, only on a smaller scale. Examples are the coast of southern California, including Los Angeles and San Diego; the southwestern shore of Lake Michigan, including Chicago and Milwaukee; the zone from Detroit along the western and southern shores of Lake Erie to the upper Ohio River Valley, which includes Toledo, Cleveland, and Pittsburgh; and a strip called "the Golden Horseshoe" from Toronto around the western end of Lake Ontario to Niagara Falls and Buffalo. Most of the largest cities in the United States and Canada, as indicated on Figure 13.21, are components of such conurbations.

Outside of Europe and North America, the only area with a clustering of cities in a significant conurbation is Japan. A densely urbanized zone extends along the southeast coast of Honshu that includes Tokyo, Yokohama, and Nagoya. In nearby southern Honshu along the shore of the Inland Sea is a second conurbation with Osaka and Kobe the largest cities. With its amazing industrial development since the end of World War II, Japan has become one of the most urbanized nations of the world.

Urban Patterns in the Less Developed World

Although Figure 13.19 shows that levels of urbanization in the less developed world are generally lower than in the industrialized world, we know that the higher rate of urban growth in the less developed countries is rapidly narrowing the gap. In fact, some of the countries already have attained urban percentages comparable to those of industrialized countries. The map also reveals that a substantial number of the world's largest cities are in the less developed countries, but they seldom are part of a conurbation. Instead, they are more likely to be primate cities and clearly separated from one another.

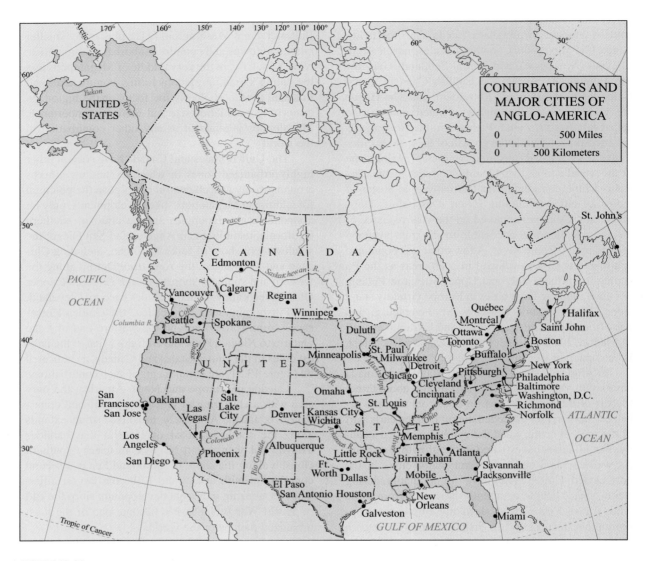

FIGURE 13.21

The major cities of the United States and Canada. Many of the largest cities in the United States are contained within conurbations, most notably the conurbation of Megalopolis.

By far the most urbanized major region in the less developed world is Latin America. The reasons are not entirely clear, but they include strong European influence in the region, a substantially higher level of economic development than most of Africa and parts of Asia, and an enormous rural-to-urban migration of long duration. Only a small minority of Latin America's countries have less than half their populations in urban settlements. By contrast, more than 70 percent of the population is urban in Argentina, Uruguay, Chile, Brazil, Venezuela, Mexico, and Cuba. São

Paulo and Rio de Janeiro in Brazil are the most notable exceptions to the general rule that Latin America's largest urban centers are primate cities. Mexico City is not only the primate city of Mexico but, as we have noted earlier, will soon become the largest city in the world.

A startling number of huge urban centers are scattered over the landscape of eastern, southeastern, and southern Asia despite the fact that most countries here have low percentages of their populations in urban settlements. Although a few countries, such as Taiwan,

FIGURE 13.22

The major cities of Monsoon Asia. Asian cities tend to stand alone; only Japan has a conurbation comparable to those in Europe and North America.

North and South Korea, the Philippines, and Malaysia, are exceptions, urban people account for less than 35 percent of the total population over most of the region. Such low percentages in a region that has an enormous total population, particularly in China and India, nevertheless result in many cities and a large absolute number (more than 750 million) of urban residents.

Among the great urban centers of Asia are Shanghai, Beijing, and Chongqing in China; Seoul in South Korea; Manila in the Philippines; Jakarta in Indonesia; Bangkok in Thailand; and Calcutta, Madras, and Bombay in India (Fig. 13.22).

Unlike the great conurbations in such industrialized areas as the United States and Japan, most of the major cities of Asia stand alone. However, geographer Norton Ginsburg has pointed out that metropolitan expansion in Asia has made it increasingly difficult to recognize urban–rural boundaries. Asian cities most commonly are situated in lowland areas where they are surrounded by dense agricultural populations in villages. With the development of transportation linkages between the cities and their surrounding rural areas over recent decades, the differences between urban and rural conditions have become obscured. Ginsburg refers to this as an "urbanization of the countryside" around the great cities.

In southwestern Asia there are few cities of substantial size, but levels of urbanization are generally higher than in most other parts of the continent. Two factors have a major bearing on the relatively high urban percentages in southwestern Asia: (1) support of rural populations is limited by the extensive deserts and mountainous terrain, and (2) economic development and living standards are generally higher in the region than in other parts of the less developed world, particularly because of the great oil wealth around the Persian Gulf.

With only 31 percent of its population in urban settlements, Africa is one of the least urbanized of all continents. (Only Asia has a lower percentage.) However, with a very high rate of natural population increase and an enormous flow of rural people to the cities now underway, Africa is the most rapidly urbanizing continent and probably will continue to be well into the future. The only city in Africa among the world's largest is Cairo. Typical of the less developed world, most African countries have an urban hierarchy dominated by a primate city.

URBAN FUNCTIONS

➤ As a general rule, the greater the population of a city, the more functions it performs and the more goods and services it provides.

What is the difference between basic and nonbasic functions?

How do threshold populations relate to the number and variety of goods and services available in an urban center?

If we are to understand why cities are such important elements of the world's cultural landscapes, we must consider the functions they perform. Perhaps the most obvious thing about cities is that they serve as places of residence for large numbers of people even though they occupy relatively small areas. Most cities did not come about merely to serve as places of residence, however. As Mark Jefferson once noted, "Cities do not grow up of themselves. Countrysides set them up to do tasks that must be performed in central places." In other words, cities typically have developed as **central places** in which functions are performed in large part to provide goods and services for the surrounding trade areas.

The number of functions performed by a place can vary enormously. Some human settlements are so small or so specialized that they involve only a single function. An agricultural village in India, a fishing village in Polynesia, or a retirement community in Florida might be examples of single-function settlements. At the other extreme are large metropolises that usually are characterized by a great variety of functions, including manufacturing, retail and wholesale trade, transportation, finance, education, recreation, and many others.

Basic and Nonbasic Functions

It is helpful to separate urban functions into two types. **Basic functions** are those performed in a city for consumers or clients located elsewhere. By contrast, **nonbasic functions** are provided to meet the needs and desires of those who reside within the city. Because basic functions bring outside money into the city, they often are considered to be more important to the city's economy. For that reason city officials tend to be particularly eager to attract to their community those firms that engage primarily in basic activities. City residents who work at nonbasic occupations sometimes are described as "taking in each other's washing" to suggest that their activities result only in the transfer of money from one segment of the community to another. (A laundry, in fact, is a good example of a nonbasic function.)

While this classification may be theoretically sound and provide an important insight into the workings of the urban economy, it is difficult to apply rigidly because activities and firms seldom are strictly basic or nonbasic. Manufacturing and wholesale trade ordinarily are designated as basic activities, yet some may be nonbasic. A firm that produces electric fans, for example, may sell 95 percent of its products outside the city where it is located, but the remaining 5 percent may be purchased by the city's residents. The manufacture of these fans therefore is not totally a basic activity. It is equally difficult to identify purely nonbasic functions. Retail stores, bakeries, law firms, and banks are a few examples of businesses that may sell most of their goods and services to residents of the city in which they are located. However, they cannot be strictly categorized as nonbasic because nonresidents who are in the city for shopping or business also may obtain some of their goods and services.

The Functional Hierarchy

The functions of urban places result in an assortment of goods and services that are hierarchical in their availability. At the bottom of the hierarchy is a limited number of goods and services that can be obtained in even the smallest communities. Included are such things as groceries, gasoline, haircuts, and church services—all commonly needed goods and services that people prefer to have available locally. The minimum population (called the **threshold population**) needed to support a grocery store, a gas station, a barber shop, a church, and similar establishments is quite small; therefore, one or more of them can exist profitably or feasibly even in a hamlet or village. At a somewhat higher level in the hierarchy might be a department store, an automobile dealership, a medical clinic, and a law firm, all of which offer more specialized and less frequently needed goods and services. Because these establishments require a large threshold population to be profitable or feasible, they are likely to exist in larger towns but not smaller villages and hamlets. Those goods and services that are even more specialized will require still larger threshold populations and therefore will be available only in larger cities at higher levels of the hierarchy. Only in a major urban center would one expect to find, for example, a furrier, a diamond cutter, the headquarters of an international corporation, a robot manufacturer, and a major league baseball club.

At each level in the hierarchy the assortment of functions is increased by the addition of more specialized goods and services to those available at lower levels. Thus, a large town will provide a combination of goods and services that are available in hamlets and villages as well as others that require a greater threshold population than that available in the smaller communities. The great cities at the top of the hierarchy therefore will possess the broadest functional variety because they offer the most specialized goods and services as well as less specialized ones that also are available in smaller centers at lower levels. The general principle of the functional hierarchy is that the available goods and services become more specialized and more varied as the size of the urban center increases.

Functional Categories of Cities

➤ The functional specialty of cities is the basis of several classification systems, one of which groups cities into three categories: central place cities, transport cities, and specialized-function cities.

What is the functional role of the cities in each of these three categories?

How do these three groups of cities differ in terms of their locational patterns?

A simple but helpful classification of cities according to their functional role has been suggested by two American geographers, Chauncy Harris and Edward Ullman. Their classification involves three categories: central place cities, transport cities, and specialized-function cities. We will summarize the distinctive characteristics of each type.

Central Place Cities   The cities and towns in this category are widespread throughout the world and particularly in regions with little or no industrial development. They serve as market places and social centers for a tributary area and may vary in size from the smallest urban agglomerations to the largest metropolitan centers. The variety of goods and services they offer and the extent of their tributary areas are generally proportional to their sizes. In regions in which land surfaces and resources are comparatively uniform, the central places tend to be spaced regularly. By contrast, they are arranged irregularly over areas with broken terrain or unevenly distributed resources.

In the United States, the trade centers of agricultural regions such as the Middle West are particularly representative of central place towns and cities. They commonly have imposing retail and wholesale districts and shopping centers. In addition to their trade,

FIGURE 13.23

The Gateway Arch in St. Louis was constructed to commemorate the city's historic role as a gateway to the Southwest. (R. Lynn Bradley)

central places also are likely to have significant social and religious functions. In the towns and cities of some less developed countries, in fact, the social and religious activities are paramount in importance. Furthermore, some central places serve as political centers; examples are county seats and state or provincial capitals.

Transport Cities These cities tend to have a linear arrangement along coasts and transportation corridors. They often have developed where an interruption in transportation is caused by a physical feature (e.g., falls on a river) or by the intersection of different modes of transportation such as a railroad and a river. These are typical break-of-bulk points (where cargo is transferred from one mode of transport to another) and therefore logical places for the processing, sorting, storage, and transshipment of goods. A good example is the Canadian city of Thunder Bay on the northern shore of Lake Superior. As a break-of-bulk point for wheat raised in Canada's prairie provinces to the west, Thunder Bay is a major grain storage and transshipment center. The *entrepôts* of Singapore and Hong Kong are particularly important transshipment centers in Asia. Transport cities also often serve as gateways linking unlike regions that produce different materials and have different needs. In the United States, St.

Louis has long functioned as a gateway between the East and the Southwest (a role commemorated by the Gateway Arch shown in Fig. 13.23). In western Africa, Timbuktu is a famous gateway city between the Sahara Desert and a tropical savanna region.

Specialized-Function Cities Cities in this category are focused on a single activity such as mining, manufacturing, or recreation for a large tributary area. Because they commonly developed their specialization on the basis of a localized resource or other physical advantage, specialized-function cities tend to occur singly or in clusters. A mineral deposit may enable a town to specialize in mining as happened in the cases of the iron ore center of Hibbing, Minnesota, and the diamond center of Pretoria, South Africa. Cities with manufacturing as their functional specialty may have a favorable location for the assembly of raw materials or good access to a power supply or markets. A picturesque coast, a beach, or an attractive climate may be the basis for the development of a resort city like Myrtle Beach, South Carolina, or Acapulco, Mexico. Once a specialized function is established, similar and related activities typically are attracted to the city in a pyramiding fashion. Whether in a resort city like Las Vegas or a manufacturing city like Detroit, this concentration of associated functions tends to occur. A recent striking example is the concentration of various elements of the electronics industry in San Jose and smaller cities of Silicon Valley in California.

The Overlap of Functions

It must be emphasized that these three functional categories of cities are not without considerable overlap. As we noted earlier, the vast majority of urban centers are multifunctional; rarely are they involved in one function to the exclusion of all others. Thus a manufacturing city also must have an adequately developed transportation system to assemble its raw materials and distribute its final products. A resort city must have good transportation linkages to make it accessible to visitors. Furthermore, nearly all urban places have, to some degree, a central place functional role. In summary, the assignment of a city to a functional category should not obscure the fact that it most likely is engaged in many other activities.

CENTRAL PLACE THEORY AND THE CHRISTALLER MODEL

➤ Central place theory is the basis for Christaller's model of the functional and spatial relationships of central places.

What are the distinctive features of Christaller's model?

Why did Christaller use hexagons to delimit trade areas?

What is the nature of areas that closely conform to the model?

What is the nature of areas that significantly depart from it?

The functional and spatial relationships of central places and their trade areas have been the objects of a considerable amount of theory in urban geography. Most of this theory, now commonly identified as **central place theory**, is based on pioneering ideas formulated in the 1930s by Walter Christaller, a German geographer. Using southern Germany as a sample area, Christaller devised a model (Fig. 13.24) that in-

corporates the basic ideas of central place theory. The model has several distinctive features:

1. Smaller central places are more frequent on the landscape than larger centers.

2. Places of the same size category are equally spaced over the landscape and have trade areas of comparable dimensions.

3. Trade areas around central places are in the form of hexagons.

4. Smaller central places and their trade areas are nested within the trade areas of large central places.

Christaller placed his model in a hypothetical setting—a featureless surface or plain containing an evenly distributed rural population with equal access to each central place from all directions.

As we described earlier, central places are market centers that serve the important functional role of providing goods and services to consumers in surrounding trade areas. To best serve the trade area's population, the optimum location of the market center is the center of the trade area (hence the name "central place"). The extent of the trade area is determined by the "range" of the market center's goods and services—that is, the maximum distance that consumers are willing to travel to a market center to obtain them. In theory, people in the countryside will travel only a short distance to the nearest market center in order to obtain the most common and frequently needed goods and services—such as groceries, gasoline, and religious services (which, as we indicated earlier, usually are available even in the smallest central places). On the other hand, they will travel farther to purchase an automobile, have a computer repaired, attend an opera, or obtain other specialized goods and services that are available only in larger cities. The extent of trade areas in the Christaller model, therefore, is proportional to the size of the market centers, with the smaller centers and their trade areas "nested" within the trade areas of larger centers.

The hexagonal shape of trade areas in the Christaller model is based on interesting logic. It might seem more reasonable that trade areas around central places should form circles. However, as Figure 13.25 illustrates, that would result in some parts of the landscape outside trade areas or contained within the overlap of adjacent trade areas (both of which are unac-

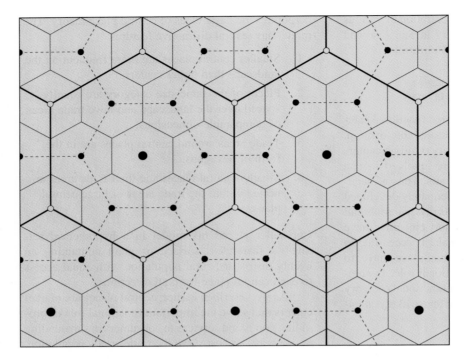

FIGURE 13.24
The Christaller model of central places and their trade areas (delimited by hexagons). Note how the trade areas of smaller places are "nested" within those of larger places.

ceptable in a model designed to represent ideal conditions). Christaller recognized that the hexagon is the closest shape to a circle that will tessellate the plane, and that hexagonal trade areas could form a perfect network that allows all parts of the landscape to be served without overlapping. The use of hexagons to represent trade areas is probably the most widely recognized aspect of Christaller's model.

Using southern Germany as a representative area, Christaller computed the typical spacing and population size of the central places at each level and the extent and population of their trade areas (Table 13.5).

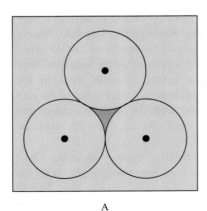
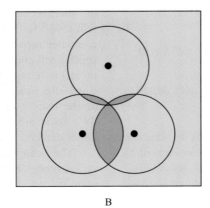
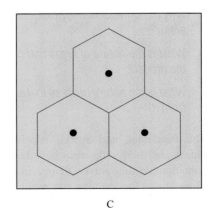

A   B   C

FIGURE 13.25
The use of circles to represent trade areas would result in either an overlap or some areas left unserved. Christaller therefore substituted hexagons, which depart little from circles but are capable of fitting together over the landscape.

TABLE 13.5   Christaller's Central Places and their Trade Areas

Central Place	Approximate Population	Distance Apart miles	(km)	Trade Area square miles	(sq km)
Market village	1000	4.5	(7)	17	(44)
Township center	2000	7.5	(12)	51	(133)
County town	4000	13.0	(21)	154	(400)
District city	10,000	22.5	(36)	463	(1200)
Small state capital	30,000	39.0	(62)	1390	(3600)
Provincial capital	100,000	67.5	(108)	4170	(10,800)
Regional capital	500,000	116.0	(186)	12,500	(32,400)

SOURCE: *Adapted from Walter Christaller,* Central Places in Southern Germany. *Englewood Cliffs, N.J.: Prentice-Hall, Inc., 1966.*

The distance separating the smallest centers, about 7 kilometers, apparently was established by the ability of a person to travel about half that far on foot or by horse to reach the nearest central place in no more than an hour. (In nearly all cases, settlements in southern Germany were established prior to the more rapid travel afforded by automobiles.) The distance between adjacent centers in each of the larger groups is greater (by the square root of 3) than that between places in the next smaller category.

After examinations of the central place network in many different parts of the world it has become apparent that Christaller's model most closely conforms to reality in uniform and thinly populated agricultural areas such as Iowa in the American Corn Belt and the Pampa region in Argentina. Any condition that disrupts uniformity of the surface or channelizes transportation—a navigable river, for example, or a railroad, a mountain range, or a lake—will alter the regularity of the central place network as portrayed in the model. Nevertheless, the model serves a valuable purpose in providing an idealized theoretical pattern against which real world conditions can be compared and thereby better understood.

THE INTERNAL ARRANGEMENT OF CITIES

➤ Most urban centers have an internal structure that features a central business district (CBD) surrounded by a variety of other districts and zones of specialized land use.

What conditions led to the establishment and development of the CBD?

What other districts and zones are common components of cities?

Why do similar urban land uses tend to be located near each other?

In addition to the spatial arrangement of urban settlements over the landscape, the patterns of land use within cities are important aspects of urban geography. All settlements have an internal geography, and that of large multifunctional cities is extremely complex. Within a major metropolis is a large assortment of districts, zones, neighborhoods, parks, and corridors that reflect the functional and social character of the city and the nature of changes through time. Some areas may be distinguished by stagnation, deterioration, or decay, while others are marked by renewal, new development, or growth. Each provides a distinctive cultural landscape.

The internal structure of cities, particularly those in the industrialized world, has been enormously altered during the twentieth century by the automobile. Individuals greatly increased their mobility as they acquired automobiles, and the growth in numbers of vehicles made necessary the improvement of streets and roads and eventually the construction of intricate highway networks and extensive parking facilities. The purchase of automobiles in the United States was so rapid after World War II that more than 100 million cars were in service by the 1960s (a ratio of one vehicle to fewer than three people), and a magnificent interstate highway system was constructed to link the nation's major cities. Within the cities, attempts were made to keep up with the burgeoning number of automobiles by building a basic network of multilane, limited-access, high-speed freeways often elevated above street level. In addition, valuable space in downtown areas was taken up by parking facilities, including multilevel garages, that had to be built to accommodate the daytime gathering of great numbers of vehicles.

Perhaps the most important impact of the automobile on cities has been the growth of suburbs to the detriment of older districts. As they acquired the ability to commute to work in private cars over greater distances than ever before, urban people in large numbers began abandoning older residential areas in favor of the many developing suburbs on the margin of the city. Soon inner-city retail stores, offices, and industries followed, taking advantage of the decentralization that the new highway system allowed. The result has been a drastic and in some ways unfortunate rearrangement of urban populations and businesses.

The Central Business District

In economic terms, the most important functional area of all urban centers—small and large—is the commercial core or **central business district** (CBD). The CBD usually is at or near the geographic center of the city or town, but that may not be true of settlements founded on a seacoast, the shore of a lake, or the banks of a river. Where the original commercial activity of urban centers was attracted to a navigable waterway, the CBD usually became established on the waterfront and remained in that location even in cases where the water transportation declined in relative importance or was totally interrupted at a later time. Once a community's largest and most expensive buildings are erected on a particular site, inertia comes into play. The CBD may expand in area, but it seldom is relocated to an entirely new site within a city or town. Individual stores or businesses may relocate, but the CBD tends to remain anchored to its original site because of the enormous expense required to move the entire district.

The desire of businesses to be accessible to the greatest number of people is the reason for their original concentration—and the reason for formation of the CBD—in the center of an urban place (or on the waterfront in cases where water transportation was a factor in accessibility). Optimum accessibility has always been of utmost importance in order for the CBD to maximize its number of customers, to obtain an adequate workforce, and to facilitate the arrival and shipment of goods. Over time, linkages of the CBD with increasingly distant parts of the city and even beyond have been strengthened by the building of streetcar lines, railroads, highways, subways, and mass transit systems. These ongoing measures to maximize the CBD's accessibility caused it to become the focus for the entire urban transportation network.

The CBD typically contains the most valuable land within a city. The high prices to buy and rent property are a consequence of competition among businesses, agencies, and firms to acquire the most accessible land on which to place their buildings. In large cities with limited space and many competitors for the available land, prices can be astronomical. This has motivated vertical development such as the construction of multistory buildings, skyscrapers, subways, tunnels, and even underground shopping facilities as means of maximizing the use of scarce and expensive lots and blocks within the CBD. The value of urban land generally decreases with distance away from the CBD. However, it is not a steady decrease because land along the highways and major streets, particularly at intersections, is usually of higher value than other areas the same distance away from the CBD. This pattern is portrayed in a model of urban land values shown in Figure 13.26.

Despite the concentration of commercial buildings, much land in the CBD is used for other purposes. Some is taken up by the sidewalks, streets, and parking facilities necessary for the movement of people within, to, and from the CBD. In addition, however, there are malls, plazas, monuments, civic centers, museums, and even parks contained within the CBDs of many large cities. (See *Cultural Landscapes: Moscow's Kremlin and Red Square.*) Most of these elements of the CBD are usually the results of formal programs implemented by cities to improve the attractiveness of their downtown areas. In small towns in the United States, buildings of the CBD often surround a public park or "square." The county courthouse is likely to occupy the center of the square and be the focal point of the CBD in towns and cities that serve as county seats.

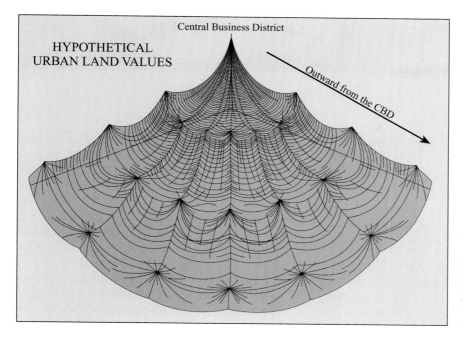

HYPOTHETICAL
URBAN LAND VALUES

Central Business District

Outward from the CBD

FIGURE 13.26

A model of urban land values, representing the most valuable land in the CBD and secondary peaks that usually characterize the intersections of major transportation arteries.

Unlike cities in most other countries that have many apartment buildings in their CBDs, relatively few people reside in the downtown area of American cities. The contrast between daytime and nighttime is astounding. Streets and sidewalks typically are jammed with shoppers, businesspeople, and other workers during the day, but nearly all of these individuals are commuters who are gone from the CBD at night. They flood into the downtown in the morning, if not by public transportation, then by car, which they commonly park in multilevel parking garages. They then rejoin the rush-hour traffic in the late afternoon to return to their homes in the suburbs and other outlying housing districts. This leaves the streets and sidewalks of the CBD virtually abandoned at night except around a few special facilities that offer entertainment, usually for tourists. Many people avoid the downtown at night because they consider the streets dangerous after dark. If they must shop at night, they visit suburban shopping centers or neighborhood stores. By constructing new luxury apartment buildings and attractive condominiums and by renovating and converting other buildings to provide high-quality housing, attempts have been made to attract people back to residential quarters in the center of some American cities. With few exceptions, these efforts have met

with little success. Abandonment of the urban core by residents who have been lured by the perceived safety, spaciousness, and attractiveness of the suburbs is now a decades-old trend that has proved nearly impossible to reverse. Furthermore, the accompanying migration of stores, offices, and industries to the suburbs has threatened the commercial viability of the CBD in many American cities.

Other Districts and Zones

Beyond the CBD are other districts and zones—each identifiable by a distinctive land use—that form additional components of the typical city. In general, similar land uses tend to agglomerate in an urban setting. This often is the result of spatial variations in land values; relatively expensive land is attractive for certain uses while other uses are practical only where the land is less valuable. In addition, there is the need to keep incompatible land uses separated. It would not be satisfactory, for example, to have a factory that generates a good deal of noise and smoke adjacent to a nursing home for elderly people. To ensure the spatial separation of incompatible land uses and to preserve the homogeneity of land use in each district, most cities employ zoning regulations.

CULTURAL LANDSCAPES

Moscow's Kremlin and Red Square

Prominent features in the central core of Moscow, Russia's capital city, are the historic Kremlin and Red Square. Originally a fortress, the Kremlin was established during the Middle Ages at a point where the Moscow River was easily crossed. Walls were built around the Kremlin during the fifteenth century, with cathedrals and palaces subsequently erected on the grounds for use by later generations of czars. As Moscow grew around it, the Kremlin became increasingly devoted to political functions. The Grand Palace within the Kremlin walls was rebuilt during the communist era to house the country's Supreme Soviet (parliament). Still surrounded by its brick walls and towers, the Kremlin retains the outward appearance of a medieval fortress. Nikolsky Tower, about 330 feet (70 m) tall, houses the gate through which revolutionary forces stormed the Kremlin in 1917 and brought an end to czarist control of the Russian government.

Red Square is an enormous public plaza that was created in the fifteenth century when old buildings were torn down just outside the east wall of the Krem-

A line of people on Red Square to enter the Lenin Mausoleum. The Kremlin wall and towers are on the right. (Swersey-Liaison)

lin. With a length of about 2300 feet (695 m) and an average width of about 425 feet (130 m), it covers an area of more than a half million square feet (70,000 sq m). Originally paved with cobblestones, it was resurfaced with stone blocks in 1930.

Since its establishment, Red Square has been the site of many historic events. The leaders of popular revolts against the czarist government were executed in Red Square before the Revolution of 1917. It was from Red Square that V. I. Lenin, the father of Bolshevik communism, inspired and dispatched his followers to defeat the enemies of the new communist state. For decades Red Square was used for Soviet military parades in which the country's latest sophisticated weapons were displayed. Also, important national events and ceremonies, including speeches by political leaders, celebrations of victories and the accomplishments of heroes, and state funerals traditionally have been held on Red Square.

Adjacent to Red Square are some of the most famous buildings of Moscow. To the north is the State History Museum, a red brick building constructed in 1878–1883, which is a major depository of historical documents and relics. On the south is St. Basil's Cathedral, distinguished by its colorful, onion-shaped domes. Built in the sixteenth century, it is considered to be an architectural masterpiece. The east side of Red Square is marked by what was GUM, the State Department Store of the Soviet Union. It continues to be the largest retail establishment of the country in the post-Soviet period.

Probably the most well-known building associated with Red Square is the Lenin Mausoleum, a granite structure just outside the Kremlin wall. The preserved body of Lenin is on display in a crystal sarcophagus within the building. During the communist era, thousands of people lined up daily to enter the mausoleum and view Lenin's body. Now that the Communist Party no longer controls the government and Lenin's fame has diminished, controversy surrounds the mausoleum. Many Russians feel that the body of Lenin should be removed to a less prominent location.

THOUGHT QUESTIONS

1. Have there been any facilities in the United States that have played a role in American history similar to that of the Kremlin and Red Square in Russian history? If so, in what ways have the roles been similar?

2. Do you believe that the role or the physical character of the Kremlin and Red Square will change significantly as the post-communist period progresses in Russia? If so, what changes do you think are most likely?

Immediately adjacent to the CBD in major cities of the United States is a "zone in transition," a portion of the inner city distinguished by low-quality housing (especially old apartments and hotels), warehouses, and some manufacturing. Advanced deterioration of old buildings is characteristic of this zone, and abandonment is common. Most residents are members of minority groups and recent immigrants. To improve living conditions for the poor, many cities have constructed public housing units in this zone; however, vandalism and high crime rates have been so common in public housing facilities that alternatives for housing the urban poor are being sought. The most substantial changes in this zone have come about through urban renewal projects and encroachment of the CBD. This commonly results in the elimination of old apartments and hotels, thereby intensifying the shortage of low-cost housing available for the poor.

Various residential areas and neighborhoods occupy other parts of the typical city. They often are differentiated on the basis of such factors as the prevailing ethnicity or race of the inhabitants, the age and quality of the housing, and dominant architectural features. As one progresses from the inner city toward the margin, the housing tends to be newer and higher in quality, although exceptions to this pattern are common. Certain types of property within the city, such as a lake shore or an area of higher elevation on a hill or ridge, may be the site of some of the most prestigious housing.

"Commercial strips" have replaced housing along highways and even some of the heavily traveled streets in most American cities. A great variety of businesses are contained within these corridors, including motels, gasoline stations, automobile dealerships, fast-food restaurants, discount stores, and home improvement centers. These commercial strips are primarily oriented toward people traveling on adjacent highways and streets, and their businesses compete for attention by the use of prominent (sometimes gaudy) signs and symbols (Fig. 13.27). At interchanges and intersections there is likely to be a somewhat greater clustering of these establishments as well as sprawling malls that function as neighborhood commercial centers.

On the margins of the typical American city are suburbs and, usually somewhat farther removed, satellite cities. These components, which we described earlier in this chapter, generally consist of relatively new housing developments. However, industries, corporate headquarters, and other businesses have joined the flight to the suburban zone, relieving some workers of the need to commute to a workplace in the urban core. Industrial parks and similar areas devoted to offices and commercial establishments thus have joined housing developments as prominent features of suburban landscapes.

FIGURE 13.27

A representative commercial strip, with concentrated businesses and their signs along a major street in an American city. (Gilles Bassignac/Gamma Liaison)

Models of Internal Structure

➤ Three basic models—the concentric zone, sector, and multiple nuclei models—of the internal structure of cities in the United States were devised by scholars during the first half of the twentieth century.

What rationale was involved in the structure of each model?

How do these models reflect trends in the development of U.S. cities?

Urban specialists in a variety of fields have devised a number of models to portray theoretical arrangements of the various zones and districts within cities. From this assortment, we will briefly examine three of the earliest models (Fig. 13.28). These three reflect both increasing sophistication in the interpretation of cities by the model builders and the growing complexity of cities over time. Other models are largely derived from these three.

The Concentric Zone Model The first model of internal city structure was proposed in 1925 by Ernest W. Burgess, a sociologist. The city is divided by this model into a series of concentric rings or zones, including the central business district. Growth and change involve the expansion of land uses from each interior zone into that on its outer margin. Close to the CBD is the *zone in transition*. It is an older residential area that has seriously deteriorated, resulting in slums and ghettos populated mostly by minorities and recent immigrants. Burgess also suggested the encroachment of business and light manufacturing in this zone. Next is the *zone of independent workingmen's homes*, predominantly inhabited by blue-collar workers who with their families have chosen to leave the

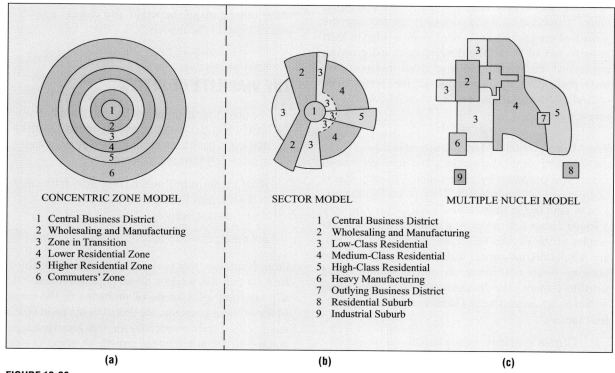

CONCENTRIC ZONE MODEL

1 Central Business District
2 Wholesaling and Manufacturing
3 Zone in Transition
4 Lower Residential Zone
5 Higher Residential Zone
6 Commuters' Zone

SECTOR MODEL

1 Central Business District
2 Wholesaling and Manufacturing
3 Low-Class Residential
4 Medium-Class Residential
5 High-Class Residential
6 Heavy Manufacturing
7 Outlying Business District
8 Residential Suburb
9 Industrial Suburb

MULTIPLE NUCLEI MODEL

(a)   (b)   (c)

FIGURE 13.28

Three models of the internal structure of cities: (a) the concentric zone model, (b) the sector model, and (c) the multiple nuclei model.

deteriorating conditions in the zone of transition. Often these people are second-generation immigrants who have improved their economic status over that of their parents. The *zone of better residences* is encountered next. It is an area of relatively expensive apartment buildings and single-family houses, often included in exclusive districts. Finally is the *commuters' zone* encompassing the upper-class residences in suburbs beyond the city limits and in satellite cities. Development in this zone is spotty, with most located along lines of rapid travel.

The Sector Model The theory that similar types of urban land use expand outward from the center of the city along transportation routes or axes of least resistance is incorporated in this model. Economist Homer Hoyt suggested the sector model in the mid-1930s. It portrays the area of a city as a circle divided into sectors of varying width that radiate out from the CBD. Each sector has been formed by a particular assortment of land uses that has originated in or near the CBD and spread along an axis toward the periphery of the city. One sector may have formed as manufacturing plants expanded along a railroad, another by the growth of upper-class residences along a ridge or high ground, and so forth. The development and growing importance during the 1930s of axial transportation lines, particularly modern highways, for certain kinds of land use clearly stimulated Hoyt's origination of the sector model.

The Multiple Nuclei Model As an alternative to the earlier more simplistic models, the multiple nuclei model was proposed by geographers Chauncy Harris and Edward Ullman in 1945. They noted that the pattern of land use in many cities is not focused on only a single center but rather on a number of nuclei. Examples of the various nuclei, in addition to the CBD, are wholesale, industrial, residential, university, and outlying business districts, as well as suburban and satellite centers. The formulation of separate nuclei within a city, according to Harris and Ullman, reflects four factors.

1. Certain activities require conditions or specialized facilities that are available only in certain parts of the city.

2. Certain activities of a similar nature benefit by clustering together.

3. Certain activities of an unlike nature are not compatible when located adjacent to one another.

4. Certain activities are not able to afford the high costs of the most desirable sites and must locate in less expensive areas.

The establishment of scattered nuclei also was facilitated by improvements in intraurban transportation, particularly the mobility provided by the automobile.

In comparing these three models, it is evident that they suggest major trends in the development of cities over time. Each should be regarded as most applicable to one stage in that development. The more recently developed multiple nuclei model best represents modern cities. However, because earlier structural patterns are seldom completely obliterated by subsequent changes, it is common for modern cities to contain traces of all three models. We should point out that the originators of all three models used Chicago as the basis for their ideas and probably intended for their models to apply only to American cities. Nevertheless, depending on their stage of development, cities in many other parts of the world also display aspects of one or more of the models.

THE VIABILITY OF CITIES

➤ The phenomenal growth of cities in the less developed world and the aging of cities in the industrialized world have been accompanied by a number of extremely serious problems.

What are the most troubling problems in the cities of the less developed countries and in those of the developed world?

Are there possible solutions to these problems?

From conditions that prevail today, it is reasonable to forecast that the world's urban population and cities will confront a multitude of problems in the future. Many of these problems are linked to the great size of many cities and—especially in the less developed world—to the accelerating growth of urban centers. Some authorities feel that many of the world's cities already are too large for officials to exercise effective control and guidance. Cities have a reputation as the main nodes in which each society's greatest cultural achievements have been attained. Can they continue in this role in the future, or is their viability at risk?

The gathering of the world's people in urban centers is progressing at a rate never experienced before in history. Unlike in the past when most urban growth was associated with industrialization and the creation of jobs in cities, the present increase is largely in less developed countries where little economic modernization is underway. Even with scarce employment opportunities for new residents in cities of the less developed world, their growth rates in the future are not likely to decelerate. The great migrations from rural areas that are unable to support more people, together with persistent increases in the general population, assure high rates of urban growth in the less developed world for decades to come. As these cities balloon in size, some by hundreds of thousands of people annually, critical questions are yet to be answered. How will essential needs of the people—pure water supplies, shelter, sewage and garbage disposal, education, health care, and police and fire protection—be met? How will the inhabitants, including many who are poorly educated and unskilled, be gainfully employed? If these needs continue to be unfulfilled, what will be the consequences?

Although the growth of cities is less rapid in the industrialized world, their problems continue to be serious. Deterioration in the urban environment is a worldwide problem, but certain facets of it are of greater magnitude or more widespread in the industrialized countries. Traffic congestion, waste disposal, and water, air, and noise pollution are urban problems that the industrialized countries have not yet solved. Several countries, especially the United States, have implemented programs and enacted legislation to reverse environmental deterioration with some success. However, the problems persist because the legislation often is inadequate and not vigorously enforced, and the cost of remedial action usually is enormous.

Racial and ethnic conflicts also are serious matters in the crowded urban centers of many industrialized countries. Prejudice and discrimination often are involved in housing and employment practices, despite official policies to ensure equal opportunity and access. Although illegal, discriminatory practices of real estate firms in the United States to prevent integration of urban residential areas have been common. While legislation to prevent discrimination obviously is important, educational programs probably have the greatest potential to solve the problem.

Inadequate financing is a crippling obstacle for major cities in the United States and many other countries. Sufficient funds simply are unavailable to maintain the cities' physical facilities and provide the many public needs of urban residents. This problem has been intensified in the United States by the massive migration of the more affluent classes to suburbs, where they are able to avoid central city taxes. Cities in the future must find a more effective means of obtaining operational funds if they are to reverse their physical decay and deterioration of social services. Perhaps the importance of cities to the general society justifies a greater commitment of federal financial support for their rejuvenation.

KEY TERMS

Metropolitan Statistical Area (MSA) An urbanized area identified by the United States Bureau of the Census. It consists of a county or group of contiguous counties that fulfill certain demographic and economic criteria and usually contain a central city with a minimum population of 50,000. **485**

Site The specific area occupied by a city or other feature. It usually is described in terms of its physical characteristics, such as its bedrock, drainage, and local relief. **485**

Situation The regional setting of a city or other feature on the landscape. **488**

Grid pattern town A nucleated settlement in which the blocks are rectangular or square and the streets cross at right angles. The streets commonly are aligned according to the cardinal points of a compass. **492**

Squatter settlement A community consisting of primitive shelters erected and occupied by people without obtaining formal approval of the landowner. Squatter settlements are common on the margins of cities in the less developed world. **500**

Gentrification A process in which inner-city dilapidated buildings or neighborhoods are rehabilitated and their lower-income inhabitants are replaced by members of the middle or upper class.   **503**

Rank–size rule   Identifies a common relationship between a city's rank in the urban hierarchy of a country and its population size. The rule is that the *n*th-ranked city will have a population 1/*n*th that of the largest city.   **503**

Primate city   A country's dominant city in size, economic importance, and cultural influence. Paris, France, is a classic example of a primate city.   **503**

Central place   A market center or community in which goods and services may be obtained by consumers in the surrounding trade area.   **512**

Basic functions   The functions of a city that provide goods and services for sale to consumers in other areas, thereby earning income for the city from outside sources.   **512**

Nonbasic functions   The functions of a city that provide goods and services for consumers within the city. As a consequence, these activities bring no income to the city from outside sources.   **512**

Threshold population   The minimum number of people required to support an economic facility or activity and make possible its presence in a market center.   **513**

Central place theory   The theory concerned with the hierarchy of market centers and their distributional patterns in an area.   **515**

Central business district (CBD)   The core area of a town or city that contains a concentration of prominent multistory buildings housing offices, retail stores, banks, and other commercial establishments.   **518**

REVIEW QUESTIONS

1. What are the major differences that distinguish urban centers from rural settlements?

2. Why are urban centers considered places exhibiting great contrasts? How are each of the following defined: legal city, physical city, central city, urbanized area, Metropolitan Statistical Area, conurbation?

3. What is the difference between an urban center's site and situation? How might each influence the location and growth of a city?

4. Where and why did the first urban centers appear? Why were the earliest cities closely associated with the hearths of civilization?

5. What characteristics did the earliest cities have in common? What were some of the special features of early Greek cities? What were some of the features of Roman cities?

6. How did the progress of European and Moslem cities differ during the Middle Ages? What events renewed the growth of European cities, and what impact did colonization have on the spread and growth of urban centers?

7. Why did the Industrial Revolution accelerate the growth and increase the number of urban centers? What factors most influenced urban growth in the United States?

8. Where is urban growth most rapid in the world today? How does urban growth in the less developed world differ from that in the industrialized world?

9. What explanations can be given for the rapid growth of suburbs on the periphery of cities in the developed world? What explanations can be given for such growth in the less developed world?

10. What is the general relationship between the population of an urban center and the assortment of functions it performs? What is the rank–size rule?

11. What is a primate city and in what parts of the world are most primate cities found?

12. On a world map of urbanization, what regions are the most and least urbanized? What explains the extent of urbanization in these regions?

13. What factors other than population may influence the number and variety of functions associated with urban centers? What are basic functions? What are nonbasic functions?

14. How is the concept of threshold population related to the goods and services available in a particular city?

15. What three types of cities are included in the Harris-Ullman functional classification of cities? What weakness exists in their classification system?

16. What are the major features of Christaller's model of *central place theory*?

17. How has the internal structure of cities in the industrialized world been altered by widespread use of the automobile?

18. What are the major internal districts or zones of the modern American city? What is the typical nature of these zones and what typical functions distinguish them?

19. What serious problems are associated with the extreme size and continued rapid growth of many cities throughout the world?

DR. CRAIG E. COLTEN,
SENIOR RESEARCH ASSOCIATE AT THE
ILLINOIS STATE MUSEUM

Craig E. Colten *Born in 1952, in the Louisiana sawmill town of Bogalusa, Dr. Craig E. Colten had a love of geography that grew from a youthful desire to travel. Today, he searches for clues to environmental mysteries. Best known for his pioneering work in reconstructing historical industrial waste disposal practices, he investigates the environmental impacts of human settlement.*

Colten is a senior research associate at the Illinois State Museum in Springfield, where he also serves as an adjunct associate professor at Sangamon State University. In his capacity as a principal investigator for a project sponsored by the Environmental Protection Trust Fund, he is conducting a geographic assessment and policy review of derelict industrial properties. His many publishing credits include co-editing THE AMERICAN ENVIRONMENT: INTERPRETATIONS OF PAST GEOGRAPHIES. (Marlin Roos)

You study the environmental impacts of industrialization. How did this interest develop?

In my second year of college, I took a break from classes because I had begun to realize that I did not want to be a business major. For the next six or eight months, I spent much of my time traveling. I hitchhiked to the east coast, then to the west coast, and I decided that traveling would be a very pleasant way to spend a lifetime.

When I began to consider which academic courses might provide me with the best opportunities to travel, geography seemed like a natural fit. Also, I had an aircraft pilot's license, so I was already fascinated by aerial map interpretation and meteorology—skills used in geography.

I returned to Louisiana State University in 1972 and stumbled, quite fortuitously, onto an excellent geography department. The LSU geography department provided a wonderful balance of the physical and human elements of geographical studies.

What are "historical hazards?"

The Resource Conservation and Recovery Act of 1976 requires any manufacturer who produces or disposes of a hazardous waste to maintain a record of that waste. Environmental agencies receive copies of those records. It is a "cradle-to-grave" system for tracking hazardous waste.

"Historical hazards" are substances that were never entered into the regulatory agency databases and information-collection inventories established after 1976. These substances were generally left behind by manufacturers before the U.S. Environmental Protection Agency put current regulations into place. Such substances might have been generated, for example, by old coal mining activities, gas works, or smelting operations.

Why is it so important to identify historical hazards?

Historical hazards are especially troublesome today because, under the Comprehensive Environmental Response, Compensation and Liability Act (or "Superfund law"), a property owner is potentially liable for all cleanup costs as well as any damage to natural resources caused by wastes. This is a big financial liability.

Huge manufacturing facilities throughout the Midwest and Northeast are obsolete, decaying, or partly dismantled. Like the old mining towns of the West, many derelict manufacturing facilities are now prime real estate, particularly those located on waterfront property. But financiers are leery of loaning money for redevelopment of industrial sites, because of possible historical hazards.

Today, an environmental site assessment (ESA) is required for anyone thinking of buying property where an industrial activity once occurred. These assessments are vitally important. Unfortunately, laws have been proposed recently to minimize the "burden" of the ESA requirement. I believe that these kinds of laws would increase the property buyer's risk of encountering contamination.

Even if the property is not catastrophically contaminated, any small hazard could result in a serious financial loss. If you are setting up a mom-and-pop business and you have to pay $100,000 to pull an old gas tank from the ground, that is a huge setback.

> "Human geographers look for a predictable pattern of human activity on the landscape. . . . To develop my model of historical waste production, I simply identified those areas in and around cities where industrial growth has traditionally occurred."

How have hazards evolved as a result of human settlement?

Some of the first types of hazardous substances produced in the United States were those associated with mining activities such as lead or gold mining and smelting. The economic lure of mining has historically drawn people from the countryside into more densely populated settlements.

Let me offer an example of a hazard that developed in Hawks Nest, West Virginia. Around the 1930s, many rural Southerners were recruited to Hawks Nest to work as miners, digging a shaft for a hydroelectric power installation. Workers were exposed to high concentrations of dust containing silica, which wrecked their lungs. Many developed a respiratory condition called silicosis. Because there were fatalities, litigation ensued. Some people said that masks or respirators would have prevented these workers from getting sick. So, this particular mining activity provided the workers with an economic livelihood, yet it also disabled them.

Many of the nation's old mining towns are now played out. Museums have been established in the gold mining towns of California and in the coal mining towns in Eastern Pennsylvania. (All these museums are going to need employees trained in human geography, by the way!)

You developed a generic "model" to help geographers determine where historical wastes might exist in any given city. How did you develop the model?

Human geographers look for a predictable pattern of human activity on the landscape. You could blindfold a bunch of geographers and turn them loose in a city, and they would be able to define these patterns instantly. They could say, "Over there, we would expect to find a financial district, and over here, we would expect to find a suburban residential area."

To develop my model of historical waste production, I simply identified those areas in and around cities where industrial growth has traditionally occurred. I also studied laws relating to hazardous waste production, and I considered what waste-disposal technologies would have been available in the past.

As early as the 1870s, cities passed "nuisance laws," which forced certain industries outside the city limits. Industries that generated smoke or bad odors, for example, were banished from cities. So you wouldn't expect to find smelters or meat packing industries or gas works to be located within the city limits after the 1870s. Historical investigations are painstaking, however, because pre-existing industries were often exempt from nuisance laws. While new industries were pushed farther and farther into the countryside, old industrial sites were left behind in the cities.

You identified historical "stages" of U.S. waste generation and disposal. Would you summarize those stages?

The pre-1870s city was fairly compact, geographically. Most industry was located near a waterfront. Fairly small volumes of waste were produced.

Between 1870 and 1930, cities began to force industries outside the city limits. Railroads became very common, so that railroad industrial districts developed. Around these districts grew working-class neighborhoods. Cities enlarged tremendously, until the Great Depression arrested urban growth. These were times of extensive industrial production, when an array of industries generated great quantities of hazardous substances.

From 1930 to the present, we have witnessed a new industrial surge outward from cities, linked to major new transportation systems in the form of interstate highways. Older industrial facilities in cities have declined and are being demolished. Old waste accumulations are being removed.

What technologies were used in the past to dispose of hazardous materials?

Technologies were available in the past to minimize environmental damage. Yet, because waste disposal wasn't regulated, disposal practices were generally inadequate, even for that era.

Industries used fairly crude incinerators to burn some waste. In the early 1900s, people in cities along the Ohio River began to complain that their drinking water had a foul taste because steel mills were dumping waste into the river. After that, the states worked with steel mills, encouraging them to dump liquid waste onto slag mounds—big heaps of processing residue. This slag was red hot. The companies would pour liquid waste onto the slag, causing steam to rise from the mound, cooling the slag and vaporizing some wastes. This technique was widely used in the 1920s.

It was also common to mix acid with alkaline wastes to neutralize them. Or, a company might put liquid waste into pits or ponds, hoping that the liquid would evaporate.

In the 1940s, recommendations were established to discourage dumping toxic materials onto bare ground. But these recommendations were very general; they merely said that companies should not pollute groundwater or surface water.

Tell me what you learned about settlement in East St. Louis.

The East St. Louis area lies on the eastern bank of the Mississippi River. It is located in the state of Illinois, across the river from its sister city, St. Louis, which is located in the state of Missouri.

East St. Louis is a classic example of a "satellite city." That is, when certain manufacturers began to be excluded from cities like St. Louis, they opened shop outside the city limits. Entire stockyards and packing plants were opened in East St. Louis, along with industries using coal, which generated smoke. There were many smelters in East St. Louis.

During industrialization, whole communities emerged along the Mississippi River floodplain. A huge industrial belt developed in the river bottoms area from Alton to East St. Louis. Many of those industries generated very toxic waste containing metals or coal by-products. Now, there are serious historical hazards in the region.

How did waste disposal practices and environmental awareness evolve over time in East St. Louis?

In the early stage of industrialization, most industries in East St. Louis took water from the ground. Often, these industries would pollute their own wa-ter supply. One industry, for instance, was refining gasoline. So much gasoline was being spilled into the groundwater system that the company drilled into the ground and pumped the gasoline back up to the surface for reuse.

A whole series of small company towns emerged. These towns were heavily dependent on industry for their livelihood. Consequently, even as environmental regulations became more common and the public became less tolerant of pollution, many people in these communities valued the economic benefits of industry far more than they feared negative health effects of pollution.

What do you think will happen to the nation's derelict industrial sites?

The trend has been to transform these old manufacturing sites into service and recreational facilities. The Baltimore Harbor is a good example of a converted industrial district. That area now includes shops, condominiums, rock-and-roll clubs, and tourist attractions. Many old industrial districts can serve this type of recreational function.

Will there be jobs in the future for students who want to follow in your footsteps?

Yes, there will be job opportunities for human geographers, especially in environmental consulting firms. Young people should also think about jobs in museums, dealing with historical patterns of human settlement. Cartography courses may be especially useful, because museums need staff with graphic skills. The U.S. Parks Service will need more employees to interpret historical and cultural landscapes.

Originally covered by a lush stand of trees that effectively held the soil in place, the land depicted in the accompanying photograph now reflects the ravages of erosion that have followed the harvesting of this area's timber. The loss of topsoil and formation of gullies obviously have drastically reduced the productive value of the area. The erosion of soil materials from such land usually results in a buildup of silt in the streams and rivers that carry away the runoff water. As their channels become increasingly reduced by silt accumulation, these water bodies are prone to overflow their banks and flood adjacent areas, causing additional damage to land and property. Furthermore, the survival of wildlife is threatened as habitats are disrupted by deforestation, erosion, and flooding.

Our example here, of course, provides only a suggestion of the growing multitude of stresses that humans are imposing on the physical environment. Others involve air pollution, reduction of the ozone layer, acid rain, global warming, desertification, depletion of

PART 6

A HUMAN-STRESSED ENVIRONMENT

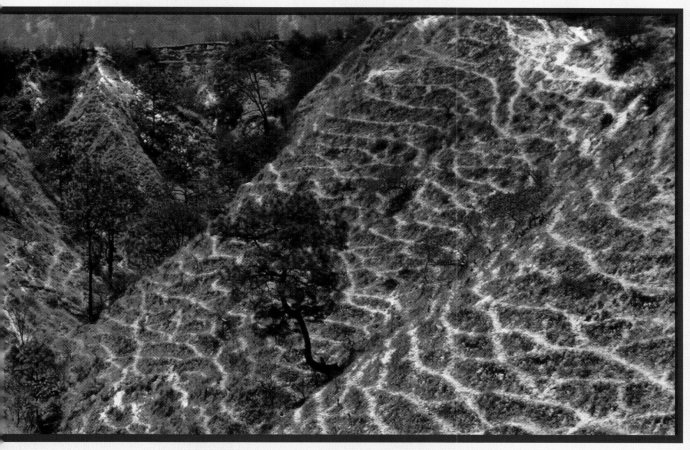

© *Eastcott/Momatiuk/The Image Works, Woodstock, NY*

mineral resources, and waste disposal, all of which represent a real or potential crisis for the earth's inhabitants. At no earlier time in human history has there been such a variety of causes for concern about threats to our environment.

In earlier sections of this book we have examined several critical global issues, including the high rate of current population growth, the need for more widespread economic development, and the new surge in urbanization of the world's population. Not only are these matters closely interrelated, they are also fundamental causes of the environmental crises we face today. It is logical, therefore, that we devote the book's final chapter to an examination of those crises and a consideration of possible remedial measures. Humans have created the planet's environmental problems, and only humans can solve them. Those individuals trained in human geography are in a particularly strong position to choose and implement the best solutions to such problems.

CHAPTER 14

CONTEMPORARY ENVIRONMENTAL ISSUES

*One generation passeth away, and another generation
cometh: but the earth abideth forever.*

—Ecclesiastes 1 : 4

*Will future generations inherit an earth environment so depleted and
polluted that their quality of life will be diminished?*
(Frank Siteman/Stock Boston)

The progression of generations and an earth forever able to provide food, shelter, and a supporting environment seemed entirely likely in biblical times, but we must question whether the opening quote is realistic today. It has already been noted that human numbers have been increasing at an unprecedented rate in the past few centuries and there is no sign that this phenomenal growth will end in the immediate future. Just as significant is the mounting evidence that contemporary societies are altering the physical environment to such an extent that the land, air, and water may be unable to support the generations to come.

Recent scientific studies have revealed some discomfiting facts. Acid precipitation has been reported in large areas of central and northern Europe, the eastern United States and Canada, and the former Soviet Union. As once productive grasslands throughout a broad belt stretching across north-central Africa are destroyed by drought and human misuse, large areas are becoming part of the Sahara Desert every year. Lush tropical forests in the Amazon Basin and the wide variety of flora and fauna associated with them are being replaced by pasture and cropland at the rate of nearly 1000 square kilometers per day. A report from National Aeronautic and Space Administration (NASA) scientists states that since 1969 the ozone layer has decreased by as much as 3 percent over heavily industrialized areas of the middle latitudes and by greater amounts near the poles. If the present rate of industrial pollution continues for another 50 years, many experts believe the amounts of carbon dioxide and similar gaseous by-products in the atmosphere will be double preindustrial levels.

Each of the previous statements is cause for concern, and together they reflect remarkable changes in the earth's environment. However, they are just a few examples of the environmental alterations that are taking place, and they are little more than lead sentences in a story that many environmentalists fear is doomed to an unhappy ending. In human geography we must seek answers to some important questions if we are to judge for ourselves the likely outcome. To what extent are humans responsible for the changes that are taking place in the environment? What are the human activities and physical processes involved in the changes? What are the present and potential impacts of the changes on humans and their societies? Are the changes inevitable and irreversible, or can humans take corrective action and have renewed confidence in an earth that will sustain generations far into the future?

We will examine in this final chapter some of the major environmental issues facing the world's societies today. The issues will be debated for years to come and the future will remain as unpredictable as it always has been. It is essential, however, that the relevant facts be understood by everyone, because in one way or another each of us has been involved in the changes that have taken place and each will be involved in any course of action that addresses the issues. Changes in relation to the earth's atmosphere will be considered first, followed by an examination of changing resources and the potential for sustaining human societies at acceptable economic levels.

AN ATMOSPHERE AT RISK

➤ Human alterations of the earth's atmosphere are so severe that the changes have become major issues with both national and global dimensions.

What are some of the most serious alterations of the atmosphere for which humans are responsible?

In what ways are these alterations international issues?

Smog has been an unwelcome companion of urban areas for decades (Fig. 14.1). Almost everyone in the technologically advanced industrial nations of the world has been exposed to it at one time or another. Although the term suggests a simple combination of smoke and fog, *smog* actually is a result of photochemical reactions that occur when radiation from the sun acts on gases emitted at the earth's surface. These reactions produce new gases, termed **photochemical smog**, that are potentially harmful to plant and animal life. It is ironic that the major gas produced by these reactions is ozone, which in the upper stratosphere forms a layer that protects life forms on earth from excessive ultraviolet radiation. Near major cities the emissions that form ozone on exposure to strong sunlight are most commonly gases associated with automobile exhaust. Recent studies of photochemical smog in cities as widely scattered as the east and west coasts of the United States, western Europe, Australia, and Japan have revealed concentrations of ozone that are ten times the level of a century ago. Smog conditions this serious can cause injury to eyes, nose, and throat, can place excessive strain on heart and lungs,

FIGURE 14.1

Two views of Los Angeles from approximately the same location in the Hollywood Hills. When the smog develops, the beautiful city is almost completely hidden in a photochemical haze. (R. Gabler)

and can severely damage natural and cultivated vegetation.

Photochemical smog is just one highly visible example of atmospheric change that has been brought about by human activity since the Industrial Revolution. Other more subtle but potentially more dangerous changes are currently in progress as humans alter the mix of trace gases in the atmosphere. Increases of nitrogen oxide gases and sulfur dioxide associated with heavy industry are the underlying cause of acid precipitation. The accumulation of chlorofluorocarbons (CFCs) in the stratosphere is seriously weakening the earth's protective ozone layer. The burning of vegetation in the tropics and the combustion of fossil fuels for heating and energy production have raised the level of atmospheric carbon dioxide (CO_2) and in turn carry the threat of global warming. These are all events of recent human history that are producing change at an accelerated pace.

Acid Precipitation

➤ Although it is natural for precipitation to be slightly acidic, an increase to damaging levels in the acid content of rain and snow has become apparent in recent years.

What are the major causes and results of acid precipitation?

What regions of the world are most affected?

The acid or alkaline nature of a solution is determined by a formula based on the presence of hydrogen ions. The measure of acidity is the **pH scale**, which ranges from a numerical value of 0 to 14, with 7 representing a solution that is neutral. Values below 7 indicate increasing acidity and values above 7 indicate increasing alkalinity. The scale is logarithmic; that is, pH 3 is ten times more acidic than pH 4, and 100 times more acidic than pH 5, and so forth. For example, lye is extremely alkaline with a pH of 13, pure water is neutral (pH 7), and battery acid is extremely acidic with a pH of 1. Because water, both in clouds and as it falls as precipitation, reacts with various gases in the atmosphere, it usually reaches the earth as a dilute acid with an average pH of 5.6. Precipitation with a pH below 5.6 is considered **acid precipitation**.

It has become increasingly apparent in recent years that acid precipitation poses a serious threat to the environment in many parts of the world. Although the chemical reactions in the atmosphere are complex, it has been established that acid precipitation is directly linked with industrial and automotive emissions of sulfur and nitrogen dioxide (Fig. 14.2). Water in the atmosphere reacts with these gases to form sulfuric and nitric acids. In addition, some industrial processes release hydrogen chloride gas, which forms a weak solution of hydrochloric acid when it comes in contact with atmospheric moisture. A study in the northeastern United States several years ago indicated that 65 percent of acid precipitation in that region was a result of

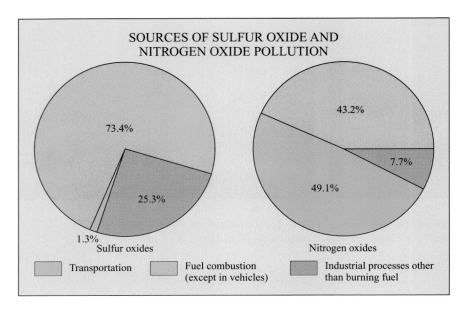

FIGURE 14.2

Motor vehicle and industrial fuel combustion are the major contributors of sulfur oxide and nitrogen oxide pollution.

sulfuric acid, 30 percent nitric acid, and 5 percent hydrochloric acid.

The primary sources of sulfur oxide in the atmosphere are thermal electric power plants burning coal of high sulfur content and mineral smelters reducing sulfide ores. For example, although coal from western U.S. states has a considerably lower average content, the sulfur content of much of the coal in the heavily industrialized eastern and midwestern United States averages close to 3 percent. Nitrogen oxides are emitted during the burning of each of the fossil fuels (coal, oil, and natural gas) but are especially associated with the internal combustion engines of automobiles. These facts help to explain why acid precipitation is an especially critical problem of the heavily populated and longer-established industrialized nations of North America and Europe. They also explain why it is a growing concern in other industrialized nations such as Japan and Korea and in the urbanized areas of the less developed countries. The less developed countries are at unusual risk as they attempt to industrialize and as their energy demands escalate. They must rely on low-quality, high-sulfur coal; furthermore, they do not have the capital to invest in pollution controls that can lower dangerous emissions.

That the pH of rain and snow has become increasingly lower (i.e., precipitation has become increasingly acidic) over the past two centuries is an established fact. Measurement of pH in snow that fell prior to heavy industrialization and is now preserved as ice in glaciers and ice caps consistently has indicated a pH well above 5. Ice in Greenland that formed nearly two hundred years ago ranges between 6 and 7. Throughout much of western Europe, the eastern United States, and southeastern Canada the pH of precipitation currently ranges between 4 and 4.5. One rainstorm in Scotland several years ago had a pH of 2.4, the acid equivalent of vinegar. Furthermore, the danger of acid precipitation has taken on regional and international dimensions. As the smokestacks of basic industries and power plants have been raised higher to ease local effects, the emissions that cause acid precipitation have been carried hundreds of kilometers from their sources by prevailing winds and migrating air masses. Acid rain that had its start in the upper Midwest may fall on New England and eastern Canada while damage to Scandinavian aquatic life may originate in Germany's industrial heartland. It is little wonder that acid precipitation has become a topic of debate and discussion among the leaders of neighboring nations.

What are the dangers of acid precipitation? Among the most obvious effects are the corrosion of outdoor machinery and equipment, the defacing of buildings, and the destruction of monuments, statues, and other works of art that occur when the atmospheric acids greatly increase the chemical weathering of exposed stone and metal surfaces (Fig. 14.3). Less apparent but far more serious is the damage done to plant and animal communities (ecosystems) that are unable to adjust to the changing conditions of the environment.

Dead Lakes In regions as distant from one another as southern Scandinavia and the Adirondack Mountains of New York, there are thousands of lakes in which crystal-clear waters set among the forested slopes of surrounding mountains have attracted generations of people engaged in freshwater fishing. However, fishing no longer attracts people to these lakes because the fish have virtually disappeared. Although it was the late 1950s before the link between acid precipitation and dying lakes was first suspected by Norwegian fishery experts, the relationship has since been well established. As atmospheric moisture in these regions has become increasingly acidic, the lakes have become acidified to such an extent that fish have been killed outright or their environments have been altered to such an extent that they can no longer reproduce. For example, records indicate that as recently as 1930 a group of 217 lakes studied in the Adirondack Mountains had pH values that approached neutrality (pH 7) and only 4 percent registered a pH lower than 5. By the mid-1970s, however, the percentage with pH below 5 had risen to 51 and the average pH was less than 4.3. Fish had disappeared completely from 90 percent of the lakes with pH below 5.

The effect on freshwater lakes of acid precipitation depends on several environmental factors and is not the same everywhere. Hence there are certain regions in which lakes are especially vulnerable. The ability of water to neutralize acid precipitation is called its *buffer capacity*, and this is generally determined by its alkalinity. Alkalinity in turn is closely related to the local bedrock. For example, if the bedrock is limestone the water will be more alkaline, the buffer capacity will be high, and lakes in the locality will be little affected by acid precipitation. In areas in which lakes are dying the underlying bedrock usually is composed of highly siliceous and slow-weathering granites, gneisses, and quartzites, which contain few minerals that contribute to alkalinity, take long periods to dissolve, and have little ability to neutralize acids.

Soils and landforms also play roles in determining which lakes are more sensitive to acid precipitation. Like bedrock, soils have the capacity to neutralize acids; the deeper the soil, the more likely that water will come in contact with soil particles as it filters downward. In mountainous regions, slopes are steep, soils are thin, and much bedrock is exposed (Fig. 14.4). In addition, air is forced to rise as it encounters landforms at higher elevations. This rising air cools, condensation takes place, and acid precipitation occurs in greater amounts. The geographic distribution of dead and dying lakes is therefore a result of a combination of environmental factors located in the path of acidified air moving out of major industrial areas. Most likely to be affected are areas with ancient crystalline bedrock (that is, *shield* areas) and eroded mountainous areas of the Northern Hemisphere continents in reach of polluted air. Such areas are most common in Norway and Sweden, in upper New York State and New England, and in Canada from southwest Ontario eastward to Nova Scotia. However, lakes and rivers acidified to below pH 5 also are found in Scotland, eastern Germany, the Netherlands, and in the United States in locations as widely separated as the Blue Ridge Mountains, the Rocky Mountains, and Florida.

Dying Forests Before the recent reunification of West and East Germany, the government in the west recognized it faced a serious ecological problem in the dying forests of the country. Extensive areas of fir, spruce, and pine showed evidence of increased loss of needles, slow and deformed growth, root deterioration, the thinning of tree crowns, and premature death. Throughout the nation, approximately one-third of all forests had been seriously damaged by the mid-1980s. In the legendary Black Forest more than 50 percent of the trees had been affected (Fig. 14.5). The major cause was identified as acid deposition from industrial pollutants, although it was clear that automobile pol-

FIGURE 14.3
This statue at the Arch of Constantine in Rome, Italy, literally has been "defaced" by the ravages of atmospheric pollution. (Donald Dietz/Stock Boston)

lution was a contributing factor as well. Before unification a West German environmental research group reported that 90 percent of East German trees were also sick, dead, or dying. The government of East Germany along with those of other eastern European nations had been using soft brown coal to fuel power plants and heavy industries in order to reduce imports of mineral fuels from the Soviet Union. Brown coal emits high levels of sulfur oxides. In addition, it takes five tons of brown coal to produce energy equivalent to that of one ton of black (bituminous) coal. Each year through the 1980s, East German smokestacks emitted nearly 4 million tons of sulfur dioxide. With the damaged forests of the East combined with those of the West, the challenge facing a united Germany today is staggering.

The fate of German forests is shared by other forests throughout the industrialized world. In some parts of the Erzgebirge and Sudeten Mountains of the Czech Republic, Poland, and eastern Germany, firs already are extinct. In Switzerland more than 40 percent of the forests—covering a quarter of the nation—are damaged or diseased by acid precipitation (Table 14.1). Trees that for centuries provided natural protection

from avalanches and landslides have been destroyed, and officials fear forced evacuation of people and damage to homes and farms. Austria, France, Italy, the United Kingdom, the Netherlands, Sweden, Norway, and many parts of the former Soviet Union report similar deterioration of their forests.

In the eastern United States and Canada the link between forest damage and acid deposition has become increasingly clear. Forests on the higher elevations of New York, the northern New England states, and southeastern Canada show the greatest signs of damage. These areas receive three to four times as much acid moisture as forests on lower slopes. In one research area of the Green Mountains in Vermont, tree growth had been reduced by half over a 15-year period in the late 1960s and 1970s. In other regions of the United States another major pollutant, ozone, competes with sulfur and nitrogen oxides as a threat to forests. As previously noted, ozone forms as hydrocarbons from automobile exhaust combine with nitrogen oxides in the presence of strong sunlight. Excessive concentrations of ozone have been directly linked to the death of large numbers of pine trees in the San Bernardino Mountains near Los Angeles and to the

FIGURE 14.4
This secluded lake in the White Mountains of New Hampshire once was a favorite destination for local people who enjoy fishing. Today the fish are gone; a deadly combination of acid precipitation and granitic bedrock has destroyed their habitat. (R. Gabler)

FIGURE 14.5
The stunted growth, thinning of crowns, and extensive loss of needles exhibited by these trees in the Black Forest region of Germany are mute evidence of the damage caused by acid precipitation. (R. Gabler)

	TABLE 14.1 Damaged Forest in Europe (1988 Estimates for Selected Countries)		

Country	Total Forest Area (1000 hectares)	Damaged Area (1000 hectares)	Percentage of Forest Area Damaged
Czechoslovakia	4,578	3,250	71
Greece	2,034	1,302	64
United Kingdom	2,200	1,408	64
Germany[a]	10,325	5,127	50
Norway	5,925	2,963	49
Poland	8,654	4,240	49
Netherlands	311	149	48
Switzerland	1,186	510	43
Finland	20,059	7,823	39
Sweden	23,700	9,243	39
Yugoslavia	4,889	1,564	32
Austria	3,754	1,089	29
France	14,440	3,321	23

SOURCE: *Air pollution and acid rain: A strategy for the nineties.* Worldwatch Paper 94, *January, 1990. Washington, DC: Worldwatch Institute.*

[a]Combined totals for former East Germany and West Germany.

damage of thousands of acres of forest in the southern Appalachians and Blue Ridge Mountains.

Western Europe, the United States, Japan, and several other developed nations have enacted a variety of laws to control automobile emissions. The expense of meeting more stringent standards for vehicle exhaust may be met through higher fuel and automobile prices but, by comparison, the cost of reducing industrial pollution is enormous. In the wealthy nations, progress in this area is slow because governments are reluctant to sacrifice economic growth in order to solve environmental problems such as acid precipitation. In economically stressed industrial nations such as some of the former Soviet states, as well as in the newly expanding industrial regions of the less developed countries, the current prospects for controlling atmospheric pollution of any type are bleak or nonexistent.

Ozone Depletion

➤ Such atmospheric change as depletion of the ozone layer is directly associated with the products and processes of industrialization.

How might depletion of the ozone layer affect humans throughout the world?

How is depletion of the ozone layer linked to industrialization?

Why is it difficult to prevent this change in the atmosphere?

Since the mid-1970s significant decreases have been recorded in the stratospheric **ozone layer** that protects the earth from excessive ultraviolet radiation. The most dramatic evidence of ozone loss occurs each spring in the Southern Hemisphere when a "hole" appears in the layer over Antarctica (Fig. 14.6). Although the shape and position of the hole varies, the area covered grows larger each year. It is estimated that ozone levels in the spring over Antarctica have declined by 50 percent since 1975. Research by NASA scientists indicates that this is not a localized problem. They report that since 1969 the ozone layer during winter and early spring in the Northern Hemisphere has decreased by as much as 3 percent over heavily industrialized areas of the middle latitudes and by as much as 10 percent in the higher latitudes.

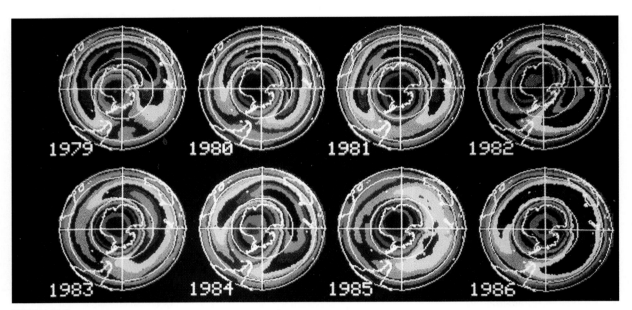

FIGURE 14.6
Progressive thinning of the Antarctic ozone layer as documented by space observations: October monthly averages, 1979–1986. Purple-violet: low levels. Yellow, brown, green: high levels. (NASA)

The ozone layer is critically important to life on earth because ozone in the stratosphere routinely absorbs large amounts of the sun's ultraviolet radiation. Any depletion of ozone and increase in ultraviolet radiation reaching the earth can increase the incidence of severe sunburn, skin cancer, and cataracts in humans, as well as damage or destroy many forms of plant and animal life. The U.S. Environmental Protection Agency (EPA) estimates that every 1 percent decrease in stratospheric ozone could result in 24,000 to 57,000 more cases of cataracts and 43,000 additional cases of skin cancer in the United States alone. Damage to plant life could seriously reduce crop yields throughout the world.

The major cause of ozone depletion has been traced directly to industrially produced CFCs. The CFCs are chemicals that have been used for several decades in refrigeration, air conditioning, insulation, and fast-food containers, and as solvents, blowing agents for foam production, and propellants for aerosol cans. These chemicals serve as a classic example of a danger to the environment that was totally unsuspected by the scientists who developed them. In fact, one reason the use of CFCs has been so widespread is

that they are chemically inactive in the lower atmosphere and are of no direct danger to plant and animal life. However, what seemed an asset has become a major environmental liability. As the products containing CFCs decompose, the chemicals are released, and they reach the stratosphere unaltered. On exposure to strong ultraviolet radiation in the stratosphere, they break apart and the liberated chlorine atoms accelerate the conversion of ozone, the triatomic form of oxygen (O_3), to diatomic oxygen (O_2). Diatomic oxygen provides no shield to ultraviolet radiation.

Some steps *have* been taken to address the issue of ozone depletion. In 1977 the United States banned the use of CFCs in most aerosol products. Ten years later representatives of 38 nations met in Montreal and signed an agreement (the Montreal Protocol) to cut the use of CFCs in half by the end of the century. But the problem is far from solved. CFCs are relatively inexpensive to produce and they have so many industrial applications that developing nations are reluctant to restrict their use. Even if everyone stopped using CFCs today it is estimated that reduction of the ozone layer would continue for a hundred years or more. It will take that long for all the products containing CFCs to decompose and for the inert chemical compounds at the earth's surface to make their way to the stratosphere. So although we may some day remove the cause, it seems we must learn to live with the effects.

Global Warming

➤ Although scientific evidence is still insufficient to prove that global warming of the atmosphere is taking place, many environmentalists believe that the greenhouse effect will have serious negative consequences within one or two centuries.

Why is it difficult to document global warming?

How does the greenhouse effect differ from the atmospheric effect?

What are some of the causes and possible consequences of global warming?

Undoubtedly the most widely debated atmospheric change that has been blamed on human activity is global warming. Much of the debate centers on the question of whether or not temperatures over the earth in fact are, on the average, undergoing a steady increase. Climatic trends are extremely difficult to predict or even to reconstruct on the basis of incomplete historical data. Predictions are made on the basis of complex computer programs that examine the entire earth. In addition, both long- and short-term climatic change is a normal occurrence and over the past 2 million years has been cyclical. Periods of lower temperatures associated with widespread glaciation have been followed by periods of warmer climate during glacial retreat (see Chapter 2). To complicate long-range climatic prediction even further, actual temperature trends associated with glaciation can only be estimated. The last major glacial period ended some 10,000 years ago, and reasonably accurate records of temperature and precipitation have been collected for only the last few hundred years, even in the more populated areas of the world.

Most atmospheric scientists believe that there is overwhelming evidence in support of a gradual warming of the earth's atmosphere, however. They also believe that this trend could have far-reaching consequences for both the environment and human populations. Their predictions are based on well-documented human alterations of a natural process called the **atmospheric effect**. This process occurs as natural gases in the atmosphere—primarily carbon dioxide,

water vapor, and other trace gases such as methane, nitrous oxide, and CFCs—permit large amounts of short-wave solar radiation to reach the earth's surface and warm it, but absorb much of the long-wave radiation given off by the heated earth. The process limits major fluctuations in atmospheric temperature and is an essential part of the heat–energy transfer that maintains global temperatures as they are.

When scientists warn about global warming they refer to the human-induced **greenhouse effect**. This occurs for the same reasons that have caused acid precipitation and deterioration of the ozone layer. The emission of gases due to industrialization, the burning of fossil fuels, and the exhaust from automobiles have increased significantly the proportion of atmospheric gases that trap outgoing radiation. The gas that plays the major role in the greenhouse effect is carbon dioxide (CO_2). Since the start of the Industrial Revolution human activity has increased atmospheric content of carbon dioxide by 25 percent. The most authoritative projections indicate that the current average annual CO_2 content of the atmosphere of 350 parts per million will nearly double and reach 600 parts per million by the middle of the twenty-first century (Fig. 14.7). It is expected that the other greenhouse gases will increase by similar amounts. These projections have convinced scientists that the greenhouse effect will magnify and that global warming is a distinct possibility.

What are the likely results of a doubling of carbon dioxide and similar increases in other trace gases in the atmosphere? The most sophisticated computer programs—global circulation models that were originally developed to project long-term weather forecasts—generally predict that global mean temperatures could rise between 5.5° and 10°F (3.0° and 5.5°C). This is approximately the same change in temperature that has occurred over many thousands of years since the last major glacial advance, but it could take place in as little as 100 to 200 years. According to the models, global warming would be more pronounced at higher than at lower latitudes, temperature increase would be greater in winter than in summer, and the interior of continents would be drier and coastal areas wetter. The impact on humans and the changes in other areas of the environment brought about by such alterations in climate could be far-reaching.

Agriculture and Food Supplies If continental interiors should become warmer and drier, especially in

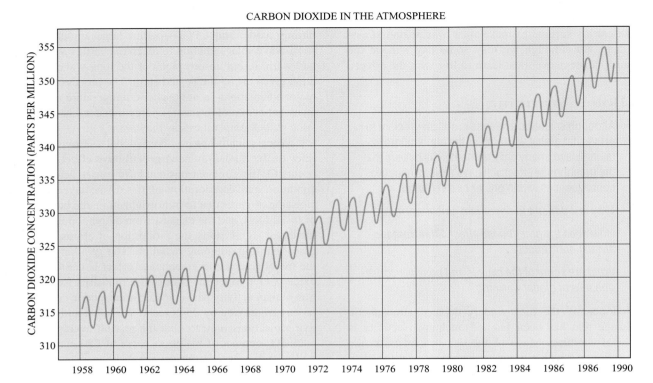

FIGURE 14.7
The increase in the amount of carbon dioxide in the atmosphere after 1958.

the Northern Hemisphere, major adjustments in agriculture would become necessary. These are precisely the regions in which are located the great grain belts of North America and Eurasia, where much of the world's surplus wheat and corn are raised and where many of its beef cattle and hogs are fattened for market. Throughout the American Midwest, for example, farmers would be forced to cope with increasing needs for irrigation, decreasing yields from traditional crops, and continual experimentation with more drought-resistant varieties of crops. Toward the interior of continents, where the climate is already subhumid, as in the North American Great Plains and the Russian steppes, the grazing of animals could be significantly curtailed and some currently productive land could well be abandoned (Fig. 14.8). As a further example, scientists estimate that a temperature increase of a few degrees in the western United States could increase evaporation and decrease runoff in the Colorado River

basin even if precipitation remained the same. Any reduction in stream flow would threaten irrigated agriculture as far from the continental interior as southern California and Mexico.

Of course, deteriorating agricultural conditions in some areas could be coupled with improving conditions in others. Rising temperatures in the higher latitudes would mean longer growing seasons in such areas as Canada, Alaska, and Siberia. It has been suggested that large areas not presently devoted to agriculture could be brought under production. However, there is serious doubt whether this would be the case or whether increases in crop production in new areas would equal losses in the old. Currently, adequate rainfall, temperatures, and growing seasons in major farming regions are matched with superior soils, many of them developed over thousands of years on thick deposits of parent material left behind by retreating glaciers. Suitable soils are thin or nonexistent in the

FIGURE 14.8
Some climatologists believe that global warming could alter these rich grasslands of the North American Great Plains to near desert conditions unable to support significant numbers of grazing animals. (R. Gabler)

higher latitudes of Northern Hemisphere continents, and climatic change is projected to be so rapid that it would be impossible for better soils to develop.

If the climatic changes associated with global warming occur as suggested, conditions would worsen for a great many of the world's people currently living with near-starvation diets and annually facing the prospect of widespread famine. Middle latitude nations such as the United States that regularly export food would have adequate supplies for themselves, but there would be limited supplies for those nations that presently must rely on imports. In addition, decreasing rainfall in continental interiors would only increase the chances of recurring drought and hasten the destruction of farmlands and pastures, and increasing amounts of coastal rainfall would accelerate the occurrence of major floods that inundate valuable croplands on river deltas and floodplains. These changes would be devastating for millions of people who have no other sources of food.

Health and Natural Hazards If 1988 provided an indication of climatic conditions that will accompany global warming as some have suggested, then climatic change may have a direct negative effect on human health. Average temperature and precipitation comprise only one aspect of climate, and they are far less noticeable than extremes such as extended periods of summer heat or serious drought. It was the extremes

that attracted attention in 1988 and provided a possible warning of things to come. In continental interiors such as the American Midwest and central China, drought and high summer temperatures combined to pose a serious threat to human health. Water supplies in the Midwest were sharply reduced as wells ran dry and reservoirs shrank to muddy lake bottoms. In some communities the remaining water became so toxic from agricultural chemicals and concentrated minerals that it was condemned as unfit to drink. In China temperatures exceeded 97°F (37°C) each day for more than a week. Heat stroke and heart attack victims flooded hospitals and hundreds of deaths were attributed to the unusual heat wave.

Although not as dramatic as the events of 1988, an increase in average global temperature could have other consequences that impact human well-being. Parasitic diseases and those diseases borne by insects that thrive in the warmth of tropical climates would migrate poleward, and the threat of these diseases in the middle latitudes would tend to increase. With dwindling food supplies, malnutrition would be more widespread, further reducing human resistance to disease. In addition, it has been suggested that global warming would increase the frequency and intensity of storms in both interior and coastal areas. Although midcontinent rainfall would be reduced in amount, it would fall as a part of more violent, high-energy atmospheric disturbances. Thunderstorms with associated lightning and high winds as well as tornadoes would affect areas further poleward and would be more frequent. The seasons for Caribbean hurricanes and Pacific typhoons would increase in length, wind speeds and precipitation amounts in these storms would increase, and they would reach coastal areas more often. Increases in both property damage and loss of life could be anticipated from these natural hazards.

Endangered Ecosystems Alterations in climatic conditions produce inevitable changes in the plant and animal life of ecosystems affected by the alterations. Each species thrives within certain ranges of temperature and precipitation, and when the ranges change within a given region the plants and animals cannot adapt. They must migrate to new regions with climatic conditions suited to their needs. The classic example of such migration occurred during the Pleistocene ice age when flora and fauna moved equatorward and poleward with the ice front as the temperatures fluctuated and the ice sheets expanded and contracted. The evergreen forests of spruce and fir that now cover much of Canada were common ecosystems Equatorward of the ice front in the central United States during major periods of glaciation. But when the climate warmed slowly during interglacial periods, the ice retreated gradually and permitted the forest ecosystems to migrate poleward. Environmentalists are concerned that the temperature change predicted to accompany global warming will be much too rapid for plants to migrate and therefore major ecosystems might simply disappear. In addition, so many natural ecosystems are isolated today by cities, farmland, transportation networks, and other products of civilization that species could not migrate even if time permitted; thus, significant climatic change could mean extinction for many species.

Another threat to ecosystems caused by global warming would accompany a rise in sea level. Many scientists believe that an increase in global temperatures of only a few degrees Celsius could cause major melting of the world's mountain glaciers and could significantly reduce the size of existing ice caps, especially the one covering much of Greenland. The additions to the earth's liquid water supply by melting

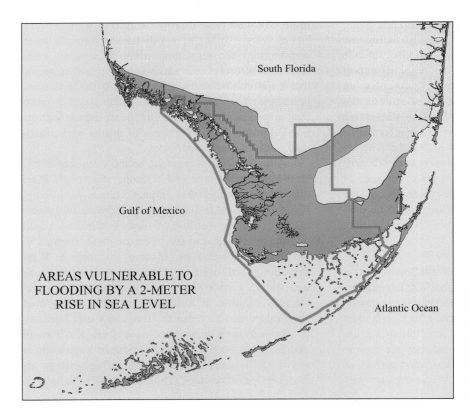

FIGURE 14.9
These areas of South Florida would be inundated by a 2-meter (approximately 6-foot) rise in sea level as a consequence of global warming and melting of glacial ice. (Florida Division of Marine Resources)

glaciers and ice caps accompanying the greenhouse effect could raise sea level nearly 6 feet (2 m). Not only would such a change create unimaginable problems and untold costs for those who occupy coastal cities or own shoreline property, but it could lead to the destruction of valuable coastal wetlands and the total disappearance of additional natural ecosystems (Fig. 14.9).

A THREATENED RESOURCE BASE

➤ A resource base sufficient to support future generations is threatened by the past use of nonrenewable resources and the present misuses of renewable resources.

Which resources are most important to the well-being of future generations?

What is the current status of these resources and how is human activity affecting the status of each?

Wherever humans have settled on the earth they have altered the physical landscape. They have considered the earth their private domain and have used its bounteous variety of flora, fauna, minerals, and soils as seemingly limitless resources provided especially for their own benefit. Although primitive societies generally adapted to their environments because the state of their technology prohibited them from behaving otherwise, the introduction of sedentary agriculture and the tools that accompanied this new way of life caused a change in human behavior. Vast areas covered by forest became farmland, grasslands disappeared under the plow, and soils were exposed to increased erosion (Fig. 14.10).

With urbanization and industrialization new threats to the earth's resource base have arisen. *Renewable resources*, such as forests, soil, and water, have been taxed to the limit. If used wisely they have the capacity to replenish themselves naturally. But humans have so overused or abused them that critical shortages or major deterioration in this group of resources are occurring throughout the world. The situation with *nonrenewable resources* might well be considered even worse. These are resources, such as the metallic minerals (iron, copper, lead, etc.) and the mineral fuels (coal, petroleum, and natural gas), that are essential to modern industry but available only in limited supplies. The most readily accessible and highest

FIGURE 14.10

The fields of corn harvested each autumn on this Illinois farm bear little resemblance to the tall prairie grasses that greeted pioneer settlers who arrived in the mid-1800s. (R. Gabler)

quality deposits of many nonrenewable resources already have been exhausted.

In the following sections we will examine tropical forests as threatened ecosystems; the deterioration of agricultural environments broadly identified by the term desertification; and two resources—water and energy—basic to life in both the developed and the less developed worlds.

Deforestation

➤ Deforestation is one of the most obvious and damaging examples of human alteration of the physical environment.

Why is the clearing of tropical forests increasing at such a rapid rate?

What are the serious consequences of tropical deforestation?

It has been estimated that prior to the beginnings of agriculture, *closed forests* with dense canopies and little undergrowth, combined with *open forests* or woodlands with open canopies and grasses between trees, covered more than 15 billion acres (6 billion ha) of the earth's land surface. Calculations provided by United Nations sources indicate that by 1980 the area covered by forests had been reduced by almost one-third, to approximately 10.5 billion acres (4.3 billion ha). Such change, however, attracted little attention

FIGURE 14.11

This tropical rainforest in the Amazon Basin of Peru is typical of nearly 50 percent of the earth's forested land. (Robert Sager)

until recently and caused even less concern because it was associated with the clearing of land for timber and the raising of crops in middle latitude nations in which industrialization was expanding rapidly. Until the twentieth century the luxuriant tropical forests remained virtually untouched except where replaced by plantation agriculture or altered by shifting cultivation. However, rapid destruction of tropical forests currently is underway, and it has become a major international issue.

Tropical closed forests comprised nearly 50 percent of the earth's forested land in the 1980 survey by the U.N., and more recent satellite data indicate that such forests still cover nearly 13 percent of the earth's total land surface (Fig. 14.11). A total forested area of more than 2 billion hectares would seem adequate to meet human needs forever until one considers the current rate of deforestation. Between 1981 and 1990 nearly 420 million acres (170 million ha) of virgin tropical forest were lost to ax, saw, and fire. Each year an area of forest somewhat larger than a football field is destroyed *every second*. To add to the problem, the rate of deforestation has steadily increased. The rate of deforestation for all tropical forests doubled between 1980 and 1989, and in tropical America, where more than half of these resources were located, the rate nearly tripled. Simple mathematics indicates that even at the present rate of deforestation, tropical forests would virtually disappear in 150 years.

There are a number of reasons for the clearing of tropical forests. Almost all such forests are located in less developed countries desperate for income to fund development and repay staggering debts owed to foreign banks. Tropical timber sales provide the prospect of short-term profit, even though in many instances as little as 15 percent of the timber is harvested before the land is cleared by burning. In addition, the governments of many less developed countries have viewed tropical forests as frontier land available for agricultural development and for resettlement of the poor from overcrowded urban areas. In the Amazon Basin of Brazil, for example, the federal government has long financed the building of roads into the forested interior and has supported the development of cattle ranches through long-term loans and tax credits sufficient to cover most investment costs (Fig. 14.12).

The irony is that clearing tropical forests for timber sales and agricultural development is economically unsound. Over a few years the income from forest products such as nuts, fruits, resins, fibers, and medicinal supplies (as opposed to the one-time sale of timber) and the selective cutting of timber far outweighs the economic gain from one-time timber sales and agricultural production. It has been estimated that the 32 million acres (12 million ha) of existing cattle ranches in the Amazon have already cost the Brazilian government more than $2 billion in income from forest products.

The tragedy is that the destruction of tropical forests exacts an almost immediate and devastating toll on the local environment. Tropical forest soils are in delicate equilibrium with the vegetation they support. Once the forests are removed, the soils are readily leached of the nutrients previously supplied by the decaying forest vegetation. In addition, serious soil erosion is often a problem. There is even evidence that deforested areas become hotter and drier, severely limiting the possibility that the original forest cover could ever return. This unfortunate situation occurs because after deforestation the tropical atmosphere loses one of its most important sources of moisture, transpiration from the forest vegetation (see Chapter 2). Less moisture means less cloud cover and less rainfall. At the surface the reduced rainfall results in drier soils. Solar energy that would have been used for transpiration is used instead to heat the soil, and it in turn heats the atmosphere.

Storing Carbon Dioxide The possible effects of increasing amounts of atmospheric CO_2 on climatic change have already been considered. However, it is appropriate at this point to explore how deforestation

FIGURE 14.12

The clearing of the Amazon rainforest has been supported by the Brazilian government to provide new land for ranching and crop agriculture. Although for a short time this clearing helps to meet the needs of a growing population, in the long run it is a poor investment. (Abril/Gamma-Liaison)

has influenced the buildup of atmospheric CO_2. There are three *natural sinks* or storage reservoirs of carbon: the oceans, the atmosphere itself, and the world's vegetation (most of this carbon is in the plants but there are additional amounts in associated soils). Recent studies have indicated that the oceans are not as important a sink as once was thought and the exchanges of carbon between oceans and atmosphere are little involved in atmospheric change. It is the exchange of carbon between vegetation and atmosphere that is significant, and because tropical forests comprise such a large proportion of the earth's biomass, they play a key role in the exchanges that take place. To give some idea of how important the vegetation–atmosphere relationship is, the carbon stored in tropical forests and

soils alone equals more than 60 percent of the carbon stored as CO_2 in the entire atmosphere.

It is estimated that tropical forests hold about 40 percent of the earth's plant carbon and tropical forest soils hold about 15 percent of the carbon in the earth's soils. If left undisturbed, a carbon balance exists between mature tropical forest ecosystems and the atmosphere. Carbon dioxide is removed from the atmosphere and converted to trunks, leaves, and roots by the forests through the process of photosynthesis. It is stored in the vegetation and only returns to the atmosphere in similar amounts when the vegetation dies. It is when the forests are removed that the balance is destroyed (Table 14.2). The carbon in the trees and organic matter of the soil is oxidized quickly through

TABLE 14.2 Carbon Added to the Atmosphere by Tropical Deforestation (1980 Estimates by World Region)

Region	Total Forest Cover (millions of ha)	Net Carbon Added (millions of tons)	Percentage of Carbon Added
Tropical America	1212	665	40
Tropical Asia	445	621	37
Tropical Africa	1312	373	23
TOTAL	2969	1659	100

Source: *Reforesting the earth.* Worldwatch Paper 83, *April 1988. Washington, DC: Worldwatch Institute.*

burning or more slowly through decay, and the carbon dioxide is added to the atmosphere. The natural or cultivated vegetation that replaces the forests continues to remove some CO_2 through photosynthesis, but the forests can hold from 20 to 100 times more carbon.

With this information, it is safe to assert that the removal of forests, especially tropical forests, can be listed with industrial and automotive emissions as a cause for potential global warming. It has been suggested that deforestation over the past 150 years has contributed almost as much carbon to the atmosphere as the burning of coal, oil, and natural gas. Even at current levels of industrialization, it has been estimated that the annual loss of tropical forests adds 20 to 40 percent as much carbon as mineral fuel combustion each year. On the other hand, preservation of existing forests and active reforestation can slow materially the accumulation of carbon in the atmosphere. One proposal for addressing the problem states that replanting 25 million acres (10 million ha) of tropical forest each year for 13 years would cut the present increase in atmospheric carbon as a result of all human activities by 10 percent. Unfortunately the current rate of tropical forest destruction is ten times that of reforestation.

Protecting Biodiversity   For some time now biologists and other environmentalists have been warning of the dangers associated with the rapid extinction of plant and animal species as a result of human activity. **Biodiversity** is the key to a healthy ecosystem because each plant and animal has a close relationship with the others and all are integrated to form a balanced biological community. Nature is so complex that there is no way to determine what role one life form plays in the nurture and support of another or how great is the loss from one extinction. Nevertheless, it is certain that the greater the variety of life forms, the stronger the ecosystem and the better the biological community can withstand environmental stress. This principle is considered to be valid whether the ecosystem is that of a small pond or the earth as a whole. Hence, decreasing diversity represents a loss to all life forms but especially to the humans that rely on plants and other animals for their survival.

Once again the destruction of tropical forests is central to an important environmental issue. Conservative estimates of worldwide plant and animal species place the number at more than 4 million, more than half of which live in tropical rainforests. Based

on studies indicating that the number of species in an ecosystem is directly proportional to the area it covers, one ecologist believes that the reduction in tropical forests leads to the extinction of as many as 4000 to 6000 species each year. This is at least 1000 times the rate of the natural extinction that took place prior to the involvement of humans in the forest ecosystem. It is impossible to calculate the true cost of such extinction. The lost species may have held secrets to increased crop production; a cure for AIDS, cancer, or other serious health problems; or a base for better insecticides that do not harm the environment. Similar services to humanity already have been provided by tropical forest species. The only way to prevent extinction and protect the treasures of the rainforest is to preserve the original tropical ecosystem. Replanting the forest cannot replace biodiversity.

Desertification

➤ When the curve of increasing population crosses the line that marks the capacity of the land to provide food on a sustainable yield basis, desertification is the inevitable result.

What is meant by desertification?

In what regions of the world is desertification a serious problem?

How is desertification related to deforestation?

Although originally coined to describe the spread of deserts in northern Africa, the term **desertification** today is used to represent deterioration of the land resource in regions of the world as far apart as interior China, northeastern Brazil, the Middle East, northwestern India, and the southwestern United States. Desertification involves a long-term loss in the productive capacity of the land and in each instance this land degradation may be traced to human activity (Table 14.3). There are multiple causes: overgrazing, the cultivation of arid lands better left in native grasses, poor farming practices leading to soil erosion and depletion, deforestation, and the accumulation of alkaline salts (salinization).

The most publicized example of desertification is the Sahel on the southern margin of Africa's Sahara Desert. In this region over the past 75 years nearly 1 million square kilometers (386,000 sq mi) have been added to the Sahara through human mismanagement of once productive agricultural and grazing lands. As

TABLE 14.3 World Desertification in Arid and Subhumid Regions: 1983–1984

Land-Use Category	Area Moderately to Seriously Degraded (millions of ha)	Percentage of Category	Amount of Land That Deteriorates to Total Degradation Annually (millions of ha)
Rangelands	3100	84	17.7
Rainfed Cropland	335	59	2.0
Irrigated Cropland	40	31	0.6
Categories Combined	3475	77	20.3

SOURCE: *Worldwatch Institute,* State of the World, *1989. New York: W. W. Norton and Co.*

might be surmised from our earlier examination of regional population trends (Chapter 6), the deterioration of the land in the Sahel and nearby areas is closely linked with rapid population growth. The number of people throughout much of the region far exceeds the capacity of the land to provide sufficient food on a sustainable yield basis. In addition, the population exceeds by several million the number of people that the region's wood resources can supply with fuel for cooking and heating.

As the rising curve of population crosses the line that marks the carrying capacity of the land, a vicious cycle begins that ultimately ends in desertification. Forests and grasslands are the first two victims of human stress on the land, but the soil resource is a close third. As areas are cleared for farmland, the ecological balance between vegetation and soil is interrupted. If crop yields are to be sustained, soil nutrients must be replaced by returning animal dung and crop residues to the fields. However, as the demand for fuelwood increases in expanding villages, farmers cut remnant trees as a cash crop and use dung and straw as fuel in their homes rather than return such materials to the land as fertilizer. The landscape is denuded, soils become further depleted, and crops fail even in years of adequate rainfall.

In areas that were originally grassland, herds tend to increase at the same pace as human numbers, and land degradation is a direct result of overgrazing. Studies in the southwestern United States and Mexico suggest that when grass is trampled, removed, or cropped too short by excessive numbers of animals, less rainfall infiltrates the soil and more runs off the land. The

greater runoff results in an increase in soil erosion and a concentration of soil moisture, nitrogen, and other plant nutrients in lower areas. Because of their deeper root systems, shrubs can compete successfully with the original grasses and they concentrate in the shallow depressions and intermittent stream beds. As the intershrub areas become barren of vegetation, the process is reinforced (positive feedback occurs in the system). There is further increase in runoff, in the loss of plant nutrients, and in erosion by water and wind. A desert landscape then replaces a productive grassland.

Some scientists believe that human-induced land degradation may be causing regional changes in climate that will make it difficult to reverse the process of desertification. As vegetative cover is removed over large areas, there is an increase in the albedo (reflected solar energy) of the bare ground. With the loss of energy through reflection, surface temperatures decrease. As a consequence of this cooling, there is more atmospheric subsidence, which in turn suppresses convection and decreases annual rainfall. As is the case when grasslands are replaced by shrubs, the lower rainfall amounts reinforce the desertification that was initiated by overgrazing and other land mismanagement practices.

Although the famine, malnutrition, and human misery associated with land degradation in sub-Saharan Africa have received the greatest publicity, there are striking examples of the abuse of the land resource in other areas of the world. In India, as in the Sahel, drought that is both normal and cyclical is coupled with rapid growth in population. Shortages of food, water, and animal fodder even in years of normal

FIGURE 14.13
Overgrazing by increasing numbers of cattle and progressive deterioration of the soil resource by lack of fertilization have hastened desertification throughout the drier portions of northwestern India. (Donald Marshall Collection)

precipitation have led to increasingly poor land use practices and land degradation. After decades of overgrazing, progressive deforestation, and mining of the soil resource through failure to return nutrients to the fields, most of India's drier regions, nearly one-fourth of the nation's total land area, have become barren landscapes (Fig. 14.13).

In the developed world (where population pressure cannot be cited as a contributing factor) mismanagement practices also have led to land degradation. As a direct result of excessive water use for irrigation, the Aral Sea in the former Soviet Union has been reduced in area by some 40 percent since 1960. It now holds only one-third of its former volume of water and, because of a threefold increase in salinity, all species of native fish have disappeared. The scarcity of water and the increasing salinization of irrigated fields threaten to destroy some of the region's most productive farmland. Meanwhile in the United States, a study conducted by the Bureau of Land Management several years ago revealed that one-third of the public rangeland in the West had been denuded of most vegetation and had lost all but a fraction of its topsoil through overgrazing. Land degradation leading to desertification is clearly a global issue as well as a problem that threatens the ability of the earth to feed, clothe, and house its inhabitants.

Basic Resources

➤ Shortages of water and energy have become critical problems over varying periods of time in almost all of the developed and less developed countries of the world.

How are humans contributing to the seriousness of these problems?

Is the continuation of such problems inevitable?

Why do the shortages differ from time to time and from place to place?

In addition to land, two other resources, water and energy, are essential to all societies. Some nations are blessed with great reserves of each of these basic resources while others have not been nearly as fortunate. However, in almost all nations critical shortages of water and energy have occurred and future demands threaten to exceed the supplies that are available on a sustainable basis.

By the choices they have made and by the careless ways they have used both water and energy, human beings are primarily responsible for the growing crises involving supplies of both these basic resources. Most of the energy that supports the developed world comes from the mineral fuels, resources that are nonrenewable. Reserves in older producing areas are nearing exhaustion or have become expensive to exploit because lack of accessibility has increased the cost of production and the remaining supplies are of low quality. In the less developed countries fuelwood has been the traditional source of energy, but soaring demands accompanying rapid population growth have outstripped the ability of forest and woodlot to replenish the supply. The case of water is even more critical because, although there are several sources of energy, there is no substitute for water.

Unreliable Water Supplies It is safe to say that no resource is more valuable than fresh water. In arid regions water shortages have always been an accepted fact and only in locations where water enters from outside these regions via surface streams or underground flow have humans used water in large amounts (Fig. 14.14). In humid regions water has been more readily available, although throughout history inhabitants have coped with drought, flood, and unreliable drinking supplies. In earlier times great civilizations flourished and then disappeared in the Tigris and Eu-

FIGURE 14.14

The water flowing through these irrigation ditches in the semiarid plains of Wyoming has traveled hundreds of miles through an underground artesian system that has its source in the central Rocky Mountains. (R. Gabler)

phrates valleys of Mesopotamia (of what is now Iraq) and in the Indus Valley of what is now Pakistan because of the use (irrigation) and misuse (excessive salinization of soils) of water. But the current concern for water is a global one, and, like other environmental issues we have discussed, it is tied to industrialization, inefficient or questionable technologies, and poor management of resources. (See *The Geographer's Notebook: The Kissimmee River–Lake Okeechobee– Everglades Ecosystem.*)

It has been estimated that 9000 cubic kilometers of the water that returns to the ocean each year throughout the world as a part of the *hydrologic cycle* is available for human use. This should be enough to sustain a total earth population more than three times the current number. However, serious water shortages occur because people and water are unequally distributed and the per capita consumption of water differs so greatly from country to country. During extended drought periods severe restrictions on water use or rationing of water have been necessary in regions as different climatically as northern China, Central America, northwestern India, the British Isles, and parts of both the Atlantic and Pacific coasts of the United States, as well as the agricultural Midwest.

Perhaps the most serious water problem is that facing agriculture. Where farmers employ carefully controlled methods, irrigated cropland (usually located

in areas favored by plenty of sunshine, long growing seasons, and soils rich in soluble nutrients) produces high yields. In recent years one-third of all the food produced in the world has come from irrigated fields that comprise only 17 percent of total world cropland. Percentages differ from nation to nation. In Egypt virtually all of the farmland is irrigated, but the estimated percentages for other countries range from 77 percent for Pakistan and 63 percent for Japan to 48 percent for China and only about 10 percent for the United States.

The greatest expansion of irrigated agriculture has taken place in the twentieth century. From an amount estimated at 125 million acres (50 million ha) in 1900, the world's irrigated land area nearly doubled by 1950 and then increased even more rapidly to the present total of more than 615 million acres (250 million ha), an area nearly the size of Argentina. Approximately 73 percent of all water withdrawn for human use worldwide is employed in irrigation and the area of irrigated farmland continues to grow at about 8 percent per year. However, even this rate of increase is not sufficient to keep pace with population expansion and increased demands for food. The amount of irrigated land per person throughout the world peaked in 1978 but has fallen by nearly 6 percent since that time.

In addition, the continued expansion of irrigated acreage may soon end. Much irrigated land is being lost to poor farming practices. Salinization affects more than 2.5 million acres (1 million ha) worldwide and some 20 percent of irrigated areas in the United States. Moreover, water for irrigation is more than ever in direct competition with water essential to industries and municipalities. All too often pumping for multiple uses removes more water from underground sources than is replaced by precipitation or underground flow. As an example, beneath Beijing on the fertile North China Plain the water table has been dropping 3 to 6 feet (1 to 2 m) per year and one-third of the city's wells have gone dry. In drought periods water already has been diverted from farmland to supply the rapidly growing capital city of China.

Water shortage in the face of rising needs is only one aspect of the water issue. Water quality is another. Regardless of source, almost all water supplies of inhabited areas are threatened by pollution. Both organic and inorganic wastes enter streams, lakes, artificial reservoirs, and underground *aquifers* (water-bearing rock layers and unconsolidated earth materials). It comes from *point sources* (such as drainage pipes, sewers, and landfills) and from *nonpoint sources* (such as run-

The Kissimmee River—Lake Okeechobee—
Everglades Ecosystem

The drainage basin that focuses on the Everglades of south Florida is a prime example of human alteration of an ecosystem without consideration of the possible results. A century ago the interconnected Kissimmee River–Lake Okeechobee–Everglades wetlands embraced one of the most valuable and stable ecosystems on earth. Its sawgrass marsh and slow-moving water stood in the way of urban and agricultural development in the region, however.

Since 1900, to facilitate development, intricate systems of ditches and canals have been built and half of the original 4 million acres (1.6 million ha) of the Everglades has disappeared. The Kissimmee River has been channelized into an arrow-straight ditch and the water-storing and purifying floodplain marshes along the river have been drained. High artificial levees have prevented excess water in Lake Okeechobee from contributing sheet flow of water to the Everglades. Natural drainage patterns also have been disrupted by the Tamiami Highway, constructed to bisect the region.

The amount of water held in the Everglades has been greatly reduced, and this reduction has pro-longed and intensified the normal yearly dry season. Fires have been more frequent and more destructive, and entire biotic communities have been eliminated by lowered water levels. It is ironic that during excessively wet periods large portions of the Everglades are deliberately flooded to prevent drainage canals from overflowing. As a result, animals drown and birds cannot nest and reproduce. With their habitats increasingly diminished over the past century, south Florida's wading bird population decreased by 95 percent. Without the natural purifying effects of wetland systems, water quality in south Florida has deteriorated, and with lower water levels salt water encroachment has become a serious problem in coastal areas.

Today south Florida is fighting an uphill battle to restore its ailing ecosystems. Agricultural land is being returned slowly to sawgrass marsh and, backed by computer models, hydraulic engineers are building culverts and spillways and notching the banks of canals to restore historic water flow patterns through the Everglades. The Kissimmee River is scheduled once again to meander across portions of its floodplain. Environmentalists hope that what humans have altered to their loss they can restore for their long-term benefit. The problems of south Florida should serve as a useful lesson. Alterations of the natural environment should not be undertaken without serious consideration of all possible consequences.

The construction of this canal and others in south Florida has disrupted the area's fragile wetland ecosystems.

THOUGHT QUESTIONS

1. In what variety of ways are natural wetlands of benefit to human populations? How might these benefits be of greater value than use of the land for agricultural or urban expansion?
2. Are you aware of any wetland ecosystems other than those in south Florida that have been disrupted or destroyed by human activities? How have they been affected? Are programs underway to restore them?
3. Does the United States now have legislation in place to protect wetlands? What does the legislation require of those proposing to develop a wetland area?

off from agricultural fields and subsurface leaching from contaminated soils). Some of the most insidious damage to water supplies, especially in association with large animal feedlot operations or in countries in which herding is a significant part of agriculture, comes from organic waste. Ammonia released from manure is converted in the soil to soluble nitrates that are readily transported to sources of drinking water in which they accumulate to undesirable levels.

Pollution of water supplies by industrial processes and products is common throughout the world. Industrial wastes have fouled the waters of the Thames, the Rhine, the Danube, and the lower Mississippi River. Toxic chemicals, heavy metals, and oxygen-depleting nutrients have accumulated where rivers empty into lakes, estuaries, and delta areas. Leaching from solid waste disposal sites and toxic waste dumps has poisoned water supplies at considerable distances from the origins of contamination (Fig. 14.15). Serious health problems have resulted and entire communities have been forced to abandon their homes.

In recent years most developed nations have passed legislation regulating the disposal of industrial wastes, and this serious commitment to decontamination is paying dividends. Lakes, rivers, harbors, and coastal areas are showing decided improvement, although pollution is still in evidence. However, coun-tries that are in the early stages of industrialization have little capital left to invest in pollution controls, and contaminated water is a serious environmental problem. In the less developed countries the situation is even worse because poor sanitation procedures permit organic wastes from both humans and animals to enter water supplies. As a result, millions of people die each year from water-borne diseases that nearly have been eliminated in the developed world.

The Recurring Energy Crisis Throughout history an abundant and reliable supply of energy—whether from human power, animal power, the direct harnessing of wind and water, or the combustion of wood and fossil fuels—has been the key to material well-being for humans and their civilizations. When energy crises developed they were primarily economic—a matter of imbalance between supply and demand or a problem of available energy but at too high a cost. In recent years, such crises occurred in the United States and many other developed nations during World War II and again in the 1970s during the oil embargo by the Organization of Petroleum Exporting Countries (OPEC), when global events disrupted petroleum supplies. A similar crisis faces less developed countries today as the cost of fuels on the world market continues to climb and these countries go heavily into debt

FIGURE 14.15

The toxic chemicals discovered in this solid waste dump near Chicago threatened local water supplies until EPA authorities ordered corrective action. (Illinois EPA)

to purchase energy in support of internal economic development. However, the current world energy crisis has a critical new dimension. The impact of energy production on the environment must now be added to the relationship that has previously existed between energy and human well-being.

In the past higher energy production almost always has had a positive effect on human living conditions. Yet time and again we have noted the link between energy production and the environmental damage that currently threatens the future of all people in numerous ways. The link began with the Industrial Revolution and the subsequent emergence of fossil fuels as the world's major source of energy. As Figure 14.16 illustrates, production of the fossil fuels, and petroleum in particular, has increased nearly fivefold since 1945. Petroleum, coal, and natural gas are now the source of nearly 80 percent of the world's energy. Petroleum alone has been the source of almost 40 percent since the early 1970s.

The present negative effects of energy production from fossil fuels are experienced worldwide and are all too easy to recount. Particulate matter and sulfurous gases from the coal-fired boilers of industrial plants and electric power facilities pollute the air, blacken cities, and lead to acid precipitation. Automobile emissions from gasoline and diesel engines cause photochemical smog and threaten the health of millions of urban inhabitants. The burning of fossil fuels is the single most important cause for the significant increases in the atmospheric percentages of CO_2 and other greenhouse gases. These increases may slowly raise earth temperatures and could lead to significant climatic changes within a few decades. It is apparent that the energy production-to-human well-being equation has changed dramatically. More energy, if it comes from the increased burning of fossil fuels, is definitely not better for humankind on a long-term basis.

There are a number of reasons why decisions regarding worldwide energy policy must be reached in the current decade. Many aspects of environmental change, such as global warming, tropical deforestation, desertification, and the acidification of lakes and groundwater, have reached critical stages. Each change is associated directly or indirectly with use of fossil fuels or traditional energy supplies. Each change may soon be at a point where the most serious environmental damage is beyond human prevention and is irreversible. The strain on national economies grows as energy demands rise and fuel reserves are depleted. It is anticipated that if present trends continue, world energy use will increase by more than 50 percent in the next twenty years, especially in the less developed countries in which population growth and energy requirements for industrialization are greatest. Yet reli-

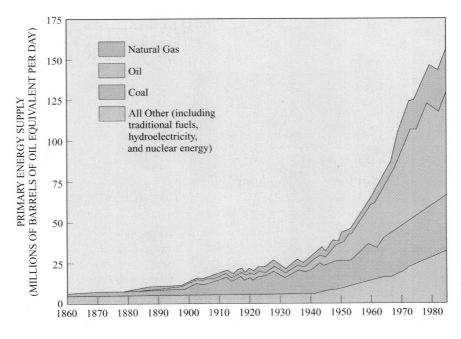

FIGURE 14.16

Changes in world sources of energy between 1860 and 1985.

able estimates indicate that remaining world supplies of fossil fuels will last less than two centuries at the current rates of consumption.

In addition, the concentration of industrial energy supplies in just a few geographical locations promises to lead to even greater economic differences and significantly increased incidents of international tension among nations. Coal reserves are the most widely distributed, although the United States, China, and the Russian and Ukrainian republics control about 60 percent of the world's total. Nearly 70 percent of all natural gas supplies are within Russia and the Middle East. The key role of the Middle East is not clearly understood until one realizes that it contains approximately three-fourths of all easily recoverable, low-cost reserves of petroleum.

Reliance on fossil fuels can be significantly reduced through greater development of nuclear power. Nuclear reactors that release energy through the *fission* or breakdown of heavy nuclei are relatively expensive to construct and operate, but they can efficiently supply much of the energy required by a nation. France, for example, produces nearly 70 percent of its electricity from nuclear power. Under normal operating conditions, nuclear power plants pose no threat to the earth's atmosphere, ecosystems, or resource base. But the accidents at Three Mile Island and Chernobyl and the unsolved problems of radioactive waste disposal have seriously weakened public confidence in nuclear power as a long-term energy source. Added to this is the concern of many thoughtful scientists and political leaders that with an increasing reliance on nuclear energy there will be a more widespread distribution of the materials and technology necessary to produce nuclear weapons.

Nuclear power nevertheless must be seriously considered as an energy source with a promising future. However, three conditions must be met if production is to expand beyond its current levels. First is the installation of advanced reactors that would eliminate the possibility of human error and have fail-safe internal controls against runaway chain reactions. Second is the development of programs to dispose of radioactive nuclear wastes without damage to the environment now or in the future. The third condition, the formation of an international authority that can halt the proliferation of weapons-grade nuclear materials, may well be the most difficult to meet. The first two require advances in technology that science can provide if society is willing to pay the economic cost. The

third requires a level of universal international agreement and political cooperation that the world has yet to achieve.

There is one additional possibility that could make nuclear power a reasonable choice for the future: the release of energy from the *fusion* of low atomic weight nuclei. Nuclear fusion would eliminate many of the problems associated with present nuclear power plants. Fusion processes could be made accident-proof and would produce little or no radioactive waste. It is also unlikely that fusion technology would lead to weapons development. Energy from fusion would be sustainable because supplies of fuel (deuterium) are virtually limitless. However, this new source of power is still in the experimental stage. It is questionable whether any nation or group of nations will be capable of developing the technology or providing the money necessary to make it commercially available.

There are steps that can be taken to ease the current energy crisis and the environmental stress for which it is an underlying cause. However, these steps are expensive, they should be part of policy decisions that collectively address all major environmental issues, and they will be of limited value unless they involve agreement and cooperation among all nations in both the developed and less developed world. Efforts can be made to increase efficiency in both the production and use of energy. In addition, alternative energy sources can be developed within the lead time available before current energy supplies are exhausted.

Some authorities believe that if a developing nation today could have access to the best technology for energy production and could make energy-efficient appliances available to its consumers, it could provide a European level of energy services with only a 20 percent increase in current energy consumption. If the United States, the world's largest consumer of energy, would employ energy conservation practices and reduce its per capita consumption to that of Germany, there would be enough unused energy to supply the current needs of Mexico and Brazil combined. If all nations had sufficient capital to institute both existing energy-efficient technology and pollution control equipment it would be possible, despite population growth, to stabilize world energy production and at the same time reduce the rate of environmental deterioration. The energy crisis would be far from resolved, but more time would be available for development of the alternative energy sources that are discussed later in this chapter.

TOWARD A SUSTAINABLE EARTH SOCIETY

➤ The essential ingredient in the perpetuation of civilization is the development of a world society that can be sustained indefinitely by the earth's resources.

What must be done if earth resources are to sustain human numbers indefinitely?

What signs indicate that humans are recognizing the need to strive for a sustainable earth society?

One lesson should have become obvious from our study of human geography. The fundamental challenge for humanity is to foster economic development and a decent standard of living for all the world's people on a sustainable basis. It is not sufficient to strive for a better quality of life today if this goal is achieved at the expense of future generations. Ways must be found to protect human well-being in the developed nations and greatly increase living standards in the less developed countries without destroying the environment on which all people depend. Human needs and environmental resources must reach a state of equilibrium that can be sustained indefinitely.

The economic, social, and political actions of all nations must be reconsidered if we are to achieve a **sustainable earth society**. If continued, our present policies and practices will only lead to further inequities in living standards among nations and additional environmental deterioration. To attain a balance between human numbers and the ability of the earth to sustain the numbers indefinitely, earth society must reach three objectives. First, world population must stabilize at a level that does not exceed the supply of resources needed to support these numbers. Second, economic development should be directed toward reducing the inequities between the developed and less developed world to ensure that the present and future needs of all human beings are met (Fig. 14.17). Third,

(a)

(b)

FIGURE 14.17
Housing is an excellent indicator of the inequality that exists between the developed and less developed worlds. (a) Condominium housing in Florida. (b) Squatter housing on the outskirts of Santo Domingo, Dominican Republic. (R. Gabler)

economic growth should be structured so that damage to the environment is minimized and environmental change does not jeopardize the quality of life in the centuries to come.

The seriousness of the environmental issues discussed in the preceding pages should not be cause for unwarranted pessimism. Sustainable economic growth leading to a sustainable earth society is well within the realm of possibility. There are a number of positive signs that indicate world society is ready for a change in direction. Environmental issues are rising to the top of the international agenda as indicated by the 1992 Earth Conference in Rio de Janeiro. Economic assistance programs in the less developed world are beginning to be structured with sustainable development in mind. Energy-efficient policies are starting to replace single-minded efforts to increase energy production in both the developed and less developed world. Most important, a "business as usual" attitude concerning the planet's future is being strongly challenged by scientific studies, political movements, educational programs, and development experimentation that demonstrates that, in the long-run, what is good for the environment is good for the world economy. As a result, several environmentally favorable courses of action are being pursued by various leaders in government, science, agriculture, and industry. If fully implemented, these could lead to a successful new relationship between humans and the planet they occupy.

Sustainable Agriculture

➤ Although conventional agriculture in the United States and the Green Revolution in parts of the less developed world have greatly increased food production, environmentalists believe these farming practices are not sustainable.

What criteria must be met for agricultural systems to be sustainable?

How have agricultural systems throughout the world failed to meet these criteria?

What developments provide hope for the future?

The remarkable productivity of American farms has been brought about by what has come to be known in the United States as **conventional agriculture**. Such agriculture is almost totally mechanized, with high energy input from fossil fuels and low labor require-

FIGURE 14.18

The spreading of chemical fertilizers, herbicides, and pesticides, as on this Illinois farm, is common agricultural practice throughout the midwestern United States. (R. Gabler)

ments. It is further characterized by the planting of hybrid seeds of one crop (monoculture) year after year in the same fields with heavy use of chemical pesticides, herbicides, and fertilizers (Fig. 14.18). The Green Revolution has introduced many aspects of American conventional agriculture to the less developed countries, although farming methods in these countries remain labor intensive. One result of implementing the newest agricultural technology has been a dramatic increase in worldwide food production. Food output per capita has increased in all world regions except Africa, in which both environmental and social circumstances have been barriers to modern agricultural practices. The production of cereals that regularly provide about half of world caloric intake has expanded at an average annual rate of 3 percent for the past 25 years. It is estimated that the world's annual food supply could support more than 6 billion people at levels recommended by United Nations agencies, if the food could be distributed evenly.

The challenge today is to preserve the recent gains in agricultural production and foster additional increases to match expanding population without severe environmental damage. The farming practices of conventional agriculture and the Green Revolution are not sustainable. They are associated with soil erosion and depletion, a deteriorating environment, and mounting hazards to natural ecosystems and human health. To be sustainable, agricultural systems must be able to maintain their productivity indefinitely. At the same time they must conserve the soil resource, be compatible with the environment, and return a reasonable profit to the farmer. Agricultural systems throughout the world do not meet these requirements. In the less developed countries soil erosion, nutrient depletion, and salinization are all serious threats to continued crop production. In the United States, underground and surface waters are polluted with nitrates from agricultural fields, and farmers handling pesticides are six times more likely to contact lymphatic cancer than other Americans. In Central America pesticide poisoning is considered one of the region's most critical health problems. In some Asian nations the overproduction of rice through monoculture has led to an actual decrease in income and standard of living for the farmer.

To achieve sustainable agriculture, new systems of farm management are emerging. They join traditional farming practices with modern methods and technology. The goal of each is to reduce the use of mineral fuels, herbicides, pesticides, and chemical fertilizers. In the United States it is estimated that the number of farmers practicing sustainable agriculture has tripled since 1980 and has grown to include nearly 3 percent of land under production. Some farmers favor **organic farming**, which totally eliminates the use of chemicals or synthetic fertilizers, but many have adopted *low-input sustainable agriculture* (LISA). With LISA the use of manufactured additives is strictly limited; they are usually applied directly to the plants along raised rows (ridge-tilling) rather than spread widely over entire fields. Animal manure is used as fertilizer wherever cattle or hogs are part of the farm operation, and winter cover crops are plowed into the soil as "green manure" in the spring. Crop rotation, as practiced generations ago, has returned as a natural method of preventing pests from increasing in numbers sufficient to cause serious crop damage. Although yields using LISA methods are often lower than those produced by conventional agriculture, the reduced costs of chemicals and fuel make sustainable agriculture highly competitive. In addition, LISA protects the soil resource. Organic fertilizers, cover crops, and crop rotation schemes prevent soil erosion, enrich the soil, and contribute to better soil structure and tilth (response to cultivation).

Because the less developed nations cannot afford to sacrifice the food production gains of the Green Revolution, they cannot abandon monoculture or risk

FIGURE 14.19
As noted in this farming village in West Bengal, India, tractors to replace animal power and diesel pumps to lift irrigation water from holding ponds are beginning to appear in some less developed countries. (R. Gabler)

a return to traditional organic farming in order to reduce side-effects that damage the environment. However, there are encouraging signs that sustainable agriculture can be achieved by protecting soils and reducing the use of chemicals in other ways. Soon there will be available controlled-release fertilizers that permit plants to make full use of chemical nutrients before they are removed by groundwater flow. Also under development are plant varieties that are resistant to new environmentally friendly herbicides. Through *biotechnology*, seeds are being genetically modified to increase resistance to insect pests and plant disease. The new generation of agricultural chemicals will be target-specific, they will be capable of being used in smaller amounts, and they will not endanger non-target organisms. Intercropping, minimum tillage, terracing, the cultivation of perennial crops, the management of forests, and improved irrigation practices can help protect the soil resource (Fig. 14.19). Sustainable agriculture is a distinct possibility even in the less developed countries, but only if the newest technology is made universally available so that all farmers can blend it with the best of current farming practices.

Alternative Energy Sources

➢ Because the fossil fuels that currently supply most of the world's energy will someday be exhausted, alternative and renewable sources of energy must be developed.

Which renewable energy sources hold the most promise?

What are the potentials and drawbacks of each?

Even if the earth's people maintain energy consumption at its current level through advanced technology and conservation by consumers, the supplies of non-renewable fossil fuels will be exhausted in the not-too-distant future. Alternative sources of energy must be developed, and it would be best if they are renewable. Renewable energy resources are self-perpetuating—in other words, capable of being constantly replenished. Hence, they are sustainable if people do not destroy the means of their renewal though overuse. Renewable energy resources already used in varying degrees include fuelwood, hydropower, geothermal energy, solar energy, tidal power, wind power, and biomass fuels.

FIGURE 14.20

Long before the advent of diesel engines, wind power served to pump water from the polders in the Netherlands. Well-preserved examples of windmills, like this one in Friesland, still stand as a reminder of earlier times. (R. Gabler)

Only a few of the energy sources we have listed hold such promise of expanded production as an alternative to fossil fuels. Fuelwood is not a reasonable choice. It is a prime energy source in less developed regions in which it already is in short supply. Major reforestation will be necessary to simply maintain production and at the same time protect the environment from more serious deterioration. Additional hydroelectric power facilities are under construction or being considered in the less developed countries, but there are few undeveloped sites remaining in the industrialized nations. In addition, growing resistance to the environmental damage caused by dam construction and reservoir formation probably will rule out significant future increases in hydropower production.

Geothermal energy sources are available wherever water is heated or converted to steam by coming in contact with rocks of high temperature deep within the earth's crust. When the water rises to the surface it is used to heat homes or produce electricity. Currently some 20 countries use geothermal heat, but sites for additional development are so restricted that the power produced will never have worldwide significance. Similarly, there are so few narrow coastal inlets where the power of tidal flow can be harnessed that this source of power will not help to meet future needs. Only four energy sources might be capable of providing a sustainable energy supply, and it is questionable if one of these, nuclear power, will ever be compatible with a sustainable earth society. The other three are wind power, biomass fuels, and solar energy.

Wind Power The wind is an inexhaustible source of clean energy. Windmills that once were used to pump water or grind grain, before electricity became available widely, can still be seen in the United States and several European countries (Fig. 14.20). As reliance on fossil fuels decreases, a new type of wind power may become a major factor in producing electricity. The United States might be able to eliminate its imports of foreign oil if it would invest sufficient money to develop its full potential for producing electrical energy from clusters of wind turbines, called *wind farms* (Fig. 14.21). Future wind farms will require sites with steady winds averaging 14 miles (23 km) per hour. One study found that 14 percent of the land area of the United States possesses such winds.

California, which has more than 15,000 wind turbines in commercial use, currently produces more than 60 percent of wind-generated electricity worldwide and 90 percent of that generated in the United States.

FIGURE 14.21

A wind farm in the Dutch polderlands. Wind farms offer significant potential for the production of electrical energy, but their disruption of the beauty of the landscape and the noise of their moving propellers have caused nearby inhabitants to protest their installation. (R. Gabler)

Only about a fifth of California's best wind sites have been developed. Other U.S. sites with equal potential are located in the western Great Plains from Wyoming to Oklahoma, the New England Coast, and the Pacific Northwest. Electricity from California wind turbines is produced at costs nearly competitive with that produced by fossil fuels, but building new facilities is expensive. Most of the new generation of wind turbines cost more than $1 million to construct. Other impediments to the rapid development of wind power include (1) the need for systems that will operate more reliably at varying wind speeds and (2) alteration of the visible landscape, sometimes for miles, by a multitude of slowly turning turbines. When the problems are solved, the wind could play a significant role in replacing fossil fuels. In the United States, for example, sixteen states have wind potential equal to or exceeding that of California.

Biomass Fuels Energy from *biomass fuels* comes from the combustion directly or in altered form of trees and other vegetation. As we mentioned previously, the increased use of wood as a biomass fuel is not a rea-

sonable alternative to fossil fuels. However, other biomass fuels already have shown considerable promise. The rising cost of petroleum has prompted nations with sizable timber reserves to use logging and sawmill wastes as fuel. Scrap wood, bark, and sawdust is pelletized and burned in industrial boilers to produce steam and electricity. Sweden is the leading nation in the use of lumber by-products as fuel. Domestic trash, consisting in large part of biomass, serves as a fuel in some thermoelectric plants in the United States, Western Europe, and Japan. Agricultural wastes also can be used as fuel, but this is done primarily in the less developed countries, not the developed nations. In Hawaii, however, a small amount of electricity is generated through the burning of bagasse, the residue left after the extraction of sugar from sugar cane.

In addition to serving as a solid fuel, biomass can be converted into liquid and gaseous biofuels. The liquid biofuels consist of two alcohols—*methanol* (wood alcohol) and *ethanol* (grain alcohol). Methanol's utility and potential as a fuel is much less than that of ethanol, but fortunately it is possible to convert wood to ethanol rather than methanol. It is easier and less costly, however, to make ethanol from grain crops rather than from wood. The U.S. government has been experimenting with wood-to-ethanol conversion processes for more than a decade, and it is possible that during the 1990s ethanol from wood will become less costly than gasoline. Surplus corn and other grains have been processed into ethanol in the United States since the 1970s. Gasolines in the 1990s often contain 10 percent ethanol. Vehicles with adapted engines can burn pure ethanol. We cannot expect that alcohol fuels will satisfy more than a small portion of the world's energy needs in the future, however. Growing trees for conversion to biofuels is not favored by environmentalists, and any soils used for the production of energy crops would have to be diverted from the important role of growing crops for livestock and human consumption. The entire corn crop of the United States—the world's largest crop by far—could supply only one-fourth of the nation's fuel needs.

Biomass that is converted into the gaseous fuel, biogas, consists of about 60 percent methane. Biogas is created naturally in landfills, and in 1990 there were more than 50 recovery systems in operation in the United States. Most were located in California, where they gathered gas for commercial and industrial use. More widespread use of such systems could take advantage of a usually wasted energy source to reduce reliance on fossil fuels. Biogas can be generated do-mestically on a small scale by converting organic wastes in *biogas digesters* to methane for home heating and cooking. The Chinese employ millions of biogas digesters, but this simple technology is rarely used in the developed world.

Solar Energy The world's future source of un-limited, pollution-free, environmentally compatible power will likely be solar energy. Through good architectural design and directional siting, energy from the sun is already being used in *passive systems* to heat homes in the winter and cool them in the summer. Passive systems involve constructing houses with well-insulated roofs and thick walls that contain large areas of double-glazed windows facing toward the sun and nearly windowless walls in the opposite direction. Overhanging roofs permit the low-angle solar rays of winter to heat interiors but protect windows from the more direct rays of summer, allowing homes to remain cool in that season. *Active systems* employ flat-plate and collector panels to heat water to as high as 160°F (70°C). The water is then circulated or stored for domestic heating purposes. Initial costs of active systems

may add 10 percent to the price of the home, but within a few years energy costs can be reduced by 60 percent or more (Fig. 14.22).

The commercial exploitation of solar energy is in its infancy but shows great promise. Photovoltaic cells that convert sunlight directly into electrical power are already in use in small instruments such as watches and calculators and in communication satellites. Through mass production of photovoltaic cells, prices have decreased dramatically in recent years to the point at which electricity can be produced at less than 30 cents per kilowatt hour. The generation of electricity from installations that convert solar energy to heat has reduced the cost even further. This type of solar technology involves a solar thermal tower and racks of tracking mirrors (a **heliostat field**) that follow the sun and focus its heat on a steam boiler perched on the tower (Fig. 14.23). Temperatures in the boiler may be raised to more than 900°F (500°C). Steam from the boiler drives turbines that generate the electricity. A solar-thermal plant, recently opened in California, is expected to produce power at less than 8 cents per kilowatt hour. This cost will soon be competitive with electricity produced by the burning of fossil fuels as their prices rise.

The earth receives, in just two weeks time, an amount of energy from the sun that equals the entire global reserves of fossil fuels. However, as people increasingly turn to this inexhaustible source of power (at least for the predicted 5 to 10 billion years remain-

FIGURE 14.22
Whether or not to build a new home with an active solar heating system similar to the one in this photograph is a decision based on many factors. These include the price of alternative mineral fuels, concern for the environment, and both the location and site of the home with respect to the duration and intensity of available solar energy. (Peter Vandermark/Stock Boston)

FIGURE 14.23
The world's largest solar electric generating system, located in Boron, California. Although the increased production of energy from the sun faces major obstacles, solar power holds the greatest promise for the future replacement of mineral fuels. (Ken Lucas, Biological Photo Service)

ing in the life of the sun), several obstacles must be overcome. Solar energy is intermittent; it is available only during the day and is greatly reduced by cloud cover. In addition, regions with the highest percentages of sunshine and the greatest potential for solar power development are often at great distances from the major consumers of electricity. Hence, storage and long distance transmission of solar-thermal generated electricity are the real problems that must be solved with improved technology. Solar-thermal installations are currently used in conjunction with pumping facilities that lift water to reservoirs that supply hydroelectric generators. In the future it should be possible to also store large quantities of solar energy as compressed air, or in batteries and current-storing superconducting coils. In addition, the challenge of economical long-distance transmission of electricity will be met when adequate resources for research and experimentation are provided. When the environmental dividends of replacing energy from fossil fuels are taken into consideration, solar power will prove to be a bargain humanity cannot refuse to accept.

Changing Value Systems

➤ Changes in value systems within both the developed and less developed countries are essential if a sustainable earth society is to be achieved.

What changes are most important?

What should be done to initiate these changes?

What can be done to solve the problem of waste and the problem of unmanageable population growth?

In the industrialized world, people value most highly the material well-being that has been gained largely by mining the resources of the earth. As we have demonstrated, this has led to a general deterioration of the environment and has brought the developed world to the point where it is questionable that current living standards can be maintained. People in the less developed countries value most the development processes that they believe will help them achieve the economic successes of the industrialized world. Their attempts to follow the development model of their wealthier neighbors is causing further environmental damage that ultimately could jeopardize the capacity of the earth to sustain their growing populations.

Significant changes in values are in order for both the industrialized countries and the less developed

countries—the rich and the poor. To achieve the goal of a sustainable earth society, people throughout the world must reconsider traditional attitudes and beliefs and reorder their individual and collective priorities. New values must replace some of the old. People need to value economic development and production that is compatible with the environment regardless of initial cost. If we do not begin to adopt such value systems, and pay the price for environmentally sound development now, in the long run the price that our descendants pay for environmental deterioration will be higher. We should value the human condition of all the earth's people, not just our own. The poor nations of the world cannot provide an acceptable standard of living for their citizens without the assistance of the wealthy nations. We should all value the *quality* of human life to such an extent that we learn to limit human numbers. The earth and its resources are finite, and they cannot support an infinite population.

Values change slowly, however, and current value systems have developed over long periods of time. To hasten change and to slow the negative impacts of humans on the environment, several initiatives are essential. Some of these are associated with environmental protection. International agreements governing acceptable levels of automotive and industrial emissions should be reached, and incentives for compliance should be included so that atmospheric pollution can be reduced. New taxes based on the amounts of fossil fuels consumed or the levels of CO_2 discharged should be considered. The tax revenues that result should be applied to the development of both more efficient energy technology and alternative energy sources. They also should be used to make environmentally safe energy production available in the less developed as well as the developed world. Because a free-market economy is now the general rule throughout the industrialized world, the environmental cost of producing goods and services must be included in the price paid for them. The developed nations must demonstrate to the less developed ones that they are serious about environmental protection, and they must make it possible for the less developed countries to be serious as well. The industrialized nations are primarily responsible for environmental problems, and only they have the funds to solve them.

Progress toward a sustainable society cannot be made in the less developed world without the cooperation and support of wealthy nations. The reality of world economics is such that the less developed countries are in no position to help themselves. Concerns for the environment in the less developed countries, therefore, must wait until their economic and social problems have been addressed.

As steps are taken to achieve environmentally sound development, there are two objectives that are equally important if a sustainable earth society is to be realized. The first is the wise use of existing resources. The second is the stabilization of world population. Both involve fundamental changes in attitudes and values.

Waste Not, Want Not The industrialized nations of the world have about one-quarter of the world's population, yet they consume nearly 80 percent of the world's goods each year. It is obvious that any discussion of conservation or the economical use of resources applies more to the developed than the less developed countries. There are many opportunities for improvement. This is especially true in the United States, the world's leading consumer of goods and services. We already have noted how waste can be reduced by improving efficiency in energy production and consumption. In the United States, for example, simple substitution of the most efficient models and products available for ones currently in use would cut energy consumption to approximately one-third for automobiles and home lighting, to one-half for refrigerators and air conditioners, and to two-thirds for gas furnaces. We also have noted similar opportunities for conservation and improved efficiency in the use of water and soil resources.

There is another aspect of developed societies where waste is the central problem. It involves the disposal of by-products of industrial processes, trash from commercial establishments, and the ordinary garbage associated with modern lifestyles. In the United States, part of the problem is economic. It often is cheaper to buy a new product than to renovate and reuse an old one. More than 200 million tires and 2 billion disposable razors are discarded each year. Millions of automobiles are rusting in junk yards. Part of the problem is convenience. Years ago cloth diapers were washed and reused; now more than 15 billion of the disposable kind add a particularly distasteful load to the nation's garbage dumps each year. Part of the problem is historical. Old toxic waste sites are being discovered faster than government funds become available to clean them up. Solid waste is accumulating so rapidly that many landfills are reaching their

capacity and new landfill sites are at a premium. Of the 9000 U.S. landfills that existed in the mid-1980s, one-third are already closed and 2000 more must be replaced over the next few years.

A number of things can be done to reduce the mounting tide of waste. New laws help to change values. Business and industrial waste decreases at its source when the penalties for improper or excessive waste disposal or the costs of toxic waste removal are greater than the prices of altering industrial processes and business practices. Similar savings occur when households are asked to pay for garbage collection based on the amount of trash they produce. The most environmentally sound remedy is recycling because it not only reduces the accumulation of waste, but it conserves natural resources as well. The United States is just beginning its recycling efforts and there is plenty of room for growth. Americans recycle about 10 percent of their trash, whereas Europeans recycle 30 percent and the Japanese a commendable 50 percent. Japan is a nation poor in natural resources, and its people learned long ago to value conservation.

Defusing the Population Bomb If there is a serious commitment and full cooperation among all the world's nations, a successful response can be made to each of the human-induced environmental issues we have discussed. But all will be for nothing and there can be no sustainable earth society if that society continues to grow indefinitely. As indicated in Chapter 6, the percentage rate of increase in population already is slowing down. It is predicted that by the year 2025 the rate will be less than half what it was in the 1980s. However, there is small comfort in this information because the population base against which this rate applies will be so large that the actual growth in numbers of people each year will be much greater than it is today. United Nations estimates indicate that there will be 8 to 9 billion people on earth by 2025. If the demographic transition model proves correct and population remains essentially stable in the developed world, the vast majority of the 3 billion or more additional people by 2025 will be living in what are now less developed countries (Fig. 14.24).

Those individuals who are most concerned about sustainable economic growth believe that the world cannot wait for birth rates in the less developed countries to decline as the countries develop. They insist that birth rates in the less developed countries must be cut in half by the turn of the century. This goal cannot

FIGURE 14.24
A crowded market outside the town of Ghatsilla in Bihar, India. The pressure of population is obvious even in the rural areas of India, a country that has experienced nearly a threefold increase in human numbers since gaining its independence in 1947. (R. Gabler)

FIGURE 14.25
Women carrying excessively heavy loads of firewood to a village near the Temple of the Sun, Kornak, India. The status of women in the less developed countries of the world is a major obstacle to the limitation of population growth. Throughout rural India, women have little or no control over their own lives and are destined at birth to lives of hard labor and the bearing of children. (R. Gabler)

be reached without major aid from the developed nations, effective education programs, and a wholesale change in values. Recent experience has demonstrated that the most effective means of slowing population growth in less developed countries is to make birth control information and free contraceptives universally available. Where religious doctrine prohibits the use of contraceptives, education in natural birth control methods can be a successful substitute. As a joint result of family planning programs and rising living standards, crude birth rates have dropped sharply over the past thirty years in Indonesia, Thailand, South Korea, and China. It has been projected by the World Bank that a threefold increase in funds currently spent each year on family planning (about $3 billion) could reduce estimated population totals for 2025 by about 2 billion people.

There is an indirect correlation in the less developed world between birth rates and the status of women. Where the status of women is low, birth rates are almost always high. Where surveys have been conducted in less developed countries, the results indicate that at least half of all currently married women do not want additional children. Yet their lack of educa-

tion, their economic status, and their role in society give them no choice (Fig. 14.25). A reasonable conclusion can be drawn from these facts. One of the primary goals of development programs in less developed countries should be to raise the status of women. Unfortunately, this will be especially difficult in sub-Saharan Africa and in many Moslem countries where a tradition of large families and conservative religious values are strong.

Of all the issues facing the world today, the ever-increasing stress on the environment as human numbers continue to grow is certainly the most critical. Can world population be stabilized at a level that can be sustained indefinitely by the earth's renewable resources? The answer is clearly yes, if we alter our value systems so that the welfare of future generations counts as much as or more than the good life today. Will we reorder our priorities and adopt new values? No one can foretell the future, but there is at least one excellent reason to be optimistic. The strongest animal instinct is the instinct to survive. As it becomes increasingly clear that human survival is at stake, habits, attitudes, and values will change. All humanity shares the goal of a better tomorrow.

KEY TERMS

Photochemical smog   A form of pollution that consists of gases produced by chemical reactions when solar radiation comes in contact with automobile and industrial emissions in the lower atmosphere. The most common gas produced is ozone.   **536**

pH scale   A scale from 0 to 14, based on a measurement of hydrogen ions, that identifies the acidity or alkalinity of a solution. A pH value below 7 indicates acidic conditions; a pH value above 7 indicates alkalinity.   **537**

Acid precipitation   Precipitation that has become abnormally acidic because of chemical reactions between atmospheric moisture and industrial or automotive emissions. Precipitation with a pH below 5.6, the average acidity of normal rainfall, is considered acid precipitation.   **537**

Ozone layer   A layer of ozone, the triatomic form of oxygen, in the upper atmosphere. It shields life forms on the earth's surface from excessive ultraviolet radiation.   **541**

Atmospheric effect   The regulation of atmospheric temperatures that occurs naturally when gases in the atmosphere permit short-wave solar radiation to reach the earth's surface and warm it, but absorb much of the long-wave radiation given off by the heated earth.   **543**

Greenhouse effect   The process whereby gases added by the burning of fossil fuels and industrial pollution to those normally in the atmosphere serve to trap abnormally high amounts of long-wave earth radiation. Many scientists believe this process will lead to slowly increasing atmospheric temperatures (global warming).   **543**

Biodiversity   The number and variety of different plant and animal species in a particular ecosystem. Studies indicate that the greater the area covered by an ecosystem, the greater its biodiversity and the better it can withstand environmental stress.   **550**

Desertification   The territorial expansion of desertlike conditions caused by human-induced deterioration of the land resource. Desertification involves a long-term loss in the productive capacity of the land.   **550**

Sustainable earth society   All the earth's people at an ideal stage in their economic and cultural development when they live in harmony with the environment and can be supported by renewable earth resources indefinitely.   **558**

Conventional agriculture   Highly mechanized agriculture characterized by heavy dependence on fertilizers, pesticides, and herbicides; by the planting of hybrid varieties of one or two cash crops; and by low labor costs.   **559**

Organic farming   A farming practice that avoids chemical fertilizers, weed killers, and pest controls by substituting the use of animal manure, crop rotation, cover crops, and other natural methods to maintain productivity and preserve the soil resource.   **560**

Heliostat field   Rows of mirrors that are preset to track the sun and focus its heat on a boiler located in a solar thermal tower. Steam from the boiler drives turbines that serve to convert solar energy to electricity.   **563**

REVIEW QUESTIONS

1. What is photochemical smog? How is it formed and in what countries of the world is it a major problem? How is it harmful?

2. What level of acidity in rain and snow is necessary to produce acid precipitation? What are the negative results of acid precipitation? What are its causes and what geographic regions are most affected?

3. What is meant by the *buffer capacity* of water? What determines a lake's buffer capacity and how is buffer capacity related to damage from acid precipitation?

4. What has been the effect of acid precipitation on middle latitude forests? What countries have been affected most?

5. What can be done to reduce acid precipitation and why have many countries been reluctant to take the necessary steps?

6. What is the major cause of damage to the ozone layer in the atmosphere? What can be the harmful results?

7. What are the reasons for differing opinions concerning global warming? Why do most scientists believe that global warming is taking place?

8. What could be some of the influences on temperatures, agriculture, human health, and ecosystems if global warming does proceed at the rate scientists predict?

9. Among coal, water, iron ore, forests, copper, and natu-

ral gas, which are considered renewable resources? Which are nonrenewable resources?

10. Why are tropical forests disappearing so rapidly? Why is the destruction of these forests harmful to humans?

11. What are the three *natural sinks* of carbon? Why are tropical forests so important in efforts to slow global warming? How do tropical forests protect biodiversity?

12. What is desertification? How and why does it occur? What are its effects on the physical environment and the humans who are involved?

13. Why do severe shortages of water exist in so many different regions despite the fact that world supplies are more than sufficient to meet the needs of all of the world's people?

14. What are the chief sources of pollution that threaten water quality? Which are examples of *point* and *non-point* sources? Why is the problem of water pollution so much greater in the less developed countries than in developed countries?

15. How has the greatly increased use of fossil fuels added a new dimension to the world's energy problems? What steps should be taken to combat the increasing likelihood of recurring shortages of energy?

16. What is meant by a sustainable earth society? What objectives must be met if a balance between human numbers and earth resources is to be reached?

17. What is the evidence that the farming practices of *conventional agriculture* and the *Green Revolution* are not sustainable? How might sustainable agriculture be reached in the developed countries? How might it be reached in the less developed countries?

18. What sources of energy are considered alternatives to fossil fuels? What is the potential and what are the limitations of each? Which sources of energy have the best chances of becoming the major energy sources of the future?

19. Why are changes in value systems essential for people throughout the world if a sustainable earth society is to be achieved? What should some of these changes be?

20. What steps can be taken to reduce the negative impacts of humans on the environment? How important to reaching the goal of a sustainable earth society are the wise use of existing resources and the stabilization of world population?

GLOSSARY

Acculturation The adoption by an individual or a cultural group of selected traits from a different cultural group.

Acid precipitation Precipitation that has become abnormally acidic because of chemical reactions between atmospheric moisture and industrial or automotive emissions. Precipitation with a pH below 5.6, the average acidity of normal rainfall, is considered acid precipitation.

Agricultural Revolution A major cultural development, beginning about 10,000 years ago, that involved domesticating plants and animals and practicing agriculture for the first time.

Animal husbandry The raising of and caring for domesticated animals as an economic activity.

Animistic religions Primitive religions that involve worship of animals or natural features such as mountains, caves, stones, and trees.

Aquaculture The production and harvesting of fish and other marine organisms in confined water bodies.

Arithmetic density A measurement of population density expressed as the average number of people per unit area (sq mi or sq km) for the total area of a country or state.

Assimilation The absorbance of an individual or a cultural group by a different cultural group to the extent that differences in their traits are no longer distinguishable.

Atmospheric effect The regulation of atmospheric temperatures that occurs naturally when gases in the atmosphere permit short-wave solar radiation to reach the earth's surface and warm it, but absorb much of the long-wave radiation given off by the heated earth.

Autarky The practice of self-sufficiency by a country.

Average life expectancy Based on current mortality levels within a population, the average number of years a newborn can expect to live.

Baby boom An abrupt increase in birth rates in the United States during the years immediately following World War II.

Basic functions The functions of a city that provide goods and services for sale to consumers in other areas, thereby earning income for the city from outside sources.

Bilingual The ability to communicate in two different languages.

Biodiversity The number and variety of different plant and animal species in a particular ecosystem. Studies indicate that the greater the area covered by an ecosystem, the greater its biodiversity and the better it can withstand environmental stress.

Biome Major terrestrial ecosystems, such as tropical rainforests or grasslands.

Boat people Refugee groups who have fled their homeland aboard vessels, often poorly equipped and marginally seaworthy. This term has been most often applied to the Vietnamese refugees of the 1970s.

Brain drain The large-scale migration of a society's most educated or talented members.

Cartography The art and science of map construction.

Central business district (CBD) The core area of a town or city that contains a concentration of prominent multistory buildings housing offices, retail stores, banks, and other commercial establishments.

Central place A market center or community in which goods and services may be obtained by consumers in the surrounding trade area.

Central place theory The theory concerned with the hierarchy of market centers and their distributional pattern in an area.

Centuriatio An orderly survey system, involving rectangular units of land, used by the Romans in classical time.

City-state A political entity that consists of a city together with the territory under its political control.

Climate The accumulated weather over a relatively long period in a place or region, usually expressed in terms of averages and deviations from the norm.

Cold War The competition between the United States and the Soviet Union (together with allies on each side) for military and technological supremacy as well as international influence following World War II.

Commercial agriculture The production of agricultural commodities primarily for sale in the marketplace rather than for providing subsistence.

Commercial grain farming A type of farming typically devoted to the large-scale production of a single grain crop for sale. Also known as cash grain farming.

Common lands Parcels of land reserved for use by all citizens. In colonial New England, certain grazing areas and wood lots were set aside as common lands to be used by all inhabitants.

Continental shelf The extension of a continental block beneath the shallow margins of an adjacent sea or ocean.

Conurbation A continuous urbanized zone that has been formed by the horizontal growth of cities and their suburbs.

Conventional agriculture Highly mechanized agriculture characterized by heavy dependence on fertilizers, pesticides, and herbicides; by the planting of hybrid varieties of one or two cash crops; and by low labor costs.

Core-periphery relationship The association or interaction between a more highly developed core area and less developed peripheral areas.

Council for Mutual Economic Assistance An organization that once linked the former Soviet Union and its Eastern European satellite states to promote their mutual economic status.

Creole language A language that has evolved from a pidgin language or a mixture of other languages. It is a more fully developed language than pidgin.

Cross-cultural fertilization The enrichment or improvement in the culture of two or more groups as they adopt selected traits from one another.

Crude birth rate The annual number of births per 1000 people in an area.

Crude death rate The annual number of deaths per 1000 people in an area.

Cultural group A society that differs from all others in terms of the unique assortment of cultural traits it possesses.

Cultural landscape A landscape or area containing material features that are the consequence of human activity.

Culture The ensemble of learned traits that distinguish individual human groups and their particular ways of life.

Culture hearth An area where a particular culture has evolved and from which its traits have diffused to other locations.

Culture region A part of the earth's surface that is defined or delimited on the basis of one or more cultural criteria.

Culture traits The individual components of a culture that have been acquired through learning.

Democratic Revolution A major cultural development, beginning in Europe two to three centuries ago, that advanced the rights and freedoms of individuals and diminished the authority and special privilege of rulers and aristocrats.

Demographic transition The changes through time in a country's birth and death rates and rate of natural increase that theoretically accompany its modernization.

Demography The study of human populations through use of vital statistics.

Dependency ratio The proportion of people under 15 and over 64 years of age to the remainder of the population in an area.

Desertification The territorial expansion of desertlike conditions caused by human-induced deterioration of the land resource. Desertification involves a long-term loss in the productive capacity of the land.

Dialect The spoken variation of a language that is associated with a particular region or socioeconomic group.

Diffusion The progressive spread of a phenomenon or idea from a place of origin to other locations on the earth's surface.

Dispersed settlement The settlement of people on the land in scattered farmsteads.

Ecumene The effectively settled or populated parts of the earth.

Ejidos In Mexico, agricultural villages that control the surrounding land. As part of Mexico's agrarian reform program, the village allocates land for use by its inhabitants but retains ownership of the land.

Empire An extensive territory or a number of territories and peoples under the control of a single political authority.

Enclosure movement In western Europe following the Middle Ages, the enclosure movement involved consolidating land into individual farms and the relocation of rural people to those farms.

Environmental determinism A conviction that the activities and attainments of humans are highly influenced or controlled by one or more elements of the physical environment.

Equinox The date (approximately March 21 and September 23) when the noon sun is vertical at the Equator and on which the periods of daylight and darkness are of equal length over the entire earth.

Ethnic group A human group that is distinguished by its unique cultural and, in some cases, racial characteristics.

Ethnic religions Associated with a particular ethnic group, these religions do not seek converts outside of the group.

European population axis The most extensive zone of relatively high population densities in Europe. It extends in a general west–east pattern from southern Britain to western Russia.

European Economic Community An organization formed in Western Europe in 1958 to promote free trade among member countries and eventually bring about their complete economic integration.

Evapotranspiration The transfer of water at the earth's surface into water vapor in the atmosphere by the combination of evaporation and transpiration.

Extractive industries Economic activities that involve extracting natural resources from the physical environment. Important examples are forestry, fishing, and mining.

Flow resources Resources such as flowing water, wind, and solar radiation that must be used as they flow past a particular location or their potential at that time is lost.

Forced (involuntary) migrations Those migrations conducted by people against their will.

Generic boundaries A group of boundary types identified on the basis of inherent characteristics of the boundaries themselves.

Genetic boundaries A group of boundary types identified on the basis of their genesis, that is, when and where they were established relative to the human occupance of the area.

Gentrification A process in which inner-city dilapidated buildings or neighborhoods are rehabilitated and their lower-income inhabitants are replaced by members of the middle or upper class.

Geographic information systems (GIS) Programs to perform tasks and solve spatial problems by use of computer cartography and database management.

Geopolitics The use of geographic information and concepts to attain political goals.

Greenhouse effect The process whereby gases added by the burning of fossil fuels and industrial pollution to those normally in the atmosphere serve to trap abnormally high amounts of long-wave earth radiation. Many scientists believe this process will lead to slowly increasing atmospheric temperatures (global warming).

Green Revolution A major increase in food grain production in parts of the less developed world, made possible by the development of high-yielding hybrids and the application of agricultural chemicals.

Grid Pattern Town A nucleated settlement in which the blocks are rectangular or square and the streets cross at right angles. The streets commonly are aligned according to the cardinal points of a compass.

Gross national product The total value of all goods produced and services provided annually within a country.

Growth pole theory A theory that economic development, when stimulated in selected (usually urban) centers, will spread subsequently to surrounding areas.

Guest workers Foreign workers who have immigrated to a more economically developed country for temporary employment. This term is applied most commonly to foreigners who are temporarily employed in the industrialized countries of Europe.

Habitat The environment inhabited by humans or other organisms.

Heliostat field Rows of mirrors that are preset to track the sun and focus its heat on a boiler located in a solar thermal tower. Steam from the boiler drives turbines that serve to convert solar energy to electricity.

High-tech industries Those industries engaged in the development and manufacture of the most technically sophisticated industrial products such as computers and robots.

Hillforts Small hilltop settlements with fortifications dating from the Iron Age in western Europe.

Holistic A focus on the whole rather than individual parts.

Human carrying capacity The maximum number of people that an area theoretically can support at an acceptable standard of living.

Hydrologic cycle The transfer of water between the earth's surface and atmosphere in a general cycle involving evaporation, condensation, precipitation, and runoff.

Idiographic The focus of a field of study on description of unique phenomena rather than identification of scientific laws.

Import substitution The practice by a country of avoiding the importation of needed goods by producing identical or similar products itself, even if it is ill suited to do so.

Industrial location factors An assortment of factors that influence where manufacturing establishments are located.

Industrial Revolution A major cultural development, beginning in Europe during the eighteenth century, that consisted of innovations in manufacturing procedures and the invention of machines to make possible the first large-scale production of industrial goods.

Infant mortality rate The annual number of deaths of infants less than one year old per 1000 live births in an area.

Intensive subsistence agriculture Subsistence farming that is distinctive in terms of large labor input and high yields per unit of land. It is most common in densely populated areas of Asia.

Internal (domestic) migrations Those migrations conducted within the territory of a single country.

International migrations Those migrations that involve the crossing of a border separating countries.

Köppen classification A widely used classification of climates developed by Wladimir Köppen.

Land bridges Land exposed by the lowering of the sea level during Pleistocene glaciation that then connected areas normally separated by water bodies. Land bridges facilitated migrations by prehistoric peoples.

Land development Any program or scheme, usually designed and implemented by a national government, to develop and settle people on land in a frontier zone.

Language family A group of related languages that have evolved from a common ancestral tongue.

Latifundia Landholdings of unusually large size, such as estates and plantations. Where latifundia exist, only a small number of people own most of the land.

Lingua franca A common language used over a wide area by speakers of different tongues, usually for diplomatic or commercial purposes.

Livestock ranching The grazing of livestock for commercial purposes, usually on a relatively large landholding.

Local relief The difference in elevation between the highest and lowest points of land in a specified area.

Long lot A relatively long and narrow parcel of land, usually with one end of the property adjacent to a river or road. In North America, long lots are found in areas originally settled by the French.

Manufacturing belts Zones or regions containing high concentrations of manufacturing activities.

Map grid The network of parallels and meridians (or similar lines) on a map or globe.

Map projection On a map, the orderly arrangement of parallels and meridians to facilitate representation of the earth's curved surface.

Map scale The ratio of distance on a map to the distance it represents on the earth's surface.

Material culture The material or physical items, such as clothing, buildings, and crops, produced by humans in conducting their particular way of life.

Mathematical (absolute) location The location on a globe or map of a place or feature by latitude and longitude.

Mediterranean agriculture A variant of specialty agriculture that is distinguished by a combination of crops raised in all regions of Mediterranean climate.

Megalopolis A particularly extensive conurbation that extends from southern Maine to the shores of Chesapeake Bay along the East Coast of the United States.

Mercantilism An economic policy of the major trading nations in Europe during the sixteenth through eighteenth centuries. It was based on the theory that national strength is attained by increasing exports of finished goods and imports of raw materials and precious metals.

Mestizo A person whose ancestors were both Amerindian and European. Mestizos are the most common individuals in extensive parts of Latin America.

Metes and bounds A land survey system in which natural features such as trees, boulders, and water bodies are used to establish property boundaries.

Metropolitan Statistical Area (MSA) An urbanized area identified by the United States Bureau of the Census. It consists of a county or group of contiguous counties that fulfill certain demographic and economic criteria and usually contain a central city with a minimum population of 50,000.

Microclimates The climates of relatively small areas or precise locations.

Microstates Countries distinguished by their unusually small size in land area.

Minifundia Landholdings of unusually small size, often too small to adequately support a family.

Mixed farming A type of farming in which both crops and livestock are raised.

Monotheism The worship of one god.

Nation A group of people occupying a specific area and united by a common cultural or ethnic background.

National core The area in which a state originated; typically it contains the country's greatest population, principal city, and greatest economic development.

Nation-state A state whose territory coincides with that occupied by a particular nation.

Natural increase of population The growth in total population as a consequence of the crude death rate being exceeded by the crude birth rate.

Neolithic Period The New Stone Age, a period distinguished by human production and use of refined stone tools and domestication of plants and animals to initiate farming and herding.

Neutrality A policy of impartiality or refusal to support either side of an issue or conflict. Some national governments have a tradition of neutrality, thereby avoiding participation in conflicts or wars.

Newly industrial countries (NICs) Countries in the less developed world that are undergoing significant development of their industrial economy.

Nomothetic The focus of a field of study on identification of scientific laws.

Nonaligned movement A joint policy among the nonaligned states to oppose the Cold War and colonialism and promote economic development in the less developed world.

Nonbasic functions The functions of a city that provide goods and services for consumers within the city. As a consequence, these activities consequently bring no income to the city from outside sources.

Nonmaterial culture The components of culture that are not material in nature, such as religion and language.

Nonmetropolitan turnaround A reversal of the population decline in some rural settlements in the United States during the 1970s and 1980s.

Nonrenewable resources Resources such as mineral ores and fuels that exist in finite amounts and are subject to total exhaustion when exploited.

Nucleated settlement Any human settlement, ranging in size from a hamlet to a major metropolis, in which the houses and other buildings are in close proximity or highly concentrated.

Official language The language specified by a government to be used for all official or formal communication.

Organic farming A farming practice that avoids chemical fertilizers, weed killers, and pest controls by substituting the use of animal manure, crop rotation, cover crops, and other natural methods to maintain productivity and preserve the soil resource.

Ozone layer A layer of ozone, the triatomic form of oxygen, in the upper atmosphere. It shields life forms on the earth's surface from excessive ultraviolet radiation.

Paleolithic Period The Old Stone Age, a period distinguished by the human production and use of crude stone tools and survival by hunting, gathering, and fishing.

Pastoral nomadism An ancient form of livestock herding most commonly practiced by wandering tribes and bands in Old World dry lands. Frequent movement is required to locate adequate pasturage for the livestock.

Patriotism Loyalty and devotion to one's country or political system.

Photochemical smog A form of pollution that consists of gases produced by chemical reactions when solar radiation comes in contact with automobile and industrial emissions in the lower atmosphere. The most common gas produced is ozone.

pH scale A scale from 0 to 14, based on a measurement of hydrogen ions, that identifies the acidity or alkalinity of a solution. A pH value below 7 indicates acidic conditions; a pH value above 7 indicates alkalinity.

Physiological density A measurement of population density expressed as the average number of people per unit area (sq mi or sq km) of arable land in a country or state. Also known as *nutritional density.*

Pidgin language Used for communication between speakers of different languages primarily for the purpose of conducting trade; a simplified tongue formed by intermixing elements of other languages.

Plantation agriculture The use of a relatively large landholding, commonly in a tropical or subtropical area, to produce a commercial crop such as sugar cane, cotton, or coffee.

Plate tectonics The independent movement and deformation of segments (plates) of the earth's crust.

Polyglot A country or society in which many different languages are in use.

Polytheism The worship of many gods.

Population pyramid A compound bar graph that portrays the distribution of a population by age and sex categories.

Possibilism A belief that the physical environment offers people a variety of possibilities from which to select ways of using their habitat.

Post-industrial society A stage of development reached by a society or country when service activities exceed manufacturing in economic importance and as a source of employment.

Primary economic activities Such economic pursuits as agriculture, fishing, forestry, and mining that involve the exploitation of natural resources.

Primate city A country's dominant city in size, economic importance, and cultural influence. Paris, France, is a classic example of a primate city.

Pull factors Characteristics of a place that attract migrants from other locations.

Push factors Conditions or circumstances in a place that stimulate a resident to migrate elsewhere.

Rank-size rule A principle that identifies a common relationship between a city's rank in the urban hierarchy of a country and its population size. The rule is that the nth-ranked city will have a population $1/n$th that of the largest city.

Refugees People who flee their homelands because of conditions (often political or environmental) that they perceive to be threatening to their personal safety.

Region A specific part of the earth's surface that is defined or delimited by one or more criteria.

Relative location The location of a place or feature in relation to an adjacent or nearby place or feature that may be more prominent or generally known.

Remote sensing The gathering of information about the earth by use of relatively distant instruments, usually cameras and radar devices aboard aircraft and space vehicles.

Renewable resources Resources such as soil and timber that can replenish themselves or return to their original state after being exploited. Use of such resources normally does not involve the risk of their total exhaustion.

Secondary economic activities Manufacturing activities that consist of processing raw materials into a finished product of higher value.

Sex ratio The proportion of males to females in a population.

Shifting cultivation A type of subsistence crop farming, now most common in tropical rainforest regions, that involves the clearing and temporary cultivation of an area until its soil is depleted (usually within a few years). The area is then abandoned as the clearing and cultivation activities are shifted to a new location.

Site The specific area occupied by a city or other feature. It usually is described in terms of its physical characteristics, such as its bedrock, drainage, and local relief.

Situation The regional setting of a city or other feature on the landscape.

Small farmers Individuals who cultivate only relatively small- or modest-sized landholdings.

Solstice The date when the noon sun is vertical at the Tropic of Cancer (about June 22) and the Tropic of Capricorn (about December 22).

Specialty agriculture A type of commercial farming focused on production of specialty crops rather than major food grains.

Squatter settlement A community consisting of primitive shelters erected and occupied by people without obtaining formal approval of the landowner. Squatter settlements are common on the margins of cities in the less developed world.

State An area organized as a political unit over which an established government exercises sovereign control.

Sustainable earth society All the earth's people at an ideal stage in their economic and cultural development when they live in harmony with the environment and can be supported by renewable earth resources indefinitely.

Tertiary economic activities Service activities such as retail sales, teaching, government work, and mechanical repair.

Theocracy A country in which the government is controlled by one or more religious leaders.

Threshold population The minimum number of people required to support an economic facility or activity and make possible its presence in a market center.

Townships Units of land in the United States that were surveyed according to provisions in the Land Ordinance of 1785. An ideal township is square and contains 36 sections, each of which is a square mile in area.

Traditional (tribal) religions Relatively early and primitive religions that served to explain the unknown and offer protection from threatening natural events.

Transhumance The movement of herders with their livestock to seasonal grazing lands, usually alpine pastures in summer and valley locations in the winter.

Troposphere The lowest general layer of the atmosphere; most weather activity occurs in this layer.

U.S. Corn Belt A highly productive agricultural region of the United States that emphasizes the production of grain crops, especially corn and soybeans, and livestock.

Universalist religion Religions that strive to convert all people and gain universal following.

Völkerwanderung The westward migration of groups from central Asia that displaced people in eastern and central Europe during the early Christian era.

Voluntary migrations Those migrations willingly undertaken by the participants.

Wagner's law A theory promulgated by a German economist named Adolph Wagner that governments progressively assume responsibility for the economic welfare of their citizens and thereby diminish the role of the private sector.

Weather The condition of the atmosphere at a specific place and time.

Women's movement A loosely coordinated effort to protect the rights and improve the status of women.

Zero population growth (ZPG) The attainment of a stable population total as a consequence of the equalization of birth and death rates.

Zionist movement The effort among Jews to reconstitute a Jewish state in Palestine.

INDEX

Use of italic type for page numbers indicates reference to a figure; t *indicates reference to a table.*